The Predictive Airliner

ANDREW PEARSON

ANDREW PEARSON

THE PREDICTIVE AIRLINER

Intelligencia Limited
www.intelligencia.co

Copyright © 2018 Andrew W. Pearson. All rights reserved.

No part of this book may be reproduced, stored in a retrieval system, or transmitted by any means without the written permission of the author, excepting brief quotes used in reviews.

Limit of Liability/Disclaimer of Warranty: While the publisher and author have used their best efforts in preparing this book, they make no representations or warranties with respect to the accuracy or completeness of the contents of this book and specifically disclaim any implied warranties of merchantability or fitness for a particular purpose. No warranty may be created or extended by sales representatives or written sales materials. The advice and strategies contained herein may not be suitable for your situation. You should consult with a professional where appropriate. Neither the publisher nor author shall be liable for any loss of profit or any other commercial damages, including but not limited to special, incidental, consequential, or other damages.

Intelligencia Limited also publishes its books in a variety of electronic formats. Some content that appears in print may not be available in electronic books. For more information about Intelligentsia's products, visit our website at www.intelligencia.co.

First published by Intelligencia.

All rights reserved

ISBN-13: 978-1979079570
ISBN-10:1979079579

CONTENTS

ACKNOWLEDGMENT i
PREFACE iii
INTRODUCTION 1
CHAPTER ONE **45**
   Customer Intelligence 45
   Overview 45
   Customer Relationship Management (CRM) 52
   Customer Loyalty 63
   The Customer Journey 66
   Data & Marketing 75
      Early Analytics 78
   Mobile Marketing 81
      Digital Interactive Marketing: The Five Paradigms 85
      Proximity Marketing 89
   Geofencing Applications 91
   Facial Recognition 94
   Gamification 98
   New Distribution Capability 100
   Near Field Communication 103
   Smart Tones 104
   Conclusion 105
CHAPTER TWO **113**
   Analytics 113
   Overview 113
   Data Mining 127
   Artificial Intelligence & Machine Learning 130
   Deep Learning 136
      Tensorflow 137
      Caffe2 140
      Torch 141
      Keras 141
      Pytorch 141
      Deeplearning4j 142
      CNTK 142
   Analytics 142
      Analytical Models 146
         Decision Trees 146
         k-Means Cluster 148

  k-Nearest Neighbors 150
  Logistic Regression 152
  A/B Testing 153
  Time Series Model.. 155
  Neural Networks 156
  Discriminant Analysis 160
  Survival or Duration Analysis... 161
 Airline Analytical Models 163
  Customer Segmentation 163
  Customer Acquisition Model... 164
  Recency-Frequency-Monetary (RFM) Models 165
  Propensity to Respond Model.. 167
  Customer Conversion Model 169
  Customer Worth Model 169
  Customer Churn Model... 170
  Optimizing Offers 171
  Chronological View of a Airline's Analytics Implementation 172
 Edge Analytics 173
 Sentiment Analysis.. 174
 Clickstream Analysis.. 178
 Location Analytics 183
 Conclusion 184
CHAPTER THREE 189
 Social Media 189
 Overview 189
  Social Proof 195
 Mobile and Social Media in China.. 199
 The Four Steps of Social Media 206
 Six Types of Social Media 209
  Collaborative Projects 209
   List of Collaborative Projects Websites........................... 212
  Blogs.. 213
   List of Blogging Websites 217
    Microblogs... 218
   List of Micro-blogging Websites 220
  Content Communities 221
   Instagram 222
   List of Content Community Sites..................................... 225
  Social Networks... 229
   Facebook 230
   WeChat... 233
   Google+ 237

    List of Social Network Sites 239
  Virtual Game Worlds 242
    Girl Gamer eSports Festival 242
  Virtual Social Worlds 245
    List of Virtual Social World Websites 247
  Videocasting/Livestreaming 248
  Podcasting 250
  Conclusion 251
Tips **255**
CHAPTER FOUR **261**
  Social Business 261
  Overview 261
  The Uses of Social Media 266
    Add Interactivity to a Website 269
    Brand and Anti-Brand Management 270
    Build Fanbases and Communities 276
    Crisis Management 280
    Develop a Virtual Social World Presence 286
    Discover a Customer's Psychological Profile 287
    Discover Important Brand Trends 291
    Engage Customers and Potential Customers 292
    Harvest Customer Feedback 294
    Influencer Marketing 297
      Micro-Influencers 299
    Reputation Management 301
  Social Media Analytics 303
  Social Media Monitoring 307
    Social Media Monitoring Tools 311
  Conclusion 315
  Tips 320
CHAPTER FIVE **327**
  The Connected Aircraft 327
  Overview 327
  Hadoop 333
    HDFS Schema Design 339
    Managing Metadata 341
    Data Ingestion Considerations 342
    Compression 344
    Relational Database Managment Systems (RDBMS) 344
    Keeping Hadoop Updated 345
    Flume 345
    Kafka 346

    Data Extraction 349
        Hadoop Machine Learning Solutions 350
   Streaming Analytics 352
        Comparison of Stream Processing Services 358
   Internet of Things (IoT) 362
   Augmented and Virtual Reality 367
   Wearables 371
   Inventory Optimization 372
   Waste Management 374
   e-Commerce 376

CHAPTER SIX **383**
   The Predictive Airliner 383
   Overview 383
   Singapore Airlines: Continuing Excellence 387
   The Customer Journey 393
        Listening 395
        Rules Engine 398
        Automation 398
        Moderation 399
        Messaging 400
        Data & Analytics 406
   The Future 409
ABOUT THE AUTHOR **415**
INDEX **417**

ANDREW PEARSON

ACKNOWLEDGMENT

鄭慧琪: you know who you are.

ANDREW PEARSON

PREFACE

The idea for the *Predictive* series of books came about when I signed on to become a partner of the analytics and IoT provider Hitachi Data Systems (HDS). They wanted help organizing an event in Macau for C-level execs within the casino industry and I not only opened my Rolodex (I know that dates me, but why not, it shows experience!), but I also decided a book that delved into the details of the technology we were showcasing would be a great companion piece. So was born my first book in this series, *The Predictive Casino*. Once that book was complete, I decided to tackle other industries, and this is the fourth book to focus on other trades.

I always envisioned *The Predictive Airliner* to be a series of books that would grow and evolve with the changes in technology. This one, the first in the series, is mostly about cutting-edge technology and, as is its want, cutting-edge technology, literally, changes by the second—that's why it's cutting edge, after all. Needless to say, there should be several more in the series. And soon. Many of the topics I discussed in the other predictive books are relevant for the airline industry, but it is a highly unique industry that does require a book of its own.

The airline industry is a low margin industry, an industry that is highly affected by price fluctuations in commodity prices. Most major airlines have entire departments dedicated to hedge things like fuel costs, but the players in the industry long ago realized that they had to be far more creative than other companies in the travel industry if they were to succeed, or, in some cases, even survive. Investments in planes run into the hundreds of millions of dollars and the cost of service, staff, and maintenance for these planes runs into the tens of millions of dollars for a major airline. It could be argued that analytics are needed in the airline industry more than any other industry and it is an industry that has seen a lot of development in the analytics field.

As I detail throughout this book, history shows us that the airline industry has been on the cutting edge of technology for quite a while now. This book is an attempt to help it stay there. After all, it is an industry that, literally, took flight; over a century ago, when Orville Wright roared into the sky on *Flyer I*, flew across 120 feet of wet sand for 12 seconds at Kitty Hawk in North Carolina. The distance is shorter than the wingspan of one of today's large passenger planes, but that historic flight led to today's aviation industry, an industry that each day sends millions of passengers packed like sardines in large metal tubes hurtling towards the sky, literally, ferrying them halfway across the world. A rudimentary search of flightradar.com shows that there are more than 190,000 tracked flights per day, which is a staggering number of trips and people being moved from one part of the globe to another.

ANDREW PEARSON

One can only marvel at the complex set of circumstances and dynamics that led to this industry's creation and it is easy to understand how difficult it must be to keep all of the people, planes, parts, and commodities aligned so an airline can turn a profit and keep flying. This book is an attempt to add to the library of books on technology in the airline industry. I hope it elucidates a few things on how this most high-tech of industries can keep leading the technological way.

Parts of this book have been written on the Macau-Hong Kong ferry, 30,000 feet above both the Pacific and the Dark Continent of Africa, on the Guangzhou-Macau high-speed rail line, on islands off the Korean Peninsula, within a taxi stuck in the smog-choked streets of Manila, as well as on the London Underground and in a café around the corner from Moscow's Red Square, to say nothing of all the hotel and motel rooms I've been scribing in; planes, trains, automobiles, ferries, and Tuk-tuks, too. If you find this book instructive, please keep up to date with my latest work on social media, a list of social sites that I can be found on are on my author page at the end. For now, enjoy...

INTRODUCTION

"Aviation is proof that—given the will—we can do the impossible."
– Eddie Rickenbacker

When Eddie Rickenbacker said those inspirational words about aviation almost a century ago, the renowned WW I American flying ace made a good point. How on earth does a plane that weighs several tons lift off the ground and fly through the air? It seems physically impossible. However, when you understand how lift, thrust, weight, and drag all work in concert together to produce the aerodynamics of flight, it is quite simple to understand how a thin metal tube can lift off from a runway in Perth, Australia, fly across oceans and continents as fast as a speeding bullet, then land in London, England, seventeen hours later. The impossible, as Rickenbacker sees it, has become a daily occurrence.

The airline industry is notoriously low margin, which means business innovation is not only necessary, but imperative. Besides the global armaments business, the airline industry is the industry most susceptible to geopolitical risks. Oil is a huge cost to an airline's bottom line and a spike in oil has cost many an airline to go defunct.

According the International Air Transport Association (IATA), a trade association that represents about 290 worldwide airlines, these are "good times for the global air transport industry."[1] In its December 5th, 2017 press release *Strong Airline Profitability Continues in 2018*, IATA claims that, "Safety performance is solid. We have a clear strategy that is delivering results on environmental performance. More people than ever are traveling. The demand for air cargo is at its strongest level in over a decade. Employment is growing. More routes are being opened. Airlines are achieving sustainable levels of profitability."[1] However, it is still "a tough business, and we are being challenged on the cost front by rising fuel, labor and infrastructure expenses," said Alexandre de Juniac, IATA's Director General and CEO.[1]

Some highlights of the expected 2018 performance point to that fact, including:

- A slight decline in the operating margin to 8.1% (down from 8.3% in 2017)
- An improvement in net margin to 4.7% (up from 4.6% in 2017)
- A rise in overall revenues to $824 billion (+9.4% on 2017 revenues of $754 billion)

- A rise in passenger numbers to 4.3 billion (+6.0% on the 4.1 billion passengers in 2017)
- A rise in cargo carried to 62.5 million tonnes (+4.5% on the 59.9 million tonnes in 2017)
- Slower growth for both passenger (+6.0% in 2018, +7.5% in 2017) and cargo (+4.5% in 2018, +9.3% in 2017) demand
- Average net profit per departing passenger of $8.90 (up from $8.45 in 2017)

The last statistic is quite striking—only $8.90 profit per passenger—reveals just how much of a volume-based business the airline industry is and should continue to be.

In her article *How Airlines Get Customer Experience So Wrong with So Much Data*[2], Sarah Steimer writes about the conundrum of the airline industry, which "may be the only place where segmentation determines whether customers receive the service they paid for. Imagine purchasing a meal at a restaurant but being denied that food because there isn't enough for everyone. The more loyal customers receive the meal; you have to come back and eat at a less-convenient hour."

According to Investopedia[3], "airlines receive about 60 percent of their revenue from consumers directly and the other 40 percent from selling frequent-flier miles to credit card companies, repairing aircraft and offering other services." Of this 60%, "business travelers make up 12% of passengers, but they are typically twice as profitable for airlines."[3] Business passengers sometimes represent 75% of an airline's profits, while first-class and business tickets can cost as much as 10 times the price of coach tickets.[3] "Luring and keeping business customers makes more economic sense than focusing equally on all passengers—or so it would seem," argues Steimer.[2]

The forced removal of David Dao from United Express Flight 3411 on April 9th, 2017[4], although apparently "justified by the company's algorithm that identified him as one of the least valuable people on the flight, highlighted the negative cost of such competitive customer segmentation,"[2] had enormous consequences. "United Airlines' social sentiment fell almost 160% within 48 hours of the incident, according to Brandwatch, and United Continental Holdings' stock was off about 4% in the immediate aftermath, knocking close to $1 billion off the company's market value," notes Steiner.[2]

"Yet airlines continue to focus on how they can slash conveniences for those unwilling to pay a premium," says Steiner.[2] "Data support this strategy," contends Steiner, like the Reuters/Ipsos opinion poll released in mid-2017 that found "83% of Americans put ticket prices among their top considerations when booking personal travel, outweighing travel perks or airline reputation."[2] "Sixty percent said they would not pay extra to avoid being assigned a middle seat, and

52% said they would not pay more to fly on their preferred airline," adds Steiner.[2]

"Armed with this knowledge, airlines have unbundled the services that were previously included when purchasing a single ticket. Booking a flight now means choosing from an a la carte group of products. Carrying on luggage, extra leg room and in-flight entertainment are now considered extras on some flights," says Steiner.

"Airlines have gotten pretty refined in their analysis of how much they can charge for add-ons, whether it's checked baggage, overhead bins, advanced boarding, preferred seat selection and so on," says John Strong, an aviation expert at the College of William and Mary's business school.[2]

"This phenomenon has been referred to as 'calculated misery,' a term coined by Tim Wu, an author and professor at Columbia Law School," says Steiner.[2] In 2014, Wu wrote in *The New Yorker* about the decline in quality of commercial airline service, explaining: "For fees to work, there needs be something worth paying to avoid. That necessitates, at some level, a strategy that can be described as 'calculated misery.' Basic service, without fees, must be sufficiently degraded in order to make people want to pay to escape it. And that's where the suffering begins."[2]

Strong says "customer data show that airlines can take their cheapest ticket and add or subtract some nuances because people are willing to pay or save a bit, whether on leg room, reserved seating or baggage."[2] "What data has let [airlines] do is divide economy seating into three classes now: premium economy, economy and economy-minus," he says.[2]

Oddly, at a time when most companies are aiming to delight their customers, airlines appear to be doing just the opposite.[2] "These companies are instead marketing their products as a reduction to discomfort, instead of incremental improvements to baseline quality, adds Steiner, which is an odd way to look at things.[2]

The concept of calculated misery is best exemplified by leg room.[2] The *New York Times* reported that seat width at the time of airline deregulation in the 1970s was 18 inches, compared with about 16.5 inches today. Seat pitch, or the distance between a point on one seat and the same point on the seat in front of it, fell from 35 inches to 31 inches. Meanwhile, the average American has grown in size," notes Steiner.[2]

"The unbundling of flight products and online booking presents airlines with an abundance of customer data," notes Steiner.[2] "For the occasional traveler, the airline may be able to track credit cards used, flight frequency, typical destinations and spending behaviors," adds Steiner.[2]

Frequent flyers and high-status loyalty members are tracked more closely.[2]

"They may receive a personal apology from a gate attendee if he notices the passenger's previous flight was delayed. A flight attendant may offer the flyer his or her favorite beverage once the flight is in progress," explains Steiner.

These and other gestures, which were once typically reserved only for high-value customers, are becoming more common as airlines upgrade their technology and combine multiple data and customer touch points.[2] It's a customer personalization world and airlines know they have to join the wave. "For example," Steiner explains, "Delta Air Lines introduced software last spring called SkyPro, which may be accessed on its flight attendants' Nokia Lumia mobile devices to track basic customer information."[2] Also, American Airlines is soon expected to launch iSolve, "an app on its flight attendants' Samsung Galaxy Note devices that will allow them to offer frequent-flyer miles or a travel voucher as immediate compensation for customer service issues onboard."[2]

Singapore Airlines, which is considered the gold standard in customer experience, not just in the airline industry, but in the greater hospitality sector, recently "worked with Accenture to develop an app that can track customer data from check-in at the airport through the flight and on to baggage retrieval."[2]

Rohit Deshpande, a professor of marketing at Harvard Business School, who has authored two case studies on Singapore Airlines explains it how detailed the customer service can be: "Let's say you go from Sydney to Singapore to change flights from Singapore to London, you decide when you're going to Singapore that instead of drinking your normal gin and tonic, you're going to ask for a vodka and tonic. They will record that, and when you reboard in Singapore to go on to London, the flight attendant will ask if you will continue with vodka and tonic or go back to gin and tonic."[2] This might, of course seem intrusive, but SIA feels that people want to know that they're cared for and recognized with not just customer service but personalized customer service."[2] He is probably right.

"This isn't the only high-tech way airlines are collecting customer data," explains Steiner.[2] "Delta has used heart rate monitors on volunteer customers to track their heartbeats at 11 stressful moments during the travel experience, such as finding a parking spot at the airport, moving through security and boarding the plane."[2]

"We do focus groups with biometrics and biodata on where customers are looking at things on screens, where their eyes are on the airplanes to make things more intuitive," says Andrew Wingrove, Delta's managing director of product and customer experience.[2] "The heart monitor was one of the tests we used for focus groups to better understand where their anxiety is."[2]

"The monitoring extends to the web via social media," Steiner says, as social channels offer "a real-time opportunity for airlines to react to customers, regardless of their status."[2] "We've created a robust social listening platform to react in the moment when things are going right or going wrong," Wingrove says.[2] "[Customers] use it to reach out directly or to mention us. Our goal is to be where customers are, and while that may have been solely over the phone in the past, we're thinking about it as more engagement with multiple channels."[2]

Most major airlines have tens of thousands of employees, some, like America Airlines, even have over a hundred thousand.[5]

Singapore Airlines is one of the major carriers that has faced the onslaught of low-cost carriers. The emergence of low-cost carriers in just about every corner of the world . From my recent travels to such far flung places as Cape Town, Lisbon, Guangzhou, Cyprus, Hyderabad, Moscow, and the Philippines, I have come to realize that low cost carriers have replaced long distance trains and overnight buses just about everywhere in the world. Why drive for eight hours when you can jump on a plane for about the same price, and get there in $1/5^{th}$ the time?

In her book *Strategic Marketing Approaches Within Airline Management: How the Passenger Market Causes the Business Concepts of Full Service Network Carriers, Low Cost Carriers, Regional Carriers and Leisure Carriers to Overlap*[6], Susanne Bölke argues that, "in general, the airline industry can be divided into four main market segments: Low-cost carriers, regional carriers, leisure carriers, and full-service network carriers." She adds, "Each segment is characterized by service level as well as number of flight routes. While low cost carriers provide little service and few routes to achieve lower cost, full-service network carriers provide a dense network of flight routes with a high level of service. Leisure carriers focus mostly on popular holiday locations. Their service is often slightly better compared to low-cost carriers. Finally, regional carriers commonly operate in a geographically bounded area with few flights."[6]

According to Boland, Morrison, and O'Neill's article *The Future of CRM in the airline industry: A new paradigm for customer management*[7], "Low-cost carriers have attracted customers through substantially lower fares enabled by high-efficiency operating models. Operational efficiency has thus become the top priority across an industry struggling to maintain profitability."

That article was written in 2002, a time when the industry was reeling financially because of a multitude of reasons, including 9/11 the previous year. Today, the aviation industry is on much stronger footing, but low margin businesses are always at risk for potential economic downturns more so than high margin businesses and the airline industry must remain vigilant and keep innovating or bankruptcies could ensue.

As for low cost carriers, the world's major airlines quickly took notice of these successful startups and several created low-cost airlines of their own; Qantas has Jetstar; Singapore Airlines has Scoot; Cathay Pacific has Dragon Air; United has Ted (perhaps the lamest named airline around).

Boland et al. add that, "Many airlines have taken a 'fast follower' approach, learning from the experience of competitors to reduce cost."[7] This, of course, means you are not going to lead, but with technological advances proving quite costly, it might be advantageous to keep a close eye on one's competition to see what they creating. In this book, I will detail as much new technology as I possibly can and so airline executives can keep up with some of them here.

As Woodrow Bellamy III explains in his article *Data Analytics Driving Efficiency in Commercial Aviation*[8], Boeing CEO Dennis Muilenburg believes "that the airplane services market will be valued at more than $2.6 trillion over the next 10 years." "The majority of those airplane services that are performed in that time will be due to decisions about part failures, replacements, upgrades and software updating provided by data analytics software," said Muilenburg.[8]

"At the 2017 Paris Air Show, Boeing unveiled a new division completely devoted to providing airplane data analytics expertise for Boeing aircraft operators. That divsion, 'AnalytX,' in 2017 alone already saw 200 new sales of advanced data and collection processing, fleet performance and reliability analytics and maintenance and engineering optimization to new operators," explains Bellamy.[8]

"What's happening today with data analytics is not much different than what's occurred in the past," Bellamy says, adding, "Operators do not need to equip with much more data acquisition technology than what is standard on today's in-service airplanes."[8]

For example, Bellamy states that, "Boeing's 737 MAX, which entered commercial service in 2017, features an onboard network system (ONS) capable of digitally storing entries about irregularities associated with aircraft components and systems. Previously, doing so required a paper logbook."[8]

"Original equipment manufacturers, such as Pratt & Whitney, are increasingly embracing the IOT concept by taking advantage of cloud computing and customized advanced analytics applications," says Bellamy.

"Lynn Fraga, manager of business analytics and engine services at Pratt & Whitney, said the company is expanding its advanced diagnostics and engine management (ADEM) system, a suite of algorithms and web tools that customers can access via its customer portal," notes Bellamy.[8]

"Operators have options. They can receive very simple reports to review on their own, or they can have Pratt & Whitney monitor their fleets," said Fraga.[8] "With the geared turbofan engine, we have expanded the number of reports that we get off the aircraft by about three times as much as what's traditionally been possible," adds Fraga.[8]

"The GTF, which features more than 5,000 sensors capable of producing up to 10 GB of data per flight, sends performance snapshots from engine start to engine shut down, explains Bellamy.

"We're also expanding the use of sensors, giving us insight into other systems on the engine," added Fraga.[8] "Today's geared turbofan will track temperatures, pressures, multiple types of low-end and high-end rotor speeds and vibration across the full-flight profile. As we look at getting more sensor data, we can look at other systems and components that are non-traditional gas path systems."[8]

"Continued expansion in the improvements in flight efficiencies provided by data analytics will depend on how well the two worlds of data science and airplane operation and engineering can continue to merge," predicts Bellamy. Personally, I would make a hefty bet that the two worlds merge quite successfully.

In his *Forbes* article *How Airlines Decide What You'll Pay To Fly Is About To Change Dramatically*[9], Dan Reed explains that "A new ticket-selling technology, made possible by the ability to harness and analyze the unfathomably huge amounts of data airlines collect and retain about every traveler and every possible routing, will make it possible for airlines to provide every travel shopper a unique, customized price for any given trip about which they may inquire."

According to Reed, New Distribution Capability (NDC) is a "new ticket-selling approach uses airlines' enormous Big Data capturing abilities in concert with new artificial intelligence or 'machine learning' methods to present to each travel shopper a unique, all-in price that includes not only the basic cost a seat but also the cost of many (or even all) of the travel services the traveler will need or want."[9] That price includes the cost of basics like seat selection, check-in baggage, as well as, potentially, current standard services like ground transportation, hotel rooms as well as services like dinner reservations, and purchase of items like concert tickets or retail goods.[9]

Veteran travel industry analyst Henry Harteveldt of Atmosphere Research says airlines in the coming years "will move away from terms like 'fare' and 'ticket' and toward terms like 'price,' 'journey' and 'experience.'"[9] Reed argues that, "the long-held notion of there being one 'fare' (or, more accurately, one set of fares priced at multiple levels) for a particular flight on a particular route quickly is eroding."[9]

The new selling approach will work this way: instead of a customer searching online travel sales website, or talking to a travel agent, the customer will simply inform one or more airlines, or his or her favorite online travel site the intended destination and then wait for a few seconds to receive a price quote unique to the recipient that takes into account highly personalized information.[9]

As Reed notes, the "price quote will be based not only on the cost of flying from A to B but also on your freshly stated and/or your previously known travel preferences. Your frequent flier status also will likely have an impact on the price you're quoted. And, if your travel is for business, and if you work for Company X, which has in place a sweet volume-of-travel discount deal with one or more airlines, that too will be factored into the price you're quoted."[9]

In chapter one, I delve into detail about how NDC technology will radically affect the travel and airline industry, as well as explain how other technologies will affect customer intelligence, including NFC, digital marketing, smart tones, facial recognition, and more. I also give a background of the use of data in marketing, as well as a brief history of analytics. From this base, I will build

In December 2014, Amazon was awarded a patent for what it calls a "method and system for anticipatory package shipping,"[10] and, according to Lance Ulanoff's article *Amazon Knows What You Want Before You Buy It*[10], "The patent summary describes a method for shipping a package of one or more items 'to the destination geographical area without completely specifying the delivery address at time of shipment,' with the final destination defined en route."[10]

According to the patent, this forecasting model uses data from a customer's "prior Amazon activity, including time on site, duration of views, links clicked and hovered over, shopping cart activity and wish lists."[10] When possible, "the algorithm also sprinkles in real-world information gleaned from customer telephone inquiries and responses to marketing materials, among other factors. Together, this can provide 'decision support for speculative shipping of items,' per the patent," explains Ulanoff.[10]

All of this may sound a little fanciful, but Ulanoff's thesis that predicting customers' orders could unquestionably increase sales as well as potentially reduce shipping, inventory and supply chain costs holds true.[10] For these reasons alone, Amazon is probably onto something here. Obviously not the sexiest part of an airline's business, supply chain and logistics is, however, an imperative and expensive part of it. Anticipatory shipping can be utilized to ensure parts are needed for the right aircraft at the right location right when it is needed.

Ulanoff quotes H. Donald Ratliff, Ph.D., executive director of the Supply Chain and Logistics Institute, who argues that optimization is "the biggest opportunity for most companies to significantly reduce their cost and improve their performance."[10] "For most…operations, there is an opportunity to reduce cost by 10% to 40% by making better decisions," Ulanoff argues.[10] This amounts to substantial savings for airline companies, who spend millions of dollars in supplies and products every year.

Amazon utilizes predictive analytics, including Machine Learning (ML) to make very sophisticated supply chain, logistics and even customer delivery decision. *The Predictive Airliner* wants to infuse this anticipatory concept throughout its entire operation, not just in logistics, but also for customer interactions. Optimization in item pricing, demand forecasting, replenishment shipping, marketing, data governance, security, sales, advertising, and labor management can all utilize the anticipatory concept, which can make an airline smart, predictive, optimized, and probably more profitable than it would otherwise be.

Human beings are, first and foremost, creatures of habit and, if an airliner can understand these habits on both a micro and macro level, it can not only predict what its customers are going to want, but also what they will do, so the airline can, potentially, shape that behavior.

Marketing has always been about influencing people's actions, what could be different here is *The Predictive Airliner's* ability to understand how one customer's actions will affect the company's entire operation. With this insight extrapolated over a million customers over 365 days of the year, the airliner can take the most appropriate—and optimized—action to reap the highest profit. That is essentially *The Predictive Airliner's* goal.

According to IBM[11], 2.5 quintillion bytes of data are created each day. That is 10 to the power of 18 and that number is growing exponentially each year; 90% of the world's data was created over the past two years and data creation is certainly not going to slow down any time soon. This data—which has been dubbed "Big Data"—comes from everywhere; our daily financial transactions; our personal online shopping history; our social media uploads; our mobile downloads, even, more and more, sensor data coming off machines and even people.

The social nature of sharing personal content with family, friends and associates may be the driver behind this growth and it is a growth that several studies[12][13] suggest will soon outpace revenue generated by commercial media, such as music downloads, video clips, and games. This is the kind of growth that an airline operator ignores at its own peril and when an airliner delves into this Big Data world, it needs to ensure that what it's opening up is a treasure chest of information and not a *Pandora's Box* full of pain.

Today's major airlines have plane engines that are fitted with hundreds of sensors that record every tiny detail about their operation and report any changes in data in real time to engineers, who then decide the best course of action. An airline's engineers need to analyze the data being fed back from their engines. They can amalgamate the data from their engines to highlight factors and conditions under which engines may need maintenance. In some situations, humans can then intervene to avoid or mitigate whatever is likely to cause a problem. Increasingly, an airline should expect their computers to carry out the intervention themselves.

As Woodrow Bellamy III explains in his article *Data Analytics Driving Efficiency in Commercial Aviation*[14], "Qantas Airways is one international carrier using data analytics as such through a platform for pilots. The new technology, called 'FlightPulse,' provides automated updates on ways that pilots can fly better to reduce fuel burn and emissions."

Currently, FlightPulse is used by more than 1,700 pilots.[14] "After manpower, fuel (even with the current low prices) is still the largest expenditure for any airline," explains John Mansfield, VP and chief digital officer for GE Aviation. "Qantas realized a 1% reduction in fuel spend as a result of the work done with GE in 2016 and is on track to double fuel savings for 2017," Mansfield added.[14]

Bellamy explains that, "The technology is designed to provide vivid imagery that is easy to interpret so pilots can quickly access actionable information. Pilots can see and review snapshots of their performance at takeoff, cruise, landing, descent and ascent at different times to see where they could be saving fuel. They're also able to see the performance of other pilots."[14]

With civil aero engines as reliable as they are, the emphasis shifts to keeping them performing to their maximum, saving an airline fuel and meeting their flight schedules.

Big Data analytics can help airlines predict maintenance issues that might become problematic days or weeks in advance, so an airline can schedule maintenance in plenty of time to limit passenger disruption.

The Predictive Airliner is an airline company that takes into account all kinds of data that is created throughout its company by its employees, vendors, patrons, and customers (we'll consider these the people who haven't signed up for a loyalty card yet and aren't, therefore, as trackable as patrons who are in the airline's database), and even potential customers through channels like social media.

The Predictive Airliner utilizes all of a company's data to make better business decisions for the company as a whole. *The Predictive Airliner* is viewed holistically and the proverbial butterfly's wing that flaps somewhere inside a company's faraway international branch can set off a chain of events that can either help or hurt the company's bottom line months, even years, down the road. Captured and analyzed the data will be, so that surprises and negative impacts can be mitigated, if not reversed.

Descriptive analytics, diagnostic analytics, predictive analytics, prescriptive analytics and the newest field of analytics—edge analytics—are delved into throughout the book. One of the goals of *The Predictive Airliner* is to try to reach as real-time an IT environment as possible. The data I will be focused on throughout this book will be culled from the following airline's data sources:

. The data this book will be focusing on will be culled from the following sources:
- Operational systems
- Customer Relationship Management (CRM) software
- Transaction data from Point-of-Sales (POS) systems
- Airline reservation system

- Clickstreams from the various airline websites
- Call center systems
- Surveillance and security systems, including facial and emotional recognition datasets
- IoT sensors and tracking devices
- Geo-location data from in-house Wi-Fi systems
- Social media data from WeChat, Facebook, Weibo, Twitter, Jeipang, Instagram, YouTube, Twitch, and other mobile and social media apps
- Ticket revenue management systems
- Social media listening hub
- Google analytics and web tracking information
- HR and ERP systems
- Transportation data
- Weather data
- Aircraft maintenance systems
- Website operations data
- Google analytics and web tracking information.

All of this information can be fed into a data lake or an Enterprise Data Warehouse (EDW), where it can be utilized by a multitude of departments, including security, call center/customer service, HR, marketing, including social media marketing, all the way up to the top executive branches, including individuals in the C-suite.

In recent years, businesses in general and airline companies in particular have come to the realization that data warehouses, while perfectly able to handle the BI and analytics needs of yesterday, don't always work in today's complex IT environments, which contain structured, unstructured, and semi-structured data, some of which can be streaming into systems through social media and mobile or IoT devices.

Normal relational databases work fine when business users are restricted to proprietary databases and the scope of work is limited to canned reports and modest dashboards that include limited drill down functionality. Today, however, with the inclusion of so much unstructured data coming from mobile, social, web logs, etc., and semi-structured data originating from a multitude of sources, limitations abound. Standard data warehouses require built-in, understandable schemas, but unstructured data, by definition, doesn't have a definable schema that is accessible and understandable in every case. Data lakes were a response to these limitations.

James Dixon, "Chief Geek" at Pentaho, is credited with coining the phrase "Data Lake" and Dixon posted that each specialized data mart in a data warehouse could be likened to a bottle of water. The data was ready for use in a small, identifiable container. In contrast, a data "lake" was a massive, intermingled repository of all data in its raw form.

A data lake is a hub or a repository of all the data that an airline has access to, where the data is ingested and stored in as close to the raw form as possible, without enforcing any restrictive schema on it. This provides an unlimited window into the data for anyone to run ad-hoc queries and perform cross-source navigation and analysis on the fly. Successful data lake implementations respond to queries in real-time and provide users an easy and uniform access interface to the disparate sources of data. Data lakes retain all data, support all data types and all users, as well as adapt easily to changes, while providing faster insights than normal EDWs.

Today's IT environment is nothing like the IT environment of even three years ago. Real-time data management capabilities have brought a whole new level of data available to customer intelligence, customer interaction, customer management and social media systems. For the airline industry, in particular, this has created a massive change as sensors fitted throughout an airplane can collect information that can be utilized in a multitude of ways to decrease cost and increase service.

One of the biggest challenges for IT departments worldwide is scalability. With a Hadoop back-ended data lake, businesses can dynamically scale up and down according to their storage needs. Over the past few years, the cost of storage has plummeted, and virtual servers can be spun up very quickly, as well as quite inexpensively (relative to the outright purchase of hardware). With this instant access to data, a whole new world of real-time interactions can flourish, and I will detail how an airline can set up a real-time stream processing environment in both chapter one and chapter five.

The concept of "Edge Analytics"—i.e., the processing of analytics at the point or very close to the point of data collection—exponentially increases the ability to use predictive analytics where they can be utilized best—at the point of interaction between the business and the consumer. In short, edge analytics brings analytics to the data rather than vice-versa, which, understandably, can reduce cost and increase its usage as the data is analyzed close to where it can make the most difference. This also reduces latency, which could be the difference between useful and useless analytics.

Today, the analytics space is more crowded than it has ever been; Standard ETL-solution providers are adding analytics to their multitude of offerings. Many new players in the Master Data Management (MDM) field have BI platforms that combine integration, preparation, analytics and visualization capabilities with governance and security features. Such standard analytics processes as column dependencies, clustering, decision trees, and recommendation engines are all included in many of these new software packages.

Instead of forcing clients to frustratingly purchase module on top of module on top of module, new software companies are creating packages that contain many pre-built analytical functions. Open source products like R, Python, and the WEKA collection in Vantara (fka Pentaho) can easily be added to many of these software solutions as well, thereby reducing the need for expensive analytics layers.

The fact that many of these analytical packages are open source is a further advantage because, since they are free to download and use, they have a robust user base and consultants are sometimes easier to find than analysts with highly developed SAS or SAP Predictive Analytics Library skills, for example. However, open source doesn't mean free and building something from scratch has its own cost of implementation, which can be quite high. However, the lack of yearly software maintenance costs can make this a profitable choice in the long run.

Before going any further, I believe one of the first questions that needs to be answered here is, "What is analytics?" The standard answer is that there are four types of analytics. They are:

- Descriptive analytics—What happened?
- Diagnostic analytics—Why did it happen?
- Predictive analytics—What will happen?
- Prescriptive analytics—How can we make it happen again?

An airline should use Master Data Management (MDM) techniques to communicate important customer preference information to staff that sit at the customer interaction points. MDM is the processes, governance, policies, standards and tools that consistently define and manage the critical data of an organization to provide a single point of reference. One of the benefits of using MDM is that when that single point of reference is a customer profile, the master data can ensure that the treatment of a passenger is consistent, and that preference information reaches all customer points of contact.

Descriptive analytics, diagnostic analytics, predictive analytics, prescriptive analytics and the newest field of analytics—edge analytics—should be used by an airline to try to reach as real-time an IT environment as possible.

All of airline's information can be fed into a data lake and an airline's EDW, where it can be utilized by a multitude of operational departments, including security, call center/customer service, HR, ticketing agents, marketing, social media marketing, customer management, all the way up to the top executive branch, including individuals in the C-level suite.

Simple cluster segmentation models could divide customers into their preferred choice of apparel purchases. Market basket analysis, which utilizes association rules, would also be considered a descriptive analytics procedure. Airlines should use market basket analysis to bundle and offer promotions as well as gain insight into its customer's buying habits. Detailed customer shopping and purchasing behavior could also be used to develop future products. I will go into full detail on this topic in chapter two.

Diagnostic analytics could be used to mine website data to determine what caused a spike in web traffic.

As to the why of analytics, in her article *How Much ROI Can Data Analytics Deliver?*, Annie Eissler makes quite a compelling case: according to Nucleus Research "analytics and business intelligence solutions deliver, on average, $13.01 for every dollar spent."[15] Leading companies have been achieving double-digit return on investment (ROI) from their analytics investments for several years now."[15] In chapter two I will delve deeper into how an airline can utilize analytics to both reduce costs and increase customer satisfaction.

As Bernard Marr argues in his article *Will 'Analytics on The Edge' Be The Future Of Big Data?*[16], "Rather than designing centralized systems where all the data is sent back to your data warehouse in a raw state, where it has to be cleaned and analyzed before being of any value, why not do everything at the 'edge' of the system?"

Marr uses the example of a massive scale CCTV security system that is capturing real-time video feeds from tens of thousands of cameras.[16] "It's likely that 99.9% of the footage captured by the cameras will be of no use for the job it's supposed to be doing—e.g. detecting intruders. Hours and hours of still footage is likely to be captured for every second of useful video. So what's the point of all of that data being streamed in real-time across your network, generating expense as well as possible compliance burdens?"[16]

The solution to this problem, Marr argues is for the images themselves to be analyzed within the cameras at the moment the video is captured.[16] Anything deemed out-of-the-ordinary will trigger alerts, while everything considered to be unimportant will either be discarded or marked as low priority, thereby freeing up centralized resources to work on data of actual value.[16]

Using edge analytics and real-time stream processing engines, airlines can "analyze point-of-sales data as it is captured, and enable cross selling or up-selling on-the-fly, while reducing bandwidth overheads of sending all sales data to a centralized analytics server in real time."[16]

An example from the airport industry shows

In its press release *CUHK Develops Real-time Trolley Monitoring System with AI-based Video Content Analytics Enhancing Service Quality of Honk Kong International Airport*[17], The Chinese University of Hong Kong notes:

> "The Department of Systems Engineering and Engineering Management at The Chinese University of Hong Kong (CUHK), in collaboration with Hong Kong R&D Centre for Logistics and

> *Supply Chain Management Enabling Technologies (LSCM R&D Centre) and Airport Authority Hong Kong (AA), has successfully developed a Real-time Trolley Supply Monitoring System at the Hong Kong International Airport (HKIA) with the use of artificial intelligence techniques for analysing video content. The system has reached an accuracy of 92%, enabling frontline staff to make proper and timely allocation of trolleys for passengers."*

As Professor Cheng Chun Hung explains, "A camera network infrastructure normally incur high installation cost which covers building, cabling and engineering works. To minimize costs, our team has devised a data network with edge processing capability to eliminate the need of high bandwidth video transfer while at the same time, maintaining the image quality and data quantity."[17]

Edge analytics, of course, goes hand-in-hand with the Internet of Things—"the network of physical objects that contain embedded technology to communicate and sense or interact with their internal states or the external environment."[18]

In his seminal 2009 article for the *RFID Journal, That 'Internet o Things' Thing*[19], Kevin Ashton made the following assessment:

> *Today computers—and, therefore, the Internet—are almost wholly dependent on human beings for information. Nearly all of the roughly 50 petabytes (a petabyte is 1,024 terabytes) of data available on the Internet were first captured and created by human beings—by typing, pressing a record button, taking a digital picture, or scanning a bar code. Conventional diagrams of the Internet include servers and routers and so on, but leave out the most numerous and important routers of all—people. The problem is, people have limited time, attention and accuracy—all of which means they are not very good at capturing data about things in the real world. And that's a big deal. We're physical, and so is our environment. Our economy, society and survival aren't based on ideas or information—they're based on things. You can't eat bits, burn them to stay warm or put them in your gas tank. Ideas and information are important, but things matter much more. Yet today's information technology is so dependent on data originated by people that our computers know more about ideas than things. If we had computers that knew everything there was to know about things—using data they gathered without any help from us—we would be able to track and count everything, and greatly reduce waste, loss and cost. We would know when things needed replacing, repairing or recalling, and whether they were fresh or past their best. The Internet of Things has the potential*

to change the world, just as the Internet did. Maybe even more so.

One of the key points of that quote for the airline industry is "greatly reduce waste, loss and cost"[19] and sensors can help keep track of inventory, it can help keep airplane parts, it can keep food fresh or provide alerts when stocks need to be filled. Sensors are inexpensive enough that strong ROI justifications can be made to implement these types of systems. I delve into more detail on this subject in chapter five.

The term "Big Data" has become a way-too-common and enormously prevalent term and it is being thrown around a lot in the world of IT these days as it has become a kind of catch-all for analytics, IoT, social media, etc., etc. Although not a comprehensive list, Big Data analytics techniques can include association, classification, cluster analysis, crowdsourcing, data fusion, data mining, machine learning (ML), modeling, network analysis, optimization, predictive, regression, rule learning, special analysis, text analytics, time series analysis, amongst many, many others. Which techniques should an airliner use, well that all depends on what type of data is being analyzed, the available technology, the skills of the business users, and the business problems it tries to solve.

In chapter two, I break down how these analytical processes would work in the concept of the customer journey, and I will specifically explain in what circumstances decision trees, time series, discriminant analysis, *K-means clustering,* and *K-Nearest Neighbor* processes, amongst others, would be best utilized.

None of these techniques, however, will amount to anything if the underlying data environment isn't robust and cleansed properly; "junk in, junk out", as most analysts warn. Enormous attention must be paid to ensure the data is prepped and cleansed, otherwise nothing of value will be achieved, no matter how fast and/or robust your chosen analytics software might be able to crunch the numbers and build the models.

IoT technology costs are coming down, broadband's price has dropped, while its availability has increased, and there is a proliferation of devices with Wi-Fi capabilities and censors built into them. Even clothes and footballs are now equipped with censors, as the World Cup ball given to Donald Trump by Valdimir Putin showed.[20] Smart phone penetration is also exploding. All of these individual technological advances were good for the IoT environment, together, however, they have created a perfect storm for it.[21] With less than 0.1% of all the devices that could be connected to the Internet currently connected[21], there is tremendous growth potential here and those who embrace it now should have the first mover advantage, an advantage that could prove enormously valuable in terms of ROI over the next few years.

How can an airliner utilize IoT technology? Well, today's airports are massive structures and sensors have become so small and cheap that they can be put almost anywhere. IoT sensors can be used for smart parking, smart lighting, or as part of a mini smart grid. They can also be used for silo stock calculation—measuring the emptiness level and weight of goods—as well as waste management, and perimeter access control tools.

Liquid presence detection in places like data centers can help ensure the integrity of the airline's IT backbone. IoT can also help with supply chain control, NFC payment systems, inventory shrinkage, as well as smart product management.

For an airline's logistics department, IoT aids quality of shipment conditions, item location, storage incompatibility detection, and fleet tracking. IoT sensors can even be installed to ensure a building's structural health.

Combining IoT data with other structured and unstructured data isn't easy, though. Previous attempts at broad-based data integration has forced users to build data sets around common predetermined schema, or a unifying data model, but this becomes impossible when unstructured and semi-structured data are included in the mix. This is where a data lake can come in.

Unlike the monolithic view of a single enterprise-wide data model, the data lake relaxes standardization and defers modeling, resulting in a nearly unlimited potential for operational insight and data discovery. As data volumes, data variety, and metadata richness grows, so, too, do the benefits.

Today, data is coming from everywhere, from business mainframes, from corporate databases, from log files, cloud services, APIs, RSS feeds, as well as from social media feeds; most of this information does contain meaning, if one knows what, where, and how to look for it. A data lake makes it easier to read and understand the data, at least that's the theory which is being tested out by several forward-thinking companies right now. Using and understanding all of this data is going to be the challenge, however.

In Tableau's *Top 8 Trends for 2016 Big Data*,[22] one of the leading visualization software vendors writes:

> "We noted the increasing adoption of NoSQL technologies, which are commonly associated with unstructured data, in last year's version of Trends in Big Data. Going forward, the shift to NoSQL databases becoming a leading piece of the Enterprise IT Landscape becomes clear as the benefits of schema-less database concepts become more pronounced."

Tableau also sees the following eight trends affecting IT departments[22]:

1. The NOSQL Takeover—the benefits of schema-less database concepts are becoming harder and harder to ignore and the proof is in Gartner's

latest *Magic quadrant for Operational Database Management Systems*, which is dominated by vendors like MongoDB, DataStax, Redis Labs, MarkLogic and Amazon Web Services (with DynamoDB), rather than entrenched players like Oracle, SAP, IBM and Microsoft.

2. Apache Spark lights up big data—according to its originator, Matei Zaharia, Apache Spark is becoming the largest big data open source project on the market because its processing speeds are dramatically faster than Hadoop's.
3. The Hadoop project matures—"In a recent survey of 2,200 Hadoop customers, only 3% of respondents anticipate they will be doing less with Hadoop in the next 12 months. 76% of those who already use Hadoop plan on doing more within the next 3 months and, finally, almost half of the companies that haven't deployed Hadoop say they will within the next 12 months."[22]
4. Big Data grows up: Hadoop adds to enterprise standards—the "Apache Sentry project provides a system for enforcing fine-grained, role based authorization to data and metadata stored on a Hadoop cluster."[22] Apache is taking the demands of the enterprise-grade RDBMS very seriously.
5. Big data gets fast: Options expand to add speed to Hadoop—As Hadoop gains more traction in the enterprise market, the need for fast data exploration capabilities is growing. To meet this demand, Tableau sees further "adoption of technologies such as Cloudera Impala, AtScale, Actian Vector and Jethro Data that enable the business user's old friend, the OLAP cube, for Hadoop—further blurring the lines behind the 'traditional' business intelligence concepts and the world of 'Big Data.'"[22]
6. The number of options to discover all forms of data grows—Because of data discovery tools like Tableau and Qlik, self-service data preparation tools are increasing in popularity. Now that business users have gotten a taste of data discovery and like it, they want to be able to reduce the time and complexity of data preparation—the most important part of the analytics process—and there's been considerable innovation in this space from companies like Alteryx, Trifacta, Paxata and Lavastorm.
7. Massively Parallel Processing (MPP) data warehouse growth heats up in the cloud—Perhaps the death knell of the data warehouse has been overhyped and now the trend seems to be towards a hybrid mix of standard DWs and on-demand cloud data warehouses. "Analysts cite 90% of companies who have adopted Hadoop will also keep their data warehouses and with these new cloud offerings, those customers can dynamically scale up or down the amount of storage and compute resources in the data warehouse relative to the larger amounts of information stored in their Hadoop data lake."[22]

8. Buzzwords converge—Internet of Things, Cloud, and Big Data come together. Although it is in its infancy, IoT technology will soon become one of the "killer apps" for the cloud, resulting in a data explosion unlike we've ever seen before. For this reason, Tableau sees "leading cloud and data companies such as Google, Amazon Web Services and Microsoft bringing Internet of Things services to life where the data can move seamlessly to their cloud based analytics engines."[22]

With a normal data warehouse, an airline needs to decide on the structure (schema) of the data when creating the warehouse—before anything is even populated with data (schema-on-write). With a Hadoop-based data lake, however, an airline must store the data and structure it later, at a time when it is needed for each query or use case (a schema-on-read framework). Table 1 reveals the main differences between the two systems.

DATA WAREHOUSE	vs.	DATA LAKE
Structured, processes	DATA	Structured / semi-structured / unstructured, raw
Schema-on-write	PROCESSING	Schema-on-read
Expensive for large data volumes	STORAGE	Designed for low-cost storage
Less agile, fixed configuration	AGILITY	Highly agile, configure and reconfigure as needed
Mature	SECURITY	Maturing
Business professionals	USERS	Data scientists, et al

Table 1: Differences between a Data Warehouse and a Data Lake

With a data lake, the data is ingested and stored in as close to the rawest form as possible, without enforcing any restrictive schema on top of it. No OLAP cubes are used to manipulate the data. This provides an unlimited view of the data for anyone within the organization who has been given access to it. The user will be able to run ad-hoc queries and perform cross-source navigation and analysis on the fly. Successful data lake implementations respond to queries in real-time and provide users an easy and uniform access interface.

A data lake can improve an airline's business in the following ways:
- Airline operations:
    o Gain visibility on all operational events, inside and outside of the airline, particularly events that impact operational flight schedules.

- View all sources of operational disruptions that affect fuel burn in a seamless way to quickly explain and triage fuel burn related issues.
- Avoid costly aircraft maintenance delays by utilizing predictive asset maintenance analytical data and inventory optimization.
- Real time cabin crew locator, as well as live airplane information to assist customer experience and customer service initiatives.
- Account for the impact of special events, which are likely to have an impact on the availability of staff.
- Gain the ability to see spend by supplier within each category so that procurement can negotiate the best price for the airline.
- Associate online ad marketing with customer conversions.
- Identify the greatest drivers of customer value and project how those drivers will affect profitability and revenue projections months into the future, with enough lead time to take corrective actions, if necessary.
- Create highly effective personalized promotions that are tailored to appeal to a unique customer by automating and personalizing marketing campaigns on a recurring basis; i.e., marketing to the customer of one continuously.
- Maximize customer satisfaction and profitability by optimizing valuable resources to meet the customer's needs at every airline touch point.
- Get valuable customer insights into the hands of customer-facing employees, decision makers, and others who can exploit it, with high-end reporting and data visualization capabilities.
- Understand real-time airline floor traffic flows and heat maps so that airline personnel can be utilized more efficiently.
- Capture fraudulent and Anti-Money Laundering (AML) activity in real-time, thereby reducing costs and creating solid evidence to catch and even lock-up criminals.
- Add social media as a customer service and marketing channel.

- Customer Intelligence:
  - Gain visibility on a customer's true identity at loyalty card sign-up by culling through government and social media records during the actual sign up process.
  - Identify and recognize high value customers.
  - Identify and understand how each customer contributes to the individual accounts and overall business revenue.
  - Identify customers affected by service failures.
  - Understand a customer's activity and behaviors—using segmentation to analyze data gathered at multiple touch

- points and then segmenting customers according to their subtle purchasing differences.
- Single Customer View across the airline's entire business, including freight.
- Ability to access full customer details as well as provide appropriate responses on the airline's social channels.
- Discover travel behavior of a company and its trends.
- Visibility of all customer interactions within the company.
- Create marketing segments for non-frequent flyers based on insights derived from frequent flyer activities.
- Dynamic pricing in order to tailor fares in customer marketing.
- Understand the current point in the customer's journey with real-time interaction and alerting.
- Understand customer interactions through social media listening channels.
- Determine a customer's current journey information (Inbound, Outbound, Stopovers) in order to serve personalised offers.
- Determine and apply Group Customer Value to a customer, for insights analytics.
- Ability to provide surveys in real-time in-flight.
- Make customer complaints a simple and seamless process.
- Freight:
  - Develop a single customer view (SCV) to ensure the airline is correctly servicing a customer based on his or her total customer relationship with the airline.
  - Identify high value freight customers who have had a recent negative experience, such as a disruption or a baggage issue.

For this book, I will consider CRM as a two-part process that allows an airline to track and organize its current and prospective customers, as well as to manage the endpoints of customer relationships through its marketing promotions. When done right, CRM systems enable data to be converted into information that provides insight into customer behavior and, from these insights, some form of behavioral influencing can occur.

Although widely recognized as an important element of most business' customer experience platform, there is no universally accepted definition of CRM. In his paper *Accepting customer relationships: Using CRM and relationship technology*[23], R. Swift defines CRM as an "enterprise approach to understanding and influencing meaningful communications in order to improve customer acquisition, customer retention, customer loyalty, and customer profitability."

In his paper *Customer relationship management: Getting it right*[24], J. Kincaid concurs, seeing CRM as "the strategic use of information, processes, technology and people to manage the customer's relationship with your company (Marketing, Sales, Services, and Support) across the whole customer lifecycle."

In their paper *Customer Relationship Management: Emerging Practice, Process, and Discipline*[25], Parvatiyar and Sheth claim CRM is "a comprehensive strategy and process of acquiring, retaining, and partnering with selective customers to create superior value for the company and the customer. It involved the integration of marketing, sales, customer service, and the supply chain functions of the organization to achieve greater efficiencies and effectiveness in delivering customer value."

In their comprehensive article on the subject, *Application of Data Mining Techniques in Customer Relationship Management: a Literature Review and Classification*[26], Ngai et al. argue that these varying definitions emphasize the importance of "viewing CRM as a comprehensive process of acquiring and retaining customers, with the help of business intelligence, to maximize the customer value to the organization."

In this book, we will consider CRM as a two-part process that allows a company to track and organize its current and prospective customers, as well as to manage the endpoints of customer relationships through its marketing promotions. When done right, CRM systems enable data to be converted into information that provides deep insight into customer behavior.

In their paper *The future of CRM in the airline industry: A new paradigm for customer management*[7], Declan Boland, Doug Morrison and Sean O'Neill argue that:

> "Through the development and implementation of customer analytics and decision-support technologies, airlines can begin to use customer information not only to differentiate service levels based on customer value, but also to drive crucial operational decisions. In the end, an airline's CRM program becomes a platform for achieving both near-term operational efficiency and long-term relationship management and growth."

Boland et al. conclude that, although operational efficiency is the top priority amongst the players in the industry, "competitive advantage in the long term will be based in large part on solid differentiated customer relationships."[7]

The process of segmenting a market is deceptively simple; seven basic steps describe the entire process, including segmentation, targeting, and positioning. In practice, however, the task can be laborious since it involves poring over loads of data, and it requires a great deal of skill in analysis, interpretation and some person al judgment.

Data coming from mobile and social media sources like WeChat, Weibo,

Facebook, YouTube, Twitter, YouKu, etc., tend to be highly unstructured, while data coming from CSVs, XML and JSON feeds are considered semi-structured. NoSQL databases are also considered semi-structured, while text within documents, logs, survey results, and e-mails also fall into the unstructured category. Structured data coming in from the plethora of an airline's source system, undoubtedly, can feed into a data lake, where it can be merged with unstructured data and then utilized in ways that are almost impossible for a normal relational DW to handle.

Today, personalized web pages can be rendered during the web page load and elements of the page can take into account past purchase history, clickstream behavior, as well as a whole host of other data points. For an airline, its website is its customer center. 90% of the time when I look to book a flight, I start with my airline of choice's website, then I work my way down my airline options. I'll double-check flight costs on websites like Orbitz, Expedia, and C-trip, but I usually start with my preferred airline and that's probably quite common. I believe an airline that isn't utilizing customer personalization at this first point of contact is missing out on a lot of potential sales.

Highly structured customer data could be combined with unstructured data coming in from social media to reveal deep customer insights. If a customer tweets that he or she is heading to an overseas trip, why shouldn't the airline's marketing department be alerted? Setting up JSON feeds for Twitter user accounts is a very simple process and many other social media companies offer APIs that allow similar access to customer accounts. These are two-way systems as well, and the airline's marketing department could include social media as a channel to connect with customers and potential customers. These and other social media marketing campaign ideas will be discussed further in chapters three and four.

So how does an airline get a customer's WeChat, WhatsApp, Facebook, Twitter, Weibo, YouTube, or even Twitch account? Simple, they just ask for it. In today's digital world, more and more people are willing to hand over their mobile information because they prefer to communicate with people—and companies—via social channels.

By utilizing the complex web of customer data coming in from several different channels—mobile, social media, customer loyalty programs, transaction data, e-commerce website, sensors, amongst others—an airline can also work more productively. By understanding customer patterns and customer behavior across the whole spectrum of the business, an airline can use these customer behavioral patterns to map out its inventory and human capital needs as well.

Today, airline loyalty programs are everywhere, even on low-cost carriers, and these programs are making the airline industry a fortune. As Wikipedia explains[27]:

> "Although United Airlines had tracked customers as far back as the 1950s, the very first modern frequent-flyer program was created in 1972 by Western Direct Marketing for United. It gave plaques and promotional materials to members. In 1979, Texas International Airlines created the first frequent-flyer program that used mileage tracking to give 'rewards' to its passengers, while in 1980 Western Airlines created its Travel Bank, which ultimately became part of Delta Air Lines' program upon their merger in 1987. American Airlines' AAdvantage program launched in 1981 as a modification of a never-realized concept from 1979 that would have given special fares to frequent customers. It was quickly followed later that year by programs from United Airlines (Mileage Plus), Delta (Delta Air Lines Frequent Flyer Program), which later changed to SkyMiles), Continental Airlines (OnePass), Air Canada (Altitude), and in 1982 from British Airways (Executive Club)."

In her article *Airlines to rake in record $57 billion in passenger fees this year*[28], Leslie Josephs write that, "airlines around the world will bring in a record $82.2 billion in fees to passengers and revenue from selling frequent flier miles to banks, among other sources aside from ticket costs, said the study by consulting firm IdeaWorks Company and online car-rental site Cartrawler. The amount is more than triple the sum of airlines' ancillary revenue in 2010, according to the study."

In his article *How airline loyalty programs seduce and abandon you*[29], Jeffrey Pfeffer notes that, "Mileage programs are big business for the airlines, which sell miles to credit card companies and other vendors such as hotels to in turn give away to their own customers." The mileage business is huge. Pfeffer adds,

"In 2012, United sold $5.1 billion in frequent flier miles compared to $25.8 billion in actual airfare revenue, and there has been talk of airlines spinning off their mileage arms as separate companies. Better yet, airlines get a lot of that money for nothing! For instance, United expects that 25% of the miles that it is selling will never be redeemed." Like a gym that oversells memberships in January knowing full well that by Feburary those New Year's resolutions about working out will be forgotten, the airline industry has a built-in buyer who isn't expected to utilize the miles it sells. For the airline industry, loyalty certainly does have a price and other people are paying nicely for it.

However, there are some warning signs on the horizon for airline loyalty programs. In their article *Customers are driving the need to evolve airline loyalty programs*[30], Mark Drusch, Austin Horowitz, and Alex Severin note that, "Airline loyalty programs began as simple plans to create product differentiation following airline industry deregulation in the late 1970s", but they have morphed into massive businesses, adopted by nearly every corner of the travel industry.[30]

Drusch et Al. note a recent report that, "found that consumers have amassed more than $48 billion worth of rewards—the vast majority of which are not earned from flying. Airlines discovered that selling miles to other companies, credit card companies in particular, is a highly lucrative business."[30] Although airlines do not separate out the value of miles sold on their corporate statements, "it is estimated that the total sold by U.S. carriers is between $15-18 billion annually, at disproportionately high margins."[30]

"In essence, airline loyalty programs have transformed massive mileage sales businesses," argue Drusch et al. state.[30] "While this shift has provided significant economic value to airlines, recent changes in the accrual and redemption of rewards has put at risk the implied economic value and attractiveness of the programs to the majority of travelers, which may ultimately challenge the volume of mileage sales to which airlines have become accustomed," the writers argue.[30]

"Despite rapid growth, there is a growing sense that these programs have grown fundamentally flawed and out of touch with modern customer behavior," argue Drutsch et al.[30] Some believe the "competitive miles-for-sale business or the growing segment of customers who travel fewer than three times per year"[30] are at fault, claim Drutsch et al.[30] The data seems to reflect this this: according to Drutsch et al., "on U.S. airlines, less than 50% of onboard customers on any given U.S. airline flight are members of that airline's frequent flyer program." This would seem to be quite a low percentage.

For Drutsch et al. this raises a profound question— "do today's airline loyalty programs achieve their original purpose of engendering brand loyalty, driving a higher share of ticket sales and increased ancillary revenues from their customers?"[30]

This question becomes even more important today because travelers have access to online ticket pricing information, on-time performance statistics, and customer reviews.[30]

"The stakes are high. If the perceived consumer value of airline miles declines, sales could follow suit," argue Drutsch et al argue. In addition, "if airline loyalty programs do not focus on appealing to a wider spectrum of their customers, they risk handing over even more control to tech and information behemoths like Google, Amazon, and Facebook."[30]

Today airlines are transitioning from a mileage-based earnings model to a currency-spend earnings models.[30] Drutsch et al. argue that, "while the currency-spent earning model makes economic sense for airlines, the shift threatens to alienate both low to mid-frequent fliers and the growing number of infrequent or occasional travelers, due to the significantly longer period required to earn the same rewards as before."[30]

"Had the programs originally followed a spend-based metric from the start—hotels and retailers, for instance, have always used this model—frequent fliers would not have perceived a significant loss in value," claim Drutsch et al. "Infrequent or occasional travelers (who make up the majority of travelers in terms of volume, not revenue) now feel that a reward is most likely out of their reach, limiting the desire to join the program or stay loyal to one airline."[30] "All but the most frequent travelers are questioning the value of the programs," argue Drutsch et al., which will also affect their loyalty.[30] "This negative perception will eventually erode the desire for the majority of travelers to collect airline miles and therefore the value to outside purchasers, like credit card companies."[30] This could have a corrosive effect on the airline industry in general. The key will be to foster emotional loyalty and not simply transactional habits.[30]

Drutsch et al. believe that, "it is time for the airline industry to reassess its approach to loyalty, incorporating the current customer dynamic and technologies to engender loyalty from a greater share of their customers with a greater opportunity to increase knowledge about their total customer set and the marketing opportunities that hold."[30] In chapter one, I will further delve into how *The Predictive Airliner* can best utilize its loyalty program by utilizing the latest technological innovations in CRM, social, and real-time streaming technology.

As Kai Wähner explains in his article *Real-Time Stream Processing as Game Changer in a Big Data World with Hadoop and Data Warehouse*[31], "Stream processing is required when data has to be processed fast and/or continuously, i.e. reactions have to be computed and initiated in real time." Wähner continues[31]:

> "'Streaming processing' is the ideal platform to process data streams or sensor data (usually a high ratio of event throughput versus numbers of queries), whereas "complex event processing" (CEP) utilizes event-by-event processing and aggregation (e.g. on potentially out-of-order events from a variety of sources—often with large numbers of rules or business logic). CEP engines are optimized to process discreet 'business events' for example, to compare out-of-order or out-of-stream events, applying decisions and reactions to event patterns, and so on. For this reason, multiple types of event processing have evolved, described as queries, rules and procedural approaches (to event pattern detection)."

Stream processing acts on real-time streaming data feeds, using "continuous queries" (i.e., SQL-type queries that operate over time and buffer windows).[31] With its ability to continuously calculate mathematical or statistical analytics on the fly within the stream, streaming analytics is an essential part of stream processing. "Stream processing solutions are designed to handle high volume in real time with a scalable, highly available and fault tolerant architecture," adds Wähner.[31]

"In contrast to the traditional database model where data is first stored and indexed and then subsequently processed by queries, stream processing takes the inbound data while it is in flight, as it streams through the server," explains Wähner.[31] Stream processing can also connect to an external data source, thereby adding a whole new dimension to analytical processes.

For airline companies, real-time streaming can help in the following ways:

- Customer Service:
    - Geo-locating a customer when he or she signs onto an airline's Wi-Fi system (in an airline lounge for instance).
    - Video analytics with facial recognition technology can spot and/or confirm a customer's true identity.
    - Social media customer service can cut down on normal customer service expenses, as well as connect with customers on the channels that they prefer, i.e., Facebook, WhatsApp, WeChat, Instagram.
- E-Commerce
    - Clickstream analysis could allow personalized offers to a potentially returning passenger when he or she is browsing the airline's website to make a reservation.
    - Website data restructuring, which will be discussed in chapter six.Bellam
- Human Capital Management:
    - Employee schedules can be adjusted in real time according to labor management's needs, as well as the airline's predictive and anticipatory needs.
- Customer Management:
    - The ecommerce department can get more accurate attribution analysis—"the process of identifying a set of user actions ('events') that contribute in some manner to a desired outcome, and then assigning a value to each of these events"[32]—so that it understands which advertising is associated with which user, making it more quantifiable and, therefore, more actionable.
    - Customer Relationship Management (CRM) systems can add social media as a channel feeding targeted messages to only those customers who are most likely to respond to them.
    - The amount of promotions available and channels through which to market through increases considerably as campaign

lift can be assessed in terms of hours rather than in days, or weeks.
- Customer acquisition is accelerated because business users throughout the company can quickly derive answers to the following questions:
  - Which combinations of campaigns accelerate conversion?
  - What behavior signals churn?
  - Do web search key words influence deal size?
  - Which product features do users struggle with?
  - Which product features drive product adoption and renewal?
  - What drives customers to use costly sales channels?
- Customer interaction data can be turned into business opportunities quickly.
- Powerful recommendation engines can ingest data from a multitude of sources and then be made available to frontline staff, who can react in near real-time.

• Airport lounge stage:
  - Facial recognition technology allows for immediate knowledge of customers entering the airline store, which can improve customer service for both VIPs and high-end buyers.

• Point-of-Sale:
  - Outliers in a data set can uncover potentially fraudulent activity on POS systems.
  - Airlines can better target merchandise, sales, and promotions and help redesign store layouts and product placement to improve the customer experience.

• Security:
  - Uncover AML activity.
  - Spot suspicious activity.

In chapter five, I detail several different stream processing engines currently available, laying out each one's pros and cons, as well as explaining the required components for a stream processing system.

Since these are highly complex system, there are few market-ready products available, and a lot of custom coding is required to implement them.[31] However, products like Apache Storm, Apache Spark, IBM InfoSphere Streams, Hitachi's Streaming Data Platform, TIBCO StreamBase, and Apache Samza are all interesting platforms to explore. In chapter five, I detail how a stream processing engine would actually work for a digital marketing platform as the marketing department is one of the best places to use these systems.

In his article *How Real-time Marketing Technology Can Transform Your*

Business[33], Dan Woods makes an amusing comparison of the differing environments that marketers face today as compared to what their 1980s counterparts might have faced[33]:

> "Technology has changed marketing and market research into something less like golf and more like a multi-player first-person-shooter game. Crouched behind a hut, the stealthy marketers, dressed in business-casual camouflage, assess their weapons for sending outbound messages. Email campaigns, events, blogging, tweeting, PR, ebooks, white papers, apps, banner ads, Google Ad Words, social media outreach, search engine optimization. The brave marketers rise up and blast away, using weapons not to kill consumers but to attract them to their sites, to their offers, to their communities. If the weapons work, you get incoming traffic."

Successful mobile advertising requires three things—reach, purity and analytics. Reach can be fostered by accessing accounts through multiple platforms like blogs, geofencing applications, OTT services, mobile apps, QR codes, push and pull services, RSS feeds, search, social media sites, and video-casting, amongst others.[34] "Purity" refers to the message and its cleanliness; if the data is unstructured and untrustworthy it is, basically, useless and data governance is paramount for real-time advertising to work properly.[34] The third ingredient, analytics, "involves matching users' interests—implicit and explicit, context, preferences, network and handset conditions—to ads and promotions in real time."[34]

Knowing what might interest a costumer is only half the battle to making the sale and this is where customer analytics comes in. Customer analytics has evolved from simply reporting customer behavior to segmenting a customer based on his or her profitability, to predicting that profitability, to improving those predictions (because of the inclusion of new data), to *actually manipulating customer behavior* with target-specific promotional offers and marketing campaigns. These are the channels that real-time thrives in and this is where an airline can gain a powerful competitive advantage.

Real-time stream processing is an integral part of this rapidly changing marketing environment and if airlines don't join the real-time marketing world, they will be left behind, I have no doubt.

Composing the marketing message, however, is probably the easiest part of the process. In its *Delivering New Levels of Personalization In Consumer Engagement*[35], Forrester Research found that survey participants believed that personalization had the potential to increase traffic, raise customer conversion rates, and increase average order value. Surveyed marketers felt that personalization capabilities could improve a variety of business metrics, including customer retention (75%), lifetime customer value (75%), and customer conversion rates (71%).[35]

Today, "Personalization" is becoming the optimum word in a radically different business environment and even though this personalization comes at a price—privacy—it is a price most consumers seem more than willing to pay if a recognized value is received in return.

For an airline operator, "personalization" requires an investment in software analytics, but airlines should recognize that this price must be paid because highly sophisticated consumers will soon need an exceptional flying experience to keep them from going over to a competitor. This kind of personalization also gives the airline powerful information to build optimization models that can reduce cost and increase productivity.

These survey participants see email, call centers, corporate websites, mobile websites and physical locations (such as stadiums, sporting venues and hospitality sites) as today's key customer interaction channels, but any future marketing efforts to reach them should be "focused on mobile websites, applications, and social media channels."[35] Airline operators should keep these channels in mind while devising their customer experience (CX) campaigns.

Understanding customer-specified preferences is imperative for personalization; "80% of marketing executives currently use them in some or all interaction channels."[35] "In addition, 68% of marketers personalize current customer interactions based on past customer interaction history. Other commonly used personalization methods used by nearly 60% of firms in some or all of their interaction channels are based on the time of day or day of the week of customer interactions."[35] Forrester Research states that the difficulties of personalization include[35]:

1. Continuously optimizing campaigns in response to a customer's most recent interactions.
2. Optimizing content or offers for each person by matching identities to available products, promotions, messages, etc.
3. Creating a single repository containing structured and unstructured data about a consumer.
4. Delivering content or offers to a customer's chosen channel in real time for purposes of conversion.
5. Analyzing all available data in real time to create a comprehensive, contextually sensitive consumer profile.

The executives pooled by Forrester Research expected there to be a "huge rise in personalization using consumer's emotional state, social media sentiment, and context"[35] as well. "Only 29% of respondents claim today to use inferences about the consumer's emotional state in some or all channels. But 53% expect to do this in two to three years' time."[35] Forester's report goes on to add, "Only

52% of marketers currently use sentiments that consumers express in social media to personalize interactions today, but fully 79% expect to do this in two to three years. In addition, only 54% capitalize on the consumer's current contextual behavior, but 77% expect to do so in two to three years' time."[35]

Today, mobile apps, mobile commerce, mobile chat, and mobile gaming have revolutionized the way people do business, seek entertainment, and gamble. Mobile commerce has now evolved into what has become known as "omni-commerce", a seamless approach to selling that puts the shopper's experience front and center, giving that shopper access to what he or she wants through these multiple channels.

As behavioral economist Susan Menke explains in *Humanizing Loyalty*[36], "Decision fatigue and cognitive fatigue are the opposite of flow and seamlessness. We are making too many decisions that tax our cognitive bank account. We dole it out on important things and not on things that are already operating well." Here, Menke touches upon the concept of psychological scripts—the idea that the mind doesn't have to focus on many day-to-day activities as they can be handled without much thought. The more seamless a company makes the interaction process, the more likely a customer will continue to do business with them.

Mobile marketing via Bluetooth, NFC, OTT, SMS, MMS, CSC and/or QR codes has become some of the most effective marketing available, while social media has turned the normal channels of marketing on its head. By accessing the Web through a wifi connection, mobile users can surf the Internet as seamlessly as if they were using a PC at home. With little more than the touch of a button, photos and videos can be uploaded seconds after they are taken, then shared with the most intimate of friends or the most distant of peoples. Live streaming channels allow cheap video streams that can be viewed almost anywhere in the world as well.

The mobile platform is so robust, and it holds so much promise that if a marketing executive had been asked to dream up the perfect device to connect to, market to, and sell its company's products and/or services to its customers and potential customers, he or she could hardly have come up with something more superior to it. One of mobile's best features is its ability to cross-pollinate the marketing message through several mediums, which include social media—and I will expound upon this throughout the book.

In its paper *5 Marketing Prediction for the Next 5 Years*[37], the B2C marketing cloud company Emarsys argues that, "Smart marketers need real-time insights into mobile marketing performance in order to understand how end users are (or aren't) engaging with their mobile marketing programs or applications."

Emarsys argues that[37]:

> "We will move from a world focused on designing for mobile as a secondary approach, to designing for mobile first. E-commerce organizations will finally fully alter the online shopping experience from responsive to completely mobile experiences. This mobile-only approach will be different, as it won't just be a smaller design but will also include more responsive websites and shopping experiences. The mobile-only experience will lead to fully tailored shopping experiences primarily designed for engagement on a mobile device."

Emarsys goes on to add that: "Within the next five years, consumers will be able to swipe right, up, and down to make their selections, all via their mobile devices. And when the consumer is ready to complete the transaction? Easy. It just takes one click; the purchase is complete, and the items arrive at the consumer's house."[37]

In their *5 Marketing Predictions For the Next 5 Years,* Emarsys concludes that, "In an effort to remain competitive and innovative in today's digital and always-connected world, marketers should continually be piloting and testing mobile strategies with a small subset of their users or target audience."[37] However "If a brand slows mobile innovation, or pauses testing and optimization for mobile devices, the brand is risking the loyalty of current users as well as jeopardizing new user acquisition," warns Emarsys.[37]

Much more than a wireless transmitter optimized for voice input and output, a mobile phone, a tablet is an always-on, anytime, anywhere marketing and sales tool that follows a mobile user throughout his or her digital day. It is also an entertainment, CRM, and social networking tool, which makes it, potentially, the most powerful device in the history of marketing and customer relations. The mobile device is, literally, a marketing tool that can—and usually is—personalized by its owner, and it is within reach of that owner almost every hour of every single day—once again a marketer's dream.

Push technology even puts the power of communication into the hands of the marketer, allowing airline operators to both initiate contact with an opted-in customer and then send him or her a wide variety of products and content. As long as a customer is opted into a CRM system, an airliner can foster a two-way dialogue with that customer and this dialogue can grow more sophisticated over time as more is learned about the customer's wants, desires, habits, and needs.

Push technology has moved from clumsy blanket SMS blasts to the sophisticated use of mobile apps that allow customers to interact with their personal customer information, including looking up points balances, checking in, and even purchasing upgrades or even items in an online mall.

I didn't want this book to only focus on developments in the United States, as I believe some of the most interesting things happening right now in the mobile, social media occur in Asia. I had thought this before I moved to Macau in 2011 and my suspicions were confirmed after I made a few trips into China during the ensuing years.

Corporations of all kinds now use WeChat to connect with their customers or potential customers in highly imaginative and sometimes very lucrative ways. WeChat has also introduced WePay, an in-app payment system that allows users to make one-click payments from their bank accounts. A scanning feature lets users get pricing information from bar codes as well.

In Hong Kong, China, and Macau, the WeChat green and white logo is almost as ubiquitous as the blue and white Facebook logo and I would argue that, as a marketing vehicle, it is just as effective, if not more so. Small mom and pop stores are using WeChat to market their wares, filling up the "Moments" thread with their latest offerings, whether they are clothes, food, shoes, handbags, etc., etc.

Since WeChat accepts payments, oftentimes buyers can purchase directly from their mobile phones; there's an entire ecosystem built within WeChat that means buyers never have to leave the app to make purchases and/or comment on them.

One of the most important elements of social media is its inter-connectedness. An upload to YouTube can go viral through Twitter, Facebook, LinkedIn, WeChat, WhatsApp, Youku, as well as a whole host of other social media and mobile media platforms. Within seconds, something uploaded onto a social media website in the US can end up on a mobile application in China or Japan or Korea, or almost anywhere else in the world that has mobile or Wi-Fi access. United Airlines knows all too well about the pitfalls of social media, it takes the crown in terms of social media crises for airlines, with Dave Carroll's United Breaks Guitars[38] song, as well as the forcible removal of David Dao from Express Flight 3411 on April 9, 2017[39] serious stains on the company's reputation. We are truly living in an interconnected world and this interconnectedness is creating a whole host of channels that airlines need to monitor for customer issues and comments.

Social media will also be explored in depth throughout this book. It is quite ironic that, in one sense, engaging in social media can be one of the most anti-social behaviors one can do; sitting alone in a room, typing away on a computer was once the realm of solitary computer geeks, but it has now become an activity that most people engage in almost every single day, both at home and on the go. Perhaps this is because human beings are, first and foremost, social beings and we crave an interconnectedness that social media offers, even if it is just a virtual connection.

It should be of no surprise that one of the greatest inventions of the twentieth century—the internet—would became the watering hole of the twenty-first century; a place where human beings can quickly gather to socialize and connect with friends, family members, and acquaintances in a way that was almost inconceivable only 20 years ago. Smart airlines marketers can tap into this interconnectedness to get their marketing message out far and wide.

Almost a decade ago, "most consumers logged on to the Internet to access e-mail, search the Web, and do some online shopping. Company Web sites functioned as vehicles for corporate communication, product promotion, customer service, and, in some cases, e-commerce. Relatively few people were members of online communities"[40] and "Liking" something had no social relevance at all. How times have changed.

"Today, more than 1.5 billion people around the globe have an account on a social networking site, and almost one in five online hours is spent on social networks—increasingly via mobile devices."[40] In little more than a decade, social technology has become a cultural, social, political and economic phenomenon.[40] More importantly, "hundreds of millions of people have adopted new behaviors using social media—conducting social activities on the Internet, creating and joining virtual communities, organizing political activities"[40], even, as with the case of Egypt's "Twitter Revolution", toppling corrupt governments.

In his article *Understanding social media in China*[40], C. I. Chui argues that the secret to social media's growth is right there in its name—"Social"—as in the fundamental human behavior of seeking "identity and 'connectedness' through affiliations with other individuals and groups that share their characteristics, interests, or beliefs."[40]

For Chui, "Social media taps into well known, basic sociological patterns and behaviors, sharing information with members of the family or community, telling stories, comparing experiences and social status with others, embracing stories by people with whom we desire to build relations, forming groups, and defining relationships to others." [40]

Social technologies allow individuals to interact with large groups of people at almost any location in the world, at any time of the day, at marginal, if not no cost at all.[40] With advantages like these, it is not surprising that social media has become so widespread that almost one in four people worldwide uses it. It is actually surprising that the figure is so low, although with mobile technology rolling out in some of the most remote locations on earth, that figure is sure to climb rapidly over the next few years.

Businesses are quickly recognizing the power of social media. In his article *The Social Economy: Unlocking Value and Productivity Through Social Technologies*[41], M. M. Chui argues that, "Thousands of companies have found that social technologies can generate rich new forms of consumer insights–at lower cost and faster than conventional methods."[41] In addition to this, businesses can watch what "consumers do and say to one another on social platforms, which provide unfiltered feedback and behavioral data (i.e., do people who "like" this movie also "like" this brand of vodka?)."[40] This can be a treasure trove of company competitive analysis and I believe airline operators would profit from spending more on their social media listening efforts rather than holding expensive and not always completely trustworthy focus groups.

Social technologies also "have enormous potential to raise the productivity of knowledge workers,"[41] a very significant development in a world where knowledge workers are becoming highly sought-after assets. "Social technologies promise to extend the capabilities of such high-skill workers (who are increasingly in short supply) by streamlining communication and collaboration, lowering barriers between functional silos, and even redrawing the boundaries of the enterprise to bring in additional knowledge and expertise in 'extended networked enterprises.'"[41]

In this book, I will use Chui et al.'s definition of "social technologies" as the "products and services that enable social interactions in the digital realm, and thus allow people to connect and interact virtually."[41] These include[41]:

> "A message to be communicated (a tweet or a blog), adding content to what is already online, or adding information about content ('liking' a piece of content). Content creation also includes performing an action that an individual knows will be automatically shared (e.g., listening to a piece of music when you know your music choice will be displayed to others). Social technologies allow anyone within a group to access and consume content or information. They include technologies that also have been described as 'social media,' 'Web 2.0' and 'Collaboration tools'."

In their book *Marketing Communications: Integrating Offline and Online with Social Media*[42], P.R. Smith and Ze Zook show just how powerful social media marketing can be. The authors looked at the target audiences for three different types of marketing platforms—broadcast network, telephone and email networks, and social media.[42]

According to Smith and Zook, "Broadcast network is based on a 'one to many' model (e.g., old TV advertising).[42] It is the Sarnoff network (after David Sarnoff, the broadcasting legend).[42] A hypothetical Sarnoff network with 20 viewers has a score of 20.[42] The network score is simply the number of nodes (i.e., audience members)" and this equates to a paltry sum of twenty individuals.[42]

The telephone and email network is based on the Metcalf model (named after Bob Metcalf, one of the inventors of the Internet) and this is a "many to each other" model.[42] This model allows everyone in the group to connect with everyone else.[42] Because any member of the group can contact anyone else in the group, the total number of potential contacts is 20 squared, or 400.[42] Obviously, this is a much more powerful communication model than the Sarnoff model as the network score is the node number to the power of 2, which is 400.[42] A good number, but it still pales in comparison to the social network model.

Named after David Reed (who noticed that people in social situations usually belong to more than just one network), the social network model is a "many belong to numerous networks" model.[42] "The possible value of a Reed network is two to the power of the number of nodes on the network," explain Smith and Zook.[42] If you take the same group of 20 people in a social situation, a "Reed network generates a score of 2 to the power of the node"[42], which generates a network score of over one million people; obviously, this is a number exponentially higher than the number of people reached by the Sarnoff and Metcalf models. This is the power of social media and it cannot be underestimated. When coupled with mobile, that number can be even greater and, just as importantly, the reach can be lightning fast.

In China, users spend more than 40 percent of their time online on social media websites, a figure that is expected to continue its rapid rise over the next few years.[40] "This appetite for all things social has spawned a dizzying array of companies, many with tools that are more advanced than those in the West: for example, Chinese users were able to embed multimedia content in social media more than 18 months before Twitter users could do so in the United States."[40]

Companies like WeChat are revolutionizing social networks, adding malls as part of their platforms, while Taobao has teamed up with Weibo to allow instant commentary and blogging on purchased items. yy.com has inverted the concept of reality TV, by taking a singing competition and broadcasting it over the internet, while allowing viewers to directly remunerate the contestants.

There is an old adage in social media marketing that says, "Content is king" and, with social media, that adage has never been truer. Those destined to succeed in the social media world won't be the ones with the most content; they will be the ones with the best and most searchable content. And that content will drive eyeballs unlike any other form of marketing in the history of advertising. To succeed in this new environment, airlines should think of themselves first and foremost as creators and syndicators of content.[43] Although content is important, the ultimate goal here is conversions, lead generation, and sales.

Chapter three delves into the world of social media, including a breakdown of Kaplan and Haenlein's six types of social media.[44] In their influential article *Users of the world, unite! The challenge and opportunities of Social Media*[44], Kaplan and Haenlein show how all social media websites can be broken down into one of six different types; collaborative projects; blogs and micro-blogs; content communities; Social networking sites; virtual game worlds; and virtual social worlds.[44] Anyone devising a social media marketing plan for an airline should find this chapter particularly helpful in understanding how to use each separate social channel and platform, both singularly and combined together.

As I break down each individual type of social media platform, I also include information about the most important websites and social channels within their group, but please keep in mind that social media literally changes by the day and companies come and go faster than in almost any other industry, so some might be extinct by the time you are reading this book.

Throughout the book, I will discuss mobile and social media in China as well. I am looking at that country individually, not only because it is the biggest social media market in the world, but also because its censorship rules make it highly unique and a potential minefield for businesses to navigate through.

Facebook might be the biggest social network in the world, but its penetration in China is minimal and it will probably remain so for a long time to come, not only because China sensors Facebook, but also because Facebook's Chinese competitors are creating some very technologically savvy products.

WeChat, in particular, has proven to be highly successful, and it is growing rapidly, both in China and throughout the rest of the world, but companies like QQ, Weibo, Hexun, Youku, Jiepang, Qieke, Ushi and Ku6 are all experiencing exponential growth. With a base of 1.3 billion people, it isn't too hard for services that catch on in China to rapidly get to tens of millions of users within a year or even sooner.

In August 2017, Steven Millward noted in his article *Facebook's new China app is reliant on WeChat*[45] that Facebook launched a photo-sharing app to test the waters in a market that Facebook has been locked out of since 2009. As Millward writes, "Facebook's new app, a China-segregated photo-sharing service called Colorful Balloons, is reliant on WeChat for its viral growth.[45] The app is not connected to Facebook and it cannot tap into a user's Facebook contacts.[45] "Hit the WeChat button, and you will send your friend an invite to your photo album within Facebook's new app. It's made up of an album preview plus a QR code, sent via a WeChat message, which takes your buddy either to the Colorful Balloons app or to the iOS App Store," notes Millward.[45] Going forward, Facebook's road in China is not going to get any easier and piggy-backing off Chinese social apps like WeChat might be the best way to get a foothold in that vast market. Facebook is trying its best to break into the market, but its most recent problems with fake news in the US might mean its road into China just got a lot tougher.

In chapter four, I explain how an airline can use social media to succeed in today's cutthroat airline business environment, answering such questions as:

- How can an airline measure the benefits of social media?
- How should an airline organize its social media presence or presences?
- How should an airline spread social media usage throughout its organization?

- How has social media changed the relationship between a customer and an airline?

In this chapter, I will also break down the ways in which an airline should use social media, including:

- Adding interactivity to a Website
- Brand and Anti-brand management
- Building fanbases and communities
- Crisis management
- Discovering a customer's psychological profile
- Discovering important brand trends
- Driving traffic to a Website
- Engaging customers and potential customers
- Harvesting customer feedback
- Influencer marketing
- Marketing to consumers
- Reputation management

Starbucks has developed a metric it believes quantifies the value of its social media marketing in terms of media spend—the "company's 6.5 million Facebook fans are worth the equivalent of a US $23.4 million annual spend, according to calculations by social media specialists Virtue, reported in Adweek."[46] Virtue claims that, on average, "a fan base of 1 million translates to at least $3.6 million in equivalent media over a year, or $3.6 per fan. Virtue arrived at its $3.6 million figure by working off a $5 CPM, meaning a brand's 1 million fans generate about $300,000 in media value each month."[46] That's quite a significant amount of money and, if a coffee company can find success in social media, airlines should be able to get similar ROI.

One company that is certainly doing analytics and customer service right is Disney. As Cliff Kuang explains in his article *Disney's $1 Billion Bet on a Magical Wristband*[47], Disney has created wristbands they call "MagicBands" that look like simple, stylish rubber wristbands, but they are anything but simple. They contain an RFID chip and a radio transmitter that connects the wearer to a vast and powerful system of sensors within the Disneyworld park.[47]

If visitors sign up in advance for the so-called "Magical Express", the MagicBand replaces all of the details and hassles of paper once the visitor touches-down in Orlando.[47] Express users can board a park-bound shuttle, and check into the hotel wirelessly.[47] Visitors don't have to mind their luggage, because each piece gets tagged at their home airport.[47] Upon arrival at the park, there are no tickets to hand over, visitors just have to tap their MagicBand at the gate and swipe for the rides they've already reserved.[47] For Disney, this technology also helps them cut down on the need for hotel check-in staff, thereby saving considerable labor expense.[47]

As Kuang explains, with the MagicBand, "there's no need to rent a car or waste time at the baggage carousel. You don't need to carry cash, because the MagicBand is linked to your credit card. You don't need to wait in long lines. You don't even have to go to the trouble of taking out your wallet when your kid grabs a stuffed Olaf, looks up at you, and promises to be good if you'll just let them have this one thing, please."[47] Disney has, obviously, thought of everything.

For Disney, the MagicBands are nothing less than thousands of sensors that communicate directly with the park's IT databases that basically turns the park into a giant computer—streaming real-time data about where guests are, what they are doing, and what they want.[47] Most importantly, the system is designed to anticipate the guest's desires, i.e., predicting their granular behavior.[47]

In chapter five, Hadoop takes center stage. A Hadoop database is the cornerstone of any data lake and throughout this chapter I will explain how to design an HDFS schema, what to consider regarding data ingestion, compression, and extraction. Hadoop can get very complicated, very quickly, so any company wishing to implement a Hadoop database should understand all of the components it is made of; from A (Avro) to Z (Zookeeper), and a bunch of products in-between.

I will also explain the current stream processing and machine learning (ML) solutions available on the market so that an airline can build a powerful EDW that ingests social media data and then fires off a marketing coupon to the right person at the right time, at the right price, to be used at the right location, at just the right moment, at just the right ROI; A worthy goal, if ever there was one.

Chapter six brings everything together; Using real world examples from some of the biggest airlines on the world, I will reveal ways to increase website traffic and I will offer some suggestions on how airlines can build up customer profiles by tracking IP addresses, then associating those with browser footprints, device IDs, social IDs, email addresses, and, ultimately, with passenger transactions. Creating an holistic view of one's customers reveals the true value of that customer and once a true value has been created, marketing offers can be better tailored to the individual, which usually means they are more likely to be used.

In this chapter, I will give examples that reveal how social networks like Instagram, Facebook, Snapchat, et al are pushing into the airline industry, both on the advertising and the commerce side. "Facebook wants to be a solution not just at the very bottom of the marketing funnel for solutions like retargeting, we actually want to create new purchase intent and consideration further up," claims Graham Mudd, product marketing director at Facebook[48] and the company is spending a fortune on its efforts to break into a market that has, so far, eluded them.

Facebook believes that in 2018 and beyond, video will drive more online sales and its new dynamic ads features will allow brands and airlines to upload videos to show-off their products catalogues.[48] Facebook is also introducing overlays for dynamic ads and the largest social network site in the world is set to let airlines and brands target consumers based on households, rather than just as individuals.[48]

For its part, Snapchat, which has hit a rough patch in terms of revenue, is looking to snap out of its conundrum with its two new forms of ads: "Promoted Stories which string together multiple Snaps into longer-form slideshows openable from a tile on the Stories page that's shown to everyone in a given country, and Augmented Reality Trial ads that let people play with an AR version of a product overlaid on the world around them."[49]

I will detail these and other changes on all the other types of social media channels in his chapter. I will also include real like examples that airlines both large and small can utilize immediately, as well as showcase what is on the marketing horizon.

What has become known as the "Dark Social", i.e., "one-on-one social sharing that is happening where analytics tools cannot track it,"[50] makes it increasingly difficult for social channels to track full attribution. In the coming years, there might be a way to track this type of attribution, and this might be stepping into 1984 territory, but we might have no choice but to go there and this does seem to be a place that China is more than willing to go.

Chapter five delves into the connected airline. According to sitaonline.com's *The Connected Aircraft: Airline's 2020 vision*[51], "More than 90% of airlines are set to ramp up investment in advancing wireless services for cabin crew and pilots over the three years to 2020 – an 18% increase since SITA's 2016 Airline IT Trends survey."

The report goes onto add, "Enhancing the passenger experience is far and away the connected aircraft's biggest encountered and perceived benefit, according to 43% of airlines. A combined 31% meanwhile, cited operational benefits across maintenance and aircraft health monitoring, cockpit and cabin, as the chief advantages of a connected aircraft. In testament to this, 78% of surveyed carriers reported automatic aircraft data management as an investment priority – 33% through major programs, 45% in R&D programs – by 2020."[51]

As Bernard Marr explains in his article *How Big Data Drives Success At Rolls-Royce*[52] today's airplane "engines and propulsion systems are all fitted with hundreds of sensors which record every tiny detail about their operation and report any changes in data in real-time to engineers who will decide the best course of action such as scheduling maintenance or dispatching engineering teams should the problem require it."

I agree with Marr that "Big Data is about much more than the volume of data which is generated. It's also about the increasingly sophisticated methods of computer analysis which can be applied to this data—in the hope of drawing out insights which can drive efficiency and progress."[52]

With civil airplane engines being as reliable as they are, "the emphasis shifts to keeping them performing to their maximum, saving airlines fuel and meeting their schedules."[52] "Big Data analytics helps Rolls-Royce identify maintenance actions days or weeks ahead of time, so airlines can schedule the work without passengers experiencing any disruption," explains Marr.[52] "To support this, analytics on-board the engines crunch through terabytes of data each flight, and transmit just the pertinent highlights to ground for further analysis. Once at the gate, the whole flight data is available for engineers to examine and detect the fine margins of performance improvement," says Marr.[52] "Data analytics are run across all of those data sets," says Paul Stein, chief scientific officer. "We are looking for anomalies—whether pressure, temperatures or vibration measurements are an indicator that an engine needs to be services," adds Stein.[52]

The next generation of aircraft and engines will be permanently connected to a data center, which will allow "engineers to turn the dial up or down on the data transmitted in-flight or even deploy a new analytic across the whole fleet in seconds."[52]

In chapter six, I reference Lozio Heracleous and Jochen Wirtz's *Harvard Business Review* article *The Globe: Singapore Airlines' Balancing Act*[53], which details how Singapore Airlines (SIA) "has combined the supposedly incompatible strategies of differentiation—which it pursues through service excellence and continuous innovation—and cost leadership." The article might be a decade old but many of SIA's methods are worth studying as they are a leader in both customer service and profit.

As Heracleous and Wirtz explain, "Few enterprises have executed a dual strategy profitably; indeed, management experts such as Michael Porter argue that it's impossible to do so for a sustained period since dual strategies entail contradictory investments and organizational processes. Yet pursuing dual strategies is becoming an imperative."[53] The demand for value-for-money products and services increased after the 2008 recession and has remained in full effect to this day, especially in the airline industry, and particularly in developing countries, which is where SIA generally operates in.[53] Cost conscious consumers have forced producers of premium offerings to figure out how to grab opportunities in the middle and the low end of the market and SIA has succeeded enormously in this area.[53]

SIA executes "a dual strategy by managing four paradoxes: providing service excellence cost-effectively; innovating in both a centralized and a decentralized manner; being a technology leader and a follower; and achieving standardization and personalization in its processes."[53] I will delve further into each of strategies in chapter six.

According to SIA, "Strategic alignment, not financial returns, must guide investment decisions. Executives should ask: What investments should we undertake to achieve both strategies? This mind-set should prevail even when rates of return are difficult to calculate or when investments are large."[53] SIA lives by its words and one interesting example from the article proves this: Amongst airline chefs, it is a known fact that a "person's ability to taste food declines by about 40% at an altitude of 30,000 feet because of the dry air."[53] To ensure the food on its flights take this change into account, "SIA invested $700,000 to build a facility that enables chefs to taste food under pressurized flight conditions," which is quite an investment to ensure your customers are cowith their food.[53]

I started this introduction with an allusion of Big Data being either a treasure chest or a Pandora's Box of pain and it can certainly be either one but going down the Big Data road requires a commitment that is all encompassing and an acceptance that it could require radical changes in corporate thinking.

State of the art technology is required and that always means there is the potential for severe bumps in the road along the way. However, it is a road that must be traveled as today's consumers have become highly sophisticated and they demand a level of personalization for their continuing patronage; if a company's marketing efforts aren't personal enough, these consumers will easily find another company that does provide the level of service they demand.

Throughout the book, I will try to avoid what has become known as "wish casting", a useful term that the field of meteorology has recently given us. As Rob Tracinski explains in his article *How Not to Predict the Future*[54], "It started with the observation that weathermen disproportionately predict sunny weather on the 4th of July and snow on Christmas Day. Their forecasts are influenced not just by the evidence, but by what they (or their audience) want to hear." The writer of any book that delves into current and future technology will, obviously, be susceptible to wish casting, but I will try to temper my enthusiasm and add a dash of skepticism to all I write here.

I will also try to avoid "Zeerust" — "The particular kind of datedness which afflicts things that were originally designed to look futuristic."[55] Taken from *The Meaning of Liff* by Douglas Adams, *TV Tropes* explains it this way: "datedness behind zeerusty designs lies in the attempt of the past designers to get an advantage over the technology of their time, only to find out that more mundane designs are actually far more efficient if advanced engineering and craftsmanship are used on them."[55]

Throughout this book, I will offer my honest assessment of the technology I discuss, trying to be as agnostic and objective as possible. Personally, I prefer not to go down rabbit holes of technology that, while proving quite colorful, exciting and interesting, really lead to nowhere, so I will try to point out paths that I think advisable to both take and not to take, always keeping a firm eye on the airliner's fiscal bottom line.

In French, "ROI" (or "Roi" more precisely) literally means "King" and in this book, ROI is king; every piece of technology I discuss will be looked at through the lens of ROI. As I detail in this book, positive ROI can be created with AI and machine learning, all forms of analytics, marketing, and social media, amongst other channels. I will provide detailed examples of this throughout.

It is my hope that this book can help airlines of every size and shape drive up their sales and helps them build stronger customer relationships, because that is ultimately what will increase ROI.

---

1 IATA. (2017). Strong Airline Profitability Continues in 2018. 5 December 2017. (Accessed 17 August 2018).
https://www.iata.org/pressroom/pr/Pages/2017-12-05-01.aspx (Accessed 17 August 2018).
2 Steimer, Sarah. (2018). How Airlines Get Customer Experience So Wrong with So Much Data. 24 January 2018. American Marketing Association. https://www.ama.org/publications/MarketingNews/Pages/how-airlines-get-customer-experience-so-wrong-with-so-much-data.aspx (Accessed 6 August 2018).
3 Investopedia. How much revenue in the airline industry comes from business travelers compared to leisure travelers? https://www.investopedia.com/ask/answers/041315/how-much-revenue-airline-industry-comes-business-travelers-compared-leisure-travelers.asp (Accessed 15 August 2018).
4 https://en.wikipedia.org/wiki/United_Express_Flight_3411_incident (Accessed 16 August 2018).
5 https://en.wikipedia.org/wiki/American_Airlines (Accessed 9 August 2018).
6 Bölke, Susanne. (2014) Strategic Marketing Approaches Within Airline Management: How the Passenger Market Causes the Business Concepts of Full Service Network Carriers, Low Cost Carriers, Regional Carriers and Leisure Carriers to Overlap. Anchor Academic Publishing, 2014.
7 Boland, Declan, Morrison, Doug, O'Neill, Sean. (2002). The Future of CRM in the airline industry: A new paradigm for customer management. IBM Institute for Business Value. 12-02-2002.
8 Bellamy III, Woodrow. (2017). Avionics. December 2017/January 2018. http://interactive.aviationtoday.com/avionicsmagazine/december-2017-january-2018/data-analytics-driving-efficiency-in-commercial-aviation/ (Accessed 3 August 2018).
9 Reed, Dan. (2018). How Airlines Decide What You'll Pay To Fly Is About To Change Dramatically. Forbes. 7 June 2018.

https://www.forbes.com/sites/danielreed/2018/06/07/airline-fares-ndc/ (Accessed 10 August 2018).
10 Ulanoff, Lance. Amazon Knows What You Want Before You Buy It. January 27, 2014. Predictive Analytics Times. http://www.predictiveanalyticsworld.com/patimes/amazon-knows-what-you-want-before-you-buy-it/3185/ (Accessed February 16, 2017).
11 http://www-01.ibm.com/software/data/bigdata/ (Accessed December 6, 2016)
12 Anderson, C. (2004). Wired. The Long Tail, pp. 171-177.
13 Berman, S. J. (2007). Executive Brief: Navigating the media divide: Innovating and enabling new business models. IBM Institute for Business Value.
14 Bellamy III, Woodrow. (2017). Avionics. December 2017/January 2018. http://interactive.aviationtoday.com/avionicsmagazine/december-2017-january-2018/data-analytics-driving-efficiency-in-commercial-aviation/ (Accessed 3 August 2018).
15 Eissler, Annie. 25 April 2017. How Much ROI Can Data Analytics Deliver? MITS Blog. https://www.mits.com/blog/how-much-roi-can-data-analytics-deliver (Accessed 22 August 2017)
16 Marr, Bernard. August 23, 2016. Will 'Analytics on The Edge' Be the Future of Big Data? Online: http://www.forbes.com/sites/bernardmarr/2016/08/23/will-analytics-on-the-edge-be-the-future-of-big-data/#124af7ea2b09
17 CUHK Develops Real-time Trolley Supply Monitoring System with AI-based Video Content Analytics Enhancing Service Quality of Hong Kong International Airport. (2017). Chinese Universtiy of Hong Kong. 11 September 2017. https://www.cpr.cuhk.edu.hk/en/press_detail.php?id=2589&t=cuhk-develops-real-time-trolley-supply-monitoring-system-with-ai-based-video-content-analytics-enhancing-service-quality-of-hong-kong-international-airport&id=2589&t=cuhk-develops-real-time-trolley-supply-monitoring-system-with-ai-based-video-content-analytics-enhancing-service-quality-of-hong-kong-international-airport (Accessed 5 August 2018).
18 Gartner. (2013, December 12). Gartner Says the Internet of Things Installed Base Will Grow to 26 Billion Units By 2020. Retrieved from Gartner.com: http://www.gartner.com/newsroom/id/2636073
19 Ashton, K. (2009, June 22). That 'Internet of Things' Thing. Retrieved from RFID Journal: http://www.rfidjournal.com/articles/view?4986
20 Silver, Vernon. (2018). Putin soccer ball for Trump had transmitter chip, logo indicates. Bloomberg.com. 25 July 2018. https://www.bloomberg.com/news/articles/2018-07-25/putin-soccer-ball-for-trump-had-transmitter-chip-logo-indicates
21 Morgan, J. (2014, May 13). A Simple Explanation of 'the Internet of Things'. Retrieved from Forbes.com: http://www.forbes.com/sites/jacobmorgan/2014/05/13/simple-explanation-internet-things-that-anyone-can-understand/
22 Top 8 Trends in Big Data for 2016. http://www.tableau.com/about/blog/2015/12/top-8-trends-big-data-2016-47846
23 Swift, R. (2001). Accelerating customer relationships: Using CRM and relationship technologies. Upper Saddle River: Prentice Hall.
24 Kincaid, J. (2003). Customer relationship management: Getting it right. Upper Saddle River, NJ: Prentice Hall.

25 Parvatiyar, A. &. Sheth, JN (2001). Customer relationship management: Emerging practice, process, and discipline. Journal of Economic & Social Research, 3, 1 - 34.

26 Ngai, N. X. (2009). Application of data mining techniques in customer relationship management: a literature review and classification. Expert systems with applications, 2592-2602.

27 https://en.wikipedia.org/wiki/Frequent-flyer_program (Accessed 4 August 2018).

28 Josephs, Leslie. Airlines to rake in record $57 billion in passenger fees this year. CNBC.com. 27 November 2017. https://www.cnbc.com/2017/11/27/airlines-to-rake-in-record-57-billion-in-passenger-fees-this-year.html (Accessed 4 August 2018).

29 Pfeffer, Jeffrey. (2014). How airline loyalty programs seduce and abandon you. Fortune. 1 October 2014. http://fortune.com/2014/10/01/airline-loyalty-programs/ (Accessed 5 August 2018).

30 Drusch, Mark, Horowitz, Austin, and Severin, Alex. (2018). Customers are driving the need to evolve airline loyalty programs. 11 April 2018. ICF Inc. https://www.icf.com/blog/aviation/airline-loyalty-program-timeline (Accessed 5 August 2018).

31 Wähner, Kai (2014, September 10). Real-Time Stream Processing as Game Changer in a Big Data World with Hadoop and Data Warehouse. InfoQ. https://www.infoq.com/articles/stream-processing-hadoop/

32 Interactive Advertising Bureau. (2012). Attribution Primer. Retrieved from iab.net: http://www.iab.net/media/file/AttributionPrimer.pdf

33 Woods, D. (2011, May 6). How Real-time Marketing Technology Can Transform Your Business. Retrieved from Forbes.com: http://www.forbes.com/sites/ciocentral/2011/05/06/how-real-time-marketing-technology-can-transform-your-business/

34 Sharma, C. H. (2008). Mobile Advertising: Supercharge Your Brand in the Exploding Wireless Market. John Wiley & Sons, Inc.

35 Forrester Research. (2013, November). Delivering New Levels Of Personalization In Consumer Engagement. Retrieved from sap.com: https://www.sap.com/bin/sapcom/he_il/downloadasset.2013-11-nov-21-22.delivering-new-levels-of-personalization-in-consumer-engagement-pdf.html

36 Humanizing Loyalty A road map to establishing genuine emotional loyalty at scale. Olson1to1.com. https://go.icf.com/rs/072-WJX-782/images/Humanizing%20Loyalty%20-%20Olson%201to1.pdf (Accessed 6 August 2018).

37 Emarsys. 5 E-Commerce Marketing Predictions for the Next 5 Years. https://www.emarsys.com/en/resources/whitepapers/5-e-commerce-marketing-predictions-for-the-next-5-years/

38 https://en.wikipedia.org/wiki/United_Breaks_Guitars (Accessed 5 August 2018).

39 https://en.wikipedia.org/wiki/United_Express_Flight_3411_incident (Accessed 5 August 2018).

40 Chiu, C. I. (2012, April). Understanding social media in China. Retrieved from www.mckinsey.com: http://www.mckinsey.com/insights/marketing_sales/understanding_social_media_in_china

41 Chui, M. M. et al. (2012). The social economy: Unlocking value and productivity through social technologies. McKinsey Global Institute.
42 Smith, P. Z. (2011). Marketing Communications: Integrating Offline and Online with Social Media; Third Edition. Kogan Page.
43 Black, L. M. (2012, November 11). 7 social media marketing tips for artists and galleries. Retrieved from Mashable: http://mashable.com/2012/11/10/social-media-marketing-tips-artists-galleries/
44 Kaplan, A. H. (2010). Users of the world unite! The challenges and opportunities of social media. Business Horizons, Vol. 53, Issue 1.
45 Millward, Steven. August 12, 2017. Facebook's new China app is reliant on WeChat. Techinasia.com. https://www.techinasia.com/facebook-china-app-reliant-on-wechat (Accessed August 18, 2017).
46 Woodcock, N. G. (2011). Social CRM as a business strategy. Database Marketing & Customer Strategy Management, Vol. 18, 1, 50-64.
47 Kuang, Cliff. March 3, 2015. Disney's $1 Billion Bet On A Magical Wristband. Wired. https://www.wired.com/2015/03/disney-magicband (Accessed 19 January 2017).
48 Dua, Tanya. (2017). Facebook wants to become the new mobile storefront, unveils new ad tools for brands and airlines. Business Insider. 27 June 2017. http://www.businessinsider.com/facebook-wants-to-become-the-new-mobile-storefront-2017-6 (Accessed 25 November 2017).
49 Constine, Josh. (2017). Snapchat seek salvation in long-form and "hands-on" AR ads. Techcrunch.com. https://techcrunch.com/2017/11/24/anything-for-arpu/ (Accessed 25 November 2017).
50 Teeters, Nicole. 2017. 10 Social Meida Trends Giving Brands New Ways to Engage in 2017. Adweek. http://www.adweek.com/digital/nicole-teeters-wire-stone-guest-post-10-social-media-trends-2017/#/ (Accessed 24 November 2017).
51 Sitaonair. (2017). The Connected Aircraft: airline's 2020 vision. https://www.sitaonair.aero/two-thirds-of-airlines-new-connected-service-era-2020/
52 Marr, Bernard. (2015). How Big Data Drives Success At Rolls-Royce. Forbes 1 June 2015. https://www.forbes.com/sites/bernardmarr/2015/06/01/how-big-data-drives-success-at-rolls-royce/#2973cc741d69 (Accessed 17 August 2018).
53 Heracleous, Loizos and Wirtz, Jochen. (2010). Harvard Business Review. July-August 2010. https://hbr.org/2010/07/the-globe-singapore-airlines-balancing-act (Accessed 6 August 2018).
54 Tracinski, Rob. October 13, 2016. How Not to Predict the Future. Real Clear Future. http://www.realclearfuture.com/articles/2016/10/13/how_not_to_predict_the_future_111945.html
55 http://tvtropes.org/pmwiki/pmwiki.php/Main/Zeerust (Accessed 15 November 2017).

CHAPTER ONE

Customer Intelligence

"If you're competitor-focused, you have to wait until there is a competitor doing something. Being customer-focused allows you to be more pioneering."

~ Jeff Bezos,
CEO of Amazon

Overview

We live in an instant gratification world and the companies that are likely to thrive in this new environment will be the ones who can both keep up with the requirements of their discerning and demanding customers and also predict what these customers will be wanting throughout their customer journeys. Today, companies need every advantage they can get so that they provide better service than their competitors, airlines more so than most industry because the customer experience is paramount to their customer's loyalty.

According to the IATA December 5th, 2017 press release[1], "Passenger numbers are expected to increase to 4.3 billion in 2018. Passenger traffic (revenue passenger kilometers or RPKs) is expected to rise 6.0% (slightly down on the 7.5% growth of 2017 but still ahead of the average of the past 10-20 years of 5.5%), which will exceed a capacity expansion (available seat kilometers or ASKs) of 5.7%." "Revenues from the passenger business are expected to grow to $581 billion (+9.2% on $532 billion in 2017)."[1]

Throughout this chapter and the rest of this book, I will break down the different technologies that I believe can be utilized by *The Predictive Airliner* to speed up the operation process; everything from old standards, like Customer Relationship Management (CRM), facial recognition, and mobile marketing technology, to some of the most interesting and innovative technologies around, including IoT, stream processing, and cutting edge technology like AI and Machine Learning (ML). In the airline industry, AI has been used to drive mobile sales and social commerce, to promote products, to create personalized recommendations, as well as to understand sentiment analysis.

This book is an attempt to chart the next course of analytics for the airline industry by utilizing IoT, geo-location capabilities, A.I., ML, facial recognition, AR, as well as many of the other technologies discussed here. It could be argued that the most valuable use of predictive analytics for an airline would be in its marketing and sales department, but that's not the whole story.

Being able to accurately predict not only who an airline's best leads and prospects are, as well as how and when it is best to engage them is nice but understanding how their acceptance of these marketing offers will affect the overall airliner's bottom line is what *The Predictive Airliner* is all about.

This ability will not only empower marketers and salespeople in the coming seasons to be radically more productive and profitable than they are today, but also give multiple airline departments visibility on their micro and macro needs. Used properly, predictive analytics can transform the science of sales forecasting from a dart-throwing exercise to a precision instrument.

The concept of sales and marketing automation has already produced some of the highest-flying successes in high-tech. Companies like Salesforce.com have been wildly successful in automating the sales process for salespeople and sales managers. Big software vendors like SAP, Microsoft, and Oracle are vying for supremacy, while smaller players like Pegasystems, SugarCRM, Netsuite, and Sage are offering interesting products at highly affordable prices.

Today, "Personalization"—the process of utilizing geo-location, mobile app, Wi-Fi, and OTT technology to tailor messages or experiences to an individual interacting with them—is becoming the optimum word in a radically new customer intelligence environment. Even though this personalization comes at a price—privacy—it is a price most consumers seem more than willing to pay if a recognized value is received in return. For an airliner, "personalization" requires an investment in analytical software, but carriers should recognize that this price must be paid because highly sophisticated consumers will soon need an exceptional customer shopping experience to keep them from visiting another competitor (who will, undoubtedly, offer such services).

Adobe's *2018 Digital Trends in Retail*[56] revealed that "the most exciting prospect through the lens of the retailer is *delivering personalized experiences in real time*, cited by 37% of retail respondents compared to 36% for client-side respondents in other sectors."[56] Airlines are not retailers, obviously, but this is an interesting survey to keep in mind a retailers are often on the cutting edge of technology and retail customers will, once they receive personalization marketing from their retail providers, expect similar service from just every other business they deal with going forward.

"Figure 1 compares the top digital-related 2018 priorities for retailers across regions, with *targeting and personalization* leading the way in both North America and Europe. While not explicitly mentioned, the theme of data again looms large for retailers seeking to personalize and target effectively."[56]

Adobe's *2018 Digital Trends in Retail* reveals that "retailers in Asia are much more focused on *social media engagement* and *brand-building/viral marketing* that their counterparts in the West, suggesting that the social and viral marketing opportunity is disproportionally higher in Asia where social uptake has not hit the same kind of plateau as it has in Western markets."[56]

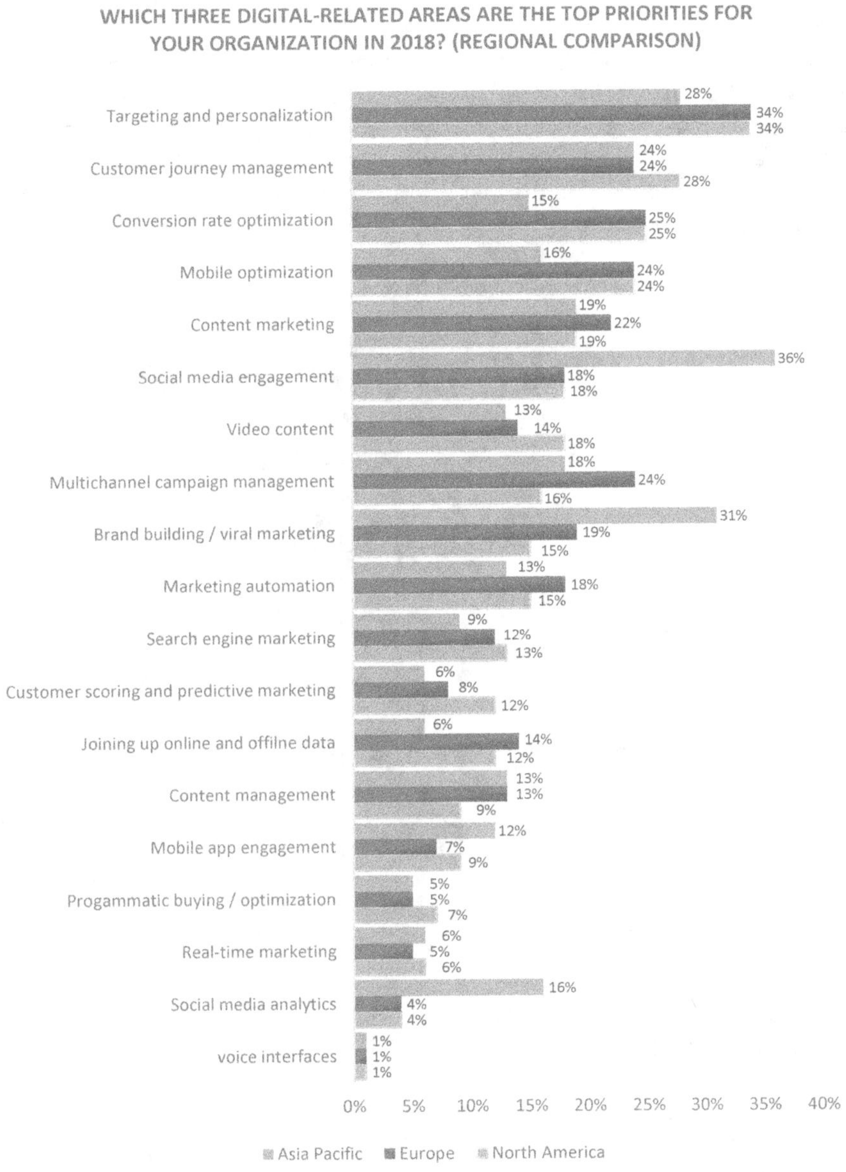

Figure 1: Organizations top priorities in 2018?
Source: *Adobe 2018 Digital Trends in Retail*

One big cultural difference between the Asian and North American markets is the impact of messaging apps.[56] "Prompted by the launch of brand-friendly Official Accounts on WeChat in 2013, the potential of messaging apps in retail has been embraced more quickly by brands and consumers in China than in the United States, where conversational commerce has been relatively slow to get off the ground."[56]

As Adobe's *2018 Digital Trends in Retail* discovered, "Retailers recognize that the quality of the customer experience will increasingly depend on being able to serve up the most relevant content and messaging at the right moment, with companies embracing predictive analytics to help them anticipate the most effective way of converting prospects into customers, and then meeting their needs on an ongoing basis."[56]

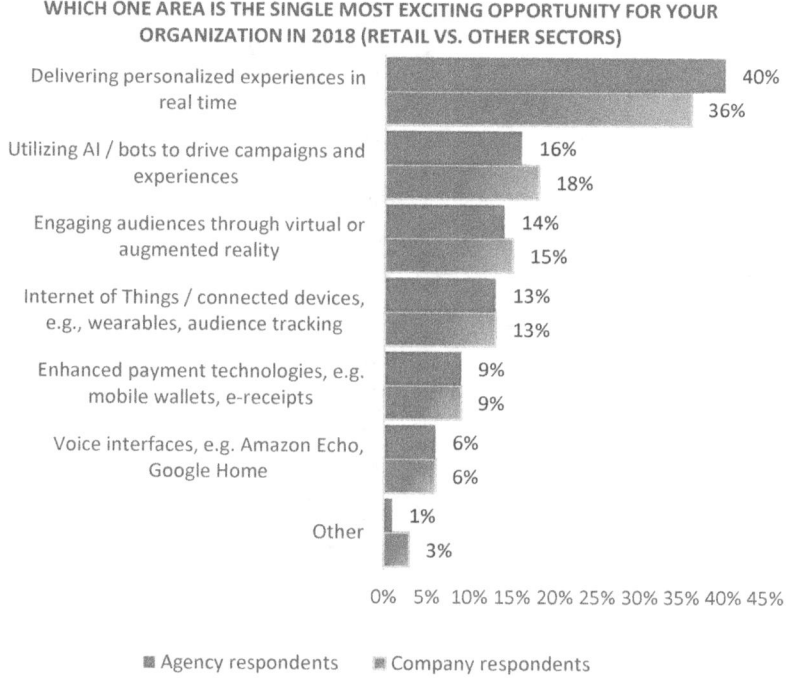

Figure 2: Most Exciting Prospects in Three Years' Time?
Source: Adobe 2018 Digital Trends in Retail

Adobe's *2018 Digital Trends in Retail* reveals that, "The appeal of real-time personalization suggests a focus on providing the most engaging and relevant experiences, a trend that cuts across numerous digital marketing techniques, including analytics, marketing automation, programmatic ad buying and dynamic content."[56]

"While a range of potential game-changing technological trends in Figure 2 will undoubtedly have a powerful impact, from the Internet of Things and connected devices, to voice interfaces and augmented reality, retailers are predominantly focused on creating a relevant, timely and engaging experience to each of their users, to maximize sales and efficiency."[56]

AI is an example of an emerging technology that can itself help to make the experience more relevant and personalized.[56] "AI-powered machine learning can increasingly help retailers comb through vast quantities of data to provide the best possible content and recommendations to consumers as they progress through the shipping journey from awareness and discovery to conversion."[56] This process can also help airlines as well.

One thing that was surprising is the lack of interest in voice technology, with only 6% of respondents pointing to voice interfaces as the most exciting opportunity.[56] "The popularity of voice assistants offered by the likes of Amazon, Google, Microsoft and Apple give retail brands the chance to increase their presence, including in homes and cars, provided that they can find the right kind of utility to consumers at the right time."[56]

To compete in this highly competitive industry, airlines are recognizing the importance of personalization when it comes to customer interactions. Most airlines today have customer loyalty programs that are a part of a CRM and/or a SCRM initiative to provide their customers with an intimate experience that will make them want to return to the airline again and again and again. Mobile and social media channels are some of the best ways to reach these customers.

One of the key demographic findings of the *2018 Adobe Digital Insights (ADI) State of Digital Advertising* report was that Millennials and Gen Zers differ from Generation X, Baby Boomers, and older generations in that, "social channels are where these generations see the most relevant content in their lives."[56] According to Taylor Schreiner, "social advertising is clearly a key part of a paid/owned/earned media strategy, especially if your audience is under 40."[56] This is a fact that airlines should keep in mind going forward as Millennials and Gen Zers are now reaching an age when they will travel considerably.

Currently, however, there is a big disconnect between what companies think they are delivering in terms of personalization and what consumers are actually experiencing. In his article *Study finds marketers are prioritizing personalization... but are further behind then they realize*[57], Andrew Jones states that, "Although two-thirds of the marketers surveyed rate their personalization efforts as 'very good' or 'excellent,' just 31 percent of consumers reported that companies are consistently delivering personalized experiences."[57]

"Aside from this disparity, the report finds that personalization strategies today are immature. It shows that 91 percent of the marketers surveyed are prioritizing personalization over the coming year, yet many still rely on basic segmentation strategies," Jones notes.[57] This isn't that surprising as many companies are struggling with the ability to not just capture the information necessary for personalization, but also creating DWs that can silo the data properly, then deliver it to highly complex analytical programs that can make sense of all that data. It is like finding a needle in a haystack for each and every customer in a massive database; a herculean task, no doubt.[57]

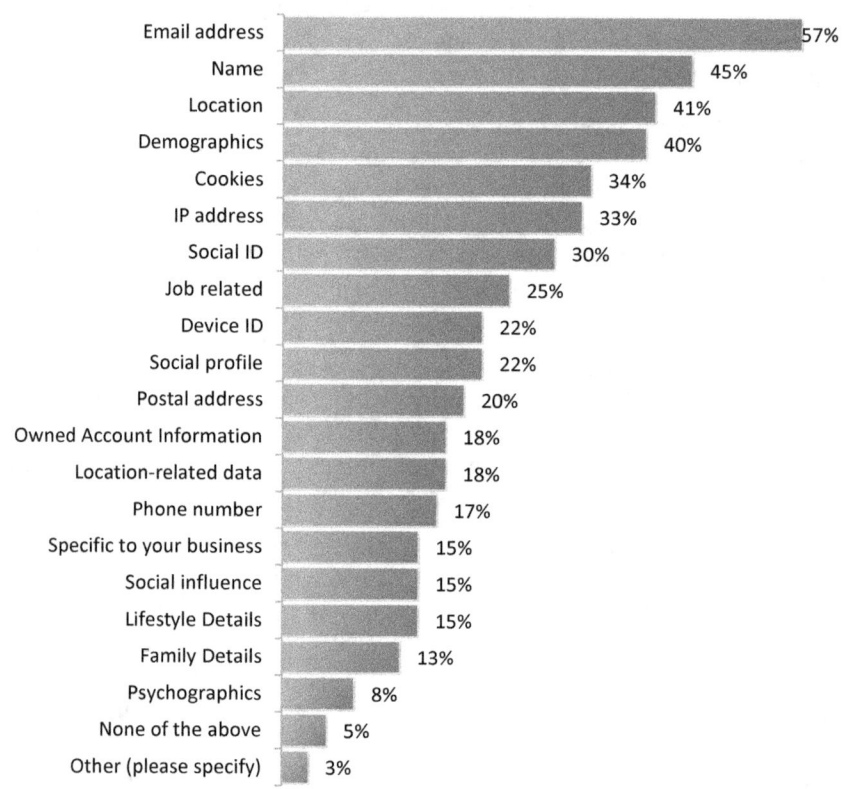

Figure 3: Identity-related data sources used for personalization
Source: VB Insights[58]

It is obvious that creating a consolidated customer view is a necessary component of personalization, but, unfortunately, "most marketers today are working with customer data that is decentralized, spread across the organization in multiple databases that are updated in batch processes. To find success, marketers must prioritize consolidating data into a single database," states Jones and this is where a data lake can come in.[57]

THE PREDICTIVE AIRLINER

Another important step to bringing personalization efforts up to a user's expectation level will be by using behavioral data. "In order to create these types of customer experiences, marketers must strategically collect and utilize customer data, including real-time signals of intent, which are typically not captured today," argues Jones.[57] Figure 3 lists out the identity-related data sources that can be used for personalization and it is a considerable amount of data that must be culled through, siloed, and understood.

Figure 4 shows the current data types that travel companies are collecting and utilizing and it does reveal that the industry has a long way to go in terms of developing personalization systems that will create powerful customer insights.

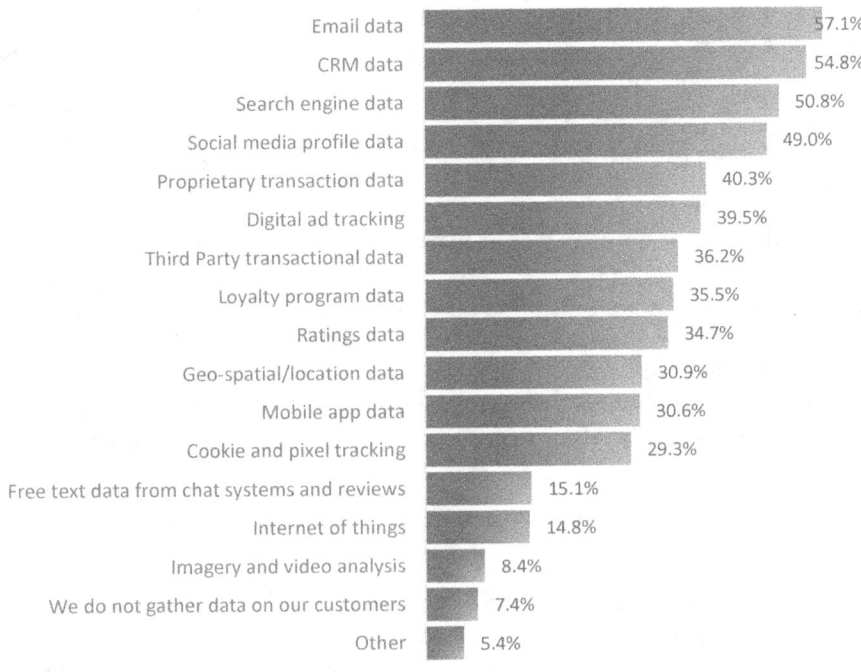

■ Which of the Following Do You Gather to Generate Insight into Your Customers?

Figure 4: State of Data in Travel Survey, 2017

With customer attitudes towards personalized content being shaped by recommendation engines like Amazon, Pandora, and Netflix, consumers are becoming more used to receiving what they want, when they want it, and on whatever channel they want it on.[57] Airlines must keep this in mind when developing personalization programs. The consumer has become highly sophisticated and he or she expects the level of sophistication received on platforms like Amazon and Pandora to filter over to all their other company communications; don't waste his or her time with non-matching offers or he or she will go down the street or into the air with another competitor.

Customer Relationship Management (CRM)

CRM is a strategy used to learn more about a customer's needs and behaviors in order to develop a stronger relationship with him or her, thereby creating a value exchange on both sides. CRM is perhaps more important for the airline industry than any other industry because customer interactions exist on a long continuum. From airport check-in, to boarding, to flying, to baggage pickup and leaving the airport, customers can interact with no less than twenty members of an airline's staff.

As Lovelock and Wirtz state in *Services Marketing, People, Technology, Strategy*[59], "from a customer perspective, well-implemented CRM systems can offer a unified customer interface that delivers customization and personalization."

Lovelock and Wirtz argue that at each transaction point, such relevant customer data as a customer's personal preferences, as well as his or her overall past history transactions are available to the clerk serving the customer, giving them valuable information about how to interact with that person.[59] This is not an easy thing to do, however, especially when unstructured data like social media feeds are added to the equation. However, currently, it is a necessity as consumers expect personalized service of this level from the companies with whom they interact.

According to Lovelock and Wirtz, most CRM solutions contain the following stages[59]:

- Data collection: the system captures customer contact details, such as demographics, purchasing history, service preferences, etc.
- Data Analysis: data captured is analyzed and categorized into a unique set of criteria. This information is then used to tier the customer base and tailor service delivery accordingly.
- Sales force automation: sales leads, cross-sell, and up-sell opportunities can be effectively identified and processed, and the entire cycle from lead generation to close of sales and after-sales service can be tracked and facilitated through the CRM system.
- Marketing automation: the mining of customer data can help a company achieve one-on-one marketing to each one of its customers. Loyalty and retention programs can reduce costs, which can result in an increase of marketing expenditure ROI. By analyzing campaign

responses, CRM systems can easily assess a marketing campaign's quantifiable success rate.
- Call center automation: with customer information available right at their fingertips, call center staff can improve customer service levels because they will be able to immediately identify a customer's tier level, as well as compare and contrast him or her against similar customers so that only promotions that are likely to be accepted are offered.

Most airlines will have plenty of data collection, data analysis, sales force automation, marketing automation, and call center automation software to help them in their CRM endeavors, but it is not easy getting all of these complicated systems and processes working together to provide a level of personalized service that wows a customer.

Beyond simple CRM (which, I guess, is never really *that* simple), Social CRM (SCRM) adds a whole new level of sophistication to the mix. SCRM is the use of "social media services, techniques and technology to enable organizations to engage with customers."[60] In his article *Time to Put a Stake in the Ground on Social CRM*[61], Paul Greenberg argues that:

> "Social CRM is a philosophy and a business strategy, supported by a technology platform, business rules, workflow, processes and social characteristics, designed to engage and react accordingly in a collaborative conversation in order to promote mutually beneficial value in a trusted and transparent business environment. It's the company's response to the customer's ownership of the conversation."

One aspect of "Social CRM" is "Social Media Monitoring," the process by which companies monitor sites like Facebook, Twitter, LinkedIn, Weibo, YouTube, Instagram, and others for relevant brand and anti-brand comments and mentions. Social media monitoring tools allow for continuous customer engagement and, in chapter three and four, I go into detail about how an airline can use these types of social media monitoring tools to build strong, two-way customer relationships.

"SCRM is the connection of social data (wherever it is) with existing customer records (customer database) that enable companies to provide new forms of customer insight and relevant context."[46] With SCRM, marketers can "understand the mood, find new sales leads, respond faster to customer needs and maybe even anticipate needs by listening into their conversations and taking action"[46] wherever appropriate.

SCRM doesn't replace CRM systems; it adds value by augmenting traditional systems.[46] As Woodcock notes, "SCRM is a great hunting ground for businesses to find and acquire consumers to full 'traditional' CRM programs as well as identify key influencers who can be considered as high value customers. It offers companies an organized approach, using enterprise software that connects business units to the social web giving them the opportunity to respond in near real time, and in a coordinated fashion."[46]

Social media can help amplify the "relationship" in "Customer Relationship Management", thereby enabling organizations to connect and engage consumers in a unique way, as well as personalize and monetize customer relationship on a sustained basis, which should increase profitability.[153] "Social media also provides a path to richer customer analysis, using technologies capable of funneling and consolidating customer insights."[153] Insights derived from this analysis can help companies to "dynamically calibrate, anticipate, and offer products and services that meet perpetually shifting consumer demands in a hyper-competitive marketplace."[153]

Marketers can also "listen into what customers are saying, to better understand their needs, their voices and tie it back to actual customer profiles"[46], which could contain their Facebook or WeChat pages or Twitter handles. "In addition, marketers will be able to catch leads in 'mid-air' by listening for keywords that suggest a customer is getting ready to buy, then sending real-time alerts to sales teams to respond."[46]

Specifically, for an airline, it would be advantageous to link a customer's account with his or her social media accounts so that the airline could get a heads-up on what a customer might be saying about them on social media.

In a lot of cases, ROI is an enormously tricky thing to measure, but social media is providing unique ways for businesses to quantify their social media spend. Gone are the days of wasting endless amounts of money to build up a useless following of thousands of Facebook fans. "Short-term campaign ROI as the main measure for individual campaigns will evolve into correlation analysis between activities, engagement and sales. This will be unsettling for many traditional marketers."[46] "The explicit use of active and control groups, and experimentation of using different treatments will help marketers understand the impact of specific SM activities."[46] More direct marketing type disciplines will be required, in a world where there is real-time feedback on attitude and behavior and a plethora of data."[46] This has become a much more demanding world in terms of capturing and utilizing all of this data, but making the effort to turn this data into actionable intelligence will be noticed by fickle consumers, I have no doubt.

For the rest of this chapter, I will list out the many different technologies that are relevant to *The Predictive Airliner* and, in the ensuing chapters, I will explain how they all come together to produce an unrivaled customer and corporate experience.

Airlines should also feel compelled to reward their customers through Facebook,

Twitter, WeChat, and Weibo, or any number of social network, blogging, and/or micro-blogging services. The beauty of using these channels is the ability of the customer to share these awards or stories of these awards with friends and family; the Reed Network[42] will do its magic from there. It wouldn't be that hard to get customers to share their social media accounts, either, as an airline can ask customers for their social media accounts at sign up through methods like social bridging. Social media is now often a preferred contact channel and it does make connecting with users in a real-time way exceptionally easy.

Airline need to empower their customers to post on Facebook or WeChat or Weibo or Twitter or comment about their retail experiences and, hopefully, turn them into apostles. In Jones and Sasser's *zone of affection*, satisfaction levels are high and "customers may have such high attitudinal loyalty that they don't look for alternative service."[75] It is within this group that "Apostles"—members who praise the firm in public—reside and this is the group that is responsible for improved future business performance.[62] *The Predictive Airliner* will not only be able to spot these apostles, but also understand them on such a unique and personal level that their loyalty and patronage will almost be guaranteed.

As Darrell Rigby explains in Bain & Company's *Management Tools 2015 An Executive's Guide*[63], CRM "is a process companies use to understand their customer groups and respond quickly—and at times, instantly—to shifting customer desires. CRM technology allows firms to collect and manage large amounts of customer data and then carry out strategies based on that information."[63]

Retail operators can utilize CRM to:

- Create databases of customers segmented into buckets that allow more effective marketing.
- Generate more accurate sales leads.
- Gather market research on customers.
- Rapidly coordinate information between the sales and marketing staff and front-facing hosts and reps, increasing the customer experience.
- Accurately gauge the return on individual promotional programs and the effect of integrated marketing activities, and redirect spending accordingly.
- Accumulate data on customer preferences and problems for product and service designers.
- Increase sales by systematically identifying, managing, and automating sales leads.
- Improve customer retention by uncovering the reason(s) for customer churn.
- Design proactive customer service programs.

Today, CRM is evolving into what has been dubbed "Customer Centric

Relationship Management" (CCRM), a style of CRM that focuses on customer preferences above all else. CCRM attempts to understand the client in a deep, behavioral way, and it engages customers in individual, interactive relationships through tailored marketing and one-to-one customer service. This personalization can help an airline retain customers, build brand loyalty, provide customers not only with the information that they really want, but also with the rewards that they might use. Today's technology allows airlines to not only surface the information that they need to know about their customers, but it can also provide front-facing employees with offers that these clients will like and, therefore, probably use.

CRM is ultimately a strategy used to learn more about a customer's needs and behaviors in order to develop a stronger relationship with him or her, thereby creating a value exchange on both sides of the equation.

In their comprehensive article on the subject, *Application of Data Mining Techniques in Customer Relationship Management: a Literature Review and Classification*[26], Ngai et al. state that CRM "comprises a set of processes and enabling systems supporting a business strategy to build long term, profitable relationships with specific customers."

In Bain & Company's *Management Tools 2015 An Executive's Guide*[63], Darrell K. Rigby claims, CRM requires managers to:

1. "Start by defining strategic 'pain points' in the customer relationship cycle. These are problems that have a large impact on customer satisfaction and loyalty, where solutions would lead to superior financial rewards and competitive advantage.
2. Evaluate whether—and what kind of—CRM data can fix those pain points. Calculate the value that such information would bring the company.
3. Select the appropriate technology platform and calculate the cost of implementing it and training employees to use it.
4. Assess whether the benefits of the CRM information outweigh the expense involved.
5. Design incentive programs to ensure that personnel are encouraged to participate in the CRM program. Many companies have discovered that realigning the organization away from product groups and toward a customer-centered structure improves the success of CRM.
6. Measure CRM progress and impact. Aggressively monitor participation of key personnel in the CRM program. In addition, put measurement systems in place to track the improvement in customer profitability with the use of CRM. Once the data is collected, share the information widely with employees to encourage further participation in the program."[63]

Once an airliner starts implementing a CRM program, data segmentation can begin. According to Wikipedia, market segmentation "is the process of dividing a broad consumer or business market, normally consisting of existing and potential customers, into sub-groups of consumers (known as *segments*) based on some type of shared characteristics."[64]

In dividing or segmenting markets, airlines can look for shared characteristics, common spend, similar lifestyles choices, or even similar demographic profiles. Market segmentation tries to identify *high yield segments*—i.e., those segments that are likely to be the most profitable or that have outsized growth potential—so that these can be selected for special attention (i.e., become target markets).

Rigby states that customer segmentation "is the subdivision of a market into discrete customer groups that share similar characteristics. Customer segmentation can be a powerful means to identify unmet customer needs. Companies that identify underserved segments can then outperform the competition by developing uniquely appealing products and services."[63] Rigby adds that customer segmentation is most effective when a company can discover its most profitable segments and then tailor offerings to them, thereby providing the customer with a distinct competitive advantage.[63]

As Rigby explains, customer segmentation requires managers to:

- *"Divide the market into meaningful and measurable segments according to customers' needs, their past behaviors or their demographic profiles.*
- *Determine the profit potential of each segment by analyzing the revenue and cost impacts of serving each segment.*
- *Target segments according to their profit potential and the company's ability to serve them in a proprietary way.*
- *Invest resources to tailor product, service, marketing and distribution programs to match the needs of each target segment.*
- *Measure performance of each segment and adjust the segmentation approach over time as market conditions change decision making throughout the organization."*[63]

For an airliner, the pain points might be things like customer loyalty and the marketing department should be asking things like, "Why does it cost so much money to retain customers?" "Can we not find cheaper but more meaningful offers that show understanding of the customer?" Also, "How can we drive customer loyalty to such a degree that our customers rave about us on social media?"

Beside the above methods, customer segmentation can be used to:

- Prioritize new product development efforts.
- Develop customized marketing programs.
- Choose specific product features.

- Establish appropriate service options.
- Design an optimal distribution strategy.
- Determine appropriate product pricing.

Market segmentation assumes that different market segments require different marketing programs—that is, different offers, prices, promotion, distribution or some combination of marketing variables. Market segmentation is not only designed to identify the most profitable segments, but also to develop profiles of key segments in order to better understand their needs and purchase motivations. Insights from segmentation analysis are subsequently used to support marketing strategy development and planning.

Many marketers use the S-T-P approach; **S**egmentation→ **T**argeting → **P**ositioning to provide the framework for marketing planning objectives. That is, a market is segmented, one or more segments are selected for targeting, and products or services are positioned in a way that resonates with the selected target market or markets. With real-time technology, segmentation can reach a whole new customer experience level.

The process of segmenting the market is deceptively simple. Seven basic steps describe the entire process, including segmentation, targeting and positioning. In practice, however, the task can be very laborious since it involves poring over loads of data, and it requires a great deal of skill in analysis, interpretation and some judgment. Although a great deal of analysis needs to be undertaken, and many decisions need to be made, marketers tend to use the so-called S-T-P process as a broad framework for simplifying the process outlined here:

- Segmentation:
    - Identify market (also known as the universe) to be segmented.
    - Identify, select and apply base or bases to be used in the segmentation.
    - Develop segment profiles.
- Targeting:
    - Evaluate each segment's attractiveness.
    - Select segment or segments to be targeted.
- Positioning:
    - Identify optimal positioning for each segment.
    - Develop the marketing program for each segment.

Markets can be broken down into the following segments:

- Geographic segment
- Demographic segment
- Psychographic segment
- Behavioral segment
- Purchase/usage occasion

- Generational segment
- Cultural segmentation

Although customer segmentation is a common business practice, it has received the following criticisms:

- That it fails to identify sufficiently meaningful clusters.
- That it is no better than mass marketing at building brands.
- That in competitive markets, segments rarely exhibit major differences in the way they use brands.
- Geographic/demographic segmentation is overly descriptive and lacks sufficient insights into the motivations necessary to drive communications strategy.
- Difficulties with market dynamics, notably the instability of segments over time and structural change that leads to segment creep and membership migration as individuals move from one segment to another.

Market segmentation has many critics, but, in spite of its limitations, it remains one of the most enduring concepts in marketing and it continues to be widely used in practice.

As Wikipedia explains[64], there are no formulas for evaluating the attractiveness of market segments and a good deal of judgment must be exercised. Nevertheless, a number of considerations can be used to evaluate market segments for attractiveness, including:

- Segment Size and Growth:
    - How large is the market?
    - Is the market segment substantial enough to be profitable?
    - Segment size can be measured in number of customers, but superior measures are likely to include sales value or volume.
    - Is the market segment growing or contracting?
    - What are the indications that growth will be sustained in the long term? Is any observed growth sustainable?
    - Is the segment stable over time?
- Segment Structural Attractiveness:
    - To what extent are competitors targeting this market segment?
    - Can we carve out a viable position to differentiate from any competitors?
    - How responsive are members of the market segment to the marketing program?
    - Is this market segment reachable and accessible?
- Company Objectives and Resources:
    - Is this market segment aligned with our company's operating philosophy?

- Do we have the resources necessary to enter this market segment?
- Do we have prior experience with this market segment or similar market segments?
- Do we have the skills and/or know-how to enter this market segment successfully?

When it comes to analytics and Big Data, Caesars was the first casino company to collect and analyze it for Customer Intelligence (CI) purposes and, since the inception of its Total Rewards programme, the company has grown from "being able to trace the journey of 58% of the money spent in their casino to 85%."[65] Caesars also credits the widespread adoption of Big Data analytics as the driving force behind its rise from an "also ran" chain to one of the largest casino groups in the U.S.[66]

The gaming company Caesars is one company that has been able to use social media to measure marketing data quite successfully. In his article *At Caesars, Digital Marketing Is No Crap Shoot*[67], Al Urbanski explains that[67]:

> "While social media networks like Facebook provide metrics that measure activity within its platform, integrating that data to enable visibility across a brand's entire marketing organization is difficult. Caesars, however, unites information from customers coming through social channels across business units, program teams, time zones, and languages. A content-building component allows Caesars' marketers to listen in and respond in real time."

No matter where the customer interaction originates, engagement is a key factor in moving those interactions from the top of the sales funnel to an eventual purchase.[67] "It doesn't matter where customers come in or leave or reenter," says Chris Kahle, Caesars Web Analytics Manager, "if they come to your social page and click your button, or if they go into your content or email and click on that, it's all the same app and you've got them."[67] Caesars IDs a cookie and, if the prospects come back around on paid search three days later, Caesars tracks them.[67] "We can track them on every website, even if they came in on a Las Vegas site and then jump markets to Atlantic City," adds Kahle.[67]

Caesars also tracks activity in real time, while responding to customer cues.[67] Unsurprisingly, different types of customers are more responsive to different interactions from Caesars. Aside from dividing customers into categories such as "Frequent Independent Traveler"—or FITs and Total Rewards members, the Caesars team uses tracking data to further segment customers by property or market as well as determine how each of their various segments respond to content.[67]

Using this data, Caesars evaluates campaigns in regard to KPIs, such as number of nights booked, and adjusts them on the fly to ramp up conversion rates.[67]

"When Caesars sponsored free concerts by top artists at several of its properties last year, for instance, it streamed the events live on the Web and used its new analytics suite to fine-tune loyalty program offers on its websites. It resulted in a dramatic spike in Total Rewards program sign-ups during the concerts."[67]

"What's really dramatic about this is that you can determine what is engaging individuals and target them with it," Adobe's Langie says.[67] "The high-roller segment, for example. They might respond to a very different Web design than the casual visitor and Caesars tailors the page view to who is visiting. Think of the website as a canvas. You can paint a still life of a fruit for one person and something different for another. The canvas is dynamic."[67]

"The speed and the manner with which the chosen website designs and digital marketing tactics are implemented across the Caesars network may well be the most transforming development of the company's new data culture," Kahle adds.[67] And this was no easy task as the Caesars landscape extends over 60 websites for its various properties and services as well as 40 Facebook pages.

"Prior to implementing a data-centric approach to the decision-making process, it could take as long as two weeks to furnish the field with actionable data. They now get it done in a matter of hours," Kahle adds.[67] In 2013, Caesars' implemented Adobe's Digital Marketing Suite, which "includes real-time tracking and segmentation of digital site visitors, analysis of social media's role in purchasing, and content testing by segment or individual visitor."[67]

"The people at the individual properties who are managing the content of the websites are not all technically sophisticated, but Adobe system provides them with built-in capabilities," Kahle says.[67] "Say one of our properties wants to track social. Before, they'd have to spend a lot of time manually adding tracking codes. With Adobe, tracking codes are integrated," Kahle adds.[67]

"Right now we can assign a percentage value to social media if a booking doesn't result right away," Kahle says.[67] "But with social we're going to be experimenting with a longer funnel, maybe a two-week time frame."[67] "Values are ascribed to social media for being the site of initial contact with a new customer, for instance, or for numbers of positive reviews by current customers."[67]

Currently, Caesars can't measure the total value of a reservation booked online and also can't determine how much an online booker spends at the tables during his or her stay.[67] This is important information when it comes to truly understanding a customer's value. Caesars would also like to know if, for example, "customers left the Caesars' casino in Las Vegas and went to dinner at Gordon Ramsay's restaurant at the Paris Las Vegas, so they could offer them a free dinner at the restaurant to close the deal on a future booking."[67]

"Eventually we're going to set a time frame that will never expire [on the sales funnel]," Kahle says.[67] "But for now we've built a sales allocation model that goes beyond the last click, and that's OK. Most organizations using multiple marketing channels are still stuck on that last click."[67]

Going forward, mobile and social media are going to be important channels for an airline's CRM, marketing and operations departments for years to come. The mobile phone's ubiquity, however, could be a double-edged sword. It allows an airline to market directly to its customers while they are not just on their property, but also anywhere they might be standing. In this changing digital world, if an airline isn't constantly marketing to its customers, some other competitor might be the customer might be lost for good.

Companies like Adobe, IBM, Oracle, Microsoft, SAP, Salesforce.com, and SugarCRM all have products that not only include contact management systems that integrate emails, documents, jobs and faxes, but also integrate with mobile and social media accounts as well, so the market doesn't lack product, but this will be a case where one side doesn't fit all. A deep understanding of the airline's current systems and pain points should be explored before any solution is chosen and implemented.

Boland et al. recommend that airlines empower their employees, "At every stage in the employee lifecycle, airline staff should be provided with the tools and incentives to deliver a high level of service."[7] They add[7]:

> First, customer-facing employees should be hired based on their service capabilities. Training should provide the employee with a vision of the airline as a "service organization," with every employee having a customer, even if that customer is internal, a philosophy espoused by profitable Southwest Airlines.[68] The airline should constantly collect employee feedback on service issues. Technological tools should be provided to employees to give them better knowledge about the customer, enabling them to tailor their interactions with each customer regardless of channel or point in the travel experience. Finally, employees should be evaluated on their ability to deliver a high level of service, with additional incentives used to encourage employees to exceed customer expectations.

CRM is, ultimately, a backward-looking technology, i.e., you're only dealing with information about past behavior. Adding predictive technology onto this CRM technology can turn a CRM system into a lead generation tool and this is where *The Predictive Airliner* should be. In T_HQ Technology and Business' article *What does the CRM of the future look like?*[69], Insightly's Founder and CEO Anthony Smith, "Overlay a business' unique CRM process, combined with deep analytics, and you have tailored customer engagement playbooks that enable businesses to treat every customer like they are their only customer."

Customer Loyalty

According to Kivetz and Simonson,[70] loyalty in the airline industry is defined as the likelihood of a customer becoming a repeat customer and that customer's willingness to behave as a partner to the airline. In his article *Are loyal visitors desired visitors?*[71], James F. Petrick argues that, while repeat visitation or repeat purchase might infer loyalty, it is should be understood that true loyalty is a two-dimensional concept that encompasses both a psychological attachment and emotional commitment.

Loyalty is so important to an airliner because, as repeated studies have shown, customers become more profitable over time. In their study *Zero Defections: Quality Comes to Service*[72], Reichheld and Sasser demonstrated that a customer's profitability increases as his or her loyalty increases. In their study, the authors found that it usually took more than a year to recoup any customer acquisition costs, but then profits increased as customers remained with the service or firm. Reichheld and Sasser believe there are four factors for this growth and, in order of their importance, they are[72]:

1. Profit derived from increased purchases: as a customer ages, he or she will probably become more affluent, therefore will have more money to spend for company products and/or services.
2. Profit from reduced operating costs: as customers become more experienced, they should make fewer demands on the business, perhaps taking advantage of available self-service options.
3. Profit from referrals to other customers.
4. Profit from price premiums: long-term customers are more likely to pay regular prices for services rather than being tempted into using a businesses' lower profit products and/or services.

Here are a few other facts and figures regarding customers and their loyalty:

- On average, loyal customers are worth up to 10 times as much as their first purchase.[73]
- It is 6-7 times more expensive to acquire a new customer than it is to keep a current one.[73]
- News of bad customer service reaches more than twice as many ears as praise for a good service experience.[73]
- For every customer who bothers to complain, 26 other customers remain silent.[73]

In their paper, Lovelock and Wirtz introduce the concept of the *Wheel of Loyalty* as an organizing structure to help businesses build customer loyalty. Its three sequential steps are[59]:

1. Build a foundation for loyalty, including "targeting the right portfolio of customer segments, attracting the right customers, tiering the service, and delivering high levels of satisfaction."[59]
2. Create loyalty bonds that "either deepen the relationship through cross-selling and bundling or add value to the customer through loyalty rewards and higher level bonds."[59]
3. Identify and reduce the factors that result in "churn"—the need to replace lost customers with new ones.

The number one thing that creates loyalty in *anybody* (that includes your customers) is the social construct of reciprocity—the social norm that's been evaluated and debated since the days of Aristotle. Many scholars believe it to be one of the single most defining aspects of social interaction that keeps society whole. Reciprocity doesn't have to be a bar of gold, like some casinos in Macau like to offer their high rollers, it could simply be an acknowledgement of poor customer service along with the promise to do better the next time.

A consumer's engagement with a brand can be measured along a continuum from no awareness, through early engagement, and, hopefully, if everything goes right, into advocacy.[46] As for the customer-company relationship, "the strength of feeling will develop and vary over time and, as in any healthy relationship, both parties should be aware of feelings so they can react accordingly," Woodcock advises.[46]

As was shown in Nielsen's 2012 *Global Trust in Advertising*[74] survey, consumers trust their friends and colleagues much more than they trust TV advertising or corporate communications. Today, consumers communicate with each other like never before through a multitude of social and mobile media channels[46] and these channels should be exploited as much as possible.

CRM is an integral part of what businesses hope will be a value exchange on both sides of the customer-company equation, one that will, hopefully, create loyal customers who become apostles for the business. Lovelock and Wirtz created the "Wheel of Loyalty" as an organizing structure to help businesses build customer loyalty and it is highly relevant to the airline industry.[59] The first of its three sequential steps include building a foundation for loyalty, including "targeting the right portfolio of customer segments, attracting the right customers, tiering the service, and delivering high levels of satisfaction."[59]

The second step—creating loyalty bonds that either deepen the relationship through cross-selling and bundling or adding value to the customer through loyalty rewards and higher level bonds—can be achieved by the airline gaining a fuller understanding of its customers.[59] It is important to understand as much about the customer as possible, his or her wants, desires and needs, all the way down to his or her preferred shopping items, styles, spend amount, as well as preferred time to shop.

The third factor—identify and reduce the factors that result in "churn"—is also extremely important to an airline's bottom line.[59] Engagement is paramount here and mobile apps and social media are great channels to keep customers interested.

Customer satisfaction is the foundation of true customer loyalty, while customer dissatisfaction is one of the main reasons why customers leave.[59] This may sound obvious, but its importance cannot be stressed enough.

According to Jones and Sasser, "the satisfaction-loyalty relationship can be divided into three main zones: Defection, indifference, and affection. The *zone of defection* occurs at low satisfaction levels. Customers will switch unless switching costs are high or there are no viable or convenient alternatives."[75] This, obviously, isn't the case with airlines, where switching often constitutes little more than walking to a competing airline's store across the way. With the vast echo chamber of social media against them, losing only one disgruntled customer could be the least of the airline's problems—to say nothing of having one dragged off a plane!

Jones and Sasser warn that, "Extremely dissatisfied customers can turn into 'terrorists,' providing an abundance of negative feedback about the service provider."[75] Through social media channels, negative feedback can reverberate around the world within seconds. Today, more than ever, airlines must spot dissatisfied customers and approach them before they do irreparable harm to the company's image and reputation and social media is one of the best channels in which to engage them. Like the proverbial canary in the coal mine, *The Predictive Airliner* will have systems in place that can warn the business about these customers before they become figurative terrorists.

In the *zone of indifference*, customers willingly switch if they can find a better alternative, while in the *zone of affection*, satisfaction levels are high and "customers may have such high attitudinal loyalty that they don't look for alternative services."[75] It is within this group that "Apostles"—members who praise the firm in public—reside and this is the group that is responsible for improved future business performance.[62] In the social media world, these people are more likely to be known as "influencers" and I will go into much more detail about these people in chapter four.

Drutsch et al. argue that airline loyalty programs are putting potential customers off and this could be a big problem in the future.[30] For example, "When an airline's loyalty program fails to attract new customers and keep current customers engaged, the airline does not collect relevant and actionable customer data, misses opportunities for more effective and relevant merchandising, and forgoes opportunities to build new revenue streams."[30]

"Online companies fight to build online 'eyeballs', a significant portion of those 'eyeballs' being specious, upon which they build multi-billion dollar businesses," note Drutsch et al.[30] "Airlines have the opportunity to do the same, with 'real' people, if they embrace the need to attract and retain the vast majority of their customers, not just the highest frequency customers," recommend Drutsch et al.[30] This short term thinking might be getting in the way of long term profit.

"In *Forrester's* latest *Loyalty Wave*™, it is clear that loyalty marketers aspire to evolve their programs to address current and future customer needs."[30] Airline loyalty programs are no exception," Drutsch et al. argue. The writers add that the "need to evaluate the next steps necessary to succeed and grow, based on the changes in both consumer expectations/behavior and earnings/rewards restructuring by the airlines."[30] "Unlike their predecessors, today's loyalty programs are ubiquitous across almost all business verticals, regardless of size, service, or product type," warn Drutsch et al.[30] They seem to argue that the time to differentiate oneself in the eyes of the consumer may have passed.

Additionally, the disrupters who have raised the bar when it comes to customer service have transformed instant gratification from a luxury into an expectation.[30] Down the line, delivering on those expectations are going to be harder and harder. "For infrequent fliers, the long-term earnings structure of airline loyalty programs can feel like an eternity compared to many other daily commercial experiences," warn Drutsch et al.[30]

Drutsch et al. argue that, "to prevent the loss of customer loyalty and data to disrupters like Amazon and Google, airlines need to adapt and evolve their loyalty programs."[30] The writers provide the following ways to do just that:

1. Offer lower-cost travel rewards to appeal to less-frequent travelers.
2. Reward less frequent travelers for flying within a specified time period.
3. "Expand the attractiveness and uniqueness of the points/currency by creating a fiat currency for purchase towards anything an airline offers (checked bag fees, in-flight beverage purchases, in-flight connectivity, etc.)." [30]
4. "Proactively collect self-reported customer data by rewarding loyalty currency, allowing more accurate targeting and both customer and airline-relevant offers."[30]
5. "Partner with consumer-positive companies that want access to real 'eyeballs' to create new revenue opportunities.
6. "Embrace the confluence of CRM and loyalty platforms—the two should no longer be considered separate but rather part of the same customer cultivation and engagement continuum."[30]

The Customer Journey

Today, I think we can safely say that the mass marketing experience is over. According to Gartner, there are five stages of customer experience maturity—

initial, developing, defined, managed and optimizing. The goal here is to improve the customer experience through a systematic process to improve customer satisfaction, loyalty and advocacy.

For airlines, customer information housed in an EDW would include things like transactional data, customer and CRM data, mobile, social, and location data, as well as information from web logs that track its user's web behavior, and online advertising bid management systems. It would also give the airliner the ability to do analytics on the fly, which could help the customer's experience in a multitude of ways.

Today, most major airlines have customer loyalty programs that are part of a CRM and/or an SCRM initiative and these should provide their customers with an intimate experience that will make them want to return to the airline again and again and again. That is the goal of it, at least.

Obviously, creating a consolidated customer view is a necessary component of personalization. Another important step of bringing personalization efforts up to a user's expectation level will be using behavioral data in the process. In order to create these types of customer experiences, airlines will strategically collect and utilize customer data, including real-time signals of intent, which aren't typically captured today.

In their article *Knowing What to Sell, When, and to Whom*[76], authors V. Kumar, R. Venkatesan, and W. Reinartz showed how, by simply understanding and tweaking behavioral patterns, they could increase the hit rate for offers and promotions to consumers, which then had an immediate impact on revenue.

By applying statistical models based on the work of Nobel prize-winning economist Daniel McFadden, researchers accurately predicted not only a specific person's purchasing habits, but also the specific time of the purchase to an accuracy of 80%.[76] In the world of instant and real-time communication, capturing a person intent to purchase can be a powerful weapon in making a sale. An offer pushed out at just the moment of interest could actually be the act that pushed a buyer to make a purchase.

Obviously, the potential to market to an individual when he or she is primed to accept the advertising is advantageous for both parties involved. By utilizing data from past campaigns and measures generated by a predictive modeling process, airlines can track actual campaign responses versus expected campaign responses, which can often prove wildly divergent. Additionally, airlines can generate upper and lower control limits that can be used to automatically alert campaign managers when a campaign is under or overperforming, letting them focus on campaigns that specifically require attention.

One of the benefits of automating campaigns is that offers based on either stated or inferred preferences of customers can be developed. Analysis can identify which customers may be more responsive to an offer. The result: more individualized offers are sent out to the airline's customers and, because these offers tap into a customer's wants, desires, needs *and* expectations, they are more likely to be used; more offers used mean more successful campaigns, which means more money coming into the airline's coffers.

With predictive analytics, airlines can even predict which low-tier and mid-tier customers are likely to become the next big spenders. In so doing, the airline can afford to be more generous in its offers as it will know that there is a high likelihood that these customers will appreciate the personalized attention and therefore become long term—and, hopefully, highly profitable—customers.

A campaign management solution can enable the airline to develop and manage personalised customer communications strategies and the delivery of offers. It will also allow users to rapidly create, modify and manage multi-channel, multi-wave marketing campaigns that integrate easily with any fulfilment channel, automatically producing outbound (contact) and inbound (response) communication history.

Users can define target segments, prioritise selection rules, prioritise offers across multiple campaigns and channels, select communication channels, schedule and execute campaigns, and perform advanced analyses to predict and evaluate the success of customer communications.

With customer attitudes towards personalized content being shaped by recommendation engines like Amazon, Pandora, and Netflix, consumers are becoming more used to receiving what they want, when they want it, and on whatever channel they prefer it on. Airlines must keep this in mind when developing personalization programs.

The consumer has become highly sophisticated and he or she expects the level of sophistication received on platforms like Amazon and Pandora to filter over to all of his or her other company communications; companies shouldn't waste their time with non-matching offers or the customer will probably go down the street to a competitor's retail outlet.

The customer journey starts a long time before the customer even enters the airline's store. It begins the moment a potential customer browses an airline's ecommerce webpage or notices an advertisement for an outfit on television, or on the internet, or in print, or on a billboard somewhere. It can even be while browsing an airline's website, connecting with its social media accounts, or even the moment a customer enters the airport.

With a few browser click strokes, an airline's ecommerce department can create a click path analysis that reveals customer interactions on the airline's websites. Descriptive analytical functionalities can then provide a deeper understanding of the customer journey. Column dependencies (standard in most of today's Data

Integration software tools) can visually display the strength of a relationship between attributes within any dataset. This helps the airline's marketing department better understand the characteristics of their data, which can be used to help target further analysis.

A recommendation engine can help predict a person's interest based on historical data from many other users. This is useful in increasing customer engagement, recommending more relevant choices and increasing customer satisfaction.

Predictive modeling is only useful if it is deployed *and* it creates an action. Taking advantage of the more powerful, statistically based segmentation methods, customers can be segmented not only by dollar values, but also on all known information, which can include behavioral information gleaned from shopping activities, as well as the customer's simple demographic information.

This more detailed segmentation allows for more targeted and customer-focused marketing campaigns. Models can be evaluated and reports generated on multiple statistical measures, such as neural networks, decision trees, genetic algorithms, the nearest neighbor method, rule induction, and lift and gains charts. Once built, scores can be generated in a variety of ways to facilitate quick and easy implementation. The projects themselves can be re-used and shared to facilitate faster model development and knowledge transfer.

In his paper *Predictive Analytics*[77], Wayne Eckerson advises creating predictive models by using the following six steps:

1. Define the business objectives and desired outcomes for the project and then translate them into predictive analytic objectives and tasks.
2. Explore and analyze the source data to determine the most appropriate data and model building approach and then scope the effort.
3. Prepare the data by selecting, extracting, and transforming the data, which will be the basis for the models.
4. Build the models, as well as test and validate them.
5. Deploy the models by applying them to the business decisions and processes.
6. Manage and update the models accordingly.

As I state throughout this book, an airline is only as strong as its weakest customer relationship and airlines should look to foster stronger relationships with their current and future customers by taking advantage of the marketing opportunities that mobile and social media offers.

One should also keep in mind Lovelock and Wirtz's *Wheel of Loyalty* when developing CRM systems and goals.[59] These include building a foundation for loyalty, creating loyalty bonds as well as identifying and reducing the factors that result in customer churn.[59] Customer satisfaction is the foundation of true customer loyalty, while customer dissatisfaction is the key factor that drives people away.[59] This may sound obvious, but its importance cannot be overstated. The *Airline Engagement and Loyalty Platform* (see Figure 5) shows how an airline would engage its customers in a loyalty platform that utilizes social media as an important part of the process.

Through mobile and social media analytics, airlines can create a single customer view that helps produce one-to-one, personalized marketing, which many would consider the Holy Grail of advertising. Marketing to the "customer of one" is one of the major slogans being bandied about by software companies these days and, although it might sound simple, it is anything but. In reality, it can be one of the hardest marketing systems to create.

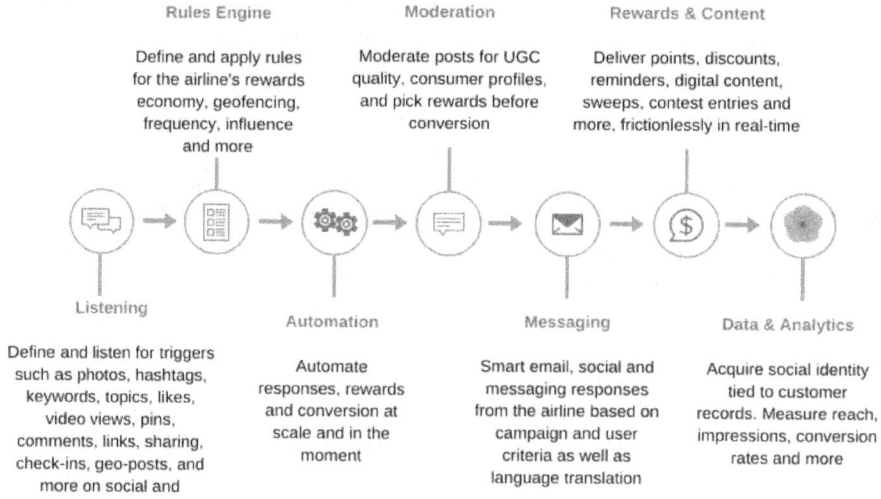

Figure 5: Airline Engagement and Loyalty Platform
Source: Based on an engagement and loyalty platform devised by Chirpify.com

The *Airline Engagement and Loyalty Platform* can be implemented in a multitude of ways. In the *Listening* part, airlines should define and look out for triggers such as photos, hashtags, keywords, likes, video views, etc., etc. This runs the gamut, from staying on top of keywords and hashtags to using image recognition technology that scans pictures of the airline's latest looks.

Check-ins and geo-posts from sites like Foursquare, WeChat, Instagram, Facebook, WhatsApp, YouTube, as well as a whole host of other social networks can help airline operators connect with a nearby audience. Airlines should also be listening to comment boards or short-term blogging sites like Tumblr or social news aggregation sites like Reddit for comments about their stores. Airline passengers are often happy to post wonderful reviews about their flights and this is gold for word-of-mouth marketing.

The *Rules Engine* step is straightforward; airlines are already creating considerable business rules for their operation and these should be extended to each company's defined rewards program, its reward's economy, and the marketing of the loyalty program.

Rewards programs are difficult to implement and costly to maintain because there are so many moving parts; each reward point and free offer has to be correlated against the department that offered it, the right budget it should be assigned to and every reward point has a monetary value that must be enumerated properly.

Building a rules engine can simplify the marketing process by defining who gets what, when he or she gets it, and through which channel it gets delivered. With mobile and social being added to the customer channel mix, things are going to get exponentially more complex very quickly, so building a rules engine that lays out things in a highly definable way is not just desirable, but absolutely necessary.

Once the rules engine is in place, automation must kick in. With some airline operators, they are handling databases filled with millions of customers and it would be impossible to market to them without considerable automation going on behind the scenes. Segmenting customers and building campaigns that market to thousands of individuals would be impossible without it. Understanding the ROI of each marketing campaign is imperative and with today's real-time personalization capabilities, airline operators can quickly understand who is accepting their marketing and how much revenue is being generated. Adding a real-time element to the process would be impossible without strict rules set in place and powerful marketing automation tools that not only send out marketing offers but also quantify them once they are utilized.

In terms of marketing and customer service, Facebook bots could be created and automated to answer standard customer service questions and this should lighten the load on an airline's customer service department.

Moderating boards and UGC posts are a great channel to connect with customers and/or potential customers. These are also good places to pick up both customer service issues and competitor information. Social media users often feel free to post stories about their bad purchases and, in some cases, will openly blast companies that have not met their expectations, and this can help an airline with competitive intel and new product development.

As Chirpify sees it: "Moderation allows brands to increase social efficiency and effectiveness by uniting automated listening triggers while giving moderators the ability to manually review posts and user content for fit before determining their qualification for a reward. This helps brands better personalize the reward based on the user while making sure that the reward is one that the customer appreciates and/or makes them feel special."[78]

Rewards and marketing content can deliver points, discounts, reminders, as well as contest entries in real-time, but reaching today's audiences can be tricky. Marriott won the *Chief Marketer's 2017 Gold for Best Loyalty Marketing* for the development of a loyalty engagement platform that uses rewards points as social currency to incentivize engagement on Twitter, Facebook, and Instagram.[79]

In the *Chief Marketer* write up about the award, the magazine noted that, "The platform was designed as a reciprocal ecosystem where members are empowered to engage via social media and advocate on behalf of the program. The platform engages guests one-to-one at scale with personalized content and instant rewards, enabling members to engage with the loyalty program even when they aren't on property."[79]

"By connecting their social media accounts with the platform, members can earn points by engaging with a variety of triggers throughout the year. The platform is integrated directly with Marriott Rewards' member database, allowing the program to recognize and reward members the moment they post," Chief Marketer notes.[79]

Engagement was huge. "When it came time to amplify the launch of Marriott Rewards' Reward-a-Friend enrollment program, connected members helped spread the word with a simple retweet. The campaign generated 7.4M earned media impressions in four days."[79]

"Connected members generated more than 65 million positive earned media impressions in 2016 on behalf of Marriott Rewards. More than 84 million Rewards points were awarded in response to 326,000 social media engagements, equivalent to earning roughly 11,000 free nights."[79] This kind of engagement comes at a cost, obviously (the free rooms), but the enormous amount of engagement is worth the price of admission because it is a word-of-mouth type of marketing and it allows verifiable visibility on the engagement. Also, the ROI will be easy to analyze.

One thing to keep in mind when it comes to rewards is uniqueness and what has become known as "social rewards". In his article *Getting it right: mixing social and economic rewards in hotel loyalty programmes*[80], Lee Jin-soo argues that:

> "The concept of relationship marketing is prevalent in the local hotel industry, giving rise to numerous loyalty or reward programmes that offer preferential rewards for members in proportion to how often they patronise an establishment. The rewards offered—usually in the form of economic or social benefits—make members feel special, important, and appreciated. Common examples of economic benefits include free room, room upgrade and discounts. Social benefits, on the other hand, are more diverse and include any preferential treatment or personalised recognition and attention given to individual customers."[80]

Lee believes that social rewards are important in today's world, which has seen an explosion of customer loyalty programs. In comparison to typical rewards, "social rewards usually work better in building stronger relationships since social benefits enhance a customer's intrinsic reasons for sustaining and reinforcing emotional commitment, and thus his attachment to a specific hotel."[80]

The author of the article, Lee Jin-soo, is also an associate professor of the School of Hotel and Tourism Management at the Hong Kong Polytechnic University and the article discusses a study the university did exploring the impact of economic and social rewards on the relational behavior of loyalty program members.[80] The university "conducted an online survey of 334 participants privy to various hotel reward programmes in the United States to study their responses towards economic reward based initiatives versus those based on social benefits."[80]

The findings revealed that a social reward dominant programme was "more effective than an economic reward oriented programme in encouraging favourable relational behaviours toward programme providers."[80]

The relational effects were especially apparent in the following areas: "openness (e.g. "I would feel comfortable telling the hotel when I think something needs improvement."), advocacy (e.g. "I would defend the hotel to others if I hear someone speaking poorly about it."), and immunity (e.g. "Even if I hear some negative information about the hotel, I would not switch to a competing hotel")."[80]

"When program members were exposed to customised, intrinsic offerings from a loyalty programme, they tend to be intrinsically motivated to stay with a hotel by developing emotional attachment, internal enjoyment, and affective commitment," Lee noted.[80]

In short, the study concluded that financial incentives alone wouldn't prevent customers from switching over to a competing program.[80] To foster relational behaviors and gain long-term benefits from a loyalty program, hotels needed to consider offering both social and economic rewards.[80]

In the article, Lee recommends the following:

> "Loyalty programme managers should consider economic benefits as a defensive relational strategy and social rewards as an offensive relational strategy in stimulating the relational behaviours of customers. Given the limitations of financial benefits in maintaining long-lasting customer relationships, and the practical need for striving cost-effectiveness in business operation, loyalty programme operators should adopt the strategy of providing economic rewards just to the extent of merely meeting, rather than greatly exceeding, members' expectations. At the same time, they should develop and offer

more customised offers, which can intrinsically motivate customers to foster a sense of belonging and emotional attachment to their hotel."[80]

Lee uses Thailand's Phuket Marine Biology Centre and the Royal Thai Navy's annual release of "baby turtles at a leading hotel in cooperation with the governor of Phuket and that hotel's guests"[80] as an example of a customized social reward.

At the event, "only members of the hotel's superclass loyalty programme are allowed to release baby turtles into the sea, which is a rewarding and memorable experience, especially for children."[80] "Such a preferential treatment is so meaningful to customers that they become reluctant to switch to any competing hotel that offers equal or even better financial incentives," Lee concludes.[80]

Of course, this book is about airlines and it isn't rooms that airlines are selling, so releasing baby turtles onto a Thai beach isn't available to most of them, but the important take-away here is that unique social rewards are what separates run-of-the-mill customer experiences from the truly memorable ones.

To make this entire loyalty/CRM/marketing system work, we are obviously talking about a huge amount of data flowing through these systems, utilizing everything from a typical EDW, to potential Hadoop clusters, as well as real-time stream processing applications like Spark, Flink, Storm, IBM's Infosphere, Hitachi's HDS, and TIBCO's StreamBase, maybe even some deep learning tools like TensorFlow and Caffe2, amongst others.

In many cases, acquiring a social identity that is tied to a customer record is as simple as asking for it; "Like" my page, "Follow" us, "heart" this, "Pin" that, "Snap" your story, "tweet or retweet" one of our offers and/or a story about your latest vacation. These are all wonderful ways to engage an audience, either connecting with a new customer or continuing to build a relationship with a current one.

Youtube Live, Facebook Live, Twitter, Periscope, Twitch, and the Chinese channels Panda.tv, Youku, Sina, Quanmin.tv, Huya, and Iqiyi are all great channels to market content through, but a word of warning, it has to be the right content at the right time. These channels have very particular audiences, so advertisers should spend the time to understand these channels in detail before marketing through them.

As Wedel & Kannan explain in their article *Marketing Analytics for Data-Rich Environments*[81], surveys are simple to administer, and data can be collected and analyzed very easily and quite quickly. "Firms continuously assess customer satisfaction; new digital interfaces require this to be done with short surveys to reduce fatigue and attrition. For example, loyalty is often evaluated with single-item Net Promoter Scores. As a consequence, longitudinal and repeated cross-section data are becoming more common," contend Wedel & Kannan.[81] Machine

Learning can be utilized to create personalized surveys that customers are much more likely to answer because they will be based upon the customer's response to previous questions.[81]

Data & Marketing

The history of the methodical use of data in marketing begins in 1910, with the work of Charles Coolidge Parlin for the Curtis Publishing Company in Boston.[82] According to Wedel and Kannan, "Parlin gathered information on markets to guide advertising and other business practices, prompting several major U.S. companies to establish commercial research departments."[81] Questionnaire survey research, which Gallup popularized in the 1820s with its opinion polling, became increasingly common in the 1920s.[83] At about the same time, "concepts from psychology were being brought into marketing to foster greater understanding of the consumer," explain Wedel and Kannan.[81]

Starch's attention, interest, desire, action (AIDA) model[84] is a example of this, and Starch is widely considered to be one of the pioneers of marketing and consumer research. This is also the era in which eye-tracking technology debuted, including the ability to collect data that followed the movements of the eye.[85] Interestingly it is a technology that is making a strong comeback almost a century later.

"In 1923, A.C. Nielsen founded one of the first market research companies. Nielsen started by measuring product sales in stores, and in the 1930s and 1950s, he began assessing radio and television audiences."[81] Today, Nielsen is a household word in the US and many places around the world and it dominates TV ratings in the US and several other countries. It is also moving into social media measurement today, although it didn't have the first mover advantage in this particular area, so only time will tell how successful it can be when challenging the dominate Internet companies on their own terms.

Beginning in the late 1970s, the market research firm Claritas started collecting geo-demographic data from government databases and credit agencies.[81] "The introduction of the Universal Product Code and IBM's computerized point-of-sale scanning devices in food retailing in 1972 marked the first automated capture of data by airlines."[81]

Companies like Nielsen "quickly recognized the promise of using point-of-sale scanner data for research purposes and replaced bimonthly store audits with more granular scanner data," notes Wedel and Kannan.[81] Shortly after the start of the data collection process, individual customers could be traced through their loyalty cards use, which led to the emergence of scanner panel data.[86]

The introduction of IBM's personal computer in 1981 enabled the collection of customer data on a massive scale.[81] Personal computers allowed marketers to store data on current and potential customers[81], contributing to the emergence of database marketing, which was pioneered by Robert and Kate Kestenbaum and Robert Shaw.[87]

"In 1990, CRM software emerged, for which earlier work on sales force automation at Siebel Systems paved the way."[81] Personal computers simplified survey research through personal and telephone interviewing.[81]

In 1995, after more than two decades of development at the Defense Advanced Research Projects Agency and several American universities, the internet was born, and this meant large volumes of marketing data were suddenly accessible to researchers.[81]

Clickstream data extracted from server logs allowed businesses to track page views and website clicks using cookies.[81] Click-through data revealed the true effectiveness of online advertising.[81] "The Internet stimulated the development of CRM systems by firms such as Oracle, and in 1999 Salesforce was the first company to deliver CRM systems through cloud computing," write Wedel and Kannan.[81]

Founded in 1998, Google championed keyword search and the capture of search data.[81] Google emerged from the highly competitive 1990s search environment, beating out the likes of Alta Vista, Yahoo!, Infoseek, and Lycos.

The launch of Facebook in 2004 opened up an era of social network data and it quickly eclipsed MySpace as the dominant social platform.[81] The arrival of User Generated Content (UGC), including pictures, online product reviews, blogs, and videos, resulted in an explosion in the volume and variety of data.[81]

"With the advent of YouTube in 2005, vast amounts of data in the form of user-uploaded text and video became the raw material for behavioral targeting," explains Wedel and Kannan.[81] Twitter, with its much simpler 140-character messages, appeared in 2006. While the social network, blogging, and micro-blogging scene solidified in the early 2000s, another important step for marketing measurement appeared in 2007 when Apple introduced the iPhone. With its global positioning system (GPS) capabilities, the first iPhone meant one could capture consumer location data at an unprecedented rate.[81]

In his article *This is How User's Data is Collected, Used and Even Sold On the Internet*[88], Hernaldo Turrillo explains that, "User's data has become gold in this new digital realm, a precious asset that needs to be harvested, gathered or forcedly grabbed whatever the cost."

Liam Hanham, director of data science at Elicit, explains that, "Customer data can be collected in three ways—by directly asking customers, by indirectly tracking customers, and by appending other sources of customer data on your own."[88] "A robust business strategy," Hanham argues, "needs all three."[88]

For example, "Facebook and Twitter collect data from tracking a user's precise location through the phone's Global Positioning System (GPS)," explains Turillo, adding that, although a user can refuse this, Facebook still has the means to see where the phone is going.[88]

In their article *What tech giants really do with your data*, BBC News' Tom Calver and Joe Miller claim that, "Many apps ask permission to track your precise location through your phone's Global Positioning System (GPS), which users can refuse. But even if you refuse the app permission, they can still see where you are."[89]

Calver and Miller give the example of Facebook collecting "location-related information aside from your phone's GPS. It still tracks where you are through IP addresses, 'check-ins or events you attend.'"[89]

Twitter also "requires" information about a user's current location, which it gleans from signals such as a user's IP address or device settings.[88] It claims this is so it can securely and reliably set up and maintain a user's account, at least according to official policy.[88]

Surprisingly, some companies even keep track of deleted search history because they want to build up the most accurate profile possible; messages, pictures, meta-data, and other manually entered information is kept.[88] "Having access to this 'old' data gives companies valuable information about what worked and didn't in previous ad campaigns," notes Turrillo.[88] A user's behavior can be tracked over time, adds Turrillo.[88] This can reveal interesting psychometric, demographic, and geolocation data that helps with segmentation, upsell and cross-sell marketing, and churn behavior. Data Director Liam Hanham argues that through this method, "they are incorporating direct feedback about what worked and what didn't, what a customer liked and disliked, on a grand scale."[88]

"Twitter also 'requires' information about your current location,"[89] Calvin and Miller add, which it gets from signals such as a user's IP address or device settings.[89] According to Twitter, this is so it can securely and reliably set up and maintain a user's account.[88]

The Tinder app collects data from a user's "phone's accelerometers (for measuring movement), gyroscopes (which measure the angle you're holding your phone at), and compasses,"[88] which all seems rather odd and slight overkill. Tinder refuses to explain what it is doing with the data, but this is an example that shows how people will sign just about any privacy policy that is put in front of them. This isn't really surprising because, as BBC Research found out, it takes about 40 minutes to read Apple's privacy policy.[88] Knowing this, it is unsurprising that few people bother reading the policy and they simply accept it, implicitly acknowledging that just about anything they do on their phone can and will be tracked.

Facebook offers the option of deleting searches from a user's history, which gives the user the false impression that these search records are wiped clean.[88] That isn't the case, however. Facebook's "data policy states that while search history can be deleted at any time, 'the log of that search is deleted after 6 months.'"[88]

Facebook even tracks what you do when you're not signed into the app—or even when you don't have an account. According to its data policy, Facebook works with "'advertisers, app developers and publishers', who can send them information 'about your activities off Facebook', through something called Facebook Business Tools," explains Turrillo.[88]

These partners apparently provide information about a user's activities off Facebook, including information about a user's device, websites a person has visited, purchases made, and ads viewed.[88] This happens "whether or not you have a Facebook account or are logged into Facebook," according to Turrillo.[88]

LinkedIn uses 'automatic scanning technology on messages', it does this, according to them, to protect users from malicious sites or spam, as well as to suggest automatic replies.[88] Most people would probably forgo the protection if offered the choice, but most people probably don't know about it, except when they click on those instant reply buttons that seem to know the full content of their LinkedIn message.

Twitter, meanwhile, uses data about whom a user has communicated with, as well as the time of the communication, but not the content. Twitter uses this data to better understand the use of its services, as well as to protect the safety and integrity of its platform.

Apple shares its user's personal data with companies who provide services such as information processing and extending credit.[88] It also uses this data to assess a user's interest in Apple products and services.[88] Turrillo ends his article with the warning that, "The EU's General Data Protection Regulation (GDPR), which came into force in May, does not order companies to list these third parties in their terms."[88]

As the reader should recognize, when it comes to data collection, almost anything goes. In the mind of the consumer, privacy has taken a backseat to data collection and this means airlines can follow the lead of the FANG companies and aggressively collect data on their customers, which can only help with customer intelligence and personalization marketing.

Early Analytics

The initiative of the Ford Foundation and the Harvard Institute of *Basic Mathematics for Applications in Business in late 1950s and early 1960s* is widely credited for providing the catalyst that introduced analytics into marketing.[90] By then, statistical methods, such as analysis of variance, had been utilized in marketing research for more than a decade[91], but the development of statistical and econometric models tailored to specific marketing problems only took off "when marketing was recognized as a field of decision making through the Ford/Harvard initiative."[92]

The development of Bayesian decision theory at the Harvard Institute[93] also played a key role, demonstrated by its successful application to, among other things, pricing decisions by Green.[94] Academic research in marketing then started focusing more on the development of statistical models and predictive analytics.[81]

New product diffusion models[95] involved applications of differential equations from epidemiology. Stochastic models of buyer behavior[96] were "rooted in statistics and involved distributional assumptions on measures of consumers' purchase behavior," add Wedel and Kannan.[81]

The application of decision calculus[97] [98] to optimize spending on advertising and the sales force became popular after its introduction to marketing by John Little in his *Models and Managers: The Concept of a Decision Calculus*.[99] Nakanishi and Cooper introduced market share and demand models for store-level scanner data in 1974, which were derived from econometric models of demand.[100]

According to Wedel and Kannan, multidimensional scaling and unfolding techniques, founded in psychometrics[101], also became an active area of research.[81] "These techniques paved the way for market structure and product positioning research by deriving spatial maps from proximity and preference judgments and choice," argue Wedel and Kannan.[81]

Conjoint analysis[102] and, later, conjoint choice analysis[103] are unique contributions that evolved from work in psychometrics by Luce on the quantification of psychological attributes.[104] Also, "The nested logit model that captures hierarchical consumer decision making, i.e., understanding the factors that influence the way a consumer shops, was introduced in marketing[105], and it recognized that models of multiple aspects of consumer behavior (e.g., incidence, choice, timing, quantity) could be integrated[106] into the marketing mix. This proved to be a powerful insight for models of recency, frequency, and monetary metrics[107], the method for analyzing customer value by looking at how recently someone has purchased an item, how often they purchase, and how much they spent. Time-series methods[108] can help airlines forecast sales, project yields and workloads, analyze budges, as well as enable researchers to test whether marketing instruments resulted in permanent or transient changes in sales.

In their paper *A Probabilistic Choice Model for Market Segmentation and Elasticity Structure*[109], Kamakura and Russell stated that heterogeneity in the behaviors of individual consumers becomes a core premise on which marketing strategy should be based, and the mixture choice model is the first to enable managers to identify response-based consumer segments from scanner data.[110]

Wedel and DeSarbo expounded upon this, arguing that the model should be generalized to accommodate a wide range of models of consumer behavior.[111] Rossi, McCulloch and Allenby concluded that consumer heterogeneity was represented in a continuous fashion in hierarchical Bayes models.[112]

Although scholars have hotly debated which of these two approaches best represents heterogeneity, i.e., the fundamental characteristic of services which result in variation from one service to another, research has revealed that the two different approaches each match specific types of marketing problems, with few differences between them.[113]

Today, it can safely be stated that the Bayesian approach is one of the most dominant modeling approaches in marketing, offering a powerful framework to develop integrated models of consumer behavior.[114] Bayesian models have been successfully applied to advertisement eye tracking[115], e-mail marketing[116], web browsing[117], social networks[118], and paid search advertising.[119]

According to Wedel and Kannan[81]:

Data-driven analytics in marketing has progressed from its inception around 1900 up to the introduction of the World Wide Web in 1995 through about three stages[81]:

1. "The description of observable market conditions through simple statistical approaches.
2. The development of models to provide insights and diagnostics using theories from economics and psychology.
3. The evaluation of marketing policies, in which their effects are predicted, and marketing decision making is supported using statistical, econometric, and OR approaches."[81]

In many cases, throughout the history of marketing analytics, once new sources of data get introduced, methods to analyze them are immediately developed. Figure 6 contains an outline of the history of data and analytical methods.

"Many of the methods developed by marketing academics since the 1960s have now found their way into practice and support decision making in areas such as CRM, marketing mix, and personalization and have increased the financial performance of the firms deploying them," note Wedel and Kannan.[81]

"Since 2000, the automated capture of online clickstream, messaging, word-of-mouth (WOM), transaction, and location data has greatly reduced the variable cost of data collection and has resulted in unprecedented volumes of data that provide insights on consumer behavior at exceptional levels of depth and granularity," explain Wedel and Kannan.[81]

Although academics have risen to the challenge of developing diagnostic and predictive models for the variety and velocity of data we've seen over the last decade, these developments are admittedly still in their infancy.[81]

On the one hand, descriptive metrics displayed on dashboards are popular in practice.[81] Perhaps because of "constraints on computing power, a need for rapid real-time insights, a lack of trained analysts, and/or the presence of organizational barriers to implementing advanced analytics."[81] In particular, unstructured data in the form of blogs, reviews, and tweets offer opportunities for deep insights into the economics and psychology of consumer behavior, which could usher in the second stage in digital marketing analytics once appropriate models are developed and applied," argue Wedel and Kannan.[81]

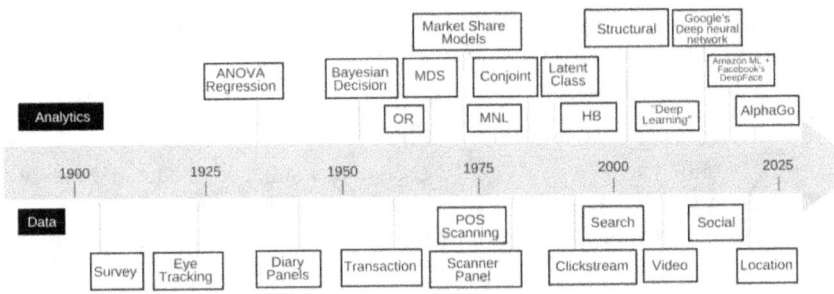

Figure 6: Timeline of Marketing Data and Analytics
Source: *Marketing Analytics for Data-Rich Environments*[81]

On the other hand, machine learning methods have become popular in practice, but have been infrequently researched in marketing academia. "It is reasonable to expect that the third step in the evolution of analytics in the digital economy— the development of models to generate diagnostic insights and support real-time decisions from big data—is imminent," conclude Wedel and Kannan.[81]

Mobile Marketing

If an advertising executive had set about to create the perfect marketing and advertising tool, she could hardly have created something more superior to the mobile phone. Not only is the mobile phone within reach of its owner almost every single hour of every single day but, because it can connect to a marketer in a highly personalized way with the simple touch of a button, it has the potential to become not only more effective than television or radio advertising but, just as importantly, more analyzable.

As the authors of *Mobile Advertising*[34] point out that, "With respect to targeting, no other medium can provide the accurate and rich user profile, psychographic, social engagement and demographic data available from mobile. No other medium has the viral capability that mobile possesses—within seconds following a simple click, a unit of advertisement can spread like wildfire."

No other media comes even remotely close to the data measurement capacity that mobile offers, which begins with exposure to the advertisement, followed by the persuasive effect of the advertisement and, finally, to the actual purchase of a product.[34] Just about every link in the marketer's chain is touched by mobile.

In 1996, the Internet advertising landscape changed forever when Procter & Gamble convinced Yahoo! that it would only pay for ads on a cost-per-click basis, rather than for banner ads.[34] Procter & Gamble realized the importance of gaining truthful user metrics for internet advertising and this move ushered in the world of internet analytics; eyeballs were no longer the goal, click-thrus that showed actual product interest were gold.

The time is right for mobile marketing. As Sharma et al., state in their book *Mobile Advertising*[34] because "the heavy lifting of measurements and metrics; of banner ad standards; of search keyword auctions; of advertising cost models and the new, digital ad networks that support them have been built. The groundwork for digital advertising in mobile is largely in place." However, because there are so many players involved, the mobile advertising value chain is incredibly complicated.[34]

As the authors point out in *Mobile Advertising*, "the mobile value chain comprises advertisers, agencies, solution providers and enablers, content publishers, operators and consumers. Phone manufacturers or original equipment manufacturers (OEMs) are enablers in this value chain rather than active participants."[34] The bottleneck in the chain arises because, even though there are only a limited number of mobile operators, the number of vendors in the value chain is exceedingly high.[34] Although this was written almost a decade ago, the complexity of the environment still remains and it is something that must be kept in mind when developing mobile marketing campaigns.

In their article *The Typological Classification of the Participants' Subjectivity to Plan the Policy and Strategy for the Smart Mobile Market*[120], Kim et al argue that the core technologies of cloud computing can greatly enhance mobile marketing efforts. Without cloud computing, it would be impossible to successfully produce targeting context-aware ads, real-time LBS ads, interactive-rich media ads, mobile semantic webs or in-app ads, advanced banner ads or incentive-based coupon ads, AR or QR codes, social network ads, and n-screen ads.[120] It would be especially difficult integrating and converging multifunctional mash-up ads involving a mix of the aforementioned.[120] "Smart mobile advertising products continuously derive combined services where two or more advertising techniques integrate and interlock due to innovative hardware or software technologies," Kim et al. conclude.[120]

Mobile advertising has the potential to give airlines the best bang for their marketing buck, but a mobile marketing campaign should not simply be viewed as an extension of a company's internet marketing brought to the mobile phone. In *Mobile Advertising*, the authors state that the three basic types of mobile advertising are[34]:

1. Broad-based brand advertising: broad-based campaigns that take advantage of user filtering and targeting. These can include subsidized premium content, sponsorships, video pre-rolls or intromercials, post-roll video, on-demand mobile media and contextual or behavioral advertising.
2. Interactive, direct response campaigns: these are opt-in campaigns in which the mobile user usually exchanges some personal information for some type of content. TXT short codes, mobile subscription portals, and user registration campaigns are all examples of this type of campaign.
3. Highly targeted search advertising: mobile's ability to inform advertiser of the user's basic age, sex, and address information is far better than any other form of advertising around. These campaigns include content targeted search advertising and paid placement or paid inclusion search.

Although there were hints that a marketing revolution was underway at the beginning of the 21st Century, few people would have predicted the radical changes that have transformed the industry—and the world—today. In their article *Interactivitys Unanticipated Consequences for Marketers and Marketing*[121], Deighton and Kornfeld argue that:

> "Mass communication technology empowered marketers with marketer-to-consumer tools such as radio, television and database-driven direct marketing. The digital innovations of the last decade made it effortless, indeed second nature, for audiences to talk back and talk to each other. They gave us peer-to-peer tools like Napster, eBay, Tivo, MySpace, YouTube, Facebook, Craigslist and blogs, and information search tools like Google and Wikipedia. Mobile platforms have given us ubiquitous connectivity, context-aware search, and the ability to tag and annotate physical spaces with digital information that can be retrieved by others. In sum, new traffic lanes were being built, not for the convenience of marketers, but for consumers."

Successful marketing is about reaching a consumer with an interesting offer when he or she is primed to accept it. Knowing what might interest the consumer is half the battle to making the sale and this is where customer analytics comes in.

Customer analytics have evolved from simply reporting customer behavior to segmenting customers based on their profitability, to predicting that profitability, to improving those predictions (because of the inclusion of new data), to *actually manipulating customer behavior* with target-specific promotional offers and marketing campaigns. Chapter two will detail this and other types of analytics an airliner can use in deep detail, but I thought it advisable to describe it here, to set up the scene as it were.

Data must be gathered from disparate sources and seamlessly integrated into a data warehouse that can then cleanse it and make it ready for consumption.[122] Trends that surface from the data mining process can help in monetization, as well as in future advertising and service planning.[34] As the authors state in *Mobile Advertising*[34]:

> *"The analytical system must have the capability to digest all the user data, summarize it, and update the master user profile. This functionality is essential to provide the rich user segmentation that is at the heart of recommendations, campaign and offer management, and advertisements. The segmentation engine can cluster users into affinities and different groups based on geographic, demographic or socio-economic, psychographic, and behavioral characteristics."*

Of course, with all of this data collection comes justified privacy concerns and the most important aspect of mobile marketing is ensuring the consumer has control of the advertising, especially in the US.[34] Without this, it is doubtful mobile marketing will reach its true potential.[34] If mobile advertisers do allow users to configure and control the ads depending on where they are, what mood they are in, who they are with, and what their current needs and desires happen to be, mobile marketing could prove to be one of the most successful forms of advertising available to airline marketers.[34]

The potential to market to an individual when she is primed to accept the advertising is advantageous for both parties involved. Marketers don't waste time making offers to consumers when they aren't primed to accept the advertisements but do market to consumers when and where they might want to use the advertisements.

One of the most interesting companies working in the digital marketing space right now is the customer experience management company Sitecore, whose platform Sitecore 8 was released in late summer of 2014. In her article *Sitecore 8 Aims to Add Context To Customer Connections*[123], Ginger Conlon explains that Sitecore 8 helps marketers enhance the customer experience by delivering consistent, integrated experiences across multiple channels, while responding to customer cues in real time.

"The more you know about someone and the context they're in, the better experience you can provide for them," Sitecore CEO Michael Seifert said during his Sitecore conference keynote.[123] "Seifert emphasized that experiences are unique to each individual, so it's essential that marketers understand customers' context and preferences at an individual level."[123] "The mass experience won't last much longer," he warned.[123]

Sitecore 8's new features—enhanced data collection, automated testing and optimization, improved customization, and real-time reporting—are designed to make it easier to gather data from such disparate sources as CRM, ERP, and customer service systems to create a holistic view of a customer.[123]

The "automated testing and optimization tools are designed to recommend the ideal content to present, the best segments to target, and the optimal paths to conversion."[123] "Real-time reporting shows customer decision points, and highlights what's working and what's not."[123] Seifert argues that technology is failing the marketer because each technology gives only a keyhole view of the customer rather than a holistic view, which means marketers aren't getting the full picture.[123]

According to Seifert, "experience marketing tools are the next generation of marketing technology, designed to provide a single view of the customer in real time to enable marketers to deliver personalized experiences."[123] By using these tools, marketers will get the full picture of their customers, rather than only disparate fragments.[123] "Only when you see the full experience can you predict optimally," Seifert added.[123]

Seifert argues that customer experience can make or break a brand.[123] "Brands must provide the right experience at the right time to get the attention and loyalty of today's modern consumer," he says.[123] "Experience is the magic. It's what ultimately matters, the lasting impression. As you get that single view of the customer you'll know things about your customers that no computer alone can tell you. Imagine the kind of personalization you can do; the experiences you can create," Conlon marvels.[123]

Although I am describing Sitecore here, all of the other major players, including Adobe, IBM, SAP, SAS, HDS, Microsoft, Oracle, etc., are jumping aboard the customer context bandwagon as it is an integral part of any customer experience solution. You're going to find they generally all do the same thing, but with slight variations and I detail some of the differences in this book.

Digital Interactive Marketing: The Five Paradigms

Deighton and Kornfeld believe that in this new media environment, there are five emerging marketing paradigms that are responses to the decrease of marketing's power relative to the consumer.[121] Digital interactive marketing has little use for words such as "viewer" and "listener".[121] Even the label "consumer" is of limited value because today's interactions with a person will include encounters that have nothing to do with consuming or being part of a "target market." Deighton and Kornfeld see this new digital interactive marketing breaking down into five different paradigms[121], as per Table 2.

Today, when a user searches for information or entertainment on sites such as Google, she leaves a trail (also known as a "clickstream") that reveals what is on her mind.[121] This information, which Deighton and Kornfeld refer to as "thought tracing", may be "available to marketers in exactly the sense that it is available to marketers through Google, as a clue to our thoughts, goals and feelings."[121]

Mobile and social media alter the marketing landscape because the ubiquitous nature of computing makes it an "always on" proposition; both the thought *and* the activity are being traced.[121] "The argument is that when a person is always connected to the Internet, the person is always in the market, always available to be communicated with, and always an audience," contend Deighton and Kornfeld.[121]

Of course, most people don't like to be marketed to continuously throughout the day so technology that allows people to filter out messages that don't interest them needs to be developed.[121] However, customized marketing messages will be allowed to get through. Just as television demands its audience to sit through commercials in order to enjoy free programming, Deighton and Kornfeld contend that, "we will enjoy ubiquitous computer connectivity for the price of voluntary exposure to context-specific persuasion efforts."[121]

If businesses want to succeed in this new marketing environment they must become an ally to the marketed individual, someone who is actually sought out as a person with cultural capital.[121] "Property exchanges", "social exchanges" and "cultural exchanges" are all paradigms that are "built on peer-to-peer interactivity motivated by the desire to exchange, to share information, or to express one's self" state Deighton and Kornfeld.[121]

Interactive marketing paradigm	How people use interactive technology	How firms interpose themselves to pursue marketing goals	Resulting digital media markets
Thought tracing	People search the web for information and browse for entertainment.	Firms infer states of mind from search terms and Web page content and serve relevant advertising.	A market in search terms develops.
Activity tracing	People integrate always-on computing into everyday life.	Firms exploit information on proximity and pertinence to intrude.	A market in access and identity develops.
Property exchanges	People participate in anonymous exchanges of goods and services.	Firms compete with these exchanges, rather than participating with them.	A market in service and reputation and reliability develops.
Social exchanges	People build identities within virtual communities.	Firms sponsor or co-opt communities.	A market in community develops, competing on functionality and status.
Cultural exchanges	People observe and participate in cultural production and exchange.	Firms offer cultural products or sponsor their production.	Firms compete in buzz markets.

Table 2: Digital Interactive Marketing: Five Paradigms
Source: Journal of Interactive Marketing[121], 23 pg. 4-10

Arguably, internet property exchanges were introduced on a mass scale by Napster, which was the first company to allow users to share and exchange files in an anonymous way.[121] Unsurprisingly, Napster ran into trouble with copyright holders and quickly left the content exchange business, but sites such as eBay, Flicker and YouTube allow users to share and even sell their property over the Internet. This is a trend that is not going to go away any time soon, if ever.

While the property exchange deals in things, the social exchange deals in identities and reputations.[121] In general, social networking sites let a person present a face to the world, "including information about whereabouts and action and a 'wall' on which friends can post short, often time-sensitive notes, allows people to exchange digital gifts, provides a marketplace for buying and selling, and allows posting of photographs and video clips."[121]

These sites allow for contextually relevant advertising because friends can share information amongst each other and some of this information can include a marketer's message. Since this messaging is coming from a trusted source, the message is considered much more trustworthy and enticing and, therefore, much more likely to be acted upon. For example, "a recent Nielsen analysis of 79 campaigns on Facebook over six months showed that, on average, social ads—those that are served to users who have friends that are fans of or have interacted with the advertised brand and prominently call the relationship out—generate a 55 percent greater lift in ad recall than non-social ads."[124]

One of the key criteria of mobile marketing is that a consumer must opt-in to the service. Mobile marketing is primarily a "pull" media model, meaning a consumer must sign up for the service rather than the traditional "push" media model, which gives the consumer no choice in whether they want to be advertised to or not.

Airline mobile marketers must spend money to get users to sign up, but, if they do, the potential market for mobile marketing is huge. It is also a market that is rapidly evolving, and its advantages include:

- Ubiquity: mobile devices and their users are everywhere.
- Effective: over 90% of received text messages are read by the recipient.
- Powerful two-way dialogue: an instantaneous link between the business and its customer is generated.
- Economical: compared to other marketing channels, mobile marketing is incredibly cheap per marketed individual.
- Spam-free: in the U.S. (but not in many other parts of the world) it is illegal to send a text message to someone who hasn't opted-in to a marketing campaign.

In her book, *The Mobile Marketing Handbook*[125], Kim Dushinski lists eight types of advertising campaigns that a mobile marketer can engage in:

1. Voice: this includes text-to-call messages in which users are sent a link that, when clicked upon, initiates a phone call to the company sending out the message. These days, Apple's SIRI, Microsoft's Tellme, Alexa, and Google's Now are adding a whole new dimension to voice.
2. Text messaging: this used to be the "now" marketing tool of mobile, and it is still one of the most important tools available. Text messaging includes both SMS and Common Short Codes (CSC), which are abbreviated phone numbers. Text messages are sent to mobile users, the content of which are limited only by SMS character limitations and the marketer's overall imagination.
3. Mobile web: most smart phones have the ability to connect to the web and many of them have graphic capabilities that rival computer screens.

4. Mobile search: a mobile user can search company listings through his or her mobile phone, just as he or she can find this information on the Internet.
5. Mobile advertising: placing banner ads and text ads on mobile websites can build brand awareness.
6. Mobile publicity: presenting a company's executives as experts in his or her field can be useful to members of the media who need instant information for fast approaching deadlines.
7. Social networking: done right, this can help marketers tap into word-of-mouth campaigns, which will, hopefully, have their marketing messages lighting up social media websites.
8. Proximity marketing: Bluetooth and geofencing campaigns that invite users to accept a multimedia message can deliver unique and location-specific marketing messages.

To these eight, I would add another two—OTT and mobile apps marketing—and I will break each of these campaigns down throughout the rest of this book.

Proximity Marketing

Proximity marketing "is the localized wireless distribution of advertising content associated with a particular place. Transmissions can be received by individuals in that location who wish to receive them and have the necessary equipment to do so," explains Wikipedia.org.[126] There are four main systems used for proximity marketing; Bluetooth-based systems; NFC-based systems; GSM-based systems (via SMS); and iBeacon-based systems.

Considered the "killer-app" for mobile commerce, the commercial viability for proximity marketing or "location-aware advertising" (LAA) is enormous. In location-aware advertising, a cellular subscriber receives an advertising message based on his or her location, so a shopper wandering through a mall could set his or her mobile phone to accept all available mobile offers or just offers from a specific store.

In their article *Foundations of SMS Commerce Success: Lessons from SMS Messaging and Co-opetition*[127], Xu et al. argue that LAA allows advertisers to deliver highly customized promotions, coupons and offers to an individual, specifically taking into account their geographical location, as well as the time of day of the offer. LAA also allows advertisers to reach their customers when they are primed to make a purchase.

iBeacon is the trademark for an indoor proximity marketing system that Apple calls, "A new class of low-powered, low-cost transmitters that can notify nearby iOS 7 devices of their presence. The technology enables an iOS device or other hardware to send push notifications to iOS devices in close proximity. Devices running the Android operating system can receive iBeacon advertisements but cannot emit iBeacon advertisements."[128]

According to Wikipedia, the iBeacon system uses "Bluetooth low energy Proximity sensing to transmit a universally unique identifier picked up by a compatible app or operating system that can be turned into a physical location or trigger an action on the device such as a check-in on social media or a push notification."[128]

In her article *Your iPhone is Now a Homing Beacon (But It's Ridiculously Easy to Turn it Off)*[129], Kashmir Hill warns that this technology opens the door to more aggressive monitoring, tracking and communication from people with apps on their phone, which will vary from convenient to invasive. In those lengthy terms of service and privacy (that few people read), app makers can slip in tracking permission warns Hill.[129] "Hypothetically, an airline with its app on your phone could tell iBeacon to turn the app on when you're in or near the store, send information about your being there to a database and then pop up some advertising," Hill warns.[129]

"At this point, every party that wants to communicate with you needs its app on your phone. Inevitably, some monster advertising network will develop a one-stop-iBeacon-shop app that will allow it to act as the conduit for lots of different people to ping your phone," Hill claims.[129] But that day is probably still a few years away.

Currently, as Shane Paul Neil explains in his article *Is iBeacon Marketing Finally Taking Off?*[130], "McDonald's has seen an increase in sales from a test run using the iBeacons, and Virgin Atlantic is among the first to use them as thermostats to supply cold passengers with blankets. iBeacons also have the potential to enhance B2B marketing with its ability to target users' smartphones at trade shows or other events."

However, as Shane Paul Neil warns, the delay in implementing beacon technology probably has to do with one of the following four possible reasons[130]:

1. Installing, managing, and maintaining beacons can be a struggle.
2. Beacon signals are often obstructed by physical objects.
3. Beacon marketing requires user opt-in.
4. Consumers aren't sold on the benefits of beacons.

In his *Washington Post* article *How iBeacons could change the world forever*[131], Matt McFarland sees a world where iBeacon technology can do the following:

1. Send a coupon to a consumer because they have entered an area.
2. React when a user walks into his or her home, turning on lights or televisions.
3. Provide tours of museums.
4. Automatically send concert or sporting events tickets to a phone that approaches an arena's turnstiles.

5. Win something for visiting a car dealership or a retail outlet.
6. Be warned when someone's car or bike is no longer in his or her garage.

These and many other examples can be created for proximity marketing and even though each upcoming year is claimed to be the "Year of iBeacons technology", betting against Apple is often a losing proposition, eventually.

Geofencing Applications

Today, most smart phones have geofencing capabilities that tap into GPS or RFID technology to define geographical boundaries. Basically, geofencing programs allow an administrator to set up triggers—usually SMS push notifications or email alerts—so when a device crosses a "geofence" and enters or exits a set area, a user is notified. Applications such as Facebook, Foursquare and China's WeChat and Jiepang use geofencing to locate users, as well as help them find their friends and/or check into places.

As TechTarget explains, geofencing has many uses, including[132]:

- Mobile Device Management—When a host's tablet PC leaves the airline property an administrator receives a notification, so the device can be disabled.
- Fleet management—When a truck driver breaks from his route, the dispatcher receives an alert.
- Human resource management—An employee smart card will send an alert to security if an employee attempts to enter an unauthorized area.
- Compliance management—Network logs record geofence crossings to document the proper use of devices and their compliance with established rules.
- Marketing—A retail business can trigger a text message to an opted-in customer when the customer enters a pre-defined geographical area.
- Asset management—An RFID tag on a pallet can send an alert if the pallet is removed from the warehouse without authorization.

With geofencing applications, "users can also offer peer reviews of locations, which add a layer of user-generated content. In exchange for loyalty, more and more businesses—from local airlines to larger organizations like Bravo TV, Starbucks and The History Channel—are offering coupons, discounts, free goods and marketing materials."[133]

SERVICES	EXAMPLES	ACCURACY NEEDS	APPLICATION ENVIRONMENT
EMERGENCY SERVICES	Emergency calls	Medium to High	Indoor/Outdoor
	Automotive Assistance	Medium	Outdoor
NAVIGATION SERVICES	Traffic Management	High	Outdoor
	Indoor Routing	Medium	Outdoor
	Group Management	Lot to Medium	Indoor
INFORMATION SERVICES	Travel Services	Medium to High	Outdoor
	Mobile Yellow Pages	Medium	Outdoor
	Infotainment Services	Medium to High	Outdoor
MARKETING SERVICES	Banners, Alerts, Advertisements	Medium to High	Outdoor
TRACKING SERVICES	People Tracking	High	Indoor/Outdoor
	Vehicle Tracking	Low	Outdoor
	Personnel Tracking	Medium	Outdoor
	Product Tracking	High	Indoor
BILLING SERVICES	Location-sensitive billing	Low to Medium	Indoor/Outdoor

Table 3: Taxonomy of mobile location services
Source: Durlacher Research

As users continue to enter personal details as well as update and check-in to their locations, geofencing applications like Foursquare can "collect a historical view of consumer habits and preferences and, over time, possibly recommend a much larger variety of targeted marketing materials in real time—as a consumer walks into a store to look for a specific item or service."[133]

In their paper *On the Potential Use of Mobile Positioning Technologies in Indoor Environments*[134], Giaglis et al. claim that there are six different types of service uses for mobile positioning technology (see Table 3).

Geofencing applications (aka Location Based Services (LBS)) like Jiepang and Foursquare are useful services for airline marketers as well. Although the article *LBS Opportunities for Casino Marketers in Macau*[135] is about casinos in Macau, the ideas Chris Wieners offers are also useful for the airline industry. For example, to get their LBS promotions rolling[135]:

1. Pick your LBS service and claim your location.
2. Offer tips to customers via LBS.
3. Reward loyalty creatively. Start by offering your most loyal customers rewards, special access, and other promotions. Those that become your

"Mayor"—or any other significant title—should be rewarded for their loyalty. This is a great way to identify potential social influencers and utilize them to further promote your venue.
4. Reward new customers: First time check-ins should receive special promotions or incentives as it is important to give people a reason to continuously check in to your establishment.
5. Understand who your loyal customers are online, and work with them. Develop a plan to utilize these 'influencers' and tap into their social networks. "Casinos do it offline all of the time; develop a similar approach for high-valued customers online through social connections. Encourage your followers to promote their checked-in status to their friends via social networks and micro blogs like Sina and Twitter."[135]
6. Promote your services both online and off-line.

In May of 2013, Lighthouse Signal Systems launched its indoor positioning system as an open service for Android app developers.[136] Developers can use the technology to create Android apps that will help users find their way through the vast indoor terrain of Las Vegas' hotels and airlines.[136]

Although global positioning systems have made outdoor navigation as simple as following directions on a mobile device, indoor navigation isn't so simple, it is actually one of the last major hurdles that smartphones have yet to truly conquer.[136] However, Cambridge, Mass.-based Lighthouse Signal Systems has launched a service that covers 20 million square feet of entertainment and retail space at leading airlines and hotels on the Las Vegas Strip.[136]

Lighthouse is "making its service freely available to Android app developers, resort operators, airlines, and others seeking to enhance the visitor experience in Las Vegas. Indoor navigation is the Holy Grail for the mobile industry, and Lighthouse says it is the first to provide GPS-like indoor positioning on a wide scale in a major U.S. metro."[136]

"We are excited to support app developer partners as they create new mobile experiences with indoor positioning in Las Vegas, where large resort interiors have traditionally presented a vexing challenge for visitors," said Lighthouse co-founder Parviz Parvizi.[136]

Lighthouse's platform "includes indoor geofencing: a hosting platform for location-based offers and user analytics."[136] The app includes user opt-in agreements and developers cannot use the service to track mobile phone users without their consent.[136]

The technology uses "a combination of WiFi fingerprinting and sensor data. As long as there are WiFi networks in the area, Lighthouse can provide positioning info."[136] Google, Cisco, Ekahau, Euclid, Shopkick, PointInside, Aisle411, Sensionlab, Indoor.rs, Yfind, and CSR are all developing similar systems.[136]

Mobile marketing in general and OTT, MMS and SMS marketing in particular can help airlines create a one-to-one, two-way interactive experience with its customers. These channels are not just about sending out a simple message, but rather they are about starting a customer relationship that can be analyzed so that the airline has a 360-degree understanding of its customer. It is an understanding that should include his or her wants, desires and needs.

Besides geo-fencing applications, social media channels like Facebook, Foursquare, Instagram, Twitter, WeChat, as well as many others can reveal a customer's location. Instagram tracks a user's photos even if he or she doesn't geo-tag them. As Cadie Thompson warns in her article *Social media apps are tracking your location in shocking detail*[137], "While the picture sharing app does give users the option to name the location of where they are uploading an image, it also geotags an uploaded pic regardless if the user has selected the 'Add to Photo Map' function."[137]

Foursquare's check-in app Swarm also broadcasts users' location even if they have not selected a specific location for check-in.[137] Many live-streaming apps like Periscope, YouTube, and several Chinese ones will also show the location of the user and this is information that can be utilized by an airline's marketing department if it can exploit the information quickly enough. Although YouTube doesn't have a filter for location, websites like geosearchtool.com allows users to search by location. Advanced filters allow searching by keyword and within a certain designated area.

Besides the normal geo-location apps, airlines should also look into the smaller ones such as Bizzy, Glympse, Neer (neerlife.com), and social gaming app Scvngr.

Facial Recognition

Facial recognition technology is the capability to identify or verify a person from a digital image or a video frame from a video source by comparing the actual facial features of someone on camera against a database of facial images, or faceprints, as they are also known.

Rapid advancements in facial-recognition technology have reached the point where a single face can be compared against 36 million others in about one second.[138] A system made by Hitachi Kokusai Electric and reported by DigInfo TV shown at a security trade show recently was able to achieve this blazing speed by not wasting time on image processing.[138]

Using edge analytics, the technology takes visual data directly from the camera to compare the face in real time.[138] The software also groups faces with similar features, so it can narrow down the field of choices very quickly. The usefulness to the airline's security enforcement is pretty obvious, but it can be used by multiple departments; facial recognition technology can be set up to send alerts to airline clerks, managers, or just about anyone needing to identify people.

Once a face has been recognized, alerts can be sent to an airline clerk through a mobile app or an SMS message. A screen can display the passenger's name, or a photo just taken from the video feed can be sent to a first-class lounge host.

As customers enter an airline lounge, "security cameras feed video to computers that pick out every face in the crowd and rapidly take many measurements of each one's features, using algorithms to encode the data in strings of numbers,"[139] as explained in the *Consumer Reports* article *Facial Recognition: Who's Tracking Who in Public.*[139] These are called faceprints or templates.[139] The faceprints are compared against a database, and when there's a match, the system alerts the VIP department or sales people. Faceprints could also be used to allow people to purchase tickets or as part of a boarding system.

Currently, facial recognition technology can be more useful for security departments than customer service.[139] At the 2014 Golden Globe Awards, facial recognition technology was used to scan for known celebrity stalkers.[139] The technology has also been used to bar known criminals from soccer matches in Europe and Latin America.[139] "Police forces and national security agencies in the U.S., the United Kingdom, Singapore, South Korea, and elsewhere are experimenting with facial recognition to combat violent crime and tighten border security."[139]

Facial recognition technology is becoming second nature to consumers, who are used to tagging themselves in photos on Facebook, Snapchat, Picasa, and/or WeChat. In 2015, Google launched a photo app that helped users organize their pictures by automatically identifying family members and friends.[139] Google, however, suffered a public relations and social media disaster when its system labeled a photo of two black people as gorillas.[139] The search giant quickly apologized profusely and promised to fix its algorithms[139], but this does show that the technology isn't foolproof and sensitivity is important.

Currently, MasterCard is "experimenting with a system that lets users validate purchases by snapping a selfie. Like fingerprint scanners and other biometric technologies, facial recognition has the potential to offer alternatives to passwords and PINs."[139]

This technology is moving so fast, privacy advocates are having trouble keeping up it all. In this regard, today's facial recognition technology is reminiscent of the World Wide Web of the mid-1990s.[139] Back then, few people would have anticipated that every detail about what we read, watch, and buy online would become a commodity traded and used by big business and sometimes, more sinisterly, hacked and used by nefarious individuals to perpetrate crimes.[139]

Facial recognition technology "has the potential to move Web-style tracking into the real world, and can erode that sense of control."[139] Experts such as Alvaro

Bedoya, the executive director of Georgetown Law's Center on Privacy & Technology, and the former chief counsel to the Senate's subcommittee on privacy, technology, and the law finds this attack on privacy alarming.[139]

"People would be outraged if they knew how facial recognition" is being developed and promoted, Bedoya states.[139] "Not only because they weren't told about it, but because there's nothing they can do about it. When you're online, everyone has the idea that they're being tracked. And they also know that there are steps they can take to counter that, like clearing their cookies or installing an ad blocker. But with facial recognition, the tracker is your face. There's no way to easily block the technology," Bedoya warns.[139]

Right now, facial recognition is largely unregulated, and few consumers seem to even be aware of its use. "Companies aren't barred from using the technology to track individuals the moment we set foot outside. No laws prevent marketers from using faceprints to target consumers with ads. And no regulations require faceprint data to be encrypted to prevent hackers from selling it to stalkers or other criminals," Bedoya warns.[139] This is true in the United States, Asia, and in Europe.

Users might be happy to tag their face and the faces of their friends and acquaintances on a Facebook wall, but they might shudder if every mall worker was jacked into a system that used security-cam footage to access their family's shopping habits.[139]

This could, however, be the future of retail, according to Kelly Gates, associate professor in communication and science studies at the University of California, San Diego.[140] In her article *Our Biometric Future: Facial Recognition Technology and the Culture of Surveillance*[140], Gates argues that "Regardless of whether you want to be recognized, you can be sure that you have no right of refusal in public, nor in the myriad private spaces that you enter on a daily basis that are owned by someone other than yourself." Gates concluded that by entering an establishment filled with facial recognition technology, you are tacitly giving your consent to the airline to use it, even if you are unaware of its use.[140]

Facial recognition technology in the offline world is now becoming more and more prevalent, particularly in the hospitality industry. "On Disney's four cruise ships, photographers roam the decks and dining rooms taking pictures of passengers. The images are sorted using facial recognition software so that photos of people registered to the same set of staterooms are grouped together. Passengers can later swipe their Disney ID at an onboard kiosk to easily call up every shot taken of their families throughout the trip."[139]

Starting in 2010, the 1,200-room Hilton Americas-Houston in Texas used a facial recognition system that was mainly designed as a security tool to identify VIP guests so the hotel staff could greet them by name.[139] The hotel won't confirm if the system is still active, but similar technology is being rolled out at retail locations worldwide.[139]

Apparently, some surprising uses of facial recognition technology are also popping up. In 2015, a company called Churchix revealed it had installed facial recognition systems in dozens of churches around the world to track service attendance.[139] Once made public, the technology received a wave of bad publicity, which is hardly a surprise as if there's one place where people should expect privacy, it is within the confining walls of their church. Hearing that it isn't God watching over them, but rather, literally, their priest, one would expect church goers to feel as though their privacy had been violated and the churches that are using the technology seem to concur as none of them agreed to go on record to explain their position.[139]

Surveillance in the pews may seem like a particularly egregious violation of privacy, but evidence suggest facial recognition does tend to make people uncomfortable wherever it appears.[139] "In a recent study of 1,085 U.S. consumers by research firm First Insight, 75 percent of respondents said they would not shop in a store that used the technology for marketing purposes. Notably, the number dropped to 55 percent if it was used to offer good discounts."[139] Airlines should take this in account if it chooses to implement facial recognition technology.

However, consumers may warm to facial recognition technology once it becomes more widespread, especially if airlines offer enough incentives to make it worth their while. In some cases, full facial recognition isn't needed, some marketers just want to determine the age, sex, and race of shoppers, although many vendors are now rolling out technology that not only recognizes the face but also the emotion.

In Germany, the Astra beer brand recently created an automated billboard directed solely at women, even to the point of shooing men away.[139] The billboard approximated the women's age, then played one of 80 pre-recorded ads to match.[139] For an airline, this could help if they want to direct specific advertising towards women, or to men, or to a certain age group.

In 2014, Facebook announced a project it called DeepFace, "a system said to be 97.35 percent accurate in comparing two photos and deciding whether they depicted the same person—even in varied lighting conditions and from different camera angles. In fact, the company's algorithms are now almost as adept as a human being at recognizing people based just on their silhouette and stance."[139]

"Entities like Facebook hold vast collections of facial images," says Gates, the UC, San Diego professor.[139] "People have voluntarily uploaded millions of images, but for their own personal photo-sharing activities, not for Facebook to develop its facial recognition algorithms on a mass scale."[139] Unfortunately for privacy advocates, there is no difference between the two.

Potentially Facebook, Instagram, WeChat, Pinterest, Snapchat, Google, and a whole host of other social media platforms could use their vast databases of faceprints to power real-world facial recognition.[139] "Hypothetically, a tech giant wouldn't need to share the faceprints themselves. It could simply ingest video feeds from a store and let salespeople know when any well-heeled consumer walked through the door."[139] It could also, potentially, do this for an airliner as well, to prevent money laundering, as well as for Know Your Customer (KYC), or AML activities.

Gamification

In his article *Earn Your Wings: Air Canada's Successful Gamification Venture into Loyalty*[141], Gabe Zichermann states that "There's little question that the loyalty 'industry' has an innovation problem." "With few exceptions," Zichermann notes, "the world's largest loyalty programs (mostly in travel, finance and retail) are mostly the same as they were 20 years ago. Social, mobile, gamification have struggled to find a footing, even as they are the entire foundation of next-gen loyalty systems such as those developed by Square, Belly or any number of gamified providers."[141]

In their paper *Defining Gamification - A Service Marketing Perspective*[142], Huotari and Hamari define 'Gamification' as "a process of enhancing a service with affordances for gameful experiences in order to support user's overall value creation."

Zichermann considers Air Canada's *Earn Your Wings* campaign a prime example of a company using gamification the way it was intended to be used. The program "created a leaderboard of top flyers during the promotional period that were ranked based on a range of activities. These included, but weren't limited to, miles flown and were supported by a series of badges awarded for different activity loops."[141] According to Zichermann, "Top players split a large pot of 10 million miles at the end of the promotion period, and that activity seemed especially fierce, which is what really excited me."[141]

Ian Di Tullo, Director of Loyalty for Air Canada (AC) explained that the company had been experimenting with socializing loyalty for a while, but a 'big win' had remained elusive.[141] "The company's business objectives however mandated that they try innovative ways to get people to be 'cross activated', meaning: fly further, fly more often, and spend more to fly. Their competitive market dictated that they needed to keep trying, and gamification was the obvious solution," claimed Di Tullo.[141]

In Di Tullo's words, "gamification's principal purpose was to vastly simplify this promotion's inherent complexity, adding 'badges, in particular, make it very easy to focus customers on pretty complicated tasks, and those are the foundation for lasting behavior change.'"[141] For example, Di Tullo explains, "if you want users to visit 3 new cities, fly to both coasts and go in first class twice, it's much easier to create 'incomplete badges' for each activity and display them on a page than to explain each one separately in text."[141] Once users understand the simple concept "that each badge represents a challenge to be completed, it acts as a valuable shorthand for behavior."[141]

Competition amongst members is also fostered, which is an example of social proof and I discuss that in chapter three. "Another element of the Air Canada leaderboard campaign that was attention grabbing was the competitive nature of the program, as leaderboards are inherently competition oriented."[141] Di Tullo explained "that the company sees loyalty program users divided into two groups: regular users, and highly-engaged users with a competitive streak."[141] The goal "was not to shy away from the competitive elements of loyalty—as most other programs have done—but rather to embrace them."[141] "By ensuring that competition could occur with some privacy protection (user handles and blended point systems aided this), the idea was to activate that competitive desire," notes Di Tullo.[141]

According to Air Canada, the program was a huge success.[141] "Although Di Tullo couldn't disclose specific revenues, the program's registration levels were double the forecast, and engagement levels for both active and inactive users were better than expected," says Zichermann.[141] Not only did the program achieve a positive ROI, but it got people to share their loyalty activity with others on social media, which isn't always something people tend to crow about.[141]

In a guest editorial titled *Gamification of Loyalty—improving customer engagement*[143] for Airlineinformation.org, Aaron Carr, CEO of Friendefi writes that, "loyalty marketers are increasingly viewing gamification as a complementary approach that can help strengthen their own customer engagement efforts."

Carr adds that, "the opportunities to boost loyalty program member engagement don't end with better data capture. In an increasingly digital world, gamification also offers a framework for motivating members to learn about your program, interact with partner offers, and to share (or even compete) with their friends."[143]

Carr provides an example from the American Airlines' AAdvantage Passport Challenge, which offers "loyalty members the opportunity to earn stamps for their digital passport as well as miles for completing various AAdvantage program and partner games and trivia from their computer or mobile phone."[143] "Customers reported spending 15-20 minutes playing the various games and trivia, which tested their knowledge of American's AAdvantage program and partner offers," explains Carr.[143]

Gamification is still a young and fast-moving practice, especially amongst loyalty marketers.¹⁴³ It is a technology airlines should look at because it has multi-channel engagement possibilities, can connect with a user on his or her mobile device, and it can add an element of excitement that will prove enticing to a passenger's competitive spirit.

New Distribution Capability

As I previously mentioned, New Distribution Capability (NDC) is a "new ticket-selling approach uses airlines' enormous Big Data capturing abilities in concert with new artificial intelligence or 'machine learning' methods to present to each travel shopper a unique, all-in price that includes not only the basic cost a seat but also the cost of many (or even all) of the travel services the traveler will need or want."⁹

For example, if you could be a customer who likes "sitting in a right-hand aisle seat near the front of the coach cabin where there's extra leg room, will want one cocktail and a meal featuring fish, plus will be checking two bags and will need a town car to pick you up at your destination airport and take you to your preferred hotel where you'll require a concierge floor room for two nights, you will get one price quote including all of those services."⁹ This price takes into consideration "your company's volume discount deals negotiated with both the airline and the hotel company, and the deal your company has with a local ground transportation company in your destination city."⁹ Your quote wouldn't be considered a "fare quote," *per se,* but rather a "travel experience" or "journey" price quote.⁹ Eventually, retail items, like a swimsuit if you're headed to Cancun, or ski goggles if on your way to snowy Aspen could also be included.⁹

It all sounds like a hyper-concierge offering and it is made available because of the high level of data collection that has been going on over the past few decades. All of it will happen without a user "having to calculate the cost of 'extras' in his or her head.⁹ Indeed, buyers should be blissfully unaware of the technology that all of these "dynamic pricing" calculations are taking place behind the scenes almost instantaneously, notes Reed.⁹ All of the needed technology is currently available so it should be a surprise to anyone that this pricing structure is about to be rolled out.

Harteveldt jokingly gripes that the system should be called 'New Retailing Capabilities' instead of 'New Distribution Capabilities' because, above all else, the new opportunities NDC technology opens up is the selling of a huge array of services and products, many of which are not travel-related.⁹

Reed notes that, "Clearly, airlines see the new approach to how they sell their seats and other services as a way of tapping into a new, rich vein of revenue and profits."⁹ Reed warns that some travel consumer watchdogs are wary of this because NDC has the potential of making air travel pricing, which is an already opaque process even more.[9]

"But airlines, analysts and even some consumer watchdogs themselves see NDC as a way of providing many travelers, especially frequent fliers, with more accurate and understandable prices early in the travel purchasing process while allowing consumers to buy the services they truly value without today's exasperating 'nickel and dime' process of paying more for each additional service desired," adds Reed.[9]

Also, proponents of NDC selling argue that no-frills buyers that don't want extra services will still have access to the low-priced fares through existing sales channels, which aren't expected to be going anywhere.[9]

"Some will be concerned, and will be right to be concerned, that consumers will struggle to understand what's being offered," Harteveldt says.[9] "So it will be essential for airlines to be clear and unambiguous about what's included in each package offered so the consumer can make a fully-informed decision."[9]

About 15 years ago big carriers, in an effort to remain competitive in a new price-conscious market, began to unbundle their services to the point where, by the early 2010s, the quoted 'fare' price that consumers received was drastically different from the real cost of travel.[9]

Unbundling 'extra services' from the basic fare gave airlines "a way of advertising prices that were the same as, or reasonably competitive with discount airlines' fares," notes Reed.[9] "Only after purchasing such an unbundled ticket did consumers then have to pay for any extra services they wanted from conventional airlines," adds Reed.[9]

"Unbundled fares have been an unqualified hit with very price sensitive leisure travelers. Yet many other travelers, especially high mileage business travelers, quickly grew weary with, and resentful of being 'nickeled and dimed' with additional fees for services beyond the basic fare," argues Reed.[9]

At the same time, "airline executives quickly came to believe that they were missing opportunities to extract more money from business travelers for services that they willingly would have paid more to receive because those services would make their travels more pleasant and productive."[9]

"But because airlines didn't control the means of selling their seats to a huge percentage of such customers they could not provide those customers with immediate relief from such irritants. Nor could they properly offer their preferred customers the kind of value-added services such customers are believed to really want and are willing pay more to get," warns Reed.[9]

"Increasingly, business travelers and others who fly frequently enough to have very specific wishes for their travel accommodations will be able to get price quotes not for a "fare," in the classic sense of the word, but for a whole array of value-added travel services," write Reed.⁹ Convenience will be key as travelers will be able to decide in advance which services they want included, or excluded, in his or her package of services, while will be priced for them as a package deal.⁹

Neil Geurin, director of distribution strategy at American Airlines claims American has been working on NDC for 10 years, and has always been the most aggressive in pushing the NDC technology.⁹ It has done, Guerin claims, "not because American believes NDC distribution itself will lower its currently high costs of selling tickets but because consumers will rather quickly come to prefer doing business in an NDC environment."⁹ Geurin might have a good case as, in many cases, consumers consider convenience above all else.

"Our feeling is that if we are the easiest airline to do business with then customers will choose to fly with us more often," Geurin says.⁹

At its core, NDC is "a way for airlines once again to offer bundled services, but on a very specific and individualized basis. And the general belief is that consumers – especially business travelers and other frequent fliers – quickly will become big fans of the new selling channel, concludes Reed.⁹

Travelport, a global distribution system used by travel sellers, has been the first seller to get its NDC service certified by IATA.⁹

"Look, it has taken time to do this," Harteveldt says. "It's very complex. A lot of software code had to be written, tested, revised and confirmed to make it work as intended. And it's adoption by the public isn't going to happen overnight either. Even five years from now we'll still be in the early year of adoption and acceptance of NDC."⁹

"As with any new technology, once you get through the early teething pains, follow-on updates are going to be easier to add. Ten years from now it'll be in widespread use," Harteveldt believes.⁹ He acknowledged that, "There'll be airlines around the world that choose not to use NDC; maybe smaller or midsize carriers, or those less likely to connect with other airlines or be in one of the big global alliances. Budget airlines may continue to get most of their customers through their own (private sales) channels."⁹

"But those bigger, conventional airlines that choose not to embrace NDC will lose out," Harteveldt predicts.⁹ "They won't have the flexible selling platform that they will need to meet an ever-more sophisticated traveling public's expectations."⁹ In a world where personalization marketing surrounds us both online and off, from companies that have accumulated so much information about our wants, desires and needs, we might just be ready to jump into a bundled world like this.

Near Field Communication

According to nearfieldcommunication.org[144], Near field Communication (NFC) "is a form of contactless communication between devices like smartphones or tablets. Contactless communication allows a user to wave the smartphone over a NFC compatible device to send information without needing to touch the devices together or go through multiple steps setting up a connection."

In her article *NFC: The bridge between IoT and the consumer*[145], Paula Hunter is convinced that "NFC technology will be the technology of choice for enabling IoT devices and that NFC tags embedded in IoT objects will provide us 'connectivity on our terms.'" "NFC technology enables simple and safe two-way interactions between electronic devices, at a distance of less than 10 centimeters, allowing consumers to perform contactless transactions, access digital content and connect electronic devices with a single tap. Best of all, NFC technology now comes standard on smartphones," Hunter adds.[145]

"NFC technology is very secure and designed for sensitive uses, such as IoT applications in payment systems, transport, ticketing, corporate access and cloud computing authentication," says Hunter.[145] "NFC is a tested, proven, sophisticated, easy-to-use technology that 2.2 billion people on the planet already have access to," adds Hunter[145]

In Dignited's article *5 Great uses of NFC Technology*[146], Kikonyogo Douglas Albert states that, NFC "is multiplying into a feature that almost every smartphone comes embedded with. This wireless radio communication technology that allows users to use tags with their smartphones when close enough, is of great use when pairing and transferring data from one device to another."

Quick Tap utilizes NFC "to do the business of delivering secure, easy, fast and efficient payments and access to control services. They install NFC tap to pay terminals at the client premises which users with NFC devices such as phones, cards, wristbands, and stickers can tap to make payment or access premises," explains Albert.[146]

In his article *9 Surprising Real-Life Uses For NFC, The Technology Transforming Mobile Payments*[147], Alex Heber adds a few other NFC ideas, including:

- Use as a bus or train ticket—"In Australia, the NSW government has spent a substantial amount of money rolling out its Opal card system. NFC has the capability of taking this system one step further."[147]
- It can remember passwords—NFC technology can be used to scan and log a device onto a network.
- Payment device—NFC users can tap a reader to pay for things an NFC-compatible payment device.

- Car radio connector—a Bluetooth-compatible car radio can be used with an NFC tag.
- Tour guide. "NFC can be used to guide tourists around a city. They can wave their devices in front of tags to give them information about iconic landmarks, download maps or coupons. The tech doesn't require wifi and can transfer small bits of data to keep tourists informed, explains Heber.[147]
- Use to connect with interactive advertising—An NFC-enabled chip can be implanted in a multitude of items, including clothes, sports equipment, and advertising. "NFC chips and stickers are tiny, and also relatively cheap. Their increasing prevalence in both mobile handsets and in retailers means people are rapidly becoming used to the idea, so it's a space to watch for consumers, and fertile ground for innovators," says Heber.[147]

Smart Tones

According to Lisnr, an American company launched in 2012, "Smart Tones are a revolutionary and proprietary data-over-audio communication protocol."[148]

In her CNBC article *Lisnr wants to make airline and concert tickets a thing of the past using sound waves*[149], Kellie Ell notes that, "Smart tones are an alternative to WiFi and Bluetooth-based communications, so you don't need an internet connection to send data. Lisnr's software, a near-ultrasonic, low-power data transmission technology, can transmit data between devices by way of a speaker and a microphone."[149]

Lisnr plans to disrupt the entire ticketing industry.[149] "That industry has chosen to go to mobile ticket," says Rodney Williams, co-founder of Lisnr, adding, "Every time you use a ticket or at an airline, they've chosen a QR code. But it's a fraudulent vehicle. I can screenshot it. I can share it. It's one of the reasons why you still have to use your ID."[149]

"QR codes are the real issue," Williams explained, noting that "China implemented a ban on mobile payments, over certain amounts, that use QR codes at the end of 2017 due to the security risks."[149]

"One company that Lisnr is disrupting but at the same time working with is Live Nation Entertainment's Ticketmaster, which is using the sound-based technology as an alternative to conventional ticketing methods," says Ell.[149]

"Apple Pay, as another example, uses NFC chip technology, which is more secure than QR codes but is expensive to deploy, as it requires more costly hardware," adds Ell.[149]

Lisnr's wants to be "as flexible as a QR code but more secure, while less expensive than NFC chips but still scalable."[149]

"We imagine a world where sound is more seamless," Williams said.[149] "Better consumer experience. But we're matching the security element of an NFC-type transaction."[149]

Lisnr has over "100 partnerships and customers, including Intel Amdocs, JLR, and Visa, and the technology is used in about 100 million devices worldwide.[149]

"What Google has proved is that there is a value in the technology, and we are proving it's bigger than a single platform," Williams said.[149]

Google's has been using the technology in India, where it works as a mobile wallet payment solution.[149] "India has security issues and data constraints because it costs a lot to transfer data. Sound is less data-intensive and more secure than a QR code," states Williams.[149]

"The Lisnr CEO expects the personal artificial intelligence and home assistant market led by Amazon Echo, Google Home and Apple HomePod to push into this area."[149] However, security issues will surface because data from cloud-based voice services, such as Alexa, can be hacked.[149]

"There [are] always bad actors," Williams said on CNBC.[149] "But a bad actor still has to intrude your device. And that intrusion happens through USB and any other methods of downloads to a particular device. That intrusion could use Bluetooth, WiFi or any other way to cause mischief on your device."[149]

"Lisnr's data transmission through ultrasonic audio bypasses this process."[149] "Voice-enabled services should detect you using something else. That's us," Williams said, adding, "It's actually a standard that could apply significant security to the entire world of ultrasonic use."[149]

Conclusion

The mobile ad of the future will be created by a sophisticated analytical-driven mobile advertisement system that juxtaposes relevant advertiser content that corresponds to the mobile user's personal profile and context variables.[34]

If airlines want to succeed in this new marketing environment, they must become an ally to the marketed individual, someone who is actually sought out as a person with cultural capital.[121] "Property exchanges", "social exchanges" and "cultural exchanges" are all paradigms that are "built on peer-to-peer interactivity motivated by the desire to exchange, to share information, or to express one's self," contend Deighton and Kornfeld.[121] Deighton and Kornfeld argue that of all the paradigms, "the most potent of the new media are those that enable cultural exchange, media currently exemplified by the functionality of YouTube and Facebook."[121]

In the next couple of chapters, I will look at how these technologies can shape the customer experience so that true personalization can be delivered to a market of one. Capturing a first-time visitor's IP address can be an important—and necessary—first step in the customer relation and once a user signs up for a loyalty card all of his or her customer information becomes relevant.

Analyzing clickstream data, customer card data, marketing data, as well as social media data can help airlines develop three dimensional profiles on each of their customers and, once these profiles are perfected, the behavioral marketing work can begin to ensure that the airline is bringing in customers that will produce the highest ROI. Matching customer needs with the airline's staffing and operational requirements then becomes an added cost reduction perk.

---

56 Vatash, Prateek. (2018). 2018 Digital Trends I Retail. Adobe. https://wwwimages2.adobe.com/content/dam/acom/uk/modal-offers/pdfs/Econsultancy-2018-Digital-Trends-Retail_EMEA.pdf (Accessed 6 August 2018).
57 Jones, Andrew (2015, December 15). Study finds marketers are prioritizing personalization...but are further behind than they realize, http://venturebeat.com/2015/12/14/study-finds-marketers-are-prioritizing-personalization-but-are-further-behind-than-they-realize/ (Accessed 26 November 2017).
58 http://insight.venturebeat.com/report/marketing-personalization-maximizing-relevance-and-revenue?utm_source=vb&utm_medium=refer&utm_content=editorial-post&utm_campaign=personalization-report (Accessed 26 November 2017).
59 Lovelock, C. a. (2010). Services Marketing, People, Technology, Strategy, Seventh Edition. Prentice Hall.
60 https://en.wikipedia.org/wiki/Social_CRM (Accessed 25 November 2017).
61 Greenberg, P. (2009, July 6). Time To Put a Stake in the Ground On Social CRM. Retrieved from ZDnet.com: http://www.zdnet.com/blog/crm/time-to-put-a-stake-in-the-ground-on-social-crm/829
62 Wangenheim, F. v. (2005). Postswitching Negative Word of Mouth. *Journal of Service Research*, 8, No. 1, 67-78.
63 Rigby, Darrell. 2015. Management Tools 2015. An Executive's Guide. Bain & Company. http://www.bain.com/publications/articles/management-tools-customer-relationship-management.aspx (Accessed 25 November 2017).
64 https://en.wikipedia.org/wiki/Market_segmentation (Accessed 25 November 2017).
65 Britt, P. (2013) Big Data Means Big Benefits for Entertainment: Caesars Exec, http://loyalty360.org/resources/article/big-data-means-big-benefits-for-entertainment-caesers-exec, accessed 5 January 2016.
66 Marr, Bernard. May 2, 2016. Big Data in Practice. John Wiley & Sons.
67 Urbanski, A. (2013, February 1). At Caesars, Digital Marketing Is No Crap Shoot. Retrieved from DM News: http://www.dmnews.com/at-caesars-digital-marketing-is-no-crap-shoot/article/277685/ (Accessed 25 November 2017).

68 Customer Loyalty – Not for Sale, for Rent. (2001). CRMGuru.com. 31 May 2001. www.crmguru.com.
69 T_HQ Technology and Business. (2018). What does the CRM of the future look like? 17 July 2018. https://techhq.com/2018/07/what-does-the-crm-of-the-future-look-like/ (Accessed 8 August 2018.
70 Kivetz, R. & Simonson, I. (2003). The idiosyncratic fit heuristic: Effort advantage as a determinant of consumer response to loyalty programs. Journal of Marketing Research, 40(4), 454-467.
71 Petrick, J. F. (2004). Are loyal visitors desired visitors? Tourism Management, 25(4), 463-470.
72 Reichheld, F. a. (1990). Zero defections: quality comes to services. Harvard Business Review, 105-111.
73 White House Office of Consumer Affairs.
74 Nielsen Company. (2012). Global Trust in *Advertising and Brand Messaging.* Nielsen Company.
75 The Customer Satisfaction-Loyalty Relationship from Thomas O. Jones and W. Earl Sasser, Jr., "Why Satisfied Customers Defect" Harvard Business Review, Nov.–Dec. 1995, p. 91. Reprinted by permission of Harvard Business School.
76 Kumar, V. V. (2006). Knowing What to Sell, When, and to Whom. Harvard Business Review.
77 Eckerson, Wayne. 2007. Predictive Analytics, Extending the Value of Your Data Warehouse Investment. TDWI Best Practices Report. https://www.sas.com/events/cm/174390/assets/102892_0107.pdf (Accessed 25 November 2017).
78 https://www.chirpify.com/announcing-chirpify-moderation-brands-can-now-moderate-social-triggers/ (Accessed September 7, 2017).
79 http://www.chiefmarketer.com/pro-awards-winners-2017 (Accessed September 7, 2017).
80 Lee Jin-soo. 24 March, 2017. Getting it right: mixing social and economic rewards in hotel loyalty programmes. South China Morning Post. http://www.scmp.com/business/companies/article/2081624/getting-it-right-mixing-social-and-economic-rewards-hotel-loyalty (Accessed 25 November 2017).
81 Wedel, Michel and Kannan, P.K. (2016) Marketing Analytics for Data-Rich Environments. Journal of Marketing: November 2016, Vol. 80, No. 6, pp. 97-121. https://www.rhsmith.umd.edu/files/Documents/Departments/Marketing/wedel-kannan-jm-2016-final.pdf (Accessed 4 November, 2017).
82 Bartels, Robert (1988), The History of Marketing Thought, 3rd ed. Columbus, OH: Publishing Horizons.
83 Reilly, W.J. (1929), Marketing Investigations. New York: Ronal Press Company.
84 Starch, Daniel (1923), Principles of Advertising. Chicago: A.W. Shaw Company
85 Nixon, H.K. (1924), "Attention and Interest in Advertising," Archives de Psychologie, 72 (1), 5–67.
86 Guadagni, Peter M. and John D.C. Little (1983), "A Logit Model of Brand Choice Calibrated on Scanner Data," Marketing Science, 2 (3), 203–38.

87 Shaw, Robert (1987), Database Marketing, Gower Publishing Co.

88 Turrilo, Hernaldo. (2018). This is How User's Data is Collected, Used and Even Sold On the Internet. IntelligentHQ. 8 August 2018. https://www.intelligenthq.com/social-media-posts/this-is-how-users-data-is-collected-used-and-even-sold-on-the-internet/ (Accessed 9 August 2018).

89 Calvin, Tom, and Miller, Joe. (2018). What tech giants really do with your data. BBC News. https://www.bbc.co.uk/news/business-44702483 (Accessed 9 August 2018).

90 Winer, Russell S. and Scott A. Neslin, eds. (2014), The History of Marketing Science. Hackensack, NJ: World Scientific Publishing.

91 Ferber, Robert (1949), Statistical Techniques in Market Research. New York: McGraw-Hill.

92 Bartels, Robert (1988), The History of Marketing Thought, 3rd ed. Columbus, OH: Publishing Horizons.

93 Raiffa, Howard and Robert Schlaifer (1961), Applied Statistical Decision Theory. Boston: Clinton Press.

94 Green, Paul E. (1963), "Bayesian Decision Theory in Pricing Strategy," Journal of Marketing, 27 (January), 5–14.

95 Bass, Frank (1969), "A New Product Growth for Model Consumer Durables," Management Science, 15 (5), 215–27.

96 Massy, William F., David B. Montgomery, and Donald G. Morrison (1970), Stochastic Models of Buying Behavior. Cambridge, MA: MIT Press.

97 Little, John D.C. and Len M. Lodish (1969), "A Media Planning Calculus," Operations Research, 17 (1), 1–35.

98 Lodish, Leonard M. (1971), "CALLPLAN: An Interactive Salesman's Call Planning System," Management Science, 18, P-25–40.

99 Little, John D.C. (1970), "Models and Managers: The Concept of a Decision Calculus," Management Science, 16 (8), B-466–485.

100 Nakanishi, Masao and Lee G. Cooper (1974), "Parameter Esti- mation for a Multiplicative Competitive Interaction Model: Least Squares Approach," Journal of Marketing Research, 11 (August), 303–11.

101 Coombs, Clyde (1950), "Psychological Scaling Without a Unit of Measurement," Psychological Review, 57, 148–58.

102 Green, Paul E. and Srinivasan, V. (1978), "Conjoint Analysis in Consumer Research: Issues and Outlook," Journal of Consumer Research, 5 (2), 103–23.

103 Louvie´re, Jordan J. and Woodworth, George. (1983), "Design and Analysis of Simulated Consumer Choice or Allocation Ex- periments: An Approach Based on Aggregate Data," Journal of Marketing Research, 20 (November), 350–67.

104 Luce, R. Duncan and John W. Tukey (1964), "Simultaneous Conjoint Measurement: A New Scale Type of Fundamental Measurement," Journal of Mathematical Psychology, 1 (1), 1–27.

105 Kannan, P.K. and Gordon P. Wright (1991), "Modeling and Testing Structured Markets: A Nested Logit Approach," Marketing Science, 10 (1), 58–82.

106 Gupta, Sunil (1988), "Impact of Sales Promotions on When, What, and How Much to Buy," Journal of Marketing Research, 25 (November), 342–55.

107 Schmittlein, David C. and Robert A. Peterson (1994), "Customer Base Analysis: An Industrial Purchase Process Application," Marketing Science, 13 (1), 41–67.
108 DeKimpe, Marnik G. and Dominique M. Hanssens (1995), "The Persistence of Marketing Effects on Sales," Marketing Science, 14 (1), 1–21.
109 Kamakura, Wagner A. and Gary J. Russell (1989), "A Probabilistic Choice Model for Market Segmentation and Elasticity Structure," Journal of Marketing Research, 26 (November), 379–90.
110 Kamakura, Wagner A. and Gary J. Russell (1989), "A Probabilistic Choice Model for Market Segmentation and Elasticity Structure," Journal of Marketing Research, 26 (November), 379–90.
111 Wedel, Michel and Wayne S. DeSarbo (1995), "A Mixture Likelihood Approach for Generalized Linear Models," Journal of Classification, 12 (1), 21–55.
112 Rossi, Peter E., Robert E. McCulloch, and Greg M. Allenby (1996), "The Value of Purchase History Data in Target Marketing," Marketing Science, 15 (4), 321–40.
113 Andrews, Rick L., Andrew Ainslie, and Imran S. Currim (2002), "An Empirical Comparison of Logit Choice Models with Dis- crete Versus Continuous Representations of Heterogeneity," Journal of Marketing Research, 39 (November), 479–87.
114 Rossi, Peter E. and Greg M. Allenby (2003), "Bayesian Statistics and Marketing," Marketing Science, 22 (3), 304–28.
115 Wedel, Michel and Pieters, Rik (2000), "Eye Fixations on Advertisements and Memory for Brands: A Model and Findings," Marketing Science, 19 (4), 297–312. White, Percival (1931), Market
116 Ansari, Asim and Mela, Carl F. (2003), "E-Customization," Journal of Marketing Research, 40 (May), 131–45.
117 Montgomery, Alan L., Shibo Li, Kannan Srinivasan, and John C. Liechty (2004), "Modeling Online Browsing and Path Analysis Using Clickstream Data," Marketing Science, 23 (4), 579–95.
118 Moe, Wendy W. and Trusov, Michael (2011), "The Value of Social Dynamics in Online Product Ratings Forums," Journal of Marketing Research, 48 (June), 444–56.
119 Rutz, Oliver J., Michael Trusov, and Randolph E. Bucklin (2011), "Modeling Indirect Effects of Paid Search Advertising: Which Keywords Lead to More Future Visits?" Marketing Science, 30 (4), 646–65.
120 Kim, K. L. (2012). The typological classification of the participants' subjectivity to plan the policy and strategy for the smart mobile market. Korean Management Review, 367-393.
121 Deighton, J. &. (2009). Interactivity's Unanticpated Consequences for Marketers and Marketing. *Journal of Interactive Marketing*, 23, 4 - 10.
122 Sharma, R. S. (2009). The Economics of Delivering. *Journal of Media Business Studies*, 1-24.
123 Conlon, G. (2014, September 15). *Sitecore 8 Aims to Add Context to Customer Connections*. Retrieved from dmnews.com: http://www.dmnews.com/sitecore-8-aims-to-add-context-to-customer-connections/article/371420/ (Accessed 25 November 2017)
124 Nielsen Company. (2012). *Global Trust in Advertising and Brand Messaging*. Nielsen Company.
125 Dushinski, K. (2012). *The Mobile Marketing Handbook.* Information Today, Inc.

126 https://en.wikipedia.org/wiki/Proximity_marketing (Accessed 25 November 2017)
127 Xu, H. T. (2003). "Foundations of SMS Commerce Success: Lessons from SMS Messaging and Co-opetition." *Proceedings of 36th Hawaii International Conference on System Sciences* (pp. 90-99). Los Angeles: IEEE Computing Society Press.
128 https://en.wikipedia.org/wiki/IBeacon (Accessed 25 November 2017).
129 Hill, K. (2013, December 10). Your iPhone Is Now a Homing Beacon (But It's Ridiculously East to Turn Off). Retrieved from forbes.com: http://forbes.com/sites/kashmirhill/2013/12/10/your-iphone-is-now-a-homing-beacon
130 Neil, Shane Paul. June 17, 2016. Is iBeacon Marketing Finally Taking Off? The Huffington Post. http://www.huffingtonpost.com/shane-paul-neil/is-ibeacon-marketing-fina_b_10508218.html (Accessed 25 November 2017).
131 McFarland, Matt. How iBeacons could change the world forever. January 7, 2016. Washington Post. https://www.washingtonpost.com/news/innovations/wp/2014/01/07/how-ibeacons-could-change-the-world-forever/?utm_term=.182e91de201b (Accessed 25 November 2017).
132 TechTarget. (2011). *Geofencing definition*. Retrieved from TechTarget: http://whatis.techtarget.com/definition/geofencing (Accessed 25 November 2017).
133 Berman, S. J., Battino Bill, Feldman, Karen. 2007. *Executive Brief: Navigating the media divide: Innovating and enabling new business models*. IBM Institute for Business Value.
134 Giaglis, G. M. (2002). On the Potential Use of Mobile Positioning Technologies in Indoor Environments. 15th Bled Electronic Commerce Conference eReality: Constructing the eEconomy. Bled, Solvenia.
135 Weiners, C. (2012, March 30). *LBS Opportunities for Casino Marketers in Macau*. Retrieved from clickz.com. https://www.clickz.com/lbs-opportunities-for-casino-marketers-in-macau/38526/ (Accessed 23 October 2017).
136 Takahashi, D. (2013, May 22). Lighthouse's new Android location service could give you indoor navigation for Las Vegas' airlines. Retrieved from Venturebeat.com: http://venturebeat.com/2013/05/22/lighthouse-signal-systemss-android-app-will-let-you-find-your-way-inside-the-biggest-las-vegas-airlines/ (Accessed 25 November 2017).
137 Thompson, Cadie. May 28, 2015. Social media apps are tracking your location in shocking detail. Business Insider. http://www.businessinsider.com/three-ways-social-media-is-tracking-you-2015-5 (Accessed 25 November 2017).
138 Bea, Francis. March 25, 2012. Goodbye, anonymity: latest surveillance tech can search up to 36 million faces per second. www.digitaltrends.com http://www.digitaltrends.com/cool-tech/goodbye-anonymity-latest-surveillance-tech-can-search-up-to-36-million-faces-per-second/ (Accessed 25 November 2017).
139 Facial recognition: Who's Tracking You In Public. (December 30, 2015) Consumer Reports. Online: http://www.consumerreports.org/privacy/facial-recognition-who-is-tracking-you-in-public1/ (Accessed 25 November 2017).
140 Gates, Kelly A. January 23, 2011. Our Biometric Future: Facial Recognition Technology and the Culture of Surveillance. NYU Press.

141 Zichermann, Gabe. Earn Your Wings: Air Canada's Successful Gamification Venture into Loyalty. Gamification.co. 8 July 2013. http://www.gamification.co/2013/07/08/earn-your-wings-air-canadas-successful-gamification-venture-into-loyalty/ (Accessed 16 August 2016).

142 Huotari, Kai, and Hamari, Juho. (2012). Defining Gamification - A Service Marketing Perspective. Proceedings of the 16th International Academic MindTrek Conference 2012, Tampere, Finland, October 3–5. https://www.researchgate.net/profile/Juho_Hamari/publication/259841647_Defining_ Gamification_-_A_Service_Marketing_Perspective/links/0c96052e13e865be0 http://www.gamification.co/2013/07/08/earn-your-wings-air-canadas-successful-gamification-venture-into-loyalty/ 0000000/Defining-Gamification-A-Service-Marketing-Perspective.pdf (Accessed 16 August 2018).

143 Carr, Aaron. Gamification of Loyalty—improving customer engagement. Airlineinformation.org. http://www.airlineinformation.org/opinion/loyalty-a-crm/785-gamification-of-loyalty-improving-customer-engagement.html

144 http://nearfieldcommunication.org/

145 Hunter, Paula. (2018). NFC: the bridge between IoT and the consumer. 18 July 2018. TechTarget. https://internetofthingsagenda.techtarget.com/blog/IoT-Agenda/NFC-The-bridge-between-IoT-and-the-consumer (Accessed 9 August 2018).

146 Albert, Kikonyogo Douglas. (2017). 5 Great uses of NFC Technology. Dignited.com. 10 November 2017. https://www.dignited.com/25763/great-uses-nfc-technology/ (Accessed 9 August 2017).

147 Heber, Alex. (2014). *9 Surprising Real-Life Uses For NFC, The Technology Transforming Mobile Payments.* Business Insider Australia. 19 August 2014. https://www.businessinsider.com.au/7-surprising-real-life-uses-for-nfc-the-technology-transforming-mobile-payments-2014-8 (Accessed 9 August 2018).

148 http://lisnr.com/resources/blog/what-is-a-smart-tone/

149 Elle, Kellie. (2018). Lisnr wants to make airline and concert tickets a thing of the past using sound waves. CNBC. 23 May 2018. https://www.cnbc.com/2018/05/23/making-airline-concert-tickets-a-thing-of-the-past-using-sound-waves.html (Accessed 9 August 2018).

CHAPTER TWO

Analytics

"The better I shoot, the less I have to maneuver."
~Eddie Rickenbacker

Overview

The above quote by the World War I ace Eddie Rickenbacker could be a motto for the analytics process of personalization marketing, i.e., the better I aim at my target, the better my marketing hit-ratio. During World War I, machine guns were attached to the ariplane and had limited movement, so it was the pilot's job to line up an opponent in his sights and stick as close to his target as possible, which obviously wasn't an easy thing to do.

According to his *New York Times obituary*[150], "Rickenbacker was officially credited with shooting down 22 planes and four balloons," so he knew what he was talking about in terms of aim. A common trick of WWI pilots was to position themselves so that they would come out of the sun, which isn't a bad philosophy for companies to conduct business today, i.e., surprise attacks from a blindside.

In her article *How Much ROI Can Data Analytics Deliver?*, Annie Eissler states that, according to Nucleus Research, "analytics and business intelligence solutions deliver, on average, $13.01 for every dollar spent."[15] Eissler adds that, "We're at a point where the hype surrounding data analytics has converted into real, documented returns for companies of all sizes and across all industries. But the truth is, leading companies have been achieving double-digit return on investment (ROI) from their analytics investments for several years now."[15]

Nina Sandy, a Nucleus Research analyst, argues that, "Companies don't have the luxury anymore to wait weeks for reports on the profitability of business decisions in increasingly fast paced markets."[15] "New analytics solutions are being developed around this need where businesses can make better decisions, faster," adds Sandy.[15]

The fact that so many software vendors are adding analytics to their standard data mining, data integration, CRM, social media, marketing automation, and other offerings is reducing prices for analytics software across the board. When it comes to price, you obviously can't beat open source prices, i.e., free, but there is no free lunch in the software industry, and these open source products do require skilled consultants to write the code and build the systems. This does often mean the sting of the yearly license/maintenance fee that comes with commercial software is removed, but there are other high costs involved.

Eissler warns that, "You need the technology to enable analytics, but if you don't understand the technology that enables the analytics—or the business application—then it won't provide any value,"[15] which is an accurate assessment; "junk in, junk out," as any good analyst will tell you. Eissler concludes that, "The real value comes when you take the technological component of analytics and apply it to a business component that—once optimized—produces a solid ROI that continues to pay off over time."[15]

Analytics is, of course, a huge field and, in this chapter, I will mostly focus on customer analytics, which, when coupled with insights from social media data, can enable organizations to make faster strides in predicting retention, attrition, and return rates, with the goal of reducing customer churn, raising customer lift, and/or increasing a whole host of other metrics.[151]

The airline industry is a data-rich industry and most people in the industry would probably agree with the assessment that, although there are many data sources needed, they are disconnected and under-analyzed. Yang and Borowczak recognize this problem in the retail industry in their paper *Assessing Retail Employee Risk Through Unsupervised Learning Techniques*.[152] It is worth reviewing the issues that the writers find as the airline industry faces similar problems, which pose both challenges and big opportunities to an airline.

Sources such as transactional data, clickstream data, as well as service and call center records are highly important for customer analytics.[151] These can both improve how a retail organization decides on characteristics for customer segmentation, and also provide clues to emerging characteristics for the definition of new segments.[151] As David Stodder explains in his article *Customer Analytics in the Age of Social Media*[151], "Firms can employ predictive modeling to test and learn from campaigns so that they are able to select the most persuasive offers to put in front of the right customers at the right time."[151]

As Webopedia.com explains, customer analytics "exploits behavioral data to identify unique segments in a customer base that the business can act upon. Information obtained through customer analytics is often used to segment markets, in direct marketing to customers, predicate analysis, or even to guide future product and services offered by the business."[151]

In the most basic sense, customer analytics is made possible by combining elements of business intelligence, software such as IBM's Cognos, SAP's Lumira and Business Object's suite, and Qlik's QlikView and Qlik Sense, amongst a whole host of others, with predictive analytics solutions like SAP's and SAS's suite of analytical tools, as well as R, Python, WEKA, etc., etc.

In IBM's *Achieving Customer Loyalty with Customer analytics*[153], IBM argues that customer analytics can uncover "patterns and trends in customer behavior and sentiment hidden among different types of customer data such as transactions, demographics, social media, survey and interactions." "The results of the analysis are then used to predict future outcomes so businesses can make smarter decisions and act more effectively."[153] Results from these models can then be presented back to the business users in easily digestible dashboards and scorecards.[153] "Self-learning predictive models ensure that each new iteration of customer analytics insight and the business decisions it drives become more accurate and effective," argues IBM.[153]

Customer analytics can also help determine which of an airline's advertising campaign or advertising partner's pages have the highest landing rates, as well as show conversion rates for all of a retailing company's advertising and marketing budgets. Mobile analytics can also display how many visitors downloaded material from a site, which can help in factoring a company's advertising and marketing budgets. And, finally, mobile analytics can display which pages have the highest exit rates. With this type of analysis, marketers can rapidly adjust marketing campaigns to exploit the most effective ones and, conversely, trim the non-performing ones.

The biggest problem with any analytics procedure is filtering out the noise associated with the data. Without clean data, "the trends, patterns, and other insights hidden in the raw data are lost through aggregation and filtering."[151]

Organizations need an unstructured place "to put all kinds of big data in its pure form, rather than in a more structured data warehousing environment."[151] This is because what might be considered just "noise" in the raw data from one perspective could be full of important "signals" from a more knowledgeable perspective.[151] "Discovery, including what-if analysis, is an important part of customer analytics because users in marketing and other functions do not always know what they are looking for in the data and must try different types of analysis to produce the insight needed."[151] As per Stodder, among the most frequent targets for analysis are the following[151]:

- Understanding sentiment drivers.
- Identifying characteristics for better segmentation.
- Measuring the organization's share of voice and brand reputation compared with the competition.
- Determining the effectiveness of marketing touches and messages in buying behavior, i.e., attribution analysis.
- Using predictive analytics on social media to discover patterns and anticipate customers' problems with products and/or services.

TWDI's research[151] about the general purpose of customer analytics technology and methods (see Figure 7) discovered that "the business functions or operations for which respondents considered customer analytics most important were marketing (81%, with 52% indicating "very important"), sales and sales reporting (79%, with 45% "very important"), and campaign management (74%, with 47% "very important").[151] Market research (43% "very important") and customer services and order management (also 43% "very important") were also high among business functions regarded as critical to developers and consumers of customer analytics.[151]

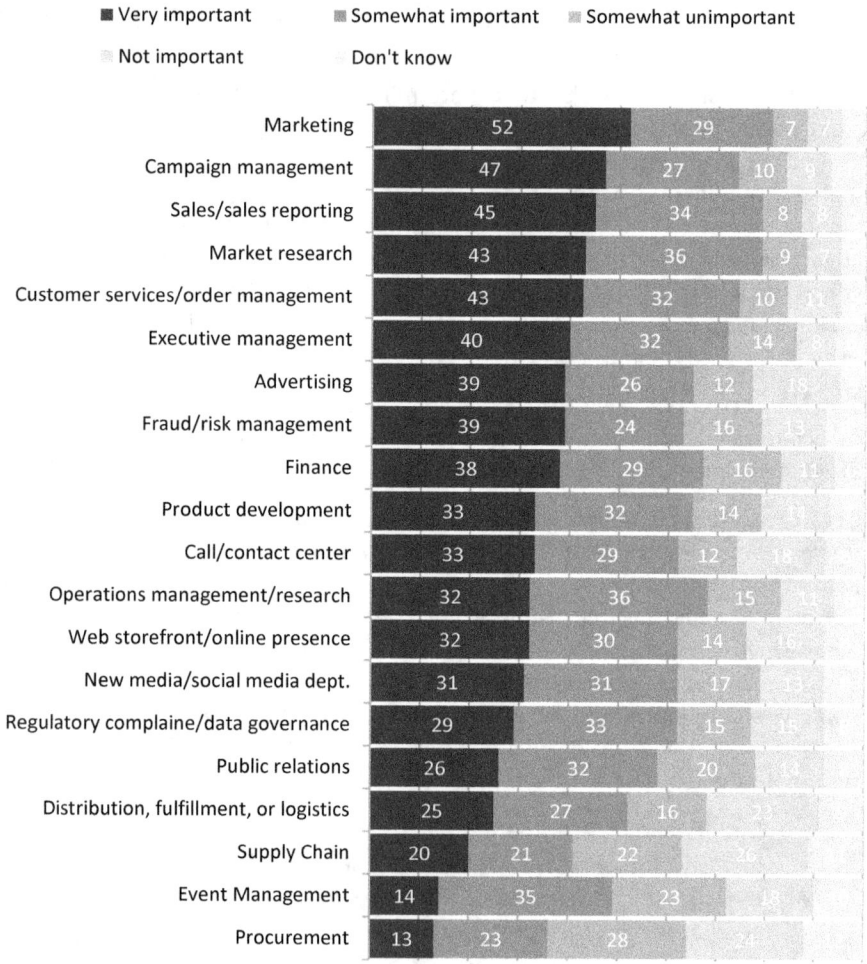

Figure 7: Importance of Customer Analytics Technology
Based on one answer per business function from 452 responses.
Source: TWDI Research[151]

The marketing department, "which in most organizations is empowered with the responsibility for identifying, attracting, satisfying, and keeping customers, is clearly the main stage for customer analytics."[151] Marketing departments and functions are becoming increasingly qualitative.[151] "Gut feelings" are being replaced by data-driven decision-making.[151] "Data drives the pursuit of efficiency and achievement of measurable results. Marketing functions are key supporters of 'data science,' which is the use of scientific methods on data to develop hypotheses and models and apply iterative, test-and-learn strategies to marketing campaigns and related initiatives."[151]

Customer analytics can be a very effective tool for micro-targeting customers with customized marketing offers and promotions.[153] Obviously, when an organization "attempts to cross-sell or up-sell a customer, a product or service they desire, it can enhance satisfaction."[153] However, unwanted marketing campaigns can do just the opposite, annoying customers, thereby eroding loyalty and, potentially, hurting sales.[153] Even worse, unwanted marketing campaigns can give customers the impression that the organization doesn't care about their wants, desires, needs and preferences."[153]

Customer analytics can help determine which marketing interactions are likely to please individual customers and which will not."[153] Sales functions can be important beneficiaries of customer analytics as well.[151] Stodder argues that, "Sales reports typically focus on providing visibility into the pipeline. Managers can use data insights to improve sales forecasting of potential revenues based on deeper knowledge of priority opportunities, most valued customer segments, and more."[151]

Customer service and order management departments "can use customer analytics to get a more subtle and substantial view of what actions impact customer experiences and satisfaction."[151] Contact centers can utilize "customer analytics to help tune performance metrics closer to real time, so that each day's agents are guided, if not incentivized, to interact with customers in beneficial ways."[151]

Analytics can also "help service and order management functions move away from one-size-fits-all approaches to customers and instead tune and tailor interactions more personally based on knowledge of particular types or segments, such as regions or nationalities."[151] "Finally, through integrated views of customer data and analytics, service and order management functions are able to work in better synchronicity with the organization's marketing, sales, and other business functions."[151] Customer analytics can be used to understand where marketing campaigns are working as well.

In the words of business management guru Thomas Davenport, "Organizations are competing on analytics not just because they can—business today is awash in data crunchers—but also because they should."[154] Although these words were said more than ten years ago, they might be more relevant today than ever before. Davenport adds, "Business processes are among the last remaining points of differentiation. And analytics competitors wring every last drop of value from those processes."[154] "Customer analytics helps organizations determine what steps will give them competitive advantages, increase profitability, and identify waste in business processes," Davenport argues.[154]

With the steep drop in RAM prices, in-memory solutions are all the rage these days and they allow analytics to reach a whole new level of speed and effectiveness. Today, creativity is becoming the differentiator; today's overriding philosophy might be "Those who analyze best win."

With products and services being commoditized at such a rapid rate today, customer loyalty has become more elusive than ever before.[151] "Innovation must be constant and must immediately address why an organization is losing customers. Information insights from analytics can help an organization align product and service development with strategic business objectives for customer loyalty."[151] In addition, these insights can help airline organizations be selective in how they deploy marketing campaigns and customer-touch processes so that they emphasize features in new products and services that are important to customers.

When TDWI Research examined the business benefits sought from customer analytics (see Figure 8), respondents cited giving executive management customer and market insight as the most important (71%).[151]

The second highest benefit was being able to react more quickly to changing market conditions (62%).[151]

Improving customer satisfaction and gaining a complete picture of a customer's activity across business channels—two areas that would be considered a part of the "Customer Experience Management" (CEM) process—are critical to identifying what steps an organization must take to build and retain customer loyalty.[151] The remaining items fall mainly into the categories of business intelligence, marketing, and brand management and they are extremely important to an airliner as well.

Organizations are becoming open to customer analytics because they are interested in discovering how a marketing department can be more effective, not just more efficient.[151] "Whereas other types of applications for e-commerce, fulfillment, or marketing automation help organizations determine how to get things done (e.g., getting goods delivered at the right time, executing a marketing campaign), customer analytics helps organizations answer who, what, when, where, and why questions," argues Scott Groenendal, program director of customer analytics market strategy for IBM Business Analytics.[151] "They can find answers to questions such as: What channel should I communicate through? When is the best time to target this person, and why would they be receptive to this message?" adds Groenendal.[151]

Figure 8: What Are the Important Business Benefits of Customer Analytics?
Based on 2,573 responses from 454 respondents; almost six responses, on average.
Source: TDWI Research[151]

Individual creativity, personal experiences, customer behavior and marketing context are critical components of consumer marketing decisions.[151] "The role of customer analytics is not necessarily to replace these, but to help decision makers come to fact-based conclusions through better knowledge of the organization's customers and markets."[151] Just as importantly, analytics are needed for scalability.[151] "Just as automation is necessary to run hundreds or thousands of marketing campaigns, customer analytics processes are important for supplying intelligence and guidance to those automated routines. Customer analytics can provide the brains to match the marketing systems' brawn."[151]

With the commoditization of products and services, customer loyalty can be elusive; innovation must be constant and it should help to reveal why an organization might be losing its customer base.[151] "Information insights from analytics can help organizations align product and service development with strategic business objectives for customer loyalty."[151] These insights can also help an organization be selective about how they deploy their marketing campaigns and customer-touch processes so that they emphasize features in new products and services that are important to each specific customer.[151]

In its *Achieving Customer Loyalty with Customer Analytics*[153], IBM describes one of its studies that asked some of the world's leading company CEOs and CMOs what their number one priority was.[153] The CEOs answered that it was to engage customers, while the CMOs said it was to enhance customer loyalty.[153] The study argued that forward-thinking companies were using customer analytics to[153]:

- Guide front-line interactions with customers.
- Create and execute customer retention strategies.
- Prompt people or systems to proactively address customer satisfaction issues.
- Guide product planning to fulfill future customer needs.
- Hire and train employees to act upon customer insights and improve loyalty.
- Align operations to focus on satisfying customers.

The *Customer Analytics in the Age of Social Media*[151] report concluded that the importance of customer analytics is in the boardroom; "overwhelmingly, respondents cited giving executive management customer and market insight (71%) as the most important business benefit that their organization seeks to achieve from implementing customer analytics."[151] "This percentage rises to 81% when survey results are filtered to see only the responses from those who indicated 'strong acceptance' of data-driven customer analytics over gut feel."[151] The second highest benefit cited at 62% was "the ability to react more quickly to changing market conditions, which speaks to the need for customer data insights to help decision makers address competitive pressures from rapid product or service commoditization."[151]

Customer analytics can also provide answers to questions like, "When in the life cycle are customers most likely to churn? What types of products or services would prevent them from churning, and when should they be offered complimentary items? When is it too costly to try to keep certain customers?[151]

Businesses can realize significant ROI from investing in customer analytics as it can improve the marketing department's efficiency and effectiveness.[151] However, customer analytics ROI is a difficult thing to fully quantify. Better customer knowledge equates to more optimized marketing spend because a business can focus its resources on those campaigns that have the highest predicted chances of success for particular segments, as well as cutting off or avoiding those that have the least.[151]

"By using analytics to eliminate mismatches of campaigns targeting the wrong customers or using the wrong messages and offers, marketing functions can reduce wasteful spending and increase gains relative to costs."[151] Customer segmentation allows organizations to move "away from one-size-fits-all, brand-level-only marketing and toward the 'market of one': that is, personalized, one-to-one marketing."[151]

Reaching a customization and customer service level that makes a customer feel as though he or she is a preferred customer is not easy, scaling that up so that an entire database of customers feel that they are unique and receiving outstanding customer service is even more challenging, but, in this day and age, it is almost a necessity if a company wants to provide good and engaging customer service.

Figure 9: Which Are the Most Important Business Objectives When it Comes to Customer Analytics?
Source: TWDI Research[151], Based on 1,625 responses from 432 respondents; almost four responses per respondent, on average.

TDWI Research[151] examined the importance of accomplishing various objectives for gaining positive ROI from customer analytics (see Figure 9). "Using customer analytics to target cross-sell and up-sell opportunities was the objective cited by the biggest percentage of respondents (54%)."[151] This objective is about gaining more value from existing customers by understanding their purchasing habits and trying to get them to buy more products more often.[151]

"Some organizations (18%) are implementing an advanced technique called 'uplift modeling' (also called incremental or true-lift modeling), which enables marketers to use data mining to measure the impact and influence of marketing actions on customers."[151] Insights such as these allow marketers to develop new kinds of predictive models to determine the best prospects for up-sell and cross-sell offerings.[151] "As firms scale up to execute large numbers of campaigns across multiple channels, the efficiency gained from predictive modeling can be critical to marketing spending optimization," Stodder argues.[151]

Analytics can improve marketing performance by quantifying a customer's lifetime value as well as customer worth at the many different stages in the customer's life cycle.[151] "If organizations can identify their most valuable customers they can determine if they are worthy of retention efforts and resources because of the returns they will provide."[153] For instance, it may not be worth the time, effort, and expense to retain a low value customer, unless customer analytics reveals that this low-spend customer actually has a lot of social influence.[153] Armed with this information, managers can align their deployment of resources to achieve the highest value, as well as avoid the costs and inefficiencies of marketing to the wrong people at the wrong time.[151]

Organizations have long used demographics such as gender, household size, education, occupation, and income to segment customers.[151] Data mining techniques let organizations segment much larger customer populations and, perhaps, more importantly, determine whether to apply new characteristics that refine segmentation to fit the specific attributes of the organization's products and services.[151]

"Customer analytics using data mining tools improves the speed of segmentation analysis over manual and spreadsheet efforts that are often used in less mature organizations."[151] Speed is a vital ingredient for marketing initiatives that are time sensitive, particularly for those companies that need to provide real-time cross-sell and up-sell offers to customers clicking through Web pages.[151] Today, personalized web pages can be rendered during the web page load and elements of the page can take into account past purchase history, clickstream information, as well as a whole host of other things.

In its *Achieving Customer Loyalty with Analytics*[153], IBM argues that customer analytics can provide businesses with the ability to:

- Analyze all data types to gain a 360-degree view of each individual

customer.
- Employ advanced algorithms that uncover relevant patterns and causal relationships that impact customer satisfaction and loyalty.
- Build predictive models that anticipate future outcomes.
- Learn from every customer interaction and apply lessons to future interactions and strategies.
- Deploy customer insights to decision-makers and front-line systems.
- Improve sales forecasting and help minimize sales cycles.
- Measure and report on marketing performance.

"The next most common objectives in the research were predicting retention, attrition, and churn rates (47%) and determining lifetime customer value (42%)."[151] Churn can cost organizations heavily, both from the loss of profits from existing customers as well as in the high price of attracting new ones. "Attrition or churn analysis methods are aimed at discovering which variables have the most influence on customers' decisions to leave or stay."[151]

With data mining and predictive analytics, organizations can learn which attrition rates are acceptable or expected for particular customer segments and which rates could be highly detrimental to the bottom line.[151] "Predictive customer analytics can play a major role in enabling organizations to discover and model which customers are most likely to leave, and from which segments."[151]

With social media added to the mix, as well as clickstreams, and other behavioral data, the volume and variety of data is exploding.[151] "Social networking sites such as Facebook, Twitter, LinkedIn, and MySpace have files containing petabytes of data, often in vast Hadoop clusters."[151] Weibo and WeChat add another hundreds of millions of users into the mix and with it petabytes of data.

"Advertising concerns are recording tens of millions of events daily that organizations want to mine in near real time to identify prospects," Stodder notes.[151] Businesses of all kinds want to use predictive models and score event and transaction details as fast as they come in so that they can gain insight into individual shopping behavior.[151] Insights that they hope will give them a competitive advantage over their competitors, but this is dangerous and expensive territory to chart, especially if done incorrectly.

The "data sources most commonly monitored for customer analytics are customer satisfaction surveys (57%) and customer transactions and online purchases (55%). Just under half (44%) are monitoring Web site logs and clickstream sources. In addition to monitoring customer satisfaction surveys, about half (48%) of organizations surveyed are studying call and contact center interactions."[151]

Customer satisfaction surveys are usually conducted in person, on a website, over the phone or through traditional mail and e-mail channels.[151] Because this includes both semi-structured data and unstructured comments, data collection can be difficult.[151] "Standard questions inquire about a customer's satisfaction with purchases, the services they received, and the company's brands overall. Other questions address the customer's likelihood of buying from the company again and whether they would recommend the firm to others."[151]

Text analytics can be used to increase the speed, depth, and consistency of unstructured content analysis far greater than what can be done manually.[151] "More advanced analytics can look for correlations between satisfaction ratings, commented sentiments, and other records, such as first-call-resolution metrics."[151]

In-memory computers can handle these large clusters of data culled both from the significant volumes of customer behavior data, as well as data from the multiple social media channels available.[151]

"To analyze data generated by social media networking services such as Twitter, Facebook, Weibo, and LinkedIn, many organizations are implementing Hadoop and NoSQL technologies, which do not force a schema on the source data prior to storage, as traditional BI and data warehousing systems do."[151] Because of this, the discovery analytics processes can run against the raw data.[151] "Customer analytics tools need to be able to consume data from sources such as Hadoop clusters and then integrate the insights into overall customer profiles," advises Stodder.[151]

The data sources can be varied for these technologies and methods; "they include transaction data, clickstreams, satisfaction surveys, loyalty card membership data, credit card purchases, voter registration, location data, and a host of [other] demographic data types."[151]

In its *Retail Analytics: Game Changer for Customer Loyalty,* Cognizant argues that in the retail industry, "predictive models can be used to analyze past performance to assess the likelihood that a customer will exhibit a specific behavior in order to improve marketing effectiveness."[155] This can help with "predicting customer reactions to a given product and can be leveraged to improve basket size, increase the value of the basket and switch the customer to a better and more profitable offering"[155] Predictive models can also help tailor pricing strategies that take into account both the need for competitive pricing and the bottom line.[155]

Predictive analytics and data mining are used to discover which variables out of possibly hundreds are most influential in determining customer loyalty within certain segments.[151] "Advanced analytics generally involves statistical, quantitative, or mathematical analysis and centers on developing, testing, training, scoring, and monitoring predictive models."[151]

Models can be created that will uncover patterns, affinities, anomalies, and other useful insights for marketing campaigns and for determining cross-sell and up-sell opportunities.[151] "The tools and techniques are also used for developing and deploying behavioral scoring models for marketing, deciding whether to adjust customers' credit limits for purchases, and a variety of highly time-sensitive analytic processes," Stodder notes.[151]

"As more online customer behavior is recorded in Web logs and tracked through cookies and other observation devices, sizeable amounts of information are becoming available to organizations that seek a more accurate view of a customer's path to purchase," states Stodder.[151] Attribution analysis is, first and foremost, a big-data problem, given the quantity and variety of data available from today's multiple platforms.[151]

Businesses that are performing attribution analysis will frequently employ Hadoop, MapReduce, with analytic software solutions such as R, SAS's eMiner, SAP's InfiniteInsights, Python, and IBM's SPSS, amongst others.[151] This allows a business to run sophisticated algorithms against detailed data to find the correct path to purchase. This analysis can then be integrated with analysis from other data types and sources, including those that might have been generated by any offline customer activity.[151]

Attribution analysis can reveal such things as what kinds of campaigns most influence customer behavior.[151] "The analysis can help organizations determine where to allocate marketing resources to gain the highest level of success, as well as how to more accurately assign the percentage of credit due to specific marketing and advertising processes," Stodder concludes.[151]

On August 13, 2014, Facebook announced a major step forward in the area of attribution analysis. It said that it "would start telling advertisers on what device people saw an ad and on what device they took an action, such as buying a product or signing up for a test drive, as a result of seeing that ad. That means Facebook will be able to credit mobile ads that lead to desktop sales and desktop ads that result in mobile purchases."[156]

Peterson notes that, "Advertisers can already track conversions through Facebook on desktop and on mobile, but to date Facebook hasn't broken out conversions by device type for advertisers to see. For example, advertisers have been able to see if their desktop and mobile ads lead to conversions, but they didn't know on which device type those conversions were taking place."[156]

However, Facebook's new cross-device conversion measurement only works for advertisers who place specific Facebook trackers on their websites and mobile apps.[156] "Without sharing users' personal information with the advertiser, those trackers can see that a Facebook user is checking out the advertisers' site or app and whether they've converted in the advertiser-specified fashion."[156] If the person does convert, "Facebook's trackers can trace back to see if that person has seen an ad from that advertiser on Facebook, which may have directly or indirectly led to the conversion."[156] Of course, nothing is 100% certain when it comes to attribution analysis, but this is a big step in the right direction.

With many of the following analytical marketing models, airlines should keep in mind that it is important to create control groups to measure the true effects of their models and marketing campaigns. Control groups are typical components in marketing analysis and are fundamental to statistical studies.[157] In his article *Control Group Marketing—With or Without CRM Software Systems*[157], Rick Cook states that:

> *"The basic idea of a control group is simple. Select a random (or nearly random) sample from your campaign's marketing list and exclude them from promotion. Then measure the control group's activity and compare it to the activity of the group targeted via a campaign. The difference between the control and campaign group gives you a pretty good notion of how effective—and profitable—the campaign is.*

"The theory is that a certain fraction of the customers in the campaign are going to purchase from you anyway during the campaign period. The control group lets you filter out that effect, as well as the effects of other channels which may be influencing behavior, such as display advertising, and shows you how much the campaign has affected customer behavior," explains Cook.[157]

Although they should be used to test out the effects of marketing campaigns, few companies include them in their marketing process.[157] "Marketing control groups become even more effective when combined with the customer analytics found in most marketing automation or customer relationship management systems," notes Cook.[157]

Cook argues that, "With a CRM system and a control group you can also detect the halo effect of your campaign. These are purchases and other actions which are influenced by the campaign but don't come in through the normal campaign channels."[157] For example, a customer could be so inspired by one particular campaign that he or she picks up the phone and orders products directly from the company instead of going through the call-to-action channel.[157] "Another example is the customer who doesn't use the promotional coupon you included in your marketing campaign but who purchases the product anyway."[157] Cook notes that airlines "can assume that customers in the test group who respond in unconventional methods are still influenced by the campaign and so should be counted as part of the campaign effect."[157]

"Because CRM software lets you track all points of customer contact, and not just the direct response to the campaign, it can capture these halo customers," concludes Cooks.

The size of the control group is usually 10 percent of the size of the campaign or test group.[157] Ideally you want the control group to be a truly random sample from the airline's campaign list, but this is difficult to attain in practice as complete randomness is hard to achieve.[157] "Many companies select their control group by a simpler process, such as selecting every 10th name on the list to make up the control group," but there are other more scientific ways to choose the participants, which should be utilized.

Data Mining

In his paper *The CRISP-DM model, the new blueprint for data mining*[158], C. Shearer introduces the concept of the "Cross-industry standard process for data mining", which is more commonly known by its acronym CRISP-DM. It is a "data mining process model that describes commonly used approaches that data mining experts use to tackle problems."[158] It is currently the de facto standard for developing data mining and data discovery projects.[158]

In their paper *Methods for mining HTS data*[159], Harper and Pickett break the CRISP-DM process of data mining into the following six major phases:

1. Business understanding—focuses on understanding the project objectives and requirements purely from a business perspective, and then "converting this knowledge into a data mining problem definition, and a preliminary plan designed to achieve the objectives."[159] "A decision model, especially one built using the Decision Model and Notation standard can be used."[159]
2. Data understanding—this starts with an "initial data collection and proceeds with activities in order to get familiar with the data, to identify data quality problems, to discover first insights into the data, or to detect interesting subsets to form hypotheses for hidden information."[159]
3. Data preparation—this phase covers "all activities to construct the final dataset (data that will be fed into the modeling tool(s)) from the initial raw data. Data preparation tasks are likely to be performed multiple times, and not in any prescribed order. Tasks include table, record, and attribute selection as well as transformation and cleaning of data for modeling tools."[159]
4. Modeling—various modeling techniques are selected and applied in this phase, and their parameters are calibrated to optimal values.[159] "Typically, there are several techniques for the same data mining problem type. Some techniques have specific requirements on the form of data. Therefore, stepping back to the data preparation phase is often needed."[159]
5. Evaluation—At this project stage, model (or models) that appear to have high quality from a data analysis perspective should have been

made.¹⁵⁹ "Before proceeding to final model deployment, it is imperative to more thoroughly evaluate the model, and review the steps executed to construct the model, to be certain it dovetails with the business objectives."¹⁵⁹ A key objective here is to determine if any important key business objective has been left out.¹⁵⁹ At the end of this phase, a decision on whether to use the data mining results should be reached.¹⁵⁹

6. Deployment—Creation of the model is generally not the end in and of itself.¹⁵⁹ "Even if the purpose of the model is to increase knowledge of the data, the knowledge gained will need to be organized and presented in a way that is useful to the customer."¹⁵⁹ "Depending on the requirements, the deployment phase can be as simple as generating a report or as complex as implementing a repeatable data scoring (e.g. segment allocation) or data mining process."¹⁵⁹ "In many cases it will be the customer, not the data analyst, who will carry out the deployment steps. Even if the analyst deploys the model it is important for the customer to understand up front the actions which will need to be carried out in order to actually make use of the created models."¹⁵⁹

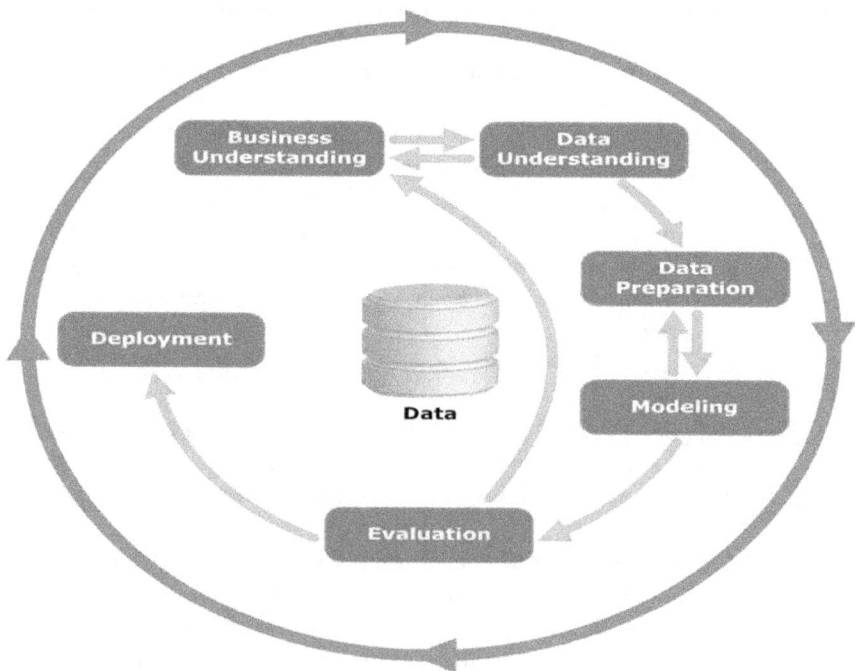

Figure 10: CRISP DM
Source: Wikipedia

The sequence of the phases (see Figure 10) is not strict and Harper and Pickett

argue that moving back and forth between different phases is often required so flexibility is important.[159] "The arrows in the process diagram indicate the most important and frequent dependencies between phases," contend Harper and Pickett.[159] "The outer circle in the diagram symbolizes the cyclic nature of data mining itself," add Harper and Pickett.[159] The data mining processes continues long after a solution has been deployed, argue Harpet and Pickett.[159] The "lessons learned during the process can trigger new, often more focused business questions and subsequent data mining processes will benefit from the experiences of previous ones," they conclude.[159]

In the SAS Institute Best Practices paper *Data Mining and the Case for Sampling*[160], SAS defines data mining "as the process used to reveal valuable information and complex relationships that exist in large amounts of data."[160] For SAS, data mining is an iterative process, divided into five stages that are represented by the acronym SEMMA.[160] "Beginning with a statistically representative sample of data, the SEMMA methodology—which stands for Sample, Explore, Modify, Model, and Assess—makes it easy for business analysts to apply exploratory statistical and visualization techniques, select and transform the most significant predictive variables, model the variables to predict outcomes, and confirm a model's accuracy," argues SAS.[160] According to SAS, the SEMMA methodology is broken down into the following steps[160]:

- "Sample the data by creating one or more data tables. The samples should be big enough to contain the significant information, yet small enough to process quickly."[160]
- "Explore the data by searching for anticipated relationships, unanticipated trends, and anomalies in order to gain understanding and ideas."[160]
- "Modify the data by creating, selecting, and transforming the variables to focus the model selection process."[160]
- "Model the data by allowing the software to search automatically for a combination of data that reliably predicts a desired outcome."[160]
- "Assess the data by evaluating the usefulness and reliability of the findings from the data mining process."[160]

SEMMA is itself a cycle, with the internal steps can be performed iteratively as needed.[160] SAS advises that projects following SEMMA "can sift through millions of records and reveal patterns that enable businesses to meet data mining objectives such as" [160]:

- "Segmenting customers accurately into groups with similar buying patterns
- Profiling customers for individual relationship management
- Dramatically increasing response rate from direct mail campaigns
- Identifying the most profitable customers and the underlying reasons

- Understanding why customers leave for competitors (attrition, churn analysis)
- Uncovering factors affecting purchasing patterns, payments and response rates
- Increasing profits by marketing to those most likely to purchase
- Decreasing costs by filtering out those least likely to purchase
- Detecting patterns to uncover non-compliance."[160]

Artificial Intelligence & Machine Learning

According to Wikipedia, Machine Learning (ML) is the subfield of computer science that "explores the construction and study of algorithms that can learn from data. Such algorithms operate by building a model based on inputs and using that to make predictions or decisions, rather than following only explicitly programmed instructions."[161]

ML "evolved from the study of pattern recognition and computational learning theory in artificial intelligence" and it "explores the study and construction of algorithms that can learn from and make predictions on data—such algorithms overcome following strictly static program instructions by making data driven predictions or decisions, through building a model from sample inputs."[161]

As per Wikipedia, ML can be broken down into the following three categories[161]:

1. Supervised learning: The computer is presented with example inputs and their desired outputs, given by a "teacher", and the goal is to learn a general rule that maps inputs to outputs.
2. Unsupervised learning: No labels are given to the learning algorithm, leaving it on its own to find structure in its input. Unsupervised learning can be a goal in itself (discovering hidden patterns in data) or a means towards an end (feature learning).
3. Reinforcement learning: A computer program interacts with a dynamic environment in which it must perform a certain goal (such as driving a vehicle), without a teacher explicitly telling it whether it has come close to its goal or not. Another example is learning to play a game by playing against an opponent.

There are so many use cases for ML and deep learning in the airline industry that it is impossible to create an exhaustive list here, but it is particularly useful for marketing personalization, customer recommendation, spam filtering, network security, optical character recognition (OCR), voice recognition, computer vision, fraud detection, predictive asset maintenance, optimization, language translations, sentiment analysis, and online search, amongst many others uses. Figure 11 reveals how ML can be broken down into supervised and unsupervised learning, as well as reinforcement learning that is specific to the airline industry.

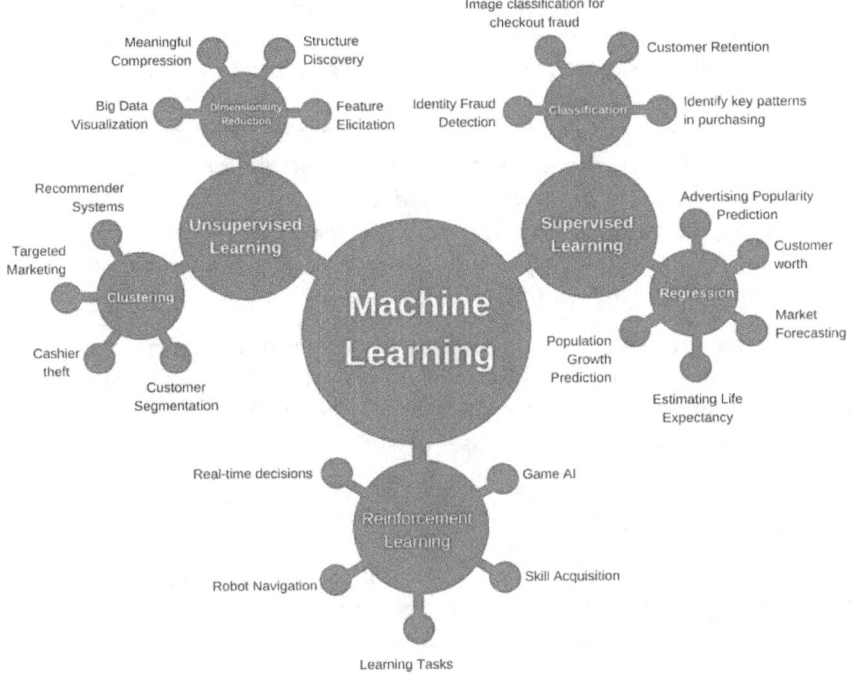

Figure 11: Machine Learning for the airline industry
Source: Intelligencia.co

Machine-learning can be used to spot credit card or transaction fraud while it is happening; ML can build predictive models of credit card transactions based on their likelihood of being fraudulent and the system can compare real-time transactions against these models. When the system spots potential fraud it can alert either the bank or the airline outlet where the transaction occurred.

Although ML and data mining often employ the same methods and overlap significantly, they do differ markedly. As Wikipedia explains[161]:

> "While machine learning focuses on prediction, based on known properties learned from the training data, data mining focuses on the discovery of (previously) unknown properties in the data (this is the analysis step of Knowledge Discovery in Databases). Data mining uses many machine learning methods, but with different goals; on the other hand, machine learning also employs data mining methods as 'unsupervised learning' or as a preprocessing step to improve learner accuracy. Much of the confusion between these two research communities (which do often have separate conferences and

separate journals, ECML PKDD being a major exception) comes from the basic assumptions they work with: in machine learning, performance is usually evaluated with respect to the ability to reproduce known knowledge, while in Knowledge Discovery and Data Mining (KDD) the key task is the discovery of previously unknown knowledge. Evaluated with respect to known knowledge, an uninformed (unsupervised) method will easily be outperformed by other supervised methods, while in a typical KDD task, supervised methods cannot be used due to the unavailability of training data.

Table 4 shows the general use cases for AI broken down by industry. I have included industries other the airline industry as I believe it is important for airline executives to understand what is going on in other industries, as that will give them a better sense of the holistic uses of AI.

GENERAL USE CASE	INDUSTRY
Sound	
Voice recognition	UX/UI, Automotive, Security, IoT
Voice search	Handset maker, Telecoms
Sentiment analysis	CRM
Flaw detection	Automotive, Aviation
Fraud detection	Finance, Credit cards
Time Series	
Log analysis/Risk detection	Data centers, Security, Finance
Enterprise resource planning	Manufacturing, Auto, Supply Chain
Predictive analytics using sensor data	IoT, Smart home, Hardware manufacturing
Business and Economic analytics	Finance, Accounting, Government
Recommendation engine	E-Commerce, Media, Social Networks
Text	
Sentiment analysis	CRM, Social Media, Reputation mgmt.
Augmented search, Theme detection	Finance
Threat detection	Social Media, Government
Fraud detection	Insurance, Finance
Image	
Facial recognition	
Image search	Social Media

GENERAL USE CASE	INDUSTRY
Machine vision	Automotive, Aviation
Photo clustering	Telecom, Handset makers
Video	
Motion detection	Gaming, UX, UI
Real-time threat detection	Security, Airports

Table 4 AI use cases
Source: deeplearning4j.org

WEKA, a comprehensive collection of machine-learning algorithms for data mining tasks written in Java and released under the GPL, contains tools for data pre-processing, classification, regression, clustering, association rules, and visualization. It has a very minimal learning curve compared to products like SAS's Enterprise Miner. However, unlike SAS, it can become quite inefficient with larger datasets.

Python and R are the most popular open sources solutions used for ML and they both have a large user base community. Scikit-learn combined with Pandas, Numpy, Seaborn and Matplotlib make implementing ML algorithms in Python very versatile and these provide more customization and utilization than R.

The R community has a large and active user base. R's libraries contain a wide variety of statistical and graphical techniques as well. These include linear and nonlinear modeling, classical statistical tests, time-series analysis, classification, clustering, amongst others. Due to its S heritage, R also has strong object-oriented programming capabilities.

Other ML software includes Matlab, Scikit, Accord, Apache's Mahout, Spark's MLLib, H2O on Hadoop, ConvNteJS, SPSS, SAP's Predictive Analytics library, even SQL Server is powerful enough to build some ML models.

ML can help an airline discover customer segments that they may not realize were there. Armed with this kind of information, airlines can understand what matters most to its customers at the individual and personalization level, which will enable them to anticipate their customer's needs before even the customers are aware of them. Even more, airlines can understand key characteristics of their most profitable customers and recognize the next important customer when he or she happens to log onto the airline's ecommerce site or step in a branch.

The use of deep neural networks and image classifiers can analyze and parse images, which can enable retail marketers to monitor the images that provide the highest selling and conversion rates through each ecommerce channel.

ML can also be used to compute dynamic clusters of customers to create fluid segmentation in real-time. As consumer buying habits or booking patterns evolve, fluid segmentation ensures the airlines continue to reach the right guests, at the right time, at the right price, through the right channels, with the right offer.

Today, the importance of personalization in customer experience initiatives can't be underestimated. In his article *5 Ways AI Will Boost Personalization in Digital Marketing*[162], Dirk Vogel argues that AI will radically change the marketing landscape by allowing the following:

- Personal shopping for everyone.
- Utilizing chatbots to increase customer service.
- Seamless programmatic media buying.
- Predictive customer service.
- Optimizing marketing automation.

According to Vogel, "Shopping online creates rich data footprints regarding the individual preferences, spending habits and preferred channels of individual consumers. Feeding these digital breadcrumbs into an AI-engine helps bring curated shopping journeys to mass audiences."[162]

As Amazon, Pandora, and Netflix have proven, personalized shopping for everyone is a winning formula[162] "Using an advanced recommendation-AI, e-commerce leader Amazon creates more than 35% of its total revenues with personalized shopping recommendations," states Vogel.[162] "Taking personalization to the next level, artificial intelligence also allows for predicting the kinds of purchases consumers are going to make before they even know it," notes Vogel.[162]

"Customer service is still where today's brands are dropping the ball," Vogel believes, adding that "Only 35% of companies are able to identify their customers at the moment of contact (Selligent survey)—with customers potentially unfriending brands and taking their business elsewhere," argues Vogel.[162]

It may sound counter-intuitive, Vogel says, "but automated bots can create lifelike, seamless customer service experiences, addressing the consumer on their purchase history and known preferences."[162] One of the standouts, Vogel notes is Facebook's "M" technology, which is embedded in the Messenger app.[162] "The AI delivers personalized product, travel and restaurant recommendations, while troubleshooting technical problems," Vogel explains.[162]

Although chatbots are cheaper than handling customer service inquiries over the phone, there is a catch as chatbots can only deliver highly personalized and contextual assistance if they have access to universal consumer profiles that are populated by real-time data.[162] This means, done correctly, developing chatbots is an expensive upfront investment, it is an investment that should be done company-wide, not siloed by just the marketing or customer service department as information that chatbots tap into are useful throughout the organization.

On the marketing side, AI may deliver that extra dash of relevancy programmatic advertising has been waiting for all these years.[162] "On the consumer side, AI helps create individualized display ads that website visitors want to see," [162] while on the accounting side, "bots handle invoicing and payment for these ad transactions, giving marketers more time to focus on the big picture."[162]

With AI, predictive customer service and marketing could be just around the corner.[162] "What may sound like a scenario from the *Minority Report* movie is already in beta testing: Intel subsidiary Saffron has created an artificial intelligence that is able to predict with 88% certainty why, on which channel, and for which product individual customers will seek help next. 'We've been expecting your call,' never rang truer," Vogel predicts.[162]

One of the biggest problems in corporate marketing is hitting the customer with automated marketing offers too often.[162] In the future, AI will analyze a consumer's purchase history and email habits to choose the optimal time for hitting the inbox with content that's bound to boost open rates and conversions," Vogel contends.[162]

Another interesting use of AI is what Pinterest is doing with its visual search technology. According to Lauren Johnson's Adweek article *Pinterest Is Offering Brands Its Visual Search Technology to Score Large Ad Deals*[163], "The visual search technology is Pinterest's version of AI and human curation that lets consumers snap a picture of IRL things and find similar items online. Taking a picture of a red dress for example, pulls up posts of red dresses that consumers can browse through and shop," states Johnson.[163]

"The idea is to give people enough ideas that are visually related so that they have a new way to identify and search for things," said Amy Vener, retail vertical strategy lead at Pinterest.[163] "From a visual-discovery perspective, our technology is doing something similar where we're analyzing within the image the colors, the shapes and the textures to bring that to another level of dimension," Vener adds.[163]

Utilizing the technology, someone who points his or her phone's camera at a baby crib will receive recommendations for similar baby products.[163] "Eventually, all of Target's inventory will be equipped with Pinterest's technology to allow anyone to scan items in the real world and shop similar items through Target.com," states Johnson. "Target is the first retailer to build Pinterest's technology into its apps and website, though the site also has a deal to power Bixby, Samsung's AI app that works similarly."[163]

"We're now in a place where we're using Pinterest as a service to power some visual search for other products," Vener said. "I think there's an opportunity for retailers to be a little more of a prominent player when it comes to visual discovery."[163]

Deep Learning

Deep Learning is a branch of Machine Learning and it seeks to imitate the neural activity of the human brain. Deep learning architectures have been applied to fields of computer vision, speech recognition, NLP, audio recognition, social network filtering, machine translation, bioinformatics and drug design, amongst others. In most cases, results have proven to be comparable, if not superior to human experts.[164]

In the ensuing pages, I'll break down the current offerings available in deep learning technology and try to give you the pros and cons of each offering. This is, however, technology that changes by the day although I'll keep the discussion as updated as possible, much of this information will need to be updated in six months. (All the more reason to keep an eye on these editions, I usually update the book once every six months, at minimum!)

In their paper *Caffe2 vs. TensorFlow: Which is a Better Deep Learning Framework?*[165], Baige Liu and Xiaoxue Zang focus on the two most used deep learning programs, Caffe2 and Tensorflow, comparing five aspects of the software: the expressiveness, the modeling capability, the performance, help & support, and the scalability.[169] The authors chose "TensorFlow because it is currently the most widely-used deep learning framework."[169] The authors recognize that Caffe was an extremely popular framework before TensorFlow was introduced and the Caffe2 framework can build upon that potential, while gaining a lot of user preference in the near future.[169]

However, as Liu and Zang conclude:

> "in many aspects and as a result we find neither of these two has an [sic] dominating advantages over the other. Therefore, in practice, the choice between these two actually depends on the specific user tasks and the user preferences. Overall if the user need [sic] to pursue speed and has limited space restricted by the device, Caffe2 is a better choice since our experiments' results revealed that Caffe2 has a significant advantage over TensorFlow both in speed and space. Nevertheless, TensorFlow is still powerful and useful because there is a large number official [six] and third-party resources, services, debugging tools, and a big supportive community that makes it easier to find reference codes."

With software, there is rarely a binary answer, i.e., "Is *x* piece of software better for my problem than *y* piece of software?" Caveats abound. Always.

Tensorflow

In his article *Google Just Open Sourced TensorFlow, Its Artificial Intelligence Engine*[166], Cade Metz explains that at its 2015 Google I/O conference Google open sourced its deep learning engine known as TensorFlow. In open sourcing TensorFlow, Google is freely sharing the underlying code with the world at large.[166] "In literally giving the technology away, Google believes it can accelerate the evolution of AI. Through open source, outsiders can help improve on Google's technology and, yes, return these improvements back to Google," explains Metz.[166]

"What we're hoping is that the community adopts this as a good way of expressing machine learning algorithms of lots of different types, and also contributes to building and improving [TensorFlow] in lots of different and interesting ways," says Jeff Dean, and a key player in the rise of Google's deep learning technology.[166]

Open sourcing AI has been a common practice over the past few years.[166] Facebook, Microsoft, and Twitter have all made huge strides in AI and some have open sourced software that is similar to TensorFlow, including Torch—a system originally built by researchers in Switzerland—as well as systems like Caffe and Theano.[166] However, Google's move is highly significant because Google's AI engine is considered to be the world's most advanced—and because, well, it is Google after all.[166]

Google, however, isn't giving away all its secrets.[166] As Metz explains[166]:

> "At the moment, the company is only open sourcing part of this AI engine. It's sharing only some of the algorithms that run atop the engine. And it's not sharing access to the remarkably advanced hardware infrastructure that drives this engine (that would certainly come with a price tag). But Google is giving away at least some of its most important data center software, and that's not something it has typically done in the past."

In the past, Google only shared its designs until after it had moved onto other designs, but it had never open sourced code.[166] With TensorFlow, however, the "company has changed tack, freely sharing some of its newest—and, indeed, most important—software."[166] Google does open source parts of its Android mobile operating system and several other smaller software projects, but this is far different.[166] With TensorFlow's release, "Google is open sourcing software that sits at the heart of its empire," states Metz.[166]

Deep learning relies on neural networks and Google typically "trains these neural nets using a vast array of machines equipped with GPU chips—computer processors that were originally built to render graphics for games and other highly visual applications, but have also proven quite adept at deep learning," explains Metx.[166]

GPUs are good at processing lots of little bits of data in parallel, and that's what deep learning need, but after they've been trained, these neural nets run in different ways[166], often running on "traditional computer processors inside the data center, and in some cases, they can run on mobile phones," notes Metz.[166] The *Google Translate* app is a prime example of this. It runs entirely on a mobile device without a data center connection, letting users translate foreign text into their native language.[166]

TensorFlow is a way of building and running neural networks that are required for computations like this, both at the training stage and the execution stage.[166] It is basically a set of software libraries that users "can slip into any application so that it too can learn tasks like image recognition, speech recognition, and language translation."[166]

The underlying TensorFlow software was built in C++[166], but "in developing applications for this AI engine, coders can use either C++ or Python, the most popular language among deep learning researchers," adds Metz.[166] Google hopes that developers "will expand the tool to other languages, including Google Go, Java, and perhaps even Javascript, so that coders have more ways of building apps."[166]

According to Google's Jeff Dean, "TensorFlow is well suited not only to deep learning, but to other forms of AI, including reinforcement learning and logistic regression."[166] Tensorflow is twice as fast as Google's previous system, DistBelief, Dean adds.[166]

In open sourcing the tool, Google provides some sample neural networking models and algorithms, "including models for recognizing photographs, identifying handwritten numbers, and analyzing text."[166] "We'll give you all the algorithms you need to train those models on public data sets," Dean says.[166]

The major caveat to Google's seeming generosity is that the initial open source version of TensorFlow only runs on a single computer, you can't train models across a vast array of machines.[166] "This computer can include many GPUs, but it's a single computer nonetheless," notes Metz.[166] "Google is still keeping an advantage," Chris Nicholson, Chief Executive of AI startup Skymind, says.[166] "To build true enterprise applications, you need to analyze data at scale," he adds. "At the execution stage, the open source incarnation of TensorFlow will run on phones as well as desktops and laptops, and Google indicates that the company may eventually open source a version that runs across hundreds of machines," notes Metz[166], so the technology is something to keep an eye on in terms of AI and ML options.

So why the change of heart at Google? Well, part of it has to do with the very nature of how the machine learning community operates.[166] "Deep learning originated with academics who openly shared their ideas, and many of them now work at Google—including University of Toronto professor Geoff Hinton, the godfather of deep learning," explains Metz.[166]

"TensorFlow was built at a very different time from tools like MapReduce and GFS and BigTable and Dremel and Spanner and Borg," notes Metz.[166] "The open source movement—where Internet companies share so many of their tools in order to accelerate the rate of development—has picked up considerable speed over the past decade. Google now builds software with an eye towards open source," adds Metz.[166] Many of Google's earlier tools were just too closely tied to Google's IT infrastructure to make them easily useful for outside developers.[166]

Unlike its competitors, Google has not handed the open source project to an independent third party, but will manage the project itself at Tensorflow.org.[166] The code is shared under an Apache 2 license, meaning anyone can use the code free of copyright issues.[166]

Any goodwill this generates for Google is less important than the projects it could potentially feed.[166] According to Dean, "you can think of TensorFlow as combining the best of Torch and Caffe and Theano. Like Torch and Theano, he says, it's good for quickly spinning up research projects, and like Caffe, it's good for pushing those research projects into the real world."[166]

However, even some within Google might disagree.[166] "According to many in the community, DeepMind, a notable deep learning startup now owned by Google, continues to use Torch—even though it has long had access to TensorFlow and DistBelief," notes Metz.[166] But, the writer concludes, "at the very least, an open source TensorFlow gives the community more options. And that's a good thing."[166]

Even utilizing TensorFlow's powerful AI and ML capabilities, building a deep learning app still requires some serious analytics and coding skills.[166] But this too may change in the years to come, Metz adds.[166] As Dean points out, "a Google deep-learning open source project and a Google deep-learning cloud service aren't mutually exclusive."[166]

For now, Google merely wants to generously share the code.[166] As Dean says, "this will help the company improve this code."[166] At the same time, other benefits will result from this, including improving machine learning as a whole, which will undoubtedly find its way back to the source—Google. The circle of code continues...

"Google is five to seven years ahead of the rest of the world," argues Chris Nicholson, adding, "If they open source their tools, this can make everybody else better at machine learning."[166] Casinos and sports books included.

According to its article *Comparing Top Deep Learning Frameworks: Deeplearning4J, PyTorch, TensorFlow, Caffe, Kera, MxNet, Gluon & CNTK*[167], TensorFlow's pros and cons include:

- Python + Numpy
- Computational graph abstraction, like Theano
- Faster compile times than Theano
- TensorBoard for visualization
- Data and model parallelism
- Slower than other frameworks
- Much "fatter" than Torch; more magic
- Not many pretrained models
- Computational graph is pure Python, therefore slow
- No commercial support
- Drops out to Python to load each new training batch
- Not very toolable
- Dynamic typing is error-prone on large software projects

Caffe2

At its F8 developer conference in San 2018, Facebook announced the launch of Caffe2, an open source framework for deep learning.[168] In his article *Facebook-Open Sources Caffe2, a New Deep Learning Framework,* Jordan Novet explains that the announcement "builds on Facebook's contributions to the Torch open source deep learning framework and more recently the PyTorch framework that the Facebook Artificial Intelligence Research (FAIR) group conceived."[168] However, Caffe2 does have several differences from PyTorch.[168]

"PyTorch is great for research, experimentation and trying out exotic neural networks, while Caffe2 is headed towards supporting more industrial-strength applications with a heavy focus on mobile," explains Yangqing Jia, Facebook AI Platform engineering lead.[168] "This is not to say that PyTorch doesn't do mobile or doesn't scale or that you can't use Caffe2 with some awesome new paradigm of neural network, we're just highlighting some of the current characteristics and directions for these two projects," notes Jia. "We plan to have plenty of interoperability and methods of converting back and forth so you can experience the best of both worlds," adds Jia.

In their paper *Caffe2 vs. TensorFlow: Which is a Better Deep Learning Framework?*[169], Baige Liu and Xiaoxue Zang focus on Caffe2 and Tensorflow and make compare five aspects of the software: the expressiveness, the modeling capability, the performance, help & support, and the scalability.[169] The authors chose "TensorFlow because it is currently the most widely-used deep learning framework."[169] The authors recognize that Caffe was an extremely popular framework before TensorFlow was introduced and the Caffe2 framework can build upon that potential, while gaining a lot of user preference in the near future.[169]

Liu and Zang discovered that while Caffe2 and TensorFlow do not differ much in expressiveness, modeling capability, and scalability, Caffe2 significantly performs better than TensorFlow in both speed and space aspects, therefore it is a better choice for people who pursue speed or are limited by the device restrictions.[169] However, "TensorFlow provides more services and tools, such as Tensorboard, TensorFlow serving, TensorFlow Lite,"[169] and it has a strong advantages in help&support.[169] "It is a better choice if people want to implement new or complicated models and do not know how to implement exactly yet," argue Liu and Zang.[169]

Torch

Officially released in October 2002, Torch is an open source machine learning library, computing framework, and a script language based on the Lua programming language. According to Collobert, Kavukcuoglu and Farabet, "Its goal is to provide a flexible environment to design and train learning machines

According to its article *Comparing Top Deep Learning Frameworks: Deeplearning4J, PyTorch, TensorFlow, Caffe, Kera, MxNet, Gluon & CNTK*[167], deeplearning4j states that while Torch is powerful, "it was not designed to be widely accessible to the Python-based academic community, nor to corporate software engineers, whose lingua franca is Java."

Keras

Created by Google software engineer Francois Chollet, Keras is a deep-learning library that sits atop TensorFlow and Theano, providing an intuitive API inspired by Torch.[167] According to Deeplearning4j it is "perhaps the best Python API in existence."[167] Deeplearning4j "relies on Keras as its Python API and imports models from Kera and through Keras from Theano and TensorFlow."[167]

- Intuitive API inspired by Torch
- Works with Theano, TensorFlow and Deeplearning4j backends (CNTK backend to come)
- Fast growing framework
- Likely to become standard Python API for NNs

Pytorch

According to its article *Comparing Top Deep Learning Frameworks: Deeplearning4J, PyTorch, TensorFlow, Caffe, Kera, MxNet, Gluon & CNTK*[167], deeplearning4j states that "A Python version of Torch, known as Pytorch , was open-sourced by Facebook in January 2017. PyTorch offers dynamic computation graphs, which let you process variable-length inputs and outputs, which is useful when working with RNNs, for example." Since it's introduction, Deeplearning4J claims that "PyTorch has quickly become the favorite among machine-learning researchers, because it allows certain complex architectures to be built easily."[167]

According to Deeplearning 4J, these are the pros and cons of Torch and PyTorch[167]:

- Lots of modular pieces that are easy to combine.
- Easy to write your own layer types and run on GPU.
- Lots of pretrained models.
- You usually write your own training code (Less plug and play).
- No commercial support.
- Spotty documentation.

Deeplearning4j

Deeplearning4j was written in Java to reflect its focus on industry and ease of use.[167] Deeplearning4J believes "usability is the limiting parameter that inhibits more widespread deep-learning implementations."[167] "They believe scalability ought to be automated with open-source distributed run-times like Hadoop and Spark. And we believe that a commercially supported open-source framework is the appropriate solution to ensure working tools and building a community."[167]

CNTK

The "Computational Network Toolkit" or CNTK is an open-source deep-learning framework from MIcrosoft.[167] "The acronym stands for The library includes feed-forward DNNs, convolutional nets and recurrent networks. CNTK offers a Python API over C++ code."[167]

Analytics

Today, the software analytics space is more crowded than it has ever been before. Standard ETL-solution providers are adding analytics to their multitude of offerings. Many of the new players in the Master Data Management (MDM) field have BI platforms that combine integration, preparation, analytics and visualization with data governance and security features.

Such standard analytics processes as column dependencies, clustering, decision trees, and recommendation engines are all included in many of these software offerings. Instead of forcing clients to purchase modules on top of modules on top of modules, new software companies are creating packages that contain many built-in analytical functions. Thanks to software connectors, open source products like R, Python, and the WEKA collection can easily be slotted into many

ETL, MDM, BI, CI and MA software solutions, thereby reducing costs the need for expensive translation layers.

Before going any further, I believe one of the first questions that needs to be answered in this chapter is: "What exactly is analytics?" The standard answer is that there are four different types of analytics and they are:

- Descriptive analytics – What happened?
- Diagnostic analytics – Why did it happen?
- Predictive analytics – What will happen?
- Prescriptive analytics – How can we make it happen again?

Figure 12 contains examples of how each of these types of analytics can be utilized by an airline.

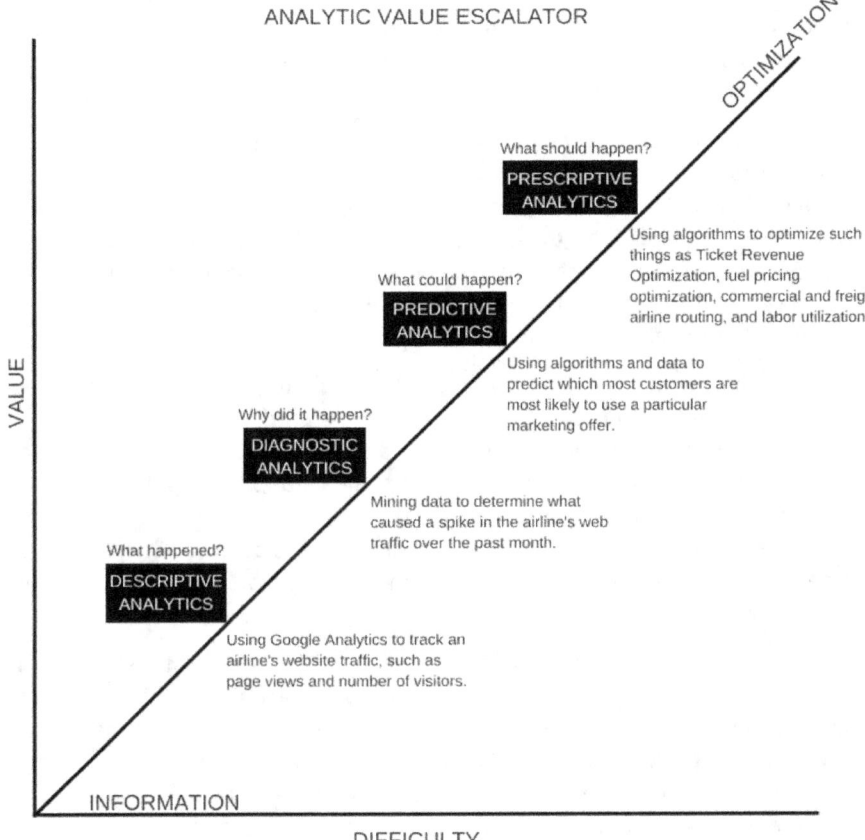

Figure 12: Analytics Value Escalator
Source: www.intelligencia.co

For an airliner, descriptive analytics could include pattern discovery methods such as customer segmentation, i.e., culling through a customer database to understand a customer's preferred game of choice. Simple cluster segmentation models could divide customers into their preferred choice of purchases.

Market basket analysis, which utilizes association rules, would also be considered a descriptive analytics procedure. Airlines should use market basket analysis to bundle and offer promotions as well as gain insight into its customers' buying habits. Detailed customer shopping and purchasing behavior could also be used to develop future products.

Diagnostic analytics is a form of advanced analytics that examines data or content to answer the question, "Why did it happen?" It attempts to understand causation and behaviors by utilizing such techniques as drill-down, data discovery, data mining and correlations. Building a decision tree atop a web user's clickstream behavior pattern could be considered a form of diagnostic analytics as these patterns might reveal why a person clicked his or her way through a website.

In his seminal article *Predictive Analytics White Paper*[170], Charles Nyce states that, "Predictive analytics is a broad term describing a variety of statistical and analytical techniques used to develop models that predict future events or behaviors. The form of these predictive models varies, depending on the behavior or event that they are predicting. Most predictive models generate a score (a customer rating, for example), with a higher score indicating a higher likelihood of the given behavior or event occurring."

Data mining, which is used to identify trends, patterns, and/or relationships within a data set, can then be used to develop a predictive model.[170] Prediction of future events is the key here and these analyses can be used in a multitude of ways, including forecasting behavior that could lead to a competitive advantage over rivals. Gut instinct can sometimes punch you in the gut and predictive analytics can help factor in variables that are inaccessible to the human mind and often the number of variables in an analytical problem are beyond human mental comprehension.

Predictive analytics (or supervised learning) is the use of statistics, machine learning, data mining, and modeling to analyze current and historical facts to make predictions about future events. Said another way, it gives mere mortals the ability to predict the future like Nostradamus. In recent years, data-mining has become one of the most valuable tools for extracting and manipulating data and for establishing patterns to produce useful information for decision-making.

Whether you love it or hate it, predictive analytics has already helped elect presidents, discover new energy sources, score consumer credit, assess health risks, detect fraud, and target prospective buyers. It is here to stay, and technology advances ranging from faster hardware to software that analyzes increasingly vast quantities of data are making the use of predictive analytics more creative and efficient than ever before.

Predictive analytics is an area of data mining that deals with extracting information from data and using it to predict trends and behavioral patterns. Often the unknown event of interest is in the future, but predictive analytics can be applied to any type of unknown, whether that is in the past, the present, or the future.

Predictive analytics uses many techniques from data mining to analyze current data to make predictions about the future, including statistics, modeling, machine learning, and artificial intelligence. For example, logistic regression can be used to turn a market basket analysis into a predictor so that an airline can understand what items are usually purchased together.

For an airline, predictive analytics can also be used for CRM, collection analysis, cross-sell, customer retention, direct marketing, fraud detection, product prediction, project risk management, amongst many other things.

Predictive analytics utilizes the following techniques:

- Regression
- Linear regression
- Discrete choice models
- Logistic regression
- Multinomial logistic regression
- Probit regression
- Time series models
- Survival or duration analysis
- Classification and regression trees
- Multivariate adaptive regression splines
- Machine learning
- Neural networks
- Naïve Bayes
- k-Nearest neighbors

Prescriptive analytics tries to optimize a key metric, such as profit, by not only anticipating what will happen, but also when it will happen and why it happens. Wikipedia states that, "Prescriptive analytics suggests decision options on how to take advantage of a future opportunity or mitigate a future risk and shows the implication of each decision option. Prescriptive analytics can continually take in new data to re-predict and re-prescribe, thus automatically improving prediction accuracy and prescribing better decision options."[171]

Prescriptive analytics can ingest a mixture of structured, unstructured, and semi-structured data, and utilize business rules that can predict what lies ahead, as well as advise how to exploit this predicted future without compromising other priorities. Stream processing can add an entirely new component to prescriptive analytics as well.

The analytics powerhouse SAS is finding its vaunted place atop the analytics pyramid challenged not just by their typical acronymic competitors—SAP, IBM, EMC, HDS, and the like—but also by the simpler visualization toolmakers like Tableau, Qlik, and Alteryx. These vendors are muscling their way into the mix, with offers that include data blending and in-memory technology that allows business users to access complete datasets at the touch of a button. These solutions offer less complex analytical capabilities, but such things as market basket analysis or simple decision tree networks can be created with them and the costs associated with them can be one quarter or one fifth of what the top echelon providers charge.

Throughout the rest of this chapter, I will break down many of the different types of analytical models that can be used to strengthen the customer experience for airlines.

In its conference paper *How Predictive Analytics is Changing the Retail Industry*[172] from the International Conference on Management and Information Systems, the writers argue that predictive models incorporate the following steps:

- Project Definition: Define the business objectives and desired outcomes for the project and translate them into predictive analytic objectives and tasks.
- Exploration: Analyze source data to determine the most appropriate data and model building approach and scope the effort.
- Data Preparation: Select, extract, and transform data upon which to create models.
- Model Building: Create, test, and validate models, and evaluate whether they will meet project metrics and goals.
- Deployment: Apply model results to business decisions or processes. This ranges from sharing insights with business users to embedding models into applications to automating decisions and business processes
- Model Management: Manage models to improve performance (i.e., accuracy), control access, promote reuse, standardize toolsets, and minimize redundant activities.

Analytical Models

Decision Trees

According to Wikipedia, a decision tree is "a decision support tool that uses a tree-like graph or model of decisions and their possible consequences, including chance event outcomes, resource costs, and utility. It is one way to display an algorithm."[173]

Decision trees are used to identify the strategy that is most likely to reach a goal. It is a decision support tool that uses a graph or model of decisions and their possible consequences, including chance event outcomes, resource costs, and utility. Decision trees are sequential partitions of a set of data that maximize the differences of a dependent variable (response or output variable). They offer a concise way of defining groups that are consistent in their attributes, but which vary in terms of the dependent variable.

A decision tree consists of three types of nodes:

1. Decision nodes—represented by squares.
2. Chance nodes—represented by circles
3. End nodes—represented by triangles

The construction of a decision tree is based on the principle of "divide and conquer": through a supervised learning algorithm, successive divisions of the multivariable space are carried out in order to maximize the distance between groups in each division (that is, carry out partitions that discriminate). The division process finalizes when all of the entries of a branch have the same value in the output variable, giving rise to the complete model. The further down the input variables are in the tree, the less important they are in the output classification (and the less generalization they allow, due to the decrease in the number of inputs in the descending branches).

For an airline, decision trees can be utilized in operations management and marketing, where they can predict whether a person will respond to an offer or not, or whether they are likely to abuse an offer.

According to Deng et al. in their paper *Building a Big Data Analytics Service Framework for Mobile Advertising and Marketing*[174], the decision tree algorithm is:

> "Used to classify the attributes and decide the outcome of the class attribute. In order to construct a decision tree both class attribute and item attributes are required. Decision tree is a tree like structure where the intermediate nodes represent attributes of the data, leaf nodes represents the outcome of the data and the branches hold the attribute value. Decision trees are widely used in the classification process because no domain knowledge is needed to construct the decision tree."

The main step in the decision tree algorithm is to identify the root node for any given set of data.[174] "Multiple methods exist to decide the root node of the decision tree. Information gain and Gini impurity are the primary methods used to identify the root node. Root node plays an important role in deciding which side of the decision tree the data falls into. Like every classification method, decision trees are also constructed using the training data and tested with the test data."[174]

Advantages	Disadvantages
• Simple and robust • Useful to predict the outcomes of future data • Little cleansing is enough to remove the missing values data • Useful for large data sets • Decision trees can handle both categorical and numerical data	• Possibility of creating complex decision trees for simple data • Replication problem makes the decision trees complex. So remove the replicated data before constructing a decision tree • Pruning is required to avoid complex decision trees • It is hard to find out the correct root node

Table 5: Advantages and disadvantages of decision trees
Source: ResearchGate[174]

k-Means Cluster

As its name suggests, the *k*-Means cluster is a clustering algorithm and it is one of the most common analytical models because of its simplicity and ease of use. The fact that it is still going strong after over 50 years of use speaks as much to its ease-of-use as it does to the difficulty of designing a general-purpose clustering algorithm.

According to Telgarsky and Vattani, "The goal of cluster analysis is to partition a given set of items into clusters such that similar items are assigned to the same cluster whereas dissimilar ones are not. Perhaps the most popular clustering formulation is *K*-means, in which the goal is to maximize the expected similarity between data items and their associated cluster centroids."[175]

In their paper *A K-Means Clustering Algorithm*[176], Hartigan and Wong explain that the:

> "aim of the k-means algorithm is to divide M points in N dimensions into k clusters so that the within-cluster sum of squares is minimized. It is not practical to require that the solution has minimal sum of squares against all partitions, except when M, N are small and k = 2. We seek instead 'local' optima, solutions that no movement of a point from one cluster to another will reduce the within-cluster sum of squares."

K Means Clustering identifies and classifies items into groups based on their similarity. *K* is the number of clusters that needs to be decided upon before the clustering process begins.[174] "The whole solution depends on the *K* value. So, it is very important to choose a correct *K* value. The data point is grouped in to a cluster based on the Euclidean distance between the point and the centroid of the cluster," explains Deng et al.[174]

For Deng et al., initial clustering can be done in one of three ways[174]:

1. Dynamically Chosen: In this method, the first K items are chosen and then assigned to K clusters.
2. Randomly Chosen: In this method, the values are randomly selected and then assigned to K clusters.
3. Choosing from Upper and Lower Boundaries: In this method, the values that are very distant from each other are chosen and they are used as initial values for each cluster."[174]

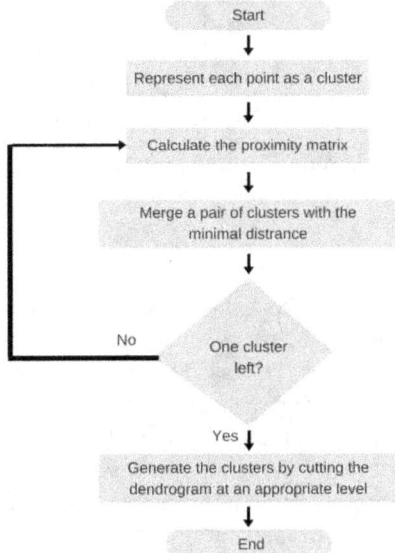

Figure 13: Clustering Algorithm
Source: Researchgate[174]

According to Deng at al., the K-Means methodology is as follows[174]:

- Step 1: Choose the initial values using one of the above three methods
- Step 2: For each additional value:
- Step 3: Calculate the Euclidean distance between this point and centroid of the clusters.
- Step 4: Move the value to the nearest cluster.
- Step 5: Calculate the new centroid for the cluster.
- Step 6: Repeat steps 3 to 5.
- Step 7: Calculate centroid of the cluster.
- Step 8: For each value:

- Step 9: Calculate the Euclidean distance between this value and the centroid of all the clusters.
- Step 10: Move the value to the nearest cluster.

Advantages	Disadvantages
<ul><li>Faster computations than hierarchical clustering</li><li>It produces tighter clusters than other clustering techniques</li><li>Gives best result when data sets are distinct</li><li>Easy to understand</li></ul>	<ul><li>Sensitive to noise</li><li>Numbers of clusters must be decided before starting clustering</li><li>Choosing correct initial clustering process</li><li>Choosing correct number of clusters</li><li>The centroid of the group changes because we calculate centroid every time a new item joins the cluster</li><li>Large data sets needed to cluster the data correctly</li></ul>

Table 6: Advantages and disadvantages of decision trees
Source: Researchgate[174]

k-Nearest Neighbors

First described in the early 1950s, the *k*-nearest neighbors method is a classification (or regression) algorithm that, in order to determine the classification of a point, combines the classification of the K nearest points. It is supervised because you are trying to classify a point based on the known classification of other points. It is labor intensive when given large training sets, and it did not gain popularity until the computer revolution in the 1960s brought processing powers that were able to handle such large data sets.[174] Today, it is widely used in the area of pattern recognition.[174]

As Deng et al. explain[174]:

> *"Nearest-neighbor classifiers are based on learning by analogy, that is, by comparing a given test tuple with training tuples that are similar to it. The training tuples are described by n attributes. Each tuple represents a point in an n-dimensional space. In this way, all of the training tuples are stored in an n-dimensional pattern space. When given an unknown tuple, a k-nearest-neighbor classifier searches the pattern space for the k training tuples that are closest to the unknown tuple. These k training tuples are the k 'nearest neighbors' of the unknown tuple. When the 'k' closest points are obtained, the unknown sample is then assigned to the most common class among those k-points. In case of k=1, the unknown sample is assigned to the closest point in the pattern space. The closeness is*

measured using the distance between the two points."

the *k*-means clustering and *k*-nearest neighbor methodologies seek to accomplish different goals; *k*-nearest neighbors is a classification algorithm, which is a subset of supervised learning, while *k*-means is a clustering algorithm, which is a subset of unsupervised learning.

K-nearest neighbor techniques can be used to prevent theft in the airline business. Modern surveillance system are intelligent enough to analyze and interpret video data on their own, utilizing k-nearest neighbor for visual pattern recognition to scan and detect hidden packages in the bottom bin of a shopping cart at check-out, for example. It could also be able to ensure parts in a warehouse don't get stolen.

As she explains in her article *Solving Real-World Problems with Nearest Neighbor Algorithms*[177], Lillian Pierson states that, "If an object is detected that's an exact match for an object listed in the database, then the price of the spotted product could even automatically be added to the customer's bill. While this automated billing practice is not used extensively at this time, the technology has been developed and is available for use."

The *K*-nearest neighbor algorithm can also be used to detect patterns in credit card usage to root out credit card fraud. "Many new transaction-scrutinizing software applications use *k*NN algorithms to analyze register data and spot unusual patterns that indicate suspicious activity," Pierson adds.[177]

"If register data indicates that a lot of customer information is being entered manually rather than through automated scanning and swiping, this could indicate that the employee who's using that register is in fact stealing customer's personal information," warns Pierson.[177] Another example would be "if register data indicates that a particular good is being returned or exchanged multiple times, this could indicate that employees are misusing the return policy."[177]

*k*NN is not just about fraud. It can also be used to increase retail sales. "Average nearest neighbor algorithm classification and point pattern detection can be used in grocery retail to identify key patterns in customer purchasing behavior, and subsequently increase sales and customer satisfaction by anticipating customer behavior," explains Pierson.[177]

Advantages	Disadvantages
• It produces tighter clusters than other clustering techniques • Gives best result when data sets are distinct • Easy to understand	• KNN neither doesn't follow any nor have any standard for selecting the value '*k*', which is one of the key factors in the success of an algorithm • As *KNN* is a Lazy Learner algorithm, it has high storage requirements and requires efficient indexing techniques

Advantages	Disadvantages
	• The efficiency of the *K*NN algorithm also depends on the choice of the distance metric used. The results of the algorithm differ for each similarity metric

Table 7: Advantages and disadvantages of decision trees
Source: Researchgate.[174]

Logistic Regression

According to Wikipedia, logistic regression is a regression model where the dependent variable (DV) is categorical, i.e., a variable that can take on one of a limited, and usually fixed, number of possible values.[178] This compares to a variable that would be continuous. Developed in 1958 by statistician David Cox, "The binary logistic model is used to estimate the probability of a binary response based on one or more predictor (or independent) variables (features). It allows one to say that the presence of a risk factor increases the probability of a given outcome by a specific percentage," explains Cox[178]

In his article *Using Logistic Regression to Predict Customer Retention*[179], Andrew Karp explains that:

> *"Logistic regression is an increasingly popular statistical technique used to model the probability of discrete (i.e., binary or multinomial) outcomes. When properly applied, logistic regression analyses yield very powerful insights in to what attributes (i.e., variables) are more or less likely to predict event outcome in a population of interest. These models also show the extent to which changes in the values of the attributes may increase or decrease the predicted probability of event outcome."*

Logistic regression techniques may be used to classify a new observation whose group is unknown, in one of the groups, based on the values of the predictor variables. According to Karp, "Logistic regression models are frequently employed to assess the chance that a customer will: a) re-purchase a product, b) remain a customer, or c) respond to a direct mail or other marketing stimulus."[179]

Karp adds that "Economists frequently call logistic regression a 'qualitative choice' model, and for obvious reasons: a logistic regression model helps us assess probability which 'qualities' or 'outcomes' will be chosen (selected) by the population under analysis."[179] As can be expected, Karp argues that, "When proper care is taken to create an appropriate dependent variable, logistic regression is often a superior (both substantively and statistically) alternative to other tools available to model event outcomes."[179]

Karp uses a health care example to make his point that the analyst has several independent variables to use in the modeling process, but this example can be illustrative of how they could be used in the airline industry.[179] Karp explains that "An analyst developing a model predicting re-enrollment in a health insurance plan may have data for each member's interaction with both the health plans administrative apparatus and health care utilization in the prior 'plan year.'"[179]

The analyst can then construct variables such as the "number of times member called the health plan for information, number of physician office visits, whether or not the member changed primary care physicians during the previous 'plan year,' and answers to a customer satisfaction survey."[179] These can be employed in the modeling process and, once the model has been constructed, the analyst must decide which variable can be employed as the "outcome" or the "dependent" variable.[179]

In logistic regression analyses "it is often the analyst's responsibility to *construct* the dependent variable based on an agreed-upon definition of what constitutes the 'event of interest' which is being modeled," explains Karp.[179]

In the health care re-enrollment example, "a health plan's management team may define 'attrition' or 'failure to re-enroll' as situations where a member fails to return the re-enrollment card within 30 days of its due date. Or, in a response modeling scenario, a direct mail firm may define 'non-response' to an advertisement as failure to respond within 45 days of mailout."[179]

Logistic regression models can be powerful tools to build models that understand customer retention.[179] "When applied properly, logistic regression models can yield powerful insights into why some customers leave and others stay. These insights can then be employed to modify organizational strategies and/or assess the impact of the implementation of these strategies," Karp adds.[179]

A/B Testing

Also known as split testing or bucket testing, A/B testing is a method of marketing testing by which a baseline control sample is compared to a variety of single-variable test samples in order to improve response rates.

A classic direct mail tactic, this method has recently been adopted within the interactive space to test tactics such as banner ads, emails, and landing pages. As Scott Sutton explains in his article *Customer Analytics in the Casino and Hospitality Industry: How the House Always Wins*[180], for airline marketers, A/B Testing is the most effective way to identify the best available marketing offer.[180] It can test "two different offers against one another in order to identify the offer that drives the highest response and the most revenue/profit."[180]

As Dan Siroker and Peter Komen explain in their book *A/B Testing: The Most*

Powerful Way to Turn Clicks into Customers[181], "The hardest part of A/B testing is determining what to test in the first place. Having worked with thousands of customers who do A/B testing every day, one of the most common questions we hear is, 'Where do I begin?'"

The mistake many companies make is they jump in head first without any detailed planning. Siroker and Komen propose the following deliberate five-step process[181]:

1. Define success
2. Identify bottlenecks
3. Construct a hypothesis
4. Prioritize
5. Test

A/B testing is particularly good for website marketing, especially for uncovering the best landing pages. As Siroker and Komen explain, "Defining success in the context of A/B testing involves taking the answer to the question of your site's ultimate purpose and turning it into something more precise: *quantifiable success metrics*. Your success metrics are the specific numbers you hope will be improved by your tests."[181]

An e-commerce site could easily define its success metrics in terms of revenue per visitor[181], but it is still important to understand such things as traffic sources, bounce rate, top pages, conversion rates, conversion by traffic source, amongst others.

Site Type	Common Conversion & Aggregate Goals
e-Commerce A site that sells things for users to purchase online.	• Completed purchase • Each step within the checkout funnel • Products added to cart • Product page views
Media/Content A site focused on article or other content consumption.	• Page views • Articles read • Bounce rate (when measuring within an A/B testing tool, this is often measured by seeing if the user clicked anywhere on the page)
Lead Generation A site that acquires business through name capture.	• Form completion • Clicks to a form page (links may read "Contact us" for example)
Donation	• Form completion • Clicks to a form page (links may read "Send a donation" for example)

Table 8: Typical A/B conversion & aggregate goals
Source: A/B Testing: The Most Powerful Way to Turn Clicks into Customers[181]

As Siroker and Komen state:

> "Part of building out your testing strategy is identifying what constitutes—and does not constitute—a 'conversion' for your particular site. In online terms, a conversion is the point at which a visitor takes the desired action on your website. Pinpointing the specific actions you want people to take most on your site and that are most critical to your business will lead you to the tests that have an impact."[181]

Once the site's quantifiable success metrics are agreed upon, attention can be paid trying to discover where the bottlenecks are.[181] These are the places where users are dropping off, or the places where momentum in moving users through the desired series of actions weakens.[181]

Time Series Model

A time series is an ordered sequence of values of a variable at uniformly spaced time intervals. A Time Series model can be used to predict or forecast the future behavior of a variable.

In his article *Time Series Analysis*[182], Muhammad Imdadullah explains that, "Time series analysis is the analysis of a series of data-points over time, allowing one to answer questions such as what is the causal effect on a variable Y of a change in variable X over time? An important difference between time series and cross section data is that the ordering of cases does matter in time series."

These models account for the fact that data points taken over time may have an internal structure (such as autocorrelation, trend or seasonal variation) that should be considered. For the airline industry, a Time Series Analysis can be used to forecast sales, project yields and workloads, as well as analyze budgets.

Time series can be broken down into two variations:

- Continuous Time Series— "A time series is said to be continuous when observations are made continuously in time. The term continuous is used for series of this type even when the measured variable can only take a discrete set of values."[182]
- Discrete Time Series— "A time series is said to be discrete when observations are taken at specific times, usually equally spaced. The term discrete is used for series of this type even when the measured variable is a continuous variable."[182]

Neural Networks

Artificial Neural Networks (ANN) or just "Neural Networks" are non-linear statistical data modeling tools that are used when the exact nature of a relationship between input and output is unknown. In their article *Neural Networks in Data Mining*[183], Singh and Chauhan claim that a neural network is:

> "A mathematical model or computational model based on biological neural networks, in other words, is an emulation of biological neural system. It consists of an interconnected group of artificial neurons and processes information using a connectionist approach to computation. In most cases an ANN is an adaptive system that changes its structure based on external or internal information that flows through the network during the learning phase."

As Jim Gao explains in his article *Machine Learning Applications for Data Center Optimization*[184]:

> "Neural networks are a class of machine learning algorithms that mimic cognitive behavior via interactions between artificial neurons. They are advantageous for modeling intricate systems because neural networks do not require the user to predefine the feature interactions in the model, which assumes relationships within the data. Instead, the neural network searches for patterns and interactions between features to automatically generate a best fit model. Common applications for this branch of machine learning include speech recognition, image processing, and autonomous software agents. As with most learning systems, the model accuracy improves over time as new training data is acquired."

There are three types of training in neural networks; reinforcement learning, supervised and unsupervised training, with supervised being the most common one. Neural Networks are data processing systems whose structure and functioning are inspired by biological neural networks. Their fundamental characteristics include parallel processing, distributed memory and adaptability to their surroundings.

In his article *A Beginners Guide To AI: Neural Networks*[185], Tristan Greene puts it in simpler terms, stating that, "Scientists believe that a living creature's brain processes information using a biological neural network. The human brain has as many as 100 trillion synapses—gaps between neurons—which form specific patterns when activated. When a person thinks about a specific thing, remembers something, or experiences something with one of their senses, it's thought that specific neural patterns 'light up' inside the brain."

Greene continues, "when you were learning to read you might have had to sound out the letters so that you could hear them out loud and lead your young brain to a conclusion. But, once you've read the word cat enough times you don't have to slow down and sound it out."[185] At that point, Greene contends, "you access a part of your brain more associated with memory than problem-solving, and thus a different set of synapses fire because you've trained your biological neural network to recognize the word 'cat.'"[185]

"In the field of deep learning a neural network is represented by a series of layers that work much like a living brain's synapses," explains Greene.[185] 'Researchers teach computers how to understand what a cat is—or at least what a picture of a cat is—by feeding it as many images of cats as they can."[185] The neural network analyzes those images and "tries to find out everything that makes them similar, so that it can find cats in other pictures," adds Greene.[185]

There are many kinds of deep learning and many types of neural networks, but I will touch upon generative adversarial networks (GANs), convolutional neural networks (CNNs), and recurrent neural networks (RNNs) here.

GANs were invented by Ian Goodfellow, one of Google's AI gurus, in 2014.[185] To put it simply, "a GAN is a neural network comprised of two arguing sides—a generator and an adversary—that fight among themselves until the generator wins."[185] Greene gives the example that, "If you wanted to create an AI that imitates an art style, like Picasso's for example, you could feed a GAN a bunch of his paintings."[185]

According to Greene, the process works in the following way, "One side of the network would try to create new images that fooled the other side into thinking they were painted by Picasso. Basically, the AI would learn everything it could about Picasso's work by examining the individual pixels of each image."[185] One side would start create the image, while the other side would determine if it was a Picasso.[185] "Once the AI fooled itself," Greene claims, "the results could then be viewed by a human who could determine if the algorithm needed to be tweaked to provide better results, or if it successfully imitated the desired style."[185]

Convolutional Neural Networks (CNNs) are among the most common and robust neural networks around, which have, at least theoretically, been around since the 1940s.[185] Thanks to advanced hardware and efficient algorithms, they're can now be used.[185] "Where a GAN tries to create something that fools an adversary, a CNN has several layers through which data is filtered into categories," explains Greene.[185] "These are primarily used in image recognition and text language processing," notes Greene.[185]

"If you've got a billion hours of video to sift through, you could build a CNN that tries to examine each frame and determine what's going on," explains Greene.[185] "One might train a CNN by feeding it complex images that have been tagged by humans," adds Greene.[185] "AI learns to recognize things like stop signs, cars, trees, and butterflies by looking at pictures that humans have labelled, comparing the pixels in the image to the labels it understands, and then organizing everything it sees into the categories it's been trained on," says Greene.[185]

RNNs are "primarily used for AI that requires nuance and context to understand its input."[185] "An example of such a neural network is a natural language processing AI that interprets human speech," such as Google's Assistant and Amazon's Alexa.[185]

"To understand how an RNN works, let's imagine an AI that generates original musical compositions based on human input," explains Greene.[185] "If you play a note the AI tries to 'hallucinate' what the next note 'should' be. If you play another note, the AI can further anticipate what the song should sound like. Each piece of context provides information for the next step, and a RNN continuously updates itself based on its continuing input – hence the recurrent part of the name," concludes Greene.[185]

Scientists use neural networks to teach computers how to do things for themselves.

Neural networks can be used to find patterns in data. A key feature of neural networks is that they learn the relationship between inputs and output through training.

For marketing purposes, neural networks can be used to classify a consumer's spending pattern, analyze a new product, identify a customer's characteristics as well as forecast sales.[183] The advantages of neural networks include high accuracy, high noise tolerance and ease of use as they can be updated with fresh data, which makes them useful for dynamic environments.[183]

In her article *How DeepMind's AlphaGo Zero Learned all by itself to trash world champ AI AlphaGo*[186], Katyanna Quach explains how neural networks can work when training computers to play board games. According to Quach, the board game *Go* is considered a "difficult game for computers to master because, besides being complex, the number of possible moves—more than chess at 10^{170}—is greater than the number of atoms in the universe."[186]

"AlphaGo, the predecessor to AlphaGo Zero, crushed 18-time world champion Lee Sedo and the reigning world number one player, Ke Jie," explains Quach.[186] The next generation of DeepMind's technology, AlphaGo Zero, beat "AlphaGo 100-0 after training for just a fraction of the time AlphaGo needed, and it didn't learn from observing humans playing against each other—unlike AlphaGo. Instead, Zero's neural network relies on an old technique in reinforcement learning: self-play."[186]

As Quach notes about the process[186]:

"Essentially, AlphaGo Zero plays against itself. During training, it sits on each side of the table: two instances of the same software face off against each other. A match starts with the game's black and white stones scattered on the board, placed following a random set of moves from their starting positions. The two computer players are given the list of moves that led to the positions of the stones on the grid, and then are each told to come up with multiple chains of next moves along with estimates of the probability they will win by following through each chain.

"So, the black player could come up with four chains of next moves and predict the third chain will be the most successful. The white player could come up with its own chains and think its first choice is the strongest.

"The next move from the best possible chain is then played, and the computer players repeat the above steps, coming up with chains of moves ranked by strength. This repeats over and over, with the software feeling its way through the game and internalizing which strategies turn out to be the strongest."

This methodology differs from the old AlphaGo, which "relied on a computationally intensive Monte Carlo tree search to play through Go scenarios."[186] "The nodes and branches created a much larger tree than AlphaGo practically needed to play."[186] "A combination of reinforcement learning and human-supervised learning was used to build 'value' and 'policy' neural networks that used the search tree to execute gameplay strategies," explains Quach.[186] "The software learned from 30 million moves played in human-on-human games, and benefited from various bodges and tricks to learn to win. For instance, it was trained from master-level human players, rather than picking it up from scratch," adds Quach.[186]

"Self-play is an established technique in reinforcement learning, and has been used to teach machines to play backgammon, chess, poker, and Scrabble," says Quach.[186] David Silver, a lead researcher on AlphaGo, explains that it is an effective technique because the opponent is always the right level of difficulty.[186]

"So it starts off extremely naive," Silver said, adding that "at every step of the learning process it has an opponent—a sparring partner if you like—that is exactly calibrated to its current level of performance. To begin with these players are very weak but over time they get progressively stronger."[186]

Tim Salimans, a research scientist at OpenAI, explains that self-play means "agents can learn behaviours that are not hand coded on any reinforcement learning task, but the sophistication of the learned behavior is limited by the sophistication of the environment. In order for an agent to learn intelligent behavior in a particular environment, the environment has to be challenging, but not too challenging."[186]

"The competitive element makes the agent explicitly search for its own weaknesses. Once those weaknesses are found the agent can improve them. In self-play the difficulty of the task the agent is solving is always reasonable, but over time it is open ended: since the opponent can always improve, the task can always get harder," adds Salimans.

Self-play does have its limitatiosn.[186] Right now, there are "problems that AlphaGo Zero cannot solve, such as games with hidden states or imperfect information, such as Starcraft, and it's unlikely that self-play will be successful tackling more advanced challenges."[186]

Self-play will be worthwhile in some areas of AI, argues Salimans.[186] "As our algorithms for reinforcement learning become more powerful the bottleneck in developing artificial intelligence will gradually shift to developing sufficiently sophisticated tasks and environments. Even very talented people will not develop a great intellect if they are not exposed to the right environment," he warns.[186]

DeepMind, the company behind AlphaGo Zero and its predecessor, believes that "the approach may be generalizable to a wider set of scenarios that share similar properties to a game like Go."[186]

Discriminant Analysis

According to Wikipedia:

> "Discriminant function analysis is a statistical analysis used to predict a categorical dependent variable (called a grouping variable) by one or more continuous or binary independent variables (called predictor variables). The original dichotomous discriminant analysis was developed by Sir Ronald Fisher in 1936. It differs from an ANOVA or MANOVA, which is used to predict one (ANOVA) or multiple (MANOVA) continuous dependent variables by one or more independent categorical variables."[187]

Discriminant or discriminant function analysis is a method used to determine which weightings of quantitative variables or predictors best discriminate between two or more than two groups of cases and do so better than chance. It is a method used in statistics, pattern recognition and machine learning to find a linear combination of features that characterizes or separates two or more classes of objects or events.

Because of its ability to classify individuals or experimental units into two or more uniquely defined populations, discriminate analysis can be used for market segmentation and the prediction of group membership. The discriminant score can be the basis on which a prediction about group membership is made. For example, the discriminant weights of each predictive variable (age, sex, income, etc.) indicate the relative importance of each variable. In other words, if age has a low discriminant weight then it is less important than the other variables.

For an airline marketing department, use of discriminant analysis can help predict why a customer frequents one airline over another. Discriminant analysis is specifically useful in product research, perception/image research, advertising research and direct marketing.

Survival or Duration Analysis

As per Wikipedia, "Survival analysis is a branch of statistics for analyzing the expected duration of time until one or more events happen, such as death in biological organisms and failure in mechanical systems. This topic is called reliability theory or reliability analysis in engineering, duration analysis or duration modeling in economics, and event history analysis in sociology."[188] Survival analysis attempts to answer questions such as[188]:

- What is the proportion of a population which will survive past a certain time?
- Of those that survive, at what rate will they die or fail?
- Can multiple causes of death or failure be considered?
- How do particular circumstances or characteristics increase or decrease the probability of survival?

A branch of statistics that deals with death in biological organisms and failure in mechanical systems, survival analysis involves the modeling of time to event data; in this context, death or failure is considered an "event" in the survival analysis literature—traditionally only a single event occurs, after which the organism or mechanism is dead or broken. Survival Analysis is the study of lifetimes and their distributions. It usually involves one or more of the following objectives:

1. To explore the behavior of the distribution of a lifetime.
2. To model the distribution of a lifetime.
3. To test for differences between the distributions of two or more lifetimes.
4. To model the impact of one or more explanatory variables on a lifetime distribution.

In her article for the Cornell Statistical Consulting Unit[189], Simona Despa explains that "In survival analysis, subjects are usually followed over a specified time period and the focus is on the time at which the event of interest occurs."[189] "Why not use linear regression to model the survival time as a function of a set of predictor variables?" asks Despa.[189] "First, survival times are typically positive numbers; ordinary linear regression may not be the best choice unless these times are first transformed in a way that removes this restriction. Second, and more importantly, ordinary linear regression cannot effectively handle the censoring of observations," explains Despa.[189]

"Observations are called censored when the information about their survival time is incomplete; the most commonly encountered form is right censoring," writes Despa.[189] She adds[189]:

> "Suppose patients are followed in a study for 20 weeks. A patient who does not experience the event of interest for the duration of the study is said to be right censored. The survival time for this person is considered to be at least as long as the duration of the study. Another example of right censoring is when a person drops out of the study before the end of the study observation time and did not experience the event. This person's survival time is said to be censored, since we know that the event of interest did not happen while this person was under observation. Censoring is an important issue in survival analysis, representing a particular type of missing data. Censoring that is random and non-informative is usually required in order to avoid bias in a survival analysis."

"Unlike ordinary regression models, survival methods correctly incorporate information from both censored and uncensored observations in estimating important model parameters," notes Despa.[189] "The dependent variable in survival analysis is composed of two parts: one is the time to event and the other is the event status, which records if the event of interest occurred or not," says Despa.[189] The two functions that are dependent on time—survival and hazard functions—can then be estiamted.[189] "The survival and hazard functions are key concepts in survival analysis for describing the distribution of event times," says Despa.[189] "The survival function gives, for every time, the probability of surviving (or not experiencing the event) up to that time. The hazard function gives the potential that the event will occur, per time unit, given that an individual has survived up to the specified time."[189] "While these are often of direct interest, many other quantities of interest (e.g., median survival) may subsequently be estimated from knowing either the hazard or survival function," says Despa.[189]

For survival studies it is often important "to describe the relationship of a factor of interest (e.g. treatment) to the time to event, in the presence of several covariates, such as age, gender, race, etc."[189] A number of models—parametric, nonparametric, and semiparametric—are available to analyze the relationship of a set of predictor variables with the survival time, claims Despa.[189]

"Parametric methods assume that the underlying distribution of the survival times follows certain known probability distributions,"[189] the most popular ones being the exponential, Weibull, and lognormal distributions.[189] "The description of the distribution of the survival times and the change in their distribution as a function of predictors is of interest. Model parameters in these settings are usually estimated using an appropriate modification of maximum likelihood," says Despa.

"A nonparametric estimator of the survival function, the Kaplan Meier method is widely used to estimate and graph survival probabilities as a function of time," notes Despa.[189] "It can be used to obtain univariate descriptive statistics for survival data, including the median survival time," says Despa. It can also be used to "compare the survival experience for two or more groups of subjects."[189] "To test for overall differences between estimated survival curves of two or more groups of subjects, such as males versus females, or treated versus untreated (control) groups, several tests are available, including the log-rank test," says Despa.[189] "This can be motivated as a type of chi-square test, a widely used test in practice, and in reality is a method for comparing the Kaplan-Meier curves estimated for each group of subjects," adds Despa.[189]

Airline Analytical Models

Customer Segmentation

As Kimberly Coffey, PhD, explains in her article *k-means Clustering for Customer Segmentation: A Practical Example*[190], clustering isn't as simple as it sounds. Coffey believes that, "Customer segmentation is a deceptively simple-sounding concept. Broadly speaking, the goal is to divide customers into groups that share certain characteristics. There are an almost-infinite number of characteristics upon which you could divide customers, however, and the optimal characteristics and analytic approach vary depending upon the business objective. This means that there is no single, correct way to perform customer segmentation."

That being said, "Customer segmentation is often performed using unsupervised, clustering techniques (e.g., *k*-means, latent class analysis, hierarchical clustering, etc.), but customer segmentation results tend to be most actionable for a business when the segments can be linked to something concrete (e.g., customer lifetime value, product proclivities, channel preference, etc.)," notes Coffey.[190] Of course, this begs the question: "if you're looking to link the segments to some sort of dependent variable, why not use an analytic technique that explicitly estimates the relationship between your possible predictors and the dependent variable?"[190]

Coffey's answer: the primary reason is that, "clustering creates groups from continuous variables (typically), so if you're looking to create groups, clustering does a really nice job of finding the boundaries between groups."[190] "In situations where there is a dependent variable of interest, it is generally included as an input variable in the cluster analysis, so the clusters can be interpreted in light of this outcome variable," explains Coffey.[190]

"Customer segmentation is the process of dividing customers into groups based upon certain boundaries; clustering is *one* way to generate these boundaries," Coffey notes.[190] There is an important caveat though—clustering assumes that there *are* distinct clusters in the data.[190] Oftentimes, customers are distributed more or less continuously in multivariate space, and they aren't in neatly defined groups.[190]

A customer segmentation model provides a view of the airline from a customer perspective: such models have many and varied applications. Customers might be segmented according to what they present to the airline. Views include:

- Interests and needs
- Gender and age
- Marital status
- Spending history
- Demographics
- Psychographics

Generally, the data is used to determine the appropriate segments for these views. The result of this analysis presents a detailed view of how the airline is populated at different times and it can allow for appropriate strategic decisions to be made by the airline. These decisions could be a function of marketing, operations or strategy. The output can also be used to build acquisition models, as I will discuss below.

Other potential for analysis would be a master segmentation model that uses the preference results described above. Customers are clustered based on their preferences to gain a global view of the airline that is concise and understandable. Furthermore, such models can help measure the impact of operational strategic decisions.

Customer Acquisition Model

Just like every other businesss, airlines are always on the lookout for new customers. With the airline business getting more and more competitive and saturated by the day, there is a constant need to know what type of customers to target and where to find them.

The results of the segmentation model described above can be used to build a predictive model that identifies likely characteristics of attractive customers. Obviously, the airline will have no internal data available on customers they don't already have on their books so the analysis becomes a data mining exercise using publicly available input variables. Airlines can then target these customers with a view to attracting those who have the traits that they see in their already valuable customers.

The best external data to use would be population census data, linked to the internal customers by a location identifier (such as postcode). It is acknowledged that in some jurisdictions robust and accurate census data may not be available, so the model would be relying on whatever information the airline records on its customers from a demographic and lifestyle point of view.

This approach becomes a classical data-mining exercise, where a pool of independent variables would be tested for the strength of association with the response variable. Once the relevant predictors are identified and the characteristics and traits are defined, marketing and acquisition campaigns could be targeted at the population towards these kinds of people.

This would be something that looks to predict a metric derived from current/past customers. Such a metric could come from a segmentation model that identified the high value customers that are most attractive to the airline. There are several approaches that can be used and once the target has been defined, this allows for a parametric equation to be derived. This equation attempts to predict the characteristics that separate out the desirable customers from the rest.

This model can only use publicly available information (although other airline information might be acceptable) as that is how a potential customer would be identified. Current information that the company would have on hand would be age, nationality, gender, and address.

Where available, third party data should be looked at to further enhance the findings. This could be census data that gives an indication of further customer demographics and this enhances the ability to hone in on customer sweet spots.

Recency-Frequency-Monetary (RFM) Models

RFM is a method used for analyzing customer value. It is commonly used in database marketing and direct marketing and has received particular attention in the gambling and retail industries. RFM stands for:

- **Recency**: How much time has elapsed since a customer's last activity or transaction with airline? Activity is usually a flight, although variations are sometimes used, e.g., the last visit to airline's website or use of its mobile app. In most cases, the more recently a customer has interacted or transacted with an airline, the more likely that customer will be responsive to communications from the airline, including marketing communications.
- **Frequency**: How often has a customer transacted or interacted with an airline during a particular period? Clearly, customers with frequent activities are more engaged, and probably more loyal, than customers

who rarely do so. A one-time-only customer is in a class of his or her own.
- **Monetary**: Also referred to as "monetary value," this factor reflects how much a customer has spent with the brand during a particular period. Big spenders should usually be treated differently than customers who spend little. Looking at monetary divided by frequency indicates the average purchase amount—an important secondary factor to consider when segmenting customers.

Most businesses will keep scores of data about a customer's purchases. All that is needed is a table with the customer name, date of purchase and purchase value. One methodology is to assign a scale of 1 to 10, whereby 10 is the maximum value and to stipulate a formula by which the data suits the scale. For example, in a service-based business like the gambling business, you could have the following:

- Recency = 10—the number of months that have passed since the customer last purchased.
- Frequency = number of purchases in the last 12 months (maximum of 10).
- Monetary = value of the highest order from a given customer (benchmarked against $10k).

RFM calculates "scores" for each customer. The customers with the highest scores will probably be those who spend the most with the airline, across the most recent and frequent dates. The idea behind RFM is that a minority of customers are responsible for most of an airline's business, i.e., the Pareto Principle, also known as the 80/20 rule. The RFM process does condenses the customers' purchasing patterns in some form of an 80/20 split, whereby 80% of the sales come from 20% of the customers and this is a further extension of analysis that airlines can derive from this RFM process.

Alternatively, one can create categories for each attribute. For instance, the 'Recency' attribute might be broken into three categories: customers with purchases within the last 90 days; purchases between 91 and 365 days; and purchases longer than 365 days. Such categories may be arrived at by applying business rules or using a data mining technique to find meaningful breaks.

Once each of the attributes has appropriate categories defined, segments are created from the intersection of the values. If there were three categories for each attribute, then the resulting matrix would have twenty-seven possible combinations (one well-known commercial approach uses five bins per attribute, which yields 125 segments).

Segments could also be collapsed into sub-segments, if the gradations appear too small to be useful. The resulting segments can be ordered from most valuable (highest recency, frequency, and value) to least valuable (lowest recency, frequency, and value). Identifying the most valuable RFM segments can capitalize on chance relationships in the data used for this analysis. For this reason, it is highly recommended that another set of data be used to validate the results of the RFM segmentation process.

The goal is to produce RFM Segments that reflect the following types of airline customers:

- Core—best customers
- Loyal—most loyal customers
- Whales—highest paying customers
- Promising—most faithful customers
- Rookies—newest customers
- Slipping—once loyal, now gone customers

Once the RFM data has been developed, an airline can utilize this data to easily develop a customer loyalty program based on the purchasing patterns of its passengers, this is one of the best reasons to develop an RFM model. Where an airline has points assigned for Recency, Frequency and Monetary Value, the airline can assign the same amount of points, or a different points concept, for loyalty to its products and/or services. Airlines should consider using a range of customer loyalty concepts to develop and measure customer loyalty, and then reward customers who choose to fly with the airline, rather than one its competitors.

Advocates of this technique point out that it has the virtue of simplicity: no specialized statistical software is required, and the results are readily understood by business people. In the absence of other targeting techniques, it can provide a lift in response rates for promotions.

Whichever approach is adopted, profiling will be done on the results to determine what makes up group membership. Categorical factors such as gender, nationality/locality can be used as well as age (or, indeed, any other demographic feature that is available) to understand the "type" of customer that resides in each group. These factors can be used for each segment and applied against the population metrics to determine how much more or less likely a segment is to exhibit a feature or type of behavior when compared to the customer base as a whole.

Propensity to Respond Model

A *Propensity to Response* model is the theoretical probability that a sampled person (or unit) will become a respondent in an offer or survey. They are specifically useful in the marketing field.

A response likelihood model can have substantial cost savings as it can lead to lower mailing costs by identifying customers who are very unlikely to respond to an offer. After segmenting these people out, the airline can then focus on only those most likely to take up the offer. A airline can identify the likelihood of response from all eligible customers.[180] After that, it can identify the most valuable customers that are most likely to respond.[180] This allows the airline to estimate the expected response from the most valuable customers and eliminate mailing(s) to the customers that are of lower worth and/or are unlikely to respond.[180]

Sutton warns that, "Occasionally, response likelihood models will lead to easy decisions, such as cutting out low worth customers with a low likelihood of responding. However, more complex situations might arise since response models are never perfect."[180] It doesn't matter how good a model is or how accurate the historical data is, there is always a chance that a customer identified as unlikely to respond will respond.[180] "Thus, when making a decision about customers identified as unlikely to respond to an offer, it is also important to balance that likelihood of response with the potential return on response," advises Sutton[180]

A propensity to respond model would be built using historical information around marketing campaigns and it looks at predicting the likelihood a customer will respond to a marketing communication. The advantage of this model is that it strengthens the marketing strategy even more, beyond purely segmenting the customer base. It can further allow for improved ROI on the marketing budget, by identifying the likely number of respondents to be returned by a campaign.

Often an aircraft's marketing department will have an expected number of respondents or an expected response rate.[180] By identifying those who are most likely to respond, the chances of meeting that expected number or rate of response is greatly improved.[180] Gone are the days of marketing to an entire customer base, once again we're back to the "marketing of one" concept. Marketing to the entire database is an unnecessary waste of the marketing budget and it also runs the risk of annoying customers by touching them too often or with the wrong offer.[180]

Again, a predictive model would be built which identifies those most likely to respond through to those least likely to respond. This would be done using customer metrics and historical campaign/marketing information that identifies those who responded and those who didn't. Variables that have a significant association with the customer action are extracted and these form part of the prediction algorithm. Every customer is then given a score according to how likely they are to respond to a marketing campaign.

This information can be used for strategies such as extracting the top 40% of customers most likely to respond, or a fixed number, such as 100,000 customers. The end result is the marketing function becomes more efficient and effective with better returns for the company's marketing dollar.

Customer Conversion Model

Historical information would be extracted from the airline's IT systems around what constitutes a desirable customer. This would include spending patterns and profitability.

To identify the relationships that may exist between how these customers come to the airline and his or her desirability metric, information would be extracted from the airline's source systems. Basically, anything that can be attributed to the initial transaction the customer has with the airline would be used as a potential input, including potential social media data.

These models might also have to be stratified by sales to identify the most relevant relationships. The major advantage of a predictive model with this intention would be that it allows the airline to identify customers that they need to interact with once the first time they fly. This would give the airline clerks the potential to get the required information they need to successfully foster a strong customer relationship.

Furthermore, if every potential customer has a score associated with them as to their long-term likelihood of being attractive, the airline can further hone in on its potentially profitable customers by monitoring their behavior once they fly. It is imperative that the airline interact with desirable customers before they finish their first flight. If customers are made to feel like they are valuable and worthwhile to the airline, the likelihood of them returning again increases significantly.

Customer Worth Model

Determining customer worth is one of the most important procedures of customer analytics for the airline industry. Of course, predicting a customer's future behavior is not easy and it is affected by several variables, many of which the airline cannot know, including total income, expendable income, reasons for a trip, etc., etc.

Even where a customer lives or information gleaned from his or her social media accounts could be very revealing to worth. There is also "plenty of information to be found with in-house data that can be used to build models and metrics to predict a customer's future worth."[180] "Once customer worth has been determined, "customers can then be segmented into groups based on other behaviors and effective marketing campaigns can be developed around those behaviors."[180]

The first thing an airline must do is "determine what worth is, as the definition of worth is critical for deciding how valuable a customer is and how much to reinvest in the customer in the future," as Sutton explains.[180] "The definition of worth will likely depend on both the various financial sources of revenue that affect the business directly and the exact business problems that are being addressed," adds Sutton.[180]

"Once customer worth has been defined, the business can then use data mining and modeling to estimate predicted worth into the future," states Sutton.[180] "There are a variety of techniques that are used to develop models to predict future worth, the most common being regression models. Multiple regression models are the most common because they utilize a variety of predictors and the relationships between those predictors to predict future worth," adds Sutton.[180]

"Regression models can also be built using such categorical variables predictors as gender, ethnicity, age range, or other demographic variables."[180] "Regression models are particularly effective because the model can be used to score historical data to predict an unknown outcome, which is worth in this case, within a certain degree of confidence," adds Sutton.[180]

All airline analytics departments should have a solid method for predicting the various types of customer worth based on the sources and time periods they need for making informed marketing decisions.

Customer Churn Model

The use of analytics and data management to help detect and avoid the act of attrition is something that can benefit airlines as well. Churn questions that airlines should be asking include:

- How is an airline detecting behavior changes in is customers?
- Does the airline have steps in place to identify when the customer experience is going wrong, or when the customer is about to leave?

Airlines can use Master Data Management (MDM) techniques to communicate important customer preference information to staff who sit at interaction points throughout the customer journey. MDM is the processes, governance, policies, standards and tools that consistently define and manage the critical data of an organization to provide a single point of reference. One of the benefits of using MDM is that when that single point of reference is a customer profile, the master data can ensure that the treatment of a customer is consistent, and that preference information reaches all customer points of contact.

To ensure customer retention is front and center, airlines should be scoring their database on a regular basis to understand the likelihood of a customer churning from their company. This kind of modeling is prevalent in the telecommunications, finance, and utilities industries, and should be utilized in the airline industry as well. Whilst a slightly different set up due to those industries mostly having their customers locked into contracts, airlines need to stay ahead of the game in retaining their customers.

One of the hardest parts for an airliner to determine—as opposed to commercial entities that have their customers on contract—is to find out if a customer has categorically churned or not. It may be that a change in location, circumstances or something else that has caused a customer to no longer fly on the airline. However, statistical measures could be used to identify customer's whose behavior has changed, with that change not being attributed to chance.

Historical internal data can be used to model the difference between a churned customer and one who is still engaged. There would be significant metrics in the data that identify the likelihood of churning. Like the acquisition model described previously, a parametric equation could be constructed that elicits the association and relationship between the target variable and the predictors.

This model would serve as an early warning system for the airline. It would also be a strategic tool used to predict whether a customer was deemed worth retaining or not. The model should be run on a regular basis across the entire customer database to understand which customers have reached or are reaching a critical value in their churn score. The theory: these customers would then be targeted with an offer to return to the airline, in the process avoiding the likelihood of them churning. Alternatively, if the customer is deemed to be of little or no value to the airline, there would be no offer forthcoming to entice them to return.

Optimizing Offers

As Sutton explains, "In addition to predicting the future worth of customers, it is important to know which marketing campaigns are the most effective for driving response, revenue, and profit. In general, certain offers are better than others, and specifically certain offers will be better for certain customers."[180]

"While knowing the probable future worth of a customer is critical for determining the reinvestment level for which a customer is eligible, customers' behaviors and interests can be used to identify the offer(s) that will be most appealing to each customer as well as the ones generating the most profitable response," explains Sutton.[180] By analyzing the likelihood that a customer will respond to a certain offer or offers, airline analysts can optimize the offer that each customer is given in order to maximize the amount of revenue and profit driven by the marketing campaigns as a whole.[180] Definable ROI becomes a set goal here.

As previously mentioned, A/B testing is one of the best ways to identify which offers work best and more "advanced statistical methods can be used to generate likelihood of response scores and classification scores."[180] "Some of the more common statistical approaches are logistic regression, decision trees, and discriminant analysis," Sutton adds.[180]

"Essentially, these statistical methods use historical data to find the factors that are related as to why a customer responds. Those factors can then be used to assess the likelihood of response based on the similarity of a customer profile to that of responders," adds Sutton.[180]

"These methods have historically been used in direct marketing analysis to identify the best types of offers and the most likely responders," says Sutton.[180] "In order to build accurate and predictive response models, historical data about response is required. The likelihood of response might be a broad measure of response that refers to the likelihood a customer will respond to any offer, or it might be specific to the likelihood of response to a specific type of offer."[180] In addition, Sutton adds, "it's a good idea to select test segments of customers for the purpose of continually testing new offers. Doing so will help to ensure that there is a large amount of response data that can be used to build models and continually improve the efficacy of marketing."[180] "Effective response models will help identify which customers are most likely to respond to an offer, and in turn to which offer customers are most likely to respond."[180]

Chronological View of an Airline's Analytics Implementation

1. Data reduction via cluster analysis and segmentation is a logical starting point and initial work should be around identifying customer preference(s). Reducing the customer database into more manageable and meaningful segments has many advantages; the preferences that can be derived are dependent on the availability of meaningful distinguishing factors.
2. *Segmentation models* use customer metrics that help reduce and profile the customer data base. These should be constructed early on as this information can be the underpinning of further analyses.
3. *First Purchase Scoring Model* would require a view of the customer across the entire business as well as a rich history of engaged customers. The airline would then need to build a modeling data set that is adequate to investigate the relationship between a metric for "valuable" and the inputs that are extracted, derived, and constructed from the first trip of each customer.
4. *A Propensity to Respond Model* is heavily dependent on the marketing data and its veracity and richness. The airline would need to develop the holistic view of the customer first. Once developed, this is one of the most powerful marketing models available.
5. *A Customer Conversion Model* could be viewed as an extension of a number of the above models, with the idea of deriving a data driven metric that scores a customer's likelihood of returning after his or her first trip.
6. *Customer Likelihood to Return Model* requires a complete view of the customer along with considerable marketing data. This would help with

offers sent, who received these offers, who responded to them, etc., etc. The derived metric on its own would have value, but it could also be a significant input in a two stage model to predict next trip value and customer worth.

7. A *Customer Worth Model* would identify the airline's most valuable customers. The assumption is that an airline would be looking to predict different metrics, such as "worth on the next trip", "worth over the next 12 months", "lifetime value", etc., etc.
8. *RFM* is a method used for analyzing customer value and it is commonly utilized in database marketing and direct marketing. It has received particular attention in the airline industry. An airline should keep scores of data about a customer's purchases that include a table with the customer name, date of purchase and purchase value. From this data, the airline can score the true value of a customer and this information can be fed to the marketing department, which can decide to send an offer to the client if it makes financial sense.
9. A *Customer Acquisition Model* would then be built by using the results of the segmentation modeling models (or a different metric for desirable customers). A deeper investigation of an airline's source systems is needed and this could be part of the analysis to help understand what is available, and what might be able to be used from external parties. Different jurisdictions would have different models.
10. *Customer Churn Models* would require preliminary analysis to extract only engaged customers. The airline would need to derive a statsitcially dirven metric that indicated whether a customer had churned or not. The airline could then build models to detect upcoming customer attrition.
11. *Ticket Revenue Optimization Model* would be useful at this stage as this is an optimization model, which is prescriptive analytics model, one of the hardest models to get right. With all of the data below this model collected, [EDIT]

Edge Analytics

The driving concept behind edge analytics is the fact that data loses its value over time. As previously mentioned, the concept of "Edge Analytics"—i.e., the processing of analytics at the point or very close to the point where the data is being collected—exponentially increases one's ability to use predictive analytics where it can be best utilized.

As Patrick McGarry explains in his article *Why Edge Computing is Here to Stay*[191], edge analytics is easier to implement than ever before because in-the-field micro data centers use a fraction of the space, power and cost of a traditional analytics infrastructure, but they can provide massive performance gains. These systems use "hybrid computing technology, seamlessly integrating diverse computing technologies, whether they are x86, GPU or FPGA technologies, or any combination thereof. They are extremely compact in space and require very little power, yet still provide performance that is several orders of magnitude more than what today's traditional systems can provide."[191] "It's a win/win situation for all involved; insights come faster than ever before, operational expenses are lower, [sic] power and administration needed to run the systems," McGarry ads.[191]

"Emergency repair work and equipment down-time can be reduced when manufacturers build edge-based analytical systems into machinery and vehicles, allowing them to decide for themselves when it is time to reduce power output or send an alert that a part may be due for replacement."[16] Airlines can connect their IoT devices into their data warehouses and enact predictive asset maintenance to reduce plant and equipment costs, as I explain in chapter 5.

Although building an edge analytics platform does require a shift in corporate thinking, the ROI benefits should far outweigh the costs. "The cost savings by scaling back central data analytics infrastructures to handle non-time sensitive analysis while installing cost-efficient platforms purpose-built for edge analytics can have a real impact on an organization's budget," McGarry notes.[191] The value of near-instant analysis and insight cannot be underestimated in a business so dependent on customer excellence like the airline business. Avoiding latency and eliminating the time and costs associated with transporting the data to and from the edge is a major step toward achieving that goal.[191]

IoT sensors can help spot customers arriving in an airport lounge, or track employees, suppliers, and supplies throughout the store, as well as help save energy and water usage. Edge analytics can help analyze airline customer behavior, as well as spot upcoming equipment malfunction as part of a predictive asset maintenance system. Other areas where IoT can help include compliance analysis and mobile data thinning, i.e., the culling of mobile data noise from social media or direct mobile streams. Personally, I believe edge analytics could be one of the top technologies that can give an airline a competitive advantage over its rivals and I will provide more detail on how this technology can be implemented within an airline's environment throughout the rest of this book.

Sentiment Analysis

In the TDWI *Customer Analytics in the Age of Social Media*[151] Research report about the same percentage (30%) of respondents sought to monitor and measure sentiment drivers. "Sentiment analysis enables organizations to discover positive and negative comments in social media, customer comment and review sites, and similar sources. Sentiment analysis often focuses on monitoring and measuring the 'buzz' value, usually through volume and frequency of comments around a topic."[151] However, it is not just the buzz that is important, many organizations want more analytical depth so that they can understand what the buzz is all about, where it comes from, and who is benefiting or not benefiting from it the most.[151]

For more sophisticated sentiment analysis, text analytics tools that use word extraction, natural language processing, pattern matching, and other approaches to examine social media users' expressions are employed.[151] "Sentiment analysis can give organizations early notice in real time of factors that may be affecting customer churn; the research shows that 14% are interested in monitoring and analyzing social activity in real time."[151]

In 2011, Toyota started testing social media monitoring and sentiment-analysis tools. After a few years of research, they discovered that by filtering for such words as "Lexus", "decide", "buy" and "BMW", they were able to quickly identify active shoppers who were choosing between theirs and their competitor's brands.[192]

Today, Toyota uses social media data analysis across many areas—sales, service, quality, marketing and product development.[192] For example, if a customer expresses interest in a car, Toyota "can determine engagement by analyzing the frequency of dealership visits via their Foursquare check-ins, understand their dealership experiences, and even understand what features may have sparked their interest in a competitor's product."[192]

Armed with this information, Toyota stratifies its leads based on their readiness to buy, moving stronger leads to the top of the funnel and weaker ones to the bottom.[192] By analyzing free-form text, Toyota can learn what customers think of specific vehicles.[192] In the quality area, "Toyota can look for information like whether new-car owners are hearing a slight rattle and pass that on to their quality engineers."[192] They are also working on using sentiment analysis to increase the accuracy of their sales predictions; an important goal, if ever there was one.[192]

Airlines should keep these ideas in mind when developing their own use cases. A "rattle" for the airline wouldn't be an engine problem, of course (except in a company bus, maybe), but rather a poor customer experience throughout the customer journey.

Toyota also wants to deepen its understanding of its customers' other interests, like what a Camry owners' favorite TV show might be, as well as which other brands they might like.[192] This can help with product placement and brand tie-ins down the line.[192]

Sentiment analysis is also key to understanding a competitors' relative strengths and weaknesses in the social sphere.[151] The TDWI research found that "18% of respondents are examining social media data to analyze a competition's 'share of voice.'"[151]

As Joe Mullich explains in his article *Opposition Research: Sentiment Analysis as a Competitive Marketing Tool*[193]:

> "When a leading bank wanted to find out how it stacked up against competitors, it assumed customers would focus on lending terms and interest rates. To the bank's surprise, the most enthusiastic discourse on blogs and specialized financial forums related to a smartphone app a competing financial institution had just put out. The bank had dismissed apps as a generic marketing gimmick, like the old custom of giving away a toaster for opening an account. After learning how much customers valued the app, the bank quickly created its own with the same prized features as its competitor."

I think it was pretty naïve and not forward-thinking at all to believe that an app was only going to be a generic marketing gimmick, but that's not the focus of this book. As Joseph Carrabis, founder of NextStage Evolution, the company that did the analysis for the bank, notes, "You get the benefits of corporate espionage without doing corporate espionage."[193]

Sentiment analysis can also provide early insight into a competitor's new product initiatives.[193] "Very often companies will test market before they release a product," says Mullich.[193] "And no matter what you get people to sign saying that they won't share information, they'll go online and talk about products they're excited about," warns Mullich.[193] You can't change human nature, but sometimes you can make it work for you.

In addition, sentiment analysis can alert companies about new competitors who are bubbling up to the surface or even coming out of left-field.[193] Ford would obviously consider Chevy a competitor, but it might not think of public transport as being threatening competition.[193] However, Carrabis argues that a car company should realize that it might want to analyze online discussion boards to try to understand why people are making different transportation choices so it can change its product offerings or marketing campaigns to emphasize their customers' growing environmental concerns and personal ecological footprints.[193] "We have to think broader and wider than we used to," Carrabis contends.[193] The lesson here: don't just look at your closest competitors as your competition, widen your view.

This is why it is so imperative for an airliner to understand how and why people discuss competitors online. "When car shoppers talk online they don't talk about 'quality,'" says Susan Etlinger, an analyst with the Altimeter Group.[193] "They'll say, 'I love the leather interior' or 'the cup holder fell out.' It takes meticulous work to roll together all the indicators of quality."[193]

Etlinger suggests that "social-media listening teams work with the groups in the organization that handle keyword search terms and search-engine optimization effort, since they have a solid grasp on how people online actually talk about the industry and products."[193]

Another thing to keep in mind: "At any point in time, the way people feel about a brand can be distorted online, because things like Twitter are so volatile and affected by the news of the day," warns Etlinger.[193] "But over time, you can get directional trends—why do people love or hate you, how do they feel about your product compared to the competitor's products."[193] Airlines in China have the added problem of Internet users who actively write fraudulent blogs and posts about a company's products and/or services; separating fact from fiction is not an easy task, but it needs to be done to get accurate measurement of sentiment.

"My belief is that the sweet spot for social media is not conversion, but nurturing," said Brian Ellefritz, vice president of global social media at SAP.[151] "Whether it's in your community, through Twitter, or through Facebook pages, you want to build an increasing conviction that your company is the one to do business with," says Ellefritz.[151] "It's about establishing a belief system that becomes robust with the support of fans and followers. The question is how you measure that and create value out of that investment," he added.[151]

When it comes to setting strategies for customer and social media analytics, Stodder recommends the following[151]:

- Use social media data to support an active, not passive social media strategy. "In competitive, fast-moving markets, organizations cannot just passively listen to and analyze social media data. The analytics should plug into strategies for engaging users and customers on social networks and comment sites. Predictive analytics can help organizations anticipate the results of active strategies. Special events such as tweet-ups can build on customer data analysis and create positive exchanges and engagement."[151]
- Take a holistic view of the potential contributions of social media data analytics. "Understanding behavior in the social sphere can have a positive impact, not just on marketing and sales functions, but also on services and other processes in the organization. Marketing executives should use social media insights to improve brand awareness and reputation throughout the organization."[151]
- Give CMOs and marketing executives the ability to understand the financial impact of certain decisions.
- Apply analytics to gain a more accurate understanding of marketing attribution. "Last-touch" attribution may be easy to affix, but it is not always reliable. Powerful analytics, along with big data, can help organizations get a better understanding of what truly affects a

customer's purchase decision.

Clickstream Analysis

When a person surfs a website, he or she leaves behind a digital trail, which is known as a "clickstream." Clickstream analysis is the process of collecting, aggregating, reporting and analyzing the browsing behavior of a web surfer to better understand the intentions of users and their interests in specific content or products on a website. Clickstream analysis is the process of collecting, analyzing and reporting aggregate data about which pages a website visitor visits—and in what order. The path the visitor takes though a website is, basically, the clickstream.

There are two levels of clickstream analysis: traffic analytics and e-commerce analytics. Traffic analytics operates at the server level and tracks how many pages are served to the user, how long it takes each page to load, how often the user hits the browser's back or stop button and how much data is transmitted before the user moves away from the website. E-commerce-based analysis uses clickstream data to determine the effectiveness of a website as a channel-to-market. It is concerned with what pages the browser lingers on, what he or she puts in or takes out of a shopping cart, what items are purchased, whether or not the buyer belongs to a loyalty program and uses a coupon code, as well as his or her preferred methods of payment.

Figure 14: Customer funnel

Utilizing clickstream analysis, an airline can help build a Master Marketing Record for each customer in real-time. This allows the airline to test scenarios and options for the website, as well as develop personalized responses for individuals. The system should include a combination of social listening, analytics, content publication and distribution, and tracking, as well as a strong workflow and rules engine that is geared around strong governance. All these applications are built to ultimately feed a Master Marketing Profile—a centralized customer record that pulls in all data based on digital activity that can be identified by a single customer ID.

Figure 14 shows the customer funnel that takes an anonymous web browser to a known customer. Through clickstream analytics, personalization marketing can begin, and associating this activity with a customer once he or she walks through the front door should be an airline's top priority. This can be done by enabling new users to log into his or her account via web or mobile applications, like an airline's app.

Of all the available marketing and customer channels, social media represents the biggest issue due to the airline's inability to track the value of social connections. In his article, *At Caesar's Digital Marketing Is No Crap Shoot*[67], Al Urbanski explains that at Caesar's, they "wanted to make better use of the social space, but one of the overwhelming problems had been, 'How do you measure the effectiveness?' Not a lot of organizations are able to measure it effectively."[67] "Caesar's marketers didn't want to create a social island that communicated with customers separately and distinctly from all other channels," Urbanski explains.[67]

"Each channel is tracked and rated for its ability to turn engagements into booked rooms, and Caesar's had been flying blind in the region of social media," explains Urbanksi.[67] "Top management wants to know, 'How did this perform?' 'What's the return on ad spend?' and how can we tell the path to purchase from first touch point to last touch point, even if the starting point was in social media," Kahle, Caesars' Web Analytics Manager, notes.[67] "Before, we couldn't understand social's role in the transaction. You could track it to a degree, but you built a social island and there was some guessing involved. You could end up double counting social's contribution," Kahle warned.[67]

"To support these efforts, Caesars invested in Adobe's Digital Marketing Suite, which includes real-time tracking and segmentation of digital site visitors, analysis of social media's role in purchasing, and content testing by segment or individual visitor," explains Kahle.[67]

The problem with driving online conversions among Frequent Independent Travelers (FITs), however, is that—based on their online behaviors—they're not loyal to a particular casino.[67] "They're on Kayak; they're on other airlines' sites. They're looking for a deal," says Kahle, who adds that Caesars regularly targets these travelers with offers, such as free meals and free gaming play.[67] This is something airlines should be actively doing as well, to cut out the Expedia, Orbitz, and/or C-trip middlemen.

As noted in the article[67]:

> "Kahle's staff conducted A/B analysis aimed at presenting the

company's individual properties with the best option for increasing Total Rewards memberships. Half the people who searched Total Rewards online were sent to the main Caesars Entertainment homepage, while the other half was sent to the homepage of a specific property. While the conversion rate for room reservations was the same for both groups, the latter group signed up for the loyalty program at a significantly higher rate. The practice was adopted across the Caesars Web network and resulted in a 10% increase in sign-ups."

"A similar test was used to maximize business from Total Rewards members, testing its old website interfaces against a new design. The difference was an eye-opener. The conversion rate for the newer interface option was 70% higher," Kahle explains.

"In the past, when planning changes to Web page design or elements, the winning design was often decided by the highest-ranking person in the office," Kahle says.[67] "With Adobe testing, people's personal opinions aren't the deciding factor. We can look at the numbers, see the results, and clearly identify the best-performing design."[67] Kahle adds that Caesars deployed these new capabilities without having to increase its IT staff.[67]

"Caesars went from a culture of opinion to a culture of data. We essentially gave them the...flexibility to test so that the [end-user's] experience is optimized," says Matt Langie, senior director of product marketing at Adobe.[67]

As per Paul Greenberg's article *Is Adobe a Marketing Player Now?*[194]:

> "First thing to know about Adobe is that they are a tools company—and this is both good and bad. For the most part and for the purposes of this discussion, the products are a good thing. The second thing to know about Adobe (and the Marketing Cloud) is that what they are currently offering is a significant piece of a digital engagement platform. Keep in mind this is for the marketing side—the first line of engagement—the first place that the customer comes into contact with the brand and either starts interacting or doesn't."

The Master Marketing Record is the core around which Adobe's Marketing Cloud is built and this goes to the heart of two Adobe themes, one of which is as old as modern man—the single view of the customer—and the other is the Real Time Enterprise.

Just to step into the MCM (Multi-Channel Marketing) arena for a moment, as Greenberg explains, The Adobe Marketing Cloud essentially consists of a basket of applications and services, including[194]:

- Adobe Analytics—A strong package focused around digital analytics, mobile and web that has predictive analytics at its core.
- Adobe Campaign—this is where the core Neolane integration has occurred.
- Adobe Target—This allows users to test scenarios and options for the web, as well as develop personalized responses for individuals. It is comparable to the functionality of Epiphany and Exact Target, two similar marketing automation products.
- Adobe Experience Manager—This is where users manage the assets and create and manage the communities needed to optimize the customer journey across all digital channels and media.
- Adobe Social—combining social listening, analytics, content publication and distribution, tracking, as well as a strong workflow and rules engine geared towards governance and strict protocols.
- Adobe Media Optimizer—helps users define an audience, as well as create ads that will appeal to individuals and outline which media mix should be used to maximize that appeal[194]

All these applications are built to ultimately feed what Adobe calls the Master Marketing Profile—a centralized customer record that pulls in all data based on digital activity that can be identified by a single customer ID. "That means that John Smith's record will have his social profile data, his transactional data, his response to campaigns, his click-throughs, his web browsing, etc. This goes to the heart of their effort—the personalization of the response to individual customers. The Master Marketing Profile is where you find all that data."[194]

To Adobe's credit, Greenberg feels that the software vendor has done some solid integration of the entire portfolio.[194] The total package, if viewed as an advanced digital marketing cloud, some believe it could very well be the best of its kind on the market. However, Adobe is "competing with other Marketing Clouds—notably, if the name Marketing Cloud is meaningful, salesforce.com and Oracle. If the name Marketing Cloud isn't—add Marketo, Microsoft, Teradata Applications, SAS, IBM Unica, and Infor to the mix. If niche players count, there are dozens and dozens out there chomping off pieces of the potential revenue stream. This is a hot competition."[194]

A word of caution here: the airline industry does seem to be struggling with CRM and marketing automation solutions because none of the big players have produced a product that fulfills all its unique needs. From my experience, airlines are cobbling together a multitude of products to capture certain elemental needs, but the addition of unstructured data and real-time streaming is only adding to the complexity and it'll be interesting to see which company, if any, can create a solution that checks off all the CRM, MA and analytics boxes for an airline client.

In his article *Google Attribution Allows Clear, Seamless Campaign Analysis for Marketers*[195], Matthew Bains explains that Google has released a new tool called Google Attribution that "uses machine learning and data to help marketers measure the impact of each of their marketing touch points, across multiple channels, and across multiple devices." "It uses data that's already there from AdWords and Google Analytics; it just takes that data and shows you how each customer moved through their buyer's journey and attributes those conversions respectively. It provides a single view of the path to purchase to help marketers learn what is actually working compared to what seems to be working," adds Bain.[195]

Wanamaker would be ecstatic as "marketers can finally begin to answer the age-old question that is typically at the forefront of their minds—is my marketing working?", as Bains puts it[195]

Moving away from the flawed last-click attribution idea, "Google Attribution uses machine learning and data to help marketers measure the impact of each of their marketing touch points, across multiple channels, and across multiple devices."[195] Google Attribution shows users how each customer moves through his or her buyer's journey and attributes those conversions respectively.[195] "It provides a single view of the path to purchase to help marketers learn what is actually working compared to what seems to be working," Bains explains.[195]

As Bains warns[195]:

> "With last click, the reward for the conversion often went to the last touch point that the user made, often with a sale after a click on an ad. This could lead to false impressions about the effectiveness of an ad campaign versus display ads, organic search, social, email affiliates, and many other interactions that a customer made with a business along the buyer's journey. Maybe organic search is actually more important than display ads or vice versa."

"The aim of Google Attribution is to simplify the complex problem of multichannel, multi-device attribution by leveraging data advertisers already have in Google Analytics, AdWords, or DoubleClick Search," adds Kishore Kanakemedela, director of product management at Google.[195]

With Attribution, users can see how effective each step of a campaign is, whether that step is a video ad, a banner ad, a carousel ad, an email, a social campaign, or any other quantifiable digital content.[195] Attribution will show users how these micro-moments worked together to spot leads and drive them to conversions.[195] Marketers will now have more transparency on what is actually driving their business, which in turn, can help them better allocate their budgets between channels[195]; quantifiable success on one channel leads to increased budget spend for that channel, that is until numbers drop off, then reallocation commences.

Location Analytics

Location analytics is a technology that enables firms to capture and analyze location data on customers who are at a physical venue. In his article *How Location Analytics Will Transform Retail*[196], Tony Costa argues that, "By leveraging connected mobile devices such as smartphones, existing in-venue Wi-Fi networks, low cost Bluetooth-enabled beacons, and a handful of other technologies, location analytics vendors have made it possible to get location analytics solutions up and running fast at a minimal cost." "Customer tracking data is typically sent to the location analytics vendor where it is analyzed and accessed via online dashboards that provide actionable data tailored to the needs of specific employees—from the store manager to the executive C-suite," adds Costa.[196]

Already, the scale of data collected by early adopters is venturing into "Big Data" territory. Location analytics firm RetailNext currently "tracks more than 500 million shoppers per year by collecting data from more than 65,000 sensors installed in thousands of retail stores. A single customer visit alone can result in over 10,000 unique data points, not including the data gathered at the point of sale."[196]

RetailNext is not alone; Euclid Analytics—one of the biggest players in this space—"collects six billion customer measurements each day across thousands of locations, and multiple location analytics firms surveyed said they are adding hundreds of new venues each month."[196]

As Costa explains, venue owners are applying insights gathered from location analytics to help in all aspects of their business, including[196]:

1. Design. "After analyzing traffic flows in their stores, a big box retailer realized that less than 10% of customers visiting their shoe department engaged with the self-service wall display where merchandise was stacked. The culprit turned out to be a series of benches placed in front of the wall, limiting customer access."[196] Simply relocating the benches to enhance accessibility increased sales in the department by double digits.[196]
2. Marketing. A restaurant chain wanted to understand whether sponsoring a local music festival had a measurable impact on customer visits. After collecting data on 15,000 visitors passing through the festival entrances and comparing it to customers who visited their restaurants two months before and after the festival, they concluded that the festival resulted in 1,300 net new customer visits.[196]

3. Operations. "A grocery store chain used location analytics to understand customer wait times in various departments and check-out registers. This data not only enabled the company to hold managers accountable for wait times, but it gave additional insight into (and justification for) staffing needs."[196]
4. Strategy. A regional clothing chain was concerned that opening an outlet store would cannibalize customers from its main stores. "After analyzing the customer base visiting each store, they discovered that less than 2% of their main store customers visited their outlet. The upside: the outlet gave them access to an entirely new customer base with minimal impact to existing store sales."[196]

Just as web analytics is an essential tool on the web, location analytics will become a must-have for designing, managing, and measuring offline experiences.[196] Location analytics is set to have a profound impact on how businesses operate in the very near future. Costa adds that, "Beyond creating more efficient, effective and meaningful services, firms will begin to rethink the notion of customer value."[196]

Costa argues that having the ability "to identify, track, and target customers in physical locations will enable companies to extend preferential status and rewards to customers based on their behaviors, rewarding them on the number and frequency of visits, where they go in venues, and their exclusive loyalty (i.e., not visiting competitor venues)."[196]

Conclusion

In this chapter, I wanted to lay out the many ways in which *The Predictive Airliner* can track and understand its customer base on both a micro and a macro level. Many of the analytical models I mention in this chapter have been around for decades and every airline should be aware that creativity with these models is what will separate them from their competitors.

With IT budgets in the millions of dollars per year, every airline can afford software that segments its customers, creates marketing campaigns, and predicts churn, but it's what it does with this information that matters. Customers want to be wowed and that is not easy to do.

Analytics can be useful for the entire customer journey process, from the initial moment a customer is picked up in a clickstream, through the descriptive analytics process of understanding website traffic, to data mining and diagnostic analytics utilized to understand customer spend. Predictive analytics can help forecast which offers a customer might use, while prescriptive analytics can optimize things like corporate budgets, and labor and stock utilization.

In her article *How Airlines Get Customer Experience So Wrong with So Much*

Data[2], Sarah Steimer tells an anecdote about JetBlue's Philadelphia coffee problem that led to consistently negative reviews. JetBlue, which tops the ACSI airline rankings by striking a balance between a positive baseline experience and added perks, has built its business on customer data and analytics.[2]

A few years ago, "JetBlue noticed that it had consistently negative trends in Philadelphia. A review of both logistical data and customer reviews showed there was a timing issue: Flights weren't late, but passengers were arriving at an hour that coffee shops in the airport weren't yet open."[2]

"All of these negative [reviews] were because people weren't getting their cup of joe before jumping on this flight from Philadelphia to their meetings and feeling prepped and primed for that," Danny Cox, director of customer support and insights at JetBlue, acknowledged.[2] "We could have just stopped at, well, people in Philadelphia, they're just angry. But, instead, we dug deeper to see what was really needed. We could easily partner with the coffee shops there and ask them to adjust their hours. Immediately the scores popped back up to a more reasonable and expected area."[2] This is perhaps one of the finest uses of analytics in the airline industry, not only did it allow an airline to raise its ratings, but it also gave JetBlue passengers access to the most important drink of all, their morning cut of joe.

---

150 New York Times. Captain Eddie Ricker is Dead. 24 July 1973. https://archive.nytimes.com/www.nytimes.com/learning/general/onthisday/bday/1008.html (Accessed 10 August 2018).
151 Stodder, D. (2012). Customer Analytics in the Age of Social Media. Retrieved from Business Times: http://www.businesstimes.com.sg/archive/monday/sites/businesstimes.com.sg/files/Customer%20Analytics%20in%20the%20Age%20of%20Social%20Media.pdf (Accessed 20 November 2017).
152 Yang, Richar R., Borowczak, Mike. (2017). Assessing Retail Employee Risk Through Unsupervised Learning Techniques. https://arxiv.org.
153 IBM. (2013). Achieving Customer Loyalty with Customer Analytics. Retrieved from adma.com: http://www.adma.com.au/assets/Uploads/Downloads/IBM-Achieving-Customer-Loyalty-with-Analytics.pdf (Accessed 20 November 2017).
154 Davenport, T. (January 2006). Competing on Analytics. Harvard Business Review.
155 Cognizant. (2014, January). Retail Analytics: Game Changer for Customer Loyalty. Retrieved from congnizant.com: http://www.cognizant.com/InsightsWhitepapers/Retail-Analytics-Game-Changer-for-Customer-Loyalty.pdf (Accessed 20 November 2017).
156 Peterson, T. (2014, August 13). Facebook Now Tells Whether Mobile Ads Lead to Desktop Purchases. Retrieved from AdAge: http://adage.com/article/digital/facebook-makes-link-mobile-ads-desktop-purchases/294568/ (Accessed 20 November 2017).

157 Cook, Rick. Control Group Marketing—With or Without CRM Software Systems. crmsearch http://www.crmsearch.com/marketing-control-groups.php (Accessed 19 November 2017).
158 Shearer C., The CRISP-DM model: the new blueprint for data mining, J Data Warehousing (2000); 5:13—22.
159 Harper, Gavin; Stephen D. Pickett (August 2006). "Methods for mining HTS data". Drug Discovery Today. 11 (15–16): 694–699.
160 SAS Institute. Data Mining and the Case for Sampling. http://sceweb.uhcl.edu/boetticher/ML_DataMining/SAS-SEMMA.pdf (Accessed November 21, 2017).
161 https://en.wikipedia.org/wiki/Machine_learning (Accessed 20 November 2017).
162 Vogel, Dirk. (6 September 2017). 5 Ways AI Will Boost Personalization in Digital Marketing. Selligent. https://www.selligent.com/blog/contextual-marketing/5-ways-ai-will-boost-personalization-in-digital-marketing (Accessed 24 October 2017).
163 Johnson, Lauren. 2017. Pinterest Is Offering Brands Its Visual Search Technology To Score Large Ad Deals. Adweek. October 2, 2017. http://www.adweek.com/digital/pinterest-is-offering-brands-its-visual-search-technology-to-score-large-ad-deals/ (Accessed 18 November 2017).
164 Krizhevsky, Alex; Sutskever, Ilya; Hinton, Geoffry. (2012). ImageNet Classification with Deep Convolutional Neural Networks. NIPS 2012: Neural Information Processing Systems, Lake Tahoe, Nevada.
165 Liu, Baige, Zang, Xiaoxue. (2017). Caffe2 vs. TensorFlow: Which is a Better Deep Learning Framework? Stanford University. http://cs242.stanford.edu/assets/projects/2017/liubaige-xzang.pdf (Accessed 1 May 2018).
166 Metz, Gade. (2015). Google Just Open Sourced TensorFlow, its Artificial Intelligence Engine. Wired.com. 9 November 2015. https://www.wired.com/2015/11/google-open-sources-its-artificial-intelligence-engine/ (Accessed 1 May 2018).
167 Deeplearning4j.org. Comparing Top Deep LearningFrameworks: Deeplearning4J, PyTorch, TensorFlow, Caffe, Kera, MxNet, Gluon & CNTK. https://deeplearning4j.org/compare-dl4j-tensorflow-pytorch (Accessed 3 May 2018).
168 Novet, Jordan. (2017). Facebook Open Sources Caffe2, a New Deep Learning Framework. Venturebeat. 18 April 2017. https://venturebeat.com/2017/04/18/facebook-open-sources-caffe2-a-new-deep-learning-framework/ (Accessed 1 May 2018).
169 Liu, Baige, Zang, Xiaoxue. (2017). Caffe2 vs. TensorFlow: Which is a Better Deep Learning Framework? Stanford University. http://cs242.stanford.edu/assets/projects/2017/liubaige-xzang.pdf (Accessed 1 May 2018).
170 Nyce, Charles. 2007. Predictive Analytics White Paper. https://www.scribd.com/document/200505883/Predictive-Analytics-White-Paper
171 https://en.wikipedia.org/wiki/Prescriptive_analytics (Accessed 20 November 2017).
172 How Predictive Analytics is Changing the Retail Industry. International Conference on Management and Information Systems. September 23-24, 2016. http://www.icmis.net/icmis16/ICMIS16CD/pdf/S154.pdf

173 https://en.wikipedia.org/wiki/Decision_tree (Accessed 20 November 2017).

174 Deng, L., Gao, J., Vuppalapatie, C. Building a Big Data Analytics Service Framework for Mobile Advertising and Marketing. March 2015. https://www.researchgate.net/profile/Jerry_Gao/publication/273635443_Building_a_Big_Data_Analytics_Service_Framework_for_Mobile_Advertising_and_Marketing/links/5508de220cf26ff55f840c31.pdf (Accessed 20 November 2017).

175 Telgarsky, Matus, and Andrea Vattani. "Hartigan's Method: k-means Clustering without Voronoi." AISTATS. 2010.

176 Hartigan, J.A., Wong, M.A. A K-Means Clustering Algorithm. Journal of the Royal Statistical Society. Series C (Applied Statistics), Vol. 28, No. 1 (1979) http://www.cs.otago.ac.nz/cosc430/hartigan_1979_kmeans.pdf (Accessed 20 November 2017).

177 Pierson, Lillian. Solving Real-World Problems with Nearest Neighbor Algorithms. www.dummies.com. http://www.dummies.com/programming/big-data/data-science/solving-real-world-problems-with-nearest-neighbor-algorithms/ (Accessed 20 November 2017).

178 https://en.wikipedia.org/wiki/Logistic_regression (Accessed 20 November 2017).

179 Karp, A. H. (2009). Using Logistic Regression to Predict Customer Retention. New York. Sierra Information Service, Inc. http://www.lexjansen.com/nesug/nesug98/solu/p095.pdf (Accessed 20 November 2017).

180 Sutton, Scott. Patron Analytics in the Casino and Gaming Industry. SAS Global Forum 2011. http://support.sas.com/resources/papers/proceedings11/379-2011.pdf (Accessed 7 November 2017).

181 Siroker, Dan, Koomen, Pete. A/B Testing: The Most Powerful Way to Turn Clicks Into Customers. Google Books.

182 Imdadullah, Muhammad, December 27, 2013. Time Series Analysis and Forecasting. http://itfeature.com/time-series-analysis-and-forecasting/time-series-analysis-forecasting (Accessed 20 November 2017).

183 Singh Y, Chauhan AS. Neural Networks in Data Mining. Journal of Theoretical and Applied Information Technology. 2009; 5:37-42 http://jatit.org/volumes/research-papers/Vol5No1/1Vol5No6.pdf (Accessed 20 November 2017).

184 Goa, Jim. Machine Learning Applications for Data Center Optimization. https://static.googleusercontent.com/media/www.google.com/en//about/datacenters/efficiency/internal/assets/machine-learning-applicationsfor-datacenter-optimization-finalv2.pdf (Accessed 20 November 2017).

185 Greene, Tristan. (2018). A Beginner's Guide to AI: Neural Networks. The Next Web. July 2018. https://thenextweb.com/artificial-intelligence/2018/07/03/a-beginners-guide-to-ai-neural-networks/ (Accessed 13 August 2018).

186 Quach, Katyanna. (2017). How DeepMind's AlphaGo Zero learned all by itself to trash world champ AI AlphaGo. The Register. 18 October 2017. https://www.theregister.co.uk/2017/10/18/deepminds_latest_alphago_software_doesnt_need_human_data_to_win/ (Accessed 21 January 2018).

187 https://en.wikipedia.org/wiki/Discriminant_function_analysis#cite_note-cohen-1 (Accessed 20 November 2017).

188 https://en.wikipedia.org/wiki/Survival_analysis (Accessed 20 November 2017).
189 Despa, Simona. Cornell Statistical Consulting Unit. Cornell University. https://www.cscu.cornell.edu/news/statnews/stnews78.pdf (Accessed 13 August 2018).
190 Coffey, PhD, Kimberly. (2016) k-means Clustering for Customer Segmentation: A Practical Example. Kimberlycoffee.com. http://www.kimberlycoffey.com/blog/2016/8/k-means-clustering-for-customer-segmentation (Accessed 7 November 2017).
191 Patrick McGarry. Why Edge Computing Is Here to Stay: Five Use Cases. https://www.rtinsights.com/why-edge-computing-is-here-to-stay-five-use-cases/ (Accessed 20 November 2017).
192 Hicks, Z. (2013, August 28). Toyota Goes All-in with Social Media Monitoring. Retrieved from CIO.com: http://www.cio.com/article/2383143/social-media/toyota-goes-all-in-with-social-media-monitoring.html (Accessed 20 November 2017).
193 Mullich, J. (2012, December 10). Opposition Research: Sentiment Analysis as a Competitive Marketing Tool. Retrieved from Wellesley Information Services: http://data-informed.com/opposition-research-sentiment-analysis-as-a-competitive-marketing-tool/ (Accessed 20 November 2017).
194 Greenberg, Paul. March 31, 2014. Is Adobe a Marketing Player Now? http://www.zdnet.com/article/is-adobe-a-marketing-player-now/ (Accessed 20 November 2017).
195 Bains, Matthew. (July 28, 2017). Search Influence. http://www.searchinfluence.com/2017/07/google-attribution-allows-clear-seamless-campaign-analysis-for-marketers/ (Accessed 25 August 2017).
196 Costa, T. (2014, March 12). How Location Analytics Will Transform Retail. Retrieved from Harvard Business Review: http://blogs.hbr.org/2014/03/how-location-analytics-will-transform-retail/ (Accessed 20 November 2017).

CHAPTER THREE

Social Media

"When you say it, it's marketing. When your customer says it, it's social proof."-

~ Andy Crestodina
web strategist

Overview

Although it is one of today's buzzwords, "Social Media" is a generic term that refers to websites that allow one or more of the following services: social networking, content management, social bookmarking, blogging and micro-blogging, live video-casting, and access into virtual worlds. Social Media—the technology as we know it today—has its roots in Usenet, a worldwide discussion system that allowed users to post public messages to it.[44]

Today, social media refers to online resources that people use to *share* content. This content can include images, photos, videos, text messages, pins, opinions and ideas, insights, humor, gossip, and news of almost any kind.[197] Drury's list of social media includes the following[197]:

> *Blogs, vlogs, social networks, message boards, podcasts, public bookmarking and wikis. Popular examples of social media applications include Flickr (online photosharing); Wikipedia (reference); Bebo, Facebook and MySpace (networking); del.icio.us (bookmarking) and World of Warcraft (online gaming).*

Unlike traditional marketing models that are nothing more than one-way delivery systems from a company to its consumers, social media is about building a relationship with an audience and starting a two-way dialogue between a company and its consumers.[197] In this new environment, marketing becomes a multi-dimensional discipline that is about receiving and exchanging perceptions and ideas.[197]

The consumer is seen as a participant rather than as a "target audience." The old Source-Message-Channel-Receiver model[198] is evolving into "a collaborative and dynamic communication model in which marketers don't design 'messages' for priority audiences but create worlds in which consumers communicate both with the company and with each other."[199]

Drury argues that confusion exists when pundits talk about social media because the emphasis is often placed on the "media" aspect of social media rather than the "social" aspect, where he feels it correctly belongs.[197] By giving people a platform to share and interact with each other, social media allows "content" to become more democratized than ever before.[197]

In their influential article *Users of the World, Unite! The Challenges and Opportunities of Social Media*[44], Kaplan and Haenlein explain that a formal definition of social media first requires an understanding of two related concepts that are often referred to when describing it: Web 2.0 and User Generated Content.[44] As Kaplan and Haenlein see it[44]:

> *"Web 2.0 is a term that was first used in 2004 to describe a new way in which software developers and end-users started to utilize the World Wide Web; that is, as a platform whereby content and applications are no longer created and published by individuals, but instead are continuously modified by all users in a participatory and collaborative fashion. While applications such as personal web pages, Encyclopedia Britannica Online, and the idea of content publishing belong to the era of Web 1.0, they are replaced by blogs, wikis, and collaborative projects in Web 2.0. Although Web 2.0 does not refer to any specific technical update of the World Wide Web, there is a set of basic functionalities that are necessary for its functioning."*

The "basic functionalities" that Kaplan and Haenlein refer to are; Adobe Flash, the popular animation tool, interactivity, and web streaming audio/video program, Really Simple Syndication (RSS), a family of web feed formats used to publish frequently updated works—such as blog entries or news headlines, as well as audio and video—in a standardized format; and Asynchronous Java Scrip (AJAX), a group of web development methods that can retrieve data from web servers asynchronously, allowing the update of one source of web content without interfering with the display and behavior of an entire page.[44] This is important because it means that a web page for an airline could, while it is loading onto a customer's computer or mobile phone, be accessing and returning specific personalized customer content, including appropriate coupons that have been chosen because they are highly likely to be used and, potentially, could cost the airline the least to redeem.

For Kaplan and Haenlein, Web 2.0 represents the ideological and technological foundation, while "User Generated Content (UGC) can be seen as the sum of all the ways in which people make use of social media. The term, which achieved broad popularity in 2005, is usually used to describe the various forms of media content that are publicly available and created by end-users."[44]

Also known as Consumer-Generated Media (CGM), User-Generated Content

(UGC) refers to a wide range of applications, including blogs, news, digital video, podcasting, mobile phone photography, video, online encyclopedias and user reviews. According to Juniper Research, User Generated Content can be broken down into the following three categories[200]:

1. Mobile dating and chat room services—destinations for people to meet.
2. Personal content distribution—audio and video files uploaded onto third party sites for other mobile users to consume.
3. Social networking—social structures made of nodes "that are tied by one or more specific types of interdependency, such as values, visions, ideas, financial exchange, friendship, kinship, dislike, conflict or trade."[201]

UGC is the sum of all the ways in which people make use of social media and, according to the Organisation for Economic Cooperation and Development, UGC needs to fulfill the following three basic requirements in order to be considered as such[202]:

1. It must be published either on a publicly accessible website or on a social networking site accessible to a selected group of individuals.
2. It must show a certain amount of creative effort.
3. It must have been created outside of professional routines and practices.

For Kaplan and Haenlein, the first condition can't include content exchanged in e-mails or instant messages; the second precludes mere replications of already existing content (e.g., posting a copy of an existing newspaper article on a personal blog without any modifications or commenting); and the third condition implies that all created content must exclude a commercial market context.[44]

Kaplan and Haenlein believe that social media isn't just "a group of Internet-based applications that build on the ideological and technological foundations of Web 2.0, and that allow the creation and exchange of User Generated Content."[44] For Kaplan and Haenlein, this general definition should be broken down further because such disparate sites as Facebook, LinkedIn, Wikipedia, Weibo, and yy.com have little in common with each other when their offered services are looked at individually.[44]

As new sites are also popping up on a daily basis, a classification system created for social media should be able to include any future applications that are developed as well.[44] To create such a classification system, Kaplan and Haenlein rely on a "set of theories in the field of media research (social presence, media richness) and social process (self-presentation, self-disclosure), the two key elements of Social Media."[44] "Regarding the media-related component of Social Media, social presence theory[203] states that media differ in the degree of 'social presence'—defined as the acoustic, visual, and physical contact that can be achieved—they allow to emerge between two communication partners."[44]

Kaplan and Haenlein argue that: "Social presence is influenced by the intimacy (interpersonal vs. mediated) and immediacy (asynchronous vs. synchronous) of the medium, and can be expected to be lower for mediated (e.g., telephone conversations) than interpersonal (e.g., face-to-face discussions) and for asynchronous (e.g., e-mail) than synchronous (e.g., live chat) communications."[44] The higher the social presence, the more social influence the communication partners will have on each other.

Media Richness Theory[204] is a framework to describe a communications medium by its ability to reproduce the information sent over it and it implies that "the goal of any communication is the resolution of ambiguity and the reduction of uncertainty."[44] For Daft & Lengel[204], Media Richness is a function of:

- The medium's capacity for immediate feedback.
- The number of cues and channels available.
- Language variety.
- The degree to which intent is focused on the recipient.

Regarding the social dimension of social media, the concept of self-presentation states that when an individual comes in contact with other people, that individual will attempt to guide or control the impression that others form of them and all participants in social interactions are attempting to avoid being embarrassed or embarrassing others.[205] "Usually such a presence is done through self-disclosure; that is, the conscious or unconscious revelation of personal information (e.g., thoughts, feelings, likes, dislikes) that is consistent with the image one would like to give."[44]

Applied to the context of social media, a classification is made based on the richness of the medium and the degree of social presence it allows.[44] Kaplan and Haenlein create the *Classification of Social Media by social presence/media richness and self-presentation/self-disclosure* table reveals (see Table 8)[44]:

- Low: Collaborative projects such as Wikipedia and blogs score the lowest, mostly because they are text based and only allow relatively simple exchanges. Blogs usually score higher than collaborative projects because the former aren't focused on specific content domains.
- Medium: Content communities and social networking sites allow users to share text-based communication, as well as other forms of media. Social network sites score higher than content communities because they allow more self-disclosure.
- High: Virtual games and social worlds attempt to replicate face-to-face interactions in a virtual environment. Virtual social worlds score higher

on the self-presentation scale as the latter are ruled by strict guidelines that users have to either follow or be kicked out of entirely.

		Social Presence/ Media Richness		
		Low	Medium	High
Self-presentation/ Self-disclosure	High	Blogs	Social networking sites (e.g., Facebook)	Virtual social worlds (e.g., Second Life)
	Low	Collaborative projects (e.g., Wikipedia)	Content communities (e.g., YouTube)	Virtual game worlds (e.g., World of Warcraft)

Table 9: Classification of Social Media by social presence/media richness and self-presentation/self-disclosure
Source: *Users of the world unite! The challenges and opportunities of Social Media.*[44]

UGC can be very useful in website Search Engine Optimization (SEO). Search engines are constantly looking for updated information on websites and adding such things as a blog and a customer forum can be a cheap and effective way to get customers and/or clients to generate new content for you, which should increase search engine rankings.

Airlines should look beyond the most well-known social platforms and try to be creative. When it comes to social media and implementing it into an airline company, the one constant question should be is, "How does this affect my ROI?" For many businesses, there is the sense that social media is an ethereal, unquantifiable thing, but this shouldn't be the case.

As Figure 15 shows, social media listening can be used in a multitude of ways, like anticipating customer problems, understanding and identifying sentiment, measuring a company's share of voice, as well as keeping track of a company's brand. All of these are important and, together, they can give an airliner deep detail into marketing campaign performances and attribution analysis, which should help with planning and implementing future marketing campaigns.

A good example of how a company can test whether a social media solution would work for it is to consider the experience of a telco company that proactively adopted social media recently as mentioned in R.E. Divol's article *Demystifying social media*.[206] "The company had launched Twitter-based customer service capabilities, several promotional campaigns built around social contests, a fan page with discounts and tech tips, and an active response program to engage with people speaking with the brand," explains Divol.[206]

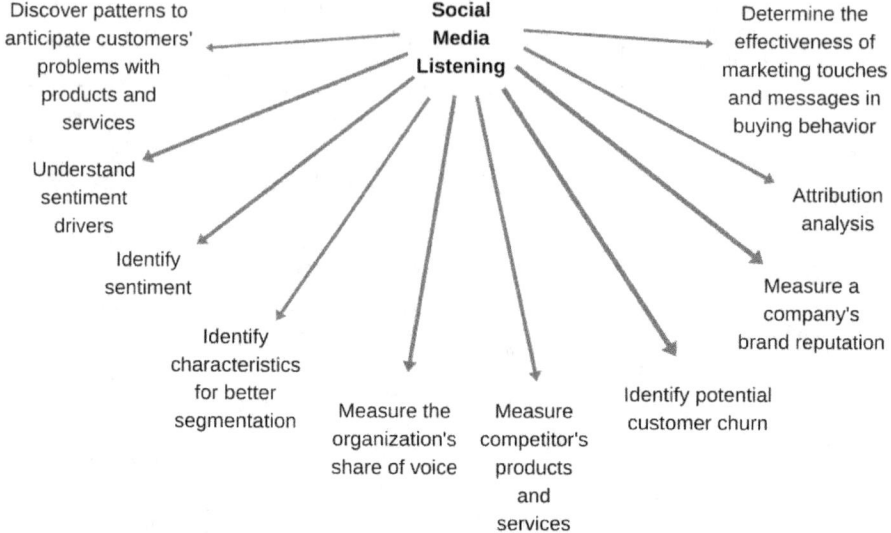

Figure 15: Social Media Listening objectives
Source: www.intelligencia.co

In social-media terms, the investment was not insignificant, and the company's senior executives wanted quantifiable ROI, not anecdotal evidence that the strategy was paying off.[206] "As a starting point, to ensure that the company was doing a quality job designing and executing its social presence, it benchmarked its efforts against approaches used by other companies known to be successful in social media."[206] According to Divol, the telecommunication company advanced the following hypotheses[206]:

- *"If all of these social-media activities improve general service perceptions about the brand, that improvement should be reflected in a higher volume of positive online posts.*
- *If social sharing is effective, added clicks and traffic should result in higher search placements.*
- *If both of these assumptions hold true, social-media activity should help drive sales—ideally at a rate even higher than the company achieves with its average gross rating point (GRP) of advertising expenditures."*[206]

The company tested its options. "At various times, it spent less money on conventional advertising, especially as social-media activity ramped up, and it modeled the rising positive sentiment and higher search positions just as it would using traditional metrics."[206] The results were quite conclusive: "social-media activity not only boosted sales but also had higher ROIs than traditional marketing did. Thus, while the company took a risk by shifting emphasis toward social-media efforts before it had data confirming that this was the correct course, the bet paid off."[206]

Just as importantly, the company had now created an analytic baseline that gave the company confidence to continue exploring a growing role for social media.[206] It is very easy to quantify search rankings and it is pretty obvious that if an airliner ranks higher in Google search rankings, it should garner more business.

Social Proof

"Think of it as building the foundation for massively scalable word-of-mouth"–these are the words of venture capitalist and blogger Aileen Lee describing the concept of social proof in her article *Social Proof Is The New Marketing*.[207] Lee believes that the best way to market a product or service "is by harnessing a concept called social proof, a relatively untapped gold mine in the age of the social web."[207] Lee contends social proof can generate sharing on a viral level through social channels that can multiply the discovery of a brand and add to its influence.[207]

Wikipedia describes social proof as "a psychological phenomenon where people assume the actions of others reflect the correct behavior for a given situation... driven by the assumption that the surrounding people possess more information about the situation."[208] In other words, "people are wired to learn from the actions of others, and this can be a huge driver of consumer behavior."[207]

Eric Hoffer's quote that, "when people are free to do as they please, they usually imitate each other," is quite amusing and, unquestionably, true. It speaks volumes about the herd mentality humans seem to succumb to as we take cues for proper behavior in most situations from the behavior of others. Psychologists call it the "conformity bias" and it is something that politicians and marketers have tapped into to enormous effect for centuries.

In his influential *Harvard Business Review* paper *Harnessing the Science of Persuasion*[209], Robert B. Cialdini looked at the science behind the power of persuasion and, since advertising is little more than persuading a person to choose one's product and/or service over another, I think it is important to explore persuasion through the lens of social media. Cialdini contends that:

> "For the past five decades, behavioral scientists have conducted experiments that shed considerable light on the way certain interactions lead people to concede, comply or change. This research shows that persuasion works by appealing to a limited set of deeply rooted human drives and needs, and it does so in predictable ways. Persuasion, in other words, is governed by basic principles that can be taught, learned and applied."

Caldini's six principles are[209]:

1. Like: People like those who like them.
2. Reciprocity: People repay in kind.
3. Social proof: People follow the lead of similar others.
4. Consistency: People align with their clear commitments.
5. Authority: People defer to experts.
6. Scarcity: People want more of what they can have less of.

For the reciprocity principle, people tend to give what they want to receive. Praise is likely to have a warming and softening effect on people because there is a human tendency to treat people they are themselves treated.[209] All kinds of companies use this concept in their marketing to customers and airlines should emulate these offerings.

For the principle of social proof, people tend to follow the lead of similar others.[209] People use peer power whenever it's available.[209] Caldini adds that, "Social creatures that they are, human beings rely heavily on the people around them for cues on how to think, feel, and act."[209] "We know this intuitively," Cialdini says because intuition has also been confirmed by experiments, such as the one first described in 1982 in the *Journal of Applied Psychology*."[209] In this study, "A group of researchers went door-to-door in Columbia, South Carolina, soliciting donations for a charity campaign and displaying a list of neighborhood residents who had already donated to the cause. The researcher found that the longer the donor list was, the more likely those solicited would be to donate as well."[209]

"To the people being solicited, the friends' and neighbors' names on the list were a form of social evidence about how they should respond. But the evidence would not have been nearly as compelling had the names been those of random strangers," explains Cialdini.[209]

The lesson here is that "persuasion can be extremely effective when it comes from peers."[209] Cialdini argues that, "The science supports what most sales professionals already know: Testimonials from satisfied customers work best when the satisfied customer and the prospective customer share similar circumstances."[209]

For the principle of consistency, businesses should make their commitments active, public, and voluntary. Cialdini states that, "Liking is a powerful force, but the work of persuasion involves more than simply making people feel warmly toward you, your idea, or your product. People need not only to like you but to feel committed to what you want them to do. Good turns are one reliable way to make people feel obligated to you. Another is to win a public commitment from them."[209]

For the principle of authority, people defer to experts, so airlines should relay their expertise and not assume things are self-evident.[209]

As Lee explains, "Approval from a credible expert, like a magazine or blogger, can have incredible digital influence."[207] Her examples include the following[207]:

- "Visitors referred by a fashion magazine or blogger to designer fashion rentals online at Rent the Runway drive a 200% higher conversion rate than visitors driven by paid search."[207]
- "Klout identifies people who are topical experts on the social web. Klout invited 217 influencers with high Klout scores in design, luxury, tech and autos to test-drive the new Audi A8. These influencers sparked 3,500 tweets, reaching over 3.1 million people in less than 30 days—a multiplier effect of over 14,000x."[207]
- "Mom-commerce daily offer site Plum District also reached mom influencers thru Klout, and found customers referred by influential digital moms shop at 2x the rate of customers from all other marketing channels."[207]

With the principle of scarcity, people want more of what they can have less of. An airline can highlight unique benefits and exclusive information, as Singapore Airlines often does with it new routes or new planes.[209] As Cialdini states, "Study after study shows that items and opportunities are seen to be more valuable as they become less available."[209] For airlines, the scarcity principle can be harnessed through the use of limited-time, limited-supply, and one-of-a-kind offers.[209]

Lee warns that[207]:

> "I don't think a social proof strategy will be effective if you don't start with a great product that delights customers, and that people like well enough to recommend. How do you know if you have a great product? Track organic traffic growth, reviews, ratings and repeat rates. And measure your viral coefficient—if your site includes the ability to share, what percentage of your daily visitors and users share with others? How is the good word about your product being shared outside your site on the social web? Do you know your Net Promoter Score, and your Klout score?"

In his *Fast Company* article *How to use the psychology of social proof to your advantage*[210], Ed Hallin argues that, "A lot of things go into a person's decision to purchase a product, and social proof is certainly one of those important factors. Studies show that 70% of consumers say they look at product reviews before making a purchase, and product reviews are 12x more trusted than product descriptions from manufacturers."[210]

One subset of social proof is celebrity social proof, this is "celebrity approval of your product or endorsements from celebrities."[210] However, Hallin warns that, "Celebrity endorsement is always a double-edged sword. If the celebrity is properly matched to the brand, it can do wonders for the company. If it's a mismatch, it may produce a bad image of the company and its brand."[210] Celebrities are also human beings and there can be a flavor-of-the-month aspect to them, especially amongst athletes, but, for every Aaron Hernandez disaster there might be a William Shatner Priceline endorsement that strikes internet and financial gold.

As Hallin explains, "To understand why celebrity endorsements work from a psychological perspective, it's important to familiarize yourself with the concept of the extended self." "The extended self," Hallin contends, "is made of up the self (me) and possessions (mine). It suggests that intentionally or unintentionally we view our possessions as a reflection of ourselves. This is why consumers look for products that signify group membership and mark their position in society."[210]

"User social proof is approval from current users of a product or service," explains Hallin.[210] This includes customer testimonials, case studies, and online reviews and it is particularly effective when storytelling is involved.[210]

Hallin believes that "We tend to imagine ourselves in other people's shoes when we read or hear a story. This is why stories are so persuasive and often more trustworthy than statistics or general trends. Individual examples stick with us because we can relate to them. Although statistics can be effective, it can be tougher to really see yourself in the aggregate the way you can with a personal account."[210]

The airline industry should exploit this as much as possible, as it offers a rich vein for storytelling unlike so many other industries because it is involved in travel and there are a million emotional stories to tell around travel; lovers uniting, grandparents meeting their grandchildren for the first time; a visit to the country of one's family roots; taking a new job in a foreign country, etc., etc., etc.

'Wisdom of the Crowds' social proof is "approval from large groups of other people. It's showing evidence that thousands, millions, or even billions have taken the action that the company wants you to take—making a purchase, subscribing, etc."[210]

Hallin argues, "We kind of joke about FOMO in pop culture, but actually the Fear of Missing Out is a real thing. It's a form of social anxiety, and it's a compulsive concern that one might miss out on an opportunity. This anxiety is especially relevant for social media, as the sharing of what's going on in our daily lives means you can constantly compare your status to others on these platforms."[210]

Unsurprisingly, Hallin contends, "Social media has sparked dozens of different ways to provide this kind of social proof. Facebook widgets that show other

Facebook friends that 'like' a brand, Twitter's display of people you follow that also follow another person, and the various ways that company offer rewards for referring others to the brand are all examples of this."[210]

It's a powerful marketing tool and one airlines need to exploit. "One study of 10,000 accounts at a German bank revealed that customers who came from customer referrals had 16% higher lifetime value than those who came from other acquisition sources. Additionally, the customers churned 18% less," Hallin relays.[210]

"The concept of implicit egotism is that most people subconsciously like things that 'resemble' them in some way," explains Hallin.[210] He adds that, "Studies show that we value the opinions of people we perceive as most like us. We tend to become friends with people that we have a lot in common with, so it makes sense that social triggers like Facebook's Like Box or referral programs are successful."[210]

Lee concludes that, "In the age of the social web, social proof is the "new marketing. If you have a great product waiting to be discovered, figure out how to build social proof around it by putting it in front of the right early influencers. And, engineer your product to share the love. Social proof is the best way for new users to learn why your product is great, and to remind existing users why they made a smart choice."[207]

Mobile and Social Media in China

I want to bring China into this discussion because it is not only home to more than 1.4 billion people, who are right next door to Macau (where I live)—many of whom are incredibly tech-savvy—but also because, I believe, China is on the cutting edge of mobile and social media technology. It also has a massive population of 1.4 billion people, who are starting to flex their travel muscles. International airports are also popping up all over the country right now.

In his *Telegraph* article *The unstoppable rise of the Chinese traveller – where are they going and what does it mean for overtourism?*,[211] Oliver Smith reveals that, "In less than two decades China has grown from travel minnows to the world's most powerful outbound market, leapfrogging the US – and leaving it in its wake." "According to the United Nations World Tourism Organisation (UNWTO) Chinese tourists overseas spent $261.1bn in 2016, up from around $10bn in the year 2000 (the figure for 2017 is likely to top $300bn). Collectively, America's globetrotters parted with a relatively paltry $123.6bn," adds Smith.[211]

Considering the fact that just "seven per cent of Chinese citizens—or 99 million people—possess a passport, compared to around 40 per cent of Americans, and 76 per cent of Britons,"[211] one can see the enormous financial potential the Chinese traveler offers.

Type	Social Media Site	Comparable Chinese site
Collaborative projects	Delicious	Baidu Bookmarks
		QQ bookmarks
		Sina viv bookmarks
	Wikipedia	Hudong
		Soso baike
		Baidu baike
		MBAlib
Blog	Blogger	Weibo
	Instablogs	Hexum
	Livejournal	Sina blog
	Tumblr	Blogus
	Wordpress	Bolaa
Micro-blogging	Twitter	Sina Weibo
		Tencent Weibo
		Netease Weibo
		Souhu Weibo
Content Community	YouTube	Youku
		Ku6
		Qivi
Social Network	Facebook	RenRen
		Kaixin
		Qzone
		Douban
	Foursquare	Jiepang
		Qieke
	LinkedIn	Ushi
		Wealink
		Jingwei
Virtual Game Worlds	League of Legends	League of Legends
Virtual Social Worlds	Stageit	yy.com

Table 10: Chinese Comparable Social Media Sites
Source: Intelligencia.co

"The China Outbound Tourism Research Institute (COTRI) predicts that overseas trips by the country's residents will increase from last year's figure of 145m to more than 400m by 2030," notes Smith.[211]

"That means that out of the 600 million additional trips in international tourism forecasted by UNWTO, bringing the total from 1.2 billion in 2017 to 1.8 billion by 2030, almost half of them will originate in China," says the COTRI.[211] By 2030, China will account for a quarter of all international tourism, they conclude.[211]

"Last year nine of the world's 50 busiest airports, and three of the 10 busiest, were found in China. Up from six and one, respectively, in 2010," notes Smith.[211] The growth is real, and airlines will be handling the brunt of this expansion.

Living in Macau, a Special Administration Region (SAR) of China, has given me a unique vantage point to witness the explosive growth of social media in China. Since it is an autonomous region like Hong Kong, Macau has no Internet censorship, but it is right next to Zhuhai, a bustling Chinese border-town of a million-and-a-half people. Censorship is very much alive there and it has been interesting to see the different types of censorship that occurs there, a city, literally—and figuratively—on the edge of China.

According to the Global Web Index[212], six out of 10 of the most widely used social systems are Chinese, including Qzone (19%), Sina Weibo (18%), Tencent Weibo (16%), RenRen (11%), Kaixin (8%) and 51.com (6%). For every one of Kaplan and Haenlein's[44] American social media types, there is a corresponding Chinese social media type that includes sites that either mimic or supersede the American original; for every Facebook in the US, there is a RenRen in China (and Qzone, and Douban, etc., etc.); for every American microblogging site like Twitter there is a corresponding site like Tencent Weibo (see Table 10). Many of the Chinese sites are offering far more complex services than their American or European counterparts.

According to Statista, China's mobile Internet users should top 650 million by the end of 2017.[213] Like their brethren in other countries, Chinese mobile subscribers do everything from make phone calls to send text and email messages, to tweeting and blogging, to watching videos and listening to music, to reading mobile books, to playing mobile games, to shopping at online stores, to checking in at physical stores through geofencing applications, as well as accessing social networking services. Basically, whatever other worldwide mobile users are doing, the Chinese are doing it too. And, probably, much, much more of it, as I will explain throughout this book. Live streamers have even figured out how to monetize eating a banana, although the Chinese government's censorship police brought a quick end to that sexually suggestive practice a few years ago.[214]

A walk through the electronics market of Huaqiangbei's commercial district in Shenzhen—reputed to be the largest electronics market in China, which, probably, makes it the largest electronics market in the world—reveals not just a bevy of counterfeit technology, but also a window into the future of mobile and social media.

China has almost half a billion social media users, who are engaging with each other on mobile. Mobile instant messaging is the most popular activity, followed by mobile search, mobile news, mobile music, mobile literature, mobile social networking sites, mobile microblogs, mobile games, mobile posts and reposts, mobile emails, mobile videos, mobile payment, mobile banking, mobile shopping, travel booking, and mobile daily deals.

To understand the popularity and the potential that social media holds for China in the future, I think it illustrative to look back at the country's long and tumultuous history. As Boye Lafayette de Mente explains in his book *The Chinese Mind: Understanding Traditional Chinese Beliefs and Their Influence on Contemporary Culture*[215]:

> "For over three thousand years the vast majority of Chinese did not have the political or social freedom to make decisions on their own. They were culturally conditioned to suppress their own personal needs and ambitions and to think and behave in terms of the collective responsibility—first for their family, then for their community, next for their clan, and ultimately for the nation at large."

Early Chinese society was built on a strong foundation of Confucian philosophy, which was "based on the already old Chinese idea that social stability was far more important than allowing people to make decisions on their own."[215] Over the ensuing centuries, "the concept and practice of collective behavior rather than personal actions became so deeply embedded in Chinese culture that individualism virtually disappeared."[215] Despite the rise and fall of one imperial dynasty after another, "the Confucian concept of collectivism continued to be the bedrock of Chinese culture until the late 1970s."[215]

When Mao Zedong rose to power in 1949, he systematically attempted to remold the Chinese into paragons of communism, but the effort was a complete failure.[215] In 1966, desperate to destroy all of the vestiges of traditional Chinese thought and behavior, Mao set in motion a violent "Cultural Revolution," whose intention was to enforce communism in the country by removing capitalist, traditional and cultural elements from Chinese society, and to impose Maoist orthodoxy within the Party.[215] During the ensuing 10-year period, agriculture and industry were mismanaged to the point where the economy became dysfunctional.[215]

Mao died in 1976 and, thankfully, that revolution died with him. However, "the damage inflicted upon the Confucian-oriented culture was profound and set the stage for a second but peaceful and entirely different kind of revolution inaugurated in the early 1970s by his successor, his former but disillusioned

Communist ally Deng Xiaoping."[215] Deng ushered in a new era that was euphemistically referred to as "socialistic capitalism."[215]

Although it seems impossible to prove Deng made the statement "To get rich is glorious!" it has been attributed to him and, whether he said those words or not, the statement embodies a philosophy he would have wholeheartedly embraced.[215] Over the next decade, Deng made it possible for ordinary Chinese people "to utilize their long suppressed ambitions and skills, to begin thinking and acting as individuals, and to help themselves for the first time in the long history of the country."[215] Incredibly, less than two decades after they went into effect, Deng's policies "freed over one billion people from a kind of cultural and political enslavement that had often treated them more like objects rather than human beings throughout their existence."[215]

There was not one area or one aspect of Chinese life in the large eastern urban areas of the country that was not fundamentally changed by the economic and social revolution initiated by Deng.[215] Today, a visit to Chinese cities like Shenzhen, Guangzhou, Dongguan and Zhuhai is an eye-opening experience. The typical London taxi cabs (painted a dull blue rather than the standard London shiny black) aren't quite as ubiquitous on the streets of Shenzhen as they are in London, but they certainly stand out as much because of their uniqueness and seemingly out-of-place oddity. Frank Gehry-esque skyscrapers pierce the smoggy skies of cities like Shenzhen, Shanghai, Chengdu and Guangzhou, turning them into modern architectural marvels. Although sometimes I think they need better translators; for example, the V hotel in Shenzhen is filled with giant 'X's on the outside, which makes for a confusingly mixed marketing message.

Many restrictions that had prevented people from changing jobs and moving away from their birthplaces have been lifted.[215] Virtually everyone in the country, from teenagers on up, tried to figure out how they could get a piece of the action.[215] Literally, for the first time in the history of the country, individual Chinese people were free to look out for number one, and millions of them began doing just that with a vengeance.[215]

In fact, the remaking of the Chinese mindset required almost no time at all.[215] The intelligence and skills the Chinese needed to start remaking their country had always been there.[215] It had just been locked down at the point of a gun or a bayonet, in some cases, literally.

The appearance of computers and the Internet in China had an equally pervasive influence on the thinking and behavior of the Chinese—further weaning them away from the traditional culture, as well as the communist culture of the Mao era.[215]

One of the key elements in the cultural changes brought on by computers was the fact that the computer itself is culturally neutral—that is, unlike human beings it does not come with any culture hardwired into it.[215] It is not preprogrammed to require any obedience to existing cultural norms.[215] Like Americans, Japanese, Koreans, and other computer users before them, large numbers of Chinese were freed for the first time in the history of the country to think like and act like individuals, without any thought of their social status, gender, or relationships with others, including with the government.[215]

One might say that computers and the Internet helped lower the Great Wall of the traditional Chinese mindset.[215] The combination of the "get rich quick" policy initiated by Mao's successor in the late 1970s and the widespread use of computers in China in the following decade resulted in a second revolution—this time one that was proposed and aided by the government, but was primarily the work of the people themselves—by individuals.[215]

The appearance of digital video games also had a profound effect on the attitudes and behaviors of the young Chinese mind.[215] Millions of children in families whose income had risen above subsistence levels began spending countless hours playing video games that had both an obvious and subtle influence on their way of thinking and acting.[215]

The role models of the first video games to hit China were not the selfless, self-sacrificing, well-mannered heroes of Confucian China.[215] They were the individualistic, independent, self-serving, fashion-oriented, sensual-minded characters embellished by the imagination and creativity of Japanese *anime* and *manga* comic masters.[215]

Unintentionally, the war that Chairman Mao set in motion in 1966 against the traditional mindset and behavior of the Chinese took one giant leap forward by the creators of these video games.[215] By the end of 2008, the number of Internet users in China had surpassed that of all the other countries in the world combined, and Chinese Internet companies started expanding globally, first into Japan and then into other neighboring countries.[215] WeChat has taken China by storm and the owner of WeChat, Tencent, is now acquiring worldwide tech and gaming companies.

As the Internet caught on in China, it gave voice to millions of people who before it had been mute and isolated, with few means beyond putting up posters on walls—a dangerous activity—to display their discontent.[215] Despite the fact that the content of the Internet was—and still is—controlled to a considerable degree by the Chinese government, the impact it had on the ability of ordinary Chinese people to make their voices heard was seminal.[215]

In the eyes of the Chinese government, Facebook has probably committed a cardinal sin—helping foment a revolution. "Given Facebook's high-profile role in mobilizing people and facilitating protests, such as those that helped topple the Egyptian government in 2011, it seems unlikely that the Chinese government would be interested in granting Facebook a license to operate locally."[216]

Unfortunately for Facebook, its time to make inroads and grow in China have probably come and gone. The local market is dominated by competitors, who have diversified business models that have helped them achieve deep mobile and social media engagement.[216] Robust startups are sprouting up in cities across China, from Shenzhen to Shanghai to Beijing and Chengdu, and many points in-between. Those cities have populations of over 10 million people, and their tech workforce are all keyed in and turned on to mobile and social.

Sina's Weibo is China's most popular and most influential social media service. It is a "mashup of Twitter and Facebook that makes money selling marketing services to business customers and offering paid memberships to individual VIPs."[216] Users post 140-character messages, which in Chinese conveys considerably more information than it does in English.[216] Images and video can be included as well as comments on post threads. "With an educated, urban audience of 368 million, Sina Weibo has become the top platform for breaking news and adding editorial commentary."[216] When Wal-Mart-backed airline 360buy.com wanted to publicize a 10% drop in prices on big home appliances, its CEO first announced it on Weibo, a sign of Weibo's growing importance to advertisers.[216]

Tencent is Sina's biggest competitor. Its platform—called QQ—today boasts 784 million accounts and it "helps Tencent attract users for its other services, such as Tencent Weibo, which has some 469 million users."[216] Tencent also owns WeChat and offers Qzone, the country's largest straight-up Facebook clone, which is "especially popular among teens, who post photos and videos, keep journal entries, and play games on it."[216] All those games and posts add up: in 2011, Tencent reported $4.5 billion in revenue, 22% more than Facebook's 2011 revenues.[216]

In China, internet users spend more than 40 percent of their time online on social media, a figure that is expected to continue its rapid rise over the next few years.[40] "This appetite for all things social has spawned a dizzying array of companies, many with tools more advanced than those in the West: for example, Chinese users were able to embed multimedia content in social media more than 18 months before Twitter users could do so in the United States."[40]

According to C.I. Chiu, "Social media began in China in 1994 with online forums and communities and migrated to instant messaging in 1999. User review sites such as Dianping emerged around 2003. Blogging took off in 2004, followed a year later by social-networking sites with chatting capabilities such as RenRen."[40]

Sina Weibo launched in 2009, offering microblogging with multimedia. Location-based player Jiepang appeared in 2010, offering services similar to Foursquare's.[40] This explosive growth should continue into the foreseeable future, "a trend that's at least partially attributable to the fact that it's harder for the government to censor social media than other information channels."[40]

The Chinese government puts the onus of censorship on the internet providers, but it is very hard for them to keep up with technologically savvy users, who are constantly on the lookout for the latest technology and newest and hippest platforms.

In China, the competition for consumers is fierce, especially in the social-media space.[40] "Many companies regularly employ 'artificial writers' to seed positive content about themselves online and attack competitors with negative news they hope will go viral."[40] "In several instances, negative publicity about companies—such as allegations of product contamination—has prompted waves of microblog posts from competitors and disguised users."[40]

Businesses trying to manage social-media crises in China should "carefully identify the source of negative posts and base countermeasures on whether they came from competitors or real consumers," warns C.I. Chiu.[40] Companies should also be aware of the impact of artificial writers when mining for social-media consumer insights and analytics.[40] They should compare "the performance of their brands against those of their competitors. Otherwise, they risk drawing the wrong conclusions about consumer behavior and brand preferences."[40] This is something that airlines should do as their competitors could potentially be creating negative reviews to affect sales.

The Four Steps of Social Media

In their book *Online Marketing Inside Out: Reach New Buyers Using Modern Marketing Techniques*[217], Eley & Tiley state that, when a company is first delving into social media, there are four steps of social media that should be followed—listen, join, participate and create—and these steps must be strictly followed in that specific order.

Listening is the most important step. People online are frequently mentioning and making comments about a company and its products, so all one has to do is listen. Even if an airliner does not choose to participate in the discussion itself, it will discover valuable information about the company by just listening.[217]

Instead of doing expensive surveys, focus groups or other experiments, the best information is often found right there in front of you at minimal or maybe even at no cost.[217] An airliner can find out what its customers think of its store and service, as well as what they might want improved.[217] Problems and frustrations that might not make it onto corporate surveys might be detailed enough on blogs to affect real change.[217] Most importantly, an airline might get the inside scoop of what is actually important to its target audience.[217]

To understand how important this process can be for a company, I'd like to take the example of one bourbon manufacturer who found itself in the midst of a self-created social media disaster. In February 2013, because it was faced with both a high demand for its product and a low supply of bourbon whiskey, Maker's Mark announced plans to cut the amount of alcohol in its drink from 45 to 42 percent.[218] Needless to say, the Internet wasn't pleased. As Laura Stampler explains in her article *Makers Mark Turned Watered Down Whiskey Debacle Into a Social Media Win*[218], "It's the age of social media, so consumers were tweeting and Facebooking their complaints to any and everyone who would listen."[218]

There were angry tweets as well as Facebook petitions against the company.[218] A normal Valentine's Day post on the company's Facebook page was flooded with negative comments about the shift.[218] Immediately realizing that it had made a huge mistake, the brand decided to embrace the social media platforms where they have been receiving such negativity and they quickly put out the message that it had made a huge mistake, it was sorry and that it was reversing its decision about lowering the alcohol content.[218] The link to the company's Facebook apology soon became a popular hashtag.[218] "Customers went from feeling abandoned to listened to and respected in record time."[218] The apology noted that even though the social media reaction was highly negative, the company wanted the conversation to continue.[218]

Maker's Mark even took this conversation into their print advertising, using the tagline line: "You spoke. We listened. Here's proof", with an arrow cleverly pointing to the label, which showed that the alcohol content (or proof) was still 45%.

By listening, joining, participating and creating, Maker's Mark built its online brand and it now has an audience to share its content with, an audience which should help them spread their content far and wide, as well as, more importantly, sell a lot more 45 proof whiskey to.

In her article *50 ways to drive traffic to your website with social media*[219], Amanda Nelson recommends, listening can be used in the following ways:

1. Monitor for buying indication terms and reply with helpful links.
2. Listen for recommendation requests and share helpful links.
3. Listen for discussions of your product or category and provide web links.
4. Share relevant web content with prospects.
5. Discover relevant blogs and ask for backlinks.

Once the airline operator understands the community and what it is all about, it is time to join a social network. Many networks require that you have an account on their site to participate in the discussions and the airline should sign up for the account as it is always better to have an account even if it is not required to have one because one always wants to claim its brand and/or company name to gain credibility.

An airline should also join communities where it is most likely to find its customers.[217] If you start out by listening, you will know where your customers tend to congregate online. Facebook, LinkedIn, YouTube, Flickr, Delicious, Digg and Twitter are big networks which should be on your radar.[217] Many of these sites can be used to listen to your audience or to start a discussion. Chinese listening social media sites include Sina Weibo, Tencent Weibo, and Netease Weibo, amongst others.

Airline operators should set up accounts at all the major social networking sites and link back to their website(s), as well as link content and similar keywords throughout their social channels.

Once the discussion has been joined, then it is time to participate in the community. Participating includes replying and posting to online forums and blogs, reviewing products and services and bookmarking sites that are like-minded.[217]

By participating, airlines will build their online brand and people will start to respect them as a valuable contributor to the community.[217] When respected, others will help to promote the company without even being asked to do so, which, as most marketers will tell you, is some of the best marketing around. Not only is word-of-mouth marketing one of the most trusted forms of marketing, but it can also spread virally. Two words of warning, however; your role models should always be very experienced and remain very active users in the community; and, most importantly of all, remember that it is never okay to spam.[217]

In her article *50 Ways to Drive Traffic to Your Website*[219], Nelson recommends using the following methods to increase participation:

1. Ask readers to sign up for an RSS feed.
2. Answer all questions and share peer referrals.
3. Feature community members on your site.
4. Share customer stories.
5. Ask influencers to share your web links.
6. Interview an influencer for web content.
7. Have an influencer guest blog.
8. Help an influencer write content about the brand.
9. Share products with influencers for feedback and web content.

Finally, it is time to create. Once an airline has built itself an online brand by listening, joining and participating, it is time to create its own content.[217] It will now have an audience to share its content with and they will help the airline spread its content far and wide.

It should be noted here that the airline operator has to create value; ads are not generally seen as valuable.[217] Posting "buy my stuff" on twitter will fail to achieve the results you want, and this practice may even get you banned.[217] By making beneficial contributions to the community, people will notice you and want to know more about the company.[217] If you have listened properly, you should have a solid idea of the type of content people would like to see.[217] Then, simply, give it to them. Nelson recommends companies be creative in the following ways[217]:

1. Divide a piece of content into multiple SlideShare presentations that link to your site.
2. Start a LinkedIn group.
3. Tie content together so an eBook links to a relevant blog post, which, in turn, links to a topical webinar.
4. Build a forum or community section on the company website.
5. Create referral programs.

The four steps of social media fit well within the six types of social media, which I will detail next. Throughout the rest of this chapter, I will explain the different types of social media and, in chapter four, I will describe how each of these social media platforms can be used individually as well as, sometimes, in combination to market the company and its services worldwide.

Six Types of Social Media

According to Kaplan and Haenlein's article *Users of the World, Unite! The Challenges and Opportunities of Social Media*[44], the writers break Social Media down into the following six different types:

1. Collaborative projects
2. Blogs and micro-blogs
3. Content communities
4. Social networking sites
5. Virtual game worlds
6. Virtual social worlds

Throughout the rest of this chapter, I will break down each of these types of social media separately, as well as explain how an airline operator can use them on their own or, preferably, combined. Chapter four goes into much more detail about how these sites should be used in a social media marketing and social media listening way, but, in this chapter, I will lay out the foundations and provide a list of sites available to the social media marketer and listener.

Collaborative Projects

Probably the most democratic form of all UGC, collaborative projects enable the joint and simultaneous creation of content by many end-users.[44] Kaplan and Haenlein believe collaborative projects can be split into two different categories[44]:

1. Wikis—these are websites that allow users to add, remove, and change text-based content; and
2. Social bookmarking applications—these enable the group-based collection and rating of Internet links or media content.

The main idea behind collaborative projects is that joint efforts can lead to a better outcome than individual action.[44] Examples of collaborative projects include the web-based encyclopedia Wikipedia and social bookmarking sites such as Delicious and StumbleUpon.

Social bookmarking is both the method of storing and the managing of web page bookmarks with individually chosen keywords, as well as the sharing of this information with others. At social bookmarking sites, users can tag, save, manage and share websites with their friends and their connections. Users can add descriptions in the form of metadata and these descriptions can be anything from free text comments, favorable or unfavorable votes, or tags that collectively form a social thread of information. This kind of thread is also known as a folksonomy— "the process by which many users add metadata in the form of keywords to shared content."[220]

In his article *How to Use Social Bookmarking for Business*[221], Lou Dubois explains that, "Social bookmarking, at its most basic form, is a simple way to organize all of the best content from around the web based off your interests, all in one place." It is a handy way to "sort the relevant from the irrelevant, according to their interests and the value of the information provided. And perhaps most importantly, the bookmarks are transferable between computers and locations."[222]

Founded in 2003, Delicious (then known as del.icio.us) coined the term *social bookmarking* and pioneered the concept of tagging.[223] The following year, similar sites such as Furl, Simpy, Citeulike and Connotea came online. StumbleUpon also appeared around the same time.

Compared to search engines and traditional automated resource location and classification software, social bookmarking systems are advantageous because the tag-based classification is done by a human being, who usually understands the content and context of a resource better than an algorithm-based computer program. Human beings are also adept at finding and bookmarking web pages that often go unnoticed by web spiders.[223] In addition, a user will probably find a system that ranks a resource based on how many times it has been bookmarked by other users more valuable than a system that simply ranks resources based on the number of external links pointing to it.

For the promotion of an airline, social bookmarking is important because it helps a website get quality backlinks. When a website is submitted for ranking by a search engine, the search engine considers the quality of the backlinks, i.e., the quality of the sites linking back to it. This means that if you bookmark popular sites, the search engine spiders will automatically follow the links back to your site. SEOMoz's Linkscape and Majestic SEO's Link Intelligence are both very good tools to discover current backlinks to a site.

Kaplan and Haenlein argue that, "From a corporate perspective, firms must be aware that collaborative projects are trending toward becoming the main source of information for many consumers. As such, although not everything written on Wikipedia may be actually true, it is *believed* to be true by more and more Internet users." This can have particularly damaging repercussions during a corporate crisis.[44] I go into specific detail about how social media should be used in crises situations in chapter four, while discussing a few examples such as the Red Cross alcohol tweet[224], the United Airlines' "United Breaks Guitars" viral video[225] and the Domino's YouTube fiasco.[226]

Collaborative projects can also be used to increase productivity, for example, the Finnish mobile manufacturer Nokia "uses internal wikis to update employees on project status and to trade ideas, which are used by about 20% of its 68,000 staff members."[44] Also, the U.S. application software company Adobe Systems "maintains a list of bookmarks to company-related websites and conversations on Delicious."[44]

Dubois explains that "From an individual consumption perspective for Internet readers, social bookmarking can make great sense to filter your news and information all into one place."[221] But it also makes great sense for businesses to utilize these tools as they can increase website traffic and grow brand recognition by curating information and disseminating client testimonials.[221]

Throughout the business world, content curators are "considered the gatekeepers to information for businesses and individuals. As a company, curating, or aggregating the best content from around the web, can make you an industry leader."[221] For companies you already work with, showing that you are on top of industry news gives you a vaunted level of credibility.[221]

"Similarly, if you think of it from the perspective of businesses who you don't already do business with, you're going to be seen as a resource for information," argues L. Dubois[221], which should give you an immediate leg up on your competition.

Another way to utilize these tools is by pulling together all of your company's best customer testimonials in a social bookmark. Just about every business gets questions about its client list and testimonials from its potential business partners and when asked the question: "What have others said about your work?", wouldn't it be better to direct potential clients to a site that has all of the company's testimonials in one place, in a simple format rather than sending them to a Yelp page, argues Dubois.[221]

Social bookmarking isn't as intuitive a process as blogging or social networking on sites like Facebook or Twitter, but it is a very valuable tool in its own right and it should be one part of an airline's social media marketing plan. Chinese collaborative projects include Baidu bookmarks, QQ Bookmarks, Sina viv, Hudong, Soso baike, Baidu baiki and MBAlib.

List of Collaborative Projects Websites

As the collaborative projects landscape changes on a daily basis, it is impossible to list all of the available Websites, but these are some of the most common and popular platforms I have found. Some of these sites might seem odd to include, but many of these sites are interesting places to market an airline's products through as well.

NAME	"ABOUT US" DESCRIPTION
A1 Webmarks	A1-Webmarks is a free service that combines the convenience of a personal webmark server with the power of social webmarking.
Blinklist	BlinkList is a powerful productivity tool that makes is much easier for anyone to share and save their links for later. With BlinkList you can save a local copy of any web page on your computer. We give you a website so that you can easily access all of the links that you saved from any computer.
Blurpalicious	Social bookmarking made simple.
Digg	Digg delivers the most interesting and talked about stories on the Internet right now. The Internet is full of great stories, and Digg helps you find, read, and share the very best ones. It's simple and it's everywhere: visit Digg on the web, find it on your iPhone, or get the best of Digg delivered to your inbox with The Daily Digg.
Diigo	If you browse or read a lot on the web, we believe you will find Diigo indispensable. Diigo is two services in one -- it is a research and collaborative research tool on the one hand, and a knowledge-sharing community and social content site on the other.
Folkd	Using social bookmarks with folkd.com will enrich your web-surfing experience. We provide a simple website and easy to use browser buttons which allow you to: Save your favourite links and bookmarks online and access them from anywhere at any time.
Google Bookmarks	Save time with quick links to your favorite websites. Use Google's Web History to find the sites you visit frequently and bookmark your favorites. Use the Google Toolbar for quick access to your bookmarks and to easily create more. Get your bookmarks on any computer. No matter where you may be surfing the web, your bookmarks can stay with you just by signing in. Keep your bookmarks organized. Add searchable labels and notes to your bookmarks to find them easily and keep them organized.
Linkroll	Linkroll is a free link blogging service. At a personal level you can bookmark, categorize and comment on all the great web pages/links you find.
Linksgutter	A complete free social bookmarking site.
Mylinkvault	online links made easy - store your links online.

NAME	"ABOUT US" DESCRIPTION
Netvouz	Netvouz is a social bookmarkingservice that allows you to save your favorite links online and access them from any computer, wherever you are. Organize your bookmarks in folders and tag each bookmark with keywords.
Oyax	Oyax is a social bookmark manager. It allows you to add web sites to your personal collection of links, categorize those sites with tags and share your collection not only with your own browsers and machine, but also with other people.
Plime	Plime is an editable wiki community where users can add and edit weird and interesting links.
Reddit	Reddit is a social news and entertainment website where registered users submit content in the form of either a link or a text. Other users then vote the submission "up" or "down", which is used to rank the post and determine its position on the site's pages and front page. Content entries are organized by areas of interest called "subreddits".
Startaid	StartAid is a Social Bookmarking site. Startaid give you the ability to make a custom homepage where you can have all your Bookmarks at your fingertips. With Startaid you can you Category and/or Tag filing systems.
Stumbleupon	StumbleUpon helps you discover and share great websites. As you click Stumble!, we deliver high-quality pages matched to your personal preferences. These pages have been explicitly recommended by your friends or one of over 15 million other websurfers with interests similar to you. Rating these sites you like automatically shares them with like-minded people – and helps you discover great sites your friends recommend.
Trendhunter	With 35,000,000 monthly views, TrendHunter.com is the world's largest, most popular trend community. Trend Hunter, Trend Hunter TV and Trend Hunter PRO feature 112,000 micro-trends and cutting-edge ideas. Routinely sourced by the media, Trend Hunter is a source of inspiration for industry professionals, aspiring entrepreneurs and the insatiably curious.
Xmarks	Xmarks was founded in 2006 under our original name Foxmarks. Our bookmark sync browser add-on is one of the most popular in the world with over twenty million downloads and counting. Our products are actively used in over four million browsers and we manage over a billion bookmarks for our users.
Zootool	Zootool is about collecting, organizing and sharing your favorite images, videos, documents and links from all over the internet. Driven by a passion for design, web, code and all kind of nerdery, we are working hard to build the most awesome bookmark tool for geeks like us and people who love the web.

Table 11: Collaborative Projects websites

Chinese collaborative projects include Baidu bookmarks, QQ Bookmarks, Sina viv, Hudong, Soso baike, Baidu baiki and MBAlib.

Blogs

In 2005, Merriam-Webster added the word "blog" to its dictionary, calling it, "a web site that contains an online personal journal with reflections, comments, and often hyperlinks provided by the writer."[227] Webopedia defines a blog as, "a web page that serves as a publicly accessible personal journal for an individual."[228] The term originated from the word "weblog", which was coined by Jorn Barger on 17 December 1997 when he used it to describe the list of links on his Robot Wisdom website that "logged" his internet wanderings.[229]

In April or May of 1999, Peter Merholz broke the word "weblog" into the two words "we blog" in the sidebar of his blog Peterme.com.[230] The term "blog" was picked up by Evan Williams at Pyra Labs who used "blog" as a noun and a verb to mean "to edit one's weblog or to post to one's weblog" and created the term "blogger" for Pyra Labs' Blogger product, which led to the term's popularity.[231]

Representing the earliest form of Social Media, blogs are the "Equivalent of personal web pages and can come in a multitude of different variations, from personal diaries describing the author's life to summaries of all relevant information in one specific content area."[44]

In its article *It's the Links, Stupid*[230], *The Economist* claims that a blog is:

> "A web page to which its owner regularly adds new entries, or 'posts', which tend to be (but need not be) short and often contain hyperlinks to other blogs or websites. Besides text and hypertext, posts can also contain pictures ('photoblogs') and video ("vlogs"). Each post is stored on its own distinct archive page, the so-called 'permalink', where it can always be found."

The Economist explains that blogging is a quintessentially social activity, highlighted by two features[230]:

> "A 'blogroll', along the side of the blog page, which is a list of links to other blogs that the author recommends (not to be confused with the hyperlinks inside the posts). In practice, the blogroll is an attempt by the author to place his blog in a specific genre or group, and a reciprocal effort by a posse of bloggers to raise each other's visibility on the internet (because the number of incoming links pushes a blog higher in search-engine results). The other feature is 'trackback', which notifies ('pings') a blog about each new incoming link from the outside—a sort of gossip-meter, in short."

According to Dave Winer, the influential software engineer who pioneered several blogging techniques and has, by his own estimate, the longest running blog of all time[230], weblogs should be:

1. Personalized: Weblogs are designed for individual use (a multi-person weblog is also possible through collaboration, such as the "team blog" offered by www.blogger.com). A Weblog style is personal and informal.
2. Web-based: Weblogs can be updated frequently. They are easy to maintain and accessible via a Web browser.

3. Community-supported: Weblogs can link to other weblogs and Websites, enabling the linkage of ideas, and hence stimulating knowledge generation and sharing between bloggers.
4. Automated: Blogging tools help bloggers to present their words without the hassle of writing HTML code or any other programming language; instead, bloggers can just concentrate on the content.

Winer argues that blogging should have a raw, unpolished authenticity to it.[230] "Blogging is all about style" and the essence of blogginess is "the unedited voice of a single person," preferably an amateur.[230] For Winer, editors do not belong in the Blogosphere, even though, today, they very much are.[230]

Blogs are incredibly popular because they are cheap, easy to set up and they provide maximum exposure with limited effort. As Jeff Jarvis, Director of the Interactive Journalism at City University of New York's Graduate School of Journalism points out, they are the "easiest, cheapest, fastest publishing tool ever invented."[229] Blogs are everywhere, affecting every sector of society and, because of their ease of use and low barrier to entry, they will continue to be a big part of the national and worldwide conversation.[229]

Blogs can take many forms, including a diary, a news service, a collection of links to Internet resources, a series of book reviews, reports of activity on a project, the journal of an expedition, a photographic record of a building project, or any one of a number of other forms.

According to Winer, a successful blog should include the following key elements[230]:

1. Great content: as the old adage goes, "Content is king" and that old axiom should be kept very much in mind when it comes to blogging. Competition is fierce so one's content better be relevant, valuable and captivating.
2. Post frequently: along with having great content, bloggers should constantly post new material. A constant stream of new material will garner more views, which should result in more followers.
3. User friendly navigation: readers prefer navigation that is simple and straightforward so have links that make logical sense.
4. Eye pleasing content: as with any other type of marketing, the prettier something looks, the more likely it is to be viewed, so keep the design element in mind when creating a blog.
5. Connect to other content: linking and back-linking is exceptionally important so feel free to add links to other content that expands upon or references your content.

Although, China censors its social media sites, Chinese consumers are some of the biggest bloggers and commentators around, and Chinese blogging sites like Weibo, Hexum, Sina blog, Blogus and Bolaa are filled with a constant stream of observations and explanations about any and everything imaginable; literally, as the Chinese love to blog about the strangest things. Stories go viral exceptionally fast in China, with friends sharing not just ideas but sometimes scams and schemes amongst their close one thousand friends in a matter of hours.

Airlines should exploit any and every available blog opportunity they have to get their message out, as well as use any and all platforms that help them to connect with their customers and potential customers anywhere they might be. There are large Chinese communities in almost every country in the world and it behooves every large airline companies to understand each unique market, especially one with the growing financial muscle of the Chinese consumer.

In his article *How the World's top 7 Airlines Use Social Media*[232], Sahail Ashraf writes a good overview of how such diverse airlines as Qatar Airways, Singapore Airlines, Cathay Pacific, Turkish Airlines, Emirates, Etihad, and All Nippon Airlines utilize social media in their own unique and expansive ways.

Qatar Airways has a strong presence on Twitter, where it offers news and information about the company.[232] Engagement is pretty constant, with retweets in the area of 25-30 per post and they focus on replying to customer comments and complaints.[232] They are adept at responding to queries as well, often turning them into effective 'upsells'.[232]

On Facebook, Qatar is all about the experience as well.[232] They don't try humor as that doesn't fit their corporate personality and there are no 'viral' aspects that they push.[232] Instead, they focus on showing videos of available inflight movies, and press releases about news, partnerships and upcoming events.[232]

The Singapore Airlines social channels are heavy on branding; its excellent Twitter account is full of gorgeous photos that are all branded with the Singapore Airlines logo.[232] Singapore Airlines has a reputation for affordable luxury, and this filters through on its images of gorgeous plane interiors, along with the delicious-looking food that the airline serves onboard.[232]

Hong Kong-based Cathay Pacific utilizes social listening to understand its customers better.[232] As Ashraf explains, "Social listening is one of the key areas that companies can excel in if they make the effort."[232] Cathay is one airline making that effort.[232] On its Twitter account, there is a significant number of retweets and, every now and then, there will be one that is a result of genuine interest.[232] In such cases, Cathay retweets it, showing that strong customer interaction can help with branding.[232]

Turkish Airlines uses hashtags to build relevance and authenticity. Arguably, hashtags are an overused social media marketing tool, but, used properly, they can provide strong brand marketing.[232] Turkish Airlines takes it to a whole new level on Twitter.[232] "The usual plush photos abound, but what this company can teach all businesses is the interaction element," explains Ashraf.[232] "One key aspect of this (that is criminally underused by many businesses) is the utilisation of the hashtag," adds Ashraf.[232] In one Twitter example, a picture of the Chicago skyline stretches below the question "Which of our destinations is known as the "Windy City'?"[232] The hashtag '#Guesswhere' follows the question and it is a call-to-action for Turkish Airlines' Twitter followers.[232]

List of Blogging Websites

As the Blogging landscape changes on a daily basis, it is impossible to list all of the available blogging Websites out there, but these are some of the most common and popular platforms I have found:

NAME	"ABOUT US" DESCRIPTION
AlterNet	AlterNet is an award-winning news magazine and online community that creates original journalism and amplifies the best of hundreds of other independent media sources. AlterNet's aim is to inspire action and advocacy on the environment, human rights and civil liberties, social justice, media, health care issues, and more.
Blog Catalog	Blog Catalog is the premiere social blog directory on the internet. Search, Browse, Rate and Review thousands of blog sites.
Blogger	Blogger is a free blog publishing tool from Google for easily sharing your thoughts with the world.
Blogigo	A free blog, quick and easy.
Blurty	Community site desgined for adults, based on livejournal source code.
Carbonmade	With Carbonmade, you can manage your online portfolio with a variety of tools that allow you to change how you display your work. The core idea behind the design of Carbonmade is to keep your images or videos at the forefront.
Disqus	Disqus (*dis·cuss • dĭ-skŭs'*) is all about changing the way people think about discussion on the web. We're big believers in the conversations and communities that form on blogs and other sites.
Instablogs	Instablogs is a news ecosystem bringing bloggers, citizen journalists and traditional media together. It's a place to discover, share, contribute and connect with the world and the people who are changing it.
IntenseDebate	IntenseDebate's comment system enhances and encourages conversation on your blog or website.
Issuu	Issuu is the leading digital publishing platform delivering exceptional reading experiences of magazines, catalogs, and newspapers. Millions of people have uploaded their best publications to create beautiful digital editions.
LiveJournal	Rooted in a tradition of global participation, LiveJournal is on the forefront of personal publishing, community involvement, and individual expression.

NAME	"ABOUT US" DESCRIPTION
Medium	Medium is a new place on the Internet where people share ideas and stories that are longer than 140 characters and not just for friends. It's designed for little stories that make your day better and manifestos that change the world. It's used by everyone from professional journalists to amateur cooks. It's simple, beautiful, collaborative, and it helps you find the right audience for whatever you have to say.
Pen.io	Pen.io is the fastest way to publish online.
Silvrback	Silvrback is a hosted, markdown-powered blog combined with a bio page. The platform is as clean and simple as Medium, while giving you complete control over your own brand.
Soup.io	Soup is a tumblelog; a super-easy blog that can do more than just text: post links; quotes; videos; audio; files; reviews and events
Svbtle	We're a network of great people mixed with an extremely simple platform for collecting and developing ideas, sharing them with the world, and reading them. Svbtle is blogging with everything else taken away.
Tumblr	Tumblr lets you effortlessly share anything. Post text, photos, quotes, links, music, and videos, from your browser, phone, desktop, email, or wherever you happen to be. You can customize everything, from colors, to your theme's HTML.
TypePad	TypePad blogs make it simple for you to share your interests and get noticed. Easily design and customize your own blog, and use our SEO (Search Engine Optimization) and SMO (Social Media Optimization) tools to promote your blog and attract an audience and following.
Wordpress	A semantic personal publishing platform with a focus on aesthetics, web standards, and usability.
WPScoop	WP-Scoop (WordPress Scoop) is website dedicated to bringing you WordPress related News, Reviews and Stories. All the latest and greatest information on the WordPress blogging platform can be found on the pages of WPscoop. We are a Social Bookmarking Site for you to use and a place for you to discover what is hot in the Wordpress world.
Zimbio	Zimbio is an interactive magazine publisher focused on entertainment, style, current events, and other pop culture topics. Zimbio.com, one of the fastest growing web publications and one of the 10 most popular magazines on the web, is now read by over 20 million people each month.

Table 12: Blogging websites

Chinese blogging sites include Weibo, Hexum, Sina blog, Blogus and Bolaa.

Microblogs

Although similar to a blogging website, a microblog site differs from a traditional blog in that its content is typically smaller in both actual and aggregate size. In his article *Visual Analysis of Microblog Content Using Time-Varying Co-occurrence Highlighting in Tag Clouds*[233], S.B. Lohmann claims: "Social networking and microblogging services such as Twitter, Facebook, or Google+

allow people to broadcast short messages, so-called micro posts, in continuous streams. These posts usually consist of a text message enriched with contextual metadata, such as the author, date and time, and sometimes also the location of origin."[233] While individual posts can be no longer than 280 characters[234], "aggregated posts of multiple users can provide a rich source of time-critical information that can point to events and trends needing attention."[233]

The most used microblog in the English-speaking world is Twitter, which, according to its website "is a real-time short messaging service that works over multiple networks and devices."[235] A free social networking and micro-blogging service, Twitter allows users to send and receive tweets—messages that can be up to 280 characters in length.

Twitter notes that, "Connected to each tweet is a rich details pane that provides additional information, deeper context and embedded media."[235] Because it is happening in near real-time, "Twitter is a 'what's-happening-right-now' tool that enables interested parties to follow individual users' thoughts and commentary on events in their lives."[236] These thoughts can, literally, be about anything and everything.

On its website, Twitter recommends building a following, increasing a businesses' reputation, and raising a customer's trust by following these best practices[235]:

1. Share: disseminate photos and behind the scenes info about your business. Even better, give a glimpse of developing projects and events. Users come to Twitter to get and share the latest, so give it to them!
2. Listen: regularly monitor the comments about your company, brand, and products.
3. Ask: question your followers to glean valuable insights and show them that you are listening.
4. Respond: reply to compliments and feedback in real time.
5. Reward: tweet updates about special offers, discounts and time-sensitive deals.
6. Demonstrate wider leadership and know-how: Reference articles and links about the bigger picture as it relates to your business.
7. Champion your stakeholders: Retweet and publicly reply to great tweets posted by your followers and customers.
8. Establish the right voice: Twitter users tend to prefer a direct, genuine, and, of course, likable tone from your business, but think about your *voice* as you tweet. How do you want your business to appear to the Twitter community?

Twitter also offers three ways to advertise on its service; promoted tweets; promoted trends; and promoted accounts. Promoted tweets are regular tweets that are amplified to a broader audience and they are offered on a Cost-per-

Engagement (CPE) basis. A business is charged when a user Retweets, replies to, clicks on, or favorites the Promoted tweet.[235] Retweeted impressions by engaged users are free, and can exponentially amplify the reach and cost-effectiveness of a marketing campaign.[235]

Twitter is a very useful tool that connects businesses to customers in real-time. It can help a business quickly share information with people who are interested in their products and/or services, as well as gather real-time market intelligence and customer feedback.[235] Using Twitter, a business can build strong relationships with its customers and partners as well as raise the profile of its brands, direct sales, and engage a primed audience.[235] Twitter can help a business build a following, increase its reputation as well as raise a customer's trust by sharing, listening, asking questions, responding to replies, rewarding customers with special offers and discounts, demonstrating wider leadership and championing the right stakeholders.

"Promoted Trends" give a business the exclusive opportunity to feature a Trend related to its business at the top of the "Twitter Trends" list.[235] When a user clicks on the "Trend", he or she is taken to the conversation for that trend and a "Promoted tweets" tag is attached to the tweet at the top of the timeline. Because of its placement, the ad receives substantial exposure, thereby initiating or amplifying a conversation on Twitter and beyond.[235]

"Promoted Accounts" can help companies quickly increase their Twitter followers.[235] Part of "Who to follow" (Twitter's account recommendation engine), "Promoted Accounts" will highlight a business account to users who will most likely find it interesting.[235] According to Twitter's Website, "Users find Promoted Accounts a useful part of discovering new businesses, content, and people on Twitter."[235]

List of Micro-blogging Websites

As the Microblogging landscape changes on a daily basis, it is impossible to list all of the available Websites online, but these are some of the most common and popular platforms I have found:

NAME	"ABOUT US" DESCRIPTION
Audioboo.fm	We're a small team based in London UK who launched Audioboo in March 2009 as a simple way of recording audio while on the move and adding as much useful data to it as possible, such as photos, tags and location. We've seen audioboo grow from a small side project in 2009 to a fully-fledged business in 2010 and we're committed to making it the platform of choice for anyone who wants to record, listen or share audio.

NAME	"ABOUT US" DESCRIPTION
Mobango	MOBANGO is the first Universal Mobile Community that allows cell phone users to publish, convert, and share with friends all kinds of user generated content -via the web and mobile devices- for personalizing and empowering the new cell phone's generation. You can publish, convert, and share Personal Content of all types for your cell phone - Videos, Photos, Ringtones, Applications, Games.
Plurk	Noun. plurk (plüer-kh) - A really snazzy site that allows you to showcase the events that make up your life in deliciously digestible chunks. Low in fat, 5 calories per serving, yet chock full of goodness. Verb. plurk (plüer-kh) - To chronicle the events of your always on, action-packed, storybook, semi-charmed kinda life.
Twitter	Twitter is a real-time information network that connects you to the latest information about what you find interesting. Simply find the public streams you find most compelling and follow the conversations.
Wadja	A simple and social way to publish web content, and connect with people who share your interests.

Table 13: List of Microblogging sites

Chinese Microblogging sites include Sina Weibo, Tencent Weibo, Netease Weibo and Sohu Weibo are useful if an airline wishes to reach the massive Chinese consumer market.

Content Communities

Content communities exist for a wide range of media types, including text, photos, videos, and PowerPoint presentations.[44] In general, users are not required to create a personal profile page or, if one is required, only basic information is needed.[44] Kaplan and Haenlein state that, "The main objective of content communities is the sharing of media content between users."[44]

Although businesses run the risk of these platforms being used for the purpose of sharing copyright-protected materials, the advantages of getting one's content into the social media community seriously outweighs the disadvantages of potential copyright infringement.[44] The popularity of these content communities make them a very attractive contact channel for many businesses. This fact isn't surprising when one considers that a site such as YouTube has over 2 billion views per day.[44]

According to its website, YouTube was founded in February 2005 and it "allows billions of people to discover, watch and share originally-created videos. YouTube provides a forum for people to connect, inform, and inspire others across the globe and acts as a distribution platform for original content creators and advertisers large and small."[237]

On 23rd April 2005, the very first video uploaded to YouTube was a video called "Me at the Zoo". Today, 72 hours of video are uploaded to YouTube every minute and *YouTube receives more than 2 billion views per day. YouTube allows users to create accounts, upload videos, "Like" or "Dislike" videos, leave comments on a video and create channels, among other things. Some other facts from the YouTube.com press centre include:*[238]

- More than 1 billion unique users visit YouTube each month.
- Over 6 billion hours of video are watched each month on YouTube.
- 80% of YouTube traffic comes from outside the US.
- YouTube is localized in 61 countries and across 61 different languages.
- According to Nielsen, YouTube reaches more US adults ages 18-34 than any cable network.
- Created in 2007, the YouTube Partner Program has more than a million partners from 30 countries around the world.
- Thousands of advertisers are using TrueView in-stream and 75% of those in-stream ads are now skippable.
- YouTube has more than a million advertisers using Google ad platforms, the majority of which are small businesses.
- YouTube's Content ID scans over 400 years' worth of video every day for any sign of copyright infringement.
- More than 5,000 partners use Content ID, including every major US network broadcaster, movie studio and record label.
- YouTube has more than 25 million reference files in its Content ID database; it's among the most comprehensive in the world.

According to its website, "SlideShare began with a simple goal: To share knowledge online. Since then, SlideShare has grown to become the world's largest community for sharing presentations and other professional content."[239] In Q4 of 2013, SlideShare averaged 60 million unique visitors a month and 215 million-page views and it is among the top 120 most-visited websites in the world.[239]

According to Wikipedia, "SlideShare is a Web 2.0 based slide hosting service. Users can upload files privately or publicly in the following file formats: PowerPoint, PDF, Keynote or OpenDocument presentations. Slide decks can then be viewed on the site itself, on hand held devices or embedded on other sites."[240]

Two of the most important things to know about SlideShare is its ability to affect the Google search engine rankings. I have been pleasantly surprised to see my SlideShare slideshows about subjects such as "predictive analytics in the gaming industry" consistently show up in the Google top ten rankings for that subject. SlideShare is also a powerful lead generator as well.

Instagram

Instagram is an online photo-sharing and social networking service that allows users to take a picture, apply a digital filter to it, and share it on various social networking sites. Unlike most other mobile device cameras, Instagram confines photos to a square shape, like a Kodak Instamatic and a Polaroid image; the old is new again. The service was launched in October 2010 and it was distributed through the App store and Google Play.

In April 2012, Facebook bought Instagram in a deal worth approximately $1 billion in cash.[241] It was the company's largest deal up to that point. As Kathleen Chaykowski explains in her Forbes article *Instagram, the $50 Billion Grand Slam Driving Facebook's Future: The Forbes Cover Story*[242]:

> "When Zuckerberg decided to shell out nearly $1 billion in 2012 to buy the photo-sharing app, which had just 30 million users, it was widely seen as a sign of a new Silicon Valley bubble. But he appears to have outsmarted everyone once again. In the four years since the purchase, Instagram has become one of the fastest-growing platforms of all time, with about as many users as Twitter (310 million), Snapchat (100-million-plus) and Pinterest (100 million) combined."

Besides the fact that Instagram is quite profitable ($630 million in sales in 2015), Instagram's true potential lies in its ability to reach a young demographic.[242] "Ask anyone under 18 (a cohort who view Facebook as their parents' social network): Instagram is that next platform," claims Chaykowski.[242]

"The combination of this visual opportunity to tell your story as a person, a marketer and a business, combined with the ability to target the audience, has been very powerful," says Facebook COO Sheryl Sandberg.[242]

Instagram's strength is its ability to cater to the hyper specific passions and obsessions of a varying range of interest groups.[242] "Users have rallied around visual hubs dedicated to Korean light shows, artisanal cheese shops, skateboarding tricks (Tony Hawk is an active user), break dancing and extreme body painting. Every day users spend more than 21 minutes on average in the app and collectively upload more than 95 million photos and videos," explains Chaykowski.[242]

"That sticky engagement is reshaping entire industries," notes Chaykowski.[242] "Look no further than fashion. Last year designer Misha Nonoo, whose modern women's clothing has been worn by Emma Watson and Gwyneth Paltrow, ditched the runways of New York Fashion Week and launched her spring 2016 collection with Aldo Shoes exclusively on Instagram," she states.[242]

"Nonoo is hardly alone among fashionistas. This year Tommy Hilfiger created an 'InstaPit,' which gave influential Instagrammers prime seating at his show, so they could capture the best shots and share them with their followers," notes Chaykowski.[242]

At this year's *Met Ball* Vogue's Anna Wintour, who has become pals with Instagram CEO Kevin Systrom, "hosted an exclusive Instagram video studio, where A-list celebrities like Madonna and Blake Lively posed for photos and clips on the app."[242] All-In-all, the synergy between the fashion world and Instagram "generated 283 million engagements—likes and comments—across 42 million accounts during four weeks of shows early this spring in New York, London, Milan and Paris," says Chaykowski.[242]

Fashion isn't the only industry Instagram can help.[242] "Brands ranging from fast food to big banks advertise on Instagram to take advantage of the site's unique features," notes Chaykowsit.[242] "At this year's Coachella, Sonic Drive-In made special square-shaped milk shakes for a single-day Instagram campaign. A 'Shop Now' button on the ads let people place an order, which Sonic delivered on the spot. More than three-quarters of festivalgoers who clicked on the 'Shop Now' button purchased a shake," explains Chaykowski.[242]

As of late 2016, more than 200,000 companies were advertising on Instagram, up from just hundreds the year before.[242] Chaykowski notes that, "A Nielsen study of more than 700 campaigns found that for 98% of them ad recall from sponsored posts on Instagram was 2.8 times higher than average for online advertising."[242]

Because it is owned by Facebook, Instagram gets access to Facebook's sales operation, including the more than three million advertisers, ad tech, relevance algorithms, spam-fighting tools and, perhaps most importantly, unparalleled user data (on interests, gender, location, occupation and more).[242] "For marketers, extending Facebook ad campaigns to Instagram is seamless—98 of the top 100 spenders on Facebook are on Instagram, too," Chaykowski notes.[242]

Instagram has now ventured beyond photo ads, "debuting video and carousel ads, opening its ad platform widely across more than 200 countries and lengthening video ads to 60 seconds."[242] According to Pinterest, "Promoted Pins are just like regular Pins—the only difference is that a business paid to have more people see it. These Pins will always be labeled 'Promoted' so they're easy to spot."[243] Pinners save Promoted Pins to their boards of wish lists, inspirations and interests—just like other Pins they discover.[243]

With an impressive 2.4 million Instagram followers, Emirates likes to use themes on Instagram, where they "have taken one of the key 'best practice' aspects and made it a mainstay of their Instagram presence."[232] Basically, they take a lot of photos and do what every business should be doing on Instagram and they upload the photos around the theme of where they fly.[232] The page is filled with people holding up an Emirates flag in different locations. Other photos contain gorgeous scenes that transport the viewer into a dream holiday they might want to have in one of Emirates far flung destinations.[232]

The brilliance is in its simplicity and it is incredibly effective, too.[232] Immediate engagement doesn't really matter because this content is long term and evergreen, how different is the Eiffel Tower in 2010 than it will be in 2020?[232] Anyone visiting this page can't help but be charmed by the themed aspect, and it certainly connects with viewers on an emotional level.[232]

Etihad Airways tries to take audience interaction to a whole new level.[232] On Twitter, Etihad have taken a light-hearted approach.[232] "They show that they genuinely care about their customer base having fun, getting caught up in the buzz of the airline and, crucially, clear audience interaction," Ashraf contends.[232] On its Twitter feed, Etihad answer questions, asks users to guess locations, and tries to engage in conversation with its followers.

For All Nippon Airways, being quirky on Instagram is paying off.[232] According to Ashraf, "All Nippon have created an Instagram account that most companies would be glad to have. It is full of pictures that are, well, slightly more unusual than others. Making sure that the Instagram account has 'different and unusual' as its theme has stood them in good stead. While they may not have the biggest engagement every time, they have a healthy follower base, and a clear focus on delivering high quality, striking imagery."[232]

List of Content Community Sites

As the Content Community landscape changes on a daily basis, it is impossible to list all of the available Websites, but these are some of the most common and popular platforms I have found:

NAME	"ABOUT US" DESCRIPTION
23h	Keep all your photos in one safe place. With 23 you can organise the photos, share them with anyone you want, and you can even order real prints of your digital photos.
Academia	Academia is a platform for academics to share research papers. The company's mission is to accelerate the world's research.
BabyCenter	BabyCenter is the voice of the 21st Century Mom® and modern motherhood. Now the Web's #1 global interactive parenting network, it has nurtured more than 100 million parents since its launch in 1997.
Bambuser	Bambuser lets you broadcast live and interactive video from your mobile phone, webcam or DV-camera — and it's free! Alert people when you go live; Shoot with almost no delay & chat with your viewers while broadcasting.
Blinkx	blinkx is the world's largest and most advanced video search engine. Now, with an index of over 35 million hours of searchable video and more than 720 media partnerships, including national broadcasters, commercial media giants, and private video libraries, it has cemented its position as the premier destination for online TV.
Blogtv	blogTV is a leading live, interactive, internet broadcasting platform that enables anyone with an internet connection and a camera to connect to their audience in an evocative, direct way.

NAME	"ABOUT US" DESCRIPTION
Brickfish	Founded in 2005, Brickfish® is based on the idea that peer to peer interactions around a brand's product and services have great value and relevance to consumers and brands alike. The Brickfish platform allows brands and agencies to launch engagement based social media programs.
Brightcove	Brightcove Inc, the cloud content services company, provides a family of products used to publish and distribute the world's professional digital media.
Bukisa	BUKISA is a one stop shop for how-to, informational & educational content. We are both an aggregator and a UGC website. We provide content in the form of articles, videos, presentations, audio recordings and image slideshows.
Clipmoon	Your online video sharing community portal. Watch, upload and share videos. Get unlimited video hosting space. It is easy, funny and free.
Clipsyndicate	Publish broadcast quality news on your web site.
Coull	Coull is the market-leading Video Performance Network. The company's platform is aimed at the video advertising market where it drives revenue generation, firstly, through capturing the attention of the customer, and secondly via product pull through.
Dailymotion	Dailymotion is about finding new ways to see, share and engage your world through the power of online video. You can find - or upload - videos about your interests and hobbies, eyewitness accounts of recent news and distant places, and everything else from the strange to the spectacular.
Dropshots	DropShots, Inc. was born from a passionate mission: To improve the interaction and strengthen the emotional connection between friends and family through the use of advanced technologies. DropShots is accomplishing this mission by becoming the leading subscription-based service for family and friends to connect, converse and share their life experiences captured on photo and video.
Flickr	Flickr - almost certainly the best online photo management and sharing application in the world - has two main goals: 1. We want to help people make their photos available to the people who matter to them; 2. We want to enable new ways of organizing photos and video.
Filmnet	Founded in May 2009 and officially launched on October 22nd, 2009, FilmNet is a social community based around video content. We bring together filmmakers and viewers through a rich content library, advanced social networking tools and an in-depth database with information about film industry professionals and web-based movie-making.
Fotki	The organic, fat-free photo and video sharing site, which uses steroids only on its technology, delivers state of the art yummy photo products and prints, and grows healthy professional photographers' business without cruelty to eyes, wallets and customers.
Fotolog	Fotolog is the world's leading photo-blogging site, one of the world's largest social networking sites and a global cultural phenomenon. More than 22 million members in over 200 countries use Fotolog as a simple and fun way to express themselves through online photo diaries or photo blogs.

NAME	"ABOUT US" DESCRIPTION
Howcast	Howcast empowers people with engaging, useful how-to information wherever, whenever they need to know how. Known for high-quality content, Howcast streams tens of millions of videos every month across its multi-platform distribution network.
Instructables	Instructables is a web-based documentation platform where passionate people share what they do and how they do it and learn from and collaborate with others. The seeds of Instructables germinated at the MIT Media Lab as the future founders of Squid Labs built places to share their projects and help others.
Issuu	Issuu is the world's fastest growing digital publishing platform. Millions of avid readers come to Issuu every day to read free publications, created by enthusiastic publishers from all over the globe.
LiveLeak	LiveLeak is a video sharing website that lets users post and share videos. Liveleak places emphasis on current events, politics and reality-based footage such as war scenes from various parts of the world.
Livestream	Livestream is the leading live video destination and platform. Event organizers, content owners, celebrities and artists around the world use Livestream's social broadcasting tools to engage and grow their audiences on the web, mobile devices, and connected TVs.
Metacafe	Metacafe is a video entertainment site that focuses on: **Short-form** - Metacafe specializes in short-form original video - content that is made for the interactive Internet medium. **Entertainment** - We're all about entertaining a large audience by featuring only those videos that amaze, inspire and make viewers laugh. **Community Auditions** - A community review panel of more than 80,000 volunteers takes a first look at each of the thousands of videos submitted to the site every day.
Netvibes	Founded in 2005, Netvibes pioneered the first personalized dashboard publishing platform for the Web. For consumers, Netvibes.com is the most awarded start page where millions of people around the world personalize and publish all aspects of their daily digital lives. For agencies and publishers, Netvibes' universal widget technology (UWA), widget distribution services and Premium Dashboards help rapidly deliver brand observation rooms and user-personalized marketing campaigns. For companies, Netvibes Enterprise delivers secure, scalable personalized workspaces, portals and industry dashboards.
Oovoo	ooVoo offers the ability to video chat face-to-face with family and friends, anytime and anywhere. With ooVoo you can have free video chats one-to-one or have a group video chat with up to 6 people at once!
Ourmedia	Welcome to Ourmedia, a community of individuals dedicated to spreading grassroots creativity: videos, podcasts and other works of personal media. Have a creative streak? This is a place where you can discuss home-brew media, store your stuff for safekeeping and show off your works to a global audience.

NAME	"ABOUT US" DESCRIPTION
Pbase	PBase was conceived in July of 1999 after observing countless camera wielding people that take cool photos but find it difficult to share their work. The primary mission of PBase is to be the best place on the web to display photos.
Photobucket	Photobucket is the premier destination for uploading, downloading, sharing, linking and finding photos, videos and graphics. Host all your images and videos for free, then share them by email or on social sites like Facebook, Twitter and MySpace.
Photopeach	Our idea is to help you tell better stories online using photos. With PhotoPeach you can create a rich slideshow in seconds to engage your friends or family. We also support background music, captions, and comments so you can elaborate on your story further.
Photoshow	Share your family's favorite stories with friends and relatives. They'll feel like they were there! Roxio PhotoShow makes it simple to combine your favorite photos and video clips from birthdays, vacations, or any other occasion with fun stickers, animations, effects, and music to create one-of-a-kind online PhotoShows they're sure to love.
Picasa.google	Picasa is free photo editing software from Google that makes your pictures look great. Sharing your best photos with friends and family is as easy as pressing a button!
Picturepush	PicturePush is a photo and video hosting service. It is built on the philosophy that you can upload everything you have in the highest quality possible and worry about what to show to whom later.
Picturetrail	PictureTrail, Inc. operates a leading photo sharing social network and widget destination. Members and visitors share photos online, host images, order prints and utilize most other options available through the top photo sharing sites.
Podomatic	PodOmatic podcast portal: Create, Find, Share Podcasts!
Prezi	Prezi is the presentation software that uses motion, zoom, and spatial relationships to bring your ideas to life and make you a great presenter.
Revision3	Revision3 has emerged as the leading special interest video network, and has attracted top Internet video talent, advertisers and distribution partners.
Skyrock	A community with blogging as well as sharing of music, videos and more
SlideShare	SlideShare is the world's largest community for sharing presentations. With 50 million monthly visitors and 90 million pageviews, it is amongst the most visited 250 websites in the world. Besides presentations, SlideShare also supports documents, PDFs, videos and webinars.
Scribd	Scribd is the world's largest digital library, where readers can discover books and written works on the Web or any mobile device and publishers and authors can find a voracious audience for their work. Launched in March of 2007 and based in San Francisco, California, more than 40 million books and documents have been contributed to Scribd by the community. Scribd content reaches and audience of 80 million people around the world every month.

NAME	"ABOUT US" DESCRIPTION
Tinychat	Tinychat is a dead-simple, live video communication platform. By providing dead simple, free to use, video chat rooms that just work!
Ustream.tv	Ustream is the leading live interactive broadcast platform. Anyone with an internet connection and a camera can start engaging with their family, friends or fans anytime, anywhere.
Videojug	Videojug is a next-generation digital media company that helps people to 'get good at life', wherever they are. Our aim is to be a world-leading factual and learning resource for the 100s of millions of global internet users hungry for knowledge on how to perform a million large and little life tasks, as well as practical and valuable information on any subject under the sun.
Vidque	Vidque is a free curation platform designed to help discover, filter and archive online video content. Controlled and curated by its users, Vidque aims to simplify the discovery of quality video content through the joint effort of the online community.
Vimeo	From the beginning, Vimeo was created by filmmakers and video creators who wanted to share their creative work, along with intimate personal moments of their everyday life. As time went on, like-minded people came to the site and built a community of positive, encouraging individuals with a wide range of video interests.
Youtube	Founded in February 2005, YouTube allows billions of people to discover, watch and share originally-created videos. YouTube provides a forum for people to connect, inform, and inspire others across the globe and acts as a distribution platform for original content creators and advertisers large and small.

Table 14: List of Content Community sites

Chinese content communities include Todou, Ku6, Sohu, Sina and Qiyi.

Social Networks

Perhaps the most familiar of all social media sites are the social networks, including platforms such as Facebook, WeChat, Foursquare, Google+, and LinkedIn, amongst hundreds of others. According to Wikipedia, "a social network is a social structure made up of individuals (or organizations) called 'nodes', which are tied (connected) by one or more specific types of interdependency, such as friendship, kinship, common interest, financial exchange, dislike, sexual relationships, or relationships of beliefs, knowledge or prestige."[244]

Boyd and Ellison define social network sites (SNS) as: "web-based services that allow individuals to (1) construct a public or semi-public profile within a bounded system, (2) articulate a list of other users with whom they share a connection, and (3) view and traverse their list of connections and those made by others within the system. The nature and nomenclature of these connections may vary from site to site."[245]

What makes a social network site unique is its "ability to enable users to articulate and make visible their social networks,"[245] which can result in connections between individuals that would otherwise not have been made.[245] These are the connections that make the Reed Network such a powerful marketing force.

Social networks can also be important platforms for airlines. In their paper *Expanding Opportunities in a Shrinking World*[246], Avimanyu Datta and Len Jessup state that "Social networks promote social entrepreneurship by means of (a) technology and knowledge transfer; (b) locating information; (c) generating entrepreneurial opportunities; (d) building entrepreneurial competency; (e) financing innovation; and (f) building effective networks for commercialization of innovations.

In her article *The Evolution of Social Media Marketing*[247], Reinaldo Calcaño states that, "Snapchat is the new kid on the block, and its user base is growing by the second." One of the reasons is its ephemeral nature: Snaps disappear forever after a while." "This newly found layer of privacy has made the app a candid, more relaxed medium to share experiences,"[247] argues Calcaño, adding that, "When consumers feel protected by a level of privacy they can feel and trust, they spend more time being themselves."[247]

Another recent addition to the social networking landscape is Snapchat. It was one of the runaway success stories of 2012.[248] Users send about 50 million pics (called "Snaps") a day on the platform. Bearing truth to the statement that copying is the highest form of flattery, the success of Snapchat prompted Facebook to release a competitor, Poke, although it met with limited success and has since been shut down.[248]

Facebook

Unlike most other SNSs, Facebook was initially built to only support distinct college networks.[245] At first, a user had to have a harvard.edu email address to join the site. As Facebook rolled out to other universities, it kept its sense of exclusivity by requiring new users to also have university email addresses.[245]

Beginning in September 2005, "Facebook expanded to include high school students, professionals inside corporate networks, and, eventually, everyone."[245] Another unique feature of Facebook was "the ability for outside developers to build 'Applications' which allow users to personalize their profiles and perform other tasks, such as compare movie preferences and chart travel histories."[245] From these humble beginnings, Facebook has grown to perhaps the most recognizable social media site in the world outside of China.

Facebook claims there are four steps to business success on Facebook, including building an audience, connecting with people, engaging an audience and influencing them through their friends and family members.

Facebook is also the perfect place for businesses to manage their brands and reputations, to understand their customers, to recruit talent, and to promote events as well as to network and build relationships. I will delve further into how Facebook and other social media sites can be used to promote businesses in chapter six. I will also explain how Facebook advertising works and how such target-specific advertising can be extremely beneficial to businesses.

In his article *Three brands still killing it on Facebook*[249], Mark Traphagen explains Jetblue's Facebook strategy. Jetblue is the sixth-largest US airline and it has consistently been named as one of the best airlines by numerous publications and consumer polls.[249]

"JetBlue's initial success came through inventing a unique niche: low fares, yet with certain amenities (e.g., extra leg room, free in-flight TV) never before offered in their market segment," explains Traphagen.[249] "They also worked hard, both in their marketing and through their actual customer experiences, to build an image as consumer-friendly and fun," Traphagen adds.[249]

Social media is an important channel for JetBlue and it is often on the cutting edge of social technology, fearless in its use of new interesting channels and networks. "The company is known for quick responses to customer inquiries on social networks, especially Twitter. JetBlue social media agents will even engage in light chit-chat with people mentioning them or using one of their branded hashtags," notes Traphagen.[249] These interactions have added a positive personality to the brand, while unquestionably contributing "to successes like JetBlue's being named as the top airline for customer loyalty in 2016 by BrandKeys."[249]

On 21st August 2017, the day of a full solar eclipse in the US, "JetBlue's marketing and social media teams created a Facebook Live video event featuring actor Skylar Astin, famous for his roles in the film 'Pitch Perfect' and its sequel. The video post earned 49,000 views, 863 reactions, 439 comments and 80 shares."[249] The share metric was probably undercounted because it "does not include the many hundreds of viewers who 'shared' the video by tagging their friends in the comments."[249]

"While not as dramatic in its metrics as the two previous examples, this is still significant engagement for a brand on Facebook and a great example of the usefulness of Facebook Live for brands," contends Traphagen.[249]

The live video opens with a view from the roof of JetBlue's corporate headquarters in New York, looking toward the east, in the general direction of the sun.[249] Traphagen writes that, "Drawn in by the tease of Skylar Astin's name in the post, and perhaps also out of curiosity over the strange billing of a 'No Blackout Non-Eclipse Non-Event,' viewers quickly tuned in by the hundreds, and then thousands, as early viewers tagged their friends to come watch the non-event."[249] Just to sweeten the pot, JetBlue added a call-to-action incentive, "promising to give away 100,000 TrueBlue points to someone who clicked 'Going' on the calendar entry for the live event."[249]

For ten full minutes, nothing happened, the feed simply contained the same static view of the sky above a rooftop.[249] What appeared to be "a social media faux pas—over 10 minutes of 'dead air'—was really just part of JetBlue's genius and their characteristic quirky sense of humor," explains Traphagen.[249] "With all of the hype building up to this solar eclipse, the JetBlue team knew there were many speculating that it would be a 'non-event,' i.e., that it would prove to be not as spectacular as the hype promised" argues Traphagen.[249] "So JetBlue intentionally—and rather cleverly—"created what appeared to be their own "non-event," teasing the appearance of a celebrity, but then seemingly having him not show up," notes Traphagen.[249]

However, JetBlue's reputation probably proceeded it and soon the gamble paid off, "as many thousands continued to tune in to the videocast, and commenters speculated wildly on what was going on. Would Skylar show up? Had JetBlue blown it? Were they pulling our collective legs?"[249]

"Finally, after more than 10 minutes, Skylar Astin popped into view, but only to further tease the audience, asking them to invite more of their friends to the video, because he would be sharing an important announcement soon," explains Traphagen.[249] "And then just the sky again," Traphagen states, adding, "A few minutes later, Skylar reappears, carrying in a large cooler... and then disappears again. By this time, the audience chatter is at a fever pitch. What in the world is going on here? Viewers accelerate their invitations to friends, telling them they've got to come see this."[249]

"When Skylar comes back, he explains to the audience (with obvious sarcastic humor) that he doesn't believe there actually will be a solar eclipse. The reason? He found out that JetBlue doesn't believe in blackout days for using their TrueBlue loyalty points, so he doesn't believe this day will be a 'blackout' either," says Traphagen.[249] As Traphagen explains, "In the airline industry, blackouts are flights for which customers cannot use their loyalty points. One of JetBlue's points of distinction is that they have no blackout restrictions."[249]

All-in-all, this was a brilliant way for JetBlue to differentiate it from its competitors, using an extremely rare event that verbally references their policy, after a solar eclipse is a blackout, in one sense.[249] As Traphagen explains, "JetBlue's 'No Blackout Non-Eclipse Non-Event' has just about every element you could want in a brand live video event."[249] Jetblue makes "use of a celebrity influencer obviously popular with the audience they attracted. But they don't just use him for his name value or his pretty face. Instead, they make him part of the prank and the inside joke shared by the audience."[249]

Just as importantly, the event overlapped with "something the brand's audience is already excited about: a major solar eclipse. This is newsjacking in real time to the extreme."[249] "The event itself is perfectly in keeping with the brand's playful and engaging character," argues Traphagen.[249] It feels organic to the brand and the JetBlue audience.[249] The video kept viewers engaged by its storytelling aspect, i.e., doing the unexpected, while building curiosity and suspense.[249] "This is exactly the kind of live video that almost guarantees users will comment, engage and keep viewing," notes Traphagen.[249]

"The design and execution of this event show that JetBlue's social media team really understands their company's personality and image, as well as why their customers like the brand so much and remain so loyal," says Traphagen.

"The tie-in with the brand is in the clever connection of JetBlue's no-blackout policy with the most famous 'blackout' in years, a solar eclipse across the heart of the US," explains Traphagen.[249] JetBlue takes it further by playing on the rampant pre-eclipse cynicism that the astronomical show would end up a non-event.[249] "So working with their influencer, they create a live 'non-event' event. The brand connection? Blackout flights are a non-event for JetBlue." [249] All-in-all, this is quite a clever message to create and pull off.

Mark Traphagen concludes the article with seven recommendations for businesses that want to increase their branding on Facebook. They are:

1. Appeal to emotions.
2. Tell a story.
3. Be active in the comments.
4. When possible, take a stand.
5. Make your audience the heroes.
6. Be surprising.
7. Be brand-relevant.

WeChat

WeChat is a Chinese mobile text and voice messaging communication service developed by Tencent. It was first released in January 2011. According to Wikipedia[250]:

> "WeChat provides multimedia communication with text messaging, hold-to-talk voice messaging, broadcast (one-to-many) messaging, photo/video sharing, location sharing, and contact information exchange. WeChat supports social networking via shared streaming content feeds and location-based social plug-ins ('Shake', 'Look Around', and 'Drift Bottle') to chat with and connect with local and international WeChat users."

WeChat is a communication platform made up of what WeChat has dubbed "The 4 Pillars"—Instant Messaging, Location Based Services, Moments and Official

Accounts.[251]

The "Instant Messaging" section is straightforward, it allows users to message other users via text, which has become many people's communication channel of choice these days, especially in China.[251] The viral marketing potential here should be obvious.

"Location Based Services" is the section that allows the user to find information that is relevant to the area they are in,[251] a good channel for airlines to disseminate information through. Beyond just finding the nearest ATM, the Radar feature launched in March 2014 allows users to find friends around them without revealing their cell phone number.[251]

In the "Moments" section, users can post pics, comments and "Like" or share their pictures or videos with the general public or simply share them with a select few.[251] Small business owners often use this feature to showcase their products to their contacts, so it can have alternative, i.e., commercial, uses. Airlines can use this like they currently use Facebook and Instagram.

The "Official Accounts" section is where large brands usually come in. WeChat has the ability to integrate into a company's CRM system so that content from the company can be posted across all its channels.[251] Official accounts allow companies to send out blanket messages to multiple users, but then it also enables individual and private conversations, too.[251] "This means that WeChat can be used to resolve issues in a private forum unlike other platforms such as Twitter."[251]

In terms of both functionality and user activity, WeChat has gone through the following three distinct phases of growth:

1. Replacement of SMS with a basic—and free—messaging function that was similar to WhatsApp.[252]
2. The addition of a social networking function through its "moments" section, where users can send status updates with pictures and short snippets of text.[252] Similar to Facebook's *News Feed*, this allows users to create a diary of personal memes. "It was an important addition because it also introduced to WeChat a more public, visible social media channel where updates can be openly shared and viewed by a wide group of connections."[252]
3. E-commerce—users can link their consumer bank cards, credit cards, and Tenpay and WePay accounts to their WeChat accounts. "The linking of these payment options allows WeChat to be a totally enclosed ecosystem where social can be linked seamlessly with sales. A user inside of WeChat never has to leave the app on their mobile phone"[252] to make a purchase.

Brands have taken advantage of WeChat's "public accounts" to create awareness and spread messages virally by teaming up with influencers, celebrities, and key opinion leaders.[252] Airlines could use these channels to sell goods through. "While WeChat's social functions are not as open as Weibo's and the structure makes it harder to create massive followings, features like 'look around' (people can add each other based on proximity), 'Shake' and 'Message Bottle' (for random connections), and 'QR Codes' (a path to the user's account from wherever they share the code) have all helped to create more growth in the number of connections."[252]

There are four e-commerce avenues inside of WeChat that brands can also exploit; subscription accounts; online-to-offline sales channels; WeChat shops; and affiliate sales.

With "Subscription Accounts", brands can create content and present new products and offers to followers. This content can be linked to an e-commerce store built inside or outside the WeChat application.[252] A "Subscription Account" is simple to build by using the tools provided by WeChat's Fengling.me service.[252] The only catch is that you have to have a company registered in China, which is, admittedly, not an easy hurdle to overcome for non-Chinese companies.[252] For companies without a China registered office, there are other ways to access the market, but they don't allow for the same control over presentation and process.[252]

As a mobile application with the GPS features of a smartphone, WeChat allows some promising location-based opportunities for airlines.[252] The app offers location-based messaging for airlines that allow one-to-one marketing to customers. Brands can take advantage of the location-based capabilities of the app by creating a loyalty card and/or by encouraging users at a specific location (a retail shop) to add (follow) the brand account.[252] "The 'Loyalty Card' account inside of WeChat is basically a CRM tool, which audiences can opt-in for and find locations nearby (of retail shops), receive discounts, promotions, points, and rewards."[252]

Today, a whole host of industries are using QR codes and other invitations to encourage customers to sign up for WeChat accounts.[252] "This is typically done on-location, taking customers from offline to online, and thereby collecting contacts within the CRM accounts of the brand. Moving from online to offline, brands are starting to experiment with creating promotions online that drive users to a retail location."[252]

For an airline this could mean sending out a "flash" alert to followers about a promotion taking place "in the next hour" for a free trial or a discount. For a fashion company it could allow them to activate a pop-up shop within a short timeframe for a launch or product demo/trial.[252] Once a user visits the pop-up shop, or on an airline's floor, he or she can pay on location, provided the payments function has been set up on his or her WeChat account.[252] It makes the airline process much more flexible as brands can take pre-payments or set up small sales without cash registers at WeChat shops.[252]

Currently, there are "a growing number of shops, malls, group-buy (TuanGou), and flash-sales (MianGou) channels being built into WeChat."[252] Companies such as Xiaomi, ONLY, and Sephora have created branded stores (as "Service Accounts") where they sell products directly"[252] to their customers. WeChat only allows access to this channel to brands that have "a plan for building awareness (traffic to their store) and to have a logistics/fulfillment capability,"[252] so this might only be an avenue for large airlines.

Most products sold on WeChat are moving through "malls" of one type or another—many of which are controlled by Tencent.[252] "Tencent has done a good job of implementing its most important companies, applications, and investments into WeChat. Grouped together inside the payments section, key WeChat/Tencent owned/invested channels are highlighted, including; 'Specials' (linked to its e-commerce mall yixun.com), Weituangou (linked to its group buy site gaopeng.cn) and Dianping for restaurants."[252]

"Tencent also has accounts for other invested companies, including eLong, JD.com, OKBuy, Tongcheng, and Sougou."[252] There are also "malls" for Dangdang, Amazon, VIP.com, Lefeng, Mougujie, Meilishou, Suning, Guomei, No1Shop, and Qunar, just to name a few.[252] The biggest challenge in selling through these channels is, firstly, gaining enough visibility in a very crowded market and, secondly, managing the presentation of the brand[252]; These are significant challenges, especially the former. To gain significant visibility in these channels, "brands often have to pay hefty fees to the 'malls' to get priority listings. Ultimately, the 'malls' control which products get sold and so there is a real loss of control for brand owners."[252]

The products OKWei currently offers are not great and the process has the potential to become very complicated, very quickly, but affiliate sales network are resilient; the invisible hand of profit is just too seductive a motivator to bet against, I believe. "Despite these hurdles, 'affiliate networks' built inside/around WeChat hold a lot of potential. It is this type of link between social and e-commerce that makes WeChat very powerful for brands, even, potentially, airline operators.[252]

In his article *How international airlines use WeChat to market to China*[253], Roy Graff explains how four different carriers have tapped into WeChat to market to the Chinese traveler. Currently, "WeChat is used by many international airlines, which have official service accounts, for marketing, ticket sales and more," explains Graff.[253]

As Graff explains, "KLM's mobile website is fully integrated into its WeChat account, so users can book a flight, search their flight status or check-in online all through WeChat."[253] "Once a flight is booked, travelers receive reminders on

WeChat when online check-in opens, and can have their boarding pass sent to their WeChat accounts, too, with a QR code to scan at the airport in place of a paper boarding pass."[253] Like many other official airline WeChat accounts, KLM also offers customer service through the app's chat interface.[253]

In 2017, WeChat launched mini-programs—micro apps accessed directly through WeChat—and, as of June 2018, there were 270 million daily active users of mini-programs.[253] "Finnair launched a mini-program in April 2018 where users upload a photo of food, and the mini-program then identifies what kind of food it is (e.g. dessert, noodles) through AI, and plays music to 'pair' with the food."[253] "This all links to an article about Finnair's Chinese in-flight dining options," explains Graff.[253]

The low-cost Singapore airline Scoot uses WeChat for branding. Graff explains that, "Service accounts on WeChat can send out a weekly newsletter with articles to their followers, and airlines' content usually focuses on promotions and sales, as well as practical tips on traveling and destination guides."[253]

"Low-haul low-cost carrier Scoot was one of the most successful international airlines on WeChat in 2017, and the airline used their articles to cultivate a fun, millennial-friendly brand image—appealing to the largest demographic of Chinese outbound tourists," notes Graff.[253] "Scoot also promoted its direct flights from Xi'an to Singapore through a FAM trip to Singapore for young and popular Chinese travel bloggers, which was also featured on WeChat," adds Graff.[253]

"In order to increase brand awareness, follower numbers and interaction with Chinese consumers, Air France launched a competition for Chinese New Year 2018 with an H5 lucky draw landing page on WeChat."[253] "Prizes included airline tickets to France, cosmetics bags and model airplanes, and the campaign encouraged sharing, converting participants into WeChat followers—and thus increasing the number of WeChat users who would be familiar with Air France and exposed to future promotional posts," says Graff.[253] To participate in the lucky draw, "users had to follow and message the Air France WeChat account, and share the campaign with least one friend. The H5 page got thousands of views, and also spurred WeChat fan growth," notes Graff.[253]

Google+

Launched on June 28, 2011, Google+ is a multilingual social networking and identity service owned and operated by Google Inc. As of December 2012, Google+ had over 500 million registered users, 235 million of whom were active on a monthly basis.[254] "Unlike other conventional social networks which are generally accessed through a single website, Google has described Google+ as a 'social layer' consisting of not just a single, but rather an overarching 'layer' which covers many of its online properties."[255]

The most compelling reason to use Google Plus is because it drives brand engagement. In his article *Why Every Marketer Should Use Google+*[256], Nate Elliott explains that when Forrester Research studied more than 3 million user interactions from more than 2,500 brand posts on seven social networks, the results were quite impressive. "Brands' Google Plus posts generated nearly as much engagement per follower as their Facebook posts—and almost twice as much engagement per follower as their Twitter posts."[256] Since users spend far less time on Google+ than on Facebook and Twitter, this is actually quite an impressive statistic.

In her article *The Plus in Google Plus? It's Mostly for Google*[257], Claire Cain Miller refers to Google Plus as a "ghost town," arguing that the platform does not bring much competition to social media giants Facebook and Twitter. However, the article goes on to explain that Google has big plans for Google Plus, seeing it as "a lens that allows the company to peer more broadly into people's digital life, and to gather an ever-richer trove of the personal information that advertisers covet."[257]

Some analysts argue that Google understands more about people's social activity than Facebook does because once a user signs up for Google Plus, it becomes his or her account for all of Google's products, including Gmail, YouTube, and maps.[257] This means Google sees who a user is and what he or she does across its services, even if he or she never returns to the social network again.[257]

"The value of Plus has only increased in the last year, as search advertising, Google's main source of profits, has slowed. At the same time, advertising based on the kind of information gleaned from what people talk about, do and share online, rather than simply what they search for, has become more important."[257]

"The database of affinity could be the holy grail for more effective brand advertising," said Nate Elliott, an analyst at Forrester studying social media and marketing.[257]

"Google says the information it gains about people through Google Plus helps it create better products—like sending traffic updates to cellphones or knowing whether a search for 'Hillary' refers to a family member or to the former secretary of state—as well as better ads."[257]

Thanks to Google Plus, Google has an enormous amount of highly valuable data on its users. This data includes such things as "people's friendships on Gmail, the places they go on maps and how they spend their time on the more than two million websites in Google's ad network."[257] Google "is gathering this information even though relatively few people use Plus as their social network. Plus has 29 million unique monthly users on its website and 41 million on smartphones, with some users overlapping, compared with Facebook's 128 million users on its website and 108 million on phones, according to Nielsen."[257]

Google is also pushing brands to "join Plus, offering them a powerful incentive in exchange—prime placement on the right-hand side of search results, with photos and promotional posts."[257] This does present a very good opportunity for brands to get in on the ground floor and get prime advertising placement.

"It is literally promotion that money can't buy," Mr. Elliott said.[257] "It is something that Google could make billions off of if they sell that space tomorrow, and they're giving it away to try to get people onto the social platform."[257]

Building and constantly updating your business's Google Plus page can lead to improved local search capability. Pages that do well on Google Plus receive a higher index on Google search. YouTube should be factored into an airline's social media plans as videos do seem to positively affect rankings in many cases. Google Plus content can also show up in search results at times when a company's website might not. Comments on content are also going to increase rankings as Google ranking algorithm factors those in too, and comments on Google+ content probably gets an extra boost.

It would be foolish to ignore the growing importance of Google+ to the airline industry, and, to be frank, many airlines are utilizing the platform already, but, since airlines now have the opportunity to get in on the ground floor of this new search service, it should be an important part of any social media marketing plan.

List of Social Network Sites

As the Social Network landscape changes on a daily basis, it is impossible to list all of the social network Websites available, but these are the most common and popular platforms in use today:

NAME	"ABOUT US" DESCRIPTION
43things	43 Things is the world's largest goal-setting community. Join over 3 million people who list their goals, share their progress, and cheer each other on.
Anobii	aNobii is an online reading community built by readers for readers allowing you to shelve, find and share books. Our mission is to bring book lovers together and encourage reading. Use the aNobii website and Apps to find your next read and tell your friends about it.
Badoo	Badoo is already the world's largest and fastest growing social network for meeting new people as proven by the millions who have joined and the hundreds of thousands who sign up daily.
Bebo	Bebo is a popular social networking site which connects you to everyone and everything you care about. Bebo combines community, self-expression and entertainment, enabling you to consume, create, discover, curate and share digital content in entirely new ways.
Blackplanet	The largest Black community online for a reason. We have music, jobs, forums, chat, photos, dating personals and groups all targeted to the specific interests

NAME	"ABOUT US" DESCRIPTION
	of the black community.
Buzznet	Find online communities featuring emo, pop, punk, rock and screamo bands. View thousands of pictures, music videos and connect with fans.
CafeMom	CafeMom is the #1 site on the internet for moms and the premier strategic marketing partner to brands that want to reach moms in a rapidly changing digital environment.
Crunchyroll	Crunchyroll is an online video service and community that offers full-length episodes and movies of the very best in Japanese anime and Asian entertainment. Crunchyroll's content is provided by Asian media leaders including TV TOKYO, Shueisha, Fuji Creative Corporation, Pony Canyon, Yomiuri Telecasting Corporation, Toei Animation, Gonzo, Munhwa Broadcasting of America, and many others.
Dailyburn	Share your training with friends and stay motivated. Find training partners, local events, routes, and groups. Social training for runners, triathletes, and cyclists.
Dailystrength	DailyStrength was created by internet veterans with more than 20 years of experience conceiving, building, and running the largest communities on the web, including Yahoo Mail, Yahoo Photos, Yahoo Personals, Yahoo Groups, GeoCities, Facebook, My Yahoo, Yahoo Message Boards and more.
Faceparty	Faceparty is a UK-based social networking site allowing users to create online profiles and interact with each other using forums and messaging facilities similar to email.
Flixster	Flixster is a social movie site allowing users to share movie ratings, discover new movies and meet others with similar movie taste.
Foursquare	Foursquare is a location-based mobile platform that makes cities easier to use and more interesting to explore. By "checking in" via a smartphone app or SMS, users share their location with friends while collecting points and virtual badges.
Goodreads	Goodreads is the largest social network for readers in the world. We have more than 5,100,000 members who have added more than 160,000,000 books to their shelves.
Google+	Google+ is a multilingual social networking and identity service owned and operated by Google Inc. It was launched on June 28, 2011. Unlike other conventional social networks which are generally accessed through a single website Google+ as a "social layer" consisting of not just a single site, but rather an overarching "layer" which covers many of its online properties.
hi5networks	Social gaming and entertainment for the worldwide market. hi5 is the world's leading social play network, focused on delivering a fun, interactive and immersive experience online to audiences around the world.
Kiwibox	Kiwibox.com is a social networking destination and online magazine for young adults, with over half a million members. Kiwibox is a social network with user profile pages, forums, blogs, and an online magazine.

NAME	"ABOUT US" DESCRIPTION
LinkedIn	LinkedIn operates the world's largest professional network on the Internet with more than 100 million members in over 200 countries and territories.
MySpace	Aimed at a Gen Y audience, Myspace drives social interaction by providing a highly personalised experience around entertainment and connecting people to the music, celebrities, TV, movies, and games that they love.
Mywebprofile	Create your free profile page and stay in touch with your friends all over the world
Nexopia	With over 1.2 million members, and hundreds of new accounts created every day, Nexopia is quickly solidifying its reputation as the online place for teens to connect and express themselves.
Pinterest	Pinterest is a Virtual Pinboard. Pinterest lets you organize and share all the beautiful things you find on the web. People use pinboards to plan their weddings, decorate their homes, and organize their favorite recipes. Best of all, you can browse pinboards created by other people. Browsing pinboards is a fun way to discover new things and get inspiration from people who share your interests.
Playlist	Playlist.com is the world's largest music community. We're here to help our 48 million music fans discover, create, organize, enjoy and share their music playlists.
Raptr	Raptr is the best place for gamers to share, interact, and discover personalized content from all over the web. Raptr is also the only platform that integrates all major gaming platforms and IM services.
QQ	QQ Chat is the new Facebook application bringing Tencent's QQ brand and instant messenger to the world's largest social network and the Web. It allows Facebook users to connect and chat with over 780 million monthly active user accounts on Tencent's instant messenger. It's the first Web-based QQ instant messenger in English with built-in live chat translations to Mandarin Chinese, Spanish and Japanese.
Tagged	Other social networks are for staying in touch with people you already know. At Tagged, we make it easy to meet new people through social games, friend suggestions, browsing profiles, group interests and much more.
Travbuddy	TravBuddy is a free site for people who love to explore the world around them. You can use TravBuddy to find travel buddies, record travel experiences in travel blogs, or share travel tips with travel reviews.
Travellerspoint	Travellerspoint is one of the web's largest and most active travel communities with members representing every country in the world. More than 30,000 blogs have shared 175,000 stories to date and over 1.2 million photos have been posted. Our forums and travel helpers answer numerous travel-related questions 365 days of the year.
Travelpod	TravelPod.com was released in 1997 when it was introduced as the web's first site to enable its members to create online travel blogs which revolutionized the way people travel and share their adventures with the world.
Viadeo	Viadeo is a Web 2.0 professional social network with over 50 million members worldwide in 2013, and a membership base that was growing by more than one million per month in 2009.[4] Members include business owners,

NAME	"ABOUT US" DESCRIPTION
	entrepreneurs and managers from a diverse range of enterprises.
WeChat	WeChat is a new and powerful mobile communication tool. It supports sending voice, video, photo and text messages. You can also do group chats, or you can find new friends nearby to talk to. WeChat works on iOS, Android, Windows Phone, Symbian and BlackBerry devices.
Xing	Get in touch with people to generate contacts that stay connected to you for a lifetime. They may well help you in your career by providing contacts, offering jobs, or coming up with ideas. Thanks to XING you can stay in touch with your contacts all the time! On top of that, you can get new contacts, find a job, events, groups, and companies.

Table 15: Social Networking sites

Chinese social networks include RenRen, Kaixin, Qzone, Douban, Pengyou and the Foursquares of China, Jiepang and Qieke, as well as Ushi, a business networking social network similar to LinkedIn.

Virtual Game Worlds

According to Wikipedia, "a virtual world is an online community that takes the form of a computer-based simulated environment through which users can interact with one another and use and create objects."[258] Wikipedia goes on to add that the term is largely synonymous with interactive 3D virtual environments, where users take the form of two-dimensional, or three-dimensional avatars visible and, through them, interact with others.

Kaplan and Haenlein claim that virtual game worlds "are platforms that replicate a three-dimensional environment in which users can appear in the form of personalized avatars and interact with each other as they would in real life. In this sense, virtual worlds are probably the ultimate manifestation of social media, as they provide the highest level of social presence and media richness of all applications discussed thus far."[44]

Girl Gamer eSports Festival

In early September 2017, I was involved with the *Girl Gamer Esports Festival* in Macau[259] and the power of social media marketing through these virtual game worlds became highly apparent. Alibaba Cloud was one of the main sponsors of the event and, early on in the process, the festival organizers decided to give the live stream to any and every channel and/or app that wanted it. The Chinese channels Panda.tv, Youku, Sina, Quanmin, Huya, and Iqiyi, as well as Twitch—the top game streaming platform in the rest of the world—streamed the entire competition live.

Over the course of the two-day competition, there were a total of 12 matches; six for *League of Legends (LOL),* the wildly popular (especially in China) MMOG game; and six for *Counter Strike: Global Offensive (CS: GO),* the first person shooter game that consistently ranks first, second, or third in worldwide popularity. Over the two-day festival, combined viewership exceeded over 200,000 views, most of which came from mainland China. Although *LOL* is huge in China, *CS: GO* viewership inside China was also extremely high.

Figure 16: Screen grab from Quanmin.tv, livestreaming CS:GO Macau Girl Gamer final

In terms of data and analytics, with social media, suddenly everything becomes highly quantifiable. For example, on Quanmin.tv, in one of the early rounds of the *League of Legends* tournament, I watched viewership rise from 5,000 views to 10,000 to 15,000, all the way up to about 24,000 views in about ten minutes as the game ramped up.

This particular game occurred early Sunday afternoon and, even though the other games were spread out over Saturday and Sunday, the viewership remained the same.

Even more impressive were the audience figures for the *CS: GO* final match, which was played between *Team Dignitas* from the US and *Team Expert* from Europe. 21,148 people tuned in for a finals match that started around 12:00 am and ended close to 1:45 am. Figures 17 and 18 show the numbers for the match on both Quanmin.tv and Twitch.

Figure 17: Detail of livestreaming viewer numbers from Quanmin.tv for CS: GO Macau Girl Gamer Festival finals broadcast

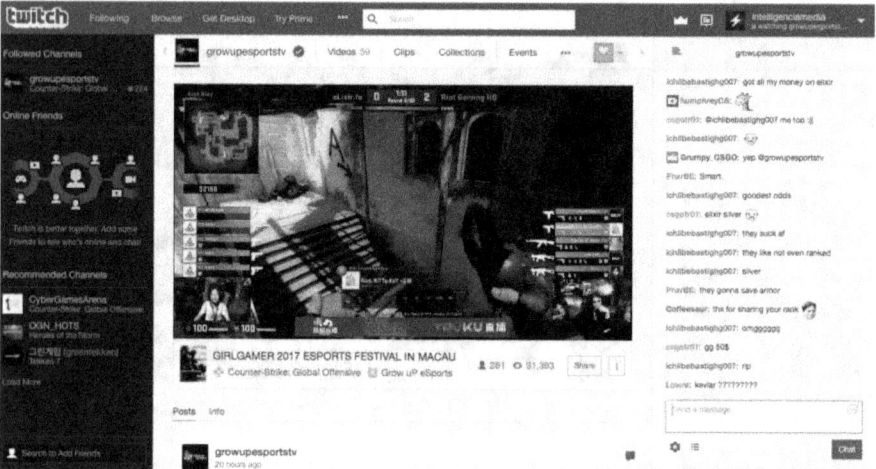

Figure 18: Twitch live stream of CS: GO finals from Girl Gamer Festival

Unfortunately, I was unable to engage with the large Chinese audience because I can't read or write simplified Chinese, but there was plenty of engagement on the English-speaking channel Twitch (see figure 15 (on the right-hand side)). However, whether the audience comes from Asia, Europe, Africa, the Middle East, or North or South America, these live streaming channels can give an airline the ability to connect with users on a one-to-one basis.

So how should airlines market through esports? Well, in this arena, it is no surprise that the Asian airline industry is leading the way. In his esports observer's article *AirAsia Potentially Planning Launch of Esports Team, League, and Center*[260], Graham Ashton writes that, "Malaysian low-cost airline, AirAsia, is looking to take its esports activities to new heights. In an Instagram post, Kamarudin Meranun—chairman of AirAsia and CEO of its parent company, Tune Group—says the company will develop its own team, league, and esports centre."[260]

Although, Taylor does add, that, "With no formal announcement made by the airline yet, it's not clear whether the company is launching own competition series, or simply become a named sponsor for an existing event."[260] However, "AirAsia CEO Tony Fernandes acquired a majority stake in *Mobile Legends* esports organization Team Saiyan, earlier this year. The squad was subsequently rebranded, but this announcement suggests the airline could even be building its own esports team subsidiary," concludes Taylor.[260]

Sponsorship opportunities abound, and this is obviously a great way to reach and young, growing and affluent demographic.

Virtual Social Worlds

For Kaplan and Haenlein, "Virtual social worlds allow inhabitants to choose their behavior more freely and essentially live a virtual life similar to their real life. As in virtual game worlds, virtual social world users appear in the form of avatars and interact in a three-dimensional virtual environment; however, in this realm, there are no rules restricting the range of possible interactions, except for basic physical laws such as gravity."[44]

China's yy.com, whose stock is listed on NASDAQ, has created a very successful business model by catering to a niche audience of online karaoke singers. According to David Goldenberg's article *Virtual Roses and the Rise of yy.com*[261]:

> YY *started in 2005 as a place for hardcore online gamers to communicate while playing games like World of Warcraft. If a group of players were planning a raid, its members would all hop on YY to talk strategy. But eventually YY administrators found that people were using the chat rooms for other reasons. Many sang karaoke. To enter certain chat rooms, you needed access codes, which YY users were selling for cash on Chinese e-commerce sites. In 2009, YY decided to keep the sales in-house by creating YY Music.*

Since it went public in November of 2012, yy.com has seen "its stock price nearly quadruple, from eleven dollars to forty-one. The growth has outpaced even that of Sina, which runs China's popular social-media site Weibo (though Sina is worth considerably more, overall).[261]

Today, visitors to YY Music can choose from thousands of live performances and each performer–and there are, literally, thousands of them–has his—or, more often, her—own theatre "in which fans' avatars cluster in seats around the main stage. A live video feed of the performer rises from the middle."[261] "Users can chat with the performer and buy all sorts of virtual gifts for her; their avatars hurl the favors onto the stage. (The performer gets pretty much the same view, along with some administrative controls.) The performances can seem something like a combination of a pop concert and a peep show."[261]

There is a revenue split between yy.com and the artists: "For every sixteen-dollar bouquet of virtual roses that a fan throws on stage, the performer keeps about five dollars; YY gets almost all of the rest."[261] "A couple of artists on YY make fifty thousand dollars a month from the platform, according to Hany Nada, a partner at GGV Capital, which invested in YY before its I.P.O."[261] Unsurprisingly, it has to do with how pretty the artists are, and "how much their fan bases want to impress them," said Nada.[261]

Some of YY Music's paying users are members of the "*diaosi*"—a once-insulting term meaning, roughly, "losers."[261] It is a term that China's underclass has embraced. Rachel Lu, the cofounder of Tea Leaf Nation, a company that analyzes Chinese social media believes these users are too poor to go to real concerts so they go to virtual ones on YY, where they bestow virtual gifts to real singers who appreciate their offerings.[261] Paying users are about one per cent of the total and each user spends an average of two hundred dollars on the site annually.[261]

In his article *Live streaming in China: boom market, business model and risk regulation*[262], Xiaocen Liu claims that, "The mature monetization model is the key for the fast growth of live streaming business in China. It goes to two parts: virtual gifts selling (i.e. IVAS) and advertising."

Liu claims that, "Virtual gifting selling is now the dominant revenue driver for all independent live streaming platforms in China."[262] Virtual gifts on Chinese live streaming platforms were first introduced by the app 9158 in 2005.[262]

Liu explains that, as more traffic goes to these live video streaming platforms, the advertising value of these platforms goes up commensurately.[262] Liu adds that live video streaming has some inherent advantages as a new form of interactive advertising; the real-time promotion element allows a direct connection between the streamer and his or her audience-members, who can immediately become consumers.[262] The direct connection between viewers and streamers, who are sometimes store owners themselves, increases the credibility of brands and boosts consumers' purchase impulse. According to a survey by Penguin Intelligence, "30.4% Chinese consumers are browsing e-commerce sites without a purpose,"[262] notes Liu, adding that "Live streaming might be the key conversion driver.[262]

Liu argues that "E-commerce is now the most promising sector for live streaming apart from online entertainment."[262] Liu believes China has an even greater opportunity in this field because not only does China have a flourishing e-commerce industry, but it is also haunted by a mistrust on the part of the consumers towards China's e-commerce brands.[262] Liu argues that this mistrust can be reduced by sufficient and comprehensive information from manufacturers.[262] Live streaming might be one of the best ways to build consumer's trust because it will allow them to get closer to the manufacturing process.[262]

Merchants & Brands	Means of marketing	Duration	Sales performance
Baby products makes Wyeth Illuma	Pop star live sreaming	60 mins	RMB 1.2 million (USD 180,000)
Cosmetics brand Maybelline	Actress and web stars live streaming	120 mins	RMB 1.4 mllion (USD 210,000)
Fashion magazine *Elle*	Actor live streaming	15 mins	7,000 prints sold
Web star Zhang Dayi's Taobao shop	Web celebrity live streaming	120 mins	RMB 20 million in GMV (USD 3 million)

Table 16: Major marketing campaigns on live streaming platforms
Source: *Live streaming in China: boom market, business model and risk regulation*[262]

China lacks copyright and IP protection and has been riddled by counterfeit technology and corporate scandals. There is no FDA per se in Chinese either, so consumers don't feel as completely comfortable purchasing things like food and drinks as they would in Western countries. Liu believes that, in the near future, "live streaming will be a standard feature for all e-commerce platforms in China."[262]

List of Virtual Social World Websites

As the landscape for Virtual Social Worlds changes on a daily basis, it is impossible to list all of the available Websites, but these are the most common and popular platforms in use today:

NAME	"ABOUT US" DESCRIPTION
Onverse	Onverse is a free online virtual world full of fun people and cool things to do. We give you an online profile, a free virtual home, clothing, furniture, tools and points to get you started. You can customize your avatar however you like and chat live in a fully 3D environment. You can play games, explore for points, go shopping, decorate your home and avatar, and meet people.
Second Life	Second Life is an online virtual world developed by Linden Lab which was launched on June 23, 2003. A number of free client programs called Viewers enable Second Life users, called Residents, to interact with each other through avatars. Residents can explore the world (known as the grid), meet other residents, socialize, participate in individual and group activities, and create and trade virtual property and services with one another. Second Life is intended for people aged 13 and over, and as of 2011 has more than 20 million registered user accounts.
SmallWorlds	SmallWorlds is a new generation of virtual world that runs inside your web browser, without the need to download or install any other software. SmallWorlds combines media, web content, and casual games into a highly accessible & compelling 3D world that integrates seamlessly with the rest of the web, bringing Virtual Worlds into the

	mainstream. SmallWorlds allows users to create and customize their own rooms and worlds and fill them with a wide variety of items and activities for them and their friends to enjoy together. With their online friends and acquaintances, they can share experiences like playing games, watching YouTube videos, listening to their favorite bands, browsing through photo galleries, and so much more. SmallWorlds brings together the best aspects of online games, instant messaging, social networks and digital media, and wraps them into a persistent virtual world that is never more than a hyperlink away.
Stageit	Stageit is an online venue where artists perform live, interactive, monetized shows for their fans directly from a laptop, offering fans unique experiences that are never archived.
Twinity	Twinity is a 3D mirror world based on real cities and real people. Virtual World is a space for an online community which looks and feels almost like the real world. virtual world People are represented by avatars, and they are able to carry our activities that they can do in real life, without the constraints of real space, such as, having a 3D chat with people who are thousands of miles away (even with voice on VOIP!), modelling without the bother of glue and paint, hanging out in virtual cities and even owning a 3D apartment in areas which would be out of reach in real life! virtual world Twinity does exactly this! Twinity is a 3D Virtual World currently spanning Virtual Berlin, Virtual London and Virtual Miami, where you travel as an avatar, own 3D Apartments and have a 3D Chat, through text or VOIP, with people from across the world!
YY	YY Inc., through its subsidiaries, operates an online social platform in the People's Republic of China. The company engages users in real-time online group activities through voice, video, and text on personal computers and mobile devices; and enables users to create and organize groups of various sizes to discover and participate in a range of activities, including online games, music activities, education, live game broadcasting, and conference calls.

Table 17: Virtual Social World

Videocasting/Livestreaming

Videocasting (aka live streaming) is the process of producing digital voice and video files and publishing them for distribution over the Internet. According to Wikipedia, streaming content refers to content delivered live over the Internet, and it requires a camera for the media, an encoder to digitize the content, a media publisher, and a content delivery network to distribute and deliver the content.[263] Streaming content can be an audio or a video file downloaded from the internet that is played live as the rest of the file is being downloaded. Online radio stations, YouTube, Periscope, yy.com, Twitch, and Youku videos are both good examples of streaming content.

On 24 June 1993, the band *Severe Tire Damage* streamed the internet's first live concert.[264] According to Experian Marketing Services, 48% of all U.S. adults and 67% of young adults watch streaming or downloaded videos during a typical week.[265] "With the explosion of smartphones and digital tablets and the steady rise of internet-connected home devices, consumers are watching more video when and where they want than ever before."[265]

Users are also creating enormous amounts of content on channels like YouTube, Twitch, yy.com (in China), Periscope, Facebook Live, amongst others. "Mobile is the first screen for watching, streaming or downloading video, with 24 percent of all U.S. adults and 42 percent of smartphone owners watching this type of video each week."[265]

"While we are seeing the way we view video drastically changing, television is likely to remain the primary device for consumer video; we just are witnessing the transition of the definition of television," said John Fetto, senior analyst, marketing and research, at Experian Marketing Services.[265] "A third of Americans live in households with Internet-connected TVs, giving them the option to stream or download video to the television either directly or with devices such as Kindle Fire TV, Roku, Apple TV and Google Chromecast," Fetto added.[265]

"While the growing trend in cord-cutting is understandably disturbing to cable and satellite companies and disruptive to the television advertising revenue model overall, the growth in online viewing creates opportunities for marketers," said Fetto.[265] "That's because online video viewers can be targeted more easily and serve up advertising that is more relevant, responsive and measurable. Marketers also can be more confident that their online ad actually was seen given that viewers typically are unable to skip ads."[265]

With cable and satellite video-on-demand (VOD), mobile video viewers in the United States and the rest of the world have become what has been dubbed as "time-shifters"—viewers who choose to watch what they want *when* they want to watch it. With mobile video, they have also become "place-shifters"—viewers who choose *where* to watch what they want to watch when they want to watch it.[266]

I am often amused by the sight of commuters on the Hong Kong subway watching what are probably pirated copies of the latest Korean, British, or US television shows on websites like Youku, Fushion and Sohu as they make their way home at the end of their day. Sights like this confirm to me that mobile video has altered the consumption of entertainment and has forever changed people's viewing habits. Other streaming services in China include Tudou, Cntv.cn, Ku6.com, Xunlei.com, Tv.sohu.com, Letv.com, Iqivi.com, Mtime.com, video.sina.com, and 56.com.

For an airline, live streaming can be used for Q&A conversations, customer support, as well as answering customer questions, special product announcements, interviews with influencer. Live events can also be broadcast, as Burberry does. These can include backstage and behind-the-scenes footage of fashion shows and other events; glimpses of after parties can show the viewer unique content as well.

Some interesting partnerships are sprouting up in the live-streaming world right now that should also be noted. In the eMarketer article *Line Teams with German Media Company for Mobile Live Streaming App*[267], Cliff Annicelli writes that, "German media company ProSiebenSat.1 has teamed with Japanese messaging app provider Line Corp. to bring its mobile live streaming platform, Line Live, to Germany—and possibly elsewhere in Europe."

Launched in December 2015, by September 2017 the app had more than 24 million active users (MAUs) in Japan.[267]

"We are building on [Line Live's success in Asia] and bringing it to Germany to begin with, because we believe in the market for user-generated live streaming and its wide reach among the young target group," said Eunjung Lee, senior vice president of business development at Line Plus Corp., a subsidiary of Line Corp.[267]

To help increase uptake, ProSiebenSat.1 and Line "launched an influencer marketing campaign for Line Live's German launch. Around 70 popular influencers will ask their followers to connect with them on the service."[267]

Several airlines are also venturing into videocasting. For example Estée Lauder's Clinique brand launched the 40 episode drama series, *Sufei's Diary*, on a dedicated Web site that broadcast daily.[273] "While skin care was part of the story line and products were prominently featured, *Sufei's Diary* was seen as entertainment—not a Clinique advertisement—and has been viewed online more than 21 million times. Clinique's online brand awareness is now 27 percent higher than that of its competitors, although social-media content costs significantly less than a traditional advertising campaign."[273]

Podcasting

In her article *How Podcasting works,* Stephanie Watson explains that, in 2004, Podcasting was developed by software engineer Dave Winer and former MTV video jockey Adam Curry, who wrote a program called iPodder that enabled the two to automatically download Internet radio broadcasts to their iPods.[268] Several developers improved upon Curry's idea, and podcasting was officially born.[268]

According to Wikipedia, "a podcast is a type of digital media consisting of an episodic series of audio radio, video, PDF, or ePub files subscribed to and downloaded through web syndication or streamed online to a computer or mobile device. The word is a neologism derived from 'broadcast' and 'pod' from the success of the iPod, as audio podcasts are often listened to on portable media players."[269]

Since its inception, podcasting has been free of government regulation and it is hard to see how this will change. "Podcasters don't need to buy a license to broadcast their programming, as radio stations do, and they don't need to conform to the Federal Communication Commission's (FCC) broadcast decency regulations. That means anything goes—from four-letter words to sexually explicit content," Watson explains.[268] Podcasts are considered copyrightable works and they are easily copyrighted under a Creative Commons licenses.[268] Just because podcasts are free of government regulation doesn't mean they will be free of every government's oversight, though, so caution should be taken in certain parts of the world.

In his article *Will the iPod Kill the Radio Star? Profiling Podcasting as Radio*[270], Richard Berry, claims that "podcasting is both a converged medium bringing together audio, the web and portable media player, and a disruptive technology that has caused some in the radio business to reconsider some of the established practices and preconceptions about audiences, consumption, production and distribution."[270] Because it is free to both listen to and create content for, which departs from the traditional model of 'gate-kept' media and production tools, podcasting can be considered a horizontal media form, i.e., producers are consumers and consumers become producers and engage in conversations with each other.[270]

Podcasts are a great way for an airline to keep control of the company's message, as well as to reach out to an audience that is engaged and probably very interested in the subject matter the airline wants to disseminate.

For those interested in setting up a blog, Keith Lock's article *Start Podcasting on Your WordPress Blog in 7 Easy Steps*[271] is a good place to start.

Conclusion

In this chapter, I have tried to lay the foundations for an understanding of the social media milieu today's airlines face. Few airlines will succeed in this new millennium without embracing social media. When first delving into social media, airlines should follow the four steps of social media—listen, join, participate and create—and these steps must be strictly followed in that order.[217]

Airlines should already be using social media to manage their brand, to enhance brand loyalty, as well as engage both their current customers and their potential customers. Today, most airlines are using social media, but in a limited way. Not only the perfect avenue to reach customers, the social media world is also the perfect place to harvest customer feedback, provide real-time customer service, build fanbases, and drive traffic to an airline's website.

Social media can have a predictive quality as well, i.e., it can be used to discover patterns that reveal upcoming customer problems with products and services. It can reveal brand sentiment, as well as show what drives that sentiment. Customer churn could be spotted early enough to head it off, as well.

Social media is a great place to get competitive intel, as well. Benchmarking a competitor's social media footprint and sentiment can help an airliner understand how its products and services measure up to its competitors and this is unfiltered information, coming directly from the voice of the customer, so it should be trustable.

Airlines should not be reluctant to dive into social media because of its unfiltered nature. These forums will exist with or without the airline's involvement, therefore it is better to stay ahead of the game rather than to be painfully stuck behind it.

Regarding social media, engagement is the key when it comes to successful ROI and profitable customer relations. To compete in this highly competitive industry, airlines are recognizing the importance of personalization when it comes to customer interactions. Most airlines today have customer loyalty programs that are a part of a CRM and/or a SCRM initiative to provide their customers with an intimate experience that will make them want to return again and again and again.

Blogs and micro-blogging sites are also important mobile and social media channels and airlines should monitor Twitter feeds for both their satisfied and dissatisfied customers. This is where brand and anti-brand management comes into play.

Real-time technology gives airlines the ability to see—and know—what is going on in real time around them, and this allows them to instantly counter negative brand perceptions. Social media marketing makes good economic sense as well. Given the explosive growth of social media sites, "these might become more cost-effective than using traditional advertising and marketing methods."[272]

To maintain credibility with customers, airlines shouldn't remove negative comments or constructive criticism from these social media sites unless the person posting the comment uses foul language or says something offensive to others.[272]

Fostering this kind of goodwill can reap many rewards. Another example of great near real-time customer service is from the MGM Mirage, which won plaudits from fans—and perhaps more business—for how it responded to a disgruntled dinner couple.[272] "After a customer posted on Facebook that he was unhappy with his meal at one of the company's Strip resorts, the property's concierge contacted the customer, who was still at the hotel, and offered to fix the problem."[272]

"In another instance, a customer who had won show tickets complained online that he couldn't use the tickets because he had a conflict. MGM Mirage gave the man free tickets for another date."[272] This kind of social media proactivity will, undoubtedly, go far in customer relations. I highly doubt, on that customer's next visit to Vegas, he or she won't think, first and foremost, of MGM when deciding where to stay and gamble. The fact is, this is the kind of service that people love to tell their friends about so, for the small price of a steak dinner and some concert tickets, MGM probably got some invaluable word-of-mouth advertising. Airlines should emulate these examples if they want to separate themselves from the competition.

Facebook should be a part of every airline's social and mobile media marketing plan, but simply putting up a Facebook page won't cut it these days; creativity and uniqueness are needed to get noticed in today's highly competitive social media landscape. Social networks and content communities require content more than anything else. Followers require constantly updated content to continue following companies but building a fan base that keeps up with an airline is invaluable as Facebook and Instagram and even YouTube, Twitter and Periscope are perfect channels to showcase new products or services.

Listening can be done on blogs, content communities, and social networks. By keeping an eye on any comments made on these blogs, or on the pages of Facebook, Instagram, Pinterest, Twitter, or a whole host of other social network pages, social media marketers can get a sense of what the community feels about its business and its products or services.

Social media is all about adding value to communities of customers and prospects by providing interesting content (blogs, podcasts, webinars, etc.). It allows immediate engagement with groups of customers and potential customers.

Today, the traditional model of blasting messages to customers and potential customers is fading as trust in corporate America is at an all-time low. In this difficult economic climate, peer referrals are becoming more and more important. Consumers are tuning out regular advertising and tapping into social media for advice. Listening and joining these conversations could prove highly lucrative to airlines.

Social Media is constrained only by the imagination of an airliner's marketers and it offers enormous potential, both creatively and financially, to any company willing to enter the arena.

In the next few chapters, I will reveal how social media can be used in an airline's mobile and social media marketing plans, as well as discuss many of the available tools one can use to track and monetize these platforms.

Continuing the journey from an anonymous customer to one who is known so well that their actions can be manipulated is the addition of a customer's IP address, user agent/browser finger print, his or her device ID, his or her digital cookies, and, finally, his or her social ID (see figure 19). But how can an airline capture a customer's social IDs? It's pretty simple actually, offer them the ability to sign in with their social media accounts. Many people enjoy the simplicity of signing into websites with their Facebook, Twitter, Pinterest, Snapchat, or other social media accounts and once the airline's marketing department can connect the customer account with a customer's social media account, a whole new world of customer interaction becomes possible.

China is an important player in social media. As Chiu et Al. state in their paper *Understanding Social Media in China*[273], "The sheer number of the more than 300 million social-media users in China creates unique challenges for effective consumer engagement," but I believe the potential market is too massive to ignore. But it is a tricky market; in China, "People expect responses to each and every post, for example, so companies must develop new models and processes for effectively engaging individuals in a way that communicates brand identity and values, satisfies consumer concerns, and doesn't lead to a negative viral spiral."[273] Other problems include the "difficulty of developing and tracking reliable metrics to gauge a social-media strategy's performance, given the size of the user base, a lack of analytical tools (such as those offered by Facebook and Google in other markets), and limited transparency into leading platforms,"[273]

Figure 19: Customer funnel

China is, unquestionably, making great strides, but they still have a long way to go before their social media analytics technology can rival the US's. However, as Chiu et al. make clear, this is not a barrier that should stand in the way of companies as "The similarity between the ingredients of success in China and in other markets makes it easier—and well worth the trouble—to cope with the country's many peculiarities."[273]

Tips

- Claim and secure your brand and/or company name. Websites like knowem.com allow you to check for the use of your brand, product, personal name on over 500 popular and emerging social media websites.
- Join communities where you are most likely to find your customers.
- Once you have joined the discussion, it is time to participate in the community; post to online forums and blogs, review products and services and bookmark sites that interest you.
- For the promotion of a business, social bookmarking is important because it helps a website get quality backlinks.
- Create a blog/blogs—they are incredibly popular because they are cheap, easy to set up and they provide maximum exposure with limited effort.
- When blogging, use lists. For some reason, lists generate more interest than long-winded diatribes.
- Although similar to a blogging website, microblog sites such as Twitter allow people to broadcast short messages, so-called microposts that can consist of text messages enriched with contextual metadata.
- Twitter can also be used to build a following, increase a businesses' reputation, and raise customer trust.
- Use social media listening tools to do highly affordable market research. Free Twitter listening tools alone can provide priceless market research.
- Use a site like Listorious to find a list of prominent tweeters in your business or industry.
- Create interest on Pinterest with their "Wish lists" feature.
- Network with other people in the community who share similar interests.
- Use SEOMoz's Linkscape and Majestic SEO's Link Intelligence to check backlinks to a site.
- Use Viralwoot to build up Pinterest followers inexpensively.
- Stay active by sharing engaging content and adding Google +1s and comments to the pages and content in your community.
- Encourage reviews from your customers on Google+, Weibo, Facebook, etc., etc.
- Download the Google+ mobile app so you can monitor and share content on the go.
- Utilize WeChat's Moments section as a sales channel.
- Research hashtags for Instagram marketing. Choose ones that have been used between 100K – 200K as this means they are active but not

overused. Businesses can get lost in the shuffle with hashtags used up to a million times.
- Constantly engage with your followers, liking or commenting on their pictures and videos. This could drive engagement from them and their followers.
- Cross promote on Instagram accounts similar to your own.
- Utilize both Pinterest's bookmarklet to quickly add content on the go.

---

197 Drury, G. (2008). Opinion piece: Social media: Should marketers engage and how can it be done effectively? Journal of Direct, Data and Digital Marketing Practice, Volume 9, pages 274-277.

198 As identified in Claude E. Shannon and Warren Weaver's *The Mathematical Theory of Communication*, the Source-Message-Channel-Receiver model is a basic model of communication; Source is the person who encodes the message and transmits it to the receiver; the Message is the intended meaning the source hopes the receiver will understand; the Channel is the medium through which the message is conveyed and it must tap into the receiver's sensory system; the Receiver is the person at the end of the communication, someone who will decode the message and create their own meaning.

199 Lefebvre, R. C. (2007). The New Technology: The Consumer as Participant Rather Than Target Audience. *Social Marketing Quarterly*, 31-42.

200 Juniper Research. (2008). *Mobile User Generated Content: Dating, Social Networking & Personal Content Deliver.* Juniper Research.

201 Juniper Research. (2008). *Mobile User Generated Content: Dating, Social Networking & Personal Content Deliver.* Juniper Research.

202 OECD. (2007). Participative web and user-created content: Web 2.0, wikis, and social networking. Organisation for Economic Co-operation and Development. Paris.

203 Short, J. W. (1976). *The Social Psychology of telecommunication.* Hoboken, NJ: John Wiley & Sons, Ltd.

204 Daft, R. &. (1986). Organization information requirements, media richness, and structural design. *Management Science*, 32(5), 554-571.

205 Goffman, E. (1959). The Presentation of Self In Everyday Life. New York: Doubleday.

206 Divol, R. E. (2012, April). Demystifying social media. Retrieved from Mckinsey.com: http://www.mckinsey.com/insights/marketing_sales/demystifying_social_media (Accessed 25 November 2017).

207 Lee, Aileen. (2011). Social Proof Is The New Marketing. Techcrunch. https://techcrunch.com/2011/11/27/social-proof-why-people-like-to-follow-the-crowd/ (Accessed 16 August 2018).

208 https://en.wikipedia.org/wiki/Social_proof (Accessed 16 August 2018).

209 Cialdini, Robert B. Harnessing the Science of Persuasion. Harvard Business Review. October 2001. http://www.coachfinder.club/downloads/Influence%20by%20Cialdini.pdf (Accessed 15 August 2018).

210 Hallin, Ed. (2014). Fast Company. How to use the psychology of social proof to your advantage. 05 May 2014. https://www.fastcompany.com/3030044/how-to-use-the-psychology-of-social-proof-to-your-advantage (Accessed 14 August 2018).

211 Oliver Smith. (2018). The Telegraph. The unstoppable rise of the Chinese traveller – where are they going and what does it mean for overtourism? 11 April 2018. https://www.telegraph.co.uk/travel/comment/rise-of-the-chinese-tourist/ (Accessed 13 August 2018.

212 https://www.globalwebindex.net/ (Accessed 25 November 2017).

213 https://www.statista.com/statistics/265146/number-of-mobile-internet-users-in-china/ (Accessed 25 November 2017).

214 http://www.bbc.com/news/blogs-news-from-elsewhere-36226141

215 De Mente, B. L. (2009). *The Chinese Mind: Understanding traditional Chinese beliefs and their influence on contemporary culture.* Tuttle Publishing.

216 Hempel, J. (2012, September 10). *Facebook's China Problem.* Retrieved from Fortune Tech: http://tech.fortune.cnn.com/2012/09/10/facebook-china-problem (Accessed 25 November 2017).

217 Eley, B & Tilley S. *Online Marketing Inside Out: Reach New Buyers Using Modern Marketing Techniques.* May 28, 2009. Sitepoint

218 Stampler, L. (2013, February 19). *How Maker's Mark turned its watered down whiskey debacle into a social media win.* Retrieved from Business Insider: http://www.businessinsider.com/makers-mark-turns-whiskey-fail-into-win-2013-2 (Accessed 25 November 2017).

219 Nelson, A. (2013, November 21). *50 ways to drive traffic to your website with social media.* Retrieved from Exact Target Cloud Blog: http://www.exacttarget.com/blog/50-ways-to-drive-traffic-to-your-website-with-social-media/ (Accessed 25 November 2017).

220 Golder, S., & Huberman, B. A. (2006). Usage Patterns of Collaborative Tagging Systems. Journal of Information Science, Volume 32 (2), pages 198-208.

221 Dubois, L. (2010, September 16). *How to Use Social Bookmarking for Business. Inc.* Retrieved from http://www.inc.com/guides/2010/09/how-to-use-social-bookmarking-for-business.html (Accessed 25 November 2017).

222 DuBois, S. (2014, July 4). Google Glass Hits the Operating Room. Retrieved from tennessean.com: http://www.tennessean.com/story/money/industries/health-care/2014/07/05/google-glass-hits-operating-room/12228547/

223 Mathes, A. (2008). Folksonomies – Cooperative Classification and Communication Through Shared Metadata. *Computer Mediated Communication – LIS590CMC.* University of Illinois Urbana-Champaign: Graduate School of Library and Information Science.

224 http://redcrosschat.org/2011/02/16/twitter-faux-pas/ (Accessed 25 November 2017).

225 http://www.davecarrollmusic.com/music/ubg/ (Accessed 25 November 2017).

226 https://www.youtube.com/watch?v=xaNuE3DsJHM (Accessed 25 November 2017).

227 https://www.merriam-webster.com/dictionary/blog (Accessed 25 November 2017).

228 http://www.webopedia.com/TERM/B/blog.html (Accessed 25 November 2017).

229 Wortham, J. (2007, December 17). After 10 Years of Blogs, the Future's Brighter Than Ever. *Wired Magazine.*

230 Economist, The. (2006, April 20). *It's the links, stupid.* Retrieved from Economist.com: http://www.economist.com/node/6794172 (Accessed 25 November 2017).

231 Baker, J. (2008, April 20). *Origins of "Blog" and "Blogger.* Retrieved from linguistlist.org: http://listserv.linguistlist.org/cgi-bin/wa?A2=ind0804C&L=ADS-L&P=R16795&I=-3 (Accessed 25 November 2017).

232 Sahail Ashraf. (2015) How the World's top 7 Airlines Use Social Media. Business2community.com. 10 July 2015. https://www.business2community.com/social-media/how-the-worlds-top-7-airlines-use-social-media-01272008 (Accessed 13 August 2018).

233 Lohmann, S. B. (2012). Visual Analysis of Microblog Content Using Time-Varying Co-occurrence Highlighting in Tag Clouds. New York, NY: AVI 2012 Conference.

234 Isaac, Mike. (2017) Twitter to Test Doubling tweet Length to 280 Characters. New York Times. 26 September 2017. https://www.nytimes.com/2017/09/26/technology/twitter-280-characters.html (Accessed October 24, 2017).

235 Twitter.com

236 Bifet, A. a. (2010). *Sentiment knowledge discovery in twitter streaming data.* Retrieved from University of Waikato, Hamilton, New Zealand: http://www.cs.waikato.ac.nz/~ml/publications/2010/Twitter-crc.pdf (Accessed 25 November 2017).

237 www.youtube.com/t/about_youtube (Accessed 5 November 2017).

238 http://www.youtube.com/t/press_statistics (Accessed 5 November 2017).

239 http://www.Slideshare.net/about (Accessed 5 November 2017).

240 https://en.wikipedia.org/wiki/SlideShare (Accessed 21 November 2017).

241 BBC. (2012, April 10). *Facebook buys Instagram photo sharing network for $1bn.* Retrieved from http://www.bbc.co.uk/news/technology-17658264 (Accessed 5 November 2017).

242 Chaykowski, Kathleen. (2016). Instagram, The $50 Billion Grand Slam Driving Facebook's Future: The Forbes Cover Story. Forbes.com. August 1, 2016. https://www.forbes.com/sites/kathleenchaykowski/2016/08/01/instagram-the-50-billion-grand-slam-driving-facebooks-future-the-forbes-cover-story/#5ddd67074a97 (Accessed 5 November 2017).

243 Pinterest Blog. An update on promoted pins. https://blog.pinterest.com/en/update-promoted-pins (Accessed 17 November 17, 2017).

244 https://en.wikipedia.org/wiki/Social_network (Accessed 25 November 2017).

245 Boyd, D. a. (2007). Social Network Sites: Definition, History, and Scholarship. Journal of Computer-Mediated Communication, Vol. 13.

246 Datta, A. J. (2009). Expanding Opportunities in a Shrinking World: A Conceptual Model explicating the Role of Social Networks and Internet-based Virtual Environments in Social Entrepreneurship. International Journal of Virtual Communities and Social Networking, 1 (4), pp. 33-49.

247 Calcano, Reinaldo. The Evolution of Social Media Marketing. Sweetiq.com. January 12, 2017. https://sweetiq.com/blog/the-evolution-of-social-media-marketing-in-retail/ (Accessed 25 November 2017).

248 Wasserman, T. (. (2013, January 3). Is Snapchat the Next Frontier for Marketers? Retrieved from Mashable.com: http://mashable.com/2013/01/02/snap-chat-marketers.com (Accessed 25 November 2017).

249 Traphagen, Mark. (2018). Three brands still killing it on Facebook. Marketing Land. 17 April 2018. https://marketingland.com/three-brands-still-killing-it-on-facebook-238303 (Accessed 15 August 2018).

250 https://en.wikipedia.org/wiki/WeChat (Accessed 25 November 2017).

251 Segev, L. (2014, March 20). *WeChat is so much more than just Instant Messaging.* Retrieved from Thetechieguy.com: http://thetechieguy.com/2014/03/20/wechat-is-so-much-more-than-just-instant-messaging/ (Accessed 25 November 2017).

252 Baker, C. (2014, May 26). 4 Ways Brands Can Use WeChat for Sales. Retrieved from clickz.com: http://www.clickz.com/clickz/column/2346596/4-ways-brands-can-use-wechat-for-sales (Accessed 25 November 2017).

253 Graff, Roy. (2018). Routes Online. 14 August 2018. https://www.routesonline.com/news/29/breaking-news/280065/how-international-airlines-use-wechat-to-market-to-china/ (Accessed 14 August 2018).

254 Gundotra, V. (2012). Google+: Communities and Photos. Retrieved from Google Blog.

255 Olanoff, D. (2012, March 8). *For the last time, let's all say this together: "Google+ is NOT a Social Network.* Retrieved from Thenextweb.com: http://thenextweb.com/socialmedia/2012/03/08/for-the-last-time-lets-all-say-it-together-google-is-not-a-social-network/ (Accessed 5 November 2017).

256 Elliott, Nate. (2014). Why Every Marketer Should Use Google+. Forbes.com. https://www.forbes.com/sites/forrester/2014/03/31/why-every-marketer-should-use-google-plus/#130e61b11e2e (Accessed 5 Novembr 2017).

257 Miller, Claire Cain. (2014) The Plus in Google Plus? It's Mostly For Google. *New York Times.* https://www.nytimes.com/2014/02/15/technology/the-plus-in-google-plus-its-mostly-for-google.html (Accessed 5 November 2017).

258 https://en.wikipedia.org/wiki/Virtual_world (Accessed 23 November 2017).

259 www.girlgamerfestival.com (accessed September 4, 2017).

260 Ashton, Graham. (2018). AirAsia Potentially Planning Launch of Esports Team, League, and Center. 31 May 2018. https://esportsobserver.com/airasia-esports-expansion/# (Accessed 15 August 2018).

261 Goldenberg, D. (2013, September 5). Virtual roses and the rise of yy.com. Retrieved from Newyorker.com: http://www.newyorker.com/online/blogs/currency/2013/09/virtual-roses-and-the-rise-of-yy-music-china.html (22 November 2017).

262 Liu, Xiaocen. Live streaming in China: boom market, business model and risk regulation. Journal of Residuals Science & Technology, Vol. 13, No. 8, 2016. DEStech Publications, Inc.

263 https://en.wikipedia.org/wiki/Streaming_media (Accessed 23 November 2017).

264 http://www.computerhope.com/jargon/s/streamin.htm (Accessed 25 November 2017).

265 Experian Marketing Services. (2014, April 21). "Cord-cutters" grew by 44 percent in the past four years, with 7.6 million households using high-speed Internet for streaming or downloading videos instead of traditional cable or satellite television. Retrieved from Experian: http://press.experian.com/United-States/Press-Release/cord-cutters-grew-by-44-percent-in-the-past-four-years-with-7-6-million-households.aspx (Accessed 25 November 2017).

266 Nielsen Company. (2009). Tuned into the Phone: Mobile Video Use in the U.S. and Abroad. Nielsen Company.

267 Annicelli, Cliff. September 6, 2017. Line Teams with German Media Company for Mobile Live Streaming App. eMarketer. https://www.emarketer.com/Article/Line-Teams-with-German-Media-Company-Mobile-Live-Streaming-App/1016430 (Accessed September 7, 2017).

268 Watson, S. (2005, March 26). *How Podcasting works*. Retrieved from Howstuffworks.com: http://computer.howstuffworks.com/internet/basics/podcasting1.htm (Accessed 25 November 2017).

269 https://en.wikipedia.org/wiki/Podcast (Accessed 25 November 2017).

270 Berry, R. (2006). Will the iPod kill the radio star? Profiling podcasting as radio. Convergence: *The International Journal of Research into New Media Technologies*, Volume 12, 143-162. Retrieved from Sage Journals.

271 Lock, K. (2014, January 4). *Start podcasting on your WordPress blog in 7 easy steps*. Retrieved from tipsandtricks-hq.com: http://www.tipsandtricks-hq.com/start-podcasting-on-your-wordpress-blog-in-7-easy-steps-6738 (Accessed 25 November 2017).

272 Benson, L. (2009, October 26). *Casinos saving face online*. Retrieved from Las Vegas Sun: www.lasvegassun.com/news/2009/oct/26/saving-face-online/ (Accessed 25 November 2017).

273 Chiu, C. I. (2012, April). *Understanding social media in China*. Retrieved from www.mckinsey.com: http://www.mckinsey.com/insights/marketing_sales/understanding_social_media_in_china (Accessed 5 November 2017).

CHAPTER FOUR

Social Business

"Social media allows big companies to act small again."
~Jay Baer

Overview

The most important thing to recognize about social media is the fact that most social media content is user generated. Social networks provide all of the tools their members require to become content producers and social network members submit photos, videos, music, and other forms of multimedia, as well as provide customer reviews, content for blogs and vlogs and links to other social networking websites that they find noteworthy.[274] The content comes from the users themselves, not from the publishers, and this is an important distinction.[274] The publisher supplies all of the necessary tools for the content's distribution, but it must remain at arm's length from the actual content to ensure the content's integrity.

Business.com's *Top Tools to Measure Your Social Media Success*[275] states that there are five Ws that must be kept in mind when devising a social media strategy. These are:

1. Who within the company will be using this tool? Will one person or several people be using the tools, and will they be inside or outside the organization? Will the primary user be tech savvy or will he or she require an intuitive interface?
2. What key performance indicators (KPI) are to be measured with this tool? It is imperative to know how you are going to measure and benchmark your social media efforts as this will dictate what social media monitoring tools are the best to use. If sales revenue is a key KPI, businesses should invest in a tool that integrates with a CRM system to track impact.
3. Where on the web will the business be engaging customers, and where does it plan to monitor its social media conversations? If a business is only interested in tracking specific channels such as Facebook or Twitter, tools such as Facebook (obviously), 48ers.com and socialmention.com can help with the former, while Twazzup, tweetEffect and Twittercounter can track the latter. All-encompassing

tools that monitor new sites and forums are useful to monitor mentions from across the entire web.
4. When should the company be alerted of conversations and mentions within the social media sphere? Options here include general reporting dashboards or instant notifications via e-mail alerts or RSS feeds.
5. Why is the company engaging in social media? This is, perhaps, the most important question of all, and an airliner must decide whether it is turning to social media to manage its online brand reputation, to engage its customers and/or potential customers, to provide real-time customer service, or simply to drive traffic to its website to influence SEO.

A company is only as strong as its weakest customer relationship and I believe that social media can help both businesses reach their customers in highly efficient and, what can be extraordinarily affordable, ways. Airlines should look to social media to help them in the following ways:

- Add interactivity to a Website
- Brand and Anti-Brand management
- Building fanbases and communities
- Crisis management
- Developing a virtual social world presence
- Discovering a customer's psychological profile
- Discovering important brand trends
- Engaging customers and potential customers
- Harvesting customer feedback
- Influencer marketing
- Marketing to consumers
- Reputation management

Studies have shown that 80% of social media users prefer to connect with brands through Facebook and 43% of people prefer Pinterest over associating directly with airlines and/or brands.[276] This fact alone underscores the importance of social media in a business context. This fact, coupled with the power of a Reed Network[42]—i.e., one million people marketed to when only 20 people are reached—should show how important marketing through social media can be. This is the true power of social media and it cannot be underestimated. And, when coupled with mobile, that number can be even greater and the reach lightning fast.

Throughout the rest of this chapter, I will go into detail about each of the different ways in which businesses should use social media. First, I will lay out the foundations for social media marketing, including a description of Jantsch's *Hierarchy of Social Marketing*[277], as well as reveal the differences between social media users.

In his article *The Hierarchy of Social Marketing*[277] John Jantsch argues that when venturing into social media, businesses should be following six distinct steps (see Figure 20). Using Abraham Maslow's *Hierarchy of Needs*[278] as a blueprint to look at social marketing, Jantsch states implicitly that each step should be fully understood and implemented before any ensuing step is undertaken.[277] Just as Maslow claimed that "Self-Actualization" can only be reached after all the needs below it have been fulfilled, so too does Jantsch believe that, without a mastery of the first five steps, the sixth step–"Micro"–will be useless because engagement with the intended audience will be shallow.[277]

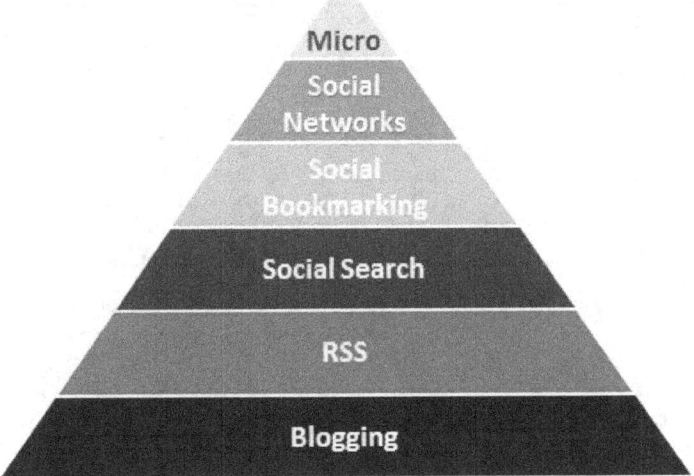

Figure 20: Jantsch's Hierarchy of Social Media
Source: *The Hierarchy of Social Marketing*[277]

Jantsch's breaks the hierarchy down into the following steps[277]:

1. Blogging: The pyramid's foundation and the doorway through which all other social marketing should flow. Airlines should read blogs, comment on blogs, and then blog themselves.
2. RSS: Aggregate and filter content around subjects and use RSS technology as a tool to help repurposing, republishing, and creating content.
3. Social Search: participation is important at this stage as is stimulating and managing one's reputation.
4. Social Bookmarking: Tagging content to and participating in social bookmarking communities can both open up more channels for an airline as well as generate extra search traffic to a site.
5. Social Networks: Creating profiles on any social networking site will prove frustrating if the steps below it haven't been completed. These

networks take time to understand and they thrive on ideas and content, therefore a lot of content is needed to build a strong business case.

6. Micro: With their instant tracking, joining, and engagement capabilities, platforms such as Twitter, Thwirl, Plurk and FriendFeed are very important elements of a social media strategy. They are atop the pyramid because, without content created below them, engagement will be superficial, at best.

Although this hierarchy is an interesting framework, it should be taken with a grain of salt. Social media is moving so fast, as well as splintering off in a thousand different directions that nothing in this field is set in stone.

TYPE OF PARTICIPATION	ACTIVITY
Creators	Publish a blog
	Publish your own Web page
	Upload video you created
	Upload audio music you created
	Write articles or stories and post them
Critics	Post ratings/reviews of products or services
	Comment on someone else's blog
	Contribute to online forums
	Contribute to/edit articles in a wiki
Collectors	Use RSS feeds
	"Vote" for Web sites online
	Add "tags" to Web pages or photos
Joiners	Maintain profiles on a social networking site
	Visit social networking sites
Spectators	Read blogs
	Listen to podcasts
	Watch video from other users
	Read online forums
	Read customer ratings/reviews
Inactives	None of the above

Table 18: Participation Ladder for Social Media
Source: Harvard Business Review[279]

To create an effective and engaging marketing campaign, a marketer must understand the individual being marketed to as best as he or she can. As there are literally billions of people using social media, categorizing them into a simple classification system is not easy, but Li and Bernoff circumvent this problem by differentiating social media users into six different categories and they have created the *Participation Ladder for Social Media* (Table 18).[279]

As the "Inactives" at the bottom rung do not use social media, they can be ignored, but the other five types should be looked at and marketed to appropriately. It should also be noted that there are two other superficial types; the "contributors", who actively participate by starting their own conversations or replying to other threads and the "lurkers", who only read and follow content created by others.[280]

It is important to recognize that the clear majority of social media users fall into the "lurkers" category and these people are highly influenced by the "contributors"[280], so reaching the contributors is imperative. Airline operators should recognize the unique symbiotic relationship between "contributors" and "lurkers" that is like a political commentator and his or her reading or viewing public.[280] These commentators do have enormous sway over their audience.

Dovetailing Li and Bernoff's participation ladder is the 1:9:90 rule, which as Paul Bates states in his article *Social Media Theory the 1:9:90 rule*[281] the 1:9:90 rule is not really a rule, but, rather, it is a useful concept to help understand how social media selling works.

The theory proposes that for a mature website, just 1% of its website or social media visitors will actually produce original material or user generated content.[281] Meanwhile, 9% of visitors "will be editors or more likely commentators on that material and 90% of visitors will only ever read the material without ever making a comment."[281] Respectively, these groups are known as:

1. Originators—1%
2. Editors (or Commentators)—9%
3. Lurkers—90%

Bates points out that, "UGC is a very desirable thing on a social media site [sic] if you can get your audience participating and creating original content, it will allow you to punch considerably above your weight and appear to have a large and active user base."[281] As previously mentioned, UGC can be a very good thing in terms of SEO and allowing users to add comments and/or create original content will go a long way to increase SEO rankings.

Bates also recommends that social media managers and professionals go out of their way to produce content that will attract comments and readership, but "it is even more profitable if social media managers or business owners can persuade others to create relevant and original content"[281]; getting such comments helps businesses gain credibility, especially if the comments are positive. A Facebook "like" is nice, but it doesn't take a lot of effort to "like" a Facebook page, whereas a comment is much more valuable because someone actually went through the process of explaining why they might recommend a product or a service, or both.[281]

The "lurker" category is the one Bates believes should not be taken for granted, though.[281] "This is the pay dirt for a social media based sales strategy," Bates argues, adding that this is where the big numbers lie.[281]

By definition, lurkers have no engagement with a business and social media theory suggests that engagement must first be developed before any sale can be made.[281] However, the good news is that, although the ratios remain relatively stable, the individuals within these groups are constantly in flux.[281] "A lurker might indeed get interested and become a commentator before eventually buying and then just disappear or go back to lurking, or your 1% of originators might suddenly stop creating content and become lurkers" argues Bates.[281] What the 1:9:90 theory fails to address is that beyond the active user base is a whole world of potential prospects that you hope one day, at the very least, become lurkers.[281]

The Uses of Social Media

Kaplan and Haenlein argue that there are several pre-conditions that should be met before a company embraces social media.[44] First, because there are so many social media sites available, it is imperative to choose social media applications based on where a target audience tends of congregate.[44]

Once the social media sites have been selected, "the next decision involves whether to make or buy."[44] In some cases, it is best to join an existing social media platform and take advantage of its popularity and built-in user base, while in other cases the right application might not be available so it is necessary to build one from scratch.[44] Whichever way an airline decides to go, "it is vital that there is an understanding of the basic idea behind social media. It's all about participation, sharing, and collaboration, rather than straightforward advertising and selling," contend Kaplan and Haenlein.[44]

Since by its very nature social media is a splintered platform, it is crucial to ensure that all social media activities are aligned with each other.[44] As an example, Kaplan and Haenlein reference Dell and its "Digital Nomads" campaign, which used "a combination of social networking sites (Facebook, LinkedIn), blogs, and content communities (YouTube videos) to show how its range of laptop computers enable individuals to become a nomadic workforce."[44] The main goal was to keep the message consistent across all channels.[44]

Social media shouldn't exist in a vacuum and it should be integrated with traditional media, contend Kaplan and Haenlein, who also argue that there is little differentiation between the two in the eyes of the consumer.[44]

Finally, a company that wants to create a social media presence should ensure that all of its employees have access to all of the company's social media platforms.

Obviously, a fine balance between giving everyone access to social media platforms and complete freedom of expression must be struck so that not everyone is wasting their time producing and uploading irreverent YouTube videos.[44] "One possible approach involves defining groups of employees whose primary objective is the management of corporate social media; all other staff members are treated as occasional participants. Under this scenario, the first group is given administrator rights—rights which allow the opening of new discussion threads and deletion of inappropriate posts—while the second group is not," Kaplan and Haenlein recommend.[44]

This is important because it could be rather embarrassing if certain people who shouldn't have access to a company's social media accounts do, as music chain HMW discovered when an employee who was about to be fired started live-tweeting about the mass firing of 190 staff members.[282]

In her article *The Top 10 corporate social media disasters*[282], Burn-Calandar explained that the first tweet announced: "'We're tweeting live from HR where we're all being fired! Exciting!!!", followed by: "There are over 60 of us being fired at once! Mass execution, of loyal employees who love the brand."[282] "Unfortunately for HMV, even its inability to lock the outgoing staff out of the social network was broadcast to the masses. The rogue @hmvtweets tweeter wrote: "Just overheard our Marketing Director (he's staying, folks!) ask 'How do I shut down Twitter?'"[282]

It is also important to inform the social media community that employees need to identify themselves before they post so that "end-consumers don't get the impression that anonymous accounts are used by employees to post fake messages and overly-positive feedback."[44] Kaplan and Haenlein warn that this could severely damage the credibility of the whole social media campaign.[44]

Once these pre-conditions have been met, Kaplan and Haenlein lay out five specific points to be aware of when going social and these include[44]:

1. Be active: keep your content fresh and constantly engage the customer, taking the lead whenever necessary.
2. Be interesting: After listening to your customers to hear what is important to them, "find out what *they* would like to hear; what *they* would like to talk about; what *they* might find interesting, enjoyable, and valuable."[44]

3. Be humble: you should engage only when you have learned the basic rules and gained the necessary understanding but remember to do so with humility. Social media has been around for quite a while now so don't claim to be an expert if you're only just wading into the waters.
4. Be unprofessional: social media is not about projecting absolute professionalism, it is about being human and that entails making mistakes. Social media consumers much prefer someone who occasionally gets his or her hands dirty than someone with a stuffy, boorish attitude.
5. Be honest: honesty is always the best policy, especially when a little dishonesty can be highly embarrassing, as well as ignite a firestorm of negativity in the blogosphere. As Kaplan and Haenlein warn, "Never expect that other participants may not find out who stands behind some anonymous user account; after all, you're dealing with some of the most technologically sophisticated people on the planet."[44]

In his article *Social Media Tips from The World's Top Airline*[283], Carmine Gallo recommends airlines create a position within the company that is 100% dedicated to social media.

"The world of social media has dramatically changed over the past few years," says Dennis Owen, group manager for social media at Cathay Pacific Airways.[283] "No longer is social media just about clever marketing campaigns or gathering as many fans as you can on Facebook," Adds Owen.[283] "Social media touches nearly every department at Cathay Pacific: marketing communications, brand storytelling, employee recruitment, reservations, customer service. Social media is not a part-time position. It's a full-time commitment," writes Gallo.[283] The job entails more than simply knowing how to open and maintain a social media account.[283] It requires "hiring people who are skilled in business, communication, storytelling, marketing, writing, service, and who have strong interpersonal skills," Gallo maintains.[283] These are a very particular set of skills, skills which aren't that easy to find in one package, but it makes sense as social media is very much about starting, maintaining and exploring a narrative.

"Cathay Pacific considers everything a customer touch point: website, reservations, phone, and social media," explains Gallo.[283] "Each touch point should be considered as an opportunity to provide exceptional service," Gallo adds.[283] "As a premium brand, Cathay Pacific must reflect its status in look, feel, and tone across each touch point," notes Gallo.[283] "As a quality carrier we look at every single touch point from the customer perspective," says Owen.[283] "If you are going to pay the extra money for a premium airline you should get more in terms of service, and that includes social media," adds Owen.[283]

"Each social media channel has its own characteristics," says Owen, adding, "On Facebook, these are our true fans. They know us, like us, and enjoy interacting on Facebook."[283] "Cathay Pacific's Facebook page includes deals, promotions, limited time specials, and photos/videos/articles about its aircraft or clubs—the type of content that resonates with loyal customers," says Gallo.[283]

According to Owen, "The Twitter audience can be our fans, but it also includes people who are generally interested in international travel, be it leisure or corporate."[283] "Twitter posts should appeal to loyal customers, as well as people who are simply interested in travel," notes Gallo.[283]

"LinkedIn, on the other hand, is more business focused and so Cathay Pacific posts content for people who are interested in the aviation industry or those looking for a premium business travel experience," says Gallo.[283] Meanwhile, "Instagram and Pinterest would be our newer platforms and those tend to skew a bit younger in age," says Owen.[283] "These are the sites where people come to be inspired. Perhaps they are planning a trip in the future and want to get more of a visual feel for what that could look like, whether it is looking at destination images, product or lounge images or even modern airplane images," adds Owen.[283]

"Since Instagram is a channel where people like to post travel photos, Cathay Pacific started a campaign inviting people to share their pictures and use the hashtag #lifewelltraveled. Today the campaign has generated over 100,000 images," writes Gallo.[283] "The future is leaning toward the visual, around images and videos, so we see great opportunity with Instagram and Pinterest," says Owen.[283]

"Above all, establishing and growing a strong social media presence requires a commitment from an organization's top leaders, a dedication to interact with a brands' fans, potential customers, and employees," concludes Gallo.[283] "We see social media as a way to build relationships with our customers through two way dialogues," says Owen. "We will always strive to be better at what we do and relationships via social media allow us to do just that."[283]

Add Interactivity to a Website

Adding social media to a static website can turn a dull website into a highly interactive destination that allows interested users and/or customers to actually become a participant in the marketing of the site and the airliner.

Adding "Like" buttons makes it easy for users to share content; sites such as Facebook, Twitter, and YouTube are some of the more well-known and highly understood social networks and these are good places to start, but other platforms such as Google+, Pinterest, Tumblr, Vimeo, Instagram, and LinkedIn can also be used to spread the company's message far and wide.

On those social media sites, airlines can add content that keeps customers interested and returning for more. All of these sites usually provide widgets that are easy to include on the company's websites. RSS feeds, blogs, and podcasts are also great platforms that can keep customers engaged. Adding videos and presentations to a website is also a great way to drive traffic. One of the most important things to remember is to update content often. This is probably the single most important rule of SEO; give the search engines a reason to keep coming back to your site with strong content.

In her article *The 12 Bookmarklets Your Social Media Life Is Missing*[284], Julie Ma explains that Bookmarklets are free, minimally invasive, time-saving applications that "make sharing and posting content while surfing the Web as easy as clicking a button—without leaving the page you're on. These tools do everything from creating Tumblr posts to tweeting links—all without requiring you to be on the social media site itself."[284] Their power lie in the fact that whenever someone has the desire to "share" an Internet gem with his or her fellow culture vultures, "the bookmarklet will get the job done in the time it takes you to open up a new tab."[284] Bookmarklets can be dragged into a browser's toolbar and they can speed up the process of social media marketing.

Airlines can also create their own bookmarklets that allow users to keep track of items on a wish list. As Ma explains, "The button reads 'Buy Later,' because you're literally building up a limitless online wish list pieced together from any store you like. Rather than racking up items in an individual store's shopping cart, Svpply compiles all your favorites on a single site. Once you click the bookmark, a lightbox shows up—all you need to do is select a category and price range."[284]

Brand and Anti-Brand Management

In 2001, Hislop defined branding as "the process of creating a relationship or a connection between a company's product and emotional perception of the customer for the purpose of generation segregation among competition and building loyalty among customers."[285]

According to the *Management Study Guide*[286], "Brand management begins with having a thorough knowledge of the term 'brand'. It includes developing a promise, making that promise and maintaining it. It means defining the brand, positioning the brand, and delivering the brand."

Although brand management can be considered to be "nothing but the art of creating and sustaining the brand,"[286] Jones and Huang note that, "unlike traditional consumer-created brand communities where the brands appear to occupy minimal presence, online brand communities are increasingly hosted by the brands."[287]

Building upon Schau et al.'s research[288] into collective value creation within brand communities, Jones and Huang found that "Social media as an interactive technology both enables and becomes a site of value creation for the individual consumers, the brand community and the brand itself."[287]

Unlike user-generated brand communities, where brands are often unwelcome, these online brand communities "revealed that brand content contributions on their brand offerings and interactions with consumers' content contributions were appreciated by the community."[287] "These consumer-brand interactions, functional and otherwise, fostered emotional bonding between the members and brands—because the brand has become individual and approachable, and the boundaries between consumer and brand interactions have somewhat blurred," Jones and Huang conclude.[287]

Jones and Huang list six different types of avenues that can be exploited by brands, including[287]:

1. Branded social networks: These are customized platforms for interacting with consumers. They often include a fusion of applications, such as discussion forums or wikis.
2. External social networks: While some brands choose to create their own community websites, others just have a presence on an external social networking site, thereby taking advantage of the network's built-in platform and audience.
3. Innovation hubs: These are unique platforms provided by the brands for users to post their ideas to the company.
4. Content aggregation sites: These are websites where users share media content with other users. They are websites such as BookCrossing, Flickr, YouTube, and SlideShare and they often include brand-sponsored "channels" through which the brand distributes media content and allows users to engage with and comment upon the content.
5. Blogs: A normal type of blog but filled with corporate information.
6. Micro-blogging: Brand-owned micro-blogging websites are normally used for data collection (i.e., a Twitter account that is used to track tweets and mentions).

Brand is one thing and anti-brand is another; when it comes to anti-brand management, businesses should be aware of the threat this unique problem entails. In his article *Negative Double Jeopardy: The Role of Anti-brand Sites On the Internet*[289], S. Umit Kucuk claims that anti-brand websites are today's "form of boycott and protest, developed through consumer activism as a result of increasing consumer power." According to Kucuk, because of the advent of the Internet, "Consumers are able to clearly broadcast their messages and organize with other like-minded consumers,"[289] which allows them to use "anti-brand websites as weapons of empowerment to battle the corporate world and its brand power on a day-to-day basis."[289]

It doesn't take much to set up a website these days and as Kucuk explains, "the corporation has a website and so does the consumer."[289] Anti-brand sites are "attacking targeted brands and corporations by using their most powerful online branding tool against them: *'domain names'*. Many such anti-brand domain names are easy to remember and catchy in nature (such as Northwest Airlines' Northworstair.org, Safeway's Shameway.com, Starbucks' Starbucked.com, Coca-Cola's Killercoke.org, etc.)."[289] Kucuk notes that, "Anti-brand sites purposefully use the targeted corporation's brand name in their domain name to insult the corporation's brand identity and to express their anger and frustration while entertaining and educating consumers and audiences"[289] alike.

Although their names can be quite humorous, these websites are no laughing matter and they must be taken very seriously. The courts in the United States have been of little help; many have found in favor of these anti-brand sites, stating that, "usage of a targeted brand's name in a domain name is not trademark infringement, but is protected under the First Amendment—as long as the site owner does not use the anti-brand site to make a profit."[289]

Like a virus living off its host, these anti-brand sites "benefit by sharing the link popularity, brand awareness and web traffic of the targeted brands' site in many search engine results and in consumer surfing decisions on the Internet."[289]

Troublingly, anti-brand sites "often show up in the top ten search results when a corporate brand is researched on major search engines," Kucuk adds.[289] Other sites are also taking "advantage of mistyping (called typo squatting) to steal traffic directed to the targeted brands as in the case of Untied.com, a hate site targeting United Airlines (United.com)."[289]

"For these oppositional consumer groups, anti-brand sites have turned out to be major message dissemination venues and a powerful communication tool. Today, hate sites exchange information, organize boycotts and coordinate lawsuits, thus revolutionizing consumer movements," Kucuk adds.[289]

The internet's tagline could almost be "Seek and ye shall find" and, in the case of disgruntled airline passengers or slighted employees, these sites are easy to discover and even easier to add complaints to, so companies should be wary of engaging on them. Another thing to keep in mind is that if one of these anti-brand websites discusses company policy and invites other employees to comment it "can be considered 'concerted activity' and is protected by the National Labor Relations Act—NLRA."[289]

Kucuk breaks down anti-brand sites into four different categories—Experts, Symbolic Haters, Complainers, and Opportunists.[289] The developers of an "Experts" website usually have detailed knowledge about a company's markets and their alternatives, as well as expertise about business practices, products and technologies.[289] "Because of their advanced level of expertise, they are capable of sensing and following market changes in real time," Kucuk notes.[289]

These websites are often sophisticated and some "apply strong expressiveness and communication strategies with unforgettably powerful images to maximize their impact on visitors to the site"[289], with the ultimate purpose of hurting brand identity.[289] "This, in effect, creates some level of economic pressure by stimulating anti-consumption against the targeted brands," concludes Kucuk.[289]

The brands targeted by "Symbolic Haters" have high brand awareness, but they are not as valuable as those targeted by the experts.[289] This group of anti-brand protesters is predominantly sustained by rumors, supposition and negative word-of-mouth and they focus more on the myths behind the brand's success.[289]

In order to create opposition to a targeted brand, "Complainers" reflect their anger by bringing negative attention to a company with service failure scandals.[289] "Complainers" are "more interested in operational and product-related problems than business philosophy or system order," notes Kucuk.[289] Acting like rejected lovers, these complainers "might have initially tried to build communication with the company regarding their concerns, but their insight was not appreciated by the company, and they chose to protest them on hate sites using 'wake-up call'-type attention grabbers to get their point across."[289]

These types of sites are not as advanced as either experts or symbolic haters sites[289], and "their expressiveness is limited to depictions of actual service failures (pictures of smashed packages, etc.) or scanned and posted documents about the unresolved communications with the targeted company rather than advanced interactive website designs."[289] The message, however, is clear and often the examples given involve personal experiences that the website's readers can empathize with, and thus the reader may develop a negative opinion of the targeted company based on another person's experience.

"Opportunists" could be considered the scavengers or hyenas of the anti-brand website world as they "rely on a company's service failures reflected in the media news as their main source of information."[289] Kucuk argues that "opportunists are fed by media, not personal expertise nor experience, but they are trying to use flashy news stories to influence potential consumers into viewing their own website in order to increase site traffic."[289] "Opportunists" are not driven by personal experience, but rather by a desire to trumpet scandalous news so that their websites gain more traction and attention.[289]

Although anti-brand sites are usually created to attempt to hurt brands, smart companies can—in a Vito Corleone "Keep your friends close, but your enemies closer" kind of way—use these websites to their advantage. Kucuk offers four basic strategies for companies to counter these anti-brand websites; work with experts; monitor symbolic haters; talk to complainers; and combat opportunists.[289]

The anti-brand "Experts" websites might actually be helpful because they can alert a company to problems they might not have known existed, and the expertise shared on the sites can be used in a company's market value creation process going forward.[289] Unlike customer-satisfaction surveys or pricey consultants, feedback gained from such sites is free to the company.[289] Some very useful information can be gleaned from an ex-employee's tell-all website, as former employees often have extensive knowledge of the inner workings of a company[289], and this is knowledge that is oftentimes overlooked by higher-level company executives.

Of course, before engaging with these experts, a company should first analyze and determine the "hostility level" and "expertise level" of such sites.[289] If the hostility level is extremely high and the expertise level low, the site should be monitored but not necessarily engaged with, until, that is, the hate generated has reached such a harmful level that it needs to be addressed.[289] "If a company reaches a somewhat manageable level of hostility along with a good level of consumer expertise through these sites, it should, however, encourage consumer involvement in the market co-value-creation process," advises Kucuk.[289]

Because symbolic haters might be under the influence of negative word-of-mouth stories, the challenge with these sites is to counter these negative stories with timely positive and credible ones.[289] Social media is actually the perfect channel to do this on. The insight symbolic haters provide on their sites isn't usually as useful or informative as that provided by experts, however.[289] Kucuk advises that, "Companies should closely monitor what these sites are talking about and be open to any communication form directed to consumers in order to control this symbolic (or sometimes even disingenuous) hate targeted towards their brands."[289] "In other words, a company cannot defend its perspectives without knowing the truth behind the news broadcasted by such sites."[289] Once again, keeping an enemy close.

"Complainers" are the consumers who "might have been satisfied with a company's products and services for a while, but have grown dissatisfied."[289] They might still be "looking for the spark or enjoyment they once felt when they met with that brand,"[289] but they have currently fallen out of favor with it. Since these sites are trying to garner attention by focusing on major service failure scandals, Kucuk recommends that companies "contact site owners to solve such consumer dissatisfaction problems before the aggression begins to impact the company's brand identity on the Internet."[289]

Because negative word-of-mouth can go viral in seconds and live on social media sites almost indefinitely, it is imperative for companies to challenge negative word-of-mouth stories and transform them into positive word-of-mouth ones as quickly as possible.[289] Airlines should keep an eye on e-complaint sites, as well as consumer blogs to monitor the type and duration of problems that can flare up.[289] When appropriate, airlines should email upset customers, perhaps attaching discount coupons or gift cards to show its remorse for poor service and/or bad quality, as well as its sincerity towards improving customer service.[289]

As their name implies, "opportunists" are mostly looking to exploit an opportunity to be recognized so that they can reach a level of awareness that will gain them public notoriety.[289] "Opportunists" "can be very harmful once they find scandalous events regarding a targeted brand, which brings the site higher visibility and traffic," warns Kucuk.[289] "Opportunists" are trying to steal web traffic from the targeted company, and will search the news media for anything they can use to gain attention by attacking brands.

"In a pre-emptive attempt to prevent the creation of such anti-brand sites, corporations can buy potential negative domain names that can be targeted on the Internet," advises Kucuk.[289] For every Facebook.com there is probably going to be a Facebooksucks.com so companies should be aware of the existence of these opportunists as well as be ready to combat them to stop any potential brand erosion.[289]

The ".sucks" web address is also available so any disgruntled customer could purchase that and quickly become a headache for any airliner by writing about their negative experiences. Airlines can help avert many potentially embarrassing anti-brand headaches in the future by snapping up possible anti-brand sites when creating their regular brand sites.

Culling through sites like Twitter, Facebook, Weibo, etc., etc., for customer complaints should be a daily, if not hourly, practice. Alerts can be set up to peg comments by known customers, with an appropriate email response automatically prepared. Approval from a customer service rep or manager would only take moments and responses could, literally, be in the hands of customers moments after they made their critical tweet, Facebook post, and/or negative Weibo comment.

Above all else, an airline should have a personality and it should be proud enough to wear that personality on its sleeve, as if it were a badge of honor. Obviously, many already do, but this is such an important part of branding that it should be reiterated. Every piece of marketing content, every brand message, every chosen marketing channel should reiterate this personality to drum it into the buyer's psyche. Think *Dollar Shave Club*, a company that went from inception to a billion dollar buyout by Unilever within about five years; it sold nothing but razors and shaving accoutrements but it had a personality that helped it go viral on social media, which made its top of the mind amongst customers who wanted cheap blades, which made its valuation go exponential to a buyer.[290]

Airlines must decide what type of brand they want to be and embrace that personality with gusto. In his article *12 Examples of Brand Personality*[291], Brendan Butler lists the options as follows:

1. Purist—companies like Dove, Disney, and Sesame Street trumpet values such as wholesomeness, ethics, simplicity, happiness, faith and purity.

2. Pioneer—companies like The Discovery Channel and Jeep push values such as freedom, adventure, self-discovery, self-reliance, bravery and ambition.
3. Source—Bloomberg, eMarketer, Forrester and Mckinsey all embrace knowledge and enlightenment as they champion values such as truth, objectivity, education, discipline, clarity and commitment.
4. Conqueror—brands like Nike and Weight Watchers push values of resilience, steadfastness, character and endurance.
5. Rebel—Harley Davidson, Red Bull and World Wrestling Entertainment champion values like independence, controversy, freedom and nonconformity. Paramount to them is the idea that rules should not just be bent, but rather completely broken.
6. Wizard—Apple and Pixar are two brands that come to mind for wizard brands, which tend to specialize in creating the extraordinary out of the ordinary. These brands foster imagination, surprise and curiosity.
7. Straight Shooter—Easy Jet and Southwest Airlines are good examples of straight shooters, who aim for authenticity, honesty and frankness above all else.
8. Seducer—DeBeers and Victoria's Secret embody the seducer's values; beauty, pleasure, passion, desire, sensuality and intimacy.
9. Entertainer—Dr Pepper and M&Ms like helping their customers see the fun side of life, championing such values as spontaneity, charm, and humor.
10. Protector—Campbell's Soup and Johnson & Johnson are examples of protectors, which promote values of compassion, kindness, care and love.
11. Imagineer—Lego, YouTube and Adobe are Imagineering companies that help customers to create, develop original thinking, and artistry.
12. Emperor—American Express, Porsche and Rolex are all brands that embody the qualities of leadership, determination, respect, dominance, influence and wealth.

Having a brand personality is important because it makes it easier for buyers and potential buyers to identify with your airliner.[291]

Build Fanbases and Communities

Whether you call them "fans", "friends", "followers" or "subscribers", building a community of users will help an airline grow its customer base, as well as help it participate in the conversation about its brand.

Facebook no longer uses the term "Fan", and, instead of becoming a "Fan", Facebook would rather users "Like" or "Find" a brand instead. Not wanting to get into too much of a semantic argument, I believe the concept of a "Fan" makes more sense when discussing the creation of user communities. "Fandom" connotes devotion, enthusiasm, advocacy, and affection and all of these positive emotions can be used to drive customer loyalty and, just as importantly, customer spend.

Few would argue that customer satisfaction is the foundation of true customer loyalty, while customer dissatisfaction is one of the key factors that drives customers away.[59] This may sound obvious but its importance cannot be stressed enough. Increasing customer loyalty is what building fanbases is all about, but an airline should be aware that building large fanbases and gaining thousands of followers shouldn't be an end-goal in itself, it is important to put in place a system that produces enough content to keep these fans engaged.

As per Jones and Sasser's *zone of affection*, satisfaction levels are high and "customers may have such high attitudinal loyalty that they don't look for alternative service."[75] It is within this group that "Apostles" or "Influencers" reside, and this is the group that is responsible for improved future business performance.[75] It is within this group of devotees that businesses can find their most vocal and valuable customers. Through social media, these people can be discovered, nurtured, and stimulated to spread the company's message far and wide.

With little marketing expenditure, a company can get its message out to the wider community and, once again, because these recommendations would be coming in through a marketed person's contacts, followers and friends, they are messages that are much more likely to be acted upon.

To increase a company's fan base, Facebook recommends doing the following:

- Encourage visitors to "like" your page.
- Partner with other brands or local organizations: this can promote viral sharing of customers between businesses. Airlines are already doing this with local charities and non-competing companies because it is highly advantageous for all parties involved.
- Expand the reach of your posts: when you mention a person or an organization in your posts, be sure to connect to them in a post so that your post will automatically appear on their wall.
- Use social plugins on your website: Installing a "Like" box on your homepage or on your newsletters will drive people to your Facebook page.
- Encourage physical check-ins at your business: these posts will appear in a customer's news feed, thereby providing more exposure for a business.
- Promote with ads and sponsored stories.

The best way to encourage engagement and interaction on Facebook is to post multimedia links on your page.[292] You should post images regularly so you have a better chance of standing out, even on status updates as images will catch the eye of your current followers and images are shared much more often than simple text.[292] Running competitions is another great way of increasing fans and fostering engagement, but be aware of Facebook's rules as they can be quite restrictive.[292]

Just as on Facebook, images are also a great way of increasing engagement on Twitter.[292] "With the likes of Instagram and Camera+ allowing Twitter integration, it's easier than ever to tweet images. There's no harm in cross posting from different social media sites so don't be afraid to link to a Facebook or Pinterest post if it's interesting. Better yet, post the image and provide the link to the other site."[292]

Twitter can also be used for competitions, but, once again, check out the rules. Twitter's rules might not be as strict as Facebook's, but you should refer to them to understand what is acceptable and what is not.

Building up a following on LinkedIn is not as easy as it is on Facebook and Twitter as there isn't as much scope for posting content.[292] However, LinkedIn recently bought SlideShare and they have made it easy to integrate SlideShare presentations on a LinkedIn page.

With LinkedIn, it is important to get involved in groups and discussions as that is a good way to get one's brand name out there.[292] In this case, you might be promoting yourself more than your actual company page, but your strategy should be about building up your own reputation, which should, subsequently, build up your brand.[292]

In her article *Six of the best travel brands on YouTube, Snapchat, Instagram, Twitter, Pinterest & LinkedIn*[293], Nikki Gilliland points out that LinkedIn is actually a good place to find potential customers. "According to a survey by MRI, LinkedIn users aged 18 to 44 are over twice as likely to join flight and hotel reward schemes compared to users of other social networks," she says.[293] "What's more," she adds, "they're also twice as likely to travel internationally and are more likely to show loyalty toward brands."[293]

Some airlines have recognized LinkedIn's power for a while now.[293] Gilliland notes that, "Back in 2014, KLM airlines was one of the first brands to offer a 24/7 service via LinkedIn, allowing users to contact the brand via the social platform."[293]

Since then, Gilliland adds that KLM "has continued to harness the platform's shift into a publishing network rather than just a professional one, using it to distribute brand content."[293] Today, KLM "publishes blogs and articles on a regular basis, aiming to push LinkedIn's large user-base towards it website, as well as position itself as an expert voice on the aviation industry."[293]

Gilliland also notes that Snapchat, although not an most obvious channel for travel brands, is utilized by some airlines to give passengers and potential passengers more of an insight into the company culture, sometimes adding sneak peek or behind-the-scenes footage through Snapchat Stories.[293] "What's more, it's also ideal for targeting the platform's young and highly-engaged user-base," Gilliland adds.[293]

"Aer Lingus is one brand that uses Snapchat in this way, posting content about what it's like to work for the company. Its Stories often provide insight into flights and company events," notes Gilliland.[293]

As it is entirely based around visuals, Pinterest has a dedicated following that is worth the time to engage with. The great thing about Pinterest is the fact that you can create boards that only vaguely relate to your company.[292] The first step an airline should take is to pin high quality images on its page. Followers are going to judge a company's pins based on their appearance, no surprise there since this is a visual medium, so airlines should use the best quality images available.[292]

"Something else worth remembering is that for each Pinterest page, each board has its own number of followers that mightn't even be following your page. If you have a number of boards, check to see just how many people are following and prioritize the boards with the most members," the digital agency Simply Zesty recommends.[292] "That doesn't mean you should neglect your other boards, but it can be useful to focus on one or two boards as you build up your following," Simply Zesty advises.[292]

Hashtag marketing is a science. "A handy way of gaining a few new followers is to use hashtags when tweeting. While there are always trending topics, you shouldn't latch onto them for the sake of it. Instead, identify hashtags that are relevant to your brand and tweet witty or useful information using it. If you provide value, you could be retweeted, which will result in more exposure and some new followers."[292]

The important thing to keep in mind while you're building fanbases is you must keep your content current, you have to make a commitment to your fans, they will not return if they have no reason to return.

In her article *Retailers Need to Master Building Shopping Communities in 2017*[294], Charlie Fusco describes Sephora's push into social media community building:

> "Through its online community, BeautyTalk, you can find thousands of other people who are interested in the same things as you, have tried stuff you wonder about, and will tell you about their experiences in one of the topic areas, where there are thousands of conversational threads about everything, including Beauty Confessions. Beauty Insiders get information and specials before anyone else, and twice a week

> *they get access to special limited time one-of-a-kind experiences, services and coveted samples. In other words, Sephora is shopping you show up for—and that experience continues inside its brick-and-mortar stores. Sephora doesn't just know its customers; it knows their names and who they talk to."*

This is a great example of a company not just understanding its customer base on a deep and intimate personal level, but also creating a space for them to come together to do nothing more than build the brand and sell the products. Of course, there is the cost of the IT infrastructure and Sephora has to pay for staff to initiate and monitor these conversations, but the ROI is probably quite substantial at both the website and in-store level. Without a reason for customers to return, they will not return, it is as simple as that.

Crisis Management

Crisis management refers to the art, technique or practice of averting or dealing with crisis situations that threaten to harm an organization, its stakeholders, or the general public. It is also the attempt to limit the damage of a known or unforeseen problem.

According to Seeger, Sellnow & Ulmer (1998), there are three elements that are common to most definitions of a crisis: (a) a threat to the organization, (b) the element of surprise, and (c) a short decision time.

In his paper *A Typology of Social Media Crisis*[295], Ashwin Malshe argues that one of the key benefits of using social media marketing is the two-way interaction it gives to both businesses and their consumers. "Consumers like it because they can engage in conversations with the brands they buy,"[295] while businesses recognize the value of keeping their customers interested and informed. However, this can be a double-edged sword as a customer can as easily complain about his or her bad brand experiences as he or she can trumpet a good one.[295]

Malshe argues that[295]:

> *"The increased efficiency of communication and intimacy with consumers come at the cost of higher riskiness of the business. Users can share an article, video, or photograph with their social network at the click of a button, thus spreading a firm's content "virally," generating wide visibility instantaneously. In exactly the same way, users can harm firms by sharing bad experiences, rumors, or events that were pure accidents."*

Malshe adds that because there is little accountability on the Internet, firms are put in a tight spot. The fact that there are no moderators on social networks monitoring the flow of information over this super highway only exacerbates the problem.[295] Because of this, social media crisis can flare up quickly and spread at the speed of light[295], turning the very viral nature of the Internet—a nature that normally makes it so appealing to marketers—into a very serious threat against them.

"There are several ways in which one can group social media crises," argues Malshe, adding that "An intuitive criterion for categorization can be the type of social medium."[295] Whether the crisis erupted on Facebook, Twitter, or YouTube will call for different strategies to be used to address and contain the crisis.[295] For example, since human beings are, first-and-foremost visual creatures, a video on YouTube will probably elicit more negative reaction than a tweet on Twitter.[295] However, Malshe argues that crises should not be viewed in a vacuum as they can quickly spread from one network to another.[295] Something initiated on Facebook can easily be shared with others on Google+, Twitter, or the hundreds of other social networks available today.[295] As Malshe notes, since a YouTube video may generate more attention on Facebook than on YouTube, it is not that important to identify which social media site the crisis first blew up on.[295] What is imperative is countering the crisis on as many social media channels and sites as it is affecting.[295]

Using the *Comprehensive Typology of Crises Model*[296] proposed by Gundel as a starting point, Malshe proposes the *Typology of Social Media Crises*. Gundel categorizes crises into "four types based on their predictability (high vs. low) and controllability (high vs. low)."[296] Gundel "puts an emphasis on predictability because, in general, organizations can design measures to proactively eliminate a crisis or at least prepare the response to a crisis based on its predictability."[296] However, for crises flaring up across multiple social media networking sites, the consideration of predictability becomes less important.[296]

Malshe argues that, "due to its open and viral nature, social media makes crises almost unpredictable. Therefore, although organizations can put in place measures to avoid crisis-like situations, the predictability of the time, place, or the nature of crisis [sic] is almost zero."[295] The global nature of social media also makes it exceptionally difficult to predict these types of crises, with language, geographical and cultural differences exacerbating not only the complexity of the problems, but also the responses necessary to deal with them.[295]

Another possible reason for low predictability of social media crises is that companies currently lack an in-depth understanding of the social media world.[295] Social media marketing still isn't very well understood and often is not considered worthy of large IT investments.[295] Although this is starting to change this underinvestment leads to two related problems.[295] "First, the employees delegated to handle social media have little resources or incentives to systematically analyze crises that have already been taking place. Second, a lack of resources leads to relatively small social media teams, which in some cases handle momentous amounts of data," warns Malshe.[295]

"Controllability is a critical factor for general crisis management as well as specifically for social media,"[295] states Malshe. "Crises with low controllability are dangerous and can scar the credibility of the firms for a long time," he adds.[295] Because content can be easily captured through screen-grabs, even small mistakes can have huge effects on a company's brand identity.

"Controversial articles that were yanked from the original websites remain alive on several blogs which display all or part of the original content," Malshe notes.[295] Even though rogue tweets can be deleted in seconds, they can still jeopardize multi-million dollar ad campaigns because screenshots of the offending tweets can encircle the globe as enthusiastic Twitter users share them with friends and followers.[295] Like a virus replicating itself, the damage can be quick and sometimes lethal.

Although it seems that all social media crises have low controllability, that is not necessarily the case.[295] By tackling a problem head-on (oftentimes with disarming humor and/or clever irreverence), a few companies have been able to avoid their own crisis-like situations turning into a full-blown disaster.[295]

An example of this is the case of the Red Cross beer tweeting fiasco: when a Red Cross social media strategist mistakenly posted a tweet about alcohol on the Red Cross's official Twitter account. The Red Cross not only removed the offending tweet quickly but also offered a witty retort on the fiasco, thereby making light of the situation.[295] Such incidences as these are not outliers and, in a few situations, social media crises can be highly controllable.[295] People are, by nature, forgiving creatures and as long as they believe one is being sincere they will give companies the benefit of the doubt.

For Malshe: "It is critical to understand the difference between the two constructs: ease of control and the degree of controllability. In some cases, the overall controllability of the crisis can be low. Within that set of cases, a few crises can be managed, to whatever limited extent, with less effort while the rest may require more effort."[295]

Malshe uses several examples to illustrate his point; including the crisis faced by United Airlines when one of its disgruntled passengers, Dave Carroll, uploaded his parody song "United Breaks Guitars" to YouTube.[295] In the song, Carroll and his band mates narrate an experience about how United broke Carroll's pricey Taylor guitar and refused to reimburse him for the damages.

The song went viral and has now garnered more than 16.2 million views.[297] United was very slow to react to this situation, which exacerbated it even more. The story was picked up by the traditional media and quickly went viral. Overall, for United, this was a situation with very low controllability, but their inaction made the problem considerably worse, turning it into a full-blown PR disaster.

Considering the triviality of the amount involved in this crisis (about US $1,500), it was a relatively "low cost solution for United to offer the money to Carroll and control the crisis," Malshe notes.[295] However, even though United may have reimbursed Carroll, there was no guarantee that he wouldn't still have uploaded the song to YouTube[295], but, at the very least, United wouldn't have looked so tin-eared.

In one television interview (more bad press for United), Carroll explained that he was emotionally attached to the guitar and, even after it had been fixed, it didn't sound as good as it had before it was broken.[295] Therefore, in this situation, there was little United could have done to control the events from getting out of hand and becoming a full-blown crisis. However, "they could have easily averted additional negative publicity by reimbursing Carroll for his troubles," argues Malshe[295], thereby mitigating the crisis to a certain extent.

After all of the social media attention the video received, United did actually offer to reimburse Carroll, but, even then, Carroll took the high road, refusing the money and asking United to give it to charity, which, once again, did little to help United's negative public perception.[295] It was a lose-lose situation for them all around—a deserved, self-inflicted lose-lose situation, admittedly—but it's an important lesson for every business; the consumer now has a megaphone that is just as loud as any company's marketing and PR department and the consumer will always be seen as the underdog in these kinds of situations.

Malshe proposes that, to some extent, the shock value of the trigger that starts the crisis can explain the ease with which the crisis can be controlled.[295] Simply put, the higher the shock value of the trigger, the more difficult the crisis is to control, although Malshe does admit that, since there has been no large scale study of this issue, it is difficult to say to what extent shock value explains the correlation.[295]

Malshe uses two dimensions to categorize social media crises. The first, "Controllability," is based on Gundel's definition[296] and is described as something that is "controllable if responses to limit or eliminate the crisis by influencing its causes are known as well as executable."[295] "Controllability" can either be high or low as can the effort required to control it.[295] This effort, Malshe argues, is a function of the shock value of the trigger, which refers to the extent to which a crisis-triggering incidence offends the social media community.[295] The amount to which the masses can be shocked by a single event is completely dependent on the context.[295]

The shock value of the trigger "refers to the degree to which an incident that is embedded in the context and time offends members of the social media community."[295] This shock value can't be isolated from the context and time, making the predictability of social media crises even more difficult to gauge.[295]

Malshe divides crises into four categories and they are based on whether a crisis has high or low levels of controllability and the shock value of the trigger is either high or low. For example[295]:

- Soft Crises: Like the Red Cross tweet previously mentioned, soft crises have high levels of controllability and low levels of shock value. Left unattended, a soft crisis is likely to turn into a full-blown crisis, so it is important to recognize the crisis, isolate the classification and immediately issue a response.
- Firefighting: This type of crises is highly controllable, but it also has a high trigger of shock value. Even though controllability is high, the high shock value of the crisis has the potential to overwhelm a company's social media department, which could mean the situation unravels very quickly.
- Wait and watch: These require patience and a thick skin. These crises are caused by less shocking triggers, but they have very low controllability. The crisis can go viral very quickly and the more an organization responds to the crisis, the more disastrous it could become.
- Disaster: These are highly uncontrollable and shocking crisis situations and they can break organizations.

The Red Cross tweet was a soft crisis because the original tweet was offensive, but its shock value was relatively low and a clarification on the origin of the tweet was enough to dissipate the tension in the social media world.[295] It is really not surprising that the Red Cross's employees think about drinking beer after work, but the tweet made it sound as if the employees were drinking on the job.[295] Once the facts were presented, the crisis was easily averted.[295]

Ashton Kutcher's November 2011 tweet stream about the firing of Penn State Football team coach Joe Paterno is one of the most celebrated examples of a firefighting crisis.[295] Kutcher, who had more than eight million Twitter followers at the time, expressed his disappointment in the firing and thought that the whole incident lacked class.[295] However, Kutcher was ignorant of the fact that Paterno had been let go because of his reluctance to fire a coach who had been accused of raping a child in the Penn State men's locker room.[295] Understandably, there was a huge backlash against Kutcher's tweet and his image was badly bruised.[295] Kutcher "immediately decided to stop engaging directly with his Twitter fans and followers."[295] He has since outsourced his social media responses.

This incident is a perfect example of a firefighting crisis. The trigger—the offending tweet—was highly shocking to the social media community.[295] Had he acted to counter his offensive tweet, Kutcher could have controlled the crisis before it had spread so wide, Malshe argues. Looking back, it is surprising to see that one person—a busy celebrity at that—insisted on communicating with his followers on a one-to-one basis, thereby so easily exposing himself to a crisis.[295]

"The crisis was controllable because Kutcher could have put in place a system to tackle such situations," Malshe concludes.[295]

The United Airlines crisis is a perfect example of a wait and watch crisis. The song was hardly shocking, but it had huge amusement value, which helped it go viral. Once the video was available on YouTube, there was little United could have done to defuse the crisis.

In April 2009, the video of two Domino's Pizza employees tainting food at a Domino's franchisee hit YouTube and, unsurprisingly, it went viral instantly.[295] Domino's Pizza immediately found itself in a classic disaster situation.[295] "The enormous shock value of the YouTube video coupled with extremely low controllability of the crisis made it the worst possible situation for Domino's," states Malshe.[295]

Domino's responded with a YouTube video of its own: Patrick Doyle, the President of Domino's USA, acknowledged that the two people in the video were, indeed, employees of a Domino's franchisee, but he explained that warrants for their arrests had been issued and that the store where they had worked had been completely sanitized since the incident.[295] This crisis became a disaster because the trigger—the YouTube video—had a very high shock value—but the crisis was highly uncontrollable.[295] The employees' actions were suicidal and completely unpredictable.[295] Domino's couldn't really be faulted for not having a plan for such an extreme scenario as the sheer bizarreness of the act of sabotage made it uncontrollable and completely unavoidable.[295]

Going forward, Domino's promised to toughen its employment hiring practices, while also hammering home the message that this was an isolated incident that didn't represent normal Domino's employee behavior.[295] Once Domino's responded, however, it could do little but hope for the situation to blow over, which, after a short while, it did. "In contrast to United Airlines, Domino's Pizza faced a highly shocking social media crisis and experienced a major damage to their brand name," states Malshe, however, neither company was able to do much about it.

As with normal crisis management, the response to a social media crisis should involve the three steps of crisis management—prevention, response, and recovery—and Malshe suggests companies use the Hale, Dulek, and Hale model[298] to mitigate crises. In this model, Hale, Dulek, and Hale propose that the response can be divided into four sub-processes: observation, interpretation, choice, and dissemination. Malshe breaks these processes down in the following way[295]:

> "Observation entails collecting all the relevant information at the onset of the crisis. Interpretation involves assessing information within the context of the current crisis to determine both its accuracy and its relevance. Choice involves assessing

viability of different alternative actions and choosing the most appropriate among them. Finally, dissemination leads to information exchange with the public."

According to Malshe, the four-step response to a social media crisis is[295]:

- Soft crises and firefighting: For soft crisis and firefighting, Malshe suggests implementing Hale, Dulek, and Hale's spiral crisis response communication model. In this model, the four steps of the crisis communication—observation, interpretation, choice, and dissemination—are repeated one after another in a kind of circle.[295] "Such a model is most appropriate for the crises with high controllability," Malshe argues, adding that, "By actively engaging in the four steps, crisis can be managed more effectively and prevented from growing into a disaster."[295]
- Wait and watch disaster: For the two crises situations where controllability is low, Malshe contends the spiral communication model is redundant.[295] By constantly changing the response based on developments within various social media avenues, an organization is very likely to make a bad situation worse. Therefore, it is more appropriate to select a linear model that follows Hale, Dulek, and Hale's four steps—observation, interpretation, choice, and dissemination. After the information is disseminated to the public, there may not be a need to actively keep on responding to the crisis as the organization doesn't have any control over the crisis.

Develop a Virtual Social World Presence

Although virtual social worlds did hold a lot of promise when they were first introduced several years ago, they have not gained much traction over the last few years. Several high-profile sites, such as Teleplace, have actually shut down, the remnants of its 3D immersive environment are now in the open source software Openqwaq, but it is too soon to give up on them altogether.

In her article *Why Virtual Worlds Suck for Business—and Some Solutions*[299], Maria Korolov makes a good case as to why virtual worlds haven't taken off when she discusses a typical virtual world scenario as such:

> *"You spend several minutes (at least!) loading up the software, finding your microphone, adjusting your sound levels, and logging into a virtual scene. If you're lucky, you have a choice of avatars, none of whom look anything like you. If you're unlucky, you show up as a big plastic Gumby-like thing or as an ugly woman in orange tights (known as 'Ruth' in OpenSim and Second Life). You already feel stupid, and then your hosts show up, also as cartoon characters. You can't make eye contact with*

> them, you can't read their body language—if they're animated at all, it's usually jerky and inappropriate to the situation. Occasionally, you'll get the tour from someone in a funky costume, or a cross-dresser, or a robot. Even when they're dressed in business clothing, the clothes are often too tight, too sexy or otherwise 'off'."

Korolov goes on to explain that even the act of walking is difficult and, for some reason, each platform does it differently.[299] This would all be worth it if there was something worthwhile to see while you were in these immersive environments, but all you get "is a screen hanging on a wall."[299] The tour guide explains that you can put anything on the screen, some video, a webpage, even share a desktop with some of the enterprise platforms but what's the use of that, Korolov asks, adding sarcastically, "You already own a screen you can put anything on, it's your own computer screen. And it already does all of those things."[299]

The argument that these worlds are so compelling because they are "immersive" as Second Life likes to point out is specious at best.[299] "The environments are bland. The clothes are bland. All virtual conference rooms look the same, anyway. And there's nothing to do there, except walk around and look at screens. You are not immersed. And if you're not immersed, then [sic] the virtual environment is, in fact, nothing more than a chat room with bad 3D graphics."[299]

Korolov does, however, make some compelling arguments for companies to use virtual social worlds as virtual work environments—fewer centralized offices, more telecommuting, lower facilities budgets, lower travel budgets, and shorter commutes that result in a better work-life balance, and, probably higher employee retention.[299] For an airline, this could be particularly compelling as they often have offices in far-flung locations throughout the world. "If a company is able to create a successful, engaging and immersive virtual workplace for its employees and managers, it will also be able to recruit from a wider pool of potential workers," offers Korolov.[299]

Discover a Customer's Psychological Profile

Since every "Like", every purchase made, every video watched, every cellphone movement, and every website visit is logged somewhere on some server, they are all analyzable.

As Hannes Grassegger and Mikael Krogerus explain in their *Das Magazin* article *I Just Showed That the Bomb Was There*[300], "Psychologist Michal Kosinski developed a method of analyzing people's behavior down to the minutest detail by looking at their Facebook activity."[300] According to Grassegger and Krogerus[300]:

> "Psychometrics, sometimes also known as psychography, is a

scientific attempt to 'measure' the personality of a person. The so-called Ocean Method has become the standard approach. Two psychologists were able to demonstrate in the 1980s that the character profile of a person can be measured and expressed in five dimensions, the Big Five: Openness (how open are you to new experiences?), Conscientiousness (how much of a perfectionist are you?), Extroversion (how sociable are you?), Agreeableness (how considerate and cooperative are you?), and Neuroticism (how sensitive/vulnerable are you?). With these five dimensions (O.C.E.A.N.), you can determine fairly precisely what kind of person you are dealing with—her needs and fears as well as how she will generally behave. For a long time, however, the problem was data collection, because to produce such a character profile meant asking subjects to fill out a complicated survey asking quite personal questions. Then came the internet. And Facebook. And Kosinski."

In 2008, with a fellow Cambridge student, Kosinski created a small app for Facebook called *MyPersonality* that asked users a handful of questions from the Ocean survey and they would receive a rating, or a "Personality Profile", consisting of traits defined by the Ocean method.[300] The researchers, in turn, got the users' personal data, which soon amounted to millions and millions of reviews.[300] "It was, literally, the then-largest psychological data set ever produced," state Grassegger and Krogerus.[300]

In the ensuing years, Kosinski and his colleagues continued the research; "first surveys are distributed to test subjects—this is the online quiz. From the subjects' responses, their personal Ocean traits are calculated. Then Kosinski's team would compile every other possible online data point of a test subject—what they've liked, shared, or posted on Facebook; gender, age, and location."[300]

Once the researchers dug into the data, they discovered that amazingly reliable conclusions could be drawn about a person by observing their online behavior.[300] For example, "men who 'like' the cosmetics brand MAC are, to a high degree of probability, gay," which isn't that surprising, but there are other interesting findings. For example, one of the best indicators of heterosexuality is liking Wu-Tang Clan.[300] Also, people who follow Lady Gaga are most probably extroverts, while someone who likes philosophy is probably an introvert.[300]

In the ensuing years, Kosinski and his team continued, tirelessly refining their models. "In 2012, Kosinski demonstrated that from a mere 68 Facebook likes, a lot about a user could be reliably predicted: skin color (95% certainty), sexual orientation (88% certainty), Democrat or Republican (85%)," explains Grassegger and Krogerus.[300] Level of intellect, religious affiliation, alcohol, cigarette, and drug use could all be calculated as well.[300] For airlines, employee Facebook pages could be scanned to screen out potentially problematic candidates.

As Kosinski continued refining his model, he discovered that with a mere ten likes as input, his model could appraise a person's character better than an average coworker.[300] With seventy, "it could 'know' a subject better than a friend; with 150 likes, better than their parents. With 300 likes, Kosinski's machine could predict a subject's behavior better than their partner. With even more likes it could exceed what a person thinks they know about themselves,"[300] which is a pretty frightening thought.

The day Kosinski published his findings, he received two phone calls, both from Facebook; one a threat to sue, the other a job offer.[300]

Since the publication of Kosinski's article, Facebook has introduced a differentiation between public and private posts so the data isn't as easily accessible now.[300] In "private" mode, "only one's own friends can see what one likes. This is still no obstacle for data-collectors: while Kosinski always requests the consent of the Facebook users he tests, many online quizzes these days demand access to private information as a precondition to taking a personality test."[300]

Kosinski and his team are now adding variables beyond Facebook Likes.[300] Offline activity is now traceable and "motion sensors can show, for example, how fast we are moving a smartphone around or how far we are traveling (correlates with emotional instability)."[300]

Flipping this idea on its head, Kosinski speculated his research could become a search engine for people.[300] By using all of this data, psychological profiles could not only be constructed, but they could also be sought and found.[300] For example, if a company, or a politician, wants to find worried fathers, or angry introverts, or undecided Democrats, these profiles could be uncovered in the data.[300]

To Kosinski's chagrin, one company he had been partnered with—Cambridge Analytica—was involved with Donald Trump's 2016 presidential election.[300] Cambridge Analytica has become infamous now and has even been shut down because of its questionable activities during the 2016 presidential election. It had bought up extensive personal data on American voters—"What car you drive, what products you purchase in shops, what magazines you read, what clubs you belong to"—and used the data in questionable and unethical ways.[300]

In America, detailed personal consumer data is available for a price and Cambridge Analytica snapped it up and the company crosschecked these data sets with Republican Party voter rolls and online data such as Facebook likes.[300] Ocean personality profiles were built from this data and, from a selection of digital signatures there suddenly emerged real individual people with real fears, needs, and interests—and home addresses.[300] By the time of the election, Cambridge Analytics had assembled psychograms for all adult US citizens, 220 million people, and they used this data to influence electoral outcomes, as was seen with the 2016 U.S. Presidential election.[300]

"Trump's conspicuous contradictions and his oft-criticized habit of staking out multiple positions on a single-issue result in a gigantic number of resulting messaging options that creates a huge advantage for a firm like Cambridge Analytica: for every voter, a different message," explains Grassegger and Krogerus.[300]

Mathematician Cathy O'Neil notes that Trump is like a machine learning algorithm that adjusts to public reactions.[300] On the day of the third 2016 presidential debate, "Trump's team blasted out 175,000 distinct variations on his arguments, mostly via Facebook,"[300] an astounding number of unique ads. "The messages varied mostly in their microscopic details, in order to communicate optimally with their recipients: different titles, colors, subtitles, with different images or videos" were utilized, explains Grassegger and Krogerus.[300] This is marketing automation at its finest.

Small towns, city districts, apartment buildings, and even individual people could be targeted, explains Grassegger and Krogerus.[300] Blanket advertising—the idea that a hundred million people will be sent the same piece of marketing collateral, the same television advert, the same digital advert—is over, note Grassegger and Krogerus.[300] Micro and personalization targeting has reached the point where companies can advertise highly detailed and personalized messages to a market of one.

Cambridge Analytica separated the entire US population into 32 different personality types, and focused their efforts on only seventeen states.[300] "Just as Kosinski had determined that men who like MAC cosmetics on Facebook are probably gay, Cambridge Analytica found that a predilection for American-produced cars is the best predictor of a possible Trump voter."[300] Among other things, this kind of information helped the Trump campaign focus in on what messages to use, and where to use them, perhaps even what channel to use them on.[300] In effect, the candidate himself became an implementation instrument of the model.[300]

As Grassegger and Krogerus note, the first results seen by *Das Magazin* were amazing: psychological targeting increased the clickthru rate on Facebook ads by more than sixty percent. And the so-called conversion rate (the term for how likely a person is to act upon a personally-tailored ad, i.e., whether they buy a product or, yes, go vote) increases by a staggering 1,400 percent."[300]

Now, what does all of this mean for an airline? How can they use Facebook Likes to gain a deeper understanding of their customers? Well, potentially, by analyzing these Likes, an airline could predict how open, conscientious, outgoing and neurotic an individual user and/or passenger was. It could be as simple as doing a Facebook graph search of "Pictures liked" or "Videos liked" and/or "Stories Liked" with the customer's name. In addition to predicting a user's personality, these tests could estimate a user/customer's age, relationship status, intelligence level, life satisfaction, political and religious beliefs, and education.

An airline's HR department would also find these personality test results interesting as matching a candidate with jobs based on their personality might make more sense than the current scattershot approach HR often takes in hiring—and firing. These personality tests could also reveal troubling traits that should not be ignored.

Discover Important Brand Trends

As Bifet and Frank explain in their paper *Sentiment Knowledge Discovery in Twitter Streaming Data*[301], Twitter is a:

> "potentially valuable source of data that can be used to delve into the thoughts of millions of people as they are uttering them. Twitter makes these utterances immediately available in a data stream, which can be mined for information by using appropriate stream mining techniques. In principle, this could make it possible to infer people's opinions, both at an individual level as well as in aggregate, regarding potentially any subject or event."

Services offered by companies like Rival iQ[302] can track a list of brands of one's choosing and monitor their activity on Facebook, Twitter, and Google. Rival IQ could not only provide insight into an airline's competitor, but also insight into the industry as a whole. For instance, airlines could learn from the "Day of the Week" chart when content from the airline industry is most likely to go viral.

Buzz Sumo[303] also has a search tool that tracks the most popular content on any given topic or website and ranks it according to shares on Facebook, Twitter, LinkedIn, and Google. Later in this chapter, I will discuss the importance of sentiment and influencers.

As Bifet and Frank note, "There are also a number of interesting tasks that have been tackled using Twitter text mining: sentiment analysis, classification of tweets into categories, clustering of tweets and trending topic detection."[301]

In their article *From tweets to polls: Linking text sentiment to public opinion time series*, O'Connor et al. found that surveys of consumer confidence correlate with sentiment word frequencies in tweets, and they proposed text stream mining as a substitute for traditional polling.[304] Free sentiment analysis services like twittersentiment.appspot.com can be used to analyze a company's sentiment.

Gilliland argues that, "Twitter can also be used as an effective tool for branding— particularly when it comes to competition between companies."[293] She notes that, "Delta Airlines is one airline that has displayed both strategies in the past, using its Twitter account to provide customer support, as well as the occasional bit of shade when necessary."[293] "For example, when a United Airlines passenger was refused to board a plane because she was wearing leggings, Delta fired back with a cheeky retort,"[293] which read: "Flying Delta means comfort. (That means you can wear your leggings." This was a brilliant piece of shade and a prime example of relevant newsjacking, a level of real-time marketing that all airlines should aspire to reach.

Engage Customers and Potential Customers

Social media has really upped the ante when it comes to customer engagement because, through social channels, customers can not only connect with the brands they like, but also with other people who like the brand as well. This also taps nicely into the social proof concept. What is now new, however, "is that customer engagement is not just a brand's connection with the customer. It is also the customers' engagement with one another in the horizontal, viral aspects," argues Macy and Thompson.[305] It is these horizontal and viral aspects that can be so important—and, potentially, so lucrative to an airline.

"Tactically, brands must begin writing and publishing content with embedded links to other content, pictures, and videos to meet the expectations of the online audience," recommends Macy and Thompson.[305] This "encourages engagement and facilitates sharing."[305] Conversely, Macy and Thompson warn that a "lack of engagement limits brand leadership effectiveness and ultimately defeats the purpose of the medium."[305]

"A smart combination of listening to the online conversation already taking place, learning what people want, and then providing what they are open to receive from the brand constitutes the winning ticket," advises Macy and Thompson.[305] Whether the engagement is through video, online polls, games, photo sharing, e-mail, blogging, PowerPoint presentations, or podcasting, "engagement strategies present an opportunity for brands to align content creation for social media with a company's priorities and involve cross-functional interaction and collaboration," state Macy and Thompson.[305] "Social media engagement can also be used for front-end campaigns and appearances to help guide the conversation and generate buzz," conclude Macy and Thompson.[305]

To engage customers and potential customers, an airline should set up blogs that provide customers a place to comment on their products and/or services. This helps an airline stay connected with its customers. An environment that keeps the dialogue open and honest should be fostered; even criticism should be welcomed, and the blog should not be censored, except for comments that are out-of-bounds or indecent, of course.

Airlines should also keep a keen eye on other blogs and websites where their customers might be blogging as this can lead to criticism that is more open and honest—and, potentially, more helpful—than criticism on the company's own social media websites.

The instantaneous nature of the blogosphere also allows companies to counteract any negative press that might be slung their way. This could be especially helpful to an airline that is hit with negative publicity or product recalls as the blogosphere allows them to immediately present their side of the story.

Today, many companies use blogs to update their employees, their customers, and their shareholders about important company developments, but anyone planning to use a blog for business should be aware that blogs do come with their own built-in risks. Customers who are dissatisfied with a company's products or services may decide to engage in virtual complaints in the form of protest websites or blogs, which could result in potentially damaging information being released online, where it can easily be read and picked up by any customer a company is trying to court.[44]

The mobile phone has added a new element to the world of blogging as well. Moblogging, m-blogging or phone blogging are blogs created or updated from a mobile phone, a tablet or a phablet. With moblogging, text updates can be sent via SMS or email from a mobile phone, while photographs and/or video files can be uploaded using the mobile device's camera feature.

Jantsch's *Hierarchy of Social Media*[277] is a good framework to consider here. Once you have set up your blog, it's time to move up to the RSS step, where aggregating and filtering content takes place. RSS can help an airline repurpose and republish content.

Content can be spread far and wide by leveraging it into other social media channels. "For those looking to feed an RSS of a blog straight to Twitter, Facebook, or LinkedIn profiles, Twitter Feed has you covered. Simply enter your feed, connect your social accounts, and send your posts complete with tracking tools for follow-up."[306] TweetDeck is another service that allows rapid sharing of content; it is a free service owned by Twitter.

The website ShareRoot has several tools that can help boost Pinterest engagement, promotion, and it measures engagement as well.[306] Pinterest's Board Cover Creator lets users create images to use as the cover for their different pin boards, which can help them stand out from the crowd.[306]

Another good example of excellent customer engagement is for the camera manufacturer GoPro, who "launched its channel four years ago and started producing videos as a way to promote its cameras. But the popularity of the campaign took [on] a life of its own, and now GoPro is taking a cue from its customers and producing many of its own videos as well. The change has tripled their amount of views so far this year."[307] GoPro's channel is now one of the most popular channels on YouTube.[307]

GoPro's videos "include the exciting dramatic events like water sports or bungee jumping, but people also used the camera to capture some emotional and personal moments up close, such as a student graduating high school or their baby falling asleep."[307]

"What they were capturing in videos were things we could not imagine to go out and shoot. They were doing things with cameras better than anything we could script," said Adam Dornbusch, GoPro's senior director of content distribution.[307] "They capture stuff we never even thought of. They're taking us to the next level of what's possible with what they're capturing."[307]

Toward the end of 2013, GoPro realized the inherent potential in this social media marketing opportunity and so launched a couple of submitted videos that received a large number of hits, Dornbusch explained.[307]

"We realized there was such an opportunity here. The users were not only using our cameras but were attaching our name (in the titles and descriptions) to incorporate with us," Dornbusch said. "Sometimes I'll get a call, and someone will say, 'That's a great video you guys did.' We have nothing to do with that. People just want to be associated with our product," explained Dornbusch.[307]

Suddenly GoPro's YouTube strategy was at a much larger scale than they had even realized, said Dornbusch.[307] "GoPro began multiplying the amount of videos they released going from a few a week—with only one or two submitted from the public a month—to as many as four a day."[307] Of the 823 videos on its page, 359—or 44%—were made since October 2014.[307]

"We get users to submit content and are able to distribute it to as many people as we can over the world," Dornbusch said.[307] "They are using their [cameras to capture] their greatest passion."[307]

GoPro has also announced a new "bonus program" for users whose videos are licensed by GoPro.[307] They will receive $1,000 if their videos reach a million views, Dornbusch said.[307] This is a very cheap way to incentivize an audience, who hardly needs to be incentivized it seems, but some of these videos do require substantial organization and expenditure.

"We want to work with users on a much larger scale," Dornbusch said. "This is the heart of GoPro. We love it. It's a surprise. We want to nurture it as much as possible."[307] Obviously, airlines aren't high-end, action camera sellers, but they are selling a lifestyle and experiences and anything they can do to help customers share those experiences should be fostered.

Harvest Customer Feedback

No other media even comes remotely close to the data measurement capacity that mobile offers, which begins with exposure to the advertisement, followed by the persuasive effect of the advertisement and, finally, to the actual purchase of a product.[34]

Today, in many cases, it is usually possible to tell if a comment, a "Like", a vote, or a blog, is coming in through a mobile or a social media platform. Facebook, YouTube, Foursquare, Twitter, WeChat, QQ, and a whole host of other apps are available for the mobile platform and it is the content that is of the utmost importance, not the platform from where it came.

Mobile analytics—the use of data collected as a visitor accesses a website from a mobile device—can effectively track unique visitors, as well as reveal a mobile user's network, device and location.

With site analysis added to a mobile analytics service, marketers can capture mobile metrics such as link tracking for campaign analysis and page tracking for site analysis. Data collected as part of mobile analytics typically includes information such as page views, length of visit as well as such mobile-specific information as mobile device, mobile network operator or carrier, country where the mobile user is calling from, language of the caller, and a unique user ID.

As He et al. argue in their article *Social Media Competitive Analysis and Text Mining: A Case Study in the Pizza Industry*[308], "The wide adoption of social media tools has generated a wealth of textual data, which contain hidden knowledge for businesses to leverage for a competitive advantage." By digging through the vast amounts of unstructured social media data, businesses can discover important brand information.[308] "Decision makers can also use the findings to develop new products or services and make informed strategic and operational decisions."[308]

Text mining is "an emerging technology that attempts to extract meaningful information from unstructured textual data."[308] It is a form of data mining that attempts to find patterns, models, and/or trends in either structured or unstructured data such as text files, HTML files, social media files as well as a whole host of other proprietary files.

Solutions such as SAP's Infinite Insights, SAS's Enterprise Miner, SPSS Modeler, and R can be used in the text mining process and they "use sophisticated computer paradigms including decision tree construction, rule induction, clustering, logic programming, and statistical algorithms to find insights and patterns from unstructured textual data."[308]

The He et al. study "examined the social media sites of the three largest pizza chains and applied text mining to analyze unstructured text content on their Facebook and Twitter sites."[308] The He et al. study attempted to answer the following questions[308]:

- What patterns could be found from their Facebook sites respectively?
- What patterns could be found from their Twitter sites respectively?

- What were the main differences in terms of their Facebook and Twitter patterns?

The results of the study revealed that the three largest pizza chains—Pizza Hut, Domino's and Papa John's—are all active in social media and have committed substantial resources for their social media efforts.[308] The data showed that each pizza chain was committed to providing a delightful experience to its customers. For example, if customer questions could not be answered immediately, the pizza chain's representatives quickly apologized and directed customers to a toll-free telephone number or customer service for further assistance.[308]

Of the three chains, the one with the smallest market share—Domino's Pizza—demonstrated a higher level of commitment and consumer engagement than the other two through the number of social media posts and user comments.[308] Perhaps the fact that they were so burned in social media previously also had a little to do with it? In particular, Domino's Pizza responded to user comments more quickly, which, the authors believe, reflects their strong efforts in monitoring and handling their social media activities.[308]

In addition, the study found that user engagement levels on Facebook were much higher than on Twitter.[308] Not only are there more Facebook fans than Twitter followers, but "the three pizza chains offered more promotional and user engagement activities on Facebook than on Twitter.[308] It was the differences in the platforms that was the key; "Facebook allows people to stay connected and supports more active user participation; Twitter is mainly used for submitting concise updates and noteworthy information."[308]

The study demonstrated the importance that social media had become in the field of customer engagement for each of these three pizza chains. "Specific staff members have been assigned to engage customers and monitor the content that customers created in their social media applications."[308] Each chain has used social media as "an additional customer services and communication tool to gain insight into consumers' needs, wants, concerns and behaviors in order to serve them better."[308] These pizza chains are using social media to listen and engage with their customers, handling customer suggestions and complaints.[308] This is something every airline should be doing.

Social media is also being used for competitor analysis. "Social media competitive analysis allows a business to gain possible business advantage by analyzing the publicly available social media data of a business and its competitors. A business can compare its social media data to the social media data of their competitors to gain perspective on their performance."[308]

He et Al. concludes the paper by offering up the following recommendations when it comes to companies establishing a social media monitoring and competitive analysis strategy[308]:

- Constantly monitor your own social media presence and your competitors' social media presence.
- Establish competitive benchmarking.
- Mine the content of social media conversations.
- Analyze the impact of social media findings and events on your business.

All-in-all social media has become a great place for companies to gain a real competitive advantage. "Correlation between social media findings (consumer sentiments and opinions) and events (e.g., price changes, rival's promotional activities) and structured data like sales data need to be examined to understand how competition affects business and provide [sic] information for decision making," state Dey et al.[309]

Influencer Marketing

Macy and Thompson explain that, "Beginning in 2008, the terms *sentiment* and *influence* were introduced into the real-time ecosystem to describe how to begin measuring the different aspects of listening. In addition to listening to mentions, companies and brands started to realize that they needed to listen to 'influencers', the leading voices whom others listen to."[305] Brands quickly realized that there were influential voices that should be listened to because they held a lot of weight amongst other members of the business community.[305]

Today's consumers are data producing machines; telco operators know every phone call an individual makes, as well as how long each phone call lasts. If signed up for their rewards program, the supermarket where an individual shops knows what foods she likes to buy and what type of shopper she is.

Visa, Mastercard, and American Express know where their cardholders like to drink, shop, and dine. Tivo and Netflix know which movies their subscribers prefer to watch. Company databases across the world house vast amounts of data about their consumers and this data can help advertisers and marketers shape unique marketing campaigns to target specific individuals with individualized offers.

All of this data falls under the umbrella of "customer analytics" and social media is the new frontier for making sense of all of this data.[151] Here, "customers are influencers, not just generators of sales transactions as seen through point-of-sale and e-commerce systems."[151] By sharing their opinions, feelings and disappointments on social networks, customers can "influence each other by commenting on brands, reviewing products, reacting to marketing campaigns and product or service introductions, and revealing shared buying interests."[151]

In the hospitality industry, Marriott has taken the lead in implementing a highly social media-savvy and YouTuber-based marketing strategy.[310] According to a company press release[311], Marriott teamed up "with the Emmy-nominated, multi-platform Internet and pop culture media brand *What's Trending* and host Shira Lazar to produce and release content videos that showcase the power of mobile check-in from Marriott."[311] Empowering travelers to experience more in cities around the world, the videos took a tongue-in-cheek approach to capturing the social influencer's personal journeys thanks to Marriott's mobile check-in system.[311]

One of the YouTube videos, which has been viewed over 4 million times, chronicles a hotel lobby dance party surprising the millionth Marriott mobile app check-in user.[310]

In another video, YouTuber Casey Neistat, shares his Marriott travel experience.[310] This resulted in a very organic and genuine campaign that resonated with Casey's audience.[310] As opposed to traditional advertising measures, marketing with Neistat ensured "a beautifully captured, day-in-the-life of experience as opposed to a scripted commercial."[310]

In an interview with David Beebe, the VP of Global Creative & Content Marketing for Marriott International, advises that "rather than dictating the topic and type of content you want from the influencers, let them come back to you with a concept that plays to their strengths and social credibility."[310]

The ad specifically showed how mobile friendly Marriott properties have become, even to the point of making the check-in process mobile. What shouldn't be lost on the reader is the fact that the use of mobile check-in is actually a win-win proposition for both parties involved; The guest doesn't have to bother with one of the industry's big pain points—waiting in the check-in line and it reduces hotel labor needs somewhat, saving money.

Another good example of the use of influencers to help in marketing is Ford's "Fiesta Movement" campaign.[206] Ford generated buzz eighteen months before it reentered the US subcompact-car market with its Fiesta model by "giving 100 social-media influencers a European model of the car, having them complete 'missions,' and asking them to document their experiences on various social channels."[206] The social media campaign included videos on YouTube, which generated more than 6.5 million views, and "Ford received 50,000 requests for information about the vehicle, primarily from non-Ford drivers."[206] The overall results: in late 2010, some 10,000 cars were sold in the first six days of the model's rollout.[206]

In the article *3 Brands Flying Ahead of Their Competitors Through Influencers!*[312] for PMYB, Tyga explains how Qantas is using influencers. "Qantas teamed up with Australian fashion, travel and lifestyle influencer Nicole Warne—also known as Gary Pepper Girl."[312] "This was a huge move for the brand, as Nicole is one of Australia's biggest influencers. She has over 1.7 million followers on Instagram alone and has worked with some of the biggest names in the world—including Dior and Vogue," notes Tyga[312]

"For the last few years, Nicole has also acted as a digital consultant for Qantas. This has allowed the airline to link the popular star directly to their brand—and to reach her millions of followers," explains Tyga.[312]

"One of Nicole's main roles as a digital consult involves creating sponsored content for her own social media platforms. This helped to promote the Qantas brand to her existing body of fans," notes Tyga.[312] Nicole's activities don't stop there, however, as she also been "involved in creating original content for Qantas' own social media channels. And this role has extended to appear in the airline's in-flight travel entertainment, as Nicole has also starred in travel guides produced by the airline."[312]

Micro-Influencers

As Yuyu Chen explains in her article *The rise of 'micro-influencers' on Instagram*[313] there is such a thing as being too popular:

> *"It turns out that once a social media influencer reaches a critical mass of followers, audience engagement actually begins to decrease. A survey of 2 million social media influencers by influencer marketing platform Markerly showed that for unpaid posts, Instagram influencers with fewer than 1,000 followers have a like rate of about 8 percent, while those with 1,000 to 10,000 followers have a like rate of 4 percent."*

According to Yuyu, as an influencer's following base increases, the like rate decreases.[313] "Instagram influencers with 10,000 to 100,000 followers see a 2.4 percent like rate, compared to 1.7 percent for those with 1 million to 10 million followers and more. Comment rate follows a similar pattern.[313]

"The findings apply to sponsored Instagram posts, too, which suggests the sweet spot for maximum impact is an influencer with a following in the 10,000 to 100,000 range. Call them 'micro-influencers'," says Yuyu.[313]

Kyla Brennan, the founder and CEO of HelloSociety, an agency that connects brands with influencers for specific campaigns, concurs in the Adweek article *Micro-influencers Are More Effective Than With Marketing Campaigns Than Highly Popular Accounts*.[314] "Just because an influencer has hundreds of thousands, or millions, of followers doesn't mean that the specific campaign will be more effective than if a marketer or brand works with an influencer with fewer followers," Brennan warns.[314] In many way, niche players can be much more influential because, "Followers of influencers who post about a niche topic, like interior design, care about the way they decorate their table"[314], not about the celebrity hawking a particular product. Experience is key here.

"Influencer marketing is still effective when they're looked at as peers,"[314] said

Brennan. "When it comes to celebrity accounts, who have maybe millions of followers nobody actually believes that a celebrity is a real fan of a product they're trying to sell,"[314] said Brennan.

HelloSociety has found that "micro"-influencers, or accounts with 30,000 or fewer followers, are more beneficial for marketers to gain exposure.[314] According to the agency, "60 percent higher campaign engagement rates are driven by micro-influencers; those campaigns are 6.7 times more efficient per engagement than influencers with larger followings, which makes them more cost effective; and micro-influencers drive 22.2 times more weekly conversations than the average consumer."[314]

The power of micro-influencers is being recognized at other agencies as well.[313] Fergus Thomas, co-founder of the social marketing agency Irban Group "used the term 'power middle influencers' to describe social media users who typically have around 100,000 to 200,000 followers."[313] For these micro-influencers creating content for a brand is still a secondary endeavor as most have full-time jobs, so they post sponsored content less often than social celebrities, which, naturally, makes their postings feel more authentic.[313] "With the same amount of budget, brands can collaborate with 20 or 40 'power middle influencers' to reach different demographics and see better engagement, compared to one or two celebrities," Yuyu adds.[313]

Social ad platform Gnack defines everyday social media users with fewer than 10,000 followers as micro-influencers.[313] "Their followers usually consist of their friends and family, so their posts are much more trustworthy and engaging," Yuyu notes. Since Instagram recently changed its algorithm to favor quality content, "micro-influencers" should become more visible because content from friends and family members is often prioritized above everything else.[313]

Micro-influencers can be found on social channels like Twitter, LinkedIn, Klout, SnapChat, Instagram, YouTube, in Facebook Groups, as well as at influencer tracking sites like Keyhole and Inkybee. Brand24, the social media monitoring company, has the following advice on how to find micro-influencers[315]:

- Find micro-influential fans from your follower list.
- User Google search to find top local bloggers.
- Use relevant hashtag research.
- Use tools like Markerly, HYPR, Insightpool and Ninja Outreach.
- Research top accounts.

To generate excitement about their routes to several beautiful destinations, Alaska Airlines enlisted eight Instagram micro-influencers –Zak Zeinert, Alex Borsuk, Jon Trend, Nick Visconti, Jovell Rennie, Emily Thomas, and Ryan Thayne—to document their trips to iconic and exotic locales using the hashtag #WeekendWanderer.[316] The travel and adventure Instagrammers have a combined social reach of 476K followers, making the influencer marketing campaign a powerful strategy for the mid-sized airline.[316]

Reputation Management

Managing one's reputation has always been a difficult and complex task, but it has become even more challenging because the internet has made it so easy to search for the reputation of a company or a person.[317] As Alison Woodruff argues in her article *Necessary, unpleasant, and disempowering: reputation management in the Internet age*[317], the internet "creates a potentially permanent record of people's alleged or actual actions that is readily accessible throughout much of the world. Online damage to one's reputation can translate into offline harm, limiting an individual's opportunities to find a job, attend college, or establish social relationships."

According to Wikipedia, reputation management is the[318]:

> "Understanding or influencing of an individual's or business's reputation. It was originally coined as a public relations term, but advancement in computing, the Internet and social media made it primarily an issue of search results. Some parts of reputation management are often associated with ethical grey areas, such as astroturfing review sites, censoring negative complaints or using SEO tactics to game the system and influence results. There are also ethical forms of reputation management, which are frequently used, such as responding to customer complaints, asking sites to take down incorrect information and using online feedback to influence product development."

Sites like Yelp, Angie's List, and Ripoff Report have become critical tools for consumers to choose a particular business or service.[317] Reviews have become the new advertisements in this 21st Century world. Expedia event rates flights now.

Airlines can utilize social media to better understand its customers and many companies do provide these kinds of social media services.

There are several reputation management systems out there, including Klout, which, according to Wikipedia uses[319]:

> "Twitter, Facebook, Google+, LinkedIn, Foursquare, Wikipedia, and Instagram data to create Klout user profiles that are assigned a unique 'Klout Score'. Klout scores range from 1 to 100, with higher scores corresponding to a higher ranking of the breadth and strength of one's online social influence. While all Twitter users are assigned a score, users who register at

> *Klout can link multiple social networks, of which network data is then aggregated to influence the user's Klout Score."*

In her article *How Your Content Strategy Is Critical for Reputation Management*, Rebecca Lieb argues that, "Monitoring—and addressing—online reputation issues boils down to search engine optimization. Creating, disseminating and promoting strong, credible, positive content is pretty much the only weapon at a marketer's disposal."[320]

In (American) football there is saying, "The best offense is a great defense" and this should be kept in mind when it comes to online reputation management. Businesses should start with a content strategy and have a content marketing plan already in place before any reputational issues come up.[320] It'll be too late to assemble the tools you need to douse the blaze once a fire has been set.[320] "Rather, you not only want those tools in place, you want to have already constructed fortifications in the form of plenty of optimized content on the web in general, as well as on blogs, social media and social networking sites," Lieb contends.[320]

"It's also critically important that all online content and digital communications be optimized for search. This includes PR, marketing, and investor relations, as well as any other digital content available on the web, anywhere. Optimized text, images, audio, and video results in more content in search engine results pages," Lieb says.[320] Fake news was a huge problem in the 2016 U.S. Presidential election and that showed just how insidious news or "news" can be if not countered quickly with facts. Even then, the damage isn't always mitigated quickly.

Businesses should also understand that content marketing is an ongoing process and it should be budgeted for accordingly.[320] "You'll always have to continue what journalists have long called 'feeding the beast,'"[320] warns Lieb, but this can actually be a good thing as getting content into the hands of journalist could help disseminate news about the company into interesting and unique channels.

Continuing with the sports analogies, even the best baseball player in history struck out more times than he hit home runs and so it could be with reviews; a business can't just expect to have nothing but happy customers. "Online reputation management isn't about obliterating any negative mention or association made with your organization, rather by mitigating those negative results with strong, positive, visible, and consistent content,"[320] the company will be able to build a strong and worthy reputation argues Lieb.

In his article *A 5-step Guide to Reputation Management Using Social Media*[321], Brynley-Jones lays out a guide to social media reputation management on a budget:

1. Decide what you want to track—define the "keywords" relating to your company that you want to track in online conversations, including:

- Company name
- Company website address
- Names of products
- Names of senior employees and directors
- Names of close competitors
- Common expressions—e.g., "[Company] sucks", "company is great."

2. Set up accounts on free social media monitoring tools, including such sites as Google Alerts, Social Mention, Whostalkin.com, Hootsuite, Trackur, Viral Heat, Scout Labs and Vocus, BackType, Blogpulse, Monitter, tweetbeep, Wholinkstome, BoardTracker, and Naymz.
3. Set up your alerts and searches through services like Google Alerts or Netvibes, as well as RSS feeds that notify you when your keywords are mentioned.
4. Set up your own social media accounts. A service like knowem.com allows businesses to search over 500 popular social networks, over 150 domain names, and the entire USPTO Trademark Database to instantly secure your brand.
5. Engage—How you respond to comments and posts made about your company is purely up to you, but there are certain rules of thumb:
   - Act quickly—take advantage of social media's most important quality—its real-time accessibility. Misconceptions can be snubbed out instantly with quick and factual replies. Never expect things to just disappear. Blog posts and forum comments can remain in search engine results forever, so you need to make sure your viewpoint is there too.
   - Be nice—the first instinct might be to get defensive and emotional, but let clearer heads prevail. Getting angry and/or making threats will likely backfire. "Try and reason with detractors and understand where they are coming from. By showing that you're listening, you'll win respect and support from others."[321]
   - Be pro-active—when industry-specific discussions arise, get involved early and often. Offer your personal perspective as this can encourage promoters to back you, while also diffusing a potential detractor's ire.

Social Media Analytics

As Melville and Lawrence explain in their article *Social Media Analytics: Channeling the Power of the Blogosphere for Marketing Insight*[322], social media analytics is "the practice of gathering data from blogs and social media websites and analyzing that data to make business decisions. The most common use of social media is to mine customer sentiment." Social media analytics evolved out of the disciplines of social network analysis, machine learning, data mining, information retrieval (IR), and Natural Language Processing (NLP).

According to Melville and Lawrence, the automotive analysis of blogs and other social media sites raise the following intriguing marketing questions[322]:

1. Given the enormous size of the blogosphere, how can we identify the subset of blogs and forums that are discussing not only a specific product, but higher-level concepts that are in some way relevant to this product?
2. Having identified this subset of relevant blogs, how do we identify the most authoritative or influential bloggers in this space?
3. How can we detect and characterize specific sentiment expressed about an entity (e.g., product) mentioned in a blog or a forum?
4. How do we tease apart novel emerging topics of discussion from the constant chatter in the blogosphere?

As Margaret Rouse explains in her article *Social Media Analytics*[323], step one of a social media analytics initiative is "to determine which business goals the data that is gathered and analyzed will benefit. Typical objectives include increasing revenues, reducing customer service costs, getting feedback on products and services and improving public opinion of a particular product or business division." Once these business goals have been identified, "KPIs for objectively evaluating the data should be defined. For example, customer engagement might be measured by the numbers of followers for a Twitter account and number of retweets of a company's name," states Rouse.[323]

Through social networks like Twitter and Weibo, organizations can pick up customer satisfaction in real time.[151] "Social media is enabling companies such as Coca-Cola, Starbucks, and Ford to go beyond standard customer satisfaction data gathering to innovate by setting up and participating in communities to gain feedback from customers."[151] A good example is MyStarbucksIdea.com, it is a website where "Starbucks customers can relate their experiences and offer ideas about how to improve the Starbucks experience, from drinks to foods to ambiance."[151]

When looking at what objectives companies were seeking when implementing customer analytics technologies with social media data (see Figure 21), TDWI Research found that gaining a "deeper customer understanding" topped the list at 56%[151] "Social media listening can provide an unprecedented window into customer sentiment and the reception of an organization's marketing, brands, and services."[151]

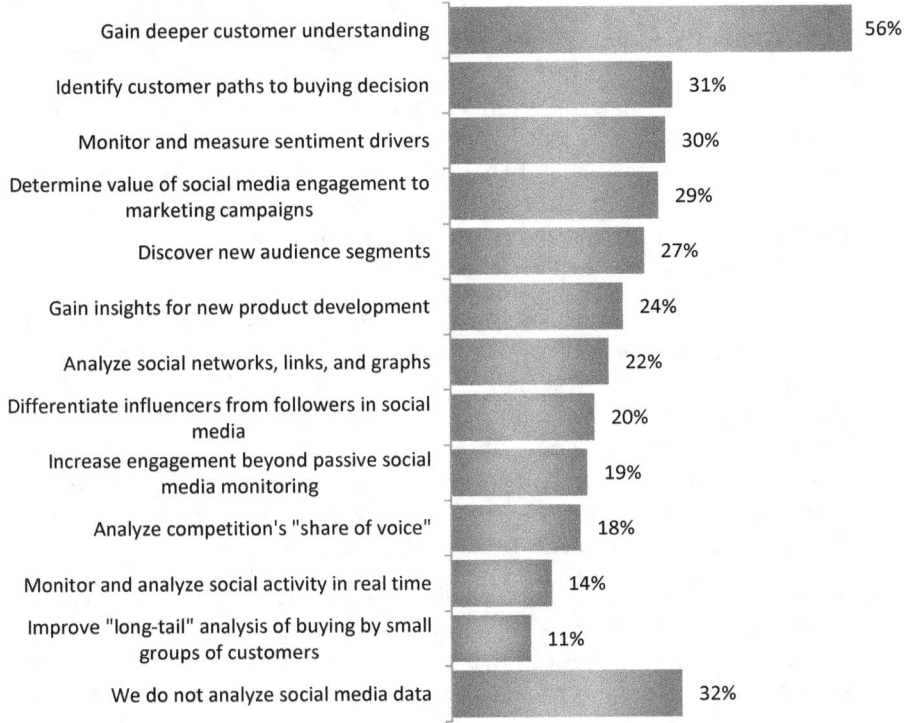

Figure 21: Customer Analytics and Social Media Objectives
Based on 1,546 respondents from 418 respondents; a bit more than three responses per respondent, on average.
Source: TDWI Research[151]

Besides the broad objective of gaining deeper customer understanding, nearly one-third (31%) of companies seek to identify attribution, or paths to buying decisions, which can be done on a limited scale with services like Google Analytics as well as other Web site analysis applications.[151] Google webmaster tools also allow airlines to understand the organic search traffic that is linking customers to them.

30% or respondents sought to discover customer sentiment, which is important because it helps companies discover positive and negative comments in social media channels, on customer comment and review sites.[151] "Sentiment analysis often focuses on monitoring and measuring the 'buzz' value, usually through volume and frequency of comments around a topic."[151]

Simply deciding which social media sites' data to analyze can be one of the biggest challenges facing businesses going down the analytics path. "Organizations have to research where their customers are most likely to express themselves about brands and products. They need to spot influencers who have networks of contacts and take it upon themselves to play an advocacy role."[151] "About 20% of respondents are interested in differentiating influencers from followers in social media.[151] "Link analytic tools and methods specialize in identifying relationships between users in social communities and enabling organizations to measure users' influence."[151] "With some tools, data scientists and analysts can test variables to help identify social communities as 'segments'. Then, as they implement segmentation models for other data sources, they can integrate these insights with social media network analysis to sharpen models and test new variables," explains Stodder.[151]

Analytics are critical in helping organizations "make the right decisions about when, where, and how to participate in social media. It isn't enough to just listen; organizations must insert themselves and become part of the conversation."[151] When doing so, however, companies should keep in mind advice from *The Cluetrain Manifesto*[324]—"Conversations among human beings sound human. They are conducted in a human voice," as well as this: "When delivering information, opinion, perspectives, dissenting arguments or humorous asides, the human voice is typically open, natural, uncontrived."[324]

One interesting strategy is for an airline operator to start viral campaigns via Twitter, using hashtags for a topic; the campaign could be a part of a larger marketing strategy. Airlines can then "monitor social media to see what people say and analyze how the campaign is playing among influencers and across networks."[121]

One example of this type of see marketing is Unilever's Dove brand series of web-integrated commercials, which attempted to fundamentally redefine the brand and Unilever's Sunsilk shampoo campaign that, according to the company, placed a "net seed" onto YouTube with the video titled "Bride Has Massive Hair Wig Out."[121] The video, which showed a bride-to-be reacting in horror to her wedding day hair, contained no brand references and quickly accumulated three million hits.[121] Later, Unilever came forward to claim the ad, saying it was intended to plant the term "wig out" in the culture, a term that was to be used in conventional advertising for Sunsilk products at a later date.[121]

Klear, a social media and social data platform that focuses on influencer marketing, offers a product that can help airlines understand the effects of their influencer marketing. Klear's campaign reports contain the following summaries[325]:

- How many influencers participated in the campaign.
- Number of updates the influencers posted during the campaign.

- Engagements metrics.
- Number of people who saw the content.

The report also includes a drill-down analysis for each and every influencer. For each influencer the report will show[325]:

- Who is the influencer.
- The influencer's expertise.
- Fanbase across different social networks.
- Top posts during the campaign.
- Engagements for these updates.
- A direct link to the influencer's profile on Klear.

This is a paid service, but most of the information is publicly available and this is something an airline could build up in-house, should they want to create a customized solution.

Influencer marketing taps directly into what Deighton and Kornfeld call the five paradigms of digital interactive marketing[121], i.e., social exchanges—building identities within virtual communities—and cultural exchanges—firms offering culture products that will compete in buzz markets.[121] This peer-to-peer interactivity should motivate the desire to exchange and share information, which should help market any airline event.[121]

Social Media Monitoring

It is high time to revise Wanamaker's oft-made quote that he didn't know which half of his marketing spend was useful, not because it is probably the most over-quoted quote in the history of marketing, but because we now have the ability to figure out which advertisement works for which customer. We can also extrapolate how that advertising will work on customers similar to the ones we might want to target.

Today, digital advertising should employ a multi-screen strategy that follows its audience throughout his or her digital day. As previously mentioned, successful mobile advertising requires three things—reach, purity and analytics. Analytics "involves matching users' interests—implicit and explicit, context, preferences, network and handset conditions—to ads and promotions in real time."[34] A retail operator can utilize analytics to enhance its marketing, campaign management, increase sales, conduct market research, ferret out fraud and for risk/management, contact center operations, supply chain management, as well as for a whole host of other things.

In their *Measuring Social Media Performance and Business Impact (Part 1)*[326], Hamill and Stevenson put forth their '6 Is' of social media monitoring framework that include:

1. Involvement—the number and quality of customers involved in your various online networks.
2. Interaction—the actions taken by online network members – read, post, comment, review, recommend, etc.).
3. Intimacy—the brand sentiments expressed, level of brand "affection" or "aversion".
4. Influence—advocacy, viral forwards, referrals, recommendations, retweets, etc.
5. Insights—the level of customer/actionable insight delivered from monitoring online conversations.
6. Impact—business impact of your social media activities benchmarked against core business goals and objectives.

In 1999, *The Cluetrain Manifesto*[324] warned, "Reviews are the new advertising." Today, this is truer than ever before. There are a multitude of platforms that allow users to rate or comment on a restaurant, a retail establishment, a hotel, or even a local handyman or plumber.

Used properly, reviews can be the new advertising currency for an airline's marketing department. Companies such as Dell, Cicso, Salesforce.com, the American Red Cross, and Gatorade are creating Social Media command centers that monitor the social conversations about their companies. These social media centers enable company employees to monitor conversations from the social web on channels such as Twitter, Facebook, and YouTube, amongst others, in an attempt to keep track of the health of a company's social brand.

In December 2010, Dell became one of the first companies to launch a social media command center. Based at company HQ in Round Rock, TX, twelve full-time employees monitor conversations about Dell and its products around the globe, responding via @DellCares or forwarding the post to the right internal Dell team.[327] Through Dell's Social Media Listening and Command Center, Dell aggregates and culls through the 25,000 conversations about Dell every day (more than 6 million every year).[327]

"We're monitoring conversations in 11 languages 24/7, and each one is an opportunity to reinforce our brand," explains Karen Quintos, Dell CMO.[327] Quintos explains that[327]:

> "With the tremendous amount of information being generated, we can track basic demographics, reach, sentiment, subject matter of the discussions, the sites where conversations are happening, and more. We leverage these analytics to identify customer support needs as they happen, influence product development, insert ourselves into conversations with IT decision makers and connect with people having the most impact on these conversations."

In his article *Taking Back The Social-Media Command Center*[328], Scott Gulbransen argues that, "To do the command-center model right, a setup has to envision a real-time workflow empowered to take action on all of the relevant content being analyzed, whether it be insights derived from real-time monitoring, opportunities to respond, or great discovered content to feature that elevates you and your fans." Gulbransen recommends breaking down a command center into the following critical functions[328]:

1. Identify trends and insights—track not only the key themes, but also how they evolve over time.
2. Review the content—monitor a wide variety of terms that are meaningful to the brand and assign employees to sort through the responses, deciding which one warrants a response, and what might interest the community at large.
3. Curate the best stuff—leverage the great content that is being said about the company as well as champion those great content providers.
4. Listen and Respond—this is a two-way conversation, listen and respond quickly and accordingly.

Unlike casual conversations, comments, updates, likes and dislikes uploaded to social networks are collected and, therefore, analyzable and measurable. This results in "a data tsunami: the actions and content generated by participants in social media create 'Big Data' sources that are full of potential for tracking and understanding behavior, trends, and sentiments."[151] Remember, this can be highly quantifiable data, especially when run through a data warehouse like Hadoop. Airlines should be studying attribution analysis for its social media campaigns on platforms like Facebook, YouTube, Twitter, Weibo, amongst others.

In its *Social Media Analytics: Making Customer Insights Actionable*[329], IBM believes that the "mistake many organizations make is to treat social media as distinct and separate from other customer data and divorced from revenue generating imperatives." IBM recommends companies venturing into the social media space do the following[329]:

- Integrate company-wide information from different data sources to drive the business through deeper consumer insight.
- Define the real value of the company's brand—its equity, reputation and loyalty—at any moment in time, in any place in the world; and
- Understand emerging consumer trends, both globally and locally and apply predictive models to determine actions with the highest probability of increasing relevance and maximizing marketing campaign ROI.

IBM recommends businesses ask the following questions when devising a social media plan[329]:

- Assess—also referred to as "listening," at this stage a company should monitor social media to uncover sentiment about its products, services, marketing campaigns, employees and partners. The questions that need to be asked at this stage include:
    - What are you company objectives? Are you looking to:
        - Attract customers?
        - Increase the value of existing customer relationships?
        - Retain customers?
    - How do customers interact with you today?
    - What are they interested in?
    - Where and when do they use social media?
    - Are there significant influencers who speak to your brand or products?
- Measure—proactive analytics can uncover hidden patterns that can reveal "unknown unknowns" in the data. Questions that businesses need to ask at this stage include:
    - Who are you targeting with your social media initiatives and why?
    - What will you be measuring:
        - Share of voice
        - Activation
        - Brand sentiment
        - Influencers
    - Sales over the life of the customer relationship?
- Integrate—social media can give businesses both a broad view of their operations as well as a detailed and intimate view of their individual customers. Questions to ask at this stage include:
    - What is your vision for social media and its integration into the company's operational marketing systems?
    - Do you have a profile of your customer advocates? Can you predict sentiment on products, services, campaigns?
    - How do you measure the effects of social media on brand equity and reputation, pipeline, and sales orders and margins?
    - How will you integrate social analytics into other customer analytics?

Regardless of the sophistication and scope of any social media initiative, the end goal, IBM argues, should be in alignment with corporate imperatives and goals, as well as produce a measurable ROI.[329]

Social media listening can provide an airline with an ongoing real-time window into customer sentiment, as well as give the business verifiable information about the company's marketing campaigns, brands, and services.

Social Media Monitoring Tools

Table 19 lists the Social Media Tools and websites available to business users to track engagement and customer feedback.

Name	Comments
Board Reader	BoardReader allows users to search multiple message boards simultaneously, allowing users to share information in a truly global sense. Boardreader is focused on creating the largest repository of searchable information for our users. Users can find answers to their questions from others who share similar interests. Our goal is to allow our users to search the "human to human" discussions that exist on the Internet.
Buffer	Buffer makes your life easier with a smarter way to schedule the great content you find. Fill up your Buffer at one time in the day and Buffer automagically posts them for you through the day. Simply keep that Buffer topped up to have a consistent social media presence all day round, all week long. Get deeper analytics than if you just post to social networks directly.
Buzzsumo	Analyze what content performs best for any topic or competitor. Find the key influencers to promote your content: • Discover the most shared content across all social networks and run detailed analysis reports. • Find influencers in any topic area, review the content they share and amplify. • Be the first to see content mentioning your keyword; or when an author or competitor publishes new content. • Track your competitor's content performance and do detailed comparisons.
Commun.it	Can help you organize, increase, and manage your followers, and can do so across multiple accounts and profiles. At a glance you can see different aspects of your community management, like the latest tweets from your stream and which new followers might appreciate a welcome message.
Crowdfire	Crowdfire is a powerful phone app and online website that helps you grow your Twitter and Instagram account reach. This tool has a variety of functions designed to understand your social analytics as well as manage your social publishing.
Cyfe	Cyfe is an all-in-one dashboard software that helps you monitor and analyze data scattered across all your online services like Google Analytics, Salesforce, AdSense, MailChimp, Facebook, WordPress and more from one single location in real-time.
Fanpage Karma	Shows a variety of valuable information related to your Facebook page, such as growth, engagement, service and response time, and of course Karma (a weighted engagement value). FanKarma also provides insight into Twitter and YouTube; the latter could be particularly valuable if you're creating a video marketing strategy.
Followerwonk	Followerwonk is a cool social media analytics tool thet lets you explore and grow your social graph. Dig deeper into Twitter analytics: followers, their locations, when do they tweet. Find and connect with influencers in

Name	Comments
	your niche. Use visualizations to compare your social graph to competitors.
Google Alerts	Google Alerts are email updates of the latest relevant Google results (blogs, news, etc.) based on your searches. Enter the topic you wish to monitor, then click preview to see the type of results you'll receive. Some handy uses of Google Alerts include: monitoring a developing news story and keeping current on a competitor or industry.
Google Trends	Trends allows you to compare search terms and websites. With Google Trends you can get insights into the traffic and geographic visitation patterns of websites or keywords. You can compare data for up to five websites and view related sites and top searches for each one.
Hootsuite	Monitor and post to multiple social networks, including Facebook and Twitter. Create custom reports from over 30 individual report modules to share with clients and colleagues. Track brand sentiment, follower growth, plus incorporate Facebook Insights and Google analytics. Draft and schedule messages to send at a time your audience is most likely to be online. HootSuite has the dashboard for your iPhone, iPad, BlackBerry and Android.
HowSocialable	Monitor and post to multiple social networks, including Facebook and Twitter. Create custom reports from over 30 individual report modules to share with clients and colleagues. Track brand sentiment, follower growth, plus incorporate Facebook Insights and Google analytics. Draft and schedule messages to send at a time your audience is most likely to be online. HootSuite has the dashboard for your iPhone, iPad, BlackBerry and Android.
Iconosquare	Key metrics about your Instagram account. Number of likes received, your most liked photos ever, your average number of likes and comments per photo, your follower growth charts and more advanced analytics. Track lead conversations, send private message as on Twitter, and improve communication with your followers.
Klear	Social media monitoring, analytics and reporting. Influencer marketing, find and create relationships with the top influencers in your sector and build your community. Competitive analysis tracks your social media landscape, see what's working for them and develop your strategy.
Klout	Klout's mission is to help every individual understand and leverage their influence. Klout measures influence in Twitter to find the people the world listens to. It analyzes content to identify the top influencers.
Kred	Kred is a social-media scoring system that seeks to measure a person's online influence. Kred, which was created by the San Francisco-based social analytics firm PeopleBrowsr, attempts to also measure a person or company's engagement, or as they call it, outreach. PeopleBrowsr hopes that that combination can offer a more informed metric for non-celebrities like entrepreneurs and those whom they follow and look to for advice.
LikeAlyzer	This Facebook analysis tool comes up with stats and insights into your page and begins every report with a list of recommendations. Keep track of where your Facebook page stands compared to other pages by following the comparison to average page rank, industry-specific page rank, and rank of similar brands.
Mention	Mention prides itself on "going beyond Google Alerts" to track absolutely anywhere your name or your company might be mentioned online. When

Name	Comments
	you subscribe to Mention's daily email you get all these wayward hits right in your inbox, and the Web dashboard even flags certain mentions as high priority.
Mentionmap	Explore your Twitter network. Discover which people interact the most and what they're talking about. It's also a great way to find relevant people to follow. The visualization runs right in your browser and displays data from Twitter. Mentionmap loads user's tweets and finds the people and hashtags they talked about the most. In this data visualization, mentions become connections and discussions between multiple users emerge as clusters.
Must Be Present	Built by the team at Sprout Social, Must Be Present searches your Twitter account to find how quickly you respond to mentions. Their engagement reports place you in a percentile based on other accounts so you can see how you stack up to the speed of others.
NeedTagger	A super-powered Twitter search tool, NeedTagger runs language filters and keyword searches to determine which Twitter users might need your products or services. The tool shows you real-time search results and sends a daily email digest of new finds.
NutshellMail	Collects your activity on Facebook, LinkedIn, and Twitter (and even places like Yelp and Foursquare) to provide an email overview of your accounts. You set how often and when you want to receive the recap emails. Put it to use: If you have a weekly metrics plan you can have NutshellMail send a message once a week with an overview of your accounts. You can then extract the data and insights straight into your weekly report.
Omgili	Omgili helps you find interesting and current discussions, news stories and blog posts. Direct access to live data from hundreds of thousands of forums, news and blogs. Very easy to use, no signup for web interface.
Pinterest Analytics	Find out how many people are pinning from your website, seeing your pins, and clicking your content. Pick a time-frame to see how your numbers trend over time. Get better at creating Pins and boards with metrics from your Pinterest profile. Learn how people use the Pin It button on your site to add Pins. See how people interact with your Pins from whatever device they use. Get a glance at your all-time highest-performing Pins.
Pluggio	Pluggio is a web-based social media tool to help marketers easily grow and manage their social media profiles (Facebook and Twitter). It includes a suite of tools to organize and keep track of multiple accounts, get more followers, and automate the finding and publishing of excellent targeted content.
Postific	The full set of social media tools. Post content to over 10 social networks with one single click of a button. Get real time click-through statistics with your domain name. Measure and analyze the best results from your social posts. Monitor the social media conversations that are important for your business.
Quintly	Quintly is the professional social media monitoring and analytics solution to track and compare the performance of your social media marketing activities. Whether you are using Facebook, Twitter or both, Quintly monitors and visualizes your social media marketing success. Benchmark your numbers against your competitors or best practice examples.

Name	Comments
Sentiment	Sentiment was born in 2007 and now boasts a team of bright enthusiastic people dedicated to provide the best social customer service and engagement platform for business.
SocialMention	SocialMention tracks areas such as sentiment, passion, reach, and strength to not just tell you what's being said about your search but how those reactions feel. While you track your brand or yourself, you can also see how your sentiment changes over time.
Social Rank	Identifies your top 10 followers in three specific areas: Best Followers, Most Engaged, and Most Valuable. Your most engaged followers are those who interact with you most often (replies, retweets, and favorites); your most valuable followers are the influential accounts; and your best followers are a combination of the two. Social Rank will run the numbers for free and show you the results today, then follow-up each month with an email report.
Social Oomph	Schedule tweets, track keywords, extended Twitter profiles, save and reuse drafts, view @mentions and retweets, purge your DM inbox, personal status feed — your own tweet engine, unlimited accounts.
This tracking tool	Keeps track of your hashtag campaign or keyword on Twitter, Instagram, or Facebook with a full dashboard of analytics, demographics, and influencers.
Tip Top	TipTop Search is a Twitter-based search engine that helps you discover the best and most current advice, opinions, answers for any search, and also real people to directly engage and share experiences with. A search on any topic reveals people's emotions and experiences about it, as well as other concepts that they are discussing in connection with the original search.
Topsy	A powerful search engine for Twitter content. Want to know how a certain term is being used on Twitter? You can search links, tweets, photos, videos, and influencers.
Twazzup	Offers real-time monitoring and analytics for Twitter on any name, keyword, or hashtag you choose. The Twazzup results page delivers interesting insights like the top influencers for your keyword and which top links are associated with your search.
Tweepi	Has a number of useful Twitter features, many of which fall into a couple categories: managing your followers and supercharging who you're following. For management, you can unfollow in batches those who don't follow you back, and you can bulk follow another account's complete list of followers or who they're following.
Tweetcaster	A Twitter management tool for iOS and Android devices and provides the basics of what you'd expect from a Twitter dashboard plus a few fun extras: enhanced search and lists, hiding unwanted tweets, and photo effects for your images.
Tweetdeck	Lets you track, organize, and engage with your followers through a customizable dashboard where you can see at a glance the activity from different lists, followers, hashtags, and more.
TweetReach	Shows you the reach and exposure of the tweets you send, collecting data on who retweets you and the influence of each. Identify which of your

Name	Comments
	tweets has spread the furthest (and why) and then try to repeat the formula with future tweets.
TwitterCounter	Twitter Counter is the number one site to track your Twitter stats. Twitter Counter provides statistics of Twitter usage and tracks over 14 million users. Twitter Counter also offers a variety of widgets and buttons that people can add to their blogs, websites or social network profiles to show recent Twitter visitors and number of followers.
Twtrland	Provides a snapshot of your Twitter profile and can even track Facebook and Instagram as well. Two of Twtrland's most helpful tools are a live count of how many followers are currently online and advanced search functionality that includes keywords, locations, and companies. Local companies can perform a location search to see which area accounts are most popular and potentially worth following.
SumAll	SumAll is a powerful social media analytics tool that allows our customers to view all of their data in one simple, easy-to-use visualization. Social media, e-commerce, advertising, e-mail, and traffic data all come together to provide a complete view of your activity.
ViralWoot	Pin Alert feature lets you track what are people pinning from your website, who is pinning the most and what images from your website are trending on Pinterest. Thousands of social media marketers and agencies use Viralwoot for their clients. You can manage & grow multiple Pinterest accounts with a single Viralwoot account.
WhosTalkin	WhosTalkin is a social media monitoring tool that lets you search for conversations surrounding the topics that you care about most. Whether it be your favorite sports team, food, celebrity, or brand name; Whostalkin will help you find the conversations that are important to you. WhosTalkin search and sorting algorithms combine data taken from over 60 of the most popular social media sites.
WhoUnfollowedMe	Who.unfollowed.me is a service that helps you track your unfollowers, in real time, without waiting for a DM, or email. It allows you to check your unfollowers on your schedule, every 15 minutes, without waiting for an email or a direct message.

Table 19: Social Media Tools
Source: Dreamgrow.com[330]

Conclusion

We live in a real-time, 24-7 world, a world where 280-character Twitter messages foment political revolutions; a world where marketers should fear not the power of the pen, but the destructive force of the critical tweet or the far-reaching viral impact of an inflammatory social media diatribe that can encircle the digital world in seconds, laying waste to a reputation that might have taken decades to develop. Conversely, it is also a world where an advertiser's message can go viral and reach more eyeballs in less than an hour than a multi-million-dollar television commercial campaign can in a year.

In chapter one, I mentioned Paul Greenberg stated that social CRM was "a philosophy and a business strategy supported by a technology platform, business rules, workflow, processes, and social characteristics, designed to engage and reach accordingly in a collaborative conversation."[61] *The Predictive Airliner* must add social media elements to its CRM systems to give customers a complete personalization experience. Continuous customer engagement can be fostered through a multitude of social channels and they are cheap to use, if not free, in some cases (excluding the airline's staff needed for social media responses, of course).

The beauty of this system is that it can be a real win-win when it comes to an airline's marketing plan as customers who are happy with a business's products and/or services will often comment and blog about the products and/or services they like, while those who aren't happy with it can be reached out to and, hopefully, converted into satisfied customers. Often, the simple act of responding to a customer's complaints can turn the tide of negativity and, as long as the remedies are constructive, can turn a hostile customer into a positive one, and, possibly, one who might even tout the company's excellent customer service at a later date.

Mullich offers the following tips on how to get the low-down on rivals[193]:

1. Understand that day-to-day online chatter can be misleading, but, over time, an airline can find directional trends important to its business and industry.
2. The deepest insights often come not from general sources, like Facebook and Twitter, but from blogs and forums that are specific to an industry.
3. Think broadly about the nature of one's "competitors"—sentiment analysis can help a business prepare for unexpected entries that might be preparing to take a piece of its business. Keyword search teams can help.
4. The information you can gain online about competitors is limited, and often must be combined with your own internal data to bring actionable insights.

There are, of course, limits to what competitive sentiment analysis can provide. "The challenges you might address, using your company's own customer, product, and transactional data, are far more extensive than those you can tackle via available competitor data," says Seth Grimes, an analyst who runs the annual Social Analysis Symposium.[193] "For instance, you're not going to have access to your competitors' contact-center notes and warranty claims, or to your competitors' customer profiles and transaction records. But with your own company's, you can create some very rich analyses," he adds.[193]

For the above reasons, competitive analysis is usually just one piece of the vast data mosaic.[193] For example, one company that noticed a drop in sales of its flagship product analyzed online chatter and found customers were talking enthusiastically about a new product a competitor had just released.[193] "When the company analyzed its contact-center data, it found that returns correlated to discontent about an attribute its own product lacked, but the new competing product offered."[193] The company was quickly able to identify the problem and by using a combination of competitive sentiment analysis, discovery from its own internal data, it was able to tweak its own product to make it much more competitive.[193]

As Grimes says, "Sentiment analysis can help you understand how the market perceives you and your competitors' products and services, but keep in mind that sentiment is only an indicator, useful in measuring and projecting market impact, not a substitute for strong human judgment."[193]

There is a dark side to all of this tracking as the case of IFA and Shopsense showed. IFA Insurance teamed up with Shopsense, a grocery chain in Midwest America, and bought their loyalty card customer data.[331] The insurance company discovered some intriguing patterns in the loyalty card data, such as the correlation between condom sales and HIV-related claims, for example.[331] It also discovered such things as households that buy cashews and bananas quarterly are the least likely to develop symptoms of Alzheimer's.[331] Although this information did prove to be highly profitable for IFA, I believe it is a clear violation of customer trust and privacy.

As Katherine Lemon explains in her article, *How Can These Companies Leverage the Customer Data Responsibly*[332], "Customer analytics are effective precisely because firms do *not* violate customer trust. People believe that retail and other organizations will use their data wisely to enhance their experiences, not to harm them. Angry customers will certainly speak with their wallets if that trust is violated."[332]

Another concern for consumers is what Lemon calls "battered customer syndrome."[332] She explains that, "Market analytics allow companies to identify their best and worst customers and, consequently, to pay special attention to those deemed to be the most valuable."[332]

"Looked at another way, analytics enable firms to understand how poorly they can treat individuals or groups of customers before those people stop doing business with them. Unless you are in the top echelon of customers—those with the highest lifetime value, say—you may pay higher prices, get fewer special offers, or receive less service than other consumers," Lemon adds.[332] "Despite the fact that alienating 75% to 90% of customers may not be the best idea in the long run, many airlines have adopted this 'top tier' approach to managing customer relationships. And many customers seem to be willing to live with it—perhaps with the unrealistic hope that they maybe reach the upper echelon and reap the ensuing benefits."[332]

"Little research has been done on the negative consequences of using marketing approaches that discriminate against customer segments. Inevitably, however, customers will become savvier about analytics. They may become less tolerant and take their business (and information) elsewhere," Lemon warns.[332]

"A smart combination of listening to the online conversation already taking place, learning what people want, and then providing what they are open to receive from the brand constitutes the winning ticket," advises Macy and Thompson.[305]

The internet has allowed companies to reach consumers in very cheap, easy, and effective ways, but the downside is that it can also give a loud and reverberating voice to unhappy customers very inexpensively, too. Because humans are, by nature, more attuned to negative messages than positive ones (think about how a raised voice in a crowded restaurant gains instant attention) businesses need to react very quickly to negative stories in the social media world.

Although anti-brand sites are usually created to attempt to hurt brands, smart companies can use these websites to their advantage as well. Kucuk offers four basic strategies for companies to counter these anti-brand Websites; work with experts; monitor symbolic haters; talk to complainers; and combat opportunists.[289]

A word of warning here: don't set up fake accounts to try to get your marketing message out. There are people out in the blogosphere who would love nothing more than to uncover the latest social media scam, especially in China, and they probably have access to some of the most sophisticated tools to ferret out dishonest behavior.

Don't pick fights with customers on social media either. Threatening customers with legal action is never a good idea. The old rule that you shouldn't whip out a gun unless you're willing to pull the trigger should be kept in mind when it comes to social media as well.

In many cases, companies seem to bring social media crises upon themselves through careless thinking and a lack of channel monitoring. In her article *The top 10 corporate social media disasters*[282], Rebecca Burn-Calandar mentions six social media crises—the "JP Morgan Snarkpocalyse," "the British Gatastrophe" (British Gas), "Mayday for British Airways," "Twitter shouts itself hoarse at Tesco," "The Qantas Bashtag," "Home Depot" (the monkey picture fiasco)—that could be considered self-inflicted wounds. A seventh, "Disobeying his master's voice," could probably have been avoided with stricter administrative controls at HMV as well.

The lesson here is to be humble when venturing into social media and understand there could be a lot of people out there who are just itching to vent their frustration at you.

Social media has really upped the ante when it comes to customer engagement because, through it, customers cannot only connect with a brand, but also with a brand's consumers. "What is new is that customer engagement is not just a brand's connection with the customer. It is also the customers' engagement with one another in the horizontal, viral aspects."[305] It is these horizontal and viral aspects that can be so important—and potentially lucrative. Conversely, Macy and Thompson warn that a "lack of engagement limits brand leadership effectiveness and ultimately defeats the purpose of the medium."[305] "A smart combination of listening to the online conversation already taking place, learning what people want, and then providing what they are open to receive from the brand constitutes the winning ticket," recommend Macy and Thompson.[305]

Tips

- Keep your user name identical on all social networking sites to allow for easy cross-posting and cross-referencing.
- Offer something to make people want to come back. It doesn't have to be something tangible, but it must be something interesting.
- Choose social media applications based on where a target audience congregates.
- Either join an existing social media platform to take advantage of its popularity and built-in user base or build a presence from scratch; both have their own unique advantages and disadvantages.
- Businesses should ensure that all of their employees have access to all of the company's social media platforms, but administrator rights should be doled out selectively.
- When stepping into the social media world, be active, interesting, humble, unprofessional (to a certain extent), and honest.
- When it comes to brand management, companies should keep an eye on e-complaint websites, as well as on consumer blogs to monitor the type and duration of problems that flare up.
- Open an innovation hub that allows users to post their ideas to the company.
- Set up Google Alerts for your company name and any of your company's products or services.
- For anti-brand management, businesses should buy potentially negative Internet domain names that could target their brand in a negative way.
- Buy up website names that are mistypes of your company name, thereby countering typo-squatters.
- There are four basic strategies for companies to counter anti-brand websites; work with experts; monitor symbolic haters; talk to complainers; and combat opportunists.
- Counter negative stories with timely positive and credible ones, with as many links to reputable sources as possible.
- When appropriate, email upset customers, perhaps attaching discount coupons or gift cards to show your remorse for poor service.
- Create an online community for your products rather than simply building an ecommerce site. Engagement sells like nothing else.
- Keep your community engaged by injecting your personality into every engagement (as long as it is not a boring personality, that is) and act as if you are interacting with friends.
- Know the interests of your consumers and build upon those interests.

- When it comes to crisis management, it is best to tackle a problem head-on. Using disarming humor and/or clever irreverence can stop crisis-like situations turning into full-blown social media disasters.
- Write and publish content with embedded links to other content, pictures, and videos to interest the potential online audience.
- Use tweeter Spy to help determine which tweets result in the most traffic back to your site.
- Use untweetme.com to find former Twitter followers who might have left because of poor service.
- Use Viralwoot to gain Instagram followers.
- Use ShareRoot's suite of free tools to get more followers on sites like Pinterest.
- Use Klear to help measure influencer engagement.
- Make customers a part of the story and use social media analysis tools to monitor and analyze your efforts.
- Allow users to log in under their social profiles, which will allow sharing of your content, increasing engagement.
- Set up accounts on free social media monitoring tools, including such sites as Google Alerts, Social Mention, Whostalkin.com, Hootsuite, Trackur, Viral Heat, Scout Labs and Vocus, BackType, Blogpulse, Monitter, tweetbeep, Wholinkstome, BoardTracker, and Naymz.
- Set up your alerts and searches through services like Google Alerts or Netvibes, as well as RSS feeds that notify you when your keywords are mentioned.

---

274 Outing, S. (2007, September). Enabling the Social Company. Enthusiast Group. Retrieved from Steveouting.com: http://www.steveouting.com/files/social_company.pdf (22 November 2017).
275 Business.com. (2010, November 8). Top Tools to measure your social media success. Retrieved from Business.com: http://www.business.com/info/social-media-monitoring-tools (22 November 2017).
276 Honigman, B. (2012, November 29). 100 fascinating social media statistics and figures from 2012. Retrieved from Thehuffingtonpost.com: http://huffingtonpost/brian-honigman/100-fascinating-social-me_b_2185281.html (22 November 2017).
277 Hierarchy of Social Marketing. John Jantsch. Duct Tape Marketing. https://www.ducttapemarketing.com/the-hierarchy-of-social-marketing/ (22 November 2017).
278 http://www.simplypsychology.org/maslow.html (22 November 2017).

279 Li, C. a. (2008). Groundswell: Winning in a World Transformed by Social Technologie. Harvard Business Press.
280 Ramirez, A. (2009). The Effect of Interactivity on Initial Interactions: The Influence of Information Seeking Role on Computer-Mediated Interaction. Western Journal of Communication, 300–325.
281 Bates, P. (2011). Social Media Theory—the 1:9:90 rule. Retrieved from Yell: http://marketing.yell.com/web-design/social-media-theory-the-1-9-90-rule/ (22 November 2017).
282 Burn-Calander, R. (2013, November 27). The top 10 corporate social media disasters. Retrieved from The Telegraph: http://www.businessinsider.com/the-top-10-corporate-social-media-disasters-2013-11 (22 November 2017).
283 Gallo, Carmine. Social Media Tips from The World's Top Airline. (2018). Forbes. 31 August 2015. https://www.forbes.com/sites/carminegallo/2015/08/31/social-media-tips-from-the-worlds-top-airline/#13b23bf2699c (Accessed 15 August 2018).
284 Ma, Julie. The 12 Bookmarkles Your Social Media Life Is Missing. March 2, 2012. The Daily Good. https://www.good.is/articles/improve-your-social-media-life-with-bookmarklets-the-one-click-wonders (Accessed 22 November 2017).
285 Shamoon, S. a. (2011). Brand Management: What Next? Interdisciplinary Journal Of Contemporary Research In Business, 435-44. Retrieved from Business Source Complete.
286 http://www.managementstudyguide.com/brand-management.htm (Accessed 1/1/2017)
287 Jones, L. a. (2011). Building Brand Communities Through Online Interaction: The Case of Social Media. (pp. 17-19). Orlando: 2nd International Colloquium on Consumer-Brand Relationships.
288 http://journals.ama.org/doi/abs/10.1509/jmkg.73.5.30?code=amma-site (Accessed 24 October 2017).
289 Kucuk, S. U. (2008). Negative Double Jeopardy: The role of anti-brand sites on the Internet. Brand Management, Volume 15, No. 3, 209-222.
290 Primark, Dan. (2016) Unilever Buys Dollar Shave Club for $1 Billion. Fortune. July 20, 2016. http://fortune.com/2016/07/19/unilever-buys-dollar-shave-club-for-1-billion/ (Accessed 18 November 2017).
291 Butler, Brendan. 2017. *12 Examples of Brand Personality.* Careeraddict.com. August 18, 2017. https://www.careeraddict.com/12-examples-of-brand-personality-to-inspire-you (Accessed 18 November 2017).
292 Simply Zesty. (2012, November). How to increase your social media following. Retrieved from simplyzesty.com: http://www.simplyzesty.com/Blog/Article/November-2012/How-To-Increase-Your-Social-Media-Following (22 November 2017).
293 Gilliland, Nikki. (2018). Six of the best travel brands on YouTube, Snapchat, Instagram, Twitter, Pinterest & LinkedIn. Econsultancy. https://www.econsultancy.com/blog/69763-six-of-the-best-travel-brands-on-youtube-snapchat-instagram-twitter-pinterest-linkedin (Accessed 15 August 2018).
294 Fusco, Charlie. Airlines Need to Master Building Shopping Communities in 2017. TotalRetail. February 7, 2017. http://www.mytotalretail.com/article/airlines-need-master-building-shopping-communities-2017-survive/ (Accessed 31 October 2017).

295 Malshe, A. (n.d.). A Typology of Social Media Crises. Retrieved from Academia.edu: http://www.academia.edu/1476436/A_Typology_of_Social_Media_Crises.
296 Gundel, S. (2005). Towards a New Typology of Crises. Journal of Contingencies and Crisis Management, Volume 13 (3), pages 106 – 115.
297 http://www.youtube.com/watch?v=5YGc4zOqozo (Retrieved: February 15, 2017).
298 Hale, J. E., Dulek, R. E., & Hale, D. P. „Crisis Response Communication Challenges - Building Theory from Qualitative Data". Journal of Business Communication, 2005, 42 (2), 112-134
299 Korolov, M. (2010, August 11). Why virtual worlds suck for business—and some solutions. Retrieved from Hypergrid Business: http://www.hypergridbusiness.com/2010/08/why-virtual-worlds-suck-for-business-and-some-solutions/ (22 November 2017).
300 Grassegger, H., Krogerus, M. December 3, 2016. I Just Showed That the Bomb Was There. Das Magazin https://www.dasmagazin.ch/2016/12/03/ich-habe-nur-gezeigt-dass-es-die-bombe-gibt/ (22 November 2017).
301 Bifet, A. a. (2010). Sentiment knowledge discovery in twitter streaming data. Retrieved from University of Waikato, Hamilton, New Zealand: http://www.cs.waikato.ac.nz/~ml/publications/2010/Twitter-crc.pdf (22 November 2017).
302 https://www.rivaliq.com (22 November 2017).
303 http://buzzsumo.com (22 November 2017).
304 . O'Connor, B., Balasubramanyan, R., Routledge, B. R. and Smith, N. A. From tweets to polls: Linking text sentiment to public opinion time series. In Proceedings of the International AAAI Conference on Weblogs and Social Media, pages 122–129, 2010.
305 Macy, B. a. (2011). *The Power of Real-Time Social Media Marketing.* New York: McGraw Hill, 2011.
306 Haden, J. (2014, April 23). 60 Awesome Social-Media Tools for Entrepreneurs. Retrieved from Inc.com: http://www.inc.com/jeff-haden/60-awesome-social-media-tools-for-entrepreneurs.html (22 November 2017).
307 Landau, J. (2014, July 22). GoPro's Viral Video Marketing Campaign Turns It Into Top YouTube Brand in the World. Retrieved from NY Daily News: http://www.nydailynews.com/news/national/gopro-marketing-turns-top-youtube-brand-article-1.1875573 (22 November 2017).
308 He, Wu, Zha, Shenghua, Li, Ling. Social media competitive analysis and text mining. A case study in the pizza industry. International Journal of Information Management 33 (2013) 464-472. http://saharbread.sahargroup.ir/Uploads/28460.pdf (22 November 2017).
309 Dey L., H. S. (2011). Acquiring Competitive Intelligence from Social Media. Proceedings of the 2011 Joint Workshop on Multilingual OCR and Analytics for Noisy Unstructured Text Data.
310 How Travel & Hospitality Brands Are Marketing With Social Media Influencers http://mediakix.com/2015/08/travel-hospitality-brands-marketing-with-social-media-influencers/#gs.rw8hqKw (22 November 2017).

311 Marriott International Partners with What's Trending and YouTube Stars to Develop Original Content Series. February 6, 2015. Marriott.com. http://news.marriott.com/2015/02/marriott-international-partners-with-whats-trending-and-youtube-stars-to-develop-original-content-series/?aff=MARUS&affname=10l1110&co=US&nt=PH (22 November 2017).

312 Tyga. (2018). 3 Brands Flying Ahead of Their Competitors Through Influencers! 29 May 2018. PMYB. https://pmyb.co.uk/3-airline-brands-competitors-influencers/ (Accessed 15 August 2018).

313 Chen, Yuyu. (2016, 27 April). The rise of 'micro-influencers' on Instagram. Digiday. https://digiday.com/marketing/micro-influencers/ (Accessed 26 August 2017).

314 Main, Sami. Micro-Influencers are more http://www.adweek.com/digital/micro-influencers-are-more-effective-with-marketing-campaigns-than-highly-popular-accounts/ (22 November 2017).

315 https://brand24.com/blog/who-are-micro-influencers-how-to-find-them/(Accessed 22 November 2017).

316 Mediakix. (2016). How Top Social Influencers Help Airlines Brands Soar 30 June 2016. http://mediakix.com/2016/06/top-social-influencers-marketing-airlines/#gs.ZzwjfDM (Accessed 15 August 2018).

317 Woodruff, A. (2014, April 26). Necessary, unpleasant, and disempowering: reputation management in the Internet age. Retrieved from www.allisonwoodruff.com: http://www.allisonwoodruff.com/publications/2014-Woodruff-CHI2014-ReputationManagement.pdf (Accessed 22 November 2017).

318 https://en.wikipedia.org/wiki/Reputation_management (Accessed 22 November 2017).

319 https://en.wikipedia.org/wiki/Klout (Accessed 22 November 2017).

320 Lieb, R. (2012, July 10). How Your Content Strategy Is Critical for Reputation Management. Retrieved from Marketingland.com: http://marketingland.com/how-your-content-strategy-is-critical-for-reputation-management-16073

321 Brynley-Jones, L. (2009, October 4). A 5-Step Guide to Reputation Management Using Social Media. Retrieved from oursocialtimes: http://oursocialtimes.com/a-5-step-guide-to-reputation-management-using-social-media/

322 Melville, P. &. (2009). Social Media Analytics: Channeling the Power of the Blogosphere for Marketing Insight. Retrieved from citeseerx.ist.psu.edu: http://citeseerx.ist.psu.edu/viewdoc/download?doi=10.1.1.157.3485&rep=rep1&type=pdf (Accessed 22 November 2017).

323 Rouse, M. (n.d.). Social Media Analytics. Retrieved from techtarget.com: http://searchbusinessanalytics.techtarget.com/definition/social-media-analytics (Accessed 22 November 2017).

324 www.cluetrain.com (Accessed 22 November 2017).

325 https://klear.com/ (Accessed 22 November 2017).

326 Hamill, J. and Stevenson, A. 2010. Step 3: *Key Performance Indicators (Post 1)*. Available at: www.energise2-0.com/2010/06/27/step-3-key-performance- indicators-post-1/ [accessed: 12 February 2011].

327 Salesforce.com. (2013). 10 Examples of Social Media Command Centers. Retrieved from Salesforce Marketing Cloud: http://www.salesforcemarketingcloud.com/resources/ebooks/10-examples-of-social-media-command-centers/ (Accessed 22 November 2017).

328 Gulbransen, Scott. January 22, 2014. Taking Back the Social-Media Command Center, Scott Gulbransen. Forbes. http://www.forbes.com/sites/onmarketing/2014/01/22/taking-back-the-social-media-command-center/#3c283a5d6513 (Accessed 22 November 2017).

329 IBM. (2013, February). Social Media Analytics: Making Customer Insights Actionable. Retrieved from IBM.com: http://www-01.ibm.com/common/ssi/cgi-bin/ssialias?infotype=SA&subtype=WH&htmlfid=YTW03168USEN (Accessed 22 November 2017).

330 Dreamgrow.com. https://www.dreamgrow.com/69-free-social-media-monitoring-tools/ (Accessed 22 November 2017).

331 Davenport, T. (2006). Competing on Analytics. Harvard Business Review.

332 Lemon, K. (2007, May). How Can These Companies Leverage the Customer Data Responsibly. Retrieved from http://blog.hansacequity.com: http://blog.hansacequity.com/Portals/11224/docs/article%20on%20Analytics.pdf (Accessed 22 November 2017).

CHAPTER FIVE

The Connected Aircraft

"In the future, every aircraft will be connected to each other. Not only will ground teams be able to see how nearly every component on the aircraft is performing, but the flight crew themselves will also be able to share information from other aircraft since they essentially will just be nodes in the network."

~Jack Jacobs
Honeywell Aerospace

Overview

In his article *The Connected Aircraft*[333], Woodrow Bellamy III states that, "Operators around the globe are deploying satellite and broadband-based connectivity solutions on their aircraft every day to keep up with passenger demand. However, these systems can also provide enhanced flight operations by enabling real time data sharing with ground-based operations teams."

"In the future," Bellamy writes, "the growing prevalence of broadband and satellite-based connectivity options will allow airlines and operators to capture data about the health of critical avionics systems and aircraft components in-flight to provide better maintenance scheduling and health trend monitoring of their aircraft fleets."[333]

Bellamy offers up the concept of the "node in the sky."[333] "Within all communication networks, a node is a connection point," Bellamy explains. "For example, within a typical office environment, every individual employee's computer could be referred to as a node within that office's Local Area Network (LAN). Air Traffic Management (ATM) modernization coupled with the data centric architectures being incorporated into modern aircraft will create this same concept in the sky in the future," says Bellamy.[333] "Aircraft will become nodes within airborne networks, sharing data with other aircraft, ground-based operational teams and Air Traffic Controllers at speeds that current ACARS and ACMS systems are not capable of producing," he predicts.[333]

Streaming data about the condition of the various aircraft systems and components to ground-based operational teams can help optimize maintenance issues, which can be handled immediately after the aircraft lands.[333]

Maintenance crews and needed mechanics can be alerted so they are at the airport ready to go to work. "This way, the operational teams get a better grasp on how the aircraft performs on certain routes, different weather patterns, and how various aircraft in their fleets perform during different phases of flight," claims Bellamy.[333]

"Currently, the technology used by airlines and operators to capture parameters of flight data and share it with their ground-based operational and maintenance teams is extremely limited and equivalent to the speed of dial up Internet connections," explains Bellamy.[333] Although hampered by limited bandwidth, this data sharing process is important because "ground-based operational teams can measure the airborne performance of various aircraft components and systems during different phases of flight, such as at cruise altitude or during adverse weather conditions."[333]

"Right now, operators are dealing with connection speeds that are ancient, with VHF connections providing on average 10 to 15 Kbps," says Jack Jacobs, vice president of marketing and product management of safety and information systems at Honeywell Aerospace.[333] "But it is getting better; the day is coming where we will see connectivity on the aircraft that is equivalent to what we're used to in our homes," Jacobs adds.[333]

"That type of connectivity can have different benefits for different parts of the aircraft, according to Jacobs."[333] For example, Bellamy notes, "the aircraft braking system on most passenger jets today is monitored by the brake control system. Maintenance teams determine whether a repair is necessary through a physical measurement of a wear device on the brakes."[333] "Introducing connectivity that provides real-time monitoring of the brakes will greatly enhance that process," explains Bellamy.[333]

"Affordable, wireless real time connectivity can allow us to monitor flight to flight and even out wear on brakes to extend life and reduce maintenance costs as well as forward stage parts proactively. We also have the ability to integrate with other information such as flight plans, weather and landing conditions to perform prognostics much more efficiently," said Jacobs.[333]

Airlines should start taking advantage of the higher speed broadband available from new satellite communication (satcom) systems "to enable more efficient and speedier sharing of real time data about the in-flight performance of their aircraft."[333] This help provide "better maintenance schedules, reduce aircraft down times and report trends back to aircraft and avionics manufacturers who can then use that data to improve future products and introduce software updates to improve existing products," says Bellamy.[333]

Bellamy notes that, "airlines flying extensively in the oceanic environment, where connectivity is a challenge, can certainly benefit from these new satcom systems."[333] According to Dan Smith, Hawaiian Airlines' manager of systems engineering and principle avionics engineer wants to use its connected aircraft to improve communication.[333] "You can save a lot of fuel with good communication," says Smith, adding that Hawaiian is looking to add a new broadband solution to its aircraft that provides free position location data offloading services.[333] The island carrier wants a solution that provides aircraft position data, latitude and longitude data, as well as heading and groundspeed data.[333]

Airframe manufacturers are about to muscle into the connected aircraft business as well, notes Bellamy.[333] Boeing, one of the industry's two heavyweights, is "evaluating the possibility of offering a satellite-based In-Flight Connectivity (IFC) system as a line-fit option on its 737s, 777s, and 787s. Having that type of connectivity on the aircraft right off of the production line could help operators of the 787—which generates up to 146,000 parameters of data per flight— capture better data about the health of the aircraft while it is being operated," say Bellamy.[333]

Boeing also believes that there is real value in enhancing connectivity options for operational and maintenance purposes. "Airlines incur billions of dollars of expenses annually, so if they're able to gain operational efficiencies in terms of reducing fuel burn, increasing flight crew situational awareness and on time performance, then 'there is some real value we can get out of connectivity,' says John Craig, Boeing's chief engineer of cabin and network systems.[333]

"Providing aircraft with more robust connectivity options is also enticing for European and Asian carriers," argues Bellamy.[333] "If these carriers can save some money on operational costs by gaining a better understanding of how their aircraft perform in-flight in real time, they surely would like to take advantage of it," claims Bellamy.[333] Boris Bubresko, head of business development at Norwegian Air Shuttle concurs this idea.[333]

"We were one of the first airlines in Europe to offer connectivity. We started in 2011 and have close to 70 aircraft installed with the service. That is around 90 percent of our fleet," says Bubresko.[333] The company first saw the connectivity as a perk for passenger-oriented, but soon recognized the importance for the airline's operational side.[333] "We believe we will have a more efficient cockpit and cabin crew," he says.[333] "We're currently in the process of connecting our cockpit to the system. We expect a more efficient flight planning and to be able to get updates during the flight."[333]

Jack Jacobs of Honeywell Aerospace "believes that the aircraft will literally become a node in the sky, and real time data sharing will be seamless."[333] "In the future, every aircraft will be connected to each other. Not only will ground teams be able to see how nearly every component on the aircraft is performing, but the flight crew themselves will also be able to share information from other aircraft since they essentially will just be nodes in the network," said Jacobs.[333] "This gives rise then to the ability to crowd source information and trends to improve safety, efficiency and reduce operational costs," Jacobs concludes.[333]

Today, airline passengers want to be able to pull up their loyalty point balances on their mobile phones and soon they will want to pay for things throughout a retail store on their phones as well, possibly, with Bitcoins or other crypto-currencies. Customers will soon expect the airline to know when they've walked through the front door.

Beyond the airline connectivity, *The Predictive Airliner* should have answers to the following questions:

- How can an airline save on it resource use?
- How can an airline improve the management of customer movements?
- How can an airline best utilize its transportation fleet?
- How can an airline reduce its labor needs?
- How can an airline cut down on waste?
- How can an airline ensure its security?

These are all important questions that need to be asked and analytics can be an answer to many of them.

UNDERSTANDING ANALYTICS
Definitions, sample applications and opportunities, and underlying techniques

	Descriptive	Predictive	Prescriptive
What the user needs to DO	What HAS happened? • Increase asset reliability • Reduce labor and inventory costs	What COULD happened? • Predict infrastructure failure • Forecast facilities space demand	What SHOULD happened? • Increase asset utilization • Optimize resource schedules
What the user needs to KNOW	• The number and types of asset failures • Why maintenance costs are high • The value of the materials inventory	• How to anticipate failures for specific asset types • When to consolidate underutilized facilities • How to determine costs to improve service levels	• How to increase asset production • Where to optimally route service technicians • which strategic facilities plan provides the highest long-term utilization
How analytics gets ANSWERS	• Standard reporting - What happened? • Query/drill down- Where exactly is the problem? • Ad hoc reporting - How many, how often, where?	• Predictive modeling - What will happen next? • Forecasting - What if these trends continue? • Simulation - What could happen? • Alerts - What actions are needed?	• Optimization - What is the best possible outcome? • Random variable optimization - What is the best outcome given the variability in specified areas?
What makes this analysis POSSIBLE	• Alerts, reports, dashboards, business intelligence	• Predictive models, forecasts, statistical analysis, scoring	• Business rules, organization models, comparison, optmization

Figure 22: Understanding analytics, definitions, applications
Source: IBM[334]

As Figure 22 shows, analytics can be used to boost service quality, reduce operating costs, as well as increase ROI. As the IBM Thought Leadership White Paper *Descriptive, predictive, prescriptive: Transforming asset and facilities management with analytics*[334] states, "As facilities and assets become more IT-like—instrumented, intelligent and interconnected—the convergence of physical and digital infrastructures makes their management increasingly complex. And in a physical world outfitted with millions of networked sensors, vast amounts of facilities- and asset-generated data make extracting meaning increasingly difficult."[334]

Airlines must tame the three Vs of big data—volume, variety, and velocity—and analytics are the best way to do so. Utilizing the right analytics in the right place can yield impressive ROI results. As IBM states[334]:

> "From basic to advanced capabilities, analytics can yield dramatic results. One study found that an organization that uses basic automation to expand its reporting capabilities can improve its return on investment (ROI) by 188 percent. But adding additional capabilities such as data management, metadata to ensure uniform data interpretation, and the ability to gather and analyze data from outside the organization, can boost ROI to as high as 1,209 percent."

IBM's specific examples include:

- "Effective facilities and asset management uses data analytics to proactively manage facilities and maintain equipment, optimize utilization, prevent breakdowns, lower occupancy and operational costs, and extend asset life."[334]
- "Utilizing analytics to monitor energy-intensive equipment across the facilities portfolio, identify operating anomalies in real time, and generate corrective work orders can dramatically reduce energy consumption."[334]
- "To help mitigate risks of failure in facilities and assets, analytics can detect even minor anomalies and failure patterns. Identifying issues early helps organizations deploy limited maintenance resources more cost-effectively, maximize equipment uptime and improve customer service levels."[334]

The rest of this chapter will focus on how to build the backbone of an IT system that will incorporate a structure that can help an airline become predictive. General sections on Hadoop, IoT, streaming analytics, amongst other, will lay out the most common questions that an airliner should ask about the data lake and predictive world. The rest of the chapter will detail specific business areas that can be improved with these technologies.

A few industry examples from *Information Week's In-memory Databases, IBM,*

Microsoft, Oracle, and SAP Are Fighting to Become Your In-memory Technology Providers. Do You Really Need the Speed?[335] might shed some light on why speed can be such an important differentiator when it comes to real-time marketing and customer interactions. These include[335]:

> "Online gaming company Bwin.party uses in-memory capabilities to handle 150,000 bets per second. This compares to their normal system rate of 12,000 bets per second. For retail services company Edgenet, 'in-memory technology has brought near-real-time insight into product availability for customers of AutoZone, Home Depot, and Lowe's. That translates into fewer wasted trips and higher customer satisfaction'"[335]

ConAgra, an $18 billion-a-year consumer packaged goods company, "must quickly respond to the fluctuating costs of 4,000 raw materials that go into more than 20,000 products, from Swiss Miss cocoa to Chef Boyardee pasta"[335] and an in-memory system assists them in material forecasting, planning, and pricing.[335]

ConAgra also taps its in-memory solution to make company promotions more relevant by using faster analysis, which allows ConAgra and its retail customers to command higher prices in an industry notorious for razor-thin profit margins.

Maple Leaf Foods, a $5 billion-a-year Canadian supplier of meats, baked goods, and packaged foods, finds that profit-and-loss reports which "used to take 15 to 18 minutes on conventional databases now take 15 to 18 seconds on their in-memory platform."[335]

Temenos, a banking software provider that uses IBM's in-memory-based BLU Acceleration for DB2 system, reports that queries that used to take 30 seconds now take one-third of a second thanks to BLU's columnar compression and in-memory analysis.

Bwin.party's advantage is a hugely important competitive advantage; not only are more bets being taken, but more customers are being made happy. In-play betting has become a huge revenue generator for sports book and speeding up the time it takes to close bets means more money flows into the company's coffers and, in some cases, better odds can be offered to bettors.

For Temenos, in particular, that difference in speed means that mobile customers will be able to quickly retrieve all of their banking transactions on their mobile devices, rather than just their last five, which could mean the difference between handling customer issues on a mobile device rather than in a company store.[335] According to *Information Week*, "Online or mobile interaction costs the bank 10 to 20 cents to support versus $5 or more for a branch visit," therefore the cost savings could be enormous.[335]

Hadoop

Perhaps one of the most interesting data warehouse developments in the last decade has been the introduction of Hadoop and its Hadoop Distributed File System (HDFS). As Grover et al. explain in their book *Hadoop Application Architectures*[336]:

> "At its core, Hadoop is a distributed data store which provides a platform for implementing powerful parallel processing frameworks on it. The reliability of this data store when it comes to storing massive volumes of data coupled with its flexibility related to running multiple processing frameworks makes it an ideal choice as the hub for all your data. This characteristic of Hadoop means that you can store any type of data as-is, and without placing any constraints on how that data is processed."

Hadoop is a *Schema-on-Read* data warehouse, meaning raw unprocessed data can be loaded into it "with the structure imposed at processing time based on the requirements of the processing application."[336] This differs from a *Schema-on-Write* DW, which is normally used with traditional data management systems.[336] "Such systems require the schema of the data store to be defined before the data can be stored in it. This leads to lengthy cycles of analysis, data modeling, data transformation, loading, testing, etc., before data can be accessed," warns Grover et al.[336] Additionally, if a wrong decision is made, or requirements change, this cycle needs to start anew.[336] "When the application or structure of data is not as well understood, the agility provided by the Schema-on-Read pattern can provide invaluable insights on data not previously accessible," adds Grover et al.[336]

Although the ability to store all a company's raw data in a Hadoop DW is a powerful option, there are still many factors that should be considered before putting this method into practice.[336] These include:

- How the data is being stored: There are several different file formats and compression formats supported on Hadoop. Each of these have particular strengths and weaknesses, which make them better suited for specific applications.[336] Additionally, although Hadoop provides the HDFS for storing data, there are several other commonly used systems implemented on top of HDFS that do allow additional functionality so these systems should also be taken into consideration.[336]
- Multi-tenancy: It is common for clusters to host multiple users, groups, and application types, so important considerations should be made when planning the management and storage of data.[336]

- Schema design: Despite Hadoop being schema-less, there are still important considerations to consider when devising the structure of data stored in Hadoop, including directory structures for data loaded into HDFS as well as the output of data processing and analysis.[336]
- Metadata: As with any data management system, cataloging and storing the metadata related to the stored data is as important as cataloging and storing the data itself.[336]

As Grover et al. point out, "One of the most fundamental decisions to make when architecting a solution on Hadoop is determining how data will be stored in Hadoop. There is no such thing as a standard data storage format in Hadoop."[336]

"Hadoop allows for storage of data in any format, whether it's text, binary, images, etc. Hadoop also provides built-in support for a number of formats optimized for Hadoop storage and processing," Grover et al. note.[336] This gives users complete control over their source data and there are a number of options on how that data can be stored, not just the raw data being ingested, but also the intermediate data generated during data processing, as well as the results of the data processing.[336] The complexity of choice obviously goes exponential as one makes one's way through the process. Major considerations for Hadoop data storage that need to be made include[336]:

- File format: These include plain text or Hadoop specific formats such as SequenceFile. There are also more complex, but more functionally rich options such as Avro and Parquet, each format comes with their own unique strengths and weaknesses, making it more or less suitable depending on the application and source data types ingested.[336] As Hadoop is customizable, It is also possible to create one's own unique file format.[336]
- Compression: Although this is more straightforward than selecting file formats, compression codecs commonly used with Hadoop have their own unique characteristics, some compress and uncompress faster, but don't compress as aggressively, others create smaller files, but take longer to compress and uncompress, and not surprisingly require more CPU power.[336] The ability to split compressed files is also a very important consideration when working with data stored in Hadoop.
- Data storage: Although Hadoop data is stored in HDFS, there are decisions around what the underlying storage manager should be, i.e. whether you should use HBase or HDFS directly to store the data.[336]

Besides HDFS there are a few alternate file systems available for Hadoop, including open-source file systems such as GlusterFS and the Quantcast File Sytem, and commercial alternatives like Isilon OneFS and Netapp.[336] Amazon's Simple Storage System (S3) is a cloud-based storage systems that is gaining traction.[336] The file system options are growing and this might become yet another architectural consideration in a Hadoop deployment.[336]

For text files like CSV and XML, or binary file types (such as images), it is preferable to use one of the Hadoop specific container formats, but in many cases you'll want to store source data in its rawest form (as that is, after all, one of Hadoop's biggest advantages).[336] "Having online access to data in its raw, source form—'full fidelity' data—means it will always be possible to perform new processing and analytics with the data as requirements change," note Grover et al.[336]

"A primary consideration when storing text data in Hadoop is the organization of the files in the file system," Grover et al. claim.[336] Since text files can very quickly consume considerable space on a Hadoop cluster, users should keep in mind that there is an overhead of type conversion associated with storing data in text formats.[336] For example, when storing *1234* in a text file and using it as an integer, a String-to-Integer conversion during read, and vice-versa during writing is required, which adds up when a lot of such conversions are being done.[336]

Selection of compression format will depend on how the end user plans to consume the data.[336] For archival purposes the most compact compression method available might be advisable, but if the data is to be used in processing in MapReduce, a splittable format might be preferable, advises Grover et al.[336] "Splittable formats provide the ability for Hadoop to split files into chunks for processing, which is critical to efficient parallel processing."[336]

It should be mentioned that in many, if not all cases, "the use of a container format such as SequenceFiles or Avro will provide advantages which makes it a preferred format for most file types, including text—among other things these container formats provide functionality to support splittable compression," state Grover et al.[336]

The structured format text files XML and JSON are especially challenging for Hadoop as splitting XML and JSON files for processing is tricky, and Hadoop does not have a built-in Input-Format for either of these formats.[336] "JSON_presents even greater challenges than XML, since there are no tokens to mark the beginning or end of a record", warns Grover et al.[336] In the case of these formats, there are a couple of options[336]:

- Use a container format such as Avro.
- Use a library designed for processing XML or JSON files; XMLLoader in the PiggyBank library for Pig for XML; the Elephant Bird project provides the LzoJsonInputFormat for JSON.

"Although text is probably the most common source data format stored in Hadoop, Hadoop can also be used to process binary files such as images. For most cases of storing and processing binary files in Hadoop, using a container format such as SequenceFile is preferred," advises Grover et al.[336]

MapReduce is a programming model used to process large data sets with a parallel, distributed algorithm on a cluster.[337] The current Apache MapReduce version is built over an Apache YARN Framework, which is a new framework that facilitates writing arbitrary distributed processing frameworks and applications.[337]

According to Wikipedia[338]:

> "MapReduce is a framework for processing parallelizable problems across large datasets using a large number of computers (nodes), collectively referred to as a cluster (if all nodes are on the same local network and use similar hardware) or a grid (if the nodes are shared across geographically and administratively distributed systems and use more heterogenous hardware). Processing can occur on data stored either in a filesystem (unstructured) or in a database (structured). MapReduce can take advantage of the locality of data, processing it near the place it is stored in order to minimize communication overhead."

There are several Hadoop specific file formats that seamlessly integrate with MapReduce, including "file based data structures such as sequence files, serialization formats like Avro, and columnar formats such as RCFiles and Parquet."[336] These file formats have differing strengths and weaknesses, but having both splittable compression as well as agnostic compression is important for Hadoop applications.[336]

As Grover et al. explain, SequenceFiles store data as binary key-value pairs in the following three formats[336]:

- Uncompressed, which, for the most part, provide no advantages over their compressed alternatives, since they're less efficient for I/O and take up more space on disk than the same data in compressed form.
- Record-compressed, which compresses each record as it's added to the file. An inefficient choice compared to block compressed.
- Block compressed, which waits until data reaches block size to compress, rather than as each record is added. Providing better compression ratios compared to record-compressed SequenceFiles, a *block* in Block compression refers to a block of records that are compressed together within a single HDFS block.

"Regardless of format, every SequenceFile uses a common header format containing basic metadata about the file such as the compression codec used, key and value class names, user defined metadata, and a randomly generated sync marker," add Grover et al.[336] "This sync marker is also written into the body of the file to allow for seeking to random points in the file, and is key to facilitating splittability. For example, in the case of block compression, this sync marker will be written after every block in the file," state Grover et al.[336] Although SequenceFiles are well supported within the Hadoop ecosystem, their support outside of the ecosystem is limited and they are commonly used as containers for smaller files.[336] "Since Hadoop is optimized for large files, packing smaller files into a SequenceFile makes the storage and processing of these files much more efficient," note Grover et al.[336]

Serialization refers to "the process of turning data structures into byte streams either for storage or transmission over a network. Conversely, deserialization is the process of converting a byte stream back into data structures," explain Grover et al.[336] "It is core to a distributed processing system such as Hadoop, since it allows data to be converted into a format that can be efficiently stored as well as transferred across a network connection."[336] Serialization is commonly associated with two aspects of data processing in distributed systems: inter-process communication (remote procedure calls, or RPC) and data storage, which is what is focused on here.

The main serialization format utilized by Hadoop is Writables, which is compact and fast, but not easy to extend beyond its natural language, Java.[336] However, Thrift, Protocol Buffers, and Avro are seeing increased use within the Hadoop ecosystem.[336] Avro was specifically created as a replacement for Writables and, of the three, it is the best suited for serialization.[336]

Developed at Facebook, Thrift is sometimes used for data serialization with Hadoop, but it has several drawbacks, including lacking support for the internal compression of records.[336] It is unsplittable and also lacks native MapReduce support.[336] There are externally available libraries to address these drawbacks, but Hadoop does not provide native support for Thrift as a data storage format.[336]

"The Protocol Buffer (protobuf) format was developed at Google to facilitate data exchange between services written in different languages."[336] "Like Thrift, protobuf structures are defined using an IDL, which is used to generate stub code for multiple languages."[336] "Also like Thrift, Protocol Buffers do not support internal compression of records, are not splittable, and have no native MapReduce support," acknowledge Grover et Al.[336]

Apache Avro is a "framework for modeling, serializing and making Remote Procedure Calls (RPC). Avro data is described by a schema, and one interesting feature is that the schema is stored in the same file as the data it describes, so files are self-describing."[337]

Avro was designed to address the major downside of Hadoop Writables: lack of language portability.[336] "Like Thrift and Protocol Buffers, Avro data is described using a language independent schema," explains Grover et al.[336] Unlike Thrift and Protocol Buffers, however, code generation is optional with Avro.[336] "Since Avro stores the schema in the header of each file, it's self-describing and Avro files can easily be read later, even from a different language than the one used to write the file."[336]

Avro is written in JSON or in Avro IDL, which is a C-like language.[336] It provides better native support for MapReduce, while also supporting schema evolution—the schema used to read a file does not need to match the schema used to write the file—which makes it superior to SequenceFiles for Hadoop applications.[336] This powerful feature makes it possible to add new fields to a schema as requirements change, which can be extremely helpful with constantly updating file systems.[336]

"Until relatively recently, most database systems stored records in a row-oriented fashion. This is efficient for cases where many columns of the record need to be fetched," explain Grover et al.[336] If your analysis relies heavily on fetching all fields for records that belong to a particular time range, row-oriented storage makes sense.[336] "This can also be more efficient when writing data, particularly if all columns of the record are available at write time since the record can be written with a single disk seek."[336] More recently, however, a number of vendors have released columnar storage systems, which provides several benefits over earlier row-oriented systems, including[336]:

- Skips I/O on columns that are not a part of the query.
- Works well for queries that only access a small subset of columns.
- Compression on columns are quite efficient and the column has few distinct values.

"Columnar storage is often well suited for data-warehousing type applications where users want to aggregate certain columns over a large collection of records," explain Grover et Al.[336] Unsurprisingly, columnar file formats, such as the RCFile format, are also being utilized for Hadoop applications.[336]

The RCFile format "was developed specifically to provide efficient processing for MapReduce applications, although in practice it's only seen use as a Hive storage format," note Grover et al.[336] Hive is a data warehouse infrastructure that was developed by Facebook to provide SQL-like language for data summarization, query, and analysis.[337] "The RCFile format was developed to provide fast data loading, fast query processing, highly efficient storage space utilization, and strong adaptivity to highly dynamic workload patterns."[336]

Similar to SequenceFiles, except data is stored in a column-oriented fashion, the RCFile format breaks files into row splits, then within each split uses column oriented storage.[336] "Although the RCFile format provides advantages in terms of query and compression performance compared to SequenceFiles, it also has some deficiencies that prevent optimal performance for query times and compression," warn Grover et al.[336] Newer columnar formats such as Parquet and Optimize Row Columnar (ORC), which I will detail next, address many of these deficiencies, and it is replacing RCFile on newer applications.[336]

The ORC format "was created to address some of the short-comings with the RCFile format, specifically around query performance and storage efficiency."[336] The ORC format provides the following features and benefits, over the RCFile format[336]:

- "Light-weight, always-on compression provided by type-specific readers and writers. ORC also supports the use of zlib, LZO, or Snappy to provide further compression."[336]
- "Allows predicates to be pushed down to the storage layer so that only required data is brought back in queries."[336]
- "Supports the Hive type model, including new primitives such as decimal as well as complex types."[336]
- "Is a splittable storage format."[336]

The main drawback of ORC is that it was specifically designed for Hive, and so "is not a general purpose storage format that can be used with non-Hive MapReduce interfaces such as Pig or Java, or other query engines such as Impala," explain Grover et al.[336] Parquet shares many of the same design goals as ORC, but it is intended to be a general purpose storage format for Hadoop, which attempts to create a format that's suitable for different MapReduce interfaces such as Java, Hive, and Pig, and also suitable for other processing engines like Impala.[336] Parquet provides the following benefits, many of which it shares with ORC:

- "Similar to ORC files, allows for returning only required data fields, thereby reducing I/O and increasing performance."[336]
- "Provides efficient compression; compression can be specified on a per-column level."[336]
- "Designed to support complex nested data structure. Parquet stores full metadata at the end of files, so Parquet files are self-documenting."[336]

For its part, the Apache-licensed Impala project brings scalable parallel database technology to Hadoop, enabling users to issue low-latency SQL queries to data stored in HDFS and Apache HBase without requiring data movement or transformation.[337]

HDFS Schema Design

As previously mentioned, Hadoop's *Schema-on-Read* model does not impose any requirements when loading data into Hadoop.[336] While many people use Hadoop for storing and processing unstructured data, some order is still desirable, especially since Hadoop often serves as a data hub for an entire organization, where the stored data is intended to be shared among many departments and teams.[337] It is important to create a carefully structured and organized repository of your data for the following reasons:

- "Standard directory structure makes it easier to share data between teams working with the same data sets."[337]
- "Often times, you'd want to 'stage' data in a separate location before all of it is ready to be processed. Conventions regarding staging data will help ensure that partially-loaded data will not get accidentally processed as if it was complete."[337]
- "Standardized organization of data will allow reusing code that processes it."[337]
- "Standardized locations also allow enforcing access and quota controls to prevent accidental deletion or corruption."[337]
- "Some tools in the Hadoop ecosystem sometimes make assumptions regarding the placement of data. It is often simpler to match those assumptions when initially loading data into Hadoop."[337]

"The details of the data model will be highly dependent on the specific use case," explain Grover et al.[337] "For example, data warehouse implementations and other event stores are likely to use a schema similar to the traditional star schema, including structured fact and dimension tables. While unstructured and semi-structured data on the other hand are likely to focus more on directory placement and metadata management," note Grover et al.[337]

When mapping out the schema design, the following specifics should be kept in mind:

- "Develop standard practices and enforce them, especially when multiple teams are sharing the data."[336]
- "Make sure your design will work well with the tools you are planning to use. For example, the version of Hive you are planning to use may only support table partitions on directories that are named a certain way. This will impact the schema design in general and how you name your table subdirectories, in particular."[336]
- "Keep usage patterns in mind when designing a schema. Different data processing and querying patterns work better with different schema designs. Knowing in advance the main use cases and data retrieval requirements will result in schema that will be easier to maintain and support in the long term as well as improve data processing performance."[336]

The first thing to understand about HBase is that it is not a Relational Database Management System (RDBMS), it is more like a huge hash table—i.e., a data structure which implements an associative array of abstract data types, or, put more simply, a structure that can map keys to values.[336] "Just like a hash table, you can associate values with keys and perform fast lookups of the values based on a given key," Grover et al explain.[336] HBase's value proposition lies in its scalability and flexibility and it works best for problems like fraud detection, problems that can be solved in a few get and put requests.[336]

Managing Metadata

As with most other data warehouses, just as important as the data itself is the metadata that relates to it.[336] As Techtarget explains, "Metadata is the data that describes other data."[339] In the Hadoop ecosystem, this can mean one of the following things[336]:

- Metadata about logical data sets. This includes information like the location of a data set, schema associated with a data set, partitioning and sorting properties of the data set itself, the format of the data set, if any are applicable. Such metadata is usually stored in a separate metadata repository.
- Metadata about files on HDFS, including permissions and file ownership information, block location on datanodes, etc., which is normally stored and managed by Hadoop Namenode.
- Metadata about tables in HBase.
- Metadata about data ingest and transformations.
- Metadata about data set statistics, i.e., number of rows in a data set, number of unique values in each column, histogram of the distribution of data, maximum and minimum values.

The concept of metadata is important to understand because metadata allows users to interact with their data through "the higher level logical abstraction of a table rather than as a mere collection of files on HDFS or a table in HBase."[336] This means that users don't need to be concerned about how or where the data is stored.[336] Metadata allows users "supply information about their data (e.g. partitioning or sorting properties) that can then be leveraged by various tools to enforce them while populating data and leveraging them when querying data", explain Grover et al.[336] Data management tools can also "hook" into this metadata, allowing users to perform data discovery and lineage analysis.[336]

Apache Hive was the first project in the Hadoop ecosystem that started storing, managing and leveraging metadata.[336] Hive, which is a data summarization, query and analysis tool, stores this metadata in a relational database called the Hive metastore.[336] "As time progressed, more projects wanted to use the same metadata that was in the Hive metastore. To enable the usage of Hive metastore outside of Hive, a separate project called HCatalog was started," explain Grover et al.[336] Today, HCatalog is included in Hive and it allows tools like Pig and MapReduce to integrate with the Hive metastore.[336] It also opens the Hive metastore up to a broader ecosystem by exposing a REST API to the Hive metastore via the WebHCat server.[336] HCatalog can be thought of as an accessibility veneer around the Hive metastore (see Figure 23).[336]

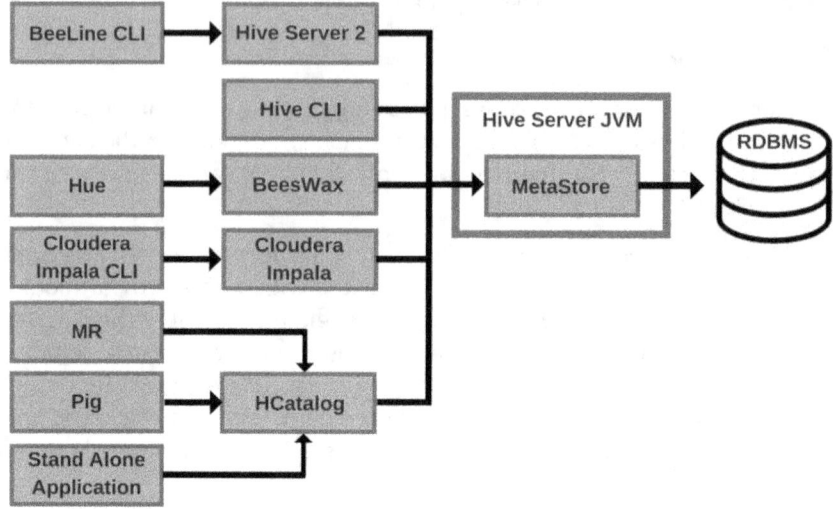

Figure 23: Metadata layer with Hive's MetaStore
Source: *Hadoop Application Architectures*[336]

MapReduce, Pig, and other standalone applications can communicate directly with the Hive metastore through their individual APIs, but HCatalog allows easy access through its WebHCat Rest APIs.[336] It also allows the cluster administrators to lock down access to the Hive Metastore, ensuring strong security measures.[336]

"The Hive metastore can be deployed in 3 modes—embedded metastore, local metastore and remote metastore," explain Grover et al.[336] MySQL, PostgreSQL, Derby and Oracle are some of the most popular Hive-supported databases around, with MySQL being the most commonly used one by far.[336]

Data Ingestion Considerations

Hadoop provides a file system client that makes it easy to copy files into and out of Hadoop, but most applications implemented on Hadoop involve the ingestion of disparate data types from multiple sources systems, with differing requirements for frequency of ingestion.[336] The most common Hadoop data sources include[336]:

- Traditional data management systems, such as relational databases and mainframes.
- Event data, including logs, and machine generated data, as well as files being imported from existing enterprise data storage systems.

There are several different factors to consider when importing data into Hadoop from differing systems, including[336]:

- Timeliness of data ingestion and accessibility:

- What are the requirements around how often data needs to be ingested?
        - How soon does data need to be available to downstream processing?
- Incremental updates:
    - How will new data be added?
    - Does it need to be appended to existing data or overwrite existing data?
- Data access and processing:
    - Will the data be used in processing?
    - If so, will it be used in batch processing jobs or is random access to the data required?
- Source system and data structure: where is the data coming from?
    - A relational database?
    - Logs?
    - Is it structured, semi-structured, un-structured data?
- Partitioning and splitting of data:
    - How should data be partitioned after ingestion?
    - Does the data need to be ingested into multiple target systems—e.g. HDFS and HBase?
- Storage format:
    - What format will the data be stored in?
- Data transformation:
    - Does the data need to be transformed in flight?

When ingesting data from a file system, the read speed of the source system devices should be considered.[336] As Grover et al note[336]:

> *"Disk I/O is often a major bottleneck in any processing pipeline. It may not be obvious, but often optimizing an ingestion pipeline requires looking at the system that the data is being pulled from. Hard drives can have read speeds of anywhere from 20MB/s to 100MB/s, and there are limitations on the motherboard or controller for reading from all the disks on the system. To maximize read speeds, make sure to take advantage of as many disks as possible on the source system. On some network attached storage (NAS) systems, additional mount points can increase throughput. Also note that a single reading thread may not be able to maximize the read speed of a drive or device. On a typical drive, 3 threads is normally required to maximize throughput."*

Data can come in any format and Hadoop can accept any file format, but not all formats are optimal for particular use cases.[336] For example, a CSV file is a very common format, and a simple CSV file can generally be easily imported into a

Hive table for immediate access and processing.[336] "However, if the underlying storage of that CSV file were converted to a columnar format such as Parquet, it very likely could be processed much more efficiently, while taking up considerably less space on disk," advise Grover et al.[336]

Another thing to consider here is that although Hadoop can accept all file formats, not all file formats can work with all of the tools within the Hadoop ecosystem.[336] An example here is of file with a variable length.[336] "Variable length files are similar to flat files in that columns are defined with a fixed length. The difference between a fixed length file and a variable length file is that in the variable length file one of the left most columns can decide the rules to read the rest of the file," explain Grover et al.[336] Variable length files may not be a good fit for Hive, but they can still be effectively processed by one of the processing frameworks available for Hadoop, such as a Java MapReduce job, Crunch, Pig, and Spark.[336]

Compression

There is a pro and a con to compressing data on the original file system. "The pro is that transferring a compressed file over the network requires less I/O and network bandwidth,"[336] explain Grover et al. "The con," warn Grover et al., "is that most compression codecs applied outside of Hadoop are not splittable, e.g. Gzip, although most of these compression codecs are splittable in Hadoop if used with a splittable container format like SequenceFiles, RCFiles, Parquet Files, or Avro Files."[336]

The normal way to do this is just to copy the compressed file to Hadoop and then convert the files in a post-processing step.[336] "It's also possible to do the conversion as the data is streamed to Hadoop, but normally it makes more sense to use the distributed processing power of the Hadoop cluster to convert files, rather than just the edge nodes that are normally involved in moving data to the cluster," advise Grover et al.

Relational Database Management Systems (RDBMS)

Hadoop easily integrates data from RDBMS vendors like Oracle, Netezza, Greenplum, Vertica, Teradata, Microsoft, and others, by utilizing tools like Sqoop.[336] Using simple SQL statements, users can define what data they wish to ingest or extract from Hadoop.[336] "Sqoop has many configuration options, with one of the most prominent being the ability to define the amount of resources used to pull the data," advise Grover et al.[336]

Although Sqoop is a very rich tool that has lots of options, it is still simple and easy to learn compared to many other Hadoop ecosystem projects.[336] "These options will control which data is retrieved from the RDBMS, how the data is retrieved, which connector to use, split patterns, and final file formats," explain Grover et al.[336]

However, Grover et al note that, "Sqoop is a batch process, so if the timeliness of the data load into the cluster needs to be faster than batch then it will likely be necessary to find an alternate method."[336] "One alternative for certain use cases is to split data on ingestion, with one pipeline landing data in the RDBMS, and one landing data in HDFS. This can be enabled with tools like Flume or Kafka, but this is a complex implementation that requires code at the application layer," warn Grover et al.[336]

A couple of important things to note about Sqoop[336]:

- Sqoop input formats are not usually the file formats desired in the long run, so a batch job will most likely be required at some point to convert the data.
- With the Sqoop Architecture the data nodes and not just the edge nodes are connecting to the RDBMS, and since this is not possible in some network configurations, then Sqoop will not be an option.

Keeping Hadoop Updated

"Ingesting data from an RDBMS to Hadoop is rarely a single event. Over time the tables in the RDBMS will change, and the data in Hadoop will require updating," note Grover et al.[336] Should the need to update arise, it is important to remember that HDFS is a read-only file system and the data files cannot be updated (except for the HBase tables, where appends are supported).[336] If a user wants to update data, he or she needs to either replace the data set, add partitions or create an entirely new dataset by merging changes.[336]

"In cases where the table is relatively small and ingesting the entire table takes very little time, there is no point in trying to keep track of modifications or additions to the table," recommend Grover et al.[336] "When we need to refresh the data in Hadoop, we simply re-run the original Sqoop import command, ingest the entire table including all the modifications, and then replace the old version with a newer one," explain Grover et al.[336]

"When the table is larger and takes a long time to ingest, we prefer to ingest only the modifications made to the table since the last time we ingested it. This requires the ability to identify such modifications," advise Grover et al.[336]

Flume

According to Apache, "Flume is a distributed, reliable and available system for the efficient collection, aggregation, and movement of streaming data."[336] "Commonly used for moving log data, Flume "can be used whenever there's a need to move massive quantities of event data such as social media feeds, message queue events, or network traffic data."[336] Flume's main components include[336]:

- Any external system that generates events, such as web servers, social media feeds, Java Messaging Service data, machine logs, etc., etc.
- Flume sources are built to consume events from specific external sources, including AvroSource, SpoolDirectorySource, HTTPSource, JMSSource, which come bundled with it.
- Flume interceptors allow events to be caught and modified in flight. Some common uses of interceptors are formatting, partitioning, filtering, splitting, validating, and/or applying metadata to events.
- Flume Selectors provide routing for events, which can be used to send events down zero or more paths, so are useful if you need to fork to multiple channels or send to a specific channel based on the event.
- Flume channels store events until they're consumed by a sink, which remove events from a channel and deliver them to a particular destination, such as the final target system for events. Common channels include the disk channel, which provides more durable storage of events by persisting to disk and the memory channel, which stores events in memory. It is important to architect the right channel as that helps balance performance with durability.
- For sinks, the destination could be the final target system for events, or it could feed into further Flume processing systems.
- The Flume agent is a container for all these components.

Kafka

Apache Kafka is a distributed publish-subscribe messaging system that maintains a feed of messages categorized into topics.[336] Grover et al. note that, "Applications can publish messages on Kafka or they can subscribe to topics and receive messages that are published on those specific topics.

Messages are published by *producers* and are pulled and processed by *consumers*."[336] "Kafka keeps track of the messages as they are consumed and guarantees that messages will not get lost even if the consumer crashes, while allowing consumers to rewind the state of the queue and re-consume messages," explain Grover et al. This rewind feature is especially helpful when troubleshooting and/or debugging.[336]

Kafka can replace a "traditional message broker or message queue in an application architecture in order to decouple services."[336] "It was designed specifically for processing high rate activity streams such as clickstream or metrics collection," say Grover et al. "Kafka can run with a large number of message brokers, while recording its common state in ZooKeeper. As a distributed service, Kafka has significant scalability and reliability advantages over traditional queuing and messaging systems such as ActiveMQ," Grover et al note.[336]

The Kafka's documentation from the Apache Kafka website provides a good explanation of Kafka's benefits[340]:

> "A traditional queue retains records in-order on the server, and if multiple consumers consume from the queue then the server hands out records in the order they are stored. However, although the server hands out records in order, the records are delivered asynchronously to consumers, so they may arrive out of order on different consumers. This effectively means the ordering of the records is lost in the presence of parallel consumption. Messaging systems often work around this by having a notion of 'exclusive consumer' that allows only one process to consume from a queue, but of course this means that there is no parallelism in processing.

> "Kafka does it better. By having a notion of parallelism—the partition—within the topics, Kafka is able to provide both ordering guarantees and load balancing over a pool of consumer processes. This is achieved by assigning the partitions in the topic to the consumers in the consumer group so that each partition is consumed by exactly one consumer in the group. By doing this we ensure that the consumer is the only reader of that partition and consumes the data in order. Since there are many partitions this still balances the load over many consumer instances. Note however that there cannot be more consumer instances in a consumer group than partitions."

Although not written specifically for Hadoop, Kafka is commonly used to store messages in HDFS for offline processing.[336] "When tracking clickstream activity on a website Kafka can be used to publish site activities such as page views and searches," note Grover et al.[336] "These messages can then be consumed by real-time dashboards or real-time monitors, as well as stored in HDFS for offline analysis and reporting," add Grover et al.[336]

"Should Kafka or Flume be used to ingest log data or other streaming data sources into Hadoop?" is a common question asked when architecting systems. The answer is not that simple as Kafka and Flume are really two different solutions that solve the following two separate problems[336]:

- "Flume is an ingest solution—an easy and reliable way to store data streaming data in HDFS while solving common issues such as reliability, optimal file sizes, file formats, updating metadata and partitioning."[336]
- "Kafka, like all message brokers, is a solution to service decoupling and message queueing. It's a possible data source for Hadoop but requires additional components in order to integrate with HDFS."[336]

Due to the lack of integration between Kafka and Hadoop, Kafka should be deployed on a separate cluster from Hadoop, but still in the same LAN.[336] According to Grover et al., "Kafka is a heavy disk I/O and memory user, and it can lead to resource contention with Hadoop tasks. At the same time, it doesn't benefit from being co-located on DataNodes since MapReduce tasks are not aware of data locality in Kafka."[336]

"It is possible and recommended to configure Kafka to use the Zookeeper nodes on the Hadoop cluster, so there will be no need to monitor and maintain two zookeeper clusters," advise Grover et al.[336] Kafka ships with a MapReduce job called Hadoop-Consumer that reads data from Kafka and writes it to HDFS, but this component is deprecated and not recommended for production use," warn Grover et al.[336] It makes more sense to use Flume to ingest messages from Kafka into Hadoop, as Flume was specifically designed to ingest streaming messages.[336] However, at the time of this writing, the Kafka source for Flume is not fully mature and not well maintained by the Flume or Kafka communities.[336] Instead Camus—a separate open source project that allows ingesting data from Kafka to HDFS—is recommended.[336]

Flexible and relatively well maintained, Camus features automatic discovery of Kafka topics from Zookeeper, the conversion of messages to Avro and Avro schema management, as well as automatic partitioning.[336] In the setup stage of the job, Camus fetches the list of topics as well as the ID of the first messages to consume from Zookeeper, and then splits the topics among the map tasks.[336] "Each map task pulls messages from Kafka and writes them to HDFS directories based on timestamps. Camus map tasks will only move the messages to the final output location when the task finishes successfully. This allows the use of Hadoop's speculative execution without the risk of writing duplicate messages in HDFS," explain Grover et al.[336] Below is a high-level diagram to help give an idea of how Camus works:

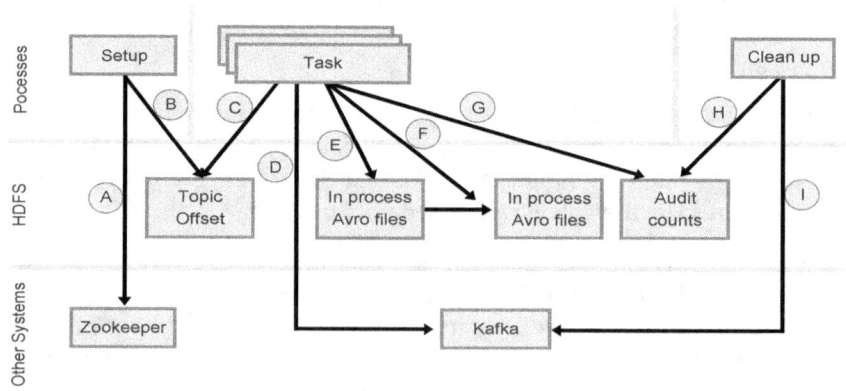

Figure 24: Camus schematic and processes
Source: *Hadoop Application Architectures*[336]

Figure 24 details the following Camus series of steps[336]:

- A—The setup stage fetches broker urls and topic information from ZooKeeper.
- B—The setup stage persists information about topics and offsets in HDFS for the tasks to read.
- C—The tasks read the persisted information from the setup stage.
- D—The tasks get events from Kafka.
- E—The tasks write data to a temp location in HDFS in the format defined by the user defined decoder, in this case Avro formatted files.
- F—The tasks move the data in the temp location to a final location when the task is cleaning up.
- G—The task writes out audit counts on its activities.
- H—A clean up stage reads all the audit counts from all the tasks.
- I—The cleanup stage reports back to Kafka what has been persisted.

One caveat: to use Camus, you may need to write your own decoder to convert Kafka messages to Avro.[336]

Data Extraction

Extracting data from Hadoop is, of course, important, and many of the considerations one makes about getting data into Hadoop also apply to getting data out of it.[336] A common pattern is to use Hadoop for transforming data for ingestion into a Data Warehouse, i.e., using Hadoop as an ETL tool.[336]

In most cases, Sqoop would be used to ingest the transformed data into the target database, but if Sqoop is not an option then using a simple file extract from Hadoop and then using a vendor specific ingesting tool is also a good option.[336] "When using Sqoop it's important to use database-specific connectors when available," recommend Grover et al.[336]

Regardless of the method used, it is imperative to avoid overloading the target database—data volumes that are easily managed in Hadoop may easily overwhelm a traditional database (that's why you're using it, after all).[336] Looking forward, it should be noted that as Hadoop matures and closes the gap in capabilities with traditional data management systems, it's likely that more workloads will be moved to the Hadoop platform, which should alleviate the need to move data out of Hadoop in the first place.[336]

"Hadoop is also a powerful tool for processing and summarizing data for input to external analytical systems and applications. For these cases a simple file transfer is probably suitable," recommend Grover et al.[336]

Data is often transferred between Hadoop clusters and DistCp provides an easy and efficient way to transfer data between those clusters.[336] DistCp leverages MapReduce to perform parallel transfers of large data volumes. DistCp is also suitable when either the source or target are a non-HDFS file system, for example when moving data into a cloud-based system such as Amazon's Simple Storage System (S3) or Microsoft's Azure.[336]

Hadoop is a complex system to implement, but it is well worth it. Any company that wants to become a data first company should look to utilize these tools, which are, in many cases, tools that were developed by the pioneers of the data and analytics industries, i.e., Facebook, Google, LinkedIn, Apple, etc.

Although there are a seemingly endless array of tools and mechanisms that can help move data into and out of Hadoop, one should carefully consider one's requirements and desired results before spinning up a cluster. The following things should be considered[336]:

- Data ingestion source systems into Hadoop, as well as the target systems should data need to be extracted from Hadoop.
- How often data ingestion or extraction needs to occur.
- What type or types of data are being ingested or extracted.
- How the data is processed and accessed once inside Hadoop.

Once these questions are answered, the full power of Hadoop becomes available and a whole host of interesting analytics and real-time stream processing enquiries can be performed.

Hadoop Machine Learning Solutions

	Machine Learning Solutions
Apache Mahout	Machine learning library and math library, on top of MapReduce.
WEKA	Weka (Waikato Environment for Knowledge Analysis) is a popular suite of machine learning software written in Java, developed at the University of Waikato, New Zealand. Weka is free software available under the GNU General Public License.
Cloudera Oryx	The Oryx open source project provides simple, real-time large-scale machine learning / predictive analytics infrastructure. It implements a few classes of algorithm commonly used in business applications: collaborative filtering / recommendation, classification / regression, and clustering.
Deeplearning4j	The Deeplearning4j open-source project is the most widely used deep-learning framework for the JVM. DL4J includes deep neural nets such as recurrent neural networks, Long Short Term Memory Networks (LSTMs), convolutional neural networks, various autoencoders and feedforward neural networks such as restricted Boltzmann machines and deep-belief networks. It also has natural language-processing algorithms such as word2vec, doc2vec, GloVe and TF-IDF. All Deeplearning4j networks run distributed on multiple CPUs and GPUs. They work as Hadoop jobs, and integrate with Spark on the slace level for host-thread orchestration.

	Machine Learning Solutions
	Deeplearning4j's neural networks are applied to use cases such as fraud and anomaly detection, recommender systems, and predictive maintenance.
MADlib	The MADlib project leverages the data-processing capabilities of an RDBMS to analyze data. The aim of this project is the integration of statistical data analysis into databases. The MADlib project is self-described as the Big Data Machine Learning in SQL for Data Scientists. The MADlib software project began the following year as a collaboration between researchers at UC Berkeley and engineers and data scientists at EMC/Greenplum (now Pivotal).
H2O	H2O is a statistical, machine learning and math runtime tool for bigdata analysis. Developed by the predictive analytics company H2O.ai, H2O has established a leadership in the ML scene together with R and Databricks' Spark. According to the team, H2O is the world's fastest in-memory platform for machine learning and predictive analytics on big data. It is designed to help users scale machine learning, math, and statistics over large datasets. In addition to H2O's point and click Web-UI, its REST API allows easy integration into various clients. This means explorative analysis of data can be done in a typical fashion in R, Python, and Scala; and entire workflows can be written up as automated scripts.
Sparkling Water	Sparkling Water combines two open source technologies: Apache Spark and H2O - a machine learning engine. It makes H2O's library of Advanced Algorithms including Deep Learning, GLM, GBM, KMeans, PCA, and Random Forest accessible from Spark workflows. Spark users are provided with the options to select the best features from either platform to meet their Machine Learning needs. Users can combine Sparks' RDD API and Spark MLLib with H2O's machine learning algorithms or use H2O independent of Spark in the model building process and post-process the results in Spark. Sparkling Water provides a transparent integration of H2O's framework and data structures into Spark's RDD-based environment by sharing the same execution space as well as providing a RDD-like API for H2O data structures.

Machine Learning Solutions	
Apache System ML	Apache SystemML was open sourced by IBM and it's pretty related with Apache Spark. If you thinking of Apache Spark as the analytics operating system for any application that taps into huge volumes of streaming data. MLLib, the machine learning library for Spark, provides developers with a rich set of machine learning algorithms. And SystemML enables developers to translate those algorithms so they can easily digest different kinds of data and to run on different kinds of computers. SystemML allows a developer to write a single machine learning algorithm and automatically scale it up using Spark or Hadoop. SystemML scales for big data analytics with high performance optimizer technology and empowers users to write customized machine learning algorithms using simple, domain-specific language (DSL) without learning complicated distributed programming. It is an extensible complement framework of Spark MLlib

Table 20: Hadoop Machine Learning Solutions
Source: The Hadoop Ecosystem[337]

Streaming Analytics

As *The Cluetrain Manifesto*[324] points out, "Real-time marketing is the execution of a thoughtful and strategic plan specifically designed to engage customers on their terms via digital social technologies." Adding to that description, Wikipedia notes that real-time marketing is[341]:

> *"Marketing performed 'on-the-fly' to determine an appropriate or optimal approach to a particular customer at a particular time and place. It is a form of market research inbound marketing that seeks the most appropriate offer for a given customer sales opportunity, reversing the traditional outbound marketing (or interruption marketing) which aims to acquire appropriate customers for a given 'pre-defined' offer."*

Real-time marketing can be inexpensive compared to the cost of traditional paid media. "Expensive research, focus groups, and awareness campaigns can be replaced with online surveys, blog comments, and tweets by anyone or any business," add Macy and Thompson in their book *The Power of Real-Time Social Media Marketing*.[305] Just to be clear, the expense of real-time marketing might be low compared to running ads through traditional media channels, but setting up an IT operation that can hit a level of personalization that will wow a customer is anything but cheap.

In his article *How Real-time Marketing Technology Can Transform Your Business*[342], Dan Woods' amusing comparison of the differing environments that marketers face today as compared to what their 1980s counterpart faced is highly instructive as today's marketing executives don't have time for a market research study in his or her sort of figurative first-person-shooter game. "The data arrives too late and isn't connected to the modern weapons of marketing. The world is now bursting with data from social media, web traffic, mobile devices, and tripwires of all kinds," Woods warns.[342]

Today, most large companies have massive amounts of data pertaining to consumer behavior coming at them constantly, from all angles. The challenge is to make sense of the data in time to matter, to understand how consumer attitudes and behaviors are changing and how they are being changed by marketing and advertising efforts; to grab the treasure and avoid the pitfalls of unleashing a figurative Pandora's box full of furies.

The challenge in understanding the modern consumer is making sense of all of the customer data, coming in from these vast unstructured sources.[342] Some of this information explains the broad fluctuations in mass opinion, while other evidence clarifies what consumers might be doing on a company website.[342] Others still explain what consumers have done, en masse or as individuals.[342] Still other data can be collected after a customer trip in the form of surveys, whether they are mobile or physical surveys.

In his article *When do you need an Event Stream Processing platform?*[343], Roy Schulte states that:

> "An event is anything that happens. An event object (or 'event,' event message, or event tuple) is an object that represents, encodes, or records an event, generally for the purpose of computer processing. Event objects usually include data about the type of activity, when the activity happened (e.g., a time and date stamp), and sometimes the location of the activity, its cause, and other information. An event stream is a sequence of event objects, typically in order by time of arrival."

Large airlines typically have three kinds of event streams:

- Copies of business transactions.[343] These are generated mostly internally and reflect the operational activities of the company.[343]
- "The second are information reports, such as tweets, news feed articles, market data, weather reports, and social media updates, including Facebook and LinkedIn posts."[343] According to Schulte, "most of these sources are external to the company, but may contain information that is relevant to a decision within the company."[343]
- "The third, and fastest growing, kind of event stream contains sensor data coming from physical assets."[343]

The reason for performing analytics on one or more event streams is to obtain information value from the data.[343] As Schulte explains, "A stream analytics application converts the raw input data (*base* events), into a form, *derived events*, that is better suited for making decisions.[343] The derived events are *complex events*, which means that they are events that are abstracted from one or more other events.[343]

Stream analytics are executed in one of two ways, push-based, continuous intelligence systems, which recalculate as new data arrives without being asked to, or pull-based systems that run when a person enters a request or a timer sends a signal to produce a batch report. Event Stream Processing (ESP) platforms are mostly relevant in highly demanding, push-based systems, but they are occasionally used for pull-based analytics on historical data.[343]

When people think of ESP, they usually think of push-based continuous intelligence systems, which ingests ongoing flows of event data and provide situational awareness, while also supporting near-real-time, sense-and-respond business processes.[343] "Continuous intelligence systems typically refresh dashboards every second or minute, send alerts, or implement hands-free decision automation scenarios," Schulte explains. "They may be used to monitor a data source, such as Twitter, or a business operation, such as a customer contact center, supply chain, water utility, telecommunication network, truck fleet, or payment process," Schulte adds.[343]

Schulte explains that[343]:

> "ESP platforms are software subsystems that process data in motion, as each event arrives. The query is pre-loaded, so the data comes to the query rather than the query coming to the data. ESP platforms retain a relatively small working set of stream data in memory for the duration of a limited time window, typically seconds to hours—just long enough to detect patterns or compute queries. The platforms are more flexible than hardwired applications because the query can be adjusted to handle different kinds of input data, different time windows (e.g., one minute or one hour instead of ten minutes) and different search terms."

According to Schulte, continuous intelligence applications are best implemented on ESP platforms if[343]:

- "A high volume of data (thousands or millions of events per second).
- Frequently recalculated results (every millisecond or every few seconds).
- Multiple simultaneous queries are applied to the same input event stream."[343]

Schulte gives the example of Twitter's ESP platforms, Storm and Heron. These DWs are "used to monitor Twitter, which averages about 6,000 tweets per second. A simple query might report the number of tweets that included the word 'inflation' in the past ten minutes. However, at any one time, there may be thousands of simultaneous queries in effect against Twitter, each looking for different key words or different time windows."[343]

"In high volume scenarios, ESP platform applications can scale out vertically (multiple engines working in parallel on the same step in a processing flow) and/or horizontally (split the work up in a sequence or pipeline where work is handed from one engine to the next while working on the same multistep event processing query (i.e., an event processing network)", explains Schulte.[343]

Schulte notes that, "On-demand analytics are pull-based applications that support ad hoc data exploration, visualization and analysis of data."[343] On-demand analytics can be used with historical event data to build analytical models.[343] In this context, "historical means stored event streams that are hours, weeks or years old."[343] Schulte explains that the "analytical models can be used for either of two purposes:

- To design rules and algorithms to be used in real-time continuous intelligence applications, or
- To make one-time, strategic, tactical and long-term operational decisions.[343]

The most common tool for on-demand analytics with historical data is a data discovery product like Qlik, Tableau, SAS, Tibco Spotfire, etc., etc., however, "companies occasionally use ESP platforms to run analytics on historical event streams by re-streaming the old event data through the ESP engine."[343] "This is particularly relevant when developing models for subsequent use in real-time, continuous intelligence ESP applications," claims Schulte.[343]

ESP platforms are not the only type of software optimized for high performance analytics on event stream data. Some stream analytics products like First Derivatives KDB+, Interana Platform, Logtrust Platform, One Market Data OneTick, Quartet ActivePivot, and Splunk Enterprise combine analytics and longer term data storage in one product.[343] "These products typically provide on-demand, pull-based analytics, but some are also used for continuous, push-based continuous intelligence. They ingest and store high volume event streams very quickly, making the 'at rest' data immediately available for interactive queries, exploration and visualization," explains Schulte.[343]

For a real-time platform to work, data must be gathered from multiple and disparate sources, which can include Enterprise Resource Planning (ERP), Customer Relationship Management (CRM), Social CRM (SCRM) platforms, geofencing applications (like Jiepang and Foursquare), Over-The-Top services (like WhatsApp and WeChat), mobile apps, augmented reality apps, and other mobile and social media systems. This data must be collected and then seamlessly integrated into a data warehouse that can cleanse it and make it ready for consumption.[122] As the authors' state in *Mobile Advertising*:

> "The analytical system must have the capability to digest all the user data, summarize it, and update the master user profile. This functionality is essential to provide the rich user segmentation that is at the heart of recommendations, campaign and offer management, and advertisements. The segmentation engine can cluster users into affinities and different groups based on geographic, demographic or socio-economic, psychographic, and behavioral characteristics."[34]

Perhaps the future of real-time marketing was on display during the 2014 World Cup. "On eight different occasions during the 2014 World Cup, Nike and Google cranked out online display and mobile ads in 15 different countries across the globe. The campaigns ran in real time—meaning they went live during the games and concluded once those games were over."[344]

For example, "on June 23, during a match between Brazil and Cameroon, Nike pumped out an ad featuring Brazil's star, Neymar da Silva Santos Júnior, who scored two goals that day."[344] Within seconds of the goal, "an ad featuring the star was featured throughout the Google Display Network, pushing it out to thousands of sites and mobile apps across the web, the search giant says."[344]

"Besides being super timely, the Neymar Jr. ad featured some unique 3D technology that utilized the gyroscope found in most smartphones. Mobile users could rotate their phones and see images of the Nike star in the ad at different angles."[344] Gimmicky, yes, but, probably, effective as fans could interact with these 3D ads as well as add personal touches. Once viewed, users could share the ads via Twitter, Facebook and/or Google+.[344] The eight different World Cup real-time campaigns generated two million fan interactions across 200 different countries.[344]

In his article *Real-Time Stream Processing as Game Changer in a Big Data World with Hadoop and Data Warehouse*[31], Kal Wähner states that:

> "Stream processing is designed to analyze and act on real-time streaming data, using 'continuous queries' (i.e. SQL-type queries that operate over time and buffer windows). Essential to stream processing is Streaming Analytics, or the ability to continuously calculate mathematical or statistical analytics on the fly within the stream. Stream processing solutions are designed to handle high volume in real time with a scalable, highly available and fault tolerant architecture. This enables analysis of data in motion."

As a batch processing framework, Hadoop can't handle the needs of real time analytics. As the first open source distributed computing environment, Hadoop has garnered a lot of attention recently, but it is not necessarily the best platform for real-time analytics of dynamic information.[345]

One recent development in stream processing methods is the invention of the "live data mart", which "provides end-user, ad-hoc continuous query access to this streaming data that's aggregated in memory," explains Wähner.[31] "Business user-oriented analytics tools access the data mart for a continuously live view of streaming data"[31] and the "live analytics front ends slices, dices, and aggregates data dynamically in response to business users' actions, and all in real time," adds Wähner.[31]

For an airline, streaming data could be coming in from facial recognition and geo-location software, fraud or anti-money laundering solutions, customer loyalty card systems, campaign management databases, redemption systems, social media feeds, IoT data, as well as wearables and employee/labor data sets.

Stream processing excels when data has to be processed fast and/or continuously. Many different frameworks and products are available on the market already, however the number of mature solutions with good tools and commercial support today is quite small.

Apache Storm is a good, open source framework, but it suffers from its open source nature and custom coding is required because of limited developer tools. The typical "commercial solution vs. open source" questions must be answered; do I want a pre-built product that will require limited—and sometimes not so limited implementation costs—or do I want to start with a solid solution and be required to customize everything?

As Wähner explains, a stream processing solution has to solve several different challenges, including:

- "Processing massive amounts of streaming events (filter, aggregate, rule, automate, predict, act, monitor, alert).
- Real-time responsiveness to changing market conditions.
- Performance and scalability as data volumes increase in size and complexity.
- Rapid integration with existing infrastructure and data sources: Input (e.g. market data, user inputs, files, history data from a DWH) and output (e.g. trades, email alerts, dashboards, automated reactions).
- Fast time-to-market for application development and deployment due to a quickly changing landscape and differing requirements.
- Developer productivity throughout all stages of the application development lifecycle by offering good tool support and agile development.

- Analytics: Live data discovery and monitoring, continuous query processing, automated alerts and reactions.
- Community (component/connector exchange, education/discussion, training/certification).
- End-user ad-hoc continuous query access.
- Alerting.
- Push-based visualization."[31]

Comparison of Stream Processing Services

From a technical perspective, Wähner explains that the following components are required for a stream processing system:

- "Server: An ultra-low-latency application server optimized for processing real-time streaming event data at high throughputs and low latency (usually in-memory)."[31]
- "IDE: A development environment, which ideally offers visual development, debugging and testing of stream processing processes using streaming operators for filtering, aggregation, correlation, time windows, transformation, etc."[31]
- "Extendibility, e.g. integration of libraries or building custom operators and connectors, is also important."[31]
- "Connectors: Pre-built data connectivity to communicate with data sources such as databases (e.g. MySQL, Oracle, IBM DB2), DWH (e.g. HP Vertica), market data (e.g. Bloomberg, FIX, Reuters), statistics (e.g. R, MATLAB, TERR) or technology (e.g. JMS, Hadoop, Java, .NET)."[31]
- "Streaming Analytics: A user interface, which allows monitoring, management and real-time analytics for live streaming data. Automated alerts and human reactions should also be possible."[31]
- "Live Data Mart and/or Operational Business Intelligence: Aggregates streaming data for ad-hoc, end-user, query access, alerting, dynamic aggregation, and user management."[31]
- "Live stream visualization, graphing, charting, slice and dice are also important."[31]

Since this is a highly complex set up and system, there are few market-ready products available and a lot of custom coding is required to implement most solutions.[31] However, the following products are a good place to start:

- Apache Storm
- Apache Spark
- IBM's InfoSphere
- Hitachi's Streaming Data Platform
- TIBCO's StreamBase

Apache Storm is "an open source framework that provides massively scalable event collection. Storm was created by Twitter and is composed of other open source components, especially ZooKeeper for cluster management, ZeroMQ for multicast messaging, and Kafka for queued messaging."[31]

Spark is a stream processing framework and it "focuses on continuous computation that can process hundreds of millions of tweets generated every day and now is an open source big data analysis system."[31] Spark is a scalable data analysis platform based on in-memory computing and it has a performance advantage over Hadoop's cluster storage method.[31] Spark is written in Scala and offers a single data processing environment. Spark also supports iteration tasks of distributed data sets.[31]

Spark is a "general framework for large-scale data processing that supports lots of different programming languages and concepts such as MapReduce, in-memory processing, stream processing, graph processing or machine learning."[31] Although Storm and Spark were not created to run on Hadoop specifically, they can be integrated into Cloudera, Hortonworks, MapR, and can be used to implement stream processing on top of Hadoop.[31]

Amazon's Kinesis is a managed cloud service that was designed for real-time processing of streaming data. Because it is Amazon owned, it integrates seamlessly with other AWS cloud services such as S3, Redshift or DynamoDB. DataTorrent is a live streaming platform that runs natively on Hadoop.[31]

The big players such as SAP and Oracle are also jumping onto the stream processing bandwagon, and open source solutions include Apache Samza—a distributed stream processing framework processor, which was developed by LinkedIn—and Esper, a major framework for Java and .NET systems.[31]

InfoSphere Streams is "IBM's flagship product for stream processing. It offers a highly scalable event server, integration capabilities, and other typical features required for implementing stream processing use cases. The IDE is based on Eclipse and offers visual development and configuration."[31]

Hitachi's Streaming Data Platform is a real-time streaming software solution that uses CQL, a popular and widely used language similar to SQL for processing and analysis. As per Hitachi Data Systems (HDS):

> "CQL (Continuous Query Language) is an extension of traditional SQL. CQL executes in memory, designed for high throughput and low latency environments. It has a 'windowing' concept that allows the system to treat each stream, packet and flow individually and allows for 'stateful' analysis unlike open source technologies where this capability has to be custom coded. Hitachi CQL provides the capability to centrally develop and globally deploy applications."[346]

TIBCO StreamBase is "a high-performance system for rapidly building applications that analyze and act on real-time streaming data. The goal of StreamBase is to offer a product that supports developers in rapidly building real-time systems and deploying them easily."[31]

Stream processing solutions can get very complicated very quickly and Wähner warns that[31], "Besides evaluating the core features of stream processing products, you also have to check integration with other products. Can a product work together with messaging, Enterprise Service Bus (ESB), Master Data Management (MDM), in-memory stores, etc. in a loosely coupled, but highly integrated way?" If the answer to these questions is negative, a lot of integration time and considerable costs could be in order.[31]

In his article *15 "True" Streaming Analytics Platforms For Real-Time Everything*[347], Mike Gualtieri, Vice President and Principal Analyst at Forrester argues that "streaming analytics analyzes data right now, when it can be analyzed and put to good use to make applications of all kinds (including IoT) contextual and smarter." In his article, Gualtieri then breaks down the offerings as follows[347]:

- Cisco Systems—The acquisitions of ParStream and Truviso give Cisco "the power to collect data as close to the edge as possible and to efficiently parse and pass it back to the center for analysis."[347]
- Data Artisans—Berlin-based data Artisans is the commercial force behind the open source Apache Flink project for distributed stream and batch processing. "While Spark uses micro-batches to enable fast processing, Flink is a true streaming engine that can also do batch processing by treating a stream of events as a data set with a beginning and an end."[347]
- DataTorrent has built a streaming platform to handle the world's biggest and fastest data.[347] "In addition to providing a distributed streaming analytics platform, the vendor also delivers accruements including a visual development tool and a library of over 400 operators. The core of DataTorrent is now open sourced as Apache Apex."[347]
- EsperTech's open source and battle tested "event processing offering provides enterprises with a flexible basis for building applications that require complex pattern matching with sophisticated time windows."[347]
- IBM Streams "can ingest and understand the always-on stream of data from applications and IoT devices needed to make the decisions that underlie cognitive solutions."[347]
- Informatica's streaming capabilities come in the form of a real-time rules engine. "Streaming data is handled by the vendor's rules engine, which includes enterprise capabilities around security, encryption, operational management, and data lineage."[347]
- Oracle's streaming solution "includes two distinct pieces that are critical for the future of analytics: Stream Explorer for ingesting and

interrogating data as it lands in the cloud or the enterprise; and Oracle Edge Analytics (OEA) for preprocessing data on IoT devices."[347]
- SAP's Smart data streaming (SDS) engine is available as an integrated add-on to SAP Hana or as stand-alone software. "SAP currently includes two machine learning algorithms—one supervised, one unsupervised—which can incrementally train on data running through the system."[347]
- SAS real time product's architecture "focuses tightly on low-latency, high-throughput complex analytics, so it is well positioned to embed many of SAS's highly regarded advanced analytics algorithms, including text analytics and machine learning."[347]
- Software AG's Apama "powers real-time, digital business transformations. Long-running pattern detection and stream enrichment is also well supported via integration with Software AG's own in-memory data grid, Terracotta, and its integration platform, webMethods."[347]
- SQLstream's Blaze "delivers a solid platform for companies to build real-time applications, especially for customers that have a lot of machine data and prefer a declarative SQL syntax to operate on streaming data."[347]
- Striim's platform "focuses equally on the continuous capture of data at its point of origin and on the upstream real-time analytics. It can ingest streaming data from many sources, including streaming change data capture (CDC) from transactions in databases."[347]
- TIBCO Software "recognizes that ideas come from human insight and domain knowledge. That's why its streaming solution includes LiveView, a real-time view of streaming data."[347]
- WSO2 is "an open source middleware provider that includes a full spectrum of architected-as-one components such as application servers, message brokers, enterprise service bus, and many others."[347]

Figure 25 shows a potential airline's DW, which contains a streams engine and stream processing unit that includes investigation, visualization and analytics systems within it.

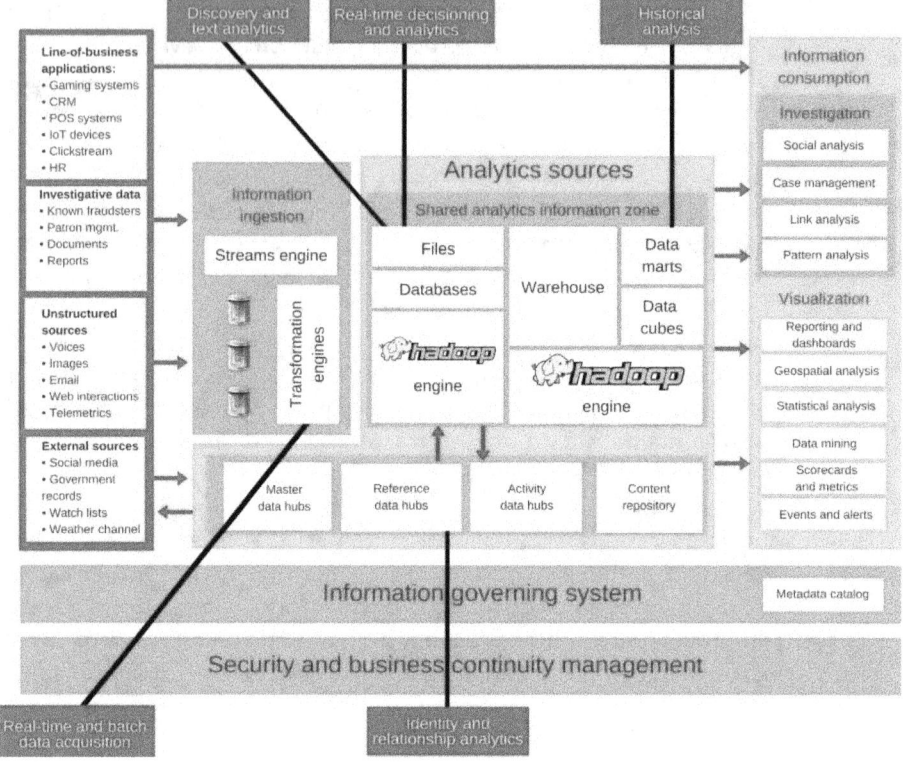

Figure 25: Potential Streams Processing engine
Source: Intelligencia.co

Internet of Things (IoT)

As previously mentioned the Internet of Things is "the network of physical objects that contain embedded technology to communicate and sense or interact with their internal states or the external environment."[18] Technology costs are down, broadband's price has dropped, while its availability has increased. There is a proliferation of devices with Wi-Fi capabilities and censors built into them, and smart phone penetration is exploding; all of these individual technological advances were good for the IoT, together they have created a perfect storm for it.[348]

According to its *Gartner Says the Internet of Things Installed Base Will Grow to 26 Billion Units By 2020*[349], Gartner claims that, "The Internet of Things (IoT), which excludes PCs, tablets and smartphones, will grow to 26 billion units installed in 2020 representing an almost 30-fold increase from 0.9 billion in 2009."

Gartner believes IoT product and service suppliers will generate incremental revenue exceeding $300 billion, mostly in services, in 2020. It will result in $1.9 trillion in global economic value-add through sales into diverse end markets."[349] Simply put, IoT is the concept of basically connecting any device with an on and off switch to the Internet, including cell phones, coffee makers, washing machines, headphones, lamps, wearable devices and almost anything else imaginable.[21]

Today, it is almost unimaginable how all-encompassing the Internet of Things will be in our daily lives in the not-too-distant future. From such life-changing technology as Google's driverless cars, which could help optimize traffic, thereby reducing traffic congestion, as well as making people more productive, to sensors that can help regulate room temperature thereby saving energy, IoT is unquestionably here to stay.

"The growth in IoT will far exceed that of other connected devices. By 2020, the number of smartphones tablets and PCs in use will reach about 7.3 billion units," said Peter Middleton, research director at Gartner.[18] "In contrast, the IoT will have expanded at a much faster rate, resulting in a population of about 26 billion units at that time," Middleton adds.[18]

An airline can utilize IoT applications in the following ways:

- Supply chain control
- NFC payment
- Intelligent shopping applications
- Smart product management
- Smart parking
- Smartphone detection
- Traffic congestion
- Smart lighting
- Waste management
- Smart Metering:
    - Smart grid
    - Silos stock calculation
    - Water leakages
- Security & Emergencies:
    - Perimeter access control
    - Liquid presence
    - Explosive and hazardous gases alerts
- Inventory optimization
- Logistics:
    - Quality of shipment conditions
    - Item location
    - Storage incompatibility detection

- Fleet tracking
- Industrial Control:
  - Smart Warehouse
  - M2M applications
  - Indoor air quality
  - Temperature monitoring
  - Indoor location tracking
  - Vehicle auto-diagnosis
- Video analytics:
  - Object detection
  - Slip fall analysis
  - People counting

IoT is faced with the typical problems of new technologies, a lack of standards as the big and small players jockey for position, although there is a movement in place to create a vendor-independent protocol that will allow devices to connect with each other under the guise of a common service layer.

Currently, IoT's growing pains are being tackled and security issues are being addressed. The addition of edge analytics, which can reduce network and connectivity costs, is also circumventing the need for cloud integration.

Improving computer processing power and memory in semiconductors and modules increases by the month. This should allow IoT devices to add an ML component, which could help IoT devices realize the potential of ambient intelligence, allowing them to grow smarter over time. However, heavy duty number crunching power is still needed when performing intensive predictive and prescriptive analytics.

In his article *The Data of Things: How Edge Analytics and IoT Go Hand In Hand*[350], Gadi Lenz explains that, although IoT data has similar characteristics to Big Data, it is much more complicated. IoT data is:

- "Messy, noisy, and sometimes intermittent because sensors are often deployed in the field. IoT data is ultimately collected by sensors sitting somewhere—for example, a sensor could be deployed on a telephone pole or street light. Sensors often cut in and out."[350]
- "Often highly unstructured and sourced from a variety of sensors (fixed and mobile)."[350]
- "Dynamic— 'data in motion' as opposed to the traditional 'data at rest'."[350]
- "Sometimes indirect—we cannot measure a certain relevant quantity directly, for example, using a video camera with video analytics to count people in a certain area."[350]

The idea of collecting all of this sensor information and bringing it into one centralized computing station is not viable over the long term, particularly as the volume of IoT devices increases exponentially.[350] "Bringing such a large amount of data into a relatively small number of data centers where it is then analyzed in the cloud, simply [sic] not scale."[350] The cost, too, would be prohibitive.[350]

"With so many devices producing so much data, a correspondingly large array of analytics, compute, storage and networking power and infrastructure is essential. Though analytics will be necessary to the growth and business value of IoT, the traditional approach to analytics won't be the right fit," Lenz argues.[350]

Edge analytics addresses these problems. Lenz argues that an airline operator can "harness the smartness of the myriad of smart devices and their low cost computational power to allow them to run valuable analytics on the device itself."[350] As Lenz explains, "Multiple devices are usually connected to a local gateway where potentially more compute power is available (like Cisco's IOx), enabling more complex multi-device analytics close to the edge."[350]

Distributed IoT analytics would work in three ways, "simple" analytics would be done on the smart device itself, more complex multi-device analytics on the IoT gateways, and finally the high computational computing—the "Big Data" analytics, if you will—would connect to and run on the cloud.[350] "This distribution of analytics offloads the network and the data centers by creating a model that scales. Distributing the analytics to the edge is the only way to progress," advises Lenz.[350]

As the DHL Trend Research and Cisco Consulting Services paper *Internet of Things in Logistics*[351] explains:

> "With the advent of IoT, Internet connections now extend to physical objects that are not computers in the classic sense and, in fact, serve a multiplicity of other purposes. A shoe, for example, is designed to cushion the foot while walking or running. A street light illuminates a road or sidewalk. A forklift is used to move pallets or other heavy items. None of these have traditionally been connected to the Internet—they did not send, receive, process or store information. Nonetheless, there is information latent in all of these items and their use. When we connect the unconnected—when we light up "dark assets"—vast amounts of information emerge, along with potential new insights and business value."

A connected shoe can reveal the number of footfalls in a given period of time, or the force with which the foot strikes the ground.[351] A connected street light can understand traffic patterns, and "provide information to drivers or city officials for route planning and to optimize the flow of traffic."[351] A connected forklift can be fitted with predictive asset maintenance alerts that can warn a warehouse manager of an impending mechanical problem.[351]

For *The Predictive Airliner* cameras immediately pick up a customer once he or she enters an airport lounge. In this case, it makes sense for the analytics to be done inside the camera itself, rather than having the data sent back to a centralized server as that can be both inefficient and it risks bottlenecking.[350] Lenz adds, "Edge analytics is all about processing and analyzing subsets of all the data collected and then only transmitting the results."[350] So, the systems is essentially discarding some of the raw data and potentially missing some insights, but it should be a calculated loss as analyzing everything is just not productive in most cases.[350]

"Some organizations may never be willing to lose any data, but the vast majority can accept that not everything can be analyzed. This is where we will have to learn by experience as organizations begin to get involved in this new field of IoT analytics and review the results," adds Lenz.[350] This is an exploding field of study and operation and the rules are, literally, been written right now, as the sensors are rolling out, but the potential for businesses to understand their businesses is enormous.

However, some trade-off must be considered with edge analytics. Lenz notes that, "Edge analytics is all about processing and analyzing subsets of all the data collected and then only transmitting the results."[350] Some of the raw data is discarded and potentially some insights are lost.[350] Lenz states that, "The question is, Can we live with this 'loss' and if so how should we choose which pieces we are willing to 'discard' and which need to be kept and analyzed?"[350]

It is also important to learn the lessons of past distributed systems. "For example, when many devices are analyzing and acting on the edge, it may be important to have somewhere a single 'up-to-date view,' which in turn, may impose various constraints," warns Lenz.[350] "The fact that many of the edge devices are also mobile complicates the situation even more," adds Lenz.[350] Although incredibly powerful devices in their own right, mobile phones and tablets will never reach the capacity and compute technology of EDWs, obviously.

In Tableau's *2018 Top 10 Business Intelligence Trends*[352], one of the leading BI companies coins a new phrase with their "Location of Things" which they believe will drive the Internet of Things. "One positive trend we are seeing is the usage and benefits of leveraging location-based data with IoT devices. This subcategory, termed 'location of things,' provides IoT devices with sensing and communicates their geographic position," argue Tableau.[352] "By knowing where an IoT device is located, it allows us to add context, better understand what is happening and what we predict will happen in a specific location,"[352] which should strengthen personalization marketing.

For companies wishing to capture this data collection, Tableau is seeing different technologies being used.[352] "For example, hospitals, stores, and hotels have begun to use Bluetooth Low Energy (BLE) technology for indoor location services, which were typically difficult for GPS to provide contextual location," claim Tableau.[352] "The technology can be used to track specific assets, people and even interact with mobile devices like smartwatches, badges or tags in order to provide personalized experiences," notes Tableau.[352]

In terms of data analysis, location-based figures can be viewed as an input rather an output of results, making it much more useful.[352] "If the data is available, analysts can incorporate this information with their analysis to better understand what is happening, where it is happening, and what they should expect to happen in a contextual area," concludes Tableau.[352]

Augmented and Virtual Reality

Not just the stuff of science fiction anymore, Augmented Reality (AR) is now a part of our everyday life. In his article *CrowdOptic and L'Oreal to make history by demonstrating how augmented reality can be a shared experience*[353], Tarun Wadhwa states that augmented reality works by "displaying layers of computer-generated information on top of a view of the physical world." It is "a technology that alters the perception of reality by distorting it, allowing escape from it, and enhancing it—all at the same time."[353]

According to Webopedia.com, Augmented Reality or AR is[354]:

> "A type of virtual reality that aims to duplicate the world's environment in a computer. An augmented reality system generates a composite view for the user that is the combination of the real scene viewed by the user and a virtual scene generated by the computer that augments the scene with additional information. The virtual scene generated by the computer is designed to enhance the user's sensory perception of the virtual world they are seeing or interacting with. The goal of Augmented Reality is to create a system in which the user cannot tell the difference between the real world and the virtual augmentation of it. Today Augmented Reality is used in entertainment, military training, engineering design, robotics, manufacturing and other industries."

According to Gartner's *Top 10 Strategic Technology Trends 2017*[355], Augmented reality (AR) and virtual reality (VR) will "transform the way individuals interact with each other and with software systems creating an immersive environment. For example, VR can be used for training scenarios and remote experiences."

AR enables a blending of the real and virtual worlds, which "means businesses can overlay graphics onto real-world objects."[355] Immersive experiences with AR and VR are reaching tipping points in terms of price and capability but will not replace other interface models."[355] In the future, AR and VR are expected to expand beyond visual immersion and they might include all of the human senses[355], although this is a very complicated thing to pull off as smell-o-vision tried and failed to do in the entertainment business in the last century.

According to its press release *Gartner Says Augmented Reality Will Become an Important Workplace Tool*[356], "Augmented reality is the real-time use of information in the form of text, graphics, audio and other virtual enhancements integrated with real-world objects." Tuong Huy Nguyen, principal research analyst at Gartner, states that "AR leverages and optimizes the use of other technologies such as mobility, location, 3D content management and imaging and recognition. It is especially useful in the mobile environment because it enhances the user's senses via digital instruments to allow faster responses or decision-making."[356]

Gartner believes "AR technology has matured to a point where organizations can use it as an internal tool to complement and enhance business processes, workflows and employee training."[356] For Gartner, "AR facilitates business innovation by enabling real-time decision-making through virtual prototyping and visualization of content."[356]

According to Deloitte, wearable AR devices can "allow users to access standardized sets of instructions for a particular task in real time, triggered by environmental factors and overlaid on the user's field of vision."[357] Research has shown that overlaying 3D instructions over a real-life process can reduce the error rate for an assembly task by 82 percent, with a particularly strong impact on cumulative errors due to previous assembly mistakes.[357]

"AR allows for improved senses and memory through the capture and enhancement of the user's perspective. By recording video/audio, capturing images and removing elements that obscure the senses, AR technology allows users' eyes to act as cameras, and can enhance the senses in ways not available naturally, such as night vision or the ability to zoom in on far-away objects," notes Deloitte.[357]

AR uses location-based data for navigation, overlaying digital maps and directions on real-world environments.[356] Through the lens of an AR device, a user can receive visual guidance based on GPS technology.[356] AR services generally fall into one of two categories—"location-based or computer vision. Location-based offerings use a device's motion sensors to provide information based on a user's location. Computer-vision-based services use facial, object and motion tracking algorithms to identify images and objects."[357]

Mr. Nguyen claims AR's benefits include the "potential to improve productivity, provide hands-on experience, simplify current processes, increase available information, provide real-time access to data, offer new ways to visualize problems and solutions, and enhance collaboration."[357]

Augmented reality has many potential applications in the airline industry as well and the following ideas might seem a little like science fiction, but they are certainly within the realm of technical possibilities, and today there is no question that they would take the concept of personalization to a whole new level.

In his article *9 Companies Using Augments and Virtual Reality in Aviation*[358], Woodrow Bellamy III describes several interesting use cases for the technology that show how it is a valuable tool for the aviation industry. Although AR can be traced back to the 1990s, it has only been in the last decade that its true potential has come through. Companies as divergent as A.

This technology is proving to be useful in all areas of an airliner's business, from pilots to mechanics, even to members of the cabin crew and passengers.

"Aero Glass has a handset that pilots can wear and view cockpit control information like altimeter readings, fuel pressure, heading and oil temperature within a display that sits in the glass portion of the headset."[358]

In March 2017, "TAE Aerospace received the Aerospace Australia Civil Industry Innovation award for its Fountx wearable technology designed to allow an on-site aviation technician to collaborate with product expert remotely."[358]

"Developed in partnership with Australian industrial research organization CSIRO, Fountx uses a real-time audio-visual system consisting of an operator headset and a station from which the expert relays guidance on how to complete specific tasks," notes Bellamy.[358]

TAE is "the largest turbine-engine maintenance provider in Australia, its technicians are on call 24 hours per day, providing assistance to airline operators, private pilots and defense forces in New Zealand, Indonesia, Taiwan, Malaysia, Thailand, Sri Lanka, Nepal, Africa and North America," explains Bellamy.[358]

"Japan Airlines first trialed the use of Google Glass for their maintenance operations at its Honolulu station in 2014 with the aim to increase work efficiency," says Bellamy.[358] "During the trial, maintenance staff could receive advice and instruction by audio during operations as well as photograph or video real-time information that could be shared with colleagues off site," he adds.[358]

"However, when Google removed Google Glass from the commercial marketplace, the Japanese carrier moved on and found a new use for Microsoft's HoloLens headset last year," notes Bellamy.[358] JAL "is using the HoloLens virtual reality headset to train new engine mechanics and flight crew members. For example, in place of traditional printouts of cockpits or engine components, mechanics in training can walk inside of an actual virtual engine or cockpit and learn how to work on them," explains Bellamy.[358]

According to Bellamy, "Air New Zealand, in collaboration with IT service-provider Dimension Data, is beta-testing the use of HoloLens for its cabin crew."[358] "The airline envisions a future where flight attendants wearing a HoloLens headset can display passenger information on the headset such as flight details, time since last served and even the emotional state of the passenger," notes Bellamy.[358]

On August 1st, 2017, Air France began testing "what it calls an 'immersive entertainment system' with the use of virtual reality headsets that passengers can wear to view 3D and 2D films or television series."[358]

"The virtual reality headset is a result of the French carrier's partnership with SkyLights, an American-French startup company that was awarded 'Les As De L'Innovation' at the Paris Air Forum in July. Under the award, SkyLights will receive funding from Air France to expand development of its headsets," says Bellamy.[358]

These ideas might be a little ahead of their time, but they are perfect for the airline industry as it might be one of the rare industries that can implement such a system because it has the financial muscle to develop AR applications, the need for in-memory computing platforms, as well as the databases that contain all of the necessary customer information that is required to make these complicated and holistic systems function properly.

So where is AR going? In his article *Augmented reality: expanding the user experience*[359], John Moore claims that "app creators have begun to engage more of a mobile device's sensors—accelerometers and gyroscopes, for example. Augmented reality apps that use detailed animations are also in the works. The objective: inject augmented reality technology in a wider range of apps to boost the user experience."[353]

Pokémon Go was the first location-based augmented reality game that hit it big. Despite mixed reviews, the mobile app quickly became a global phenomenon and it was one of the most used and profitable mobile apps of 2016, having been downloaded more than 500 million times worldwide.[360] It certainly revealed the enormous potential of AR and it proved, without a shadow of a doubt, that the barriers to AR technology were limited and easily scaled by humans seeking out little dueling pocket monsters.

Gartner believes "AR technology has matured to a point where organizations can use it as an internal tool to complement and enhance business processes, workflows and employee training."[356] Gartner also believes that "AR facilitates business innovation by enabling real-time decision-making through virtual prototyping and visualization of content."[356]

Wearables

Wearable products include smart watches, activity trackers, smart jewelry, head-mounted optical displays and earbuds. According to wearabledevices.com[361]:

> "The terms 'wearable technology', 'wearable devices', and 'wearables' all refer to electronic technologies or computers that are incorporated into items of clothing and accessories which can comfortably be worn on the body. These wearable devices can perform many of the same computing tasks as mobile phones and laptop computers; however, in some cases, wearable technology can outperform these hand-held devices entirely. Wearable technology tends to be more sophisticated than hand-held technology on the market today because it can provide sensory and scanning features not typically seen in mobile and laptop devices, such as biofeedback and tracking of physiological functions."

In general, wearable technology includes some form of communications capability that allows the wearer to access real-time information.[361] "Data-input capabilities are also a feature of such devices, as is local storage. Examples of wearable devices include watches, glasses, contact lenses, e-textiles and smart fabrics, headbands, beanies and caps, jewelry such as rings, bracelets, and hearing aid-like devices that are designed to look like earrings."[361]

Wearable technology isn't just for items that can be put on and taken off with ease, there are also more invasive and permanent versions of the concept as implanted devices such as micro-chips or even smart tattoos can be considered wearables. Ultimately, whether a device is worn on or incorporated into the body, "the purpose of wearable technology is to create constant, convenient, seamless, portable, and mostly hands-free access to electronics and computers."[361]

In its *Adoption of IoT for Warehouse Management*[362], Israel Gogle argues that wearable devices and augmented reality are some of the best technologies to help improve the performance of human operators.

John Bermudez, VP of Product Management at Infor, explains that, "In our innovation lab, we are looking into options like providing workers with wearable video cameras that can upload information to the warehouse management system or with smart glasses. This augmented reality solution will give the operator a visual confirmation on a small screen in front of his eye that he is picking the right thing."[362]

"Wearable devices will add a new layer of visibility that does not exist now. It will work in route management, showing wearers where to go via the glasses, and pick and pack verification, where bar code scans or RFID readings in real time can be used to ensure correct pick and order management," added Douglas Bellin, Global Lead for Manufacturing and Energy Industries at Cisco Systems.[362]

Another advantage of wearables is their ability to collect information that can also be used for such things as employee safety.[362] This has a doubly positive effect, not only does it ensure the employees' wellbeing, but it can also save the company money, minimizing losses due to injured employees and lost productivity, maybe even saving lives.[362]

"Our wearables platform serves as a real-time warning system. It analyzes a vast amount of information gathered from wearable sensors embedded in personal protective equipment, such as smart safety helmets and protective vests, and in the workers' individual smartphones," said Asaf Adi, Senior Manager of IoT and Wearables at IBM Research.[362] "Information from the sensors and smart protective equipment feeds directly to the worker's smartphone, which can then immediately process and analyze the personal data," explains Google.[362]

By tracking a worker's pulse rate, his movement, his body temperature, even, potentially, his hydration level, sensors can continuously monitor a worker's physical condition.[362] The noise level and/or an employees' location in relation to moving machinery and forklifts can also be monitored to guard against accidents.[362] Alerts can also be sent out in cases where sensors detect a worker that has fallen or fainted in the warehouse. [362]

Inventory Optimization

Inventory optimization—the ability to have the right inventory, in the right quantities and at the right locations, at the right time to meet the supply and demand of parts and materials in the enterprise[363]—is an important part of *The Predictive Airliner*. As Tristan O'Gorman explains in his blog *5 Inventory Analytics Best Practices to Achieve Inventory Optimization[363]*, "Significant benefits exist for organizations that optimize their inventory by reducing inventory items and stock levels, thus avoiding associated carrying costs and obsolescence write-downs." O'Gorman adds that, "Indirectly, organizations can generate savings by using time formerly spent on inventory management to ensure physical assets' reliability and availability."*[363]*

"Spare parts, an essential component of the availability of any system, have intermittent consumption patterns and usually have only one specific use, and organizations can often source them only from the system manufacturer. For these reasons, many organizations overstock spare parts to avoid costly system downtime. Unfortunately, overstocking incurs its own costs—and they can be significant," warns O'Gorman.[363]

Often, organizations use unreliable manufacturer lifetime and degradation information to stock spares, but such data can be imperfect and, therefore, unreliable.[363] Airlines can "use inventory analytics to identify items that are trending toward being out of stock, providing a means of stock management more reliable than supplier data. In addition, research has shown that monitoring technology can reduce the need for spare part inventory," O'Gorman adds[363]

As O'Gorman explains that to "maintain ideal inventory stock levels, organizations must accurately classify inventory. ABC analysis, a particularly popular classification system, classifies inventory by the relative priority of each item against other items in the inventory. A-classed items, the most important, typically make up 5 to 10 percent of inventory. B-classed items typically make up the next 15 to 25 percent of inventory. C-classed items, the least important, make up the remaining 65 to 80 percent of inventory."[363]

However, classifying inventory like this isn't as easy as it seems; ABC analysis requires ongoing review and revision to achieve optimal item distribution.[363] In addition, many organizations rely on corrective maintenance procedures that lead to unscheduled inventory demands.[363] O'Gorman recommends that organizations implement forecasting practices such as the following[363]:

- Forecasting demand and planning supply.
- Communicating, cooperating and collaborating.
- Eliminating islands of analysis.
- Using tools wisely.
- Emphasizing forecasting.
- Measuring everything.

With these practices in place, inventory analytics and predictive asset maintenance can make use of the wealth of data that an airline generates, which will help it capitalize on an analytics solution designed for asset inventory management.[363]

As O'Gorman argues, "Obsolescence is an unavoidable fact of inventory management, but unfortunately, many organizations manage it reactively. To manage obsolescence proactively, organizations must be able to answer questions such as the following: *How can we anticipate obsolescence? What contingency plans have we in place? What are our most important needs? Should we maintain items, or replace them? How do we ensure safety?*"[363]

Gorman advises airlines to, "Develop an obsolescence risk assessment process, helping inventory managers assess the probability that items will become obsolete and flag the items that are at greatest risk of becoming so. To augment the process, inventory managers can use analytics to identify already obsolete items, identify items that the organization can afford to manage reactively and reduce the manual effort involved in computing the probability of obsolescence."[363]

Adding analytics into the obsolescence process gives airlines actionable data that can be used to strengthen their bargaining position when negotiating supplier agreements, systems upgrades, or it could just help risk mitigation purchases.[363]

By optimizing reorder points for inventory items, airlines can avoid excess stock conditions. Airlines must juggle the need between having enough inventory to handle fluctuating demand, while also keeping costs down.[363] The potential benefits of doing this are huge.[363]

In her article, *Why the food and beverage industry needs to start using internet of Things technology*[364], Carolyn Heneghan argues that, "One of the most important applications for IoT in a food and beverage industry context is temperature tracking and control. Using sensors in the product, manufacturers can track shipments from afar, both where it is and how cold it is."[364] The data captured will let the airline know if products have been spoiled and possibly why, like if there's a problem with delivery truck refrigeration.[364]

"It's not really the temperature of the truck that matters, but the temperature of the food," says Jim Cerra, cofounder and CEO of PlanetTogether. "If they're opening up the truck to drop off material at various stores and warehouses, the temperatures are fluctuating in the truck."[364]

Light can also affect quality and safety as well.[364] Too much light can hasten bacteria growth.[364] "That's particularly important for companies embracing the clear packaging trend, or for producers like brewers that traditionally use glass or see-through materials as packaging," Heneghan argues.[364] "IoT technology can detect light, and can send data about when a package is first opened or how much sunlight hits a product during shipping," Heneghan explains.[364]

Waste Management

According to the Food and Agriculture Organization (FAO) of the United Nations, annual food wastage is estimated at 1.6 billion tonnes.[365] The economic impact of this waste is priced at over $750 billion, a number that doesn't include fish and seafood waste.[365] The FAO warns that it is not only the loss of money that is consequential, but the "environment is also damaged by an increased carbon footprint, additional landfill deposits and higher demand for agricultural land. Using more land for agriculture, in turn, poses a threat to various plant and animal species."[365]

In his article *Smart Food Management Utilizes IoT to reduce Cost, Waste and Pollution*[366], Shay Adar explains that multi-sensored smart devices can monitor perishable goods in storage and in transit and relay location, temperature, and humidity data to the cloud. "This provides real-time information on the precise conditions of each unit of goods and thus enables corrective actions to reduce waste and save money," Adar adds.[366] An airline can utilize this data to ensure both the quality and the amount of its purchased product is being received in a timely manner.

The transition to Ag3.0 means farmers are no longer looking to the clouds for weather patterns, but rather to the "cloud" for its big data and analytics capabilities, hoping to maximize the life and quality of their produce and livestock.

As Adar explains[366]:

> "A cold chain is the entire process that perishable goods go through, from production to market, including storage and various methods of transport. During this entire chain, temperature and other factors must be maintained to safeguard the quality of the product. Traditional monitoring systems are either stationary wired sensors, or portable temperature data loggers. The former are only suitable for warehouses, while the latter are only good for hindsight. This is due to the fact that the logged information can only be read once the goods have arrived at their destination. At that point, the only decision to make is whether to place the goods on the shelf or in the trash."

Because cold chain monitoring occurs in real-time, corrective action can be taken immediately, which could, potentially, reduce spoilage and waste.[366] Once an airline knows that the goods it is expecting will most likely arrive spoiled, the goods can be rejected, and replacements can be found. A "reduction of superfluous trips delivering spoiled goods can lead to a significant decrease in fuel and shipping costs, as well as the carbon footprint that comes with them," adds Adar.[366] The butterfly effect is in full effect and there's no reason why an airline has to pay for both unwanted product and unneeded labor.

The perishability of a product can also be tracked. A sensored cold chain adds precision into the supply chain.[366] "By placing sensors on each pallet of food, the differences in environment conditions between pallets in the same shipment can be measured and collected. This data can then be used to calculate the remaining shelf-life of the product. With this information, the traditional FIFO (First In First Out) inventory system can be replaced with the more effective FEFO (First Expired First Out)," Adar recommends.[366]

Machine learning models can also be built to discover the optimized delivery methods, or these models can help spot outliers in the supply chain. A powerful feedback loop can be created, and this information might prove valuable to other airlines so the data could, potentially, be sold to others.

GPS location can be built into products, so that an airline knows exactly where every item it is buying is located in the supply chain.[367] Every object will have its own unique identifier, and the airline will be able to pin-point each and every item or piece of equipment the company has.[368] This can "greatly decrease the number of lost or stolen products, increase management of stock shortages and overstocks, and better identify inefficiencies."[367] For example, the airline can be alerted about shipments that get stuck in traffic at a certain time of day, items that sell better at certain locations, when and, potentially, where items get damaged, how and perhaps why food arrives spoiled, amongst other things.[367]

e-Commerce

A web search engine is a software system designed to search for information on the web and the search results are generally presented in a line of results often referred to as search engine results page (SERPs).[369] "The information may be a mix of web pages, images, and other types of files. Some search engines also mine data available in databases or open directories. Unlike web directories, which are maintained only by human editors, search engines also maintain real-time information by running an algorithm on a web crawler."[369]

In the US, Google is, by far, the biggest search engine around. Google Search (or Google Web Search) is a web search engine owned by Google Inc. and it is the most-used Internet search engine in the world today, handling more than three billion searches every day.[370]

Outside the U.S., Google's main competitors are "Baidu and Soso.com in China; Naver.com and Daum Communications in South Korea; Yandex in Russia; Seznam.cz in Czech Republic; Yahoo! in Japan, Taiwan [sic]."[370]

Bit players like Bing compete with Google on standard search, but today Apple and Amazon are making inroads on Google's dominance, with Facebook set to be a challenger in the not-too-distant future. With those latter two, search is organically included within their platforms, i.e., when someone searches for an item to buy on Amazon, it gets included in the overall search rankings, ergo, an ecommerce site has become an important search engine.

Why is search so influential? Because users flock to search engines to organize the vast amounts of information most buyers need to make purchase decisions. "The main purpose of Google Search is to hunt for text in publicly accessible documents offered by web servers, as opposed to other data, such as with Google Image Search."[370] "The order of search on Google's search-results pages is based, in part, on a priority rank called a 'PageRank.'"[370] As Sharma et al. state in *Mobile Marketing*, "Search is one of the best ways to find content and the absolute best way for a marketer to determine consumer intent."[34]

Google Search "provides at least 22 special features beyond the original word-search capability, and language translation of displayed pages."[370] "In June 2011, Google introduced 'Google Voice Search' and 'Search by Image' features for allowing the users to search words by speaking and by giving images. In May 2012, Google introduced a new Knowledge Graph semantic search feature to customers in the U.S."[370]

"When Google was a Stanford research project, it was nicknamed BackRub because the technology checks backlinks to determine a site's importance."[370] As I explain in the section on collaborative projects in the social media chapter, backlinks—and the quality of them—are very important for search engine optimization (SEO). The higher the quality of backlinks, the higher a Website's ranking.

Even today backlinks count, and they likely count prominently for SEO and, although backlinks are not always within a company's control, they are highly important due to their stature as the earliest persisting Google ranking factor. According to the *Moz 2015 Ranking Survey*, "the data continues to show some of the highest correlations between Google rankings and the number of links to a given page."[371] Today, *quality* backlinks are of the utmost importance and Google is the one who decides the quality of those backlinks; links from known spammy sites or sites associated with them, or merely hosted on servers that also host spammy content negatively affect rankings.[371]

In the early days of the battle for internet search supremacy, "previous keyword-based methods of ranking search results, used by many search engines that were once more popular than Google, would rank pages by how often the search terms occurred in the page, or how strongly associated the search terms were within each resulting page."[372] Google's PageRank algorithm instead "analyzes human-generated links assuming that web pages linked from many important pages are themselves likely to be important. The algorithm computes a recursive score for pages, based on the weighted sum of the PageRanks of the pages linking to them."[372] As a result, PageRank is thought to correlate well with human concepts of importance.[372]

Today, Google wants site owners to focus on developing great content—clear, accurate, highly-readable content that other sites owners want to link to.[371] The way modern engines make this determination is by using advanced natural language processing, artificial intelligence and machine learning.[371] These evolving technologies enable the search engines to understand content without relying on a small set of specific keywords and phrases.[371] Google has invested heavily in this, as evidenced by the plethora of white papers and research posted on its 'Machine Intelligence' website.[371]

As Brian Alpert argues in his article *Search engine optimization in 2017: A new world where old rules sill matter*[373], "One aspect of today's search engines that makes them very different from their predecessors is that advances in artificial intelligence and machine learning have enabled them to understand content and its underlying concepts independently of specific keywords."[373] Alpert adds: "This renders null and void the old concept that one must focus on keywords specific to a certain kind of content in order to be found via search engines. In today's landscape, exact keyword matches are less influential than ever before as engines can understand the relationships between words that are semantically related."[373]

With the introduction of its Knowledge Graph, Google is attempting to give users answers instead of just links.[370] "If you want to compare the nutritional value of olive oil to butter, for example, Google Search will now give you a comparison chart with lots of details. The same holds true for other things, including dog breed and celestial objects. Google says it plans to expand this feature to more things over time."[370]

Knowledge Graph also allows users to filter results.[370] "Say you ask Google: 'Tell me about Impressionist artists.' Now, you'll see who these artists are, and a new bar on top of the results will allow you to dive in to learn more about them and to switch to learn more about abstract art, for example," Lardinois explains.[370]

Questions like, "Tell me about the best airline flying from Sydney to Las Vegas" could be reverse-engineered to spit out results that a particular airline wants the search engine to relay, but this requires considerable thought and engagement from multiple departments at the airline wanting to get this listing discovered by someone searching for vacations in Las Vegas, let's say.

Search is always going to be an important part of an airline's marketing plan and, for that reason alone, creating a Google+ presence is imperative. Putting a little time and energy into an airline's Google+ page can lead to improved local search capability. "Pages that do well on Google Plus receive a higher index on Google search. And that's not all, Google Plus content—meaning the posts you share on your page—can show up in search results in instances where your website may not."[374] Retail operators should take advantage of the golden opportunity Google has offered them—"prime placement on the right-hand side of search results, with photos and promotional posts."[375] This presents a very good opportunity for brands to get in on the ground floor and get prime advertising placement right now.

Search engines are constantly looking for updated information on websites and adding things like blogs and customer forums is a cheap and effective way to get customers and/or clients to generate new content for you.

Search advertising falls into two main types—natural search results, and paid sponsorship based on keywords.[376] "Natural search requires high-quality, constantly updated content and search engine optimization (SEO). Paid search requires work to optimize keyword choice and messaging, but can be phenomenally expensive."[376] When not optimized for conversion, this can be a very pricey channel to use, with low conversion rates as well.[376]

Airlines should constantly be testing their web pages for the most searched for or visited pages. As Siroker and Komen explain, A/B testing is particularly good for website marketing, especially for uncovering a website's best landing pages. "Defining success in the context of A/B testing involves taking the answer to the question of your site's ultimate purpose and turning it into something more precise: *quantifiable success metrics*. Your success metrics are the specific numbers you hope will be improved by your tests," argue Siroker and Komen.[181]

An e-commerce website could easily define its success metrics in terms of revenue per visitor[181], but it is still important to understand such things as traffic sources, bounce rate, top pages, conversion rates, conversion by traffic source, amongst others.

---

333 Woodrow, Bellamy III. The Connected Aircraft. Avionics Today. http://interactive.avionicstoday.com/the-connected-aircraft/ (Accessed 16 August 2018).
334 IBM Software Thought Leadership White Paper. Descriptive, predictive, prescriptive: Transforming asset and facilities management with analytics. October 2013. https://static.ibmserviceengage.com/TIW14162USEN.PDF (22 November 2017).
335 Henschen, D. 2014, March 2. In-Memory Databases: Do You Need the Speed? Retrieved from informationweek.com: http://www.informationweek.com/big-data/big-data-analytics/in-memory-databases-do-you-need-the-speed/d/d-id/1114076 (Accessed 25 November 2017).
336 Grover, Mark, Malaska, Ted, Seidman, Jonathan, Shapira, Gwen. Hadoop Application Architectures: Designing Real-World Big Data Applications. O'Reilly Media. July 2015.
337 https://hadoopecosystemtable.github.io/ (Accessed 27 October 2017).
338 https://en.wikipedia.org/wiki/MapReduce (accesssed 27 October 2017).
339 http://whatis.techtarget.com/definition/metadata (Accessed 29 October 2017).
340 https://kafka.apache.org/documentation/#producerapi (Accessed 13 November 2017).
341 https://en.wikipedia.org/wiki/Real-time_marketing (Accessed 13 November 2017).
342 Woods, D. (2011, May 6). How Real-time Marketing Technology Can Transform Your Business. Retrieved from Forbes.com: http://www.forbes.com/sites/ciocentral/2011/05/06/how-real-time-marketing-technology-can-transform-your-business/ (22 November 2017).
343 Schulte, Roy. (May 23, 2017). When do you need an Event Stream Processing Platform? Logtrust.com. https://www.logtrust.com/need-event-stream-processing-platform/ (Accessed 30 August 2017).
344 Shields, M. (2014, July 14). Inside Google's World Cup Real-Time Marketing Experiment with Nike. Retrieved from Wall Street Journal Blog: http://blogs.wsj.com/cmo/2014/07/14/inside-googles-world-cup-real-time-marketing-experiment-with-nike/ (22 November 2017).

345 Deng, Lei, Gao, Jerry, Vuppalapati, Chandrasekar. March 2015. Building a Big Data Analytics Service Framework for Mobile Advertising and Marketing. Online: https://www.researchgate.net/profile/Jerry_Gao/publication/273635443_Building_a_Big_Data_Analytics_Service_Framework_for_Mobile_Advertising_and_Marketing/links/5508de220cf26ff55f840c31.pdf (22 November 2017).

346 https://www.hds.com/en-us/pdf/brochure/hitachi-overview-streaming-data-platform.pdf (Accessed 30 December 2016)

347 Gualtieri, Mike. April 16, 2016. 15 "True" Streaming Analytics Platforms for Real-Time Everything. Forrester.com. https://go.forrester.com/blogs/16-04-16-15_true_streaming_analytics_platforms_for_real_time_everything/ (Accessed 2 September 2017).

348 Morgan, J. (2014, May 13). A Simple Explanation of 'the Internet of Things'. Retrieved from Forbes.com: http://www.forbes (22 November 2017).

349 Gartner. (2013, December 12). Gartner Says the Internet of Things Installed Base Will Grow to 26 Billion Units By 2020. Retrieved from Gartner.com: http://www.gartner.com/newsroom/id/2636073 (22 November 2017).

350 Lenz, Gadi. September 22, 2015. Datanami.com The Data of Things: How Edge Analytics and IoT Go Hand in Hand. https://www.datanami.com/2015/09/22/the-data-of-things-how-edge-analytics-and-iot-go-hand-in-hand/ (22 November 2017).

351 DHT Trend Research, Cisco Consulting Services. 2015. Internet of Things in Logistics. http://www.dpdhl.com/content/dam/dpdhl/presse/pdf/2015/DHLTrendReport_Internet_of_things.pdf (22 November 2017).

352 Tableau. (2017) 2018 Top 10 Business Intelligence Trends. Tableau. https://www.tableau.com/sites/default/files/pages/838266_2018_bi_trends_whitepaper_1.pdf (Accessed 17 November 2017).

353 Wadhwa, T. (2013, June 3). CrowdOptic and L'Oreal to make history by demonstrating how augmented reality can be a shared experience. Retrieved from Forbes.com: http://www.forbes.com/sites/tarunwadhwa/2013/06/03/crowdoptic-and-loreal-are-about-to-make-history-by-demonstrating-how-augmented-reality-can-be-a-shared-experience/ (22 November 2017).

354 http://www.webopedia.com/TERM/A/Augmented_Reality.html (Accessed 13 November 2017).

355 Gartner. October 18, 2016. Gartner's Top 10 Strategic Technology Trends for 2017. http://www.gartner.com/smarterwithgartner/gartners-top-10-technology-trends-2017/

356 Gartner. 2014, January 14). Gartner believes augmented reality will become an important workplace tool. Retrieved from Gartner.com: http://www.gartner.com/newsroom/id/2649315 (22 November 2017).

357 Deloitte. (2013). Augmented Government, Transforming Government Services Through Augmented Reality. Retrieved from Deloitte Development LLC: http://www.deloitte.com/assets/Dcom-UnitedStates/Local%20Assets/Documents/Federal/us_fed_augmented_government_060613.pdf (22 November 2017).

358 Bellamy III, William. (2017). 9 Companies Using Augments and Virtual Reality in Aviation. Aviation Today. 24 August 2017. https://www.aviationtoday.com/2017/08/24/9-companies-using-augmented-virtual-reality-aviation/ (Accessed 19 August 2018).

359 Moore, J. (2012). Augmented reality: expanding the user experience. Retrieved from Digital Innovation Gazette: http://www.digitalinnovationgazette.com/uiux/augmented_reality_app_development/#axzz2z8tFKN00 (22 November 2017).

360 https://en.wikipedia.org/wiki/Pokémon_Go (22 November 2017).

361 http://www.wearabledevices.com/what-is-a-wearable-device/ (22 November 2017).

362 Gogle, Israel. Internet of Things. May 2016. Adoption of IoT for Warehouse Management. A & S Internation. Asmag.com. http://www.cisco.com/c/dam/en/us/solutions/collateral/industry-solutions/iot-warehouse.pdf (22 November 2017).

363 O'Gorman, Tristan. September 14, 2015. 5 Inventory analytics best practice to achieve inventory optimization. IBM Big Data & Analytics Hub. http://www.ibmbigdatahub.com/blog/5-inventory-analytics-best-practices-achieve-inventory-optimization (22 November 2017).

364 Heneghan, Carolyn. September 6, 2016. Why the food and beverage industry needs to start using Internet of Things technology. www.fooddive.com. http://www.fooddive.com/news/why-the-food-and-beverage-industry-needs-to-start-using-internet-of-things/425693/ (22 November 2017).

365 http://www.fao.org/news/story/en/item/196402/icode/ (22 November 2017).

366 Adar, Shay. April 10, 2016. Smart Food Management Utilizes IoT to Reduce Cost, Waste and Pollution. CEVA. http://blog.ceva-dsp.com/smart-food-management-utilizes-iot-to-reduce-cost-waste-and-pollution/ (22 November 2017).

367 How the Internet of Things (IT) Will Transform Inventory Management. www.clearspider.com http://www.clearspider.com/internet-of-things-inventory-management/ (22 November 2017).

368 How the Internet of Things (IT) Will Transform Inventory Management. www.clearspider.com http://www.clearspider.com/internet-of-things-inventory-management/ (22 November 2017).

369 https://en.wikipedia.org/wiki/Web_search_engine (Accessed 13 November 2017).

370 Lardinois, F. (2013, September 26). Google improves knowledge graph with comparisons and filters, brings cards & cross-platform notifications to mobile. Retrieved from TechCrunch: http://techcrunch.com/2013/09/26/google-improves-knowledge-graph-with-comparisons-and-filters-brings-cards-to-mobile-search-adds-cross-platform-notifications/

371 Moz (2015) 'Search Engine Ranking Factors 2015 Expert Survey and Correlation Data', available at: https://moz.com/search-ranking-factors (Accessed 15th August 2017). Moz's rankings survey consists of the compiled results of 150 SEP expert opinions as to what influences Google's secret algorithm. It is largely a technical document and relies heavily on (defined) technical terms, such as 'Domain-Level-Keyword-Agnostic-Features', but it is worth a look nevertheless.

372 https://en.wikipedia.org/wiki/Google_Search (Accessed 13 November 2017).
373 Alpert, Brian. (Spring 2017). Search engine optimization in 2017: A new world where old rules still matter. Journal of Digital & Social Media Marketing, Volume 5, Number 1, Spring 2017, pp. 39 – 60 (22). Henry Stuart Publication.
374 The Bright Blue Wave Team. (2014, May 22). Why Small Businesses Need Google Plus. Retrieved from brightbluewave.com: http://brightbluewave.com/blog/small-businesses-need-google-plus/ (Accessed 13 November 2017).
375 Miller, C. C. (2014, February 14). The Plus in Google Plus? It's Mostly for Google. Retrieved from New York Times: http://www.nytimes.com/2014/02/15/technology/the-plus-in-google-plus-its-mostly-for-google.html?_r= (Accessed 13 November 2017).
376 Vindicia. (2014). Digital Age/Digital Goods. Retrieved from vindicia: http://info.vindicia.com/White-Paper---Digital-Age-Digital-Goods-9essentials_for_acquiring_subscription_and_recurring_revenue_customers.html (Accessed 15 August 2018).

CHAPTER SIX

The Predictive Airliner

"The best way to predict the future is to invent it."
~Alan Kay

Overview

As the IATA December 5th, 2017 press release notes, the biggest challenge in retaining profitability in the airline business in 2018 will be rising costs.[1] The following reasons are particularly worrying[1]:

- "Oil prices are expected to average $60/barrel for Brent Crude in 2018 (up 10.7% from $54.2/barrel in 2017). Jet fuel prices are expected to rise even more quickly to $73.8 per barrel (up 12.5% on $65.6 in 2017)."[1]
- Fuel bills are expected to be 20.5% of total costs in 2018 (up from 18.8% in 2017).[1]
- Labor costs have been accelerating strongly and are now a larger expense item than fuel (30.9% in 2018).[1]
- "Overall unit costs are expected to grow by 4.3% in 2018 (a significant acceleration on the 1.7% increase in 2017). This will outpace an expected 3.5% increase in unit revenues."[1]

Many of these costs can be mitigated by analytics and, as Annie Eissler stated in her article *How Much ROI Can Data Analytics Deliver?*, there is a compelling case for analytics, which have achieved double-digit returns on investment for several years now.[15] "We're at a point where the hype surrounding data analytics has converted into real, documented returns for companies of all sizes and across all industries," states Eissler.[15] Because the airline industry is such a data-rich industry, it is extremely important to introduce analytics into the business process.

Today, one particularly positive part of the business is cargo shipments, which is benefiting "from a strong cyclical upturn in volumes, with some recovery in yields."[1] According to IATA, "Volumes are expected to grow by 4.5% in 2018 (down from the 9.3% growth of 2017)." IATA believes that, "The boost to cargo volumes in 2017 was a result of companies needing to restock inventories quickly to meet unexpectedly strong demand."[1] Although restocking cycles tend to be short-lived, "the growth of e-commerce is expected to support continued momentum in the cargo business beyond the rate of expansion of world trade in 2018."[1] Ultimately, IATA sees cargo revenues growing robustly in 2018, up 8.6% year-over-year to $59.2 billion.[1] This strong growth should help build momentum in other areas of the business as well.

On the passenger side, since an airline is only projected to make $8.90 profit per passenger, it will need to embrace personalization at scale. This is possible with several of today's CRM, real-time personalization marketing and social media marketing and listening products.

The hill to personalization and customer understanding is steep though. "Roughly half of the people who belong to a U.S. airline loyalty program don't understand how it works," claims Justin Bachman in his Bloomberg article *These Are the Best Frequent-Flyer Programs*[377]. Considerable education initiatives are also going to be needed.

"We're not just talking about people who fly a few times a year,"[377] Bachman adds, citing a J.D. Power study that revealed "almost one-third of those who travel enough to gain status (silver, gold, platinum, etc.) may be unable to explain how they got it."[377] This is an incredible statistic considering how much interest and use there is in these programs.

"Among loyalty program members, only 55 percent of respondents said they know how to book and redeem rewards—a statistic that means the rest may be confused about how airlines structure these loyalty schemes," says Bachman.[377]

"The J.D. Power survey shows that airlines have a long way to go to make their programs more accessible and better understood by the flying public," warns Bachman.[377]

In their article *Data-Driven Transformation: Accelerate at Scale Now*[378], Gourévitch et al argue that, "Data-driven transformation is becoming a question of life or death in most industries" and more so for the airline industry than most others.

"Most CEOs recognize the power of data-driven transformation. They certainly would like the 20% to 30% EBITDA gains that their peers are racking up by using fresh, granular data in sales, marketing, supply chain, manufacturing, and R&D," Gourévitch et al claim.[378] What's not lost on these CEOs is the fact that today the top five companies with the highest market capitalization worldwide are all data-driven, tech companies—Apple, Alphabet, Microsoft, Amazon, and Facebook.[378] Five years ago, there was only one of these tech companies in the top five (Apple), whereas ten years ago there was only one in the top ten (Microsoft).[378]

CEOs are correct in worrying about how their organizations are going to handle a tenfold increase in company data when their managers are already complaining about a lack of data skills and overburdened IT systems.[378] "Transformations should start with pilots that pay off in weeks or months, followed by a plan for tackling high-priority use cases, and finishing with a program for building long-term capabilities," Gourévitch et al recommend.[378]

"It starts with small-scale, rapid digitization efforts that lay the foundation for the broader transformation and generate returns to help fund later phases of the effort," Gourévitch et al advocate.[378] "In the second and third phases, companies draw on knowledge from their early wins to create a roadmap for companywide transformation, 'industrialize' data and analytics, and build systems and capabilities to execute new data-driven strategies and processes."[378]

In terms of infrastructure and data transformation, Gourévitch et al state that companies need to ask the following questions[378]:

> "Can our current infrastructure support our future data value map? Should we make or buy? Should we go to the cloud? Do we need a data lake? What role should our legacy IT systems play in our data transformation? The company should design a data platform (or data lake) that can accommodate its product map and should use that platform to progressively transform its legacy systems."

"To progressively transform its legacy system," is an important concept here because it is imperative that companies don't bite off more than they can chew when they decide to embrace the data driven culture. The Japanese have a concept known as *Kaizen*—continuous incremental improvement—and it is an idea that should be kept in mind when a company steps into the data-driven world.

While the company architects the transformation roadmap, it needs to begin industrializing its data and analytics.[378] As Gourévitch et al explain, "This means setting up a way to standardize the creation and management of data-based systems and processes so that the output is replicable, efficient, and reliable."[378] Digital systems need to have all the attributes of industrial machinery, including reliability and consistency.[378]

For analytics, a flexible open architecture that can be updated continuously and enhanced with emerging technologies works best.[378] "Rather than embracing an end-to-end data architecture, companies should adopt a use-case-driven approach, in which the architecture evolves to meet the requirements of each new initiative," advise Gourévitch et al.[378] "The data governance and analytics functions should collaborate to create a simplified data environment; this will involve defining authorized sources of data and aggressively rationalizing redundant repositories and data flows," recommend Gourévitch.[378]

To prepare an organization for a digitized future, a company "needs to move on four fronts: creating new roles and governance processes, instilling a data-centric culture, adopting new ways of working, and cultivating the necessary talent and skills."[378]

Change starts at the top and senior leaders need to both buy into and adopt data-driven objectives, as well as instill a data-driven culture in every department throughout the organization.[378] Gourévitch et al. recommend that top management "set up data councils to extend the work to all sectors of the organization and to carry it out more effectively."[378] "The company should promote data awareness by using data champions to disseminate data-driven practices," state Gourévitch et al.[378]

"Not everyone needs to become steeped in data analytics or learn to code in order for digital transformation to work. However, everyone does need to adopt a less risk-averse attitude," advise Gourévitch et al.[378] The writers believe companies should embrace the software company model that utilizes a test-and-learn philosophy that accepts failure and is constantly changing–and learning.[378]

Businesses can also foster the desired cultural change through organizational moves, "such as creating internal startup units where employees can focus on experimentation or co-locating data labs within operating units."[378] "The company can also promote the new culture by using cross-functional teams that share data across silos, thereby encouraging openness and collaboration throughout the organization," advise Gourévitch et al.[378]

For any data-based transformation to succeed, a company needs talent with the right skills to execute data-driven strategies and manage data-based operations.[378] Airlines should start by assessing their current employees and defining their future needs and create an inventory of the talents and skills that its employees will need, as well as identify where the gaps are in the current workforce.[378]

Airlines will need to retrain current employees, hire new talent, or use a partnership to get the right capabilities. "To recruit people with digital skills, the company may need to rethink the value proposition it offers—work, opportunity, rewards, career path, and so on—in relation to what tech companies offer," advise Gourévitch et al.[378]

Airline executives should be inspired by the idea of using data to make better decisions, to create stronger customer bonds, and to digitize all sorts of processes to improve performance. They should also be motivated "by fear that they won't be able to keep up with competitors who are ahead of them in data-driven digital transformation."[378] Some caution is due; sweeping, companywide change to go digital can easily lead to counterproductive overreaching.[378] In this case, the contest will not necessarily be won by making huge bets.[378] As Gourévitch et al conclude, "The winners will be agile, pragmatic, and disciplined. They will move fast and capture quick wins, but they will also carefully plan a transformation roadmap to optimize performance in the functions and operations that create the most value, while building the technical capabilities and resources to sustain the transformation."[378]

Boland et al. provide the following five guidelines for airlines to follow to reinvigorate their customer relationships[7]:

- *Develop a vision*—understand how transformative CRM can be for customer relations.
- *Focus on customer value*—Understand each customer's profitability, each segment's profitability, each segment's customers, regardless of frequent flyer status or membership. Use that customer value to differentiate service levels and to identify opportunities that can increase the loyalty of the airline's most valuable customers. Use this knowledge to recruit new customers with similar profiles.
- *Empower the employee*—Communicate to every employee the importance of customer service. Provide key customer information at important interactions points throughout the company, whether on the web, at baggage claim, with a flight attendant, or through reservations. Incentivize employees to encourage a deepening of the customer relationship and experience.
- *Set targets and success metrics*—Quantify CRM payback. Ensure that both the business and the customers obtain value from its CRM program, allowing honest feedback from both customers and employees.
- *Address customer needs throughout the lifecycle*—recognize each customer has his or her own lifecycle and become an essential partner to those needs. Analyze information gleaned through both the company's CRM and marketing channels, refining business actions to target the customers' needs better, as well as create an even more customized and consistent experience throughout the lifecycle.

Singapore Airlines: Continuing Excellence

In their *Harvard Business Review* article *The Globe: Singapore Airlines' Balancing Act*[53], Heracleous and Wirtz state that, despite Singapore Airlines (SIA) being one of the most cost-effective airline operators, it is also renowned for its quality of service. "From 2001 to 2009, its costs per available seat kilometer (ASK) were just 4.58 cents. According to a 2007 International Air Transport Association study, costs for full-service European airlines were 8 to 16 cents, for U.S. airlines 7 to 8 cents, and for Asian airlines 5 to 7 cents. In fact, SIA had lower costs than most European and American budget carriers, which ranged from 4 to 8 cents and 5 to 6 cents respectively," note Heracleous and Wirtz.[53]

As Heracleous and Wirtz explain cost-effectiveness and award-winning service can often entail contradictory investments and organizational processes, yet SIA sees it as an imperative."[53] The demand for value-for-money products and services increased after the 2008 recession and has remained in full effect a decade later, especially in the airline industry, and particularly in developing countries, the area that SIA generally operates in.[53]

Cost conscious consumers have forced producers of premium offerings to figure out how to grab opportunities in the middle and the low end of the market .[53] Additionally, "multinational corporations face competition from rivals—many of them from emerging markets—that use new technologies and business models to provide good-enough offerings at attractive prices."[53] Of course, incumbents can fight back, but cutting prices and limiting services is often a losing battle.[53] As Heracleous and Wirtz explain, "Price wars typically hurt leaders more than they do challengers, and relentless differentiation is tough to sustain. Adopting a dual strategy is often the only choice."[53]

Heracleous and Wirtz's research suggests[53]:

> "dual strategies are embraced more readily in Asian countries. Many Western executives believe that, for instance, cost leadership and differentiation, globalization and localization, and size and agility are fundamentally contradictory and can't be reconciled. But SIA and other companies such as Banyan Tree, Haier, Samsung, and Toyota operate as though the dualities are opposites that make up a whole; that is, they complement, instead of contradicting, each other. This way of thinking is embedded in Eastern thought; the concept of yin and yang in Taoist philosophy, for instance, encapsulates the idea. To be sure, pursuing two strategies will result in organizational paradoxes, but executives in Asian markets tend to realize that opposing insights present the full picture and develop policies to manage both of them."

Heracleous and Wirtz believe that no company executes a dual strategy better than SIA. The airline has delivered healthy financial returns since its inception. It is debt free, has never posted an annual loss, funded growth through retained earnings, and has consistently paid dividends.[53]

SIA executes "a dual strategy by managing four paradoxes: providing service excellence cost-effectively; innovating in both a centralized and a decentralized manner; being a technology leader and a follower; and achieving standardization and personalization in its processes."[53] Unfortunately for competitors, "SIA's self-reinforcing system is difficult to imitate, yielding sustainable competitive advantage."[53]

"SIA has two main assets—planes and people—and it manages them so that its service is better than rivals' and its costs are lower," explain Heracleous and

Wirtz.[53] SIA always ensures that its fleet is young.[53] "For instance, in 2009, its aircraft were 74 months old, on average—less than half the industry average of 160 months," note Heracleous and Wirtz.[53] Unsurprisingly, this "triggers a virtuous cycle: Because mechanical failures are rare, fewer takeoffs are delayed, more arrivals are on time, and fewer flights are canceled."[53] Of course, this also has a follow-through effect on passengers, who appreciate the on time arrival and departures these new planes afford.

In addition, new planes are more fuel efficient and need less maintenance:[53] "In 2008, repairs accounted for 4% of SIA's total costs compared with 5.9% for United Air Lines and 4.8% for American Airlines. SIA's aircraft spend less time in hangars—which means more time in the air: 13 hours, on average, per day versus the industry average of 11.3 hours. And, of course, customers like newer planes better."[53]

SIA believes service mostly boils down to people, so it invests heavily in employee training.[53] "It schools its fresh recruits for four months—twice as long as the industry average of eight weeks—and spends around $70 million a year to put each of its 14,500 employees through 110 hours of retraining annually," explain Heracleous and Wirtz.[53]

With classes on deportment, etiquette, wine appreciation, and cultural sensitivity, SIA believes in an expansive and cultured education. "Cabin crews are trained to interact with Japanese, Chinese, and American passengers in different ways. Trainees learn to appreciate subtle issues, such as communicating at eye level rather than 'talking down' to passengers. The superior service that results not only delights customers but also reduces costs by minimizing customer turnover," note Heracleous and Wirtz.[53]

SIA is extremely cost conscious, and each training program "focuses as much on the necessity of keeping costs down as on the delivery of great service."[53] Trainers "discuss the airline industry's fiercely competitive nature with employees every year."[53] "At town hall–style meetings and in internal communications, senior executives stress the fact that SIA must become more efficient in order to remain competitive. They emphasize both parts of the company's vision: providing air transportation services of the highest quality and maximizing returns for the benefit of shareholders and employees," add Heracleous and Wirtz.[53]

In day-to-day operations, the aim is to reduce waste without compromising customer service and even SIA's employee bonus scheme serves as an incentive for employees to worry about expenses.[53] For example, "when cabin crews noticed that about a third of passengers don't eat dinner on late-night flights out of Singapore, they recommended carrying less food."[53]

Unlike other airlines, SIA offers two brands of champagne in first class, spending $8 million on champagne every year.[53] SIA's cabin attendants "minimize costs by pouring from whichever bottle is open unless a passenger specifically requests the other brand." Also, SIA decided not to place jam jars on every breakfast tray several years ago because cabin crews noticed that many people don't eat jam.[53] SIA's bonus scheme, which extends to all employees, gives employees "the opportunity to earn bonuses of up to 50% of their salary depending on how profitable the company is."[53]

Another cost cutting philosophy is, "Anything that touches the customer must be consistent with SIA's premium positioning, whereas everything behind the scenes is subject to control."[53] "The company's headquarters is atop an old hangar at Changi Airport—not in a swank downtown skyscraper—and the number of headquarters staff is small."[53]

"For its training program, SIA uses its own facilities instead of sending employees to resorts, and participants buy their lunch from company canteens. Hard-bargaining local managers negotiate hotel rates for crew members at SIA's destinations," explain Heracleous and Wirtz.[53] SIA's other costs—fuel, labor, depreciation, and aircraft rentals—is, "at 29.1%, lower than the other large airlines' average of 38.2%."[53] This flies in the face of the notion that companies delivering quality service can't be cost leaders. Of course, Singapore does have several advantages that many European and American airlines can't emulate, like employees' costs, but holistically they are doing much that can be emulated.

SIA has more than earned its serial innovator reputation, "bringing many firsts to the civil aviation industry: on-demand entertainment systems in all classes; Dolby sound systems; a book-the-cook service that allows business- and first-class customers to order their favorite meals before boarding; the widest business-class seats; and so on."[53]

SIA "follows a 4-3-3 rule of spending: 40% on training, 30% on revising processes and procedures, and 30% on creating new products and services every year."[53] "SIA sustains innovation by using a structured, rigorous, and centralized process along with an emergent, distributed, and local process. The former is the skeleton, the latter the flesh and blood; together, they provide customers with a body of novel services at a low cost."[53]

SIA's Product Innovation Department (PID) "follows a highly structured process that includes opportunity identification, concept evaluation, design and development, and launch."[53] The PID has "developed innovations such as a nonstop, all business-class service between Singapore and New York and the induction of the Airbus A380 into the fleet in 2007,"[53] although this service ended in 2013. "SIA engages frontline employees, customers, competitors, and the media to create multiple feedback channels,"[53] which, through social media, is much easier to do today compared to how it was when this article was written in 2010.

SIA also uses its distributed innovation approach for efficiency by fostering "the idea that employees—especially those in customer-facing functions such as in-flight services, ground services, and loyalty marketing—must innovate if SIA is to stay ahead."[53] Every airline function is responsible for improving the airline's service, and department heads must implement new ideas out of their own budgets.[53] This approach is both cost-effective and it ensures that innovations are developed in accordance with operational realities, making it much easy to implement them.[53] "Tensions sometimes erupt between central and local innovation," Heracleous and Wirtz concede, "but SIA encourages both because they complement each other."[53] "Distributed innovation helps sustain service excellence, which requires that every part of a customer encounter be outstanding," state Heracleous and Wirtz.[53]

"Frontline employees are particularly important in developing innovations that strengthen SIA's image—and torpedoing those that could damage it," state Heracleous and Wirtz.[53] "For example, cabin crews demurred when the idea of allowing passengers to order food and drinks by using the in-flight entertainment system was floated. The crews felt they wouldn't be able to respond to requests immediately after take-off, before landing, and during planned services, harming their ability to meet customer expectations consistently."[53] That completely derailed the idea, but for good reason.[53]

SIA doesn't try to be best in class on every count, but rather focuses on incremental innovation in the majority of places because the overall customer experience matters most.[53] "This approach enables the airline to make a profit, without pricing itself out of the market," argue Heracleous and Wirtz.[53]

According to Heracleous and Wirtz, "SIA is often the first to innovate in order to enhance the customer experience."[53] However, "unlike many market leaders that innovate in every aspect of their business, SIA engages in only small improvements in functions that don't touch the customer."[53] SIA is not afraid to execute high-risk innovation projects either.[53] For example, the introduction of the "A380 not only strengthened its image as a pioneer but also gained enormous publicity for the company. People bid for seats in one of eBay's biggest auctions, and some paid $100,000 for a seat on the flight from Singapore to Sydney."[53]

SIA's deep pockets allow it to take calculated risks. "For instance, in 1976, when it introduced slumberettes in first class, competitors demanded that it either charge more or withdraw the innovation,"[53] which isn't always a good look for a competitor. Imagine the viral marketing potential on social media today with those kinds of competitor demands—"Our competitors asked us to raise our prices, we told them our loyalty bunks with you." Of course, SIA did neither and won the 'battle of the slumberette'.

In 1991, SIA became "the first to introduce telephone and fax services on board, and in 1998, SIA was one of the first airlines to set up a website where customers could book flights, choose seats, and order meals. That was a no-brainer; SIA knew it would save costs by sending would-be travelers online."[53]

Although it has deep pockets, SIA is a pragmatic innovator, quickly halting the use of technology that causes problems or that customers dislike.[53] For example, "In 1981, it introduced slot machines in the upper decks of its Boeing 747s but removed them when the queues that formed became a safety risk."[53] In the aftermath of the SARS epidemic in the early 2000s, "SIA introduced a check-in system based on biometric technology, which enabled passengers to clear immigration, check in, and get their boarding passes in about 60 seconds. However, the airline discontinued the system's usage when data showed that few passengers were taking advantage of it and conventional immigration procedures had speeded up."[53]

Unsurprisingly, SIA's service processes, like those of many other airlines, are highly standardized so they can be easily repeatable.[53] This is "central to high-volume service operations, because it leads to predictability, safety, and lower costs," state Heracleous and Wirtz. "It also leads to customer satisfaction, but it can't deliver a 'wow' experience, partly because once customers have experienced something, they tend to discount its value. That's why SIA combines standardization with personalization to delight customers."[53]

SIA institutionalizes personalization "by creating a service culture that, as mentioned earlier, it sustains through recruitment, training, and rewards"[53] "It instills in employees a certain pride in working for the company, and they come to identify with its reputation. SIA's crew members and managers alike say that service is in their blood," Heracleous and Wirtz.[53]

"SIA personalizes the customer experience by relaying information about birthdays and preferences from its CRM system to cabin crew members,"[53] something most airlines are probably doing today. SIA cabin crew address frequent flyers by name and know their favorite drinks and magazines.[53] Usually, though, personalization is spontaneous, which makes it all the more welcome.[53] Most opportunities are unexpected—a passenger looks unwell; another may lack reading material; yet another may have a laptop that has run out of power.[53] According to Heracleous and Wirtz, "Most airlines' employees don't pay attention to these small things, but SIA's training programs such as Transforming Customer Service teach cabin crews how to anticipate customer needs and enhance employees' ability to delight customers."[53] For example, a passenger may request a vegetarian meal without having reserved one as SIA's cabin crews know how to put together a vegetarian meal from the standard food available on most flights.[53] Also, "if a passenger wants to discuss the wine he is drinking, a member of the crew who has taken a wine appreciation course will quickly materialize."[53]

"Standardization actually enables personalization," argue Heracleous and

Wirtz.[53] "Because SIA designs simple processes and trains people well, following procedures becomes second nature. Employees know their jobs so well that they have the mental space to 'read' customers and respond to them in creative ways," add Heracleous and Wirtz.[53] However, for SIA to provide such excellent service, it requires more crew members than their competitors'.[53] "That adds about 5% to costs, but these crews help the airline provide unmatched service, which allows it to charge premium prices," conclude Heracleous and Wirtz.[53]

Heracleous and Wirtz state that for other airlines to emulate SIA, it is not just about following SIA's best practices; "it's about implementing two seemingly contradictory strategies."[53] Four broad principles must be followed; harnessing the power of a company's people and culture; making good use of technology; utilizing the power of the business ecosystems; and making investment decisions strategically.

Heracleous and Wirtz conclude that, "Executing dual strategies is difficult— that's what makes the approach so valuable. By being different in ways that customers like, companies that do so rise from the pits of commoditization and make profits even in highly competitive industries."[53]

The Customer Journey

As I wrote in chapter one, successful marketing is about reaching a consumer with an interesting offer when he or she is primed to accept it. Knowing what might interest the consumer is half the battle to making the sale and this is where customer analytics comes in. Customer analytics have evolved from simply reporting customer behavior to segmenting customers based on their profitability, to predicting that profitability, to improving those predictions (because of the inclusion of new data), to *actually manipulating customer behavior* with target-specific promotional offers and marketing campaigns.

An airline needs to create a single view of the customer so that it will enable its marketers to deliver a personalized experience that wows the customer. Data can come from transactional systems, CRM systems, app impressions, operational data, facial recognition software, wearables, iBeacons, clickstream data, etc., etc. As Dan Woods explains in his amusing comparison of the different environments that today's marketers face in comparison to what their 1980's counterparts saw.[33] Today, stealthy marketers are forced to use "email campaigns, events, blogging, tweeting, PR, ebooks, white papers, apps, banner ads, Google Ad Words, social media outreach, search engine optimization."[33] Woods didn't include SMS, but that is still an integral part of the marketing chain.

As he explains in his article *Social Media Tips From The World's Top Airline*[283], Carmine Gallo states that, "Cathay Pacific considers everything a customer touch point: website, reservations, phone, and social media." This is good advice and I would include an airline's mobile app as a channel as well.

In practice, all these channels should work in concert with each other; an email campaign can promote a sale at an event, which can be blogged and tweeted about through social media. PR can also promote the event through their typical news channels. Coupons for the event can be disseminated through the airline's mobile app and SMS messaging. Banner ads will appear on the airline's website, while Google ads and SEO will drive buyers and potential buyers to the airline's website or its social channels. Hopefully, viral marketing then kicks in, with customers and potential customers sharing on Facebook, Instagram, Pinterest, Polyvore, Weibo, WeChat, etc., etc. Of course, influencer marketing can also help the viral marketing process at some point.

Seen through the lens of the *Airline Engagement and Loyalty Platform* (Figure 5), all of these activities can increase personalization to the point where it will be recognized by the customer. Lovelock and Wirtz's "Wheel of Loyalty" concept and its three sequential steps—building a foundation for loyalty, creating loyalty bonds, and identifying and reducing factors that result in churn[59] should be kept in mind when building up the foundation of *The Predictive Airliner's* CRM system. The most important part of the second step is the cross-selling and bundling of products and a real-time stream processing recommendation engine will certainly help with that.

In its article *The 5 Different Types of Influencer Marketing Campaigns*, Mediakix claims that there are probably a limitless amount of ways for brands to create effective influencer marketing campaigns, but, in general, these campaigns fall within one of the following five subcategories[379]:

1. Product Placement—this involves incorporating a company's product, services, or logo into a digital influencer's content just as it has been done in the film industry for decades. Just like actors in films, social media stars have earned the trust of their followers, so product placements are an excellent opportunity for brands to gain valuable exposure to millions of engaged consumers through the influencer's YouTube, yy.com, Instagram, Viner, or Snapchat account.
2. Contests, Giveaways, Sweepstakes—Hosting social media contests like giveaways, sweepstakes, or best-of contests, such as best photograph, video, or blog competitions can generate buzz about an airline, as well as foster goodwill among consumers. These contests compel social media users to take a specific action (like following the brand's channel or increasing company exposure by using branded hashtags). Aligning with a social media influencer, an airline can promote a contest that will leverage the social media star's large follower base and ensure that consumers participate in the campaign.
3. Theme/Hashtag Campaign—Hashtags are great ways to build a theme around a campaign. Focusing each influencer marketing campaign

around a central theme or hashtag that is leveraged throughout all of the social channels helps build cohesion and encourages consumers to get involved by using the brand's hashtag in their own content. As Mediakix recommends, "Developing and implementing an influencer marketing campaign around a memorable branded hashtag is one of the best ways brands can facilitate a genuine social conversation and increase brand exposure, especially if the hashtag happens to go viral."[379]

4. Creative Influencer Campaign—These give the social media star much more freedom to create content and these campaigns usually center around a specific concept or idea. Done right, these campaigns allow the digital influencer to interpret themes to create unique brand-sponsored content, leading to increased levels of engagement from the social media influencer's followers and/or subscribers.
5. Campaign to Build Social Followers—airlines can invite social media influencers to expose new audiences to their brand's social media accounts. Snapchat Takeovers—having a social media influencer "take over" a brand's Snapchat account for a set period of time—is one of the most effective ways for businesses to reach thousands or millions of new followers, as well as organically grow their own Snapchat follower fanbase.

Listening

In the *Listening* part, airlines should define and look out for triggers such as photos, hashtags, keywords, likes, video views, etc., etc. Hootsuite's *14 of the Best Social Media Monitoring Tools for Business*[380] lists some of the best tools for airlines to use for this listening step, including Reddit, Streamview, Reputology, and Synthesio, Crowd Analyzer, amongst others (see Table 21).

SERVICE	DESCRIPTION
Streamview for Instagram	With a community of over 700 million users it makes sense to monitor what people are posting on Instagram, especially if your audience falls in the 18 to 29 age range. With the Streamview for Instagram app you can monitor posts by location, hashtag, or username. The app within Hootsuite allows you to monitor and engage with users that are posting in your area, or an area you choose to follow. For example, you can use this tool during events to see what is being posted and to engage with attended.
Hootsuite Syndicator Pro	Manage and monitor all your favorite blogs and websites with Hootsuite Syndicator Pro. This tool provides a quick and easy way to view RSS feeds and quickly share them to your social media channels, as well as rich filtering, monitoring, and tracking tools. You can also track which stories you've shared.

Reputology	Online (and offline) reputation management is extremely important and surprisingly easy. The Reputology app lets you monitor and check major review sites, such as Yelp, Google, Facebook reviews, so that you can engage with reviewers and resolve any issues in a timely manner. You can track activity across multiple storefronts and locations and respond quickly via quick links.
Hootsuite Insights	Hootsuite Insights combines social media listening, analytics, and powerful social media monitoring capabilities. It allows you to gain powerful real-time insights about your brand, track influencers, stories, and trends, and visualize the metrics—all in one place. You can filter and tailor results by sentiment, platform, location, and language, and engage directly from your stream to take action on previously hidden results.
Brandwatch	The name says it all; the Brandwatch app in Hootsuite lets you keep watch over your brand through deep listening. You can identify key insights from more than 70 million traffic sources across the web, including major social channels, blogs, forums, news and review sites, and much more. This tool lets you make real-time, informed decisions and take action on them.
ReviewInc	Whether it's a positive or negative online review, your response should be in the same place as that review. The ReviewInc app for Hootsuite lets you view over 200 popular review sites across over 100 countries. Organize positive reviews for sharing on social media sites and resolve negative issues instantly.
Synthesio	Synthesio is a comprehensive social monitoring tool for finding the information you need to gain deeper insights and better inform business decisions. The tool lets you monitor multiple mention streams at once, so you can listen to the social media conversations most important to you. You can then analyze these conversations and join them.
Crowd Analyzer	If you or your customers are based in the Middle East, Crowd Analyzer is an invaluable analytics and social media monitoring tool. As the first Arabic-focused social media monitoring platform, Crowd Analyzer analyzes "Arabic content in terms of relevancy, dialect and sentiment." It not only monitors major social networks, but also blogs, forums, and news sites.
76Insights	If content marketing is an important aspect of your Facebook marketing strategy, consider 76Insights. This social media monitoring tool measures the resonance of your social media content and breaks down your resonance score, which measures how much social media engagement someone receives after publishing something.
Keyhole	Keyhole lets you see what's being said about you on Twitter and Instagram in real-time. You can monitor keywords, hashtags, URLs, and usernames, and see historical as well as real-time data. One cool

		feature is the heat maps that show you activity levels around the world.
Digimind		Digimind lets you track keywords in news outlets and social media platforms for mentions of your company in real-time. It also measures sentiment, so you can gauge whether what is being said about you is good, bad, or "meh." You can also compare how your company is perceived online against your competitors.
Google Alerts		Google Alerts lets you monitor the web for mentions of your company, your competitors, or other relevant topics. Just go to the Google Alerts page, type a keyword or phrase in the search box, and provide your email address to receive a notification every time Google finds results relevant to your alert criteria. You can set alerts for specific regions and languages.
Hootsuite		On top of all the social media monitoring tools mentioned above, Hootsuite Pro provides social listening capabilities right in the dashboard. Monitor specific keywords, hashtags, regions, and more. Stay on top of what people are saying about your brand and listen to your customers and competitors to gain competitive advantage.

Table 21: Hootsuite's Social Media Monitoring Tools
Source: *14 of the Best Social Media Monitoring Tools for Business*[380]

Airlines should also be listening to comment boards or short-term blogging sites like Tumblr or social news aggregation sites like Reddit for comments about their company and their services. Travelers are often happy to post wonderful reviews about their visits and purchases, and this is gold for word-of-mouth marketing, so airlines should do their best to motivate reviews.

Check-ins and geo-posts from sites like Foursquare, WeChat, Instagram, Facebook, WhatsApp, YouTube, as well as a whole host of other social networks can help airline operators connect with a nearby audience. Underlying these check-ins is a treasure-trove of collected data. As Aaron Gell explains in his *New Yorker* article *The Not-so-Surprising Survival of Foursquare*[381], "Foursquare's stockpile of location-data breadcrumbs has allowed the company to steadily augment its map of the world, and to test the fuzzy signals it receives from users' phones (the service gleans from G.P.S., Wi-Fi, and Bluetooth, and from other markers) against the eleven billion definitive check-ins provided by its users over the past seven years."

"According to Mike Boland, a chief analyst at the market-research firm BIA/Kelsey, Foursquare can now pinpoint a phone's location with an accuracy that matches, and may in some cases surpass, that of much larger rivals," notes Gell.[381] "Facebook has a much larger sample of data points," Boland says, but "Foursquare has more accurate and reliable data."[381] Foursquare claims its map now "includes more than a hundred million locations, many of them in tightly crowded areas, like office buildings and malls, that other services still struggle to identify."[381] "The accuracy of Foursquare's Places database has led more than a hundred thousand other apps and developers—including Snapchat, Twitter, Pinterest, Uber, and Microsoft—to use its application programming interface (A.P.I.) to power their own features," notes Gell.[381]

"A smart combination of listening to the online conversation already taking place, learning what people want, and then providing what they are open to receive from the brand constitutes the winning ticket," advises Macy and Thompson.[305]

Whether the engagement is through video, online polls, games, photo sharing, e-mail, blogging, PowerPoint presentations, or podcasting, "engagement strategies present an opportunity for brands to align content creation for social media with a company's priorities and involve cross-functional interaction and collaboration," state Macy and Thompson.[305] "Social media engagement can also be used for front-end campaigns and appearances to help guide the conversation and generate buzz," conclude Macy and Thompson.[305]

One trend airlines should be aware of is the penchant of users to utilize what is known as the "Dark social." As Nicole Teeters explains in her Adweek article *10 Social Media Trends Giving Brands New Ways to Engage in 2017*[49], "Users are tending to use Snapchat or messaging applications to share content, meaning that now, almost 70 percent of online shares are going on within so-called dark social (one-on-one social sharing that is happening where analytics tools cannot track it)."[49]

Rules Engine

The Rules Engine step is a pretty straightforward concept, airlines are already creating considerable business rules for their establishments and these rules should be extended to each company's defined rewards program, their reward's economy, and the marketing of the program. Rewards can be as simple as a reward for a store visit, a points threshold reached, a birthday or anniversary, loyalty card utilization, or reaching a spending tier. Reward rules engine must contain the conditions of the loyalty program, i.e., If the activity of a member fulfills the conditions, the loyalty engine executes the assigned rule actions, which could be giving the member a unique offer based on his or her spend.

Automation

One of the big benefits of automating campaigns is that offers based on either stated or inferred preferences of customers can be developed. Analysis can identify which customers may be more responsive to a particular offer. The result: more individualized offers are sent out to the airline's customers and, because these offers tap into a customer's wants, desires, needs *and* expectations, they are more likely to be used; more offers used mean more successful campaigns.

By understanding what type of customer is using its airline, why they are flying, and what they like to do in-flight, an airliner can individualize its marketing campaigns so that it can be more effective, thereby increasing the airline's ROI. "As customers gravitate towards one-on-one communication, brands should explore the use of social messaging to interact conversationally with customers, providing customer service or support while building relationships," Teeters recommends.[49]

Once the customer leaves the store, the marketing cycle begins anew. RFM models can project the time at which a customer is likely to return and social media should be checked for any comments, likes or uploads, left by a customer. All of a customer's captured information can now become part of the Master Marketing Profile that will be the basis for future marketing efforts. Combining the daily, weekly and monthly Master Marketing Profiles will also allow the airline to develop insightful macro views of its data, views that could help with facilities, labor management, and other needs as well.

Moderation

Moderating boards and UGC posts create a double whammy for airlines because, as Rachel Perlmutter explains in her article *Why You Need Social Proof on Your Website*.[382] Perlmutter believes that, "People need to see that others also enjoy that product. It's what we call social proof: the idea that buyers are influenced by the decisions and actions of others around them." Perlmutter offers the following reasons why it is so important to have UGC reviews on your site[382]:

- "Testimonials add credibility for the products and services you offer.
- People tend to trust online reviews when making purchases.
- Social proof earns better SEO: Adds more favorable language surrounding your brand online.
- When sourcing opinions from your client base, you show that you care about their experience with your brand, thus strengthening the relationship you have with your clients."[382]

Perlmutter states that airlines can gather testimonials in a variety of ways, including sending surveys to new clients.[382] Perlmutter also advises airlines to encourage buyers to post on social media.[382] Airlines should use hashtags to track customers' responses to the airline's products and services so they can be easily found and responded to.[382] Instagram should be a big part of an airline's strategy because testimonials with images trump text testimonials alone. Testimonials are powerful examples of social proof as well.[382]

Airlines shouldn't be afraid to send free products to people with large followings on platforms like Instagram, YouTube, etc. "Whether you want to call them social media influencers, bloggers, or local celebrities, consider getting meatier' testimonials from people who have already gained some amount of trust online," states Permitter.[382] "Some may ask for a small fee to review your product, but the return you get from their article, video post, Instagram picture, or even just their words and name listed on your site will likely be tremendous," advises Perlmutter.[382]

It's important to get instant reactions, too. Perlmutter recommends that "If you host events, then you have the prime opportunity to gather testimonials from attendees right on the spot."[382] Don't be afraid to set up a camera right outside the event space and ask participants to provide their opinions on the spot.[382]

Messaging

In her Digiday article *How Facebook is wooing luxury brands*[383], Bethany Biron writes that "Facebook is advocating for 'digitally influenced sales,' that assist consumers with the discovery process while still driving them to e-commerce sites and physical stores, said Narain Jashanmal, industry manager of retail at Facebook. This concept has helped major retailers like Barneys break out of the traditional retail rut and embrace e-commerce."

In her article *Engage Customers and Gain Advocates Through Social Media and Social Networking*[384], Wendy Neuberger argues that: "Social commerce is about making a retailer's brand a destination. Retailers really need to listen to what their customers are saying. Customers can provide valuable input and feedback that can be used to make more informed assortment decisions, changes to website features and enhancements to the shopping experience." What's good for the retail industry in this case is also good for the airline industry.

"When customers feel their voice is being heard, they feel a stronger connection to the retailer and are more likely to become advocates."[384] Neuberger claims it is important for airlines to identify and engage with the key influencers for several reasons, the two most important being: "to empower their advocacy or capabilities, which helps build and foster a sense of community among brand loyalists, and empowers those loyalists to better advocate on behalf of a brand, product and/or service."[384]

Neuberger recommends that airlines use the following social media platforms[384]:

- Blogs: airlines can provide additional product or category information here as well as post how-to information in the form of text, photos and/or videos. Airlines should also provide space for customers to add feedback and/or comments about their retailing experience.
- Micro-blogging: coupons, sales and promotions can be offered through these channels. Airlines can "'tweet press releases, provide exclusive tips and tricks to customers, and ask for customer feedback, suggestions or ideas for improvements. Some airlines even use Twitter as a customer service mechanism."[384]

- Co-Shopping: this is a form of social shopping and it enables two people—a customer and sales associate or two shoppers in different locations—to share a joint shopping session using live instant messaging such as Skype, WeChat or any number of other OTT services.
- Widgets: these are tiny applications that can be embedded into a website, blog or social network that are portable and relatively inexpensive to create.
- Social Bridging: anyone who has signed into a website using their Facebook, Pinterest or Twitter account knows what social bridging is. "This level of authentication provides enough credentials to participate in the social elements of the site. Additional authentication is required to complete a shopping transaction due to the sensitivity of the content included in a shopper's account. Social bridging can be used to drive traffic and engage existing and new customers. It can access a user's identity, their social graph, and stream activities such as purchases and other social participation on the retailer's site" says Neuberger.[384]
- In-Store Kiosks and Flat Panels can be provided to enable customers to use social networking tools from within a store.[384]

In her article Facebook wants to become the new mobile storefront, unveils new ad tools for brands and airlines, Tanya Dua states that Facebook is trying again to establish itself as a true shopping outlet. Facebook "believes it can play a unique role in the shopping world—helping people both discover new products and make decisions when they're ready to buy."[48]

"Facebook believes that because people spend so much time on its mobile app, it can lay claim to being able to help marketers pitch their products before people know they even want them (like TV) and then help people find products when they know they're ready to pull the trigger on purchases (like Google and Amazon)," notes Dua.[48]

"Facebook wants to be a solution not just at the very bottom of the marketing funnel for solutions like retargeting, we actually want to create new purchase intent and consideration further up," said Graham Mudd, product marketing director at Facebook.[48] "If you look at 20 to 30 years ago, that was actually done through broadcast media but in a feed-based environment we have the opportunity to do that in a much more relevant way," adds Mudd.[48]

Facebook might be onto something here as its own research has shown that shoppers increasingly rely on Facebook and Instagram to find and purchase products."[48] Facebook claims that, "Mobile-first shoppers in the U.S. are 1.7 times more likely to get inspiration for gifts or shopping ideas on Facebook, and 2.5 times more likely to research gift or shopping ideas on Instagram."[48]

In 2018 and beyond, video will drive more online sales. When Facebook surveyed 20,824 mobiles shoppers across 17 markets, 30% of them said they preferred to discover new products via video."[48] This is why the "company is enhancing its dynamic ads feature, which allows brands and retailers to upload videos to show-off their products catalogues, instead of just static images."[48]

According to Dua, "Dynamic ads automatically promote products to people who have expressed some interest in a brand, whether on its website, in its app or anywhere else on the internet. The new video feature in dynamic ads has already been trailed by retailers like made.com."[48]

"Facebook has also introduced overlays for dynamic ads, a product which enable brands to add price tags and visuals into their dynamic ads, touting discounts and other offers. Among the airlines that have tested the feature include boxed.com" adds Dua.[48]

One other item that should be noted, Facebook will now let brands target consumers on Facebook based on households, rather than just as individuals.[48] According to Dua, "Facebook will allow marketers to create a new 'household audience,' which enables marketers to target to family members in the same household, with the idea being to inspire members of their audience's household to purchase."[48] Facebook believes that advertisers will be able to "measure the impact of these ads, including whether they influence household members who didn't actually see the ads to make purchases."[48]

Snapchat should also be a part of every airline's social media marketing options, as it was for Lufthansa in 2017. As explained in Alexander Neely's article *Lufthansa Customer Engagement Soars with Snapchat Campaign*[385], "Lufthansa wanted to engage consumers by turning the camera on their own employees, by giving them an authentic, unfiltered window into the world of airline travel." The challenge was figuring out the which was the platform to reach its customers.[385]

As Neely explains, "Currently, Lufthansa operates services to 18 domestic destinations and 197 international destinations in 78 countries across Africa, the Americas, Asia, and Europe, using a fleet of more than 270 aircraft. And, in an effort to show consumers the work that goes into such an extensive airline program, Lufthansa decided the best way to launch a brand experiment for consumer engagement would be on Snapchat."[385]

In September 2016, the German airline launched "Lufthansa Crew Stories", which delivered "an intimate, behind-the-scenes window into the airline's crew members."[385] "From flight preparation, to lift off, to landing, Snapchat users would now be able to follow the crew to gain a greater respect for the career, learn about different destinations, and become 'closer to the Lufthansa family.'"[385]

Daniel Abt, marketing executive at Lufthansa, says "the company also wanted to focus on connecting with the consumer on a personal level."[385] "Some examples of crew stories included a A380 flight from Frankfurt to Los Angeles, where the crew takes you inside the crew's hidden quarters in the belly of the plane; and Crew Story to Cape Town, which is is told by a Lufthansa flight attendant who grew up in South Africa and includes a personal, guided tour of the destination."[385] "We wanted to give our consumers a perspective of the crew to inspire them to travel, and perhaps even consider certain airlines' employment," says Abt.[385]

The marketing campaign was a huge success. Lufthansa experienced "positive feedback from its employees, but the results from the consumer were even more impressive."[385] "Since the launch of Lufthansa Crew Stories, the company has experienced an 800% increase in Snap views," claims Neely.[385] And, according to Abt, "the retention rate is very strong and viewership of each episode of a crew's story is relatively constant."[385]

"We are extremely excited to have such a successful campaign," says Abt, "But I am even more curious to see what we are going to do in the future as social media continues to develop."[385]

"There is a shift in the way brands engage with their customers," argues Calcaño.[247] "Brands are now expected to produce interesting content, entertain, and provide value beyond their product offerings. Snapchat is the best example of this. Brands have to become people—a Snapchat user in this case—just like everyone else," notes Calcaño.[247] "And the communication is no longer from the position of an advertiser, but more a conversation where brands have to listen as much as they talk," adds Calcaño.[247]

"The challenge here is spontaneity. Snapchat offers brands the opportunity to show their 'behind-the-scenes,' be real and less posed. Customers, especially millennials, can smell a fake from across the web," concludes Calcaño.[247]

In his article *Snapchat seeks salvation in long form and "Hands-on" AR ads*[49], Josh Constine states that "Together, these new formats could make Snap's ads less skippable and more memorable, coaxing money out of businesses hoping to make a mark on premier audience of US teens." "Both Promoted Stories and AR Trial ads go a step beyond what Facebook can offer but could soon be copied like the rest of Snapchat," Constine adds.[49]

In the past, Snapchat's ads were either "single Snap ads inserted between Stories or Discover content that could easily be skipped with a single tap, or sponsored creative tools that let you try on goofy masks or project 3D mascots into the world but that didn't offer much utility."[49] Constine argues that these ads, which, in some cases were quite juvenile, may have left advertisers skeptical about the lasting impact on buying behavior.[49]

"Our advertising partners have been asking for ways to tell deeper stories on mobile" Snap's Director of Revenue Product Peter Sellis told TechCrunch in a statement.[49] According to Constine, "HBO is piloting the format with Promoted

Stories about why you should stay in and watch Game Of Thrones on Black Friday, while in Europe clothing brand ASOS highlights 'night-out worthy looks.'"[49]

"These Promoted Stories are labeled 'ad', get their own preview tile, and are purchased on a full-country one-day takeover basis with users having to actively tap to view."[49] Advertisers receive a range of analytics from preview tile impression through to conversions.[49] The numbers are actually quite impressive: "Snap says it can reach 88 million people in the US with Promoted Stories, surpassing the 74 million Instagram Stories users, and approaching half as many as Facebook's 190 million mobile audience members."[49] For the coveted youths 13 to 24 demographic, "Snap reaches 47 million people—supposedly 9 million more than Facebook and 15 million more than Instagram's feed."[49]

"We wanted to insert ourselves in an organic way into the Snapchat environment and its users' world. That is the most meaningful way to address our fans in a style that fits the channel" head of Digital Marketing Jörg Poggenpohl told *TechCrunch*.[49] "A previous BMW sponsored face lens ad in Europe reached 13 million Snapchatters who played with it for an average of 24 seconds," Constine notes.[49]

"That's the magic of these AR ads," Constine says, adding "Even if you never share the content with friends, you still get extended exposure to the brand just playing with the selfie mask or 3D objects."[49] "Actually resizing and walking around a car company's vehicle will probably leave a bigger impact than just scrolling past some Facebook News Feed display ad. If you reshare that content in private messages or Stories, BMW gets bonus exposure to people who see the brand enmeshed with their friends' content, so they don't just skip past it like the banners we've all grown numb to."[49]

In her article *Whatsapp For Business—What Does It Mean?*[386], Holly Turner explains that in August 2017, "WhatsApp announced it was experimenting with verified business accounts on the platform, which would offer brands the opportunity to communicate with its users; a platform the average user checks 23 times a day and which boasts 1.2 billion monthly active users."

"Businesses can gain a verified green checkmark icon to indicate the authenticity of the account, assuring users its legitimacy, alongside opening the door to the platform's previously walled off garden," Turner adds.[386]

"The platform could be following in the footsteps of other messaging apps such as Facebook Messenger and Kik, implementing a chatbot function to enable WhatsApp users to ask businesses questions, make purchases and receive instant bot responses."[386]

The opportunity is considerable. WhatsApp business accounts offer up one more channel for brands to send out simple automated messaging to users who opt into their messages.[386] "Whether it be discount codes, new products or brand news, users could stay up to date with businesses they invest in and brands would be presented with the opportunity to reach people on a platform that, sees 6 out of 10 users accessing the app on a daily basis," argues Turner.[386]

WhatsApp's history will work in its favor. Having never allowed any form of advertising previously, WhatsApp currently feels like a very intimate and private environment for its users.[386] Turner believes that "content delivered to users would, therefore, benefit from having an 'organic' feel; providing useful and totally personalised content."[386]

A good example of the potential can be seen in the Nike On Demand WhatsApp service.[386] It is a one-to-one messenger-based service that was "created to connect athletes with Nike experts on a regular basis to keep them motivated and on-track with their fitness goals."[386] The campaign delivers "personalised content in the form of images, conversation, playlists, etc. as well as providing expert advice from pacers and trainers all through the WhatsApp platform, akin to a real peer's motivational reminder," explains Turner.[386]

"Whether WhatsApp intends to follow the crowd by implementing a chatbot strategy or go against the grain to offer users something truly useful and personalised will soon become clear," adds Turner. "What is already very clear, however, is the opportunity WhatsApp business accounts presents, regardless of what strategy they choose, to reach inside the walled gardens of messaging apps," Turner concludes.

In the future, it is likely that all marketing will become interactive and the consumer will become a participant rather than a "target audience". As Shar VanBoskirk states in his article *US Interactive Marketing Forecast, 2007 To 2012*[387], "Instead of planning for a set 'search budget' or an 'online video campaign', marketers will instead organize around 'persona planning'–that is, they will plan around generating a desired response from a customer type. In response to changing customer behavior, channel optimization will take place on the fly, shifting between channels dynamically."

Airlines can use social media to manage their brand, enhance brand loyalty, as well as engage both their current customers and their potential customers. The social media world is also the perfect place to harvest customer feedback, provide real-time customer service, build fanbases, and drive traffic to an airline's website.

Blogs and micro-blogging sites are also important mobile and social media channels and airlines should monitor Twitter feeds for both their satisfied and dissatisfied customers.

Airlines should also feel compelled to reward their customers through Facebook, Twitter, WeChat, and Weibo or any number of blogging and micro-blogging services. The beauty of using these channels is the ability of the customer to share these awards or stories of these awards with friends and contacts. It wouldn't be that hard to do, either, as an airline can ask customers for their social media accounts upon sign up.

Jones and Sasser warn that, "Extremely dissatisfied customers can turn into 'terrorists,' providing an abundance of negative feedback about the service provider."[75] Through social media channels, negative feedback can reverberate around the world within seconds. Today, more than ever, airlines must spot dissatisfied customers and approach them before they do irreparable harm to the company's image and reputation and social media is one of the best channels in which to engage them.

In the *zone of indifference*, customers willingly switch if they can find a better alternative, while in the *zone of affection*, satisfaction levels are high and "customers may have such high attitudinal loyalty that they don't look for alternative services."[75] It is within this group that "Apostles"—members who praise the firm in public—reside and this is the group that is responsible for improved future business performance.[62]

Airlines need to empower their customers to post on Facebook or WeChat or Twitter or comment about their experience and, hopefully, turn them into apostles. A simple search of the Twitter feed on the multiple services I mentioned in the previous chapters will probably reveal a list of customers who could be courted for social marketing purposes.

Facebook should be a part of every airline's social and mobile media marketing plan, but simply putting up a Facebook page won't cut it these days; creativity and uniqueness are needed to get noticed in today's highly competitive social media world. Gamification is also a good way to stand out from the crowd. Facebook bots can also add a customer service channel that can answer common customer service questions quickly, efficiently and inexpensively. The best part of being on Twitter or Weibo or any of the other instant messaging services is the ability to interact with a customer in real time. A direct, two-way dialogue can be created, which helps with engagement and, probably, sales.

Data & Analytics

In this final section of the customer journey, airlines should "acquire social identity tied to customer records" and figure 26 shows how the airline can close the circle on going from the anonymous customer to known one.

Neuberger argues that it is very important to monitor the market conversation to understand what the marketplace is (or isn't) saying about an airline (their brand, products, services, etc.).[384] companies "need to understand the tone and impact of the conversation and begin to identify areas of opportunity for helping shape that conversation and gather valuable market intelligence," says

Neuberger.[384]

As previously mentioned ROI is not that tricky of a thing to measure with social media, quite the contrary. Today, the endless search for Facebook fans should be replaced by short-term campaign ROI as the main measure for individual campaigns. Airlines should look at correlation analysis between activities, engagement and sales, which might be unsettling for some traditional marketers, but the reward should be worth the time and the effort.[46] "The explicit use of active and control groups, and experimentation of using different treatments will help marketers understand the impact of specific SM activities."[46] More direct marketing type disciplines will be required, in a world where there is real-time feedback on attitude and behavior and a plethora of data."[46] This has become a much more demanding world in terms of capturing and utilizing all of this data, but making the effort to turn this data into actionable intelligence will be noticed by fickle consumers, I have no doubt.

Figure 26: Customer funnel

Airlines should look to assign a percentage value to social media so that a true attribution measurement can be created. Values should be ascribed to social media for being the site of new customer contact or for numbers of positive reviews by current customers. These are all important metrics to know because a highly followed influencer might not be spending that much on your airline, but their followers might be.

For Neuberger, "Social media metrics include sentiment, activity, share-of-voice, and thematic content of online conversations. Trends and key influencers ("mavens") and the most active sites/blogs are identified and tracked. By understanding the impact, airlines will have a way of identifying measurable progress, quantifying the return on social media investment, and enabling benchmarking against future efforts."[384]

In her article *Personalization Is Key to Converting Airlines' Mobile Traffic Into Bookings, Qubit Finds*[388], Stephanie Taylor writes that, "As part of a Qubit survey, over 4,000 consumers were asked which factors were most likely to encourage them to make a purchase on their phone. 'Finding exactly what I want more easily' and 'Easier to discover new products that I like' were the second and third most popular responses after "A faster or easier browsing experience.'"

"Daniel Bensley, Qubit's industry lead for Travel, attributes this to the fact that platforms like Netflix, Instagram, Spotify and Pinterest are re-wiring consumer expectations by using machine learning to guide visitors to content that is individually curated. He believes this kind of personalization is now essential to a brand's long-term success," says Taylor.[388]

"Much like the aforementioned media platforms, airlines offer a seemingly endless number of choices and products, so they're well-placed to cater to a broad range of customer needs. However, Qubit's March 2018 report highlighted that 'in 65% of cases, larger catalogs don't translate into explorable catalogs, meaning that often, the larger the range of products, the harder it is for users to find what they're looking for,'" warns Taylor.[388]

"Talking specifically about airlines, Bensley says that the booking process must take into account what 'state' the customer is in: 'Their state is important because the same person booking for business during the day could be booking a family holiday for leisure in the evening.'"[388]

"Successful brands are able to collect intent and preference-based information from customers as they engage and interact. Short interactive surveys and quick questions can provide data for airlines to then quickly act upon and be able to serve a relevant offer, promotion or user journey," adds Bensley.[388]

Bensley recommends airlines act on intent in such areas as "flexi-fares for business travelers; promoting trending ancillaries for each booker segment (e.g. family/couple/solo traveler); advising customers when remaining seats available are becoming scarce. The key is to focus on relevance to the customer at all times."[388]

The same techniques apply for web traffic. In a case study on Thomas Cook Airlines, Qubit said it used 'social proof messaging' tailored to specific routes.[388] "When the carrier started highlighting what other customers on the same route are buying – 'it could be that customers booking flights for ski destinations are buying insurance, whereas customers on longer-haul flights buy meals for the plane,' the study clarifies – it saw a 1.6 percent increase in purchases," Taylor notes.[388]

"For Bensley, the good news is that machine learning will allow personalization to keep improving," says Taylor.[388] "We're already seeing successful examples of airlines tying historical booking data with onsite behavioral data in order to provide more relevance to the customer," Taylor says.[388] "We believe that personalization will become more intelligent as time goes on and will be based on more data sources from across the business which add further context or value," Taylor concludes.[388]

The Future

The industry, IATA believes, faces several long-term challenges, many of which are in the hands of governments throughout the world.[1] It is hard to argue with IATA's assessment that, "Aviation is the business of freedom and a catalyst for growth and development."[1] "The benefits of aviation are compelling—2.7 million direct jobs and critical support for 3.5% of global economic activity. And the industry is ready to partner with governments to reinforce the foundations for global connectivity that are vital to modern life," said de Juniac.[1] "To continue to deliver on our full potential," de Juniac believes, "governments need to raise their game—implementing global standards on security, finding a reasonable level of taxation, delivering smarter regulation and building the cost-efficient infrastructure to accommodate growing demand."[1] With these structures in place, the global airline industry should thrive, and *The Predictive Airliner* should really take off.

The Predictive Airliner—an airline company that considers how a customer who walks through the door of an airline's retail outlet or a web surfer browsing to the airline's website will affect every facet of the airline's business.

The Predictive Airliner follows a customer before arrival, through his or her entire trip, then keeps tabs on him or her once the trip is over. As Kahle states, eventually we're going to set a time frame on the sales funnel that never expires.[67] The process starts at the moment of first contact, when the airline's systems spots the IP address of a web browser, through capturing the social ID, to understanding the social activity, all the way through to the loyalty card sign up process. The only thing remaining is to capture post-transaction information if and when it comes in.

Besides Apple and Google, Facebook is now entering the acquisition business full throttle. Along with its Instagram buy, the Oculus Rift purchase further shows that Facebook is obsessed with staying relevant by buying the next big thing argues Paul Berry, founder and CEO of New York City-based social publishing platform RebelMouse.[389] "Through this and other acquisitions, Berry thinks Facebook will become a brand-holding company in the future, similar to Viacom or Hearst."[389] "I see them, better than anyone else, using their market capitalization to create even bigger market cap for the Instagrams or WhatsApps," he says.[389]

The purchase of Oculus Rift should help Facebook grab a large piece of the advertising market.[389] In five years, Arvind Bhatia, managing director of equity research at Sterne Agee, expects Facebook's "graph search to become bigger, and the company to make more inroads in e-commerce."[389] "Then, with its ancillary networks like WhatsApp and Instagram, Facebook will be able to run its own platform, rather than operate through Android and iOS."[389] "They are being bypassed on the mobile platform," Bhatia says. "They want to be the next Android, and so the only way to do that was to start from scratch, and that's what they're doing with this virtual reality technology."[389]

Just as Facebook might morph into a complex conglomeration of services and brands, Twitter should continue to differentiate itself through its simplicity.[389] First, the network has to focus on monetization, and in "Berry's view, over the next five years Twitter's monetization will be faster than its user adoption."[389] "They are so simple and so public, and it works so much data around what you are interested in—the fact that it's all public is perfect for advertising," Berry says.[389] "I think it achieves being the short, public, status updates of the Internet," Berry adds.[389]

Meanwhile, Twitter's decelerating growth worries Bhatia. "While he thinks the network will continue to grow, he believes it won't equal Facebook's user base."[389] "And already Instagram is catching up," he says.[389] "While Facebook is going to become one of the four horsemen of technology, Twitter will be an interesting, decent-sized company, but not a mainstay, if you will."[389] What really sets Twitter apart is its openness.[389] "As data science continues to boom, this openness will give Twitter increasing utility, and because of this he sees the long-shot possibility that the service gets bought out by a giant organization, like the United Nations, for dissemination and collection of data on a scale never imagined."[389]

With their *Cluetrain Manifesto*[324], Rick Levine, Christopher Lock, Doc Searle, and David Weinberger warned that not only are markets conversations but the Internet is revolutionizing the way businesses communicate with their customers and if businesses don't adapt and treat their customers with respect, their customers will desert them. What better way to treat them with respect than to listen to them and respond accordingly, which mobile and social media channels do better than any other form of communication.

In their paper *Marketing Analytics for Data-Rich Environments*[81], Webel and Kannan, argue that there are many promising areas of research that businesses should keep on their radar. The technological developments of tomorrow might just be some of the ones discussed in Table 22.

DATA	DETAILS
Structured data	• Behavioral targeting with cross-device data; mobile, location-based, and social analytics. • Fusing data generated within the firm with data generated outside the firm; integrating "small stats. • Combining machine learning approaches with econometric and theory-based methods for big data applications; computational solutions to marketing models for big data.
Unstructured data	• Development of diagnostic, predictive, and prescriptive approaches for analysis of large-scale unstructured data. • Approaches to analyze unstructured social, geo-spatial, mobile data and combining them with structured data in big data contexts. • Using, evaluating, and extending deep learning methods and cognitive computing to analyze unstructured marketing data.
Marketing-mix modeling	• Aligning analysis of disaggregate data with that of aggregate data and including unstructured data in the analysis of the marketing mix. • New techniques and methods to accurately measure the impact of marketing instruments and their carryover and spillover across media and devices using integrated path-to-purchase data. • Dynamic, multi–time period and cross-category optimization of the marketing mix. • Approaches to incorporate different planning cycles for different marketing instruments in media-mix models.
Personalization	• Automated closed-loop marketing solutions for digital environments; fully automated marketing solutions. • Personalization and customization techniques using cognitive systems, general artificial intelligence, and automated attention analysis; personalization of content. • Mobile, location-based personalization of the marketing mix.
Security and privacy	• Methods to produce and handle data minimization and data anonymization in assessing marketing-mix effectiveness and personalization. • Distributed data solutions to enhance data security and privacy while maximizing personalized marketing opportunities.

Table 22: Area of Focus Promising and Important Issues for Research

In Greek mythology, once Pandora's box was opened and the evils of the world were let out, the only thing remaining inside was hope. It Is my hope that this book helps businesses avoid a Pandora's box full of pain that IT implementations can create if done incorrectly.

It is also my hope that this book helps narrow the gap between what businesses think they are delivering in terms of customer experience and what customers think they are delivering. Currently, the chasm is wide, and improvement is needed immediately.

Many of technology discussed in this book require considerable time, effort, and money to implement, but if companies are willing to go down the personalization, real-time streaming, and data lake road properly, I have no doubt they will be richly rewarded.

---

377 Bachman, Justin. (2018) These Are the Best Frequent-Flyer Programs. Bloomberg. 15 August 2018. https://www.bloomberg.com/news/articles/2018-08-15/these-are-the-best-frequent-flyer-programs (Accessed 15 August 2018).
378 Gourévitch, Antoine, Faeste, Lars, Baltasis, Elias, and Marx, Julien. May 23, 2017. Data-Driven Transformation: Accelerate at Scale Now. Boston Consulting Group. https://www.bcg.com/en-in/publications/2017/digital-transformation-transformation-data-driven-transformation.aspx (Accessed 8 September 2017).
379 The 5 Different Types of Influencer Marketing Campaigns. March 30, 2016. Mediakix.com. http://mediakix.com/2016/03/influencer-marketing-campaigns-5-examples/#gs.Lz0k6B4 (Accessed 13 November 2017).
380 Mathison, Rob. Hootsuite. (2017). 14 of the Best Social Media Monitoring Tools for Business. August 14, 2017. https://blog.hootsuite.com/social-media-monitoring-tools/ (Accessed 23 November 2017).
381 Gell, Aaron. (2017) The Not-so-Surprising Survival of Foursquare. The New Yorker. March 1, 2017. https://www.newyorker.com/business/currency/the-not-so-surprising-survival-of-foursquare (Accessed 23 November 2017).
382 Perlmutter, Rachel. (2016) Why You Need Social Proof on Your Website. Entrepreneur.com. July 6, 2016. https://www.entrepreneur.com/article/296644 (Accessed 23 November 2017).
383 Biron, Bethany. (2017). How Facebook is wooing luxury brands. Digiday. https://digiday.com/media/bringing-retail-speed-feed-facebooks-quest-court-luxury-brands/ (Accessed 24 November 2017).
384 Neuberger, W. (n.d.). Engage Customers and gain advocates through social media and social networking. January 24, 2013. ftp://public.dhe.ibm.com/software/solutions/soa/newsletter/2010/newsletter-mar10-article_social_media.pdf (Accessed 13 November 2017).
385 Neely, Alexander. (2017). Lufthansa Customer Engagement Soars with Snapchat Campaign. Data Strategy Technology. 18 May 2017.
386 Turner, Holly. 2017. Whatsapp For Business—What Does it Mean? M&C Satchi Mobile. http://www.mcsaatchimobile.com/whatsapp-business-mean/ (Accessed 23 November 2017).
387 VanBoskirk, S. (2007). US Interactive Marketing Forecast, 2007 To 2012 for Interactive Marketing Professionals. Forrester Research.

388 Taylor, Stephanie. (2018). Personalization Is Key to Converting Airlines' Mobile Traffic Into Bookings, Qubit Finds. Apex.aero. 29 May 2018. https://apex.aero/2018/05/29/personalization-key-converting-airlines-mobile-traffic-bookings (Accessed 13 August 2018).

389 Pullen, J. P. (2014, April 2). What Will Social Media's Giants Look Like in 5 or 10 years? Retrieved from fortune.com: http://fortune.com/2014/04/02/what-will-social-medias-giants-look-like-in-5-or-10-years/ (Accessed 13 November 2017).

ABOUT THE AUTHOR

ANDREW PEARSON was born in Pakistan, grew up in Singapore, and was educated in both England and America. With a degree in psychology from UCLA, Pearson has had a varied career in IT, marketing, mobile technology, social media, and entertainment.

In 2011, Pearson relocated from Los Angeles to Hong Kong to open Qualex Asia Limited, bringing its parent company's software consulting experience into the ASEAN region.

In 2016, Pearson founded his own consulting company, Intelligencia Limited, and he is currently the managing director of the company. Intelligencia is a leading analytics, BI, CI, digital marketing and social media company, implementing complex CX, AI, analytics and digital marketing solutions for clients like The Venetian Macau, Galaxy Macau, Genting HK, Tatts Lottery, Resorts World Casino New York, Mexico's Logrand Group, Junglee Games, and Macau Slot.

In 2010, Pearson published *The Mobile Revolution*, and, in 2013, Pearson was invited to write a chapter in *Global Mobile: Applications and Innovations for the Worldwide Mobile Ecosystem*, a book on mobile technology. The book, which was co-authored by several of the mobile industry's leading figures, was published in July 2013. The first in the *Predictive* series—*The Predictive Casino*—was published in 2017, and *The Predictive Sports Book*, *The Predictive Retailer*, and *The Predictive Airliner* followed. There are plans to tackle several other industries in 2018 and 2019.

Pearson is also a noted columnist, authoring articles on such topics such as AI, mobile technology, social, predictive analytics, real-time stream processing, esports, and cloud technology. Pearson has written for such publications as *ComputerWorld HK*, *The Mobile Marketer*, and *The Journal of Mobile and Social Media Marketing*, where he is also a contributing editor. Pearson is the president of the *Advanced Analytics Association of Macau* and one of the founders of *Grow uP eSports*, a Macau association that promotes esports throughout the world.

An avid traveler, Pearson is a sought-after speaker on such disparate topics as AI and Machine Learning, deep learning, gaming, social media, and esports. If he's not pounding the pavements of Hollywood, he's probably wandering the labyrinthine streets of Hong Kong's Lang Kwai Fong, or tearing up useless betting slips at Happy Valley (perhaps the most perfectly named racecourse in the world (for some)), or haggling in a street market in Hyderabad, or dining at a hawker center in Singapore, or marveling at the historical importance of Moscow's Red Square, or doubling down at the gaming tables in Macau. Basically, Pearson's out there trying to find the next great story that the world doesn't yet know that it desperately wants to see…

Social Media
LinkedIn: andrew-pearson-96513a3
Amazon Author Central: https://www.amazon.com/Andrew-Pearson/e/B005M5ACG0
Twitter: intelligenciaMD
Academia: PearsonAndrew
Blog: medium.com/@intelligentsiaf

ANDREW PEARSON

INDEX

51.com, 201
56.com, 249
A/B Testing, 153
Activity tracing, 86
Adobe, 46, 48, 49, 61, 62, 86, 179, 180, 181, 190, 211, 276
Advertising
  banner ads, 82
AI, 7, 14, 15, 43, 45, 49, 100, 105, 130, 132, 133, 134, 135, 137, 138, 139, 140, 145, 156, 157, 158, 160, 237, 377, 378
Air Canada, 24, 98, 99
Amazon, 8, 18, 19, 25, 45, 49, 51, 66, 68, 105, 134, 158, 236, 334, 350, 359, 376, 384, 401
American Express, 297
Analytics
  descriptive analytics, 10, 13, 143
  diagnostic analytics, 10, 13, 143, 144
  edge analytics, 12, 173, 364
  predictive analytics, 8, 10, 12, 13, 46, 68, 114, 115, 123, 143, 144, 145, 173, 177, 180, 415
  prescriptive analytics, 10, 13, 143, 145, 364
  Text analytics, 124
App store, 222
Apple, 88, 249
Ashton, Kevin, 15, 284
Astra beer, 97
Attribution analysis, 27, 115, 125, 126, 193, 309
Augmented reality, 367, 368, 369, 370, 380
  wearables, 368
Baidu, 212, 213
Bebo, 189
Behavioral information, 69
Behavioral patterns, 67
Bellamy III, Woodrow, 6, 7, 9, 10, 43, 327, 328, 329, 369, 370

Big Data, 7, 9, 10, 14, 16, 17, 18, 19, 26, 40, 41, 42, 60, 100, 147, 183, 309, 351, 356, 364, 365
Blogging, 189, 219, 292
  list of sites, 217
Blogosphere, 215, 268, 293
Blogroll, 214
Blogs, 36, 189, 261, 292
Bluetooth, 89
Boeing, 6, 329, 392
Bookmarking, 189
Bookmarking websites
  Delicious.com, 189
Brand management, 252
  Apostles, 55, 65, 277, 406
Bwin.party, 332
Caesars, 60, 61, 62, 179, 180
Caffe2, 74, 136, 140, 141
Campaign management, 68, 116, 307, 357
Carroll, Dave, 282
Casino Engagement and Loyalty Platform, 70
Chatbots, 134, 135
Chauhan, Alok S., 155
China
  Confucian society, 202
  mobile subscriber count, 201
  social media subscribers, 201
Chinese
  mindset, 203
Chinese Mind, The, 202
Cicso, 308
Classification of Social Media, 192
clickstream, 86, 114, 122, 123, 144, 178
Clickstream, 23, 86, 106
Clickstream analysis, 27, 177
Click-thrus, 82
Cloud computing, 83
Cluetrain Manifesto, The, 308, 352
Cntv.cn, 249
Collaborative projects, 36

list of websites, 212
Collaborative Projects, 377
Common Short Codes, 88
Concept of self-presentation, 192
Consumer-Generated Media, 190
   blogs, 191
   digital video, 191
   mobile phone photography, 191
   news, 191
   online encyclopedias, 191
   podcasting, 191
   user reviews, 191
Content communities, 36
   List of sites, 225
Content management, 189
CRM, 10, 21, 22, 27, 32, 45, 49, 52, 53, 54, 55, 56, 57, 62, 64, 67, 70, 85, 145, 235, 252, 261, 316, 355
CrowdOptic, 367
CSC, 31, 88
Cultural exchanges, 86, 105
Customer Acquisition Model, 164
Customer analytics, 29, 84, 114, 115, 116, 117, 118, 119, 120, 121, 122, 123, 124, 174, 297, 305, 317, 393
Customer behavior, 21, 22, 29, 84, 119, 393
Customer Centric Relationship Management, 56
Customer churn, 28, 55, 64, 65, 70, 114, 120, 123, 171, 174, 184, 251
Customer Churn Model, 170
Customer Conversion Model, 168
Customer dissatisfaction, 65, 70, 277
Customer journey, 67
Customer Loyalty, 63, 66, 73, 120, 122, 124, 167, 231, 357
Customer satisfaction, 65, 70, 277
Customer segmentation, 114, 163
Customer's Psychological Profile, 287
Das Magazin, 287
Data lake, 11, 12, 13, 17, 18, 19, 23, 51
Decision tree
   construction of, 147
Decision Trees, 146
Deep Learning, 136, 140, 141, 351
Deeplearning4j, 141, 142, 350
Deighton, John A., 83, 86, 105
Delicious.com, 210

Dell, 266, 308
   Digital Nomads Campaign, 266
   social media command center, 308
Deloitte, 368
Delta, 4, 24, 291
Deng, Xiaoping, 202
Digital Interactive Marketing: The Five Paradigms, 86
Discriminant Analysis, 160
Disney, 38, 39, 96
   MagicBand, 38
Domino's Social Media Crisis, 285
Drury, Glen, 189, 190
Dushinski, Kim, 88
Eckerson, Wayne, 69
Economist, The, 214
Eddie Rickenbacker, 1
Emarsys, 31, 32
Facebook, 11, 23, 25, 27, 33, 37, 38, 39, 53, 54, 55, 60, 61, 71, 72, 74, 76, 77, 78, 84, 88, 91, 94, 95, 96, 97, 98, 105, 123, 124, 125, 134, 137, 140, 141, 177, 189, 191, 193, 198, 199, 200, 201, 204, 205, 207, 211, 216, 218, 222, 223, 224, 228, 229, 230, 231, 233, 234, 238, 240, 241, 248, 252, 253, 254, 255, 261, 262, 266, 268, 269, 275, 276, 277, 278, 281, 287, 288, 289, 290, 291, 293, 295, 296, 300, 301, 308, 309, 311, 312, 313, 314, 315, 316, 337, 338, 350, 353, 356, 376, 384, 394, 396, 397, 400, 401, 402, 403, 404, 405, 406, 407, 409, 410
Facial recognition, 28, 94, 95, 96
Flickr, 189
Flume, 345, 346, 347, 348
folksonomy, 210
Ford, 298
Forrester Research, 29, 30
Four Steps of Social Media, The, 206
   create, 208
   join, 207
   listening, 206
   participating, 208
Foursquare, 71, 91, 92, 94, 175, 200, 205, 229, 295, 301, 313, 355, 397
Gamification, 98, 99, 406
Gartner, 17, 362, 363, 367, 368, 370

Geofencing, 91, 92, 201
Giaglis, George, 92
Girl Gamer Esports Festival, 242
Global Trust in Advertising, 64
Google, 11, 19, 25, 29, 49, 66, 76, 84, 86, 88, 93, 95, 98, 105, 137, 138, 139, 141, 157, 181, 182, 195, 212, 217, 218, 222, 228, 229, 237, 238, 239, 240, 249, 254, 255, 269, 281, 291, 300, 301, 303, 305, 311, 312, 320, 321, 337, 350, 356, 363, 369, 376, 377, 378, 393, 394, 396, 397, 401, 409
Greenberg, Paul, 53
Gulbransen, Scott, 309
Hadoop
 HDFS Schema Design, 339
Hadoop, 12, 18, 19, 26, 74, 123, 124, 125, 133, 309, 331, 333, 334, 335, 336, 337, 338, 339
Hadoop
 Data Ingestion, 342
Hadoop
 Compression, 344
Hadoop
 Data Extraction, 349
Hadoop
 Machine Learning Solutions, 350
Hadoop, 356
Hadoop, 357
Hadoop, 358
Hadoop, 359
Hadoop, 359
Hexum, 37
Hierarchy of Social Marketing, 262
High rollers, 68
Hitachi, iii, 28, 94, 358, 359
IATA, 1, 43, 45, 102, 383, 409
iBeacon, 89, 90
IBM, 9, 18, 28, 43, 62, 74, 75, 76, 86, 114, 118, 120, 122, 125, 146, 181, 309, 310, 324, 330, 331, 332, 352, 358, 359, 360, 372
InfiniteInsights, 125
In-memory computing, 124
Instagram, 71, 222, 229, 253, 269, 278, 301, 314, 315, 394, 397, 409, 410
Internet, 86
Intromercials, 83

Inventory optimization, 372
IoT, iii, 11, 15, 16, 17, 19, 45, 174, 362, 363, 364, 365, 366, 371, 372, 374, 380
Iqivi.com, 249
Jantsch's Hierarchy of Social Media, 263
Jiepang, 37, 92, 242
Jones, Thomas, 65
Juniper Research, 191
Kafka, 345, 346, 347, 348, 349, 359
Kaixin, 201, 242
k-Means cluster, 148
k-Means Cluster Regression, 148
k-nearest neighbors, 150
Knowing What to Sell, When, and to Whom, 67
Kornfeld, Leora, 83, 86, 105
Kosinski, Michal, 287
Ku6, 37, 229, 249
Kumar, R., 67
Lafayette de Mete, Boye, 202
Letv.com, 249
Lift and gains charts, 69
Lighthouse Signal Systems, 93
LinkedIn, 33, 53, 123, 124, 191, 207, 209, 229, 242, 266, 269, 278, 291, 293
Location analytics, 182, 183, 184
Location-aware advertising, 89
Logistic Regression, 152
Lovelock, Christopher, 52, 64
Loyalty, 21, 23, 32, 49, 55, 56, 57, 61, 63, 64, 65, 67, 70, 85, 91, 92, 93, 117, 118, 120, 123, 124, 178, 179, 184, 235, 251, 252, 270, 277, 309, 317, 405, 406
Machine Learning, 8, 45, 130, 156, 304
Macy and Thompson, 297
Maker's Mark, 206, 207
Malshe, Ashwin, 280, 281, 282, 283, 284, 285, 286
MapReduce, 125
Market segmentation, 57, 58, 59, 160
Marketing campaigns, 29, 69, 84, 115, 297, 393
 automating campaigns, 68, 398
Marketing promotions, 21, 22
Marr, Bernard, 14, 40, 41

Marriott
   Marriott Rewards, 72
Mastercard, 297
Media Richness Theory, 192
Message boards, 189
Metcalf model, 35, 36
Metcalf, Bob, 35
Micro-blog, 36, 218
Micro-blogging, 189
   list of sites, 220
Microsoft, 18, 19, 46, 49, 62, 86, 88, 137, 181, 332, 344, 350, 369, 384, 398
MMS, 31, 94
Mobile
   digital advertising, 82
Mobile advertising
   broad-based brand advertising campaign, 83
   campaigns, 83
   Interactive, direct response campaign, 83
   targeted search advertising, 83
Mobile Advertising, the book, 82, 83, 84, 356
Mobile analytics, 115, 295
   what it is, 295
Mobile commerce
   personalization, 30, 46
Mobile marketing, 82, 88
   advantages, 88
   location-specific marketing messages, 89
   marketing campaigns, 88
   mobile advertising, 89
   mobile publicity, 89
   mobile search, 89
   mobile web, 88
   opting-in, 88
   persona planning, 405
   proximity marketing, 89
   push media model, 88
   social networking, 89
   text messaging, 88
   types of advertising campaigns, 88
   voice, 88
Mobile Marketing, 376
Mobile Marketing Handbook, The, 88
Mobile positioning technology
   kinds of, 92
Mobile search, 376
Mobile TV, 249
Mobile value chain, 82
Mtime.com, 249
MyPersonality, 288
MySpace, 84, 123, 189, 207, 228
Napster, 87
Net seed, 306
Netflix, 51, 68, 134, 297, 408
Neural networks, 155
   types of training, 156
Neural Networks in Data Mining, 155
New Distribution Capability, 7, 100
New York Times, 3, 113
NFC, 8, 17, 31, 89, 103, 104, 105, 363
Nielsen, 64, 75, 76, 88, 222, 224, 238
Ocean Method, 288, 289
Omni-commerce, 31
Optimizing Offers, 171
Oracle, 18, 46, 62, 76, 86, 181, 332, 342, 344, 358, 359, 360
OTT, 29, 31, 89, 94, 401
Page tracking, 295
Page views, 295
Patron Worth Model, 169
Pengyou, 242
Pentaho, 11
Periscope, 248
Pinterest, 98, 229, 253, 255, 262, 269, 278, 279, 293, 313, 315, 321, 401
Podcasts, 189, 250, 251
Pokémon Go, 370
Post-roll video, 83
Predictive analytics, 124
Predictive asset maintenance, 130, 174, 365, 373
Predictive modeling, 68
   predictive models, 69
   segmentation methods, 69
Predictive models
   six steps of creating them, 69
Procter & Gamble, 82
Propensity to Respond Model, 167
Property exchanges, 86, 105
Proximity marketing, 89
Psychometrics, 287
Push technology, 32
Pyra Labs, 214

Python, 13, 114, 125, 133, 142
PyTorch, 140, 141, 142
Qieke, 37, 242
QlikView, 114
QQ, 37
QQ Bookmarks, 212, 213
QR codes, 29, 31, 83
Qzone, 201, 242
Real-time marketing, 29, 332, 352, 356
Reed network, 36
Reed, David, 36
Reichheld, Frederick, 63
Reinartz, V.K., 67
Reinforcement learning, 130
Relational Database Managment Systems, 344
RenRen, 201, 205, 242
RetailNext, 183
RFM Models, 165
Rickenbacker, Eddie, 1, 113
Salesforce.com, 62
SAP, 62, 114, 125, 332
Sarnoff model, 35
Sarnoff network, 35
Sarnoff, David, 35
Sasser, W. Earl, 55, 63, 65, 406
SCRM, 49, 53, 67, 252
Search engine, 29, 193, 210, 272, 289, 302, 303, 314, 376, 377, 378, 393
Second Life, 191, 193, 247, 286, 287
Sentiment analysis, 174, 175
SEOMoz's, 210
Severe Tire Damage, 248
Sharma, Chetan, 82
Short Message Service, 88
Sina Weibo, 201, 205
Singapore Airlines, 4, 5, 41, 197, 216, 387
Singh, Dr. Yashpal, 155
Siri, 88
Site analysis, 295
Sitecore, 85
Six Types of Social Media, 209
   Blogs, 213
   Collaborative Projects, 209, 211
   Content Communities, 221
   Social Networks, 229
   Virtual Game Worlds, 242
   Virtual Social Worlds, 245

Slideshare, 209, 222, 271, 278
Smart Tones, 104
Smith, P.R., 35, 36, 181, 323
SMS, 31, 32, 88, 91, 94, 293
Snapchat, 40, 95, 98, 230
Social bookmarking, 189, 210, 211, 255, 263
Social exchanges, 86, 105
Social marketing
   potential, 253
Social media, 89, 189, 190, 251, 253
   collaborative and dynamic communication model, 189
   The six types of, 36
   two-way dialogue, 189
Social media analytics, 303, 304, 309
Social Media Marketing
   Influencer Marketing, 297
   Micro-Influencers, 299
Social media monitoring, 53
Social Media Monitoring Tools, 311
Social Media Theory the 1:9:90 rule, 265
Social media uses
   Social Media Monitoring, 307
Social Media uses
   Add Interactivity to a Website, 269
   Brand and Anti-Brand management, 270
   Build Fanbases, 276
   Crisis Management, 280
   Develop a Virtual Social World Presence, 286
   Discover Important Brand Trends, 82, 291
   Engage Customers and Potential Customers, 292
   Harvest Customer Feedback, 294
   Reputation Management, 301
Social network analysis, 304
Social Network Sites
   Definition, 229
   List of, 239
Social networking, 89, 189, 219
Social networking sites, 36, 89
Social networks, 189
Social presence, 192
Social proof, 195, 399

Source-Message-Channel-Receiver model, 189
Spark, 18, 28, 133, 358, 359
SPSS, 125
Starbucks, 38, 91, 272, 304
Stodder, David, 115, 118, 119, 177
Stream Processing, 26, 356, 358
  comparison of services, 358
Streaming Analytics, 352, 356, 358, 360
Streaming content, 248
Stumbleupon, 210
SugarCRM, 62
Supervised learning, 130
Survival or Duration Analysis, 161
Sutton, Scott, 153, 167, 168, 169, 170, 171, 172
Tableau, 17, 18, 19, 146
TDWI Research, 174
Tencent, 201, 205
Tencent Weibo, 201
Tensorflow, 136, 137, 139, 140
Text analytics, 174
Thought tracing, 86
TIBCO StreamBase, 359
Time Series Model, 155
Tivo, 297
Toyota, 175
Tracinski, Rob, 42
Tudou, 249
Tv.sohu.com, 249
Twitter, 11, 23, 33, 34, 36, 53, 54, 55, 72, 74, 76, 77, 78, 93, 94, 123, 124, 137, 176, 177, 193, 198, 200, 201, 205, 207, 211, 216, 218, 219, 220, 221, 223, 224, 228, 231, 234, 238, 252, 253, 255, 261, 264, 267, 269, 271, 275, 278, 281, 282, 284, 291, 293, 295, 296, 300, 301, 304, 306, 308, 309, 311, 312, 313, 314, 315, 316, 318, 321, 323, 354, 355, 356, 359, 396, 398, 400, 401, 405, 406, 410, 415
  Promoted Trends, 220
  Tweets, 219
  what is it?, 219
Twitter Revolution, 34
Typology of crises model, 281
Typology of Social Media Crisis, A, 280

Ulanoff, Lance, 8
Unilever, 306
United Breaks Guitars, 282
United Express Flight 3411, 2
Unsupervised learning, 130
User Generated Content, 190
  categories, 191
  mobile dating, 191
  personal content distribution, 191
  social networking, 191
Ushi, 37, 201
VanBoskirk, Shar, 405
Venkatesan, Rajkumar, 67
Video pre-rolls, 83
video.sina.com, 249
Videocasting, 189, 248
Virtual game worlds, 36
Virtual Reality, 367
Virtual Social World
  List of Websites, 247
Virtual social worlds, 36
Virtual worlds, 189
Virtual worlds websites
  worldofwarcraft.com, 189
Visa, 297
Vlogs, 189, 261
Wähner, Kai, 26, 27, 356, 357, 358, 360
Waste Management, 374
Wearables, 371, 372
Webopedia, 213, 367
WeChat, 11, 22, 23, 33, 36, 37, 48, 55, 71, 91, 94, 95, 98, 123, 204, 205, 229, 233, 234, 235, 236, 295, 355, 397, 401, 405, 406
Weibo, 11, 22, 23, 36, 37, 53, 55, 123, 191, 200, 201, 205, 208, 215, 221, 235, 255, 275, 304, 309, 405, 406
WhatsApp, 33
Wheel of Loyalty, 64, 394
Wikipedia, 84, 189, 191, 192, 193, 210, 211, 229, 233, 242, 248, 250, 352
Wirtz, Jochen, 52, 64, 394
Xunlei.com, 249
Yahoo!, 82
Youku, 23, 33, 37, 248
YouTube, 23, 33, 84, 87, 94, 105, 193, 200, 207, 211, 221, 248, 266, 267, 269, 271, 281, 282, 283, 285, 293, 294, 295, 298, 306, 308, 309, 311,

323
YY.com, 36, 200, 245, 246, 248, 394
Zedong, Mao, 202, 204
Zone of affection, 55, 65, 277, 406

Zone of defection, 65
Zone of indifference, 65, 406
Zook, Ze, 35, 36

www.ingramcontent.com/pod-product-compliance
Lightning Source LLC
Chambersburg PA
CBHW050045230526
45470CB00004B/1412